OXFORD MATHI

CW00549317

FOUNDATION
GCSE

Authors

Jim Kirkby

Peter McGuire

Derek Philpott

Ken Smith

Course Editors

Peter McGuire

Ken Smith

Oxford
University
Press

About this book

This book will help you to learn the mathematics you need for GCSE. You will also be able to use the book for your revision, and to practise skills and techniques. Colour is used to help you find your way around the different parts of the book.

In this book you will find :

Contents

This lists each part of the book, and the mathematical skills that are explained and practised in each of the 52 Sections are given with their code. For example, the first skill in Section 4 (on page 27) is: Skill 4A Ordering Decimals.

Wordfinder

This lists, alphabetically, words and mathematical terms that you can look up quickly and easily. The colours will guide you to:
■ Section   ■ Review   ■ End points   ■ Exam-style questions

Starting points

Starting points give the mathematics you need to know, before you start on a section. There are some questions for you to try out so that you can test what you know already. See page 77 as an example of Starting points.

If you can do these questions, you should be able to start on the section.

As you work through each section, you will find things in yellow panels. In these panels are :
- ■ new mathematical ideas, and skills that are explained
- ■ worked examples
- ■ methods to help you to use what you know

There are many questions to answer for practice. More difficult questions are shown in blue. For example, on page 151:

11   a   Make a sketch of the patio and label each side with its length.
     b   Calculate the area of the patio.

In the margin of some pages you will find other things to help, such as the definitions of terms. Words in the margin that link with the words in the work are in red. For example, on page 112: distribution links the definition in the margin and how it is used in the question.

You will also see that blue text is used at times to stress things that are important. For example, on page 134: the term $3y$ is stressed.

End points

This is where the work of each stage is listed for you.
You can check that you have understood things that have been taught. See page 64 as an example of End points.

Skills breaks

Skills breaks provide a mix of questions all linked to the same data.
They are one way to revise what you have learned and already know.
You will have to decide on the skills you will need to answer each question.

Review pages

These give you the chance to revise things you have done in the last few weeks. The skills are listed for you.

Revision pages

These give you the chance to revise the work of the book as you work your way through it.

Exam-style questions

Towards the back of the book is a set of questions organised as they might be in a GCSE examination. The questions will help you to know about the sort of things to can expect at Foundation level.

Answers

You will find the numerical answers to questions at the end of the book.

This is more than just a book of questions: it is a learning pack that will help you to make the most of your mathematical talents and skills. You can be sure that you are well prepared for the examination and you will not need a separate revision book. Everything is in this book.

CONTENTS

STAGE 4

A note on accuracy

Make sure your answer is given to any degree of accuracy stated in the question, for example 2 dp or 1 sf. Where it is not stated, choose a sensible degree of accuracy for your answer, and make sure you work to a greater degree of accuracy through the problem. For example, if you choose to give an answer to 3 sf, work to at least 4 sf through the problem, then round your final answer to 3 sf.

Examination groups differ in their approach to accuracy. Some say that you should not give your final answer to a greater degree of accuracy than that used for the data in the question, but others state answers should be given to 3 sf.

If you are in any doubt, check with your examination group.

Metric and Imperial units

	Metric	Imperial	Some approximate conversions
Length	millimetres (mm) centimetres (cm) metres (m) kilometres (km) 1 cm = 10 mm 1 m = 100 cm 1 km = 1000 m	inches (in) feet (ft) yards (yd) miles 1 ft = 12 in 1 yd = 3 ft 1 mile = 1760 yd	1 inch = 2.54 cm 1 foot ≈ 30.5 cm 1 metre ≈ 39.4 in 1 mile ≈ 1.61 km
Mass	grams (g) kilograms (kg) tonnes 1 kg = 1000 g 1 tonne = 1000 kg	ounces (oz) pounds (lb) stones 1 lb = 16 oz 1 stone = 14 lb	1 pound ≈ 454 g 1 kilogram ≈ 2.2 lb
Capacity	millilitres (ml) centilitres (cl) litres 1 cl = 10 ml 1 litre = 100 cl = 1000 ml	pints (pt) gallons 1 gallon = 8 pt	1 gallon ≈ 4.55 litres 1 litre ≈ 1.76 pints ≈ 0.22 gallons

Starting points

You need to know about ...

... so try these questions

A Numbers and digits

To make **whole numbers** we use these **digits**:
0, 1, 2, 3, 4, 5, 6, 7, 8, 9

To count on from 9, we put these digits together:
10, 11, 12, 13, 14, 15, 16, 17, 18, 19, 20, 21, ... , 99, 100, 101, ... , 199, 200, ... , 999, 1000, and so on.

If we choose 4, 5, and 8 from the list of digits, they can be used to make:

three	1-digit numbers	4, 5, and 8
or six	2-digit numbers	45, 48, 54, 58, 84, and 85
or six	3-digit numbers	458, 485, 548, 584, 845, and 854

A1 Which of these is a three-digit number?

   a 26   **b** 158   **c** 8

A2 How many digits are used to make each of these numbers?

   a 4875   **b** 90 224
   c 1 034 055 **d** 882 455 106

A3 Choose from this list of digits 3, 4, 7, 8, and 9 and make:

   a a two-digit number
   b a four-digit number
   c a five-digit number that starts with the digit 7.

A4 As you count, what is the first three-digit number?

Place value and whole numbers

♦ The place a digit has in a number gives it a value. Each of these numbers has 7 as one of its digits:

   137   one hundred and thirty seven

   475   four hundred and seventy five

   726   seven hundred and twenty six

In these numbers the digit 7 has a place that gives it a value of:
  7 in 137
  or   70   in 475
  or   700 in 726

♦ The place values in whole numbers are these.

> The U in the place value table stands for Units.
>
> The units column has digits with whole number values from zero to nine.

...	...	...	1 000 000	100 000	10 000	1000	100	10	U
							1	3	7
							4	7	5
							7	2	6

♦ The place of a digit in a number gives it a value.

Exercise 1.1
Practising place value

1 Give the value of the digit 6 in each of these numbers.

a 476	**b** 565	**c** 681	**d** 1654
e 3769	**f** 6075	**g** 3644	**h** 96
i 568	**j** 6	**k** 6783	**l** 64 149
m 604 538	**n** 6 985 451	**o** 198 211 346	**p** 36 542

2 In which of these numbers does the digit 4 have a value of 4000?

a 748	**b** 4075	**c** 14 365	**d** 42 638
e 4005	**f** 43 506	**g** 5460	**h** 104 606

Exercise 1.2
Using place value

1 Give the value of each digit in the number 45 627.

2 Give the value of each digit in the number 120 043.

3 A three-digit number has:
   a digit 4   with a place value of 40
   a digit 6   with a place value of 600
   a digit 5   with a place value of 5

   What is this three-digit number?

4 A four-digit number has:
   a digit 3   with a place value of 300
   a digit 9   with a place value of 90
   a digit 2   with a place value of 2000
   a digit 4   with a place value of 4

   What is this four-digit number?

5 Write this five-digit number. It has:
   a digit 7   with a place value of 70
   a digit 8   with a place value of 8000
   a digit 3   with a place value of 3
   a digit 2   with a place value of 20 000
   a digit 6   with a place value of 600

6 Give the value of each digit in these numbers.
   a 45 236   b 512 607   c 5 821 763

Ordering whole numbers

Skill 1A
Ordering whole numbers

◆ One way to put a set of numbers, all larger than 0, in order is:

   ❖ put the numbers in the order of the number of digits; then

   ❖ put those with the same number of digits in order.

Example

Put these numbers in order. Start with the smallest.

   1247, 988, 15 754, 365, 58, 375, 1088, 255

Start in the order of the number of digits (smallest first):

   58, 988, 365, 375, 255, 1247, 1088, 15 754

Then put those with the same number of digits in order:

   3 digits   58, 255, 365, 375, 988, 1247, 1088, 15 754

   4 digits   58, 255, 365, 375, 988, 1088, 1247, 15 754

In order, the numbers are: 58, 255, 365, 375, 988, 1088, 1247, 15 754.

> There are four 3-digit numbers in the list.
> 988, 365, 375, 255
>
> In order they are
> 255, 365, 375, 988.

Exercise 1.3
Practising Skill 1A

1 Put each set of numbers in order. Start with the smallest.
   a 189, 2362, 567, 34, 58, 5332, 21
   b 495, 16, 384, 509, 14, 630, 1244
   c 636, 75, 385, 88, 592, 4425, 1304, 81
   d 846, 17, 9224, 675, 38, 112, 5, 488, 10 566
   e 18 455, 327, 4342, 565, 3224, 4553, 875, 3, 15, 88
   f 1047, 3005, 9, 7802, 11 000, 3502, 16, 12 883, 14 562

Exercise 1.4
Using Skill 1A

1 The digits 2, 5, and 7 can make six different 3-digit numbers.
   a What is the largest 3-digit number you can make from 2, 5 and 7?
   b What is the smallest?
   c List all the 3-digit numbers you can make.
   d List the numbers in order, smallest first.

2 The digits 8, 3, and 9 can make six different 3-digit numbers.
   a List the different 3-digit numbers you can make.
   b List the numbers in order, smallest first.

3 The digits 0, 0, 1, and 4 can make this set of 4-digit numbers.
   1004, 4010, 1040, 1400, 4100, 4001
   a Which is the largest of the numbers?
   b Which is the smallest?
   c List the numbers in descending order.

> Descending order is from largest to smallest.
> Start the list with the largest of the **numbers.**

4 The digits 0, 0, 5, and 9 can make 4-digit numbers.
   a What is the largest 4-digit number you can make from these digits?
   b What is the smallest?
   c List all the 4-digit numbers you can make, in descending order.

Numbers in words and digits

Skill 1B
Writing numbers in words

Place value can help when you need to write a number in words.

Example 1

Write the number 2426 in words.

The place values give:

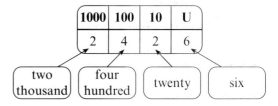

So **2426 in words is: two thousand four hundred and twenty six.**

Zeros fill places in numbers to make sure each digit shows the right value.

Example 2

Write the number 35 068 in words.

The place values give:

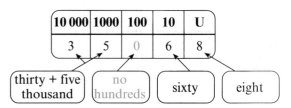

So **35 068 in words is: thirty-five thousand and sixty eight.**

Exercise 1.5
Practising Skill 1B

1 Write each of these numbers in words.
   a 675   b 1542   c 12458   d 5607
   e 1004   f 26804   g 4040   h 56410
   i 265612   j 4872453   k 1307526   l 37000002

Skill 1C
Writing numbers in digits

0 can be written as **zero** or **nought**.

There can be problems with a number written in words if one or more of the digits is zero (0).

Example 1   Write the number six thousand and forty two in digits.

The largest place value is thousands.

The number must have 4-digits

1000	100	10	U
■	■	■	■
6	■	■	■
6	■	4	■
6	■	4	2
6	0	4	2

six thousand
and   forty
two
the other digit must be zero (0)

So six thousand and forty two in digits is 6042.

Zeros (0s) are used to make sure each digit has the right place value.

Example 2   Write the number fifty two thousand and three in digits.

Largest place value is ten thousands

There must be 5 digits

10 000	1000	100	10	U
■	■	■	■	■
5	■	■	■	■
5	2	■	■	■
5	2	■	■	3
5	2	0	0	3

fifty thousand
two thousand
and   three
the other digits must be zero

So in digits, fifty two thousand and three is: 52 003.

Zeros (0s) are used to fill place values to make sure the digits show an exact number.

Four hundred and one is not written as 4 1, it is written as 4 0 1.

Exercise 1.6
Practising Skill 1C

1   Write each of these numbers in digits.

   a   three thousand and sixty seven
   b   five thousand two hundred and forty
   c   nine thousand five hundred and six
   d   eight thousand and one
   e   six thousand and twenty nine
   f   nine thousand three hundred and ten
   g   one thousand one hundred and one

2   Write each of these numbers in digits.

   a   twenty one thousand and fifty six
   b   thirty two thousand six hundred and eight
   c   seventy five thousand and forty five
   d   ninety one thousand and sixteen
   e   sixty thousand and twenty four
   f   ten thousand and ten
   g   ninety thousand nine hundred and nine

3   Rewrite this report with all the numbers in digits.

Only forty five of those on board were children. One thousand and sixty two holiday makers chose to fly the eleven thousand three hundred and five kilometres back to London.
Repairs will cost two million three hundred and forty two thousand pounds. The ship will be in dry dock for about eight thousand and forty hours and will be worked on by fifteen hundred men and women. A new ship costing three hundred and sixty seven million dollars will be started next year. The new ship will weigh about thirty five thousand tonnes.

Starting points
You need to know about ...

... so try these questions

A Vertical and horizontal

A **vertical** line goes straight up.

When you drop a stone it falls **vertically**.

A **horizontal** line goes straight across.
When you lie in bed you are lying **horizontally**.

horizontal

A1 Say if each of these is vertical or horizontal.

   a the surface of the sea
   b the wall of a house
   c the leg of a table
   d the crossbar of a goal.

A2 Why is the gutter of a house not quite horizontal?

A3 Does a plane take off vertically?
Explain your answer.

A4 Name an object which is usually:

   a vertical
   b horizontal

Line symmetry

A shape has line symmetry if one side of it is a mirror image of the other.

♦ This letter has a horizontal line of symmetry.

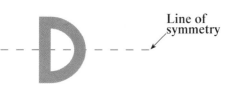

Line of symmetry

♦ This word has a vertical line of symmetry.

♦ This shape has 3 lines of symmetry. None of these lines are vertical or horizontal.

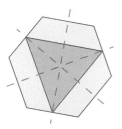

Exercise 2.1
Practising line symmetry

1 For each word say if it has a horizontal line of symmetry, a vertical line of symmetry, or no line symmetry.

a HOD	**b** ICON	**c** MADAM
d NOOSE	**e** WOW	**f** CHOICE
g ROTOR	**h** MUM	**i** TOXIC
j OXO	**k** DOE	**l** BOX

2 **a** Draw the first eight letters of the alphabet as capitals
b Show all the lines of symmetry of each letter.

3 Here are some signs. Sketch each one and draw in all its lines of symmetry.

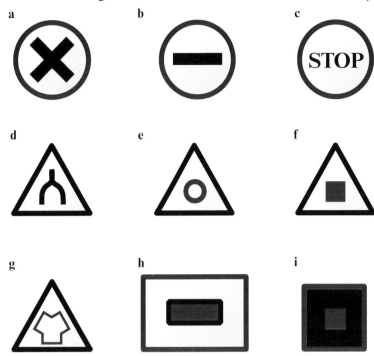

4 Invent a road sign of your own with:
a two lines of symmetry
b three lines of symmetry

Rotational symmetry

♦ **Rotational symmetry** is the symmetry of a shape that can be turned and fitted on to itself.

Example 1   This **Z** has an **order of rotational symmetry** of **2** because it can fit on to itself in two ways by turning it.

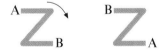

Example 2   This shape has rotational symmetry of order 4.

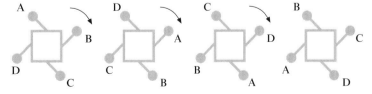

♦ A shape with no rotational symmetry has an order of rotational symmetry of 1.

Example   This shape has an order of rotational symmetry of 1 because it can only fit onto itself in one way. It does not have rotational symmetry.

Exercise 2.2
Practising rotational and
line symmetry

1   Which letters in this word have rotational symmetry?
HEADLINES

2   Give three capital letters with no rotational symmetry.

3   Give the order of rotational symmetry of each of these shapes.

a   **b**   **c**   **d**

e   **f** 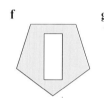   **g**   **h**

4   What is the order of rotational symmetry of a rectangle?

5   Draw a shape with an order of rotational symmetry of 3.

6   This shape has an order of rotational symmetry of 4.
   a   Copy the shape.
   b   Add one line to the shape to change its
      order of rotational symmetry to 2.

7   **a**   What order of rotational symmetry
      has this road sign?
   b   How many lines of symmetry has the sign?

8   **a**   Draw two other road signs which have rotational symmetry.
   b   Label each sign with its order of rotational symmetry.

9   For each shape:
   a   sketch it and draw in all its lines of symmetry
   b   label its order of rotational symmetry.

Tracing paper may help
when you find the order of
rotational symmetry.

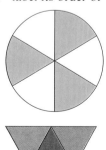

Plane symmetry

A plane is a flat surface that goes on for ever in each direction.

Plane symmetry is the symmetry of a 3D shape.
Each plane of symmetry divides the solid into two mirror images.

Example 1 This solid has plane symmetry.
It has two planes of symmetry (shown in red).

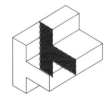

Example 2

This solid does not have plane symmetry.
It cannot be cut so that one side
is a mirror image of the other.

Exercise 2.3
Practising planes
of symmetry

1 Which of these everyday objects usually has plane symmetry?
If it does not have plane symmetry, say why.

a pair of spectacles b dining table c telephone
d mug e wrist watch f pair of headphones
g car h car wheel

2 How many planes of symmetry has this pencil?

3 This new eraser is shaped like a cuboid.
How many planes of symmetry has it?

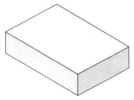

4 Say if each object usually has a vertical plane of symmetry, or a horizontal plane of symmetry, or both.

a chair b clothes hook c milk bottle
d slice of bacon e traffic cone f solid door

5 Explain why a shoe does not have plane symmetry.

6 How many planes of symmetry has each of these solids?

a  b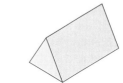

Square-based pyramid   Equilateral triangular prism

7 How many planes of symmetry has a cube?

Adding numbers without using a calculator

Skill 3A
Adding whole numbers without a calculator

> Adding numbers mentally is doing the working out in your head.

> You have to remember the running total each time. Here the running totals are (13), (17), and (24). The answer is 30.

◆ Some addition can be done mentally.
People use different methods because they find some easier than others.

Example 1

What is $8 + 5 + 4 + 7 + 6$?

You can add the numbers in order, using a running total.
$8 + 5 (13) + 4 (17) + 7 (24) + 6 = 30$

Example 2

What is $34 + 25 + 18$?

You can add the units of a number and then the tens.
So, to add 25 you add 5 first, and then you add 20

$$34 + 5 (39) + 20 (59) + 8 (67) + 10 = 77$$

25   18

Example 3

What is $148 + 79$?

One way to add 79 is: add 80, and then take away 1, as $79 = 80 - 1$
$148 + 80 (228) - 1 = 227$

◆ Use methods that work for you and you feel happy with.

Exercise 3.1
Practising Skill 3A

1 Add these mentally.
   a $8 + 4 + 9 + 5 + 6 =$ b $6 + 3 + 8 + 5 + 9 =$
   c $6 + 7 + 6 + 4 + 8 + 5 =$ d $9 + 6 + 6 + 7 + 4 + 4 + 1 =$
   e $8 + 8 + 5 + 9 + 8 + 7 + 3 =$ f $6 + 8 + 4 + 4 + 3 + 5 + 7 + 2 =$

2 Add these mentally.
   a $44 + 27 =$ b $58 + 43 =$ c $76 + 88 =$
   d $32 + 54 + 76 =$ e $75 + 46 + 38 =$ f $54 + 21 + 35 =$
   g $27 + 16 + 28 + 14 =$ h $96 + 15 + 12 + 77 + 28 =$

3 Add these mentally.
   a $54 + 79 =$ b $88 + 49 =$ c $53 + 39 =$
   d $27 + 69 =$ e $78 + 29 =$ f $18 + 37 + 49 =$
   g $45 + 59 + 12 =$ h $24 + 39 + 89 =$ i $16 + 33 + 29 + 59 =$

Skill 3B
Adding whole numbers by pencil and paper methods

> One way to line up all the place values is to line up the units as you write the numbers. The units here are 4, 7, 8, and 6.

With a pencil-and-paper method to add numbers, you must write each of the numbers so that the place values line up.

Example 1

$34 + 157 + 88 + 6$

```
  34 +
 157
  88
   6
 ───
 285
```

Example 2

$158 + 12 + 1057 + 60$

```
 158 +
  12
1057
  60
────
1287
```

Exercise 3.2
Practising Skill 3B

1 Add each of these.

a 157 + 456   **b** 675 + 16   **c** 458 + 192
d 1344 + 458   **e** 23 + 6784   **f** 34 566 + 804
g 573 + 12 609   **h** 12 875 + 157 844   **i** 30 475 + 587

2 Calculate the answer to each of these.

a 57 + 125 + 8   **b** 34 + 1056 + 355
c 1258 + 8 + 32   **d** 16 + 2536 + 1932
e 44 + 5675 + 9 + 108   **f** 385 + 8663 + 42 + 153
g 15 656 + 58 + 1595   **h** 857 + 2344 + 15 662 + 14
i 34 + 45 662 + 345 253 + 152   **j** 1662 + 45 + 8256 + 6 + 145 078

Exercise 3.3
Using Skill 3B

1 Five people using the desk at a supermarket had these items.

Customer A 7 items, Customer B 8 items, Customer C 5 items, Customer D 8 items, Customer E 9 items.

Add the number of items bought by the five people .

2 Three ferries arrived on the island of Barsay on 9 August.

Seaker 1   carried 44 cars and 185 passengers.
Islander   carried 168 cars and 456 passengers.
Amtar   carried 207 cars and 588 passengers.

a How many cars arrived by ferry?
b How many passengers were there?

3 Jake prints T-shirts. This shows the shirts he printed last week.

Mon 178   Tues 254   Wed 476   Thurs 508   Fri 437

a How many shirts, in total, did Jake print last week?
b Find the total for his best 3 days.

4 Eurolink deliver parcels.
The table shows deliveries for 5 days.

a Find the total for the first 3 days
b Calculate the total for Tuesday and Thursday
c Find the total for Monday and Friday.
d Calculate the total for all 5 days.

Day	Parcels
Mon	1575
Tues	2055
Wed	13704
Thurs	20078
Fri	1287

5 Cars using the Sasco River bridge are counted on a meter.
Readings are filled in at the end of each hour.
The table shows the start of a shift.

The cars using the bridge were:
in 1st hour   288
in 2nd hour   594
in 3rd hour   1656
in 4th hour   2807

a What did the meter read after 1 hour?
b What did it read after 2 hours?
c What did it read after 3 hours?
d What did it read after 4 hours?
e In the 4 hours, how many cars used the bridge in total?

Sasco River Bridge Records Department

Operator   Mike

Time	0800		Meter reading (cars)				
Start of shift		1	6	5	9	8	8
After 1 hour							
After 2 hours							
After 3 hours							
After 4 hours							

Subtracting whole numbers without using a calculator

Skill 3C
Subtracting whole
numbers

To subtract numbers you must line up the place values when you write the calculation.

Example 1	Example 2
1364 – 785	3005 – 947

To subtract one number from another, in most cases, you will subtract the smaller number from the larger of the two numbers.

$$
\begin{array}{r}
1364\ - \\
785 \\
\hline
579
\end{array}
\qquad
\begin{array}{r}
3005\ - \\
947 \\
\hline
2058
\end{array}
$$

Exercise 3.4
Practising Skill 3C

1 Subtract to calculate these answers.

   a 884 – 695   **b** 504 – 375   **c** 921 – 787
   d 1057 – 968   **e** 6341 – 486   **f** 6341 – 5475
   g 12345 – 8578   **h** 20504 – 13856   **i** 63002 – 37845

2 Subtract these numbers.

   a 16000004 – 12463956   **b** 2000000 – 875624
   c 125010030 – 98345627   **d** 56 million – 48621833
   e thirty one thousand – six thousand five hundred and twenty three
   f six million – five hundred and four thousand two hundred and sixty one

Exercise 3.5
Using Skill 3C

1 The miles travelled by a van, in one day are shown here.

	Mileage					
Start of day	1	0	3	8	2	7
End of day	1	0	4	3	0	1

   a Which is the larger number; the start, or end of the day?
   b How far did the van travel that day?
   c Write the number of miles travelled in words.

2 A survey asked forty two thousand students about sport. The number of females in the survey was 23762. How many males were in the survey?

3 A supermarket had six and a half thousand cartons of milk to start the day. At 12 noon there were 2883 left.
Calculate how many cartons of milk had been sold.

4 Last year Quadra Air flew 3041082 passengers to Spain.
This total includes 67856 children.
Last year, how many adults did Quadra Air fly to Spain?

5 A database holds 4650000 records of mail-order shoppers.
The records show that 1874676 shoppers made an order in July.
How many of the shoppers did not order in July?

6 Food-on-the-Move make sandwiches in brown or white bread.
Last month, they made a total of 80024 sandwiches.
Only 16485 of the sandwiches were in brown bread.
How many of the sandwiches made were in white bread?

7 In one day, Wyvern Water took 35000000 litres of water from rivers.
It took 14872565 from the River Tarn, how much came from other rivers?

Multiplying whole numbers without using a calculator

Skill 3D
Multiplying whole numbers by pencil and paper methods

♦ Multiplying numbers without a calculator can be more difficult as the numbers become larger.

Example 1 A single-digit by a single-digit $3 \times 9 = 27$

Example 2 A 2-digit by a single digit

38×7

$$\begin{array}{r} 38 \\ \times\ 7 \\ \hline 266 \end{array}$$

or you can think of it as
$8 \times 7 = 56$ and $30 \times 7 = 210$
which is $56 + 210 = 266$

Example 3 A 2-digit by a 2-digit

46×73

$$\begin{array}{r} 46 \\ \times\ 73 \\ \hline 138 \\ 3220 \\ \hline 3358 \end{array}$$

To multiply by 73 you
♦ multiply by 3
♦ multiply by 70
then add the two answers.

or you can think of it as
$3 \times 46 = 138$
and $70 \times 46 = 3220$
which is $138 + 3220 = 3358$

♦ These are just two ways to multiply without a calculator.
There are many other ways.
You need to use a way you are happy with and gives a correct answer.

Exercise 3.6
Practising Skill 3D

1
a 46×8 b 87×4 c 56×9 d 78×3
e 67×5 f 26×7 g 74×9 h 45×6

2
a 34×56 b 73×62 c 58×23 d 45×87
e 78×33 f 38×55 g 37×42 h 81×62

3
a 145×8 b 265×7 c 188×4 d 257×8
e 324×5 f 624×9 g 253×7 h 635×9

4
a 124×18 b 156×24 c 263×38 d 286×44
e 365×46 f 482×57 g 535×62 h 748×73

Exercise 3.7
Using Skill 3D

1 Trolleysure make supermarket trolleys with 8 wheels each.
They make 375 trolleys a day. How many wheels do they use in a day?

2 Carla fixes fence panels. She uses 7 nails to fix each panel. A car park fence needed 126 panels. How many nails were used to fix all the panels?

3 In a Jumbo size box, there are 480 drawing pins. Patrick bought 7 boxes. How many drawing pins were there in total?

4 A case of baked beans holds 24 cans. A supermarket orders 68 cases. How many cans is this?

5 Films are packed in boxes of 18 films.
Megaprint sold 46 boxes of films last week. How many films is this?

6 A Centrabus seats 74 people when it is full.
Fans go to a match in 41 full Centrabuses.
How many fans is this?

7 A book has 384 pages. 185 books are printed.
How many pages is this?

Dividing whole numbers without using a calculator

Skill 3E
Dividing whole numbers by pencil and paper methods

When 35 is divided by 6 there is a remainder of 5. The 5 is carried on. Then 54 is divided by 6.

♦ Dividing numbers can be done in different ways.
   When a whole number is divided there may be a remainder.

Example 1   Dividing by a one-digit number $354 \div 6$

$$6\overline{)35^54}$$
$$59$$ So **$354 \div 6 = 59$** (no remainder)

Example 2 $546 \div 8$

$$8\overline{)54^66}$$
$$68\,r\,2$$ So **$546 \div 8 = 68$ remainder** 2

Example 3   Dividing by a 2-digit number $451 \div 16$

$$16\overline{)45^{1}1}$$
$$28\,r\,3$$ So **$451 \div 16 = 28$ rem** 3

Exercise 3.8
Practising Skill 3E

1   Divide these numbers without using a calculator.

a $475 \div 5$	**b** $378 \div 7$	**c** $282 \div 6$	**d** $584 \div 8$
e $755 \div 9$	**f** $471 \div 7$	**g** $265 \div 4$	**h** $512 \div 6$
i $588 \div 8$	**j** $292 \div 5$	**k** $504 \div 9$	**l** $352 \div 4$

2   Work out:

a $812 \div 14$	**b** $912 \div 16$	**c** $855 \div 15$	**d** $936 \div 12$
e $835 \div 13$	**f** $712 \div 15$	**g** $785 \div 17$	**h** $616 \div 18$
i $962 \div 14$	**j** $665 \div 19$	**k** $908 \div 12$	**l** $792 \div 16$

3   Find:

a $1302 \div 7$	**b** $2048 \div 8$	**c** $1413 \div 9$	**d** $3512 \div 6$
e $4376 \div 8$	**f** $3818 \div 4$	**g** $4172 \div 7$	**h** $5063 \div 9$

4   Use a pencil and paper method to work out:

a $414 \div 23$	**b** $672 \div 31$	**c** $966 \div 46$	**d** $952 \div 28$
e $2210 \div 34$	**f** $4992 \div 52$	**g** $2104 \div 28$	**h** $2115 \div 34$

Exercise 3.9
Using Skill 3E

1   A volleyball team has six players.
   A school has 522 volleyball players. How many teams is this?

2   A minibus can seat 18 people. (No standing is allowed.)
   How many minibuses are needed to take 1152 fans to a match?

3   On a 476 mile cycle tour, Jan travelled 34 miles each day.
   How many days was the cycle tour?

4   1825 pens are packed in boxes of 12.

   a   How many full boxes are there?
   b   How many pens are left over?

5   The Tor Island Ferry can carry 27 passengers at a time.
   On one day, the ferry carried 1710 passengers.

   a   The ferry was full, except once. How many trips did it make?
   b   On one trip the ferry was not full. How many passengers did it have?
   c   How many trips would the ferry need for 1500 passengers?

Starting points

You need to know about ...

... so try these questions

A Tenths, hundredths and thousandths

- When one unit is divided into 10 equal parts, each part is: one-tenth or $\frac{1}{10}$.

- Each tenth can be split into 10 equal parts to give: hundredths or $\frac{1}{100}$'s.

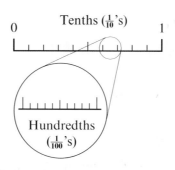

- A hundredth divided into 10 equal parts gives 10 thousandths ($\frac{10}{1000}$'s).

A1 How many hundredths are there in three-tenths?

A2 How many thousandths are there in nine-hundredths?

A3 A centimetre is one-hundredth of a metre.

    a How many centimetres are in seven-tenths of a metre?

    b How many centimetres are in twenty-three-hundredths of a metre?

Place value and decimal fractions

A decimal fraction is a way of writing a number between 0 and 1 by:

- using place values of tenths, hundredths, thousandths, ... and so on

- placing a nought in the units column 0 . 2 9 7

- placing a decimal point between the units column and the tenths column.

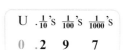

A decimal fraction is written in words by writing each of the digits.

    For example, **0.297** in words is **nought point two nine seven**,
               0.3081 in words is **nought point three nought eight one**.

Exercise 4.1
Decimal fractions

1 Write each of these in words.

    a 0.371   **b** 0.28   **c** 0.506   **d** 0.0409

2 Sam writes 0.485 in words like this:

    nought point four hundred and eighty five

    Explain what is wrong.

3 In which of these does the digit 7 have a value of seven-hundredths?
    0.72   0.372   0.717   0.9703   0.076

4 Which one of these numbers is two-hundredths greater than 0.3166?
    0.3168   0.3366   0.3186   0.5166

5 Which one of these numbers is three-thousandths less than 0.4975?
    0.4972   0.4675   0.1975   0.4945

6 How much is 0.3468 greater than 0.3418?

7 What number is twelve-hundredths greater than 0.362?

Exercise 4.2
Using place value

1 In the 1996 Olympics, Donovan Bailey set a new 100 metres world record. His time of 9.64 seconds beat the old world record by thirty-two hundredths of a second. What was the old world record?

2 In 1997, the world record for the women's 100 metres was held by Gail Devers at 10.04 seconds. What would be her time if she were to break the record by one-tenth of a second?

3 **a** Sergei Bubka raised the world record for the pole vault by three centimetres to 5.85 metres. What was the old world record?
   b He then raised the record to 5.92 metres. How many centimetres did he raise it by?

Decimal places

> A decimal is any number that is written using only place values, such as:
>
> 0.4   3.75   156.9   72
>
> $2\frac{1}{2}$ is not a decimal.

The digits in a decimal after the decimal point are called decimal places.

 0.4, 12.3 and 8.0 each have one decimal place (1 dp)
 12.965 and 8.000 each have three decimal places (3 dp)

In athletics, long jump distances are measured in metres (m). Each is given as a decimal to 2 dp.

For example, the women's long jump at the 1996 Olympics was won with a jump of 7.12 metres.

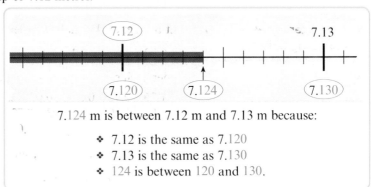

7.124 m is between 7.12 m and 7.13 m because:

❖ 7.12 is the same as 7.120
❖ 7.13 is the same as 7.130
❖ 124 is between 120 and 130.

Exercise 4.3
Decimal places

1 Which of these is between 4.35 m and 4.36 m?

   4.358 m   4.355 m   4.365 m   4.356 m

2 Which of these is between 7.1 m and 7.2 m?

   7.21 m   7.12 m   7.152 m   7.116 m

3 This line is 8.3 cm long.

> To measure these lines, you need a ruler marked in centimetres and millimetres.
>
>

Give the length, in centimetres, of each of these lines.

a ⎯⎯⎯⎯⎯⎯⎯⎯⎯⎯⎯⎯⎯⎯⎯
b ⎯⎯⎯⎯
c ⎯⎯⎯⎯⎯⎯⎯⎯⎯⎯⎯

4 Which is longer: 7 cm or 7.0 cm?
Explain your answer.

Ordering decimals

Skill 4A
Ordering decimals

Example   Put these decimals in order, smallest first.

0.07   0.318   1.491   0.6   3.4   0.009   3.18

♦ add 0s so that each decimal has the same number of decimal places

| 0.070 | 0.318 | 1.491 | 0.600 | 3.400 | 0.009 | 3.180 |

♦ use the first digit to put the decimals in order

| 0.070 | 0.318 | 0.600 | 0.009 | 1.491 | 3.400 | 3.180 |

♦ if the first digits are the same, use the second digit to order again

| 0.070 | 0.318 | 0.600 | 0.009 | 1.491 | 3.400 | 3.180 |
| 0.070 | 0.009 | 0.318 | 0.600 | 1.491 | 3.180 | 3.400 |

♦ if the second digits are the same, use the third digit to order again

| 0.070 | 0.009 | 0.318 | 0.600 | 1.491 | 3.180 | 3.400 |
| 0.009 | 0.070 | 0.318 | 0.600 | 1.491 | 3.180 | 3.400 |

♦ when no more ordering is needed, remove the added 0's.

0.009   0.07   0.318   0.6   1.491   3.18   3.4

You may need to revise:

Skill 1A: *see page 13*

Exercise 4.4
Practising Skill 4A

1   Put this set of decimals in order, smallest first.

0.729   1.82   0.2   0.006   1.905   0.75

2   Order each set of decimals, smallest first.

a   1.26   0.92   0.571   0.02   2.1   1.2175
b   0.052   0.0391   1.093   0.72   0.4   0.037   1.07
c   0.601   2.145   0.7019   0.06   2   0.706   1.2

3   Put these numbers in order, smallest first.

8.07   0.34   12.6   1.2   11.125   0.317

4   Put this set of numbers in order, largest first.

0.0613   1.053   1.51   0.0032   1.5   11   0.06

Exercise 4.5
Using Skill 4A

1   These are the batting averages of 6 cricketers.

The best batsman has the highest average.

Put them in order, best first.

Michael	32.5
Alex	52.325
John	23.75
Nasser	52.3
Graham	32.525
Mark	23.1875

2   Put these exchange rates in order, highest first.

Exchange Rates (July 1997)		
Number of **French francs** for £1	Flysave	9.0025
	Getaway	9.02
	Going Abroad	9.015
	Summer Breaks	9.0
	Travelfar	9.005

Adding decimals without using a calculator

Skill 4B
Adding decimals by
pencil-and-paper methods

To use a pencil-and-paper method to add decimals:

◆ write the numbers so that the place values line up.

Example 1

6.45 + 8.66 + 12.71

```
    6.45 +
    8.66
   12.71
   ─────
   27.82
```

Example 2

12.75 + 6.206 + 34.4

```
   12.75   +
    6.206
   34.4
   ──────
   53.356
```

Exercise 4.6
Practising Skill 4B

1 Calculate each answer.

a 4.12 + 5.65	**b** 5.73 + 2.06	**c** 1.217 + 3.202
d 3.6 + 2.5	**e** 3.52 + 1.29	**f** 4.227 + 5.465
g 12.7 + 24.9	**h** 9.28 + 2.36	**i** 7.51 + 2.85
j 6.17 + 9.84 + 2.05	**k** 16.89 + 8.07 + 3.45	**l** 23.07 + 5.64 + 12.72
m 18.124 + 7.812 + 9.999		

2 Calculate:

a 5.7 + 4.16	**b** 8.24 + 1.3	**c** 3.519 + 9.2
d 6.82 + 3.197	**e** 15.3 + 4.75	**f** 0.478 + 21.5
g 11.34 + 5.2 + 4.63	**h** 21.33 + 18.2 + 4.608	**i** 0.357 + 1.79 + 23
j 7.77 + 8 + 9.999		

Exercise 4.7
Using Skill 4B

1 Sue and Dave went shopping.
They wrote what they spent in each shop.   34.55   123.50   55.02

How much did they spend in total?

2 At the 1996 Olympics, Great Britain won silver for the relay. These are the times for the GB team.

Mens 4 × 400 metres Relay Final	
Iwan Thomas	44.91 seconds
Jamie Baulch	44.19 seconds
Mark Richardson	43.62 seconds
Roger Black	43.87 seconds

What was the teams total time, in seconds, for the race?

3 Gina is posting catalogues to customers.
This shows how much she spent on postage in one week.
What was the total for the week?

Monday	£162.46
Tuesday	£48
Wednesday	£61.90
Thursday	£142.12
Friday	£93

Subtracting decimals without using a calculator

Skill 4C
Subtracting decimals by
pencil-and-paper methods

To use a pencil-and-paper method to subtract decimals:

♦ write the numbers so that the place values line up

♦ add 0's to the number you are subtracting from, if you need to.

Example 1	Example 2
23.487 – 12.751	17 – 4.38

$$
\begin{array}{r}
23.487\ - \\
12.751 \\
\hline
10.736
\end{array}
\qquad
\begin{array}{r}
17.00\ - \\
4.38 \\
\hline
12.62
\end{array}
$$

Exercise 4.8
Practising Skill 4C

1 Calculate each answer.

a 7.82 – 4.21	**b** 23.39 – 11.14	**c** 9.75 – 5.24
d 9.34 – 6.18	**e** 18.6 – 12.9	**f** 13.55 – 7.26
g 17.63 – 12.81	**h** 0.258 – 0.173	**i** 6.258 – 6.173
j 24.56 – 18.57	**k** 34.7 – 7.9	**l** 31.065 – 18.778

2 Calculate:

a 18 – 6.5	**b** 23 – 7.4	**c** 8.9 – 5.25	**d** 7.6 – 4.81
e 35 – 12.62	**f** 12.8 – 7.23	**g** 20 – 9.95	**h** 6.72 – 1.178
i 8.7 – 3.407	**j** 5 – 2.366	**k** 11 – 0.23	**l** 11 – 0.237

Exercise 4.9
Using Skill 4C

1 These times are for the relay.

Mens 4 × 400 metres Relay Final		
	Jamie Baulch	Mark Richardson
	(seconds)	(seconds)
Round One	45.36	44.69
Semifinal	44.66	45.34
Final	44.19	43.62

a How much slower was Jamies time in the semifinal than in the final?
b How much faster did he run in the semifinal than in round one?
c How much faster did Mark run in the final than in the semifinal?
d Find the difference between Jamie's and Mark's times in Round One.
e In which round were their times the closest?

2 Great Britain's total time in the semifinal was 181.36 seconds.
These are the times:

Iwan Thomas	45.78 seconds
Jamie Baulch	44.66 seconds
Duane Ladejo	▓▓▓ seconds
Mark Richardson	43.62 seconds

Calculate the time for Duane Ladejo.

3 Sue pays for a folder costing 3.65 with a £20 note.
How much change should she get?

4 First to run a mile in under 4 minutes was Roger Bannister in 1954.

In 1997, the world mile record was 3 minutes 45.78 seconds.
How much under 4 minutes is the 1997 record time?

Starting points

You need to know about ...

... so try these questions

A Angles and turning

- ◆ An angle shows an amount of turn.

- ◆ Angles are measured with an angle measurer or protractor.

- ◆ Angles are measured in **degrees**.
  Sixty-five degrees is written as 65°.

- ◆ A full turn is 360°.

- ◆ A turn can be **clockwise** or **anti-clockwise**.

- ◆ A full turn clockwise has the same effect as a full turn anti-clockwise.

- ◆ A turn can also be to the left or to the right.

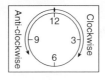

A1 How many degrees in:

 a a $\frac{1}{4}$ turn

 b a $\frac{1}{2}$ turn

 c a $\frac{3}{4}$ turn?

A2 Copy and complete this table.

Equal Turns	
Clockwise	Anti-clockwise
$\frac{1}{4}$	■
■	$\frac{1}{2}$
$\frac{3}{4}$	■

Words used to describe angles

- ◆ An angle of 90° is called a right angle.
  A right angle can be shown on a diagram like this:

- ◆ An angle between 0° and 90° is called an acute angle.

- ◆ An angle between 90° and 180° is called an obtuse angle.

- ◆ An angle between 180° and 360° is called a reflex angle.

Acute angle	Obtuse angle	Reflex angle

Exercise 5.1

Practise describing angles

1 Copy and complete this table.

Angle	Acute	Obtuse	Reflex
54°	✓		
165°			
188°			
75°			
252°			✓
104°			
16°			
304°			
179°		✓	
197°			

2 In this diagram, angle **c** is obtuse.

List each of the other angles and label them: acute *or* obtuse *or* reflex *or* a right angle.

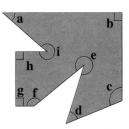

Measuring angles

Skill 5A
Measuring an angle

When you place the measurer the cross at its centre must be over the point where the two lines of the angle meet.

When you read off, make sure you use the right scale. This is an acute angle, so it is less than 90°.

This is how you measure an angle accurately with an angle measurer:

◆ Place the measurer over the angle.

◆ Line up the 0 line with the start of the angle.

◆ Look for the angle line on the scale.

◆ Read the degrees from the scale.

This angle is 35°.

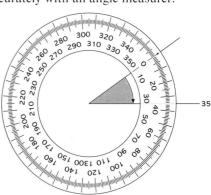

Exercise 5.2
Practising Skill 5A

1 Measure each of these angles.

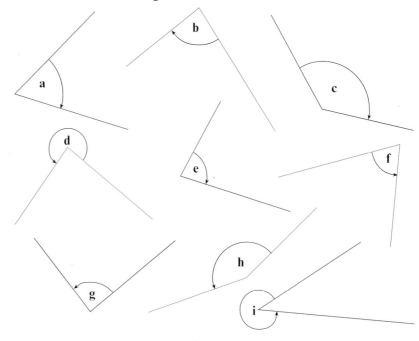

2 Measure each angle in this shape.

3 Which of the angles is obtuse?

4 Find the total of angles **a**, **b**, **c**, and **d**.

5 Calculate **a** + **b**.

6 Calculate **c** + **d**.

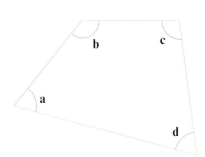

7 Measure each of the angles **a** to **k**.

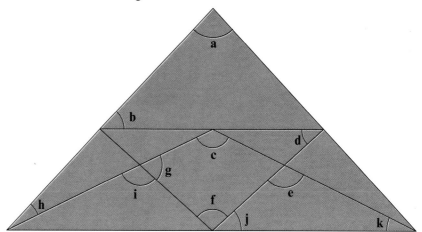

8 Which of the angles **a** to **k** are obtuse angles?

Drawing angles

Skill 5B
Drawing angles

When you place the
measurer, the cross at its
centre must be over the
point of the angle.

Example

Draw an angle of 40°.

A _____

♦ Mark the point of the angle (A).

♦ Draw a start line from A.

♦ Place the measurer over the
   start line.

♦ Line up 0° on the scale with
   the start line.

♦ Find 40° on the scale.

♦ Mark the 40° point with
   a pencil.

♦ Join the 40° mark to the point
   of the angle.

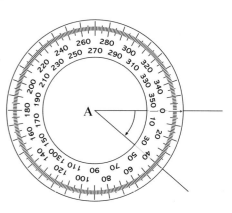

Exercise 5.3
Practising Skill 5B

1 Draw and label each of these angles.

a 50°   b 70°   c 110°   d 150°   e 200°

2 Draw and label each of these angles.

a 65°   b 35°   c 135°   d 205°   e 175°

3 Draw and label angles of:

a 38°   b 172°   c 216°   d 365°   e 17°

4 On the same diagram draw and label angles of 335° and 25°.

Starting points
You need to know about ...   ... so try these questions

A Ordering whole numbers

  Skill 1A: *see page 13*

B Using the signs > and <

  > means **greater than** and < means **less than**.

  These signs can be used to show the order of numbers

  Example   6780 > 6078 means **6780 is greater than 6078**.

C Reading scales not marked in single units

  To read some scales you will need to estimate.

  Example   What value is shown by arrow B?

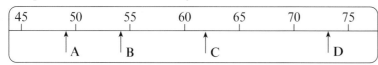

  Each gap stands for 5 units.
  Arrow B is just before 55, so it reads about 54.

A1 Put these numbers in order, smallest first.
8050, 5080, 5800, 8500, 8005

A2 What is the largest 4-digit number you can make using all the digits 8, 0, 4 and 7?

B1 Use either > or < in place of the ■ to make each correct.
a 756 ■ 2365 b 143 ■ 134
c 4564 ■ 4645 d 108 ■ 1800
e 9 million ■ 11 020 400

C1 What reading is shown by:
a arrow A
b arrow C?

C2 How many units are there between:
a arrow A and arrow D
b arrow B and arrow C?

Ordering negative numbers

Skill 6A
Ordering negative numbers

♦ To order two numbers you must know their place on a number line.

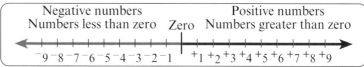

As you move to the right the numbers become greater, so:

Example 1

$^+2$ is greater than $^-3$ or $^+2 > ^-3$

Example 2

$^-8$ is less than $^-5$ or $^-8 < ^-5$

♦ To order a list of numbers from small to large:
  ❖ put them on a number line
  ❖ list them from left to right.

Example

List these numbers in order, smallest first.   5, $^-4$, $^-1$, $^-12$, 45, $^-8$

On the number line their positions are $^-12$ ... $^-8$ ... $^-4$ ... $^-1$ ... 5 ... 45

So, in order they are $^-12$, $^-8$, $^-4$, $^-1$, 5, 45

Exercise 6.1
Practising Skill 6A

1 Is each of these true or false?
a $^-4$ is less than $^+3$
b $^+2$ is greater than $^-12$
c $^-8$ is greater than $^+3$
d $^-8$ is less than $^-15$
e $^-1$ is greater than $^-5$
f $^+2$ is less than $^-14$
g $^-56$ is greater than $^-57$
h 5 is less than $^-746$

Remember that 5 is the same as $^+5$.

2 Copy each of these but change the ■ to > or < to make each true.
a $^-6$ ■ $^-4$ b 0 ■ $^-3$ c $^-3$ ■ $^-9$
d 5 ■ $^-6$ e $^-2$ ■ 2 f $^-10$ ■ $^-67$

3 Put each set of numbers in order, smallest first.
a $^-4, 2, ^-2$ b $^-2, ^-5, ^-3, ^-7, 0, ^-12$
c $6, ^-6, 5, ^-5, 4, ^-4, ^-8, 2$ d $7, ^-56, ^-4, ^-12, ^-3, 45$

4 Mark tried to put these numbers in order, smallest first.
What is wrong with his list? $^-2, ^-4, ^-6, 7, 8, 9$

5 Put these numbers in order, **largest** first. $^-7, ^-12, 5, ^-4, 0, ^-6$

Exercise 6.2
Using Skill 6A

1 Which is colder: $^-8°C$ or $^-5°C$?

2 Which is warmer: $^-2°C$ or $^-4°C$?

3 These were the temperatures in some cities on 1 January.
London $^-1°C$, Vladivostok $^-52°C$, Bombay $20°C$, Helsinki $^-12°C$,
New York $^-5°C$, Sydney $32°C$, Warsaw $^-7°C$.
Put these cities in order starting with the coldest.

4 These are the temperatures of five freezer boxes in a store.
A $^-6°C$ B $^-2°C$ C $^-18°C$ D $^-12°C$ E $^-17°C$.

Servicing is done on the warmest boxes first.
In what order will the boxes be serviced?

Temperature changes

Skill 6B
Finding temperature changes

You can use moves on a number line to work out temperature changes.

Example 1   The temperature is $^-5°C$ and rises by 8 degrees.
What is the new temperature?

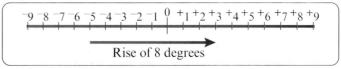
Rise of 8 degrees

So the new temperature is **3°C.**

Example 2   The temperature is $^-2°C$ and falls by 6 degrees.

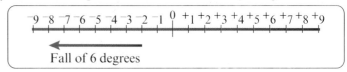
Fall of 6 degrees

So the new temperature is **$^-8°C$.**

Exercise 6.3
Practising Skill 6B

1 Find the new temperature in each of these.
a   a rise of 4 degrees from $^-1°C$ b   a fall of 7 degrees from $2°C$
c   a fall of 3 degrees from $^-5°C$ d   a rise of 7 degrees from $^-9°C$
e   a rise of 6 degrees from $^-5°C$ f   a fall of 6 degrees from $2°C$
g   a fall of 4 degrees from $^-6°C$ h   a rise of 20 degrees from $^-2°C$
i   a fall of 30 degrees from $^-5°C$ j   a fall of 16 degrees from $4°C$
k   a rise of 64 degrees from $^-50°C$ l   a fall of 38 degrees from $^-5°C$

2 Copy the table and fill in the gaps.

	Starting temperature	Change	Final
a	⁻6 °C	Rise of 4 degrees	■
b	7 °C	Fall of 15 degrees	■
c	■	Rise of 2 degrees	⁻5 °C
d	4 °C	■	⁻2 °C
e	⁻3 °C	■	2 °C
f	■	Fall of 6 degrees	⁻4 °C
g	⁻12 °C	■	⁻14 °C
h	⁻7 °C	■	5 °C
i	■	Rise of 16 degrees	6 °C

A sequence is a set of numbers written in order by a rule. For example, the sequence of the first 5 odd numbers is: 1, 3, 5, 7, 9

3 Continue each sequence for the next three terms:

a ⁻8, ⁻6, ⁻4, __, __, __   b 10, 7, 4, __, __, __

c ⁻15, ⁻11, ⁻7, __, __, __   d 17, 10, 3, __, __, __

Exercise 6.4
Using Skill 6B

1 The temperature in Moscow rose from ⁻3 °C on Monday to 4 °C on Tuesday. How many degrees did it rise?

2 The liquid was cooled from 4 °C to ⁻56 °C. How many degrees did its temperature fall?

3 The temperatures in three cities were measured at midday and midnight.

City	Midday	Midnight
Berlin	16 °C	⁻4 °C
Anchorage	⁻34 °C	⁻52 °C
New York	4 °C	⁻17 °C

In which city did the temperature change most between midday and midnight? Explain your answer.

4 These thermometers show the temperature in °C in South Georgia at different times in a day.

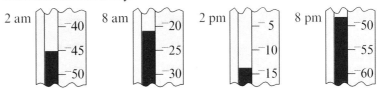

Describe how the temperature changed between each reading.

5 In an experiment the temperature of oxygen in a freezer fell by 6 degrees every hour. The oxygen started at a temperature of 13 °C.

a What was its temperature after one hour?

b Write a sequence for its temperatures after each of the first five hours.

6 The air temperature outside a plane drops by 7 degrees for every 1000 metres it climbs. The temperature at ground level is 18 °C.

What is the temperature at 5000 metres?

Adding and subtracting negative numbers

Skill 6C
Adding with negative
numbers

♦ A number line can help when you add positive and negative numbers.

❖ If you **add a positive number** the answer will be greater.
❖ If you **add a negative number** the answer will be lower.

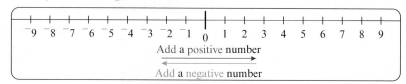

Example   Calculate the value of $7 + {}^-4$

Start from 7
Add $^-4$ ... go left by 4 spaces
So $7 + {}^-4 = 3$

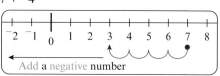

Exercise 6.5
Practising Skill 6C

1   Show the calculation $^-5 + 7 = 2$ on a number line.

2   **a**   Show the calculation $4 + {}^-6$ on a number line.
     b   What is the answer to $4 + {}^-6$?

3   Use a number line to help you give the answers to these calculations.
     a $^-4 + 2 =$ **b** $^-4 + {}^-2 =$ **c** $^-2 + 4 =$ **d** $^-2 + {}^-4 =$

4   Copy and complete these calculations.
     a $^-5 + {}^-3 =$ **b** $6 + {}^-5 =$ **c** $^-4 + 3 =$ **d** $^-4 + {}^-5 =$
     e $3 + {}^-7 =$ **f** $^-3 + 3 =$ **g** $5 + {}^-5 =$ **h** $0 + {}^-6 =$

Skill 6D
Subtracting with
negative numbers

♦ If you **subtract a positive number** the answer will be lower.
   So if you **subtract a negative number** the answer will be greater.

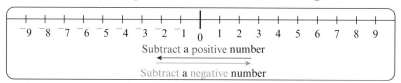

Example   Calculate the value of $^-2 - {}^-5$

Start from $^-2$
Subtract $^-5$ ... go right by 5 spaces
Then $2 - {}^-5 = 3$

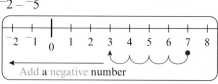

Exercise 6.6
Practising Skill 6D

1   Use a number line to help you give the answers to these calculations.
     a $^-4 - 2 =$ **b** $^-4 - {}^-2 =$ **c** $^-2 - 4 =$ **d** $^-2 - {}^-4 =$

2   Copy and complete these calculations.
     a $^-5 - {}^-3 =$ **b** $6 - {}^-5 =$ **c** $^-4 - 3 =$ **d** $^-4 - {}^-5 =$
     e $3 - {}^-7 =$ **f** $^-3 - 3 =$ **g** $5 - {}^-5 =$ **h** $0 - {}^-6 =$

Multiplying and dividing negative numbers

Skill 6E
Multiplying with negative numbers

Multiplying numbers gives either a negative or a positive answer.

Negative **answer**	Positive **answer**
Positive × Negative	Positive × Positive
Negative × Positive	Negative × Negative

Example

What is the value of $^-3 \times 7$?

This is Negative × Positive, which gives a Negative answer.

So $^-3 \times 7 = ^-21.$

Exercise 6.7
Practising Skill 6E

1 Say if each of these gives a negative or a positive answer.

    a $^-6 \times ^-4$ **b** $^-5 \times 5$ **c** $7 \times ^-4$ **d** $^-2 \times ^-1$

    e 6×7 **f** $23 \times ^-7$ **g** $^-87 \times ^-34$ **h** $^-9 \times 586$

2 Copy and complete these calculations.

    a $3 \times ^-5 =$ **b** $^-2 \times 6 =$ **c** $5 \times ^-4 =$ **d** $^-3 \times ^-6 =$

    e $^-12 \times ^-3 =$ **f** $^-8 \times 4 =$ **g** $24 \times ^-6 =$ **h** $^-40 \times 5 =$

3 Which of these calculations is not right? If the answer is wrong say why.

    a $^-5 \times ^-5 = 25$ **b** $^-2 \times ^-6 = 12$ **c** $^-5 \times ^-4 = ^-20$ **d** $^-2 \times 4 = ^-6$

    e $8 \times ^-4 = 32$ **f** $^-5 \times ^-3 = ^-15$ **g** $^-6 \times 2 = ^-12$ **h** $7 \times ^-5 = ^-25$

Skill 6F
Multiplying with negative numbers

Dividing numbers uses the same rules as multiplying.

Negative **answer**	Positive **answer**
Positive ÷ Negative	Positive ÷ Positive
Negative ÷ Positive	Negative ÷ Negative

Example

What is the value of $^-21 \div ^-7$?

This is Negative ÷ Negative, which gives a Positive answer.

So $^-21 \div ^-7 = 3.$

Exercise 6.8
Practising Skill 6F

1 Say if each of these gives a negative or a positive answer.

    a $^-6 \div ^-2$ **b** $^-5 \div ^-5$ **c** $28 \div ^-4$ **d** $^-2 \div ^-1$

    e $63 \div 7$ **f** $^-56 \div 7$ **g** $^-20 \div ^-4$ **h** $^-945 \div 5$

2 Copy and complete these calculations.

    a $35 \div ^-5 =$ **b** $^-6 \div 2 =$ **c** $16 \div ^-4 =$ **d** $^-36 \div ^-6 =$

    e $^-12 \div ^-3 =$ **f** $^-8 \div 4 =$ **g** $24 \div ^-6 =$ **h** $^-40 \div 5 =$

3 What is wrong with each of these answers?

    a $^-5 \div ^-5 = ^-1$ **b** $^-12 \div ^-6 = 6$ **c** $^-36 \div 4 = 9$ **d** $12 \div ^-4 = ^-6$

    e $^-15 \div ^-5 = ^-3$ **f** $20 \div ^-10 = 2$ **g** $^-10 \div ^-20 = 2$ **h** $^-6 \div ^-6 = ^-1$

Negative coordinates

◆ A coordinate fixes a position on a grid.

◆ It has two numbers which can be either positive or negative.
(*x* number, *y* number)

◆ *x* numbers are greater going to the right
y numbers are greater going upwards.

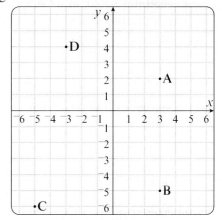

Examples

The coordinates of the points are:

A (3, 2)   B (3, ⁻5)
C (⁻5, ⁻6)   D (⁻3, 4)

Exercise 6.9
Practising coordinates

1 On this grid what are the coordinates of points P to V?

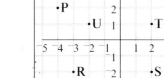

2 **a** Make a copy of the axes shown.
    b Mark and label the points:
        A (⁻2, ⁻3)   B (1, ⁻4)
        C (⁻3, 5)   D (3, ⁻2)

3 What is the coordinate of a point:

  a 2 squares straight above (3, ⁻4)
  b 3 squares right of (⁻1, ⁻3)
  c 1 square below (3, 0)
  d 4 squares left of (1, 2)?

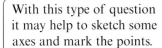

With this type of question it may help to sketch some axes and mark the points.

4 Which one of these coordinates lies straight above the coordinate (⁻5, ⁻1)?
(⁻12, 5), (5, ⁻12), (12, ⁻4), (⁻5, ⁻4), (8, ⁻5), (⁻5, 7), (7, ⁻5)

5 Which of these points lies on the same horizontal line as the point (3, ⁻2)?
(⁻2, 3), (3, 2), (4, ⁻6), (2, ⁻2), (8, ⁻2), (⁻2, 8)

6 Is the point (3, ⁻2) to the right or the left of the point (⁻2, 3)?

7 Is the point (⁻5, 4) above or below the point (7, 2)?

8 Is the point (⁻4.5, 2.5) above or below the point (2.5, ⁻4.5)?

9 This square has the coordinates of A and B given.
What are the coordinates of C and D?

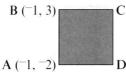

10 Put these coordinates in order, from left to right.
(5, ⁻4), (⁻6, ⁻4), (4.5, ⁻4), (⁻2.3, ⁻4), (0, ⁻4), (⁻2.9, ⁻4)

11 Put these coordinates in height order. Start from the highest one.
(⁻5, 3), (2, ⁻4), (0, 6.7), (15, ⁻2.6)

This revises the work in Sections 1 to 6

1 Give the value of the digit 4 in each number.

   a 147   **b** 408   **c** 1054

   d 4 765 001 **e** 60 451   **f** 41 567 129

2 Skill 1A

Put each set of numbers in order, smallest first.

   a 157, 63, 1053, 575, 14, 6, 1305

   b 160 504, 15 766, 150 405, 106 540, 15 677, 51, 108

3 Skill 1B

Write each of these numbers in words.

   a 863   **b** 3504   **c** 16052

   d 7 082 207 **e** 834 902 **f** 65 802 301

4 Skill 1C

Write each of these numbers in digits.

   a eight thousand and seventeen

   b one million and five

   c two million two hundred and twenty thousand

5 Does the word **HOOD** have a horizontal or vertical line of symmetry?

Copy the word and draw in the line of symmetry.

6 Sketch this road sign and draw in any lines of symmetry.

7 What is the order of rotational symmetry for this shape?

8 How many planes of symmetry has a stapler?

9 Skill 3A

Add these mentally

   a 9 + 5 + 7 + 8 **b** 76 + 58 **c** 88 + 65

10 Skill 3B

Add these by a pencil-and-paper method.

   a 58 + 44 + 138 + 9 + 204

   b 1058 + 56 + 3 + 206 + 182

11 Skill 3C

Subtract these without using a calculator.

   a 93 006 − 8457   **b** 40 502 − 26 835

12 Skill 3D

Multiply these numbers without a calculator.

   a 68×47 **b** 84×56 **c** 584×39

13 Skill 3E

Divide these numbers without a calculator.

   a $2984 \div 8$ **b** $3822 \div 14$ **c** $7633 \div 23$

14 Write each of these decimal fractions in words.

   a 0.504   **b** 0.025   **c** 0.38

15 Give the value of the digit 8 in each of these.

   a 0.185   **b** 0.3481   **c** 0.804

16 Which of these measurements is between 6.5 m and 6.6 m?

   a 6.58 m   **b** 6.601 m   **c** 5.599 m

17 Skill 4A

Put each set of decimals in order, smallest first.

   a 0.056, 0.35, 2.01, 0.6, 1.08, 0.26

   b 0.701, 0.007, 0.17, 0.71, 7.1, 1.07

18 Skill 4B

Calculate the answer to each of these.

   a 1.25 + 3.04 + 12.6   **b** 15.3 + 8.68 + 154.6

19 Skill 4C

Calculate the answer to each of these.

   a 28.63 − 14.7   **b** 50.08 − 23.395

20 Is each of these angles acute, obtuse, or reflex?

   a 76° **b** 245° **c** 27° **d** 155° **e** 6°

21 Skill 5A

   a Draw a triangle and measure each angle.

   b Find the total of the three angles.

22 Skill 5B

Draw each of these angles.

   a 75° **b** 135° **c** 210° **d** 340° **e** 8°

23 Skill 6A

Put each set of numbers in order, smallest first.

   a 5, ⁻6, 4, ⁻3 , ⁻8   **b** 23, ⁻18, 6, ⁻9, 5, ⁻1

24 Skill 6B

Find the new temperature in each of these.

   a a rise of 6° from ⁻5°C **b** a fall of 8° from 3°C

25 Is the point (3, 5) above or below (3, ⁻1)?

26 Skill 6C and Skill 6D

Copy and complete these calculations.

   a ⁻8 + 5   **b** ⁻7 + ⁻4   **c** ⁻16 + ⁻5

   d ⁻2 + ⁻18 **e** ⁻8 − 9   **f** ⁻6 − 4

   g ⁻8 − ⁻5   **h** ⁻16 − ⁻5

27 Skill 6E and Skill 6F

Copy and complete each of these.

   a ⁻5 × 4   **b** ⁻6 × ⁻8   **c** 7 × ⁻3

   d ⁻7 × ⁻9 **e** ⁻36 ÷ 9 **f** ⁻40 ÷ ⁻5

   g 35 ÷ ⁻7   **h** ⁻81 ÷ 9

Decorum Design

DDC is the favourite shop for trade and private buyers who want a new look for bathrooms, kitchens and bedrooms. Here are some of our items but come to the shop to see our full range.

■ WALLPAPER – rolls

width 53 cm, length 10 metres.

FLORAL DESIGN **£5.49** per roll.

£4.97 each for 12 rolls or more

ANTIQUE EMBOSSED **£7.99** per roll

WALLPAPER PASTE **£4.99** – covers 10 sq metres

> TRY OUR ANTIQUE EMBOSSED PAPERS TO COVER THAT TATTY WALL

> ALL PAINT PRICES REDUCED BY 25% FOR NEXT THREE WEEKS

■ EMULSION PAINTS – Top quality own brand

BRILLIANT WHITE	$1\frac{1}{2}$ litre	£3.42
	2 litre	£8.45
	5 litre	£16.99
PASTEL SHADES	$2\frac{1}{2}$ litre	£11.99
	5 litre	£19.49

A litre tin will cover about 8 m² with a single coat. Two coats needed over very dark surfaces.

When calculating how much paint to order, do not subtract the area of doors and windows.

■ WALL TILES – imported Italian and French

JARDIN RANGE – **£1.79** each or **£16.99** a box (10 tiles)

ASSISI RANGE – **£1.99** each or **£18.99** a box (10 tiles)

JARDIN

ASSISI

For those who have not caught up with metric units yet.

1 foot = 0.3048 metres   1 inch = 25.4 millimetres

All prices include VAT

TILE-FIX CEMENT – **£7.99** a tub, covers 4 sq. metres

FORRET – Box of 10 wall tiles **£12.50**

BENETIA – Box of 10 tiles **£16**

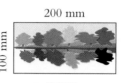

FORRE

BENETIA

■ FLOOR TILES

QUARRY TILES – terracotta, 120 mm x 120 mm, 31p each

CERAMIC REGULAR SHAPED TILES – choice of patterns

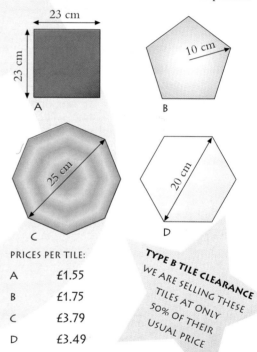

PRICES PER TILE:

A	£1.55
B	£1.75
C	£3.79
D	£3.49

> TYPE B TILE CLEARANCE WE ARE SELLING THESE TILES AT ONLY 50% OF THEIR USUAL PRICE

We also sell small square tiles to fit with our type C tile. Pack of ten **£5.75**

TILE CEMENT – 12 kg bag – **£17.89** – enough for 10 square metres of floor.

COLOURED GROUT **£7.69** per tub – enough for 15 square metres of floor.

When calculating what to order, allow one complete tile for every part of a tile you need.

■ KITCHEN BASE UNITS

SPECIAL PRICE   **£756** for 12 base units

1   How much each are Quarry tiles?

2   How much is one Jardin range tile?

3   How much is a box of Benetia tiles?

4   How much is a 12 kg bag of Tile Cement?

5   How much will you pay in total for a 5 litre tin of white emulsion and a $2\frac{1}{2}$ litre tin of coloured emulsion paint?

6   What is the cost of 6 rolls of floral design wallpaper?

7   Emma has £50 to spend.
    She buys 5 rolls of antique embossed wallpaper and one packet of wallpaper paste.
    How much money will she have left?

8   This receipt shows what Jim bought at Decorum.

DECORUM DESIGN
Westleigh

    3 Rolls Floral paper   £16.47
    2 Rolls Antique Emb.   £15.98
    1 Wallpaper Paste   £ 4.99
    1 Tilefix Cement   £ 7.99

                    ***TOTAL

    a   What was the total for this receipt?
    b   How much change did Jim have from £50?

9   Find the total cost of five 1 litre tins of white emulsion paint.

10 a   Which is cheaper:
        five 1 litre tins of white emulsion
        or one 5 litre tin of white emulsion?
    b   By how much is it cheaper?

11 How much more does one Assisi tile cost than one Jardin tile?

12 Kurt wanted 215 Jardin tiles.
    He decided to buy 22 boxes of tiles.

    a   How many spare tiles did Kurt buy?
    b   How much did he pay for all the tiles?

13 Ewan worked out that he needed exactly 432 tiles for a job. He always buys 15 tiles extra.

    a   How many tiles will he need to buy in total?

    He decides to buy boxes of Assisi tiles and some single tiles to make up the total he needs.

    b   How many boxes of tiles should Ewan buy?
    c   How many single tiles should he buy?
    d   What will these tiles cost him in total?

e   Ewan allowed £850 for the tiles.
    How much money was left over?

14 This diagram shows one corner of a type B ceramic tile.

    a   Is the angle at each corner of the tile acute, obtuse, or reflex?
    b   How many angles like this are in a type B tile?
    c   Measure the angle.
    d   Is the angle larger or smaller than 110°?
    e   What is the total of all the angles at the corners of one type B tile?

15 What do you think is the angle at each corner of a type A ceramic tile?

16 Sketch a type A tile and show how you think the angles at each corner should be marked.

17 Trace the angle at one corner of a type D tile.
    a   Measure the angle.
    b   Is the angle larger or smaller than 110°?

18 One tub of Coloured Grout is enough for how many square metres of floor?

19 How many tubs of Coloured Grout are needed for 200 square metres of floor?

20 A changing room has 180 square metres of tiled floor that needs to be grouted.
    a   How many tubs of coloured grout are needed?
    b   What will be the total cost of these tubs?

21 Paint prices are reduced by 25%. Is this $\frac{1}{2}$ off, $\frac{1}{3}$ off, or $\frac{1}{4}$ off?

22 Without using a calculator, find the cost of one kitchen base unit.

23 Without using a calculator, find the total cost of 147 boxes of Benetia tiles.

24 Decorum Design order tiles in bulk.
    Last week they ordered:

    | 104520 | Foret tiles |
    | 107050 | Benetia tiles |
    | 107500 | Type A ceramic tiles |
    | 250000 | Quarry tiles |
    | 95040 | Jardin tiles |
    | 94880 | Assissi tiles |

    a   List the number of tiles in descending order.
    b   How many tiles were ordered last week?
        Do not use a calculator for this.

Starting points

You need to know about ...   ... so try these questions

A Letters for numbers

Letters can be used to stand for numbers

Three dice a, b, and c are rolled
For the score you:
add the numbers on dice a and b
then subtract the number on dice c.

Die Die Die
a b c

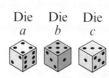

We can write: Score = $a + b - c$

So a, b and c can be any number from 1 to 6

When $a = 4$, $b = 5$ and $c = 3$
  Score = $a + b - c$
  Score = $4 + 5 - 3$
  Score = 6

A1 Score = $a + b - c$
Calculate Score when:
$a = 6$, $b = 4$, and $c = 5$

A2 Score = $p - w + y$
Calculate Score when:
  a $p = 4$, $w = 6$, and $y = 3$
  b $p = 5$, $w = 2$, and $y = 6$
  c $p = 4$, $w = 4$, and $y = 1$
  d $p = 2$, $w = 6$, and $y = 1$

A3 If $n = h - t - k$
calculate n when:
  a $h = 12$, $t = 4$, and $k = 1$
  b $h = 15$, $t = 8$, and $k = 5$
  c $h = 14$, $t = 9$, and $k = 7$
  d $h = 11$, $t = 5$ and $k = 6$

Collecting like terms

Skill 7A
Collecting like terms

Collecting like terms is when you group letters that are used.
It is sometimes called **simplifying**.

Example 1   Simplify

$a + a + b + b + a$
$a + a + b + b + a = 3a + 2b$

$3a$ is the same as:
$a + a + a$ or $3 \times a$

---

b is the same as:
$1b$ or $1 \times b$

As $3 - 17 + 9 = {}^-5$
In the same way
$3y - 17y + 9y = {}^-5y$

Example 2   Simplify

$15a + 4b - 2a - b = 13a + 3b$

Example 3   Collect like terms to simplify

$6c + 3y - 4c - 17y + 9y + c = 2c - 5y$

Exercise 7.1
Practising Skill 7A

1   In each of these, collect like terms.

  a $w + k + w + w + w + k =$
  b $h + f + f + h + h + h + f + f =$
  c $n + a + n + a + n + a + n =$
  d $y + y + a + a + a + a + y + a =$
  e $p + p + a - p - a - p + a + a =$
  f $b + c + c + b + a + b + a =$
  g $w + e + t + t + e + w + e + e =$
  h $r + t + v + w + r + w + r =$

2   Collect like terms to simplify each of these.

  a $3w + 5w + 12w - 8w =$
  b $15y - 9y + 6y - 8y =$
  c $5k - 11k + 8k - k + 2k =$
  d $23a + 5b - 19a + 3b =$
  e $55h + 32f - 13h - 29f + 2h =$
  f $14y - 42b - y + 57b + b =$
  g $67w - 15b - 38w + b + 12b =$
  h $100h + 200k - 55h - 250k =$

3   Simplify each of these.

  a $12y - 25y =$
  b $125k - 180k =$
  c $45h + 35h - 55h - 66h =$
  d $2n - 8n - 11n - n =$

4   Ian collected like terms and made an answer of $4a - 3b$.
Give an example of something that simplifies to this answer.

Collecting like terms is a skill you need not only in algebra.

Example

What is the perimeter of this shape?
Simplify your answer.

If the perimeter of the shape is P:

$$P = 3a + 3a + b + b$$

So $P = 6a + 2b$.

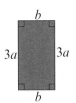

> The perimeter of a shape is the total distance around its edges.

Exercise 7.2
Using skill 7A

1 What is the perimeter of each shape?
Simplify each of your answers.

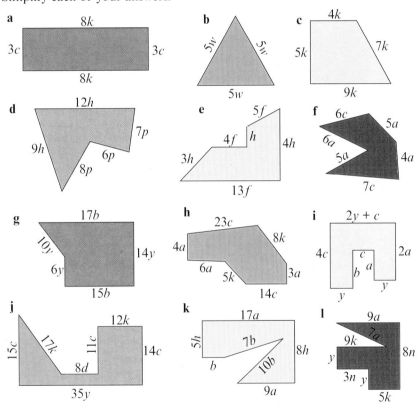

2 Find the missing length in each of these diagrams.

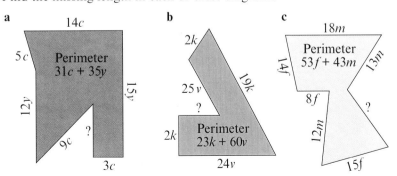

3 What does the ■ stand for in each of these?

    a $5y + 3n - ■ + n = 3y + 4n$ **b** $■ - 8w + k + 13w = 13k + 5w$

Expanding brackets

Skill 7B
Expanding brackets

> The 2 shows that there are 2 lots of 3 + 5.
>
> Or $2 \times (3 + 5)$

◆ Brackets are used to package parts of a calculation.
They are used when you have to add and multiply in the same calculation.

Example

Find the value of $2(3 + 5)$
Think of this as: $2(\blacksquare + \blacksquare + \blacksquare + \blacksquare + \blacksquare + \blacksquare + \blacksquare + \blacksquare)$
or $(\blacksquare + \blacksquare + \blacksquare + \blacksquare + \blacksquare + \blacksquare + \blacksquare + \blacksquare) + (\blacksquare + \blacksquare + \blacksquare + \blacksquare + \blacksquare + \blacksquare + \blacksquare + \blacksquare)$
or $\blacksquare + \blacksquare + \blacksquare + \blacksquare + \blacksquare + \blacksquare + \blacksquare + \blacksquare + \blacksquare + \blacksquare + \blacksquare + \blacksquare + \blacksquare + \blacksquare + \blacksquare + \blacksquare$
or $\qquad 2 \times 3 \qquad\qquad\qquad 2 \times 5$

So 2(3 + 5) is the same as $2 \times 3 + 2 \times 5$.

◆ Each term inside the bracket is multiplied by the term outside the bracket.

> Expand brackets is the same as:
> remove the brackets, or multiply out the brackets

Example 1 Expand these brackets $2(3a + 5b)$
$2(3a + 5b) = 6a + 10b$ $\qquad [6a = 2 \times 3a]$

Example 2 Remove the brackets from $3(5y - 4a + k)$
$3(5y - 4a + k) = 15y - 12a + 3k$

Example 3 Multiply out $4(c + 3f - 12n + 1)$
$4(c + 3f - 12n + 1) = 4c + 12f - 48n + 4$

Exercise 7.3
Practising Skill 7B

1 In each of these, expand the brackets.

 a $4(3y - 5k)$ b $5(6h - 3)$ c $12(4f + 7v)$
 d $9(12v + 9n)$ e $8(11y - 2)$ f $4(4h + 5k)$
 g $7(9v + 1)$ h $5(y - f)$ i $6(k + 3a - y)$

2 Remove each of these brackets.

 a $6(4n - 5v + w)$ b $7(h - 8y + 9k)$ c $7(a + y - k)$
 d $5(2n + w - 12a)$ e $15(w - a + 2b)$ f $6(12 - h + 3w + 6b)$
 g $4(5f - y - w + 1)$ h $10(5 - 3v + w - 5c)$ i $50(3a - 3 + y)$

3 Multiply out each of these brackets.

 a $5(8k - w + 1)$ b $7(9f + 3 - y + 5w)$ c $5(3 - h - k + 5w)$
 d $6(w + 3 - y + 3n)$ e $25(4 - 3a + 8n)$ f $150(3 + 4a - w)$

◆ You may have to collect like terms after expanding brackets.

Example 1

> Simplify here means to collect like terms **after** removing the brackets.

Remove the brackets and simplify $3(4a - b) + 2(a + 5b)$

$\qquad 3(4a - b) + 2(a + 5b) = 12a - 3b + 2a + 10b$

Now collect like terms $\qquad = 14a + 7b$

So 3(4a - b) + 2(a + 5b) = 14a + 7b.

Exercise 7.4
Practising Skills 7A and 7B

1 Remove the brackets and simplify each of these.

 a $2(7y + 5k) + 4(5k - 2y)$ b $5(6k - 3w) + 2(8w + 3k)$
 c $5(2w + y + 6f) + 3(f - 3w)$ d $8(2n - 6) + 5(a + 4n + 20)$
 e $6(3y + 2a) + 4(a - 5y) + 5(2y - 3a)$

Starting points

You need to know about ...   ... so try these questions

A Collecting data

A **data collection sheet** is any form or table used to collect data.

To the BDA,
10 Queen Anne Street, London W1M 0BD
Tel: 0171-323 1531

*A charity helping people with diabetes
and supporting diabetes research.*

I enclose a cheque/postal order*
payable to the BDA £ _____

Debit my Access/Visa* card
by the amount of   £ _____
Card number ☐☐☐☐☐☐☐☐☐☐☐☐☐☐☐☐
Expiry data   ☐☐☐☐
            Please send me more information
                and membership details

Name _____
Address _____

Signature _____
*Delete which is inapplicable   Reg. Charity no. 215199

Name	Length of thumb (cm)	Length of foot (cm)	Height (cm)
Sam			
Wasim			
Liz			
Shane			
Des			
Linda			
Dean			
Nisha			

Body Matters

A **questionnaire** collects data by asking questions.

Sleep Questionnaire

1 What is your name ?   _____

2 How old are you ? (years)   _____

3 What time do you usually go to bed ? _____

> **A1** Design a data collection sheet with 6 questions to use for a traffic survey.

Types of question

You can use different types of questions on a questionnaire:

◆ multi-choice questions, such as:

7 What do you sleep on ?

Please tick one box only   ☐ Back   ☐ Front   ☐ Side

◆ multi-choice questions with a scale, such as:

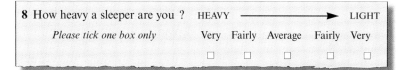

8 How heavy a sleeper are you ?   HEAVY ⟶ LIGHT

Please tick one box only   Very   Fairly   Average   Fairly   Very

☐   ☐   ☐   ☐   ☐

◆ questions with Yes or No answers, such as:

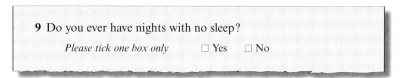

9 Do you ever have nights with no sleep?

Please tick one box only   ☐ Yes   ☐ No

Exercise 8.1
Types of question

1 Design a questionnaire about sleep with different types of question.

Surveys using data

The reason for doing a survey using data is:

♦ to test if a **statement** is true, or

♦ to answer a **question**.

For example, the start of a survey into sleep might be:
  Statement – Most people sleep more than 7 hours a night.
  Question – How long do people sleep at night?

You can carry out a survey in four stages:

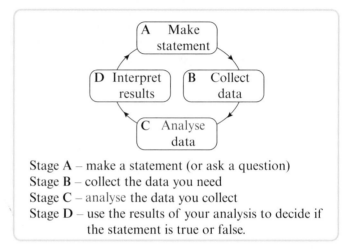

Stage A – make a statement (or ask a question)
Stage B – collect the data you need
Stage C – analyse the data you collect
Stage D – use the results of your analysis to decide if
         the statement is true or false.

> To analyse means to look at very closely.

Stage D may give you an idea for a follow-up survey.

For example, the start of a follow-up into sleep could be:
  Statement – People need more sleep in the winter.
  Question – Is there a link between sleep and time of year?

Exercise 8.2
Surveys using data

1   _Most people sleep more than 7 hours a night._

   a Decide what data to collect to test this statement.
   b Design a data collection sheet.
   c Use your sheet and collect the data.
   d Analyse the data you collect.
   e Is the statement true or false?
      Explain your answer.

2   _Do older people sleep less than younger people?_

   a Decide what data you need to test this statement.
   b Do a survey to answer this question.

3   a Make a statement, or ask a question, of your own about sleep.
   b Do a survey.

Designing and criticising questions

Skill 8A
Designing questions

For a questionnaire, the questions must be designed to:

◆ make them easy to answer

◆ make sure the answers give the data you need.

Poor question	Why it is poor	Better question
How much sleep did you get last night? ☐ Less than average ☐ About average ☐ More than average	This question is **not clear**: the words need to be more exact. (Different people have different ideas what 'average' means.)	How much sleep did you get last night? ☐ Less than 8 hours ☐ About 8 hours ☐ More than 8 hours
Do you agree that we need at least 8 hours sleep each night? ☐ Yes ☐ No ☐ Not sure	This is a **leading** question: it leads people to give one answer. (The question seems to expect the answer 'Yes'.)	Do you think we need at least 8 hours sleep each night? ☐ Yes ☐ No ☐ Not sure
What do you sleep on?	This question is **ambiguous**: it has more than one meaning. (The question is meant to be about position, but might be answered 'a bed'!)	What do you sleep on? ☐ Back ☐ Front ☐ Side

Exercise 8.3
Using Skill 8A

1　**a**　Explain why this question is not clear.
　　b　Write a better question.

> When do you usally go to bed?
> ☐ Early ☐ Late

2　**a**　Explain why this is a leading question.
　　b　Write a better question.

> You get a worse night sleep on a softbed, don't you

3　**a**　Explain why this question is ambiguous.
　　b　Write a better question.

> Where do you sleep best?

4

> ### Leisure Centre Survey
>
> **1**　Do you agree that the town needs a new leisure centre ?　☐ Yes　☐ No
>
> **2**　Would you be a frequent user of the centre ?　☐ Yes　☐ No
>
> **3**　Would you use the courts ?　☐ Yes　☐ No
>
> **4**　How much would you be prepared to pay to use the pool ?　☐ Less than £1.50
> 　　　　　　　　　　　　　　　　　　　　　　　　　　　　☐ Morethan £2.50

This questionnaire is about a new leisure centre.

a　What is wrong with each question?
b　Write a better question for each one

47

Experiments

Skill 8B
Designing experiments

Most surveys ask people to give a view on something, or ask about facts which are easy to remember.

> ## TV Survey
> 1 What is your favourite TV channel ?   □ BBC1 □ BBC2 □ ITV
>   □ Channel 4 □ Channel 5
> 2 Did you watch TV last night ?   □ Yes   □ No

The data needed for some surveys can only be collected:

◆ over a length of time

> How much time do people spend in a week watching each TV channel?

◆ by designing an experiment.

> People take longer to go to sleep when it is not dark.

The data collection sheet used for these types of survey can be called an **observation sheet.**

To design an experiment:

◆ decide what data you need

◆ decide how to collect it

◆ design an observation sheet.

Exercise 8.4
Using Skill 8B

1 Design an observation sheet to collect data on how much time people spend in a week watching each TV channel.

2 **a** Design an experiment to test this statement.
   b Do your experiment.
   c Analyse the data you collect.
   d Do you think the statement is true or false? Explain why.

> ***Body Matters***
> Your waist is roughly two times the distance around your neck.

3 **a** Design an experiment to answer this question.
   b Do your experiment.
   c Analyse the data you collect.
   d Interpret your results to answer the question.

> ***Body Matters***
> How many times do people blink in a day ?

4 **a** Design an experiment to test this statement.
   b Do your experiment.
   c Analyse the data you collect.
   d Do you think the statement is true or false? Explain why.

> ***Body Matters***
> Taller people do not have as good a sense of balance as shorter people.

Starting points
You need to know about ...

... so try these questions

A Rounding to the nearest ten

♦ Numbers can be rounded up or down to give an approximate value.

28	rounded to the nearest 10 is	30 (rounded up)
143	rounded to the nearest 10 is	140 (rounded down)
225	rounded to the nearest 10 is	230 (rounded up)

because half-way numbers are rounded up.
(225 is exactly half-way between 220 and 330.)

♦ When you round to the nearest 10 you must look at the Units digit

B Rounding to the nearest hundred

♦
245	rounded to the nearest 100 is	200 (rounded down)
388	rounded to the nearest 100 is	400 (rounded up)
1150	rounded to the nearest 100 is	1200 (rounded up)

♦ When you round to the nearest 100 you must look at the Tens digit.

A1 Round each of these numbers to the nearest ten.

a	326	**b**	675	**c**	14
d	1052	**e**	265	**f**	188
g	768	**h**	992	**i**	998
j	1275	**k**	1995	**l**	3904

B1 Round each of these numbers to the nearest hundred.

a	475	**b**	829	**c**	449
d	1550	**e**	1982	**f**	737
g	3450	**h**	9739	**i**	1067
j	205	**k**	5550	**l**	9005

B2 Give a number, rounded to the nearest 100, which gives 6700.

Rounding to the nearest 1000, 10000, 100000 or million

Skill 9A
Rounding to the nearest
1000, 10000,
100000, million

♦ Place values are important when you round large numbers.

Example 1   Round 34768 to the nearest 1000

Look at the hundreds digit
4768 rounds up to 5000

So 34768 rounded to the nearest 1000 is 35000.

10 000	1000	100	10	U
3	4	7	6	8
3	5	0	0	0

347675 rounds down to 300000

7543679 is closer to 8000000 than 7000000.

Example 2   Round 5347675 to the nearest 100000

Look at the 10000 digit.

1 000 000	100 000	10 000	1000	100	10	U
5	3	4	7	6	7	5
5	3	0	0	0	0	0

So 5347675 rounded to the nearest 100000 is 5300000.

Example 3   Round 7543679 to the nearest million.

Look at the 100000 digit.

1 000 000	100 000	10 000	1000	100	10	U
7	5	4	3	6	7	9
8	0	0	0	0	0	0

So 7543679 rounded to the nearest million is 8 million.

Exercise 9.1
Practising Skill 9A

1   Round each of these numbers to the nearest thousand.

a	6745	**b**	7489	**c**	3097	**d**	2604
e	5507	**f**	8498	**g**	2708	**h**	9399
i	12675	**j**	25478	**k**	16399	**l**	34355
m	36705	**n**	123457	**o**	344788	**p**	650575

2 Round each of these to the nearest 10 000.

a	34 675	**b**	56 788	**c**	23 854	**d**	16 403
e	48 932	**f**	44 292	**g**	25 004	**h**	66 676
i	88 609	**j**	69 001	**k**	244 878	**l**	304 909
m	135 060	**n**	252 788	**o**	535 261	**p**	624 975

3 Round each of these to the nearest 100 000.

a	365 344	**b**	424 781	**c**	722 848	**d**	564 385
e	655 024	**f**	929 898	**g**	135 600	**h**	548 867
i	1 345 066	**j**	2 542 786	**k**	2 627 833	**l**	794 001

4 Round each of these to the nearest million.

a	3 657 613	**b**	4 298 978	**c**	4 750 020	**d**	12 125 559
e	48 677 512	**f**	6 788 100	**g**	9 702 030	**h**	35 090 991
i	20 290 575	**j**	16 575 614	**k**	99 630 000	**l**	56 390 999

Exercise 9.2
Using Skill 9A

1 To the nearest ten, there were 60 people on a bus.

a What is the largest number of people there could have been?
b What is the smallest number of people there could have been?

2 There were 35 384 seats sold for a hockey final.

a Give the number of seats sold to the nearest hundred.
b Give the number of seats sold to the nearest thousand.
c Give the number of seats sold to the nearest 10 000.

3 Last year Butterfly World had 360 000 visitors (to the nearest 10 000).

a What is the largest number this could have been?
b What is the smallest number this could have been?

In 1994 Butterfly World had 282 954 visitors.

c Give the 1994 figure to the nearest 10 000.

4 Fast Packet deliver parcels. A parcel must weigh no more than 560 grams rounded to the nearest 10 grams.

a Which of these parcels are too heavy for Fast Packet?

Parcel	A	B	C	D	E	F	G	H
Weight (g)	548	564	558	566	562	567	565	563

b Calculate the total weight of all these parcels.
c Give this total weight to the nearest 100 grams.

Skill 9B
Rounding to find an
approximate answer

♦ Rounding numbers can help to find an approximate answer.

Example

A case of orange juice holds 24 boxes.
Approximately how many boxes are in 138 cases?

The number of boxes is	24×138
❖ round each number to the nearest ten	20×140
❖ do the calculation	$20 \times 140 = 2800$

There are approximately 2800 boxes of juice in 138 cases.

Rounding makes the calculation easy to do without a calculator.
You must decide whether to round to the nearest 10, or 100, or 1000, or … .

> Approximate answers are not exact. They are often calculated mentally.

> Round each number to the same rule.

Exercise 9.3
Practising Skill 9B

Do not use a calculator for this exercise.

1 By rounding, find an approximate answer to each of these. In each case round to the nearest ten.

a 38×52	**b** 27×67	**c** 45×61	**d** 78×89
e 19×76	**f** 32×69	**g** 53×57	**h** 83×29
i 23×18	**j** 97×38	**k** 149×27	**l** 198×17

2 Which of these can have an approximate answer of 2400?

| **a** 32×78 | **b** 41×56 | **c** 48×65 | **d** 18×118 |
| **e** 56×49 | **f** 21×41 | **g** 236×8 | **h** 55×82 |

3 Which of these does not have an approximate answer of 5400?

| **a** 88×64 | **b** 175×34 | **c** 93×57 | **d** 265×14 |

4 When the numbers are rounded to the nearest ten,
■ $\times 32$ is approximately 1500

a What is the largest value ■ can have?
b What is the smallest value ■ can have?

Round to the nearest 10.

5 Find an approximate answer to each of these.

| **a** $12 \times 23 \times 8$ | **b** $15 \times 26 \times 7$ | **c** $22 \times 9 \times 13$ | **d** $38 \times 11 \times 6$ |
| **e** $15 \times 13 \times 8$ | **f** $24 \times 28 \times 11$ | **g** $35 \times 19 \times 6$ | **h** $48 \times 14 \times 13$ |

Exercise 9.4
Using Skills 9A and 9B

Do not use a calculator for this exercise.

1 Find the approximate number in stock of each item.

Stock Sheet			
Item	No. of Cases	No. in a case	No. in stock Approximately
Beans	44	48	
Pears	75	36	
Peaches	116	24	
Tomatoes	152	12	
Peas	97	16	

Rounding numbers to the nearest hundred helps with numbers like 1745.
Does it help with numbers like 348?

2 Rewrite this article with each number rounded to the **nearest hundred**.

There were 1745 people on the train for the 865 mile trip. During the day a total of 2218 cans of cola, 1861 bags of crisps, and 273 gallons of coffee were sold. Ticket sales were £32 282 and the organsiers expect to give £20 805 to local charities. There were 348 children on board and 163 of them spent time with the drivers.

The train used 14 560 litres of fuel for the trip. Wessex Oil donated 12 550 litres of fuel on the day of the trip.

3 Tickets for a match were £23 each.
From one school a group of 85 students went to the match.
Approximately how much did they pay in total for their tickets?

4 Ed has a part-time job. He earns £26 each week.
Approximately how much will Ed earn in one **year**?

A year is 52 weeks.

5 Emma cycles 13 km each day to work.

a Approximately how far will Emma cycle in total over 42 working days?
b Exactly how far did Emma cycle in total?
c Was your approximation too large or too small?

Starting points

You need to know about ...

... so try these questions

A The names of triangles and quadrilaterals

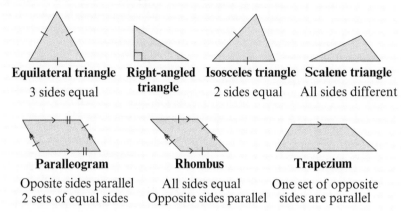

Equilateral triangle
3 sides equal

Right-angled triangle

Isosceles triangle
2 sides equal

Scalene triangle
All sides different

Paralleogram
Oposite sides parallel
2 sets of equal sides

Rhombus
All sides equal
Opposite sides parallel

Trapezium
One set of opposite
sides are parallel

◆ Lines with marks like this ┼ are equal in length.
◆ Lines with marks like this ➤ are parallel.

A1 What can you say about the angles of
   a an equilateral triangle
   b an isosceles triangle?

A2 What makes a parallelogram different from a rhombus?

A3 Draw a scalene triangle.

A4 **a** Draw a right-angled triangle.
   b Draw a right-angled triangle which is also isosceles.

A5 Look at the rhombus. What do you think is true about its opposite angles?

Constructing triangles

Skill 10A
Constructing an
equilateral triangle

Example   Construct an equilateral triangle with sides of 3 cm.

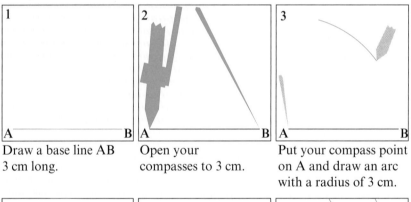

1 Draw a base line AB 3 cm long.

2 Open your compasses to 3 cm.

3 Put your compass point on A and draw an arc with a radius of 3 cm.

Make sure for
constructions that:
◆ your pencil is sharp
◆ your compasses are tight
◆ you do not rub out any construction lines.

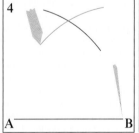

4 Put your compass point on B and draw another arc.

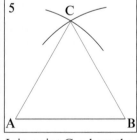

5 Join point C, where the arcs cross, to A and B.

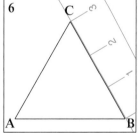

6 Measure the sides to check they are all 3 cm.

Exercise 10.1
Practising Skill 10A

1 Construct an equilateral triangle with sides of 5 cm.

2 Construct a triangle PQR where PQ = 6 cm, QR = 6 cm and PR = 6 cm.

3 Draw a 4 cm square and construct an equilateral triangle on top.

Skill 10B
Constructing a triangle
when you know 3 sides

These diagrams do not
show the triangle full size.

Example   Construct a triangle with sides of 3 cm, 4 cm and 5 cm.

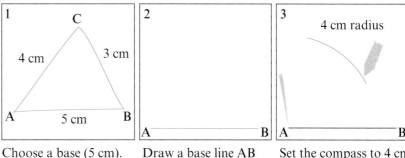

Choose a base (5 cm).
Make a rough sketch.

Draw a base line AB
5 cm long.

Set the compass to 4 cm.
Put the point on A.
Draw an arc.

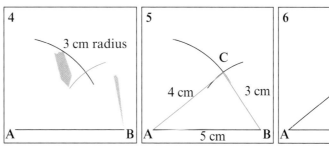

Set the compass to 3 cm.
Put the point on B.
Draw an arc.

Join point C, where the
arcs cross, to A and B.

Check that the sides are
3 cm, 4 cm and 5 cm.

Exercise 10.2
Practising Skill 10B

1 **a** Construct the above triangle but full size.
   b Measure the size of angle ACB.
       What do you find?

2 Construct accurately a triangle with sides of 4 cm, 7 cm and 6 cm.

3 **a** Construct a triangle with sides of 7 cm, 3 cm and 7 cm.
   b What name do we give this type of triangle?

4 Construct a triangle with sides of 34 mm, 57 mm and 62 mm.

5 **a** Try to construct a triangle with sides of 10 cm, 6 cm and 3 cm.
   b Why is this triangle impossible to construct?

6 Do not try to construct triangles with these sides.
   Say which ones it is impossible to construct.

   a 12 cm, 7 cm, 9 cm   **b** 4 cm, 8 cm, 5 cm   **c** 4 cm, 8 cm, 3 cm
   d 24 cm, 7 cm, 22 cm   **e** 1 cm, 9 cm, 5 cm   **f** 2 cm, 1 cm, 2 cm

Exercise 10.3
Using Skill 10B

1 A garden is triangular.
   The sides of the garden are 7 metres, 6 metres and 8 metres long.

   Use a scale of 1 cm to 1 metre to construct a scale drawing of the garden.

2 A field is shaped like a triangle.
   The lengths of its sides are 400 metres, 500 metres and 700 metres.

   Construct a scale drawing of the field. Use a scale of 1 cm to 100 metres.

3 A small oak tree and a small elm tree are 7 metres apart.
   Tony wants to plant an ash tree 6 m from the oak and 8 m from the elm.

   Construct a scale drawing of the positions of the three trees.

A scale of 1 cm to 1 metre
means that to draw a line
to stand for 4 metres you
draw one 4 cm long.

Skill 10C
Constructing a triangle
when you know 2 sides
and an angle

Example

Construct a triangle ABC, where AB = 5 cm, BC = 6, cm and angle ABC = 40°

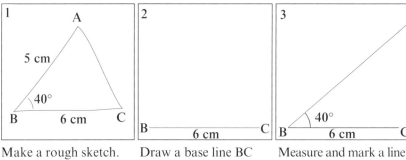

Make a rough sketch. | Draw a base line BC 6 cm long. | Measure and mark a line from B at an angle of 40°.

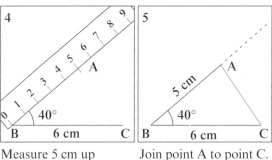

Measure 5 cm up the 40° line. Mark point A. | Join point A to point C.

Exercise 10.4
Practising Skill 10C

1 Construct the triangle ABC above, full size.

2 Construct triangle PQR where PQ = 7 cm, QR = 5 cm and angle PQR = 110°.

3 a Construct triangle RST where RS = 6 cm, ST = 6 cm and angle RST = 40°.
  b Measure angles RTS and TRS. What do you notice?
  c What type of triangle is RST?

4 This is the sketch of a right-angled triangle.

  a Construct the triangle full size.
  b On your triangle, measure the length of side AB.
  c Measure angle ABC on your triangle.

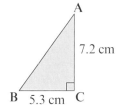

Exercise 10.5
Constructing triangles

1 Construct an equilateral triangle with sides of 8 cm.

2 a Construct a triangle ABC where AB = 4 cm, BC = 4 cm, and angle ABC = 45°.
  b What name do we give this type of triangle?

3 a Construct an equilateral triangle with sides of 7 cm.
  b Construct a triangle PQR where PQ = 7 cm, QR = 7 cm, and angle PQT = 60°.
  c Compare your two triangles. What do you find?

4 Construct a triangle with sides of 4 cm, 6 cm, and 8 cm.

Constructing quadrilaterals

Constructing a quadrilateral

♦ To construct a quadrilateral you can normally use an angle measurer, a set square, compasses and a ruler.

♦ There are two different shapes of set square.

 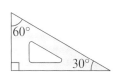

Make sure you use the right one for angles of 30°, 60° and 45°.

Exercise 10.6
Constructing quadrilaterals

1 This sketch shows two sides of a rectangle ABCD.

    a Draw the sides AB and BC full size.
    b Construct the rest of rectangle ABCD.

2 This is a sketch of a quadrilateral

    a What name do we give the shape?
    b Construct the shape full size.

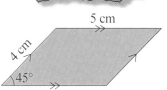

3   **a** Construct a square with sides of 6.4 cm.
    b Measure its diagonals.

4   **a** What name do we give this quadrilateral?
    b Construct the shape full size.

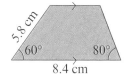

5 This sketch shows two sides of a rhombus.

    a Draw the sides AB and BC full size.
    b Construct the rest of the rhombus ABCD.

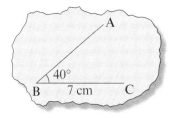

6 A parallelogram RSTU has RS = 7 cm, ST = 8 cm, and angle RST = 56°. Construct the parallelogram RSTU.

7 A field is shaped like a trapezium.

    a Make a scale drawing of the field using a scale of 1 cm to 100 metres.

    A hedge is planted along the side CD.

    b How long is the line CD on your scale drawing?
    c How long is the hedge in real life?

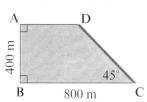

Starting points

You need to know about ...

... so try these questions

A Times in the day, am, pm, and noon

- ◆ A day spans 24 hours (1 hour = 60 minutes).

- ◆ The day starts at midnight.

- ◆ The day ends at the next midnight.

- ◆ Half way through a day is the midpoint, or the middle of the day. This half way point in a day is called **midday** or **noon**.

- ◆ We use **am** for times between the start of the day and midday.

- ◆ We use **pm** for times between midday and the next midnight.

- ◆ A day can be shown on a time line.

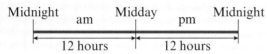

Midnight   am   Midday   pm   Midnight

12 hours   12 hours

> **A1** Write each of these times with am or pm.
>
>   **a** 6.30 Breakfast TV starts
>   **b** 3.30 School ends
>   **c** 5.30 Day–shift starts
>   **d** 2.45 Night club closes
>   **e** 8.30 Night–shift starts
>   **f** 3.00 Premier league kick–off
>   **g** 7.15 Post delivered
>   **h** 8.23 New moon seen
>   **i** 7.00 Night–shift ends
>   **j** 1.15 Cinema closes
>
> **A2 a** How many hours from midnight to midday?
>   **b** How many minutes is this?
>
> **A3** How many hours in 4 days?

The 24–hour clock system

- ◆ The 24-hour clock system does not use am and pm.

- ◆ All times in the 24-hour clock system are shown by 4 digits.

> Hours and minutes in the 24-hour clock system can be shown, where:
> a dot separates them   06.45
> two dots separate them 06:45
> space separates them   06 45

Hours   Minutes

06.45

Dot separates hours and minutes

- ◆ The day starts at 00.00, and midday is 12.00.
  After midday the hours continue: 13.00, 14.00, 15.00, and so on until 23.59.

> ### Skill 11A
> Writing times in the 24-hour clock system

- ◆ Writing am times, and pm times up to 12.59 pm, is the same in both systems, you must write 4 digits for a 24-hour clock time.

> Only add 12 hours to the pm time if the pm time is after 12.59 pm.

Example 1 Write these times in the 24-hour clock system.

	6.15 am	8.28 am	10.45 am	11.55 am
24–hour times	**06.15**	**08.28**	**10.45**	**11.55**

- ◆ Times in pm can be difficult when you try to write them as 24 hour times. From 1.00 pm onwards you can add 12 hours to the pm time.

Example 2 Write these times as 24-hour times.

> For a pm time of 1.55 pm. Add 12 hours gives 13.55.

	1.55 pm	3.40 pm	5.15 pm	11.30 pm
24–hour times	**13.55**	**15.40**	**17.15**	**23.30**

Exercise 11.1
Practising Skill 11A

1 Write each time as a 24 hour time: 4.40 pm, 5.30 pm, 6.15 am, 3.44 am.

2 Write each of these times as 24-hour times.

a	4.20 am	**b**	7.25 pm	**c**	8.19 am	**d**	12.42 pm	**e**	1.35 am
f	9.05 pm	**g**	11.47 am	**h**	7.08 pm	**i**	12.55 pm	**j**	10.18 am
k	6.04 pm	**l**	11.62 pm	**m**	6.57 am	**n**	1.10 am	**o**	12.27 pm

Exercise 11.2
Using Skill 11A

1 These are the times that three buses reached a bus stop.
    Bus A 17.52   Bus B 7.52 pm   Bus C 5.50 pm

    a Which bus reached the bus stop first?   **b** Which bus was last?

2 Jenny wanted to catch a train at 3.44 pm.
    When she got to the station the clock showed 13.35.

    a Has she missed the train?
    b Write the time of the train Jenny wanted to catch in 24–hour time.

3 Jo wanted to set his alarm for 4.20 am.
    The alarm on his clock was set for 19.30 so he had to reset it.

    What time should he set his 24-hour alarm clock for?

4 A flight from Spain was due to land Gatwick at 19.40. It landed at 9.35 pm.

    Was the flight early or late? Explain your answer.

5 Copy this report with all the times as 24-hour times.

> The team was up by 5.25 am. They had gone to bed at 11.15 pm the night before. The bus to the airport was booked for 6.40 am, this was the only bus on the island. The plane had left London at 9.45 pm to arrive here at 8.10 am. The plane was late, it got here at 1.28 pm and it finally took off at 5.30 pm. The team should be in Rome at about 3 am tomorrow.

Calculating time intervals

◆ One way to think of a time interval is that it is the length of time taken.

Example

A train leaves York at 14.00 and arrives in London at 17.00.
How long does this journey take?

The time taken is the time interval between 14.00 and 17.00.
Between 14.00 and 17.00 is 3 hours.

So the journey took 3 hours.

Exercise 11.3
Calculating time intervals

1 Copy and complete this table.

Leave at	Arrive at	Journey time
15.00	19.00	_____ hours
06.00	21.00	_____ hours
5 am	2 pm	_____ hours
8.30 am	5.30 pm	_____ hours
21.00	02.00	_____ hours

Skill 11B
Calculating time intervals

♦ Time intervals can be difficult when times are not just hours.

Example 1

A train left Leeds at 13.54 and got to Liverpool at 16.23.
How long did this journey take?

Think of these times on a time line.

The time interval is 2 hours + 6 min + 23 min

So, the journey took 2 hours 29 minutes.

Example 2

An oven is switched on at 17.25 and switched off at 21.42.

For how long was the oven on?

Show the times on a time line.

The time interval is 3 hours + 35 min + 42 min.

So the oven was on for 4 hours 17 minutes.

> 35 min + 42 min = 77 min
>
> 77 min is 1 hours 17 min

Exercise 11.4
Practising Skill 11B

1 Copy and complete this table.
Draw a time line for each
time interval you calculate.

Start time	Stop time	Time interval
16.24	19.06	■
19.42	23.07	■
06.35	09.12	■
08.47	11.28	■
09.34	17.25	■
01.17	11.04	■
10.43	19.16	■
00.18	13.04	■

Exercise 11.5
Using Skill 11B

1 Jim went to London by coach.
The coach left at 17.15 and got to Victoria Coach Station at 21.08.
For how long was Jim travelling in the coach?

2 Street lights were set to go on at 16.35 and set to go off at 23.10.
For how long were the lights on?

3 In a school the heating was set to go on at 07.15 and off at 15.05.
For how long was the heating on?

4 Emma left Dover at 15.51 and arrived in Paris at 20.06.
How many hours and minutes did this journey take?

5 An alarm was set to go on at 20.15 and off at 06.35.
For how long was the alarm on?

Reading timetables

Charing Cross is a station in London.

♦ Most timetables show times in 24-hour time.
But often the hours and minutes are not separated by a dot or a space.

♦ This timetable shows trains between Charing Cross and Margate on Saturdays.

— shows that the train does not stop at this station.

LONDON TO FOLKSTONE – DOVER – RAMSGATE – MARGATE

Saturdays

Charing Cross	d	—	0600	0700	0730	0800	0830			1900	2000
Waterloo East	d	—	0603	0703	0733	0803	0833			1903	2003
Cannon Street	d	—	—	—	—	—	—	and		—	—
London Bridge	d	—	0607	0707	0737	—	0837			—	—
Tonbridge	d	—	0657	0743	0811	0842	0911	at the same minutes		1942	2042
Maidstone East	d	—	—	0718	0918	0850	0913			—	2016
Ashford (Kent)	d	0645	0734	0834	0857	0915	0957	past		2014	2114
Westhanger	a	—	—	—	—	—	—			—	—
Sandling	a	0655	0745	0845	0908	—	1008	each		2025	2125
Folkestone West	a	0700	0750	0850	0913	—	1013	hour		2030	2130
Folkestone Central	a	0703	0753	0853	0915	0929	1016	until		2033	2133
Dover Priory	a	0715	0808	0908	0928	0941	1028			2044	2145
Martin Mill	a	0725	0819	0919	—	0952	—			2055	2155
Walmer	a	0729	0823	0923	—	0956	—			2059	2159
Deal	a	0733	0826	0926	—	0959	—			2102	2202
Sandwich	a	0740	0833	0933	—	1006	—			2109	2209
Ramsgate	a	0752	0845	0945	—	1019	—			2122	2222
Margate	a	0830	0857	1001	—	1040	—			2146	2246

♦ The timetable shows times for 8 different trains (one column each).

♦ The timetable shows 18 stations (one row each).

♦ You can follow the journey of a train by moving down a column.

Example At what time does the 0700 from Charing Cross get to Deal?

| Column starts | Charing Cross | 0700 |
| Move down to | Deal | 0926 |

So the 0700 from Charing Cross gets to Deal at 0926.

Exercise 11.6
Practising Skill 11C

1   At what time does the 0700 from Charing Cross get to:

  a Sanding   **b** Margate   **c** Tonbridge
  d Walmer   **e** Ashford   **f** Deal?

2   Copy and complete this table

Leave	at	Get to	at
Tonbridge	0842	Walmer	
Dover Priory	0941	Ramsgate	
Ashford	0734	Deal	
Martin Mill	2055	Sandwich	
Sandling	0745	Margate	
Tonbridge		Sandling	0908
Folkestone West		Deal	0826
Ashford		Ramsgate	2122
Walmer		Ramsgate	0945
Walterloo East		Sandwich	2109

Exercise 11.7
Using Skill 11C

1   At what times does the 1942 from Tonbridge get to Dover Priory?

2   When does the 0737 from London Bridge get to Folkestone Central?

3   You want to get to Ramsgate at 1019. When should you leave Ashford?

Exercise 11.8   This shows a timetable for trains between London Waterloo and Exeter.
Using skills 11B and 11C

LONDON WATERLOO, WOKING, BASINGSTOKE, ANDOVER, SALISBURY, YEOVIL JUNCTION to EXETER.
Mondays to Fridays

London, Waterloo	d	0710	0754	0835	0935	1035	1135	1235	1335	—	1435	1410	1535	1605	1635	1700	1730
Gatwick Airport	d	0625|	0722|	0740|	0854|	0954|	1056|	1156|	1256|	—	1356|	—	1456|	1524|	1556|	—	—
Clapham Junction	d	0716u	0802u	0841u	0941u	1041u	1141u	1241u	1341u	—	1441u	—	1541u	1611u	1641u	1651g	—
Heathrow Airport	d	0610k	0720k	0750k	0900k	1000k	1100k	1200k	1300k	—	1400k	—	1500k	1530k	1600k	—	—
Woking	d	0735	0822	0900	1000	1100	1200	1300	1400	—	1500	—	1600u	1630	1701	1710g	1728g
Reading	d	0725g	0755g	0825g	0936g	1050g	1150g	1250g	1350g	—	1450g	—	1550g	1620g	1650g	1711g	1722g
Basingstoke	d	0755	0842	0920	1021	1121	1221	1321	1421	—	1521	1456	1622u	1651	1721	1741	1812
Overton	d	0803	0851	—	1029	—	1229	—	1429	—	—	—	1630	1700	1730	1749	1821
Whitchurch (Hants)	d	0808	0856	—	1034	—	1234	—	1434	—	—	—	1635	1706	1735	1754	1826
Andover	d	0817	0905	0937	1043	1138	1243	1338	1443	—	1538	—	1644	1714	1743	1803	1834
Grateley	d	0824	0912	—	1050	—	1250	—	1450	—	—	—	1651	1722	1751	1810	1842
Portsmouth & Southsea	d	0707b	—	0828b	0928b	1028b	—	1228b	1328b	—	1428b	1437c	1528b	—	1628b	—	1728b
Fareham	d	0725b	—	0847b	1006b	1047b	—	1247b	1347b	—	1447b	1457c	1547b	—	1647b	—	1747b
Southampton Central	d	0754b	—	0909b	1034b	1109b	—	1309b	1409b	—	1509b	1533	1629b	—	1709b	1737b	1809b
Romsey	d	0805b	—	0920b	1045b	1120b	—	1320b	1420b	—	1520b	1544	1640b	—	1720b	1748b	1820b
Salisbury	a	0836	0924	0954	1102	1154	1302	1354	1502	—	1554	1604	1703	1737	1802	1822	1854
Salisbury	d	0839	—	0957	1116	1156	—	1357	1514	—	1557	1635	1717	—	1806	1825	1858
Tisbury	d	0853	—	1011	1130	1210	—	1411	1528	—	1611	1650	1732	—	1820	1839	1912
Gillingham (Dorset)	d	0903	—	1021	1139a	1220	—	1421	1537a	—	1622	1702a	1745	—	1830	1852	1922
Templecombe	d	0911	—	1029	—	1228	—	1429	—	—	1629	—	1752	—	1837	1859	1937
Sherborne	d	0918	—	1036	—	1235	—	1436	—	—	1637	—	1800	—	1845	1907	1937
Yeovil Junction	a	0924	—	1042	—	1241	—	1442	—	—	1642	—	1805	—	1850	1914	1943
Yeovil Junction	d	0925	—	1043	—	1242	—	1443	—	—	1643	—	—	—	1852	—	1944
Crewkerne	d	0935	—	1053	—	1252	—	1453	—	—	1653	—	—	—	1901	—	1954
Axminster	d	0948	—	1106	—	1305	—	1506	—	—	1720	—	—	—	1915	—	2007
Honiton	d	1002	—	1118	—	1317	—	1518	—	1712	1732	—	—	—	1927	—	2019
Feniton	d	1007	—	1124	—	—	—	1524	—	—	1738	—	—	—	1932	—	—
Whimple	d	1012	—	—	—	—	—	1529	—	—	1743	—	—	—	1937	—	—
Pinhoe	d	1019	—	—	—	—	—	—	—	—	—	—	—	—	1944	—	—
Exeter Central	a	1023	—	1135	—	1332	—	1537	—	1729	1753	—	—	—	1948	—	2034
Exeter St Davids	a	1030	—	1139	—	1336	—	1544	—	1733	1757	—	—	—	1954	—	2040

1 At what time does the 0710 from Waterloo get to Basingstoke?

2 If you leave Overton at 1229 when should you get to Salisbury?

3 The 1235 from Waterloo get to Salisbury at 1354.
At what time does this train leave Salisbury for Exeter?

4 Javed caught the 1635 from Waterloo to Exeter St Davids.
The train was on time. How long did the journey take?

5 How long does the 1751 from Grateley take to get to Feniton?

6 You want to be in Tisbury for 2.15 pm.
What is the latest train you can catch from Clapham Junction?

7 You caught the 0937 from Andover.
You were on the train for about an hour and a quarter.
Which station did you travel to?

8 Warren lives in Salisbury and wants to go to Honiton.
He got to Salisbury station at 1555.
  a Did he miss the next train to Honiton?
  b When will he be in Honiton if the trains are on time?
  c How long did the train journey take?

9 Marika is going by train from Woking to Templecombe.
She gets to Woking station at 3 35 pm.
  a How long will she have to wait for a train, if it is on time?
  b At what time should she get to Templecombe?
  c How long should she be on the train?

10 The 1721 from Basingstoke to Exeter Central was 23 minutes late leaving Basingstoke and arriving at Exeter Central.
  a At what time did it leave Basingstoke?
  b At what time did it get to Grateley?
  c What was the journey time for Basingstoke to Exeter Central?

This revises the work in Sections 7 to 11

1 Skill 7A

In each case, collect like terms

a $b + b + c + b + c - b$ **b** $2s + 7b + 3s - 4b$
c $6t - 2g + t + g - 2t + 5g$ **d** $26h + 5f + 3j - 7h + j$

2 Skill 7B

In each case, expand the brackets.

a $2(a + 2b)$ **b** $4(5s + 6)$
c $5(5g - 2r)$ **d** $5(3a + 6b - 4c)$

3 Remove the brackets then simplify this.

$2(3a + 2b) + 3(a + 5b + c)$

4 You design a shopping questionnaire.
You want to ask a question about a person's age.

Give two different types of question you could ask to find out a person's age.

5 Skill 8A

These questions were used in a survey.

Town Centre Survey

1 Do you come into the town centre often?   ☐ Yes ☐ No

2 Do you agree that the town centre should be free of cars?   ☐ Yes ☐ No

3 What do you think about buses?

....

a What is wrong with question **1**?
b Give a better way to ask question **1**.
c Why is question **2** not a fair question?
d In question **3** it is not clear what data is wanted. Write a better question about buses.

6 This is a statement made in a book.

> For right-handed people, their left eye is stronger than their right.

a Decide how to test this statement.
b Design a data collection sheet.
c Do the survey and decide if you think the statement is true.

7 Round 163

a to the nearest 10
b to the nearest 100.

8 Skill 9A

Round each of these to the nearest thousand.

a 4326   **b** 8572   **c** 9 754 325
d 36 824   **e** 69 653   **f** 9905

9 Skill 9A

Round each of these numbers.

a 43 745 to the nearest 10 000
b 37 845 622 to the nearest million
c 3 456 789 to the nearest 10 000
d 3 456 789 to the nearest million.

10 Skill 9B

By rounding first to the nearest ten, find approximate answers to each of these.

a 67×18 **b** 84×78 **c** 196×41 **d** 56×96

11 Skill 10A

Construct an equilateral triangle with sides of 6.5 cm.

12 Skill 10B

Construct a triangle ABC where AB = 5 cm, BC = 6.5 cm and AC = 8.5 cm.

13 Skill 10C

Construct a triangle PQR where PQ = 5 cm, QR = 6 cm and angle PQR = 90°.

14 These are two sides of a rhombus.

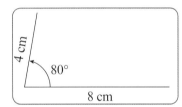

a Draw the sides full size.
b Construct the rest of the rhombus.

15 Skill 11A

Write each of these in 24-hour time.

a 4.45 pm   **b** 11.30 am   **c** 8.55 pm
d 12.15 pm   **e** 12.15 am   **f** 6.40 am

16 Skill 11A

Write each of these in am or pm time.

a 19.20   **b** 06.20   **c** 12.45
d 16.30   **e** 00.38   **f** 04.50

17 Skill 11B

How long is it between 6.30 am and 11.15 am?

18 Skill 11C

Look at the timetable on page 59.

When does the 0941 from Dover Priory arrive at Sandwich?

Southampton Evening Chronicle   Monday 15 April 1912

TRAGEDY AT SEA

Last night at 10:40 pm the Titanic hit an iceberg on her way to New York.
She sank at 2:20 am and 1497 people drowned.
It was the ship's first voyage.
On board were:
331 first-class passengers, 273 second-class, 712 third-class and 892 crew.
Each first-class passenger paid £870 for the trip to New York.
The band played on as the ship went down.
Many people were so sure the ship could not sink that they would not go in the lifeboats.

The iceberg had a height of about 100 feet above the water.
The ship's lights went out $2\frac{1}{2}$ hours after the Titanic hit the iceberg.
The sea water temperature was –2°C and the air temperature –5°C.
Survivors were picked up by the Carpathia which heard the SOS at 12:30 am.

HOW FAIR WAS THE RESCUE?

203 first-class, 118 second-class and 178 third-class passengers were rescued. Nearly a quarter of all crew were saved.

The lifeboats could hold 1170 people, not enough for all on board that night.

The average number of people to a lifeboat was only 33.6 but each one could hold nearly 60 people when full.

Strange BUT true

14 years before the Titanic sank, a story book was sold. The book was about a big ship called the Titan which sank after it had hit an iceberg on its first voyage. Compare the two ships.

	Titan (Story 1898)	Titanic (True 1912)
Flag	British	British
Month of sailing	April	April
Weight (tons)	70 000	66 000
Propellers	3	3
Max. speed	24 knots	24 knots
Length	800 feet	882 feet
No. of lifeboats	24	20
No. on board (incl. crew)	2000	2208
What happened?	Right side split by iceberg	Right side split by iceberg
Full capacity	3000 people	3545 people

The richest person on board was Colonel J.J. Astor. He had thirty million pounds in the bank and $4250 in his pocket on the night.

1 How many people in total were on board that night?

2 1497 people drowned.
   What is the value of the 4 digit?

3 How many people on board did not drown?

4 **a** How many passengers were on board?
   b How many passengers were rescued?
   c How many passengers died?

5 How many years ago did the Titanic sink?

6 **a** Copy the word
   TITANIC
   b For each letter, draw in all its lines of symmetry
   c Which letters have an order of rotational symmetry of 2?

7 In what year was the book about the Titan first sold?

8 When did the Titanic hit the iceberg in 24-hour time?

9 How was the air temperature different from the water temperature?

10 Did the Titanic have a vertical or horizontal plane of symmetry?

11 How long after the Titanic hit the iceberg did she sink?

12 The capacity of the Titanic was 3545 people.
    Write this number:
    a to the nearest hundred
    b to the nearest thousand.

13 How many tons heavier was the Titan than the Titanic?

14 Colonel Astor had thirty million pounds in the bank.
    Write this number in digits.

15 Tickets are now about 340 times as expensive as in 1912.
    Roughly, what would a first-class ticket on the Titanic cost now?

16 At what time did the ship's lights go out?

17 How many people died who were
    a first-class passengers
    b second class passengers
    c third class passengers?

18 Roughly how many of the crew were saved?

19 The Titanic had cranes to lift cargo on to the ship. This shows a crane in one position.

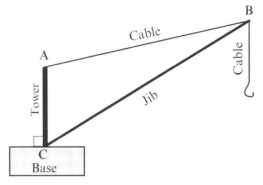

Measure these angles:

a angle ABC   **b** angle BAC
c angle ACB

20 In 24-hour time, when did the Titanic sink?

21 Passengers had to answer questions about the sinking later in New York.
    What is wrong with each of these questions?

a
> How many times have you crossed the Atlantic before?
>
> ❏ None   ❏ 1–2   ❏ 2–5   ❏ 5 or more

b
> The Titanic was the fastest ship you ever sailed on, wasn't it?
>
> ❏ Yes   ❏ No   ❏ Don't know

c
> What size was the iceberg?
>
> ❏ Enormous ❏ Big ❏ Large ❏ Gigantic

22 The average number in a lifeboat was 33.6
    In the number 33.6 what is the value of the 6 digit?

Stage 1 End points

You should be able to ...   ... so try these questions

A Use place value in whole numbers

A1 What is the value of the digit 5 in each of these numbers?
    a 103 504   **b** 25 438   **c** 5 623 412   **d** 351 208

B Order whole numbers
Skill 1A: *see page 13*

B1 Put each set of numbers in order, smallest first.
    a 104, 3252, 54 532, 206, 35 143, 4553
    b 654, 1053, 3054, 126, 564, 18, 2513, 9
    c 120, 67, 100 342, 25 182, 93, 26 654, 341, 110 020

B2 Put these numbers in descending order.
    48, 136, 17, 2304, 2403, 562, 2575, 81

C Write numbers in words
Skill 1B: *see page 14*

C1 Write each of these numbers in words.
    a 1045   **b** 23 106   **c** 3 450 002   **d** 24 000 001

D Write numbers in digits
Skill 1C: *see page 15*

D1 Write each of these numbers in digits.
    a four thousand and five
    b one hundred and sixty three thousand six hundred and sixty
    c eight million three hundred and fifty seven

E Identify a line of symmetry

E1 **a** Copy shape A.
    b Draw in all its lines of symmetry.

Shape A

E2 How many lines of symmetry has each of these letters?
    H   C   M   Y   I

F Find the order of rotational symmetry of a shape

F1 What is the order of rotational symmetry of Shape A?

F2 What is the order of rotational symmetry of a rectangle?

G Identify a plane of symmetry

G1 How many planes of symmetry has this book? (Ignore any printing.)

H Add whole numbers without using a calculator
Skill 3A: *see page 20*
Skill 3B: *see page 20*

H1 Work out:
    a 6 + 8 + 4 + 7 + 6 =   **b** 9 + 5 + 7 + 8 + 4 + 5
    c 35 + 62   **d** 74 + 68
    e 12 + 34 + 27   **f** 34 + 76
    g 385 + 466   **h** 3544 + 1068
    i 675541 + 5630   **j** 1892 + 568
    k 3506 + 121 134 + 67 + 875 + 14 + 40 056

I Subtract whole numbers without using a calculator
Skill 3B: *see page 20*

I1 Subtract these numbers.
    a 975 − 678   **b** 57 312 − 9576
    c 15 643 504 − 9 875 776   **d** 1 100 504 − 86 635
    e 9 million − three hundred thousand

J Multiply whole numbers without using a calculator
Skill 3C: *see page 22*

J1 **a** 56 × 3   **b** 67 × 8   **c** 435 × 6   **d** 54 x 76
    e 135 × 16   **f** 578 × 14   **g** 634 × 36   **h** 637 × 82

K Divide whole numbers without using a calculator
Skill 3D: *see page 23*

K1 **a** 888 ÷ 6   **b** 1430 ÷ 4   **c** 3171 ÷ 7   **d** 312 ÷ 12
    e 1944 ÷ 36   **f** 6396 ÷ 52   **g** 4118 ÷ 22   **h** 12 258 ÷ 27

L Order decimals
Skill 4A: *see page 27*

L1 Put this set of decimals in order, smallest first.
    0.403   2.271   0.6028   0.005   0.604   2   1.3

M	Add decimals **Skill 4B:** *see page 28*	**M1**	Add each of these without using a calculator.

M1 Add each of these without using a calculator.
  a $56.38 + 4.5$ **b** $17.82 + 0.054$
  c $0.5 + 0.68 + 0.0004$ **d** $0.481 + 1.87 + 17$
  e $0.4 + 0.055 + 3 + 1.05$

N Subtract decimals
Skill 4C: *see page 29*

N1 Subtract each of these without using a calculator.
  a $7.9 - 2.503$ **b** $16.4 - 7.75$ **c** $4.5 - 2.88$
  d $12 - 0.006$ **e** $6 - 4.305$

O Describe angles

O1 For each of these angles say if they are acute, obtuse or reflex.
  a $55°$ **b** $166°$ **c** $77°$
  d $288°$ **e** $33°$ **f** $330°$

P Measure angles
Skill 5A: *see page 31*

P1 Measure each of these angles.

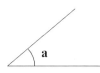

Q Draw angles
Skill 5B: *see page 32*

Q1 Draw each of these angles.
  a $65°$ **b** $145°$ **c** $255°$

R Use negative numbers
Skill 6A: *see page 33*
Skill 6B: *see page 34*

R1 Order each list of numbers, starting with the smallest.
  a $^-6, ^-4, 5, ^-1, ^-5, 3$ **b** $1, ^-3, 4, ^-6, ^-9, 12, 7, ^-2$

R2 Find the new temperature in each of these.
  a a rise of $6°$ from $^-8°C$ **b** a fall of $9°$ from $2°C$

S Add and subtract with
negative numbers
Skill 6C: *see page 36*
Skill 6D: *see page 36*

S1 Copy and complete each of these.
  a $^-7 + 5 =$ **b** $3 + ^-12 =$ **c** $^-8 + ^-5 =$ **d** $4 + ^-5 =$

S2 Copy and complete each of these
  a $^-7 - 9 =$ **b** $4 - 19 =$ **c** $^-6 - ^-9 =$ **d** $4 - ^-7 =$

T Multiply and divide with
negative numbers
Skill 6E: *see page 37*
Skill 6F: *see page 37*

T1 Copy and complete each of these.
  a $^-5 \times ^-8 =$ **b** $3 \times ^-9 =$ **c** $^-7 \times 12 =$ **d** $0 \times ^-7 =$

T2 Copy and complete each of these.
  a $45 \div ^-9 =$ **b** $^-63 \div 7 =$ **c** $^-8 \div ^-8 =$ **d** $^-124 \div 4 =$

U Collect like terms
Skill 7A: *see page 42*

U1 In each of these, collect like terms.
  a $y + 2b + 3y + + 8b$
  b $12w + 9y - y - 8w$
  c $10k + k - 2k + f$

U2 Simplify each of these.
  a $5y + y - 8y + 4y$
  b $3h - h - 5h$
  c $100k + k - 200k$

V Expand brackets
Skill 7B: *see page 44*

V1 In each of these expand the bracket.
  a $5(3k + 1)$ **b** $7(4y - 3x)$ **c** $8(3f + 4 - 5p)$ **d** $3(9y - 5 + 7x)$

W Design an experiment to
answer a question
Skill 8B: *see page 48*

W1 Design an experiment
to answer this question.

> **BODY MATTERS**
>
> For how long can people hold their breath?

W Design and criticise questions in a questionnaire
Skill 8A: *see page 47*

W1 These are some questions from a survey.

> **Bypass Survey**
>
> **1** Are you local?   Yes ❑ No ❑
>
> **2** What do you think of traffic in the village?
>
> _____
>
> **3** Do you agree that the village needs a bypass? Yes ❑ No ❑

    a What is wrong with each of the questions?
    b Write a better question for each one.

X Round numbers to the nearest 1000, 10000, etc.
Skill 9A: *see page 49*

X1 Round each of these numbers to the nearest thousand
    a 8604   **b** 12 099   **c** 9555   **d** 14 449

X2 Round each of these numbers to the nearest 10 000.
    a 38 565   **b** 62 571   **c** 14 989   **d** 27 823

X3 Round each of these to the nearest million.
    a 12 671 221   **b** 35 804 512   **c** 14 701 104   **d** 37 298 879

Y Round numbers to find approximate answers
Skill 9B: *see page 50*

Y1 Find an approximate answer to each of these.
    a 37×42 **b** 58×32 **c** 75×44 **d** 97×58

Z Construct equilateral triangles
Skill 10A: *see page 52*

Z1 Construct an equilateral triangle with sides of 6 cm.

AA Construct a triangle knowing all 3 sides
Skill 10B: *see page 53*

AA1 Construct a triangle with sides of 5 cm, 6 cm, and 7 cm.

BB Construct triangles knowing two sides and an angle
Skill 10C: *see page 54*

BB1 Construct a triangle ABC where, AB = 7 cm, BC = 6 cm, and angle ABC = 55°.

CC Write times in the 24-hour clock system
Skill 11A: *see page 56*

CC1 Write each of these in 24-hour time.
    a 6.15 am   **b** 2.35 pm   **c** 7.45 pm   **d** 12.50 pm

DD Calculate time intervals
Skill 11B: *see page 58*

DD1 A coach left Leeds at 14 25.
The coach got to Luton at 17 18.
How long was the journey time?

EE Use timetables
Skill 11C: *see page 59*

EE1 Use the timetable on page 60.
    a If you leave Andover at 0937, when should you get to Honiton?
    b When should the 1730 from Overton get to Tisbury?
    c If you leave Basingstoke at 1321, how long should you travel on the train to Feniton? (The train is on time!)

This revises the work in Stage 1

1 Give the value of the digit 3 in each of these.
   a 503 004   **b** 230 567   **c** 3 045 627

2 List these numbers in order, largest first.
   54 362, 342, 8, 55 241, 1064, 585, 16, 3058

3 Write each of these numbers in words.
   a 25 604   **b** 420 308   **c** 40 502 006

4 Write each of these numbers in digits.
   a fifty thousand and sixty two
   b two hundred and four thousand and eight
   c five million and seven

5 Copy each of these letters and draw in all lines of symmetry.
   T   A   H   M   X

6 Give the order of rotational symmetry of shape A.

Shape A

7 How many planes of symmetry has a CD box?

8 Find an answer to each of these.
   (Do not use a calculator.)
   a $9 + 5 + 8 + 6 + 7 + 4$
   b $23 + 18 + 7$
   c $1405 + 36 + 22614 + 5$
   d $23004 - 7545$
   e 34×17
   f 563×37
   g $3720 \div 15$
   h $10136 \div 18$

9 Give the value of the digit 8 in each of these.
   a 42.183   **b** 7.0708   **c** 6.1085

10 List these numbers in order, smallest first.
   2.004, 0.409, 0.094, 0.41, 2.1, 0.05

11 Find an answer to each of these.
   (Do not use a calculator.)
   a $2.345 + 12.4 + 0.02 + 0.5 + 4$
   b $327.68 + 17 + 0.004 + 3.4$
   c $46.025 - 28.74$

12 Draw each of these angles accurately.
   a 75°   **b** 155°   **c** 245°

13 Which of these angles are obtuse?
   88°, 188°, 144°, 44°, 148°, 99°

14 Copy and complete each of these.
   a $^-5 + ^-8$ **b** $^-12 + 7$ **c** $8 + ^-7$
   d $4 - 12$ **e** $^-5 - 9$ **f** $^-6 - ^-8$
   g $7 - ^-4$ **h** $^-6 \times 5$ **i** $4 \times ^-9$
   j $^-9 \times ^-7$ **k** $63 \div ^-9$ **l** $48 \div ^-8$

15 List each set of numbers in order, smallest first.
   a $^-8, 4, ^-9, 3, ^-1, 1, ^-5$
   b $4, ^-6, ^-1, 3, 0, ^-2, 12, ^-10$

16 The coordinates of two corners of a square are:
   $(^-6, ^-1)$ and $(^-6, 5)$.
   Give the coordinates of the other two corners of the square.

17 Collect like terms in each of these.
   a $k + 3w + k + 7w + k$
   b $5f + 4h + f - h - 2h$

18 Expand the brackets in each of these.
   a $4(5w + 7)$ **b** $3(4 - 6k)$

19 Expand these brackets and collect like terms to simplify.
   $4(5y + 3g + 1) + 3(4y - 2g - 1)$

20 Round each of these numbers to the nearest thousand.
   a 15 604   **b** 235 498   **c** 2 364 505

21 Round each of these to the nearest 100 000.
   a 304 788   **b** 2 562 441   **c** 1 062 000

22 Find an approximate answer to each of these.
   a 58×71 **b** 88×27 **c** 96×48

23 Construct a triangle with sides of:
   7 cm, 8 cm and 9 cm.

24 Construct triangle ABC where:
   AB = 6 cm, BC = 8 cm, and angle ABC = 65°

25 Write each of these in 24-hour time.
   a 7.55 pm   **b** 6.25 am   **c** 10.20 pm
   d 12.35 pm   **e** 2.45 am   **f** 1.56 pm

26 A train left Sheffield at 1134 and arrived in Plymouth at 1812.
   What was the journey time for this train?

27 Use the timetable on page 60.
   Jo catches the 1821 from Overton.
   She travels to Tisbury.
   a When should she get to Tisbury?
   b What is the journey time?

Starting points

You need to know about ...

... so try these questions

A The perimeter of a shape

This is the total distance around the edge of a shape.

The perimeter of this rectangle is:
5 cm + 7 cm + 5 cm + 7 cm = 24 cm

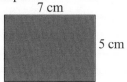

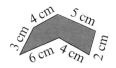

A1 Calculate the perimeter of this shape.

B The area of a shape

This is the amount of surface covered by a shape.

To find the area of Shape A:
put a centimetre grid over the shape,
it shows that the area is about 6 cm².

(cm² stands for square centimetres.)

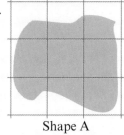

Shape A

B1 Roughly, what is the area of each of these shapes ?

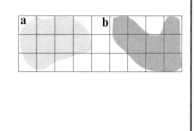

The area of a rectangle

Skill 12 A
Calculating the area of a rectangle

The area of a rectangle can be found by counting squares on a grid. You can also use the formula for the area of a rectangle.

The formula for the area of a rectangle is:
Area = Length × Width

Width

Length

Example 1

Calculate the area of ABCD.

Area = Length × Width
= 7 × 3
= 21

The area of ABCD is 21cm².

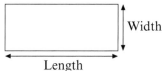

Example 2

Calculate the area of RSTV.

Area = Length × Width
= 6.5 × 3.7
= 24.05

The area of RSTV is 24.05 cm².

Exercise 12.1
Practising Skill 12 A

1 Calculate the area of each of these rectangles.

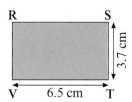

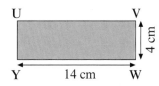

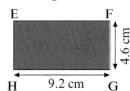

2 Calculate the area of each of these rectangles.

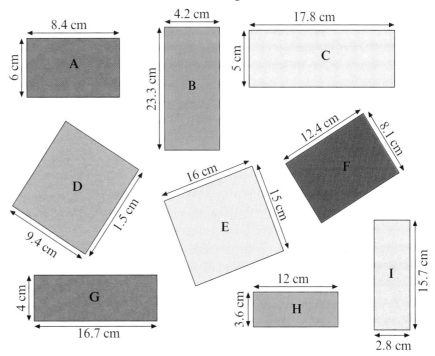

3 The area of a rectangle is 56 cm². The length of the rectangle is 7 cm.
What is its width?

4 A rectangle has an area of 96 cm². The width of the rectangle is 8 cm.
What is its length?

Exercise 12.2
Using Skill 12A

1 A lawn is a rectangle 12.4 metres long and 7.6 metres wide.
Calculate the area of the lawn.

2 A sheet of glass is a rectangle 4.2 metres long and 2.1 metres high.
One square metre of this glass costs £6.50.
a Calculate the area of the glass.
b Find the cost of the glass.

3 A map is painted on a rectangle of board that is 35 cm long and 32 cm wide.
a Find the area of the board.
b What is its perimeter?

4 A calculator screen is a rectangle 50 mm long and 14 mm wide.
a Find the area of the screen.
b What is its perimeter?

5 Dean wants to buy the computer with the biggest screen.
This is a list of the computers he can buy.

Type	Screen width (cm)	Screen length (cm)
425 ZX	28	32
616 ORCO	29	31
700 BEZ	28.5	31.5

Which computer has the biggest screen area?

6 A sticky label is 88 mm long and 35 mm wide.
Is the area of the label greater than, or less than, 3100 mm²?

The area of a triangle

Skill 12B
Calculating the area of
a triangle

♦ You can think of the area of a triangle as:
half the area of a rectangle that fits around the triangle.

The area of triangle RCD is
half the area of rectangle ABCD.

Area RCD = $\frac{1}{2}$ of (Area ABCD)

Area RCD = $\frac{1}{2}$ of (12×7)

Area RCD = $\frac{1}{2}$ of (84)

Area RCD = 42 cm²

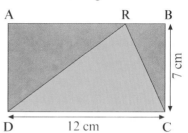

♦ Or you can use the formula for
the area of a triangle.

The formula is:

Area of triangle = $\frac{1}{2} \times$ Base $\times$ Height

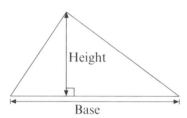

> The height of a triangle is
> the distance at right angles
> from its base to its highest
> point.

Example

Calculate the area of triangle CDE.

Area of CDE = $\frac{1}{2} \times$ Base $\times$ Height
= $0.5 \times 14 \times 9$
= 63

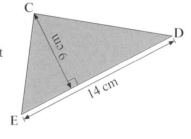

> $0.5 = \frac{1}{2}$
> 0.5 is easier when you work
> with a calculator.

The area of CDE is 63 cm².

Exercise 12.3
Practising Skill 12B

1 Calculate the area of each of these triangles.

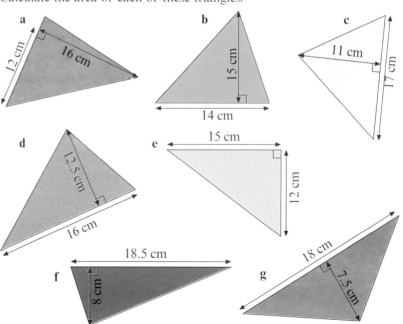

2 Calculate the area of each of these triangles.

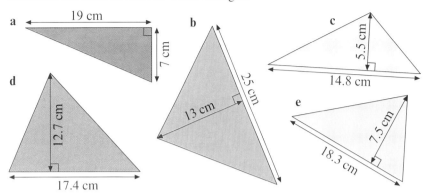

Exercise 12.4
Using Skill 12B

1 **a** Measure the base (BC) of ABC in millimetres.
b Measure the height (AC) of ABC
c Calculate the area of ABC.

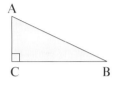

2 A triangle of carpet has a base of 8 metres and a height of 5.5 metres. One square metre of this carpet costs £8.99 at Carpetland.
a Calculate the area of the carpet.
b What will you have to pay for the carpet?

3 The diagram shows a plastic logo.
a Find the area of the red part of the logo.
b What is the area of the yellow part?
c Calculate the total area of the logo.

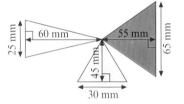

4 The diagram shows a flag.
a Calculate the area of the yellow part.
b Calculate the area of the green part.
c Calculate the area of the flag.
d What area is red or white?

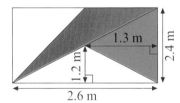

The perimeter of shapes

Skill 12C
Calculating the perimeter
of shapes

To find the perimeter of a shape you need the lengths of all the sides. In some cases you will have to work out some lengths.

Example

Calculate the perimeter of this shape.

You need to find the length of the red side
Length of red side = 12.5 cm – 3 cm = 9.5 cm

Perimeter of shape = 15.4 + 12.5 + 5 + 9.5 + 10.4 + 3
= 55.8

On the diagram:
Red side + 3 = 12.5
So Red side = 9.5 cm

The perimeter of the shape is 55.8 cm.

Exercise 12.5
Practising Skill 12C

1 Calculate the perimeter of each of these shapes.
In each one you need to find a missing length.

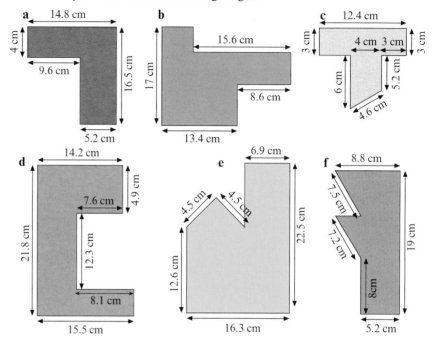

Exercise 12.6
Using Skills 12A, 12B
and 12C

1 The area of this rectangle is 54 cm².

    a Find the width of the rectangle.
    b What is the perimeter of the shape?

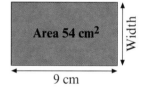

2 A square has a perimeter of 20 cm.
Find the area of the square.

3 This triangle has an area of 21 cm².

    a Find the length of the base.
    b Calculate its perimeter.

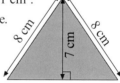

4 A rectangle has an area of 24 cm².
It has a perimeter of 22 cm.

    a What is its length?
    b What is its width?

5 A rectangle has an area of 36 cm². (All lengths of sides are whole numbers.)
Which of these cannot be its perimeter?

    20 cm   24 cm   28 cm   30 cm   36 cm   40 cm

6 A triangle has an area of 67.5 cm².
Its base is 9 cm long.

    What is the height of the triangle?

7 A rectangle is 17 cm long and 15 cm wide.
What is the area of the biggest triangle that just fits inside the rectangle?

Starting points

You need to know about ...   ... so try these questions

A Letters for numbers

Letters can be used to stand for numbers

Three dice *a*, *b*, and *c* are rolled.
For the score you:
    add the numbers on dice *a* and *c*
    then subtract the number on dice *b*.

We can write:
    Score = *a* + *c* − *b*

So *a*, *b* and *c* can be any number from 1 to 6.

When *a* = 5, *b* = 4 and *c* = 2
    Score = *a* + *c* − *b*
    Score = 5 + 2 − 4
    Score = 3

Die   Die   Die
 a   *b*   *c*

A1 Score = *c* + *b* − *a*
    Calculate Score when:
    a = 5, *b* = 6, and *c* = 3

A2 Copy and complete this table
    for Score = *a* + *c* − *b*

a	*b*	*c*	Score
5	4	2	
6	5	3	
3	4	5	
6	2	6	
5	1	3	
1	5	2	
3	6	1	
2	5		3

B Expanding brackets

Skill 7B: *see page 44*

B1 Expand the brackets in each of
    these.
    a 4(5*k* − 2) **b** 3(4 + 5*w*)
    c 7(6*w* + 4*n*) **d** 5(8*g* − 3*y*)

Using formulas

Skill 13A
Substituting values
in formulas

A formula may be called
a rule.

A formula tells you how things are linked.

A formula for the perimeter *P* of a rectangle is:
    P = 2*l* + 2*w*

Example   A formula for the perimeter of a rectangle is:

    P = 2*l* + 2*w* (*P* is the perimeter, *l* is the length and *w* the width)

    Calculate the perimeter of a rectangle 17.4 cm long and 12.5 cm wide

        P = 2*l* + 2*w*   (*l* = 17.4 and *w* = 12.5)
        P = (2 × 17.4) + (2 × 12.5)
        P = 34.8 + 25
        P = 59.8

    The perimeter of the rectangle is 59.8 cm.

Exercise 13.1
Practising Skill 13A

1 A formula for the length *l* (cm) of tape used for a parcel is:
    l = 2*w* + 5 (*w* is the width of the parcel)

    Copy and complete this table.

w	*l*
15	35
18	○
23	○
34	○

73

2   A formula that links p, r and t is:
$r = 5p - 3t$

Copy and complete this table.

p	t	r
5	2	19
7	4	⬚
12	15	⬚
35	24	⬚
6.5	4	⬚
8	7.5	⬚
6.4	8.5	⬚

3   A formula that links h, p and w is:
$w = hp - 8$

hp is $h \times p$

Find the value of w when:

a $h = 6$ and $p = 7$
b $h = 9$ and $p = 12$
c $h = 14$ and $p = 5$
d $h = 16$ and $p = 4.5$

4   A formula that links y, k and n is:
$y = 4(k + n - 2)$

Find the value of y when:

a $k = 5$ and $n = 3$
b $k = 12$ and $n = 23$
c $k = 8$ and $n = 15$
d $k = 1$ and $n = 1$

5   A formula that links t, w and y is: $y = 3w + 2t$

a $w = 5$ and $t = {}^-2$
b $w = 6.5$ and $t = {}^-9$
c $w = {}^-1$ and $t = 20$
d $w = {}^-4$ and $t = 25$

Exercise 13.2
Using Skill 13A

1   Josh rents cars. He uses this formula to work out the charge.
$C = 15d + 25$ (C is the charge in pounds, d is the number of hire days.)

Calculate the charge C for:

a   9 days hire
b   15 days hire
c   21 days hire.

2   Ella drives a cab. This is the formula she uses to work out fares.
£F = £1.40 + £0.60m (F is the fare, m is the miles covered)

Use the formula to work out the fare for:

a   a 9-mile trip
b   a 25-mile trip.

3   In a bowling match this formula is used for the scores.
$S = 3p - 5$ (S is the score, p is the number of pins knocked down)

Use the formula to work out the score when:

a   9 pins are knocked down
b   6 pins are knocked down.

Equations

◆ An equation, like a formula, shows the link between amounts.

◆ An equation is like a puzzle because we say that we solve it.

◆ We solve an equation to find the value of an unknown amount.

> The unknown is shown by a letter.

Exercise 13.3
Finding the value of an unknown

1   What is the value of n in each of these?

    a $n + 3 = 8$ **b** $n + 4 = 12$ **c** $5 + n = 19$
    d $8 + n = 33$ **e** $n + 16 = 50$ **f** $37 + n = 52$
    g $44 + n = 65$ **h** $44 + n = 100$ **i** $105 + n = 234$

2   Solve each of these.

    a $n - 4 = 7$ **b** $w - 5 = 10$ **c** $t - 12 = 3$
    d $35 - k = 30$ **e** $56 - n = 6$ **f** $108 - b = 75$
    g $a - 121 = 91$ **h** $n - 185 = 35$ **i** $210 - c = 80$

3   Find the value of n in each of these.

    a $2n = 8$ **b** $3n = 27$ **c** $4n = 48$
    d $8n = 64$ **e** $10n = 90$ **f** $9n = 72$
    g $9n = 36$ **h** $8n = 24$ **i** $6n = 90$

Skill 13 B
Solving equations

◆ The two sides of an equation are equal.

◆ To solve an equation we can think of it as being balanced.

◆ To keep the balance you must do the same to both sides.

Example 1

Solve the equation $\qquad\qquad 3n + 4 = 31$
[take 4 from both sides] $\qquad 3n + 4 - 4 = 31 - 4$
$\qquad\qquad\qquad\qquad\qquad\qquad 3n = 27$
[divide both sides by 3] $\qquad\qquad\qquad \boldsymbol{n = 9}$

Example 2

Solve the equation $\qquad\qquad 7n - 5 = 37$
[add 5 to both sides] $\qquad 7n - 5 + 5 = 37 + 5$
$\qquad\qquad\qquad\qquad\qquad\qquad 7n = 42$
[÷ both sides by 7] $\qquad\qquad\qquad \boldsymbol{n = 6}$

Exercise 13.4
Practising Skill 13B

1   Solve each of these.

    a $5n + 4 = 29$ **b** $9n + 3 = 48$ **c** $8n + 6 = 38$
    d $10n + 8 = 98$ **e** $4n + 12 = 44$ **f** $7n + 1 = 50$
    g $9n + 7 = 61$ **h** $2n + 7 = 155$ **i** $2n + 4 = 17$

2   Find the value of n in each of these.

    a $6n - 5 = 25$ **b** $7n - 3 = 32$ **c** $9n - 8 = 10$
    d $11n - 4 = 18$ **e** $4n - 5 = 27$ **f** $3n - 15 = 6$
    g $7n - 6 = 50$ **h** $2n - 3 = 6$ **i** $2n - 5 = 10$

3   Solve these to find n.

    a $5 + 8n = 53$ **b** $8 + 4n = 72$ **c** $^-9 + 3n = 15$

Skill 13C
Solving equations
with brackets

◆ Some equations have brackets

◆ The first step is to expand the brackets. Skill 7B page 44

Example 1

Solve the equation	$3(2n + 3) = 57$
[expand the bracket]	$6n + 9 = 57$
[take 9 from both sides]	$6n + 9 - 9 = 57 - 9$
	$6n = 48$
[÷ both sides by 6]	$n = 8$

Example 2

Solve the equation	$4(3n + 1) = 64$
[expand]	$12n + 4 = 64$
[− 4]	$12n + 4 - 4 = 64 - 4$
	$12n = 60$
[÷ 12]	$n = 5$

Exercise 13.5
Practising Skill 13C

1 Solve each of these.

   a $2(4n + 3) = 30$ **b** $5(2y + 3) = 75$ **c** $6(2a + 1) = 90$
   d $3(2p + 4) = 42$ **e** $2(6w + 5) = 46$ **f** $4(2h + 6) = 64$
   g $5(c + 1) = 35$ **h** $7(t + 3) = 56$ **i** $9(m + 2) = 90$

2 Solve these to find n.

   a $3(2n - 1) = 15$ **b** $5(n - 3) = 55$ **c** $2(3n - 8) = 14$
   d $4(3n - 5) = 4$ **e** $7(n - 5) = 14$ **f** $2(4n - 1) = 38$
   g $8(2n - 1) = 8$ **h** $9(n - 4) = 36$ **i** $5(2n - 4) = 70$

3 Find the value of n in each of these.

   a $3(3n + 4) = 48$ **b** $4(2n - 5) = 36$ **c** $7(n - 4) = 7$
   d $5(n + 3) = 75$ **e** $7(n - 1) = 35$ **f** $3(3n + 1) = 57$
   g $12(n + 3) = 60$ **h** $10(2n + 1) = 50$ **i** $5(5n - 6) = 70$

Exercise 13.6
Using Skills 13B and 13C

1 ABCD is a rectangle.
The perimeter of ABCD is 42 cm.

   a Copy and complete this equation
      for the perimeter P.
      $P = \bigcirc + l + \bigcirc + 9$
   b Copy and complete this perimeter equation.
      $42 = \bigcirc l + \bigcirc$
      Solve the equation to find l.

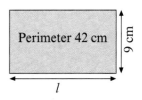

Perimeter 42 cm

9 cm

l

2 An equation that links k and w is
   $4(w - 3) = k$

   a Write the equation when $k = 12$.
   b Solve the equation to find w when $k = 12$.
   c Write the equation when $k = 4$.
   d Find w when $k = 4$.

Starting points

You need to know about ...

... so try these questions

A Odd and even numbers

An **even number** is one which has no remainder when it is divided by 2.

Ann **odd number** has a remainder of 1 when divided by 2.

Examples 34 is even because $34 \div 2 = 17$ (no remainder).
43 is odd because $43 \div 2 = 21$ remainder 1.

B Square numbers

A **square number** is one which can be shown in a square of dots.

Examples 16 is a square number.
It can be shown as a
4 by 4 square.

24 is not a square number.
It cannot be shown as a square.

A1 From Set A below, list six odd numbers?

A2 List 5 even numbers from Set A.

Set A				
20	21	22	23	24
25	26	27	28	29
30	31	32	33	34
35	36	37	38	39
40	41	42	43	44
45	46	47	48	49

B1 Give two numbers from Set A which are square numbers.

B2 What is the next square number after the last number in set A?

Multiples

Skill 14A
Finding multiples of a number

♦ A multiple of a number is made by multiplying it by any whole number.

Examples 48 is a multiple of 4 ... because $4 \times 12 = 48$
Some other multiples of 4 are 20, 4, 12, 172, ...

♦ You can tell if a number is a multiple of another one by dividing.

❖ If there is no remainder, then it is a multiple.

$35 \div 5 = 7$ (no remainder)

Examples These are multiples of 5:   35, 15, 40, 1435, ...
There is no remainder when you divide them by 5.

❖ If there is a remainder it is not a multiple.

$32 \div 5 = 6$ remainder 2

Examples These are not multiples of 5:   32, 7, 56, 71, 154, ...
There is a remainder when you divide by 5.

Exercise 14.1
Practising Skill 14A

1 List any four multiples of 7.

2 Which of these is not a multiple of 3?
   9 26 60 39 15 48 38 27

3 **a** Is 42 a multiple of 6?   **b** How can you tell?

4 **a** List the first five multiples of 9.
  b What pattern can you see in these multiples?

5 Simon thinks of a number less than 20. It is a multiple of 6 and a multiple of 4. What is the number?

6 Give a number that is a multiple of 4 and a multiple of 5.

7 How can you tell if a number is a multiple of 10?

Factors

Skill 14B
Finding factors of a number

A number divides exactly into another number when there is no remainder.

◆ A **factor** is a number which divides exactly into another number.

Examples   3 is a factor of 12   … 3 divides exactly into 12
7 is a factor of 35   … 7 divides exactly into 35

◆ A number can have many factors.

Example   The factors of 24 are 1, 2, 3, 4, 6, 8, 12, 24.
Each of these numbers will divide exactly into 24.

❖ 1 is a factor of every number.

❖ Every number has itself as one factor.

Exercise 14.2
Practising Skill 14B

1   1, 2, 4, 6 and 12 are all factors of 12.
One factor is missing. What is it?

2   List all four factors of 8.

3   Which of these numbers has 9 as a factor?
34   36   48   17   63   65   72

You can find all the factors by finding factor pairs.

Example
Find the factors of 48.

$1 \times 48 = 48$ $2 \times 24 = 48$
$3 \times 16 = 48$ $4 \times 12 = 48$
$6 \times 8 = 48$

So, all the factors of 48 are
1, 2, 3, 4, 6, 8, 12, 16, 24, 48

4   List all the factors of each of these numbers.
a   14   b   30   c   25   d   18

5   a   List all the factors of 20.
b   How many factors has 20?

6   How many factors has 33?

7   Find a number with only 2 different factors.

8   A number has only one factor.
What is it?

9   These are all the factors except two of a number.
The number is more than 40 but less than 100.
1   2   3   5   6   10   ◯   15   20   30   ◯
a   What is the number?
b   What is the other missing factor?

Prime Numbers

Skill 14C
Identifying prime numbers

◆ A prime number is a number with only two different factors.
One of its factors is always 1.
The other factor is the number itself.

Examples   17 is a prime number … 1 and 17 are its only factors (2 factors).
61 is a prime number … 1 and 61 are its only factors (2 factors).

◆ 1 is not a prime number.
2 is the first prime number and is the only even prime number.

Exercise 14.3
Practising Skill 14C

1   a   List all the factors of 11?
b   Is 11 a prime number? How can you tell?

2   Why is 1 not a prime number?

3 Is 21 a prime number? Explain your answer.

4 List all the prime numbers that are less than 10.

5 37 is a prime number. What is the next prime number after 37?

6 There is only one prime number between 90 and 100.
What is it?

7 Two of these numbers are not prime.

101   103   105   107   109   111   113

Which two are not prime numbers?

8 Some prime numbers can be made if you add two square numbers.
For example: 22 + 32 = 13 which is prime.

Show how four prime numbers can be made in this way.

Prime factors

Skill 14D
Finding prime factors

◆ A prime factor of a number is

  ❖ a prime number
  ❖ a factor of the number

◆ To find the prime factors of a number

  ❖ list all its factors
  ❖ find those factors which are prime.

Example   Find the prime factors of 60.

  ❖ The factors of 60 are 1, 2, 3, 4, 5, 6, 10, 12, 15, 20, 30, 60
  ❖ Only 2, 3 and 5 are prime.
  So, the prime factors of 60 are 2, 3 and 5.

Exercise 14.4
Practising Skill 14D

1 List the prime factors of 12.

2 Jim says the prime factors of 40 are 2, 5 and 10.
What has he done wrong?

3 Sue says the prime factors of 147 are 7 and 21.
What is wrong with this?

4 List all the prime factors of each of these numbers.

  a 56   **b** 42   **c** 28   **d** 54   **e** 64   **f** 45

5 **a** Give a number which has 2, and 5 as its only prime factors.
   b Give a different number with prime factors of only 2 and 5.

6 A number only has the prime factors 3 and 7.
Which of these could it be?

   42   63   103   121   147

7 Copy and complete this table. Choose three numbers to fit.

Number	Prime factors	No. of prime factors
15	3, 5	2
		2
		3
		4

Square roots

Skill 14E
Finding the square root of a number

25 is a square number (5 rows of 5 dots)

5 is called the square root of 25
This can be written as $\sqrt{25} = 5$
This means: the square root of 25 = 5

Example Calculate the value of $\sqrt{144} + \sqrt{49}$

$\sqrt{144} = 12$ (because $12 \times 12 = 144$) $\sqrt{49} = 7$ (because $7 \times 7 = 49$)

So $\sqrt{144} + \sqrt{49} = 12 + 7 = 19$.

Exercise 14.5
Practising Skill 14E

1 Find the value of each of these.

   a $\sqrt{100}$ **b** $\sqrt{16}$ **c** $\sqrt{81}$ **d** $\sqrt{25}$ **e** $\sqrt{64}$ **f** $\sqrt{121}$

2 If you know that $124^2 = 15\,376$, what is the value of $\sqrt{15\,376}$?

3 What is the square root of 400?

4 Calculate the value of

   a $\sqrt{9} + \sqrt{4}$ **b** $\sqrt{144} - \sqrt{121}$ **c** $\sqrt{169} - \sqrt{81}$

5 The square root of a number is 17.
   What is the number?

6 What is $\sqrt{3600}$?

Different types of number together

Exercise 14.6
Using different types of number

1 Copy the cross-number grid.
   Fill in the numbers from the clues.

Clues across
2 A factor of 36
4 The 3rd multiple of 110
6 20^2
7 $\sqrt{196}$
10 The prime number closest to 20
11 The first prime number after 140
12 $30^2 + \sqrt{81}$
14 A multiple of 21

Clues down
1 12 squared
3 A prime factor of 46
5 18^2
7 A prime factor of 66
8 The 10th multiple of 12
9 A prime number between 20 and 30
10 14 squared
13 $10^2 - \sqrt{4}$

2 On a 5 by 5 grid make up your own cross-number puzzle.
   Show the clues you use.

Starting points

You need to know about ...   ... so try these questions

A Tallying and frequency tables

In surveys, data can be recorded in frequency tables.
A tally helps when you count the items.

Example This table shows the results of a bird survey.

Bird type	Tally	Frequency
Sparrow	ＪＨＴ ＪＨＴ ＪＨＴ ＪＨＴ ＩＩ	22
Blackbird	ＪＨＴ ＪＨＴ ＩＩＩ	13
Robin	ＪＨＴ ＩＩＩ	8
Magpie	ＩＩ	2
Starling	ＪＨＴ ＪＨＴ ＪＨＴ ＪＨＴ ＪＨＴ	25
Wren	ＩＩＩＩ	4
Crow	ＪＨＴ ＪＨＴ Ｉ	11

B Bar and bar line charts

♦ These can have horizontal or
  vertical bars.

♦ There are usually gaps
  between the bars.

Horizontal   Vertical

♦ Scales may be marked in single units or 5s or 10s, and so on.

Example This **bar chart** shows the data from an animal survey.

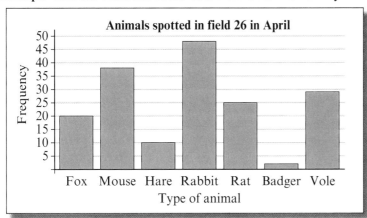

This data can also be shown in a bar-line chart.

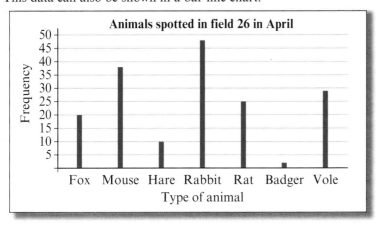

A1 Copy and complete the
frequency table for this saying.

IF YOUR BOB DOESN'T
GIVE MY BOB THE BOB
THAT YOUR BOB OWES
MY BOB, MY BOB WILL
GIVE YOUR BOB A BOB IN
THE EYE.

Letter	Tally
A	ＩＩ
B	
C	
D	
E	
F	
G	
H	
I	

B1 How many rats were seen in
the survey?

B2 For which animal were the
smallest numbers seen?

B3 Which animal had:
    a the highest frequency
    b the lowest frequency?

B4 How many voles were seen?

B5 There were 11 of one type of
animal seen. What animal was
that?

B6 How many more rabbits than
mice were seen?

B7 How many animals in total
were seen?

Other types of bar chart

◆ Where two groups are looked at a comparative bar chart can be used.
A key is used to show the colour of each group.

Example

This chart shows the birth months of people in a factory.

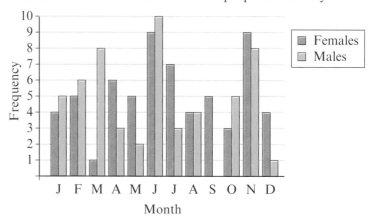

The two groups to compare here are males and females.
For instance, 7 males and 3 females were born in July.

Exercise 15.1
Comparative bar charts

1   In which two months were 5 females born ?

2   In which months were more males than females born ?

3   How many males and how many females were born in October ?

4   In which month were the same number of males and females born ?

5   How many females were born in September ?

6   In which month was there the greatest difference between births of
    males and females ?

7   **a** How many males work in the factory ?
    b How many people in total work in the factory ?

8   This frequency table gives the test marks for students in two forms.
    The test was marked out of 8.

Test mark	0	1	2	3	4	5	6	7	8
Frequency – Form 11S	0	2	3	3	7	6	2	9	1
Frequency – Form 11M	0	0	1	7	4	8	5	2	1

a On axes like these draw a comparative
bar chart to show the data.

b How many students took the test
in form 11S ?

c How many students got more than
4 marks in form 11M ?

d Which form do you think
did better in the test ?
Give reasons for your answer.

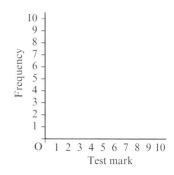

> In an exam, more marks
> might be given for your
> reasons in question **8d** than
> for your first answer.

Split bar charts are often used when data is given in percentages.

◆ A split bar chart can be used to show more than one piece of data about each entry.

Example   This chart shows how four people spend their money.

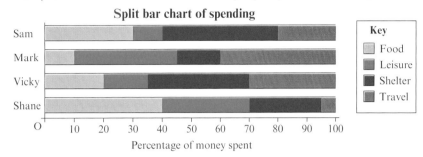

Mark spends most of his money on travel (40% on travel).

This chart is horizontal but they can also be vertical.

Exercise 15.2
Reading a split bar chart

1 **a** Who spends most on food?
   b What percentage does this person spend on food?

2 **a** Who spends least on leisure?
   b What percentage is this?

3 One person lives a long way from work.
   Who do you think this is? Explain your answer.

4 One person still lives at home.
   Who do you think this is?

5 List the percentage each person spends on shelter.

Pictograms

A pictogram uses a symbol to stand for a number of units of data.

◆ Each symbol should be the same size.

◆ It is best to use the same symbol all the way through.

◆ You have to estimate what parts of the symbol stand for.

Example

This pictogram shows the number of computers owed in each form.
For instance, 13 people have computers in form 5.

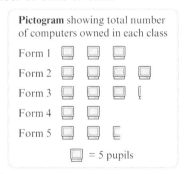

Pictogram showing total number of computers owned in each class

Exercise 15.3
Pictograms

1 How many people in each of the other forms have computers?

2 **a** Draw a pictogram for this data.

Country	UK	Nigeria	India	Iran	Spain
Male life span (years)	72	49	58	65	74

Use the symbol (⏰) to stand for 10 years.

3 This table gives the life span of women in different countries.

Country	UK	Nigeria	India	Iran	Spain
Life span (years)	78	52	58	66	80

Draw a pictogram using the symbol ⧗ to stand for 20 years

4 This table shows the number of CD's sold in a shop in a morning. Draw a pictogram to show this data. Choose a symbol to use.

Type of CD	Jazz	Folk	Indie	Rock	Reggae	Pop
Number sold	6	12	32	26	16	40

Pie charts

Skill 15A
Drawing a pie chart

♦ A pie chart gives a quick picture of the size of different parts of a total.

Action **C**oncern	Children	£58
Amount given to	Elderly	£46
charity this week	Green issues	£22
	Medical	£18

♦ To draw a pie chart:

❖ add the amounts to find the total
58 + 46 + 22 + 18 = **144**

There are 360° at the centre of a circle.

360°

The £144 is shared between the 360°.

❖ divide 360° by the total
360° ÷ 144 = **2.5°**

❖ work out the angle for each group
Children   58 × 2.5° = 145°
Elderly   46 × 2.5° = 115°
Green issues 22 × 2.5° = 55°
Medical   18 × 2.5° = 45°
                360°

❖ draw the pie chart

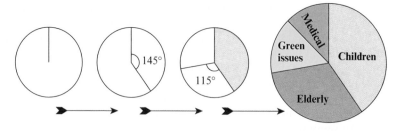

Exercise 15.4
Practising skill 15A

1 A local survey into where a group of people went for their main holiday gave this data.

Country	Spain	Greece	Turkey	Malta	UK
No. of people	6	8	5	3	2

a How many people were in the group?
b List the angles which would show each country in a pie chart.
c Draw and label a pie chart to show the data.

2 This table shows types of main meal eaten by people in Carlo's bar on Friday night. Each person had only one type.

a How many people ate at the bar?

b Draw a pie chart to show the data.

Meal type	No. of people
Meat	51
Vegetarian	25
Fish	36
Sea food	8

3 This table shows how a group of people travel to work.

Method	Car	Motorbike	Walk	Cycle	Bus	Train
No. of people	103	13	46	61	15	2

Draw a pie chart to show the data.

Exercise 15.5
Using skill 15A

1 Match each pie chart to its own table of data.

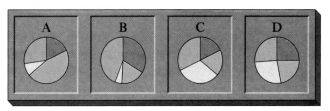

Table 1		Table 2		Table 3		Table 4	
Make	No.	Make	No.	Make	No.	Make	No.
Ford	18	Ford	34	Ford	18	Ford	25
Vauxhall	46	Vauxhall	17	Vauxhall	18	Vauxhall	22
Citroën	9	Citroën	5	Citroën	32	Citroën	27
Honda	27	Honda	44	Honda	32	Honda	26

2 These 3D pie charts show how three people spend their money.

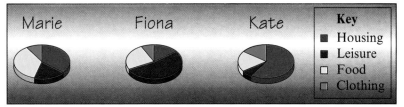

a Who spends most of their money on leisure?

b Who spends 3 times as much on housing as on food?

c Fiona spends £240 a week.
Estimate how much she spends on food.

d Marie spends £120 on housing each week.
Estimate how much she spends on leisure.

3 This pie chart shows the results of a car colour survey of 60 cars.

Estimate the number of cars that were

a blue   **b** green   **c** red

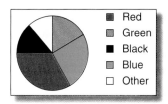

Starting points
You need to know about ...   ... so try these questions

A Powers of 10

We can write 100 as 10×10

We can use a shorthand for 10×10
we can write $10 \times 10 = 10^2$ [we say 'ten to the power of 2']

So, 10^3 is ten to the power of 3
... 10^4 is ten to the power of 4
... and so on.

We can write 100, 1000, 10000, 100000 etc. as powers of 10.

$100 = 10 \times 10 = 10^2$
$1000 = 10 \times 10 \times 10 = 10^3$
$10000 = 10 \times 10 \times 10 \times 10 = 10^4$
$100000 = 10 \times 10 \times 10 \times 10 \times 10 = 10^5$
$1000000 = 10 \times 10 \times 10 \times 10 \times 10 \times 10 = 10^6$
...

A1 Copy and complete this table:

Number	is	is
300	3×100	3×10^2
500	$5 \times$	$\times 10^2$
6000	$6 \times$	
8000	$8 \times$	
20000	$2 \times$	
50000	$5 \times$	
600000	$6 \times$	
300000	$3 \times$	
4000000	$4 \times$	
9000000	$9 \times$	

Multiplying decimals by powers of ten

Skill 16 A
Multiplying decimals by powers of ten

When you multiply a decimal value by 10, 100, 1000, 10000, ... , the answer will be a larger value.

A pattern builds up as you multiply by larger and larger values.
$5.4 \times 10 = 54$ we can write as $5.4 \times 10 = 54$
$5.4 \times 100 = 540$ $5.4 \times 10^2 = 540$
$5.4 \times 1000 = 5400$ $5.4 \times 10^3 = 5400$
$5.4 \times 10000 = 54000$ $5.4 \times 10^4 = 54000$
and so on   and so on

Look at the place values for these multiplications

10 000	1000	100	10	U		$\frac{1}{10}$	$\frac{1}{100}$	
				5	.	4		digits start here
			5	4	.			[5.4 × 10]
		5	4	0	.			[5.4 × 10²]
	5	4	0	0	.			[5.4 × 10³]
5	4	0	0	0	.			[5.4 × 10⁴]

(labels left of table: digits start here / move 1 place left / move 2 places left / move 3 places left / move 4 places left)

Zeros fill in place values as the digits move to the left.

So for $\times 10$ the digits move 1 place to the left
for $\times 10^2$ the digits move 2 places to the left
for $\times 10^3$ the digits move 3 places to the left
for $\times 10^4$ the digits move 4 places to the left
... and so on ... and so on ... and so on ...

Example

Calculate 12.6752×10^3
For '$\times 10^3$' the digits move 3 places to the left

It is the digits that move to the left.

So $12.6752 \times 10^3 = 12675.2$.

Exercise 16.1
Practising Skill 16A

1 Copy and complete each of these.

a $3.165 \times 10^2 =$	**b** $27.56 \times 10^3 =$	**c** $105.24 \times 10^2 =$
d $4.1056 \times 10^3 =$	**e** $23.155 \times 10^2 =$	**f** $34.618 \times 10 =$
g $5.44 \times 10^2 =$	**h** $153.4 \times 10 =$	**i** $1.16552 \times 10^4 =$
j $34.75 \times 10^4 =$	**k** $6.25 \times 10^3 =$	**l** $5.5451 \times 10^2 =$
m $158.75 \times 10^3 =$	**n** $8.5 \times 10^4 =$	**o** $1.6667 \times 10^5 =$

Do not use a calculator for this exercise

2 Copy and complete each of these.

a $0.6575 \times 10^2 =$	**b** $0.0545 \times 10^3 =$	**c** $0.00558 \times 10 =$
d $0.00675 \times 10^4 =$	**e** $0.0752 \times 10 =$	**f** $0.000868 \times 10^5 =$
g $0.3575 \times 10^4 =$	**h** $0.0861 \times 10^5 =$	**i** $0.175 \times 10^4 =$
j $0.0924 \times 10 =$	**k** $0.105 \times 10^2 =$	**l** $0.0050605 \times 10^3 =$
m $0.5006 \times 10^2 =$	**n** $0.004 \times 10^4 =$	**o** $0.00005 \times 10 =$

Dividing decimals by powers of 10

Skill 16B
Dividing decimals by powers of 10

When you divide a decimal value by 10, 100, 1000, 10000, … the answer will be a smaller value.

There is a pattern as you divide by larger and larger values.

$54 \div 10$	$= 5.4$	
$54 \div 10^2$	$= 0.54$	$[10^2 = 100]$
$54 \div 10^3$	$= 0.054$	$[10^3 = 1000]$
$54 \div 10^4$	$= 0.0054$	$[10^4 = 10000]$

and so on.

Look at the place values for these divisions

	100	10	U		$\frac{1}{10}$	$\frac{1}{100}$	$\frac{1}{1000}$	$\frac{1}{10000}$	
digits start here		5	4	•					
move 1 place right			5	•	4				$[54 \div 10]$
move 2 places right			0	•	5	4			$[54 \div 10^2]$
move 3 places right			0	•	0	5	4		$[54 \div 10^3]$
move 4 places right			0	•	0	0	5	4	$[54 \div 10^4]$

0's fill in place values as the digits move to the right.

So for $\div 10$ the digits move 1 place right
for $\div 10^2$ the digits move 2 places right
for $\div 10^3$ the digits move 3 places right
for $\div 10^4$ the digits move 4 places right
… and so on … and so on … and so on …

Example

Calculate $3.375 \div 10^2$
$\div 10^2$ the digits move 2 places right

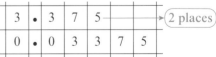

So $3.375 \div 10^2 = 0.03375$.

It is the digits that move to the right.

Exercise 16.2
Practising Skill 16B

1 Copy and complete each of these.

a $4.652 \div 10^2 =$	**b** $135.5 \div 10^3 =$	**c** $2352.65 \div 10 =$
d $12.5 \div 10^3 =$	**e** $135.75 \div 10^4 =$	**f** $385.4 \div 10 =$
g $3.65 \div 10^3 =$	**h** $27.75 \div 10 =$	**i** $3.054 \div 10^3 =$
j $12.04 \div 10^4 =$	**k** $6500.4 \div 10^5 =$	**l** $875.25 \div 10^2 =$
m $0.5 \div 10^3 =$	**n** $354.1 \div 10^4 =$	**o** $385 \div 10^5 =$

Do not use a calculator for this exercise.

2   Copy and complete each of these.

    a $0.45 \div 10 =$ b $0.125 \div 10^3 =$ c $0.275 \div 10^2 =$

    d $0.04 \div 10 =$ e $0.725 \div 10^4 =$ f $0.05 \div 10^3 =$

    g $0.755 \div 10^2 =$ h $0.4 \div 10^3 =$ i $0.15 \div 10 =$

    j $0.405 \div 10^2 =$ k $0.006 \div 10 =$ l $0.75 \div 10^4 =$

Multiplying decimals

Skill 16C
Multiplying decimals by a whole number

This way uses an estimate of the answer.

Example

Without a calculator, find the value of 13.56×7

An estimate is: $13 \times 7 = 91$

```
   13.56
 ×   7
 ───────
   94.92
```

The digits in the answer are 9492.

The estimate is 91

The decimal point is placed to give 94.92

So **13.56 × 7 = 94.92.**

> The decimal point can be put to make: 9.492, 94.92, and 949.2 from the digits.
>
> Only 94.92 is close to the estimate.

Exercise 16.3
Practising Skill 16C

1   Without a calculator find the value of:

    a 12.35×4 b 18.37×9 c 235.52×3

    d 28.75×6 e 157.8×5 f 3.075×7

    g 104.65×8 h 16.075×9 i 155.36×4

    j 88.675×5 k 907.38×6 l 4304.07×3

Skill 16D
Multiplying a decimal value by a decimal value

You can use an estimate of the answer to help.

Example   Without a calculator, find the values of 18.6×2.4

An estimate is: $18 \times 2 = 36$

```
   18.6
 × 2.4
 ──────
   744
  3720
 ──────
  4164
```

The digits in the answer are 4464.

The estimate is 36

The decimal point is placed to give 44.64

So **18.6 × 2.4 = 44.64.**

Exercise 16.4
Practising Skill 16D

1   Copy and complete this table. Do not use a calculator.

Calculate	Estimate	Answer
24.3×6.4	144	
45.2×3.6		
66.2×5.3		
78.4×6.2		
94.6×7.1		
75.5×8.5		

2 Without a calculator find the value of:

   a 17.4×9.6 **b** 34.3×5.4 **c** 54.2×7.1

   d 97.5×6.6 **e** 65.3×4.4 **f** 157.4×3.5

   g 255.3×5.4 **h** 338.5×4.2 **i** 457.3×7.5

Exercise 16.5

Using Skills 16A, 16B, 16C and 16D

1 Four students calculated 45.5×7.3 without a calculator.
These were their answers:

Jenny	33.215
Ikbal	3321.5
Ian	3.3215
Kim	332.15

   a Estimate the answer to 45.5×7.3

   b Whose answer might be right?

   c Calculate 45.5×7.3 without a calculator.

   d Whose answer was right?

2 Rob hand-makes chocolates.
It takes him 15.4 seconds to make one Celtic Coffee.

Calculate how long it should take Rob to make 8 Celtic Coffee chocolates.
Do not use a calculator.

3 The life of a battery is given as 4.5565×10^3 seconds.

   a How many seconds is this?

   b Is this more than, or less than, 5000 seconds?

4 The life of a light-bulb is given as 0.63546×10^4 hours.

Is this more or less than 6000 hours?
Explain your answer.

5 A machine takes 3674.5 seconds to make 10000 plastic spoons.

   a Copy and complete this: $10\,000 = 10^{\square}$

   b How long does it take to make one plastic spoon?

6 It takes a printer 3.585 seconds to print one label.
A firm orders one hundred thousand of these labels.

   a Write one hundred thousand in digits.

   b Copy and complete:

     One hundred thousand is ten to the power of ... .

   c How long will it take to print all one hundred thousand labels?

7 Intercity Parcels will take boxes that weigh no more than 100 kg.
One Microdesk kit weighs 12.62 kg.
8 Microdesk kits are packed in one box.

   a Will Intercity parcels take this box?

   b Explain your answer and show any calculations you did.
     Do not use a calculator.

8 These are two questions from a test.

   a Explain what you think has
     happened to give these answers.

   b What should the answers be?

16	$1345.54 \times 10^3 = 1.34554$	✗
17	$0.57541 \times 10^4 = 575.41$	✗

Dividing a decimal by a whole number

Skill 16E
Dividing a decimal by a
whole number

Remainders are carried on,
so the calculation goes:

4 into 13 is	3 rem 1
4 into 18 is	4 rem 2
4 into 27 is	6 rem 3
4 into 36 is	9

This is one way to divide a decimal by a whole number.

Example 1   Dividing by a single digit number gives $138.76 \div 4$

$$4)13^18.^27^36$$
$$\overline{3\,4.\,6\,9}$$

↖ The decimal points line up

So 138.76 ÷ 4 = 34.69

Example 2   Calculate $254.62 \div 5$ [without using a calculator]

$$5)254.^46^12^20$$ This 0 is put on to deal with the 2 rem
$$\overline{50.\,9\,2\,4}$$

So 254.62 ÷ 5 = 50.924

Example 3   Dividing by a two-digit number gives $416.52 \div 18$

$$18)41^56.^25^72$$
$$\overline{2\,3.\,1\,4}$$

So 416.52 ÷ 18 = 23.14

Example 4   Calculate $351.39 \div 15$

$$15)35^56.^63^39^90$$ This 0 is put on to deal with the 9 rem
$$\overline{2\,3.\,4\,2\,6}$$

So 351.39 ÷ 15 = 23.426

Exercise 16.6
Practising Skill 16E

1   Without a calculator find the value of:

a $57.312 \div 8$	**b** $132.104 \div 7$	**c** $381.504 \div 4$
d $578.754 \div 9$	**e** $1286.72 \div 4$	**f** $1365.75 \div 5$
g $2128.35 \div 7$	**h** $1236.4 \div 5$	**i** $579.54 \div 4$
j $7963.53 \div 6$	**k** $6534.18 \div 5$	**l** $950.52 \div 8$

2   Calculate the value of each of these (without a calculator).

a $3885.72 \div 12$	**b** $859.362 \div 14$	**c** $1988.115 \div 15$
d $4388.992 \div 16$	**e** $1983.9 \div 12$	**f** $68513.4 \div 17$
g $380.43 \div 15$	**h** $5203.22 \div 11$	**i** $4448.899 \div 13$

Exercise 16.7
Using Skill 16E

1   A long-distance relay team has 8 runners.
Each person runs the same distance.
The relay covers a total of 610.8 kilometres.

Find the distance covered by each runner. (Do not use a calculator.)

2   A display is made using 15 cans of beans.
The total weight of the cans in the display is 6095.25 grams.

Find the weight of one can of beans in the display.
Show any calculations you do to find your answer.

3   An ink-jet printer takes 290.1 seconds to print 12 copies of the same page.

At this rate, how long should it take to print one copy?

4   Kit recycles printer ink-bottles.
He uses 956.25 ml of ink to refill 18 type A bottles.

How much ink is used to refill one type A bottle?

This revises the work in Sections 12 to 16

1 Skill 12A
Find the area of each of these rectangles.

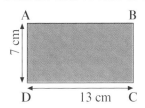
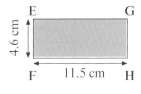

2 A rectangle is 8.3 cm long.
It has an area of 37.35 cm².
Find the width of the rectangle.

3 Skill 12B
Find the area of each of these triangles.

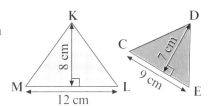

4 Skill 12C
Calculate the perimeter of this shape.

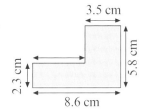

5 Skill 13A
A formula that links *l*, *t*, and *w* is: $l = 8w - 5t$

Copy and complete this table.

w	t	l
4	5	◯
7	6	◯
3.5	3	◯
50	40	◯

6 Skill 13B
Solve each of these.

a $5n + 4 = 44$ b $6 + 8y = 62$
c $7k - 3 = 32$ d $^-8 + 9n = 28$
e $6(w + 1) = 48$ f $4(h - 3) = 16$
g $8(3 + 2m) = 56$ h $2(3d - 4) = ^-2$

7 a Add all the even numbers less than 9.
b Add all the odd numbers less than 10.
c Which of these are square numbers?

56 75 81 32 49 20 88

8 Skill 14A
Which of these is a multiple of 7?

56 75 81 49 35 67 42 90

9 A number less than 20 is a multiple of 3 and a multiple of 5. What is the number?

10 Skill 14B
List all the factors of these numbers.

a 18 b 24 c 28

11 Skill 14C
List all the prime number that are less than 20.

12 Skill 14D
List the prime factors of 20.

13 Skill 14E
Calculate the value of each of these.

a $\sqrt{49} + \sqrt{25}$ b $\sqrt{81} - \sqrt{36}$ c $\sqrt{6400}$

Use these tables for questions 15 to 17.
They show the the number of hours two girls spent on different activities.

Elaine Manning		Sarah Cutts	
Activity	No. of hours	Activity	No. of hours
Work	24	Work	28
Sport	17	Sport	2
Reading	5	Reading	0
TV	10	TV	26
Eating	4	Eating	4

14 Draw a comparative bar chart to show the data.

15 Copy and complete the split bar chart to show the data for each girl.

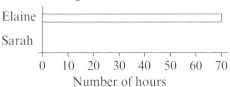

16 Skill 15A
Draw a pie chart to show the data for Elaine.

17 Skill 16A and Skill 16B
Copy and complete each of these.

a 1.384×10^4 b 0.00566×10^5
c $158.62 \div 10^2$ d $23.405 \div 10^4$

18 Skill 16C and Skill 16D
Without a calculator find the value of:

a 13.54×7 b 12.5×8.4 c 7.2×9.4

19 Skill 16E
Without a calculator find the value of:

a $273.96 \div 8$ b $192.64 \div 14$

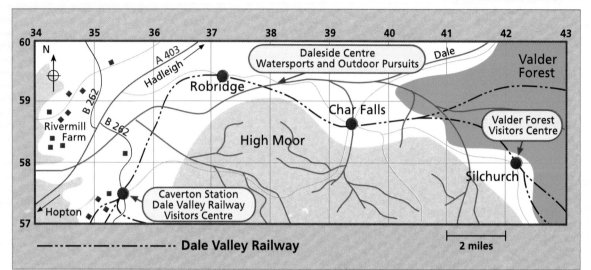

Dale Valley Railway Spring 1997

—————·—·— Dale Valley Railway

2 miles

Dale Valley Railway

Timetable 1 May to 30 September

	Depart	Depart	Depart
Caverton Station	1000	1200	1430
Robridge	1012	1212	1445
Char Falls	1025	1225	1505
Silchurch	a 1040	a 1240	a 1520

	Depart	Depart	Depart
Silchurch	1105	1330	1610
Char Falls	1120	1345	1628
Robridge	1135	1400	1645
Caverton Station	a 1145	a 1410	a 1700

a – arrival time

** Note – in May and September there is no 1200 departure

Fares

Adult	£5.50
Child (under 14 years)	£3.00
Senior Citizen	£3.50

* Note all fares are return
  no single tickets are for sale

Festival Special

Adult	£12.50
Child (under 14 years)	£6.50
Senior Citizen	£9.50

* Note all fares include lunch
  at the Railway Arms in Silchurch

Information card

Weights and Measures

Locomotive	55 tons
Type A coach	27 tons
Type B coach	37 tons
Coal	1.5 tons
Water	500 gallons

1 gallon of water weighs 10 lb

1 ton = 2240 lb

Tally for Festival Special

Adult	// ////////////////////////////
Child	/////////////////////
Senior Citizen	// // ////////////////////////////

1   What is the area of one grid square on the map?

2   Estimate the area of High Moor on the map.

3   Tony estimates the area of Valder Forest on the map as 12 square miles.
    a   Do you agree with this estimate?
    b   If your answer to part **a** is no, what is your estimate of the area?

4   When you travel from Robridge to Char Falls by road, is the railway on your left or right?

5   Which station is at the eastern end of the Dale Valley Railway?

6   a   On what date does the timetable start?
    b   On what date does the timetable end?
    c   How many days is the timetable for?

7   If you catch the 14:30 from Calverton Station:
    a   When will you arrive in Char Falls?
    b   How long will this journey take?

8   You want to go from Robridge to Silchurch by train. You arrive at Robridge station at 12 50 pm.
    a   When does the next train leave for Silchurch?
    b   How long will you have to wait for a train?
    c   When will you get to Silchurch?

9   Bob walked to Silchurch station and got there at 3.15 pm.
    a   When was the next train to Robridge?
    b   How long did he have to wait?
    c   At what time did he get to Robridge?

10   How long does the 14:30 from Calverton take to get to Silchurch?

11   Copy the Dale Valley Railway timetable and give all the times using am or pm.

12   How much lighter is a Type A coach than a Type B?

13   The trains are made up in this way.

Month	Coach A	Coach B
May	3	2
June	3	3
July	4	3
Aug	4	4
Sept	3	4

    a   In which month are fewest coaches used?
    b   In which month are most coaches used?
    c   Calculate the total weight of the coaches used each month.

14   Copy and complete:
    The water for the locomotive is $5 \times 10^{\blacksquare}$ gallons.

15   A Type A coach weighs sixty thousand four hundred and eighty pounds. Write this weight in digits.

16   a   Calculate the weight of the locomotive in lb.
    b   Write this number of lb in words.

17   This data shows the amount of coal used over ten days.

Date	Coal used (tons)
1 May	0.7
2 May	0.88
3 May	0.75
4 May	1.2
5 May	0.9
6 May	1.4
7 May	2
8 May	1.75
9 May	0.5
10 May	2.4

From the data:
    a   On which data was most coal used?
    b   When was the least amount of coal used?
    c   Find the amount of coal used in total (without using a calculator).
    d   How much more coal was used on 8 May than on 2 May?
    e   On which date was roughly twice as much coal used than on 2 May?

18   For each of these groups find the total paid in normal fares.

Group	Adult	Child	Sen. Cit.
A	2	3	0
B	2	1	1
C	1	4	1
D	3	5	0
E	4	6	0

19   How many children went on the Festival Special?

20   In total how much was paid in fares for children on the Festival Special?

21   On the Festival Special:
    a   How many adult tickets were sold?
    b   How many Senior Citizens were there?

22   What was the total paid by Senior Citizens for Festival Special tickets?

23   What was the total paid for all the tickets sold for the Festival Special?

Starting points
You need to know about ...

... so try these questions

A Angles and turning

- An angle shows an amount of turn.
- Angles are measured in degrees.
- One full turn is 360°.
- A right-angle is 90°.

- Angles are described with the terms:
  acute   (between 0° and 90°)
  obtuse   (between 90° and 180°)
  or   reflex   (between 180° and 360°)

- To measure or draw an angle use:
  an angle measurer or a protractor

A1 Label each angle acute, obtuse or reflex.

    a 125°   **b** 300°   **c** 165°
    d 58°   **e** 275°   **f** 85°

A2 How many right angles are in:

    a half a full turn
    b a full turn

A3 Draw angles of:

    a 55°   **b** 135°   **c** 26°

A4 **a** Draw a triangle.
     b Measure each angle.

Angles at a point

Skill 17 A
Calculating angles at a point

Angles at a point make one full turn.

Angles **a**, **b**, **c**, and **d**
- ❖ meet at a point
- ❖ and make one full turn

One full turn is 360° so we say that:
Angles at a point add up to 360°.

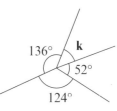

Example

In the diagram calculate angle **k**.

The angles meet at a point so:
$$136 + 124 + 52 + k = 360$$
$$312 + k = 360$$
$$k = 360 - 312$$
$$k = 48$$

Angle k is 48°.

Exercise 17.1
Practising Skill 17A

1 In each diagram calculate the angle marked with a letter.

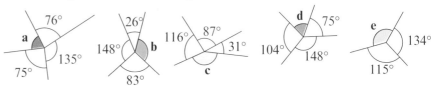

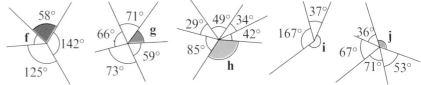

Skill 17B
Calculating angles on a
straight line

A straight line shows half a full turn.

Half a full turn is 180°.

So angles on a straight line make 180°.

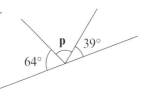

Example

Calculate the angle marked **p** in the diagram.

Angles 64, **p** and 39 make 180°.

So 64 + **p** + 39 = 180
         103 + **p** = 180
                  p = 77

The angle marked p is 77°.

Exercise 17.2
Practising Skill 17B

1   Calculate the angle marked with a letter in each of these.

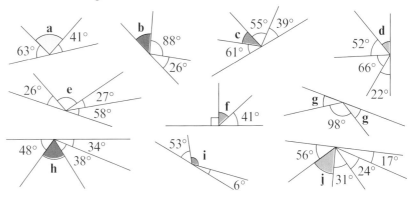

Skill 17C
Calculating angles between
intersecting lines

When straight lines intersect, they cross each other.

When these two lines intersect they make 4 angles.

We can say this about the angles:

❖ **a** + **b** + **c** + **d** = 360° (angles at a point)

❖ **a** + **b** = 180° (angles on a straight line)

❖ **c** + **d** = 180° (angles on a straight line)

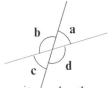

> Angles **a** and **c** are called
> vertically opposite angles.
> Vertically opposite angles
> are equal.

Also, from the diagram: angles **a** and **c** are vertically opposite each other
angles **b** and **d** are vertically opposite each other.

So we can say that **a** = **c** and **b** = **d**.

Example

In the diagram calculate angles **k**, **w**, and **t**.

36° + **k** = 180° (angles on a straight line)   **k** = 144°

36° and **w** are vertically opposite so: **w** = 36°
k and **t** are vertically opposite so: **t** = 144°

In the diagram angle k = 144°, angle w = 36°, angle t = 144°.

Exercise 17.3
Practising Skill 17C

1 Calculate the angles marked with letters in each of these.

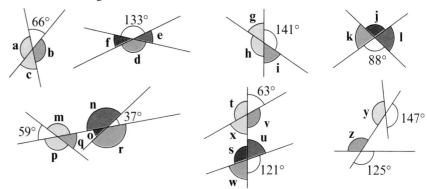

Parallel lines are lines that are always the same distance apart.

Parallel lines are shown by arrows.
In the diagram: AB is parallel to CD
         and EG is parallel to FH

Often railway lines are used as an example of parallels.

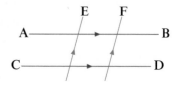

Skill 17D
Calculating angles beween
parallel lines

Alternate angles are also
known as Z-angles

Corresponding angles are
also known as F-angles.

When a line intersects (crosses) two parallels, two types of angle are made.

Alternate angles   and   **Corresponding angles**

These are alternate angles.   These are corresponding angles.

Alternate angles are equal.   Corresponding angles are equal.

Example   Example

Find angle **p**.   Find angle **w**.

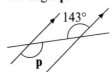   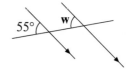

Angle **p** and 143° are alternate   Angle **w** and 55° are corresponding

So p = 143°.   **So w = 55°.**

Exercise 17.4
Practising Skill 17D

1 From the diagram calculate the angles marked with a letter.

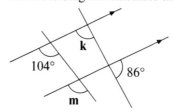

2 Calculate each angle marked with a letter.

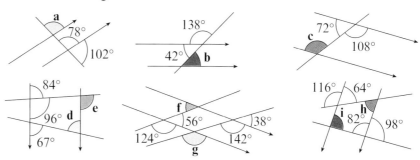

Exercise 17.5
Using Skills 17A, 17B, 17C, and 17D

1 The diagram shows four shapes that fit together.
  a Calculate the angle marked **a**.
  b Calculate the angle marked **b**.

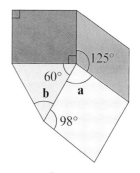

2 The diagram shows part of a roof.
  a Name two lines that are parallel.
  b Calculate the angle marked **c**.
  c Calculate angle **d**.
  d Is angle **e** more or less than 100°? Explain your answer.

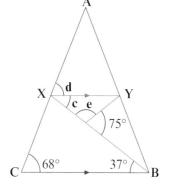

3 The diagram shows a cargo lift.
  a What type of angles are **h** and **j**?
  b Name two alternate angles.
  c What is the size of angle **g**? Give a reason for your answer.
  d What is the size of angle **h**? Give a reason for your answer.
  e Is angle **i** = 46°? Explain.

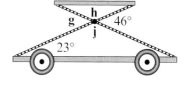

4 ABCD is a rectangle.
  a Name two alternate angles.
  b Calculate the size of angle **w**.
  c What is the size of angle **k**? Give a reason for your answer.
  d Explain why angle **y** is 51°.
  e What is the size of angle **m**?

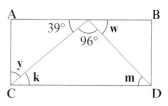

Starting points
You need to know about ...   ... so try these questions

A Adding Decimals

Skill 4B: *see page 28*

B Subtracting decimals

Skill 4C: *see page 29*

C Multiplying decimals

Skill 16C: *see page 88*

D Dividing decimals

Skill 16E: *see page 90*

A1 a $6.56 + 2.952 + 34.2 = \bigcirc$
b $5.45 + 7 + 0.234 = \bigcirc$
c $98 + 2.45 + 0.541 = \bigcirc$

B1 a $34.5 - 1.45 = \bigcirc$
b $62 - 4.356 = \bigcirc$

C1 a $2.7 \times 5 = \bigcirc$
b $4.5 \times 2.4 = \bigcirc$

D1 a $86 \div 4 = \bigcirc$
b $45.752 \div 8 = \bigcirc$

Money calculations

Skill 18A
Adding and subtracting money

To add or subtract money without a calculator:

❖ remember that 6p is £0.06 and 75p is £0.75
❖ write the amounts so that the place values line up.

Example 1

Calculate the total of
£15 + 75p + £300 + 74.63 + 6p

```
 £   p
 15.00
  0.75
300.00
 74.63
  0.06
------
390.44
```

Example 2

What is £56 - 18p?

```
 £   p
56.00
 0.18
-----
55.82
```

Exercise 18.1
Practising Skill 18A

1 Calculate the answer to each of these.
a £6.54 + £5 + £32.12   **b** £13.65 – £6.74
c 54p + £2.54 + £4 + 75p   **d** £30 – £7.46
e £86 + £4.20 + 7p + £45.32   **f** £98 – 89p
g 8p + £400 + 27p + £1.26   **h** £392 – £5.76

2 What is the missing amount in each of these?
a £45 + 78p + ■ = £54.85   **b** 4p + £3 + 95p + £432 = ■
c £645 + ■ + £14.35 = £700   **d** £56.54 – ■ = 20p
e 45p + ■ + £6.73 = £42.60   **f** ■ – £45.90 = 12p
g £9.78 + 67p + ■ + £4 = £20   **h** ■ – £5.67 = £254.12

Skill 18B
Multiplying and dividing
money

To multiply or divide money:

❖ decide if you are going to work in £ or pence
❖ do the calculation
❖ decide if your answer needs to be changed into £.

Example 1 What is 67p × 35?

Working in pence

$$
\begin{array}{r}
67 \times \\
35 \\
\hline
335 \\
2010 \\
\hline
2345 \\
\end{array}
$$

Working in £

$$
\begin{array}{r}
0.67 \times \\
35 \\
\hline
335 \\
2010 \\
\hline
23.45 \\
\end{array}
$$

So 67p × 35 = 2345pence
= £23.45

So 67p × 35 = £23.45 = £23.45

Example 2 What is £17.12 ÷ 8?

Working in pence

$$
\begin{array}{r}
214 \\
8\overline{)1712}
\end{array}
$$

Working in £

$$
\begin{array}{r}
2.14 \\
8\overline{)17.12}
\end{array}
$$

So £17.12 ÷ 8 = 214 pence
= £2.14

So £17.12 ÷ 8 = £2.14 = £2.14

Exercise 18.2
Practising Skill 18B

1 Calculate each answer without using a calculator.

   a 48p × 7 = ◯   **b** 87p × 9 = ◯   **c** 38p × 17 = ◯
   d 67p × 48 = ◯   **e** 19 × 85p = ◯   **f** 84p × 23 = ◯

2 Calculate each answer without using a calculator.

   a £18.04 ÷ 4 = ◯   **b** £51.84 ÷ 9 = ◯   **c** £18.96 ÷ 8 = ◯
   d £39.30 ÷ 5 = ◯   **e** £98.70 ÷ 6 = ◯   **f** £129.29 ÷ 7 = ◯

3 Calculate the answer to each of these.

   a £4.56 × 5 = ◯   **b** £7.56 × 12 = ◯   **c** £393.88 ÷ 4 = ◯
   d £754.20 ÷ 6 = ◯   **e** £63.68 × 23 = ◯   **f** £392.91 ÷ 7 = ◯

4 Find the missing amount in each of these.

   a £19.20 ÷ ◯ = £2.40   **b** £4.34 × ◯ = £26.04
   c 8 × ◯ = £365.76   **d** ◯ × 9 = £48.42

Exercise 18.3
Using Skills 18A and 18B

1 Copy each bill and fill in the hidden amounts.

Timber – treated
   4 items @ 2.59

means 4 pieces of timber at
£2.59 each.

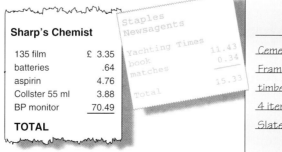

Sharp's Chemist	
135 film	£ 3.35
batteries	.64
aspirin	4.76
Collster 55 ml	3.88
BP monitor	70.49
TOTAL	

Staples
Newsagents

Yachting Times   11.43
book   0.34
matches

Total   15.33

Ringway DIY	
Cement 25 kg	2.35
Frame sealant – white	1.99
timber – treated	
4 items @ 2.59	
Slater's felt	8.49
Sale total	☐

2   Anita buys a bottle of perfume at £23.76
She hands over a £10 note and a £20 note.

What change should she get?

3   Sadie buys a CD. She hands over a £20 note.
She gets £4.58 change.

What did the CD cost?

4   This bill comes from a farming shop.

```
Vole Malley Farm Supplies
Item Ref. Description                Quantity   Each   Cost
0261      Grease - chainsaw              1       3.85   3.85
0564      Starter cord sold per metre    8       0.16   1.28
0435      Sprayer                        1      16.49
0134      Fence post                     6       5.23
0957      Spark plug BMR7A                       1.55   3.10
0963      Spark plug BPMR6Y              3       5.58
                                                Total
```

a   How was the amount £1.28 calculated by the machine?
b   Copy the bill and fill in the missing amounts.

Wages

Skill 18C
Calculating wages

♦ Wages are paid at a basic rate for each hour worked.

♦ If you work at weekends or bank holidays, you get more pay.

  ❖ Double time – means you earn 2 times as much per hour
  ❖ Time and a half – means you earn $1\frac{1}{2}$ times as much per hour.

Example

Alex works in a shop and this is part of his September pay slip.
What are the missing amounts?

Alex Daniels	Pay details		September
Basic rate = £3.96 per hour			
Rate	Number of hours	Amount/hour	Total
Basic	141	3.96	
Double time	9		
Time + $\frac{1}{2}$	31		
Total pay			

The basic rate is £3.96 per hour so:

  ❖ double time = £3.96 × 2 = £7.92 per hour
  ❖ time + $\frac{1}{2}$ = £3.96 × 1.5 = £5.94 per hour

Alex Daniels	Pay details		September
Basic rate = £3.96 per hour			
Rate	Number of hours	Amount/hour	Total
Basic	141	3.96	558.36
Double time	9	7.92	71.28
Time + $\frac{1}{2}$	31	5.94	184.14
Total pay			813.78

To work out the total you multiply the number of hours by the rate per hour.

$141 \times 3.96 = 558.36$
$9 \times 7.92 = 71.28$
$31 \times 5.94 = 184.14$

So Alex earns £813.78 in September.

Exercise 18.4
Using Skill 18C

1 This is the pay slip for Debbie who works with Alex.

Debbie Kahn	Pay details		September
Basic rate = £3.96 per hour			
Rate	Number of hours	Amount/hour	Total
Basic	136	3.96	A
Double time	8	7.92	B
Time $+\frac{1}{2}$	43	5.94	C
Total pay			D

    a Calculate the missing amounts A, B and C.
    b What is Debbie's total pay for September?

2 Carla's basic pay is £4 an hour.
How much will she earn each hour at:

    a double time
    b time and a half?

3 Andy earns a basic rate of £5.80 an hour.
How much will he earn each hour at:

    a double time
    b time and a half?

4 This pay slip is for Winston, a supervisor.

Winston Landers	Pay details		September
Basic rate = £4.50 per hour			
Rate	Number of hours	Amount/hour	Total
Basic	138	4.50	◯
Double time	10	◯	◯
Time $+\frac{1}{2}$	25	◯	◯
Total pay			◯

Copy Winston's pay slip and fill in the missing amounts.

5 This is Amanda's pay slip.

Amanda Rogers	Pay details		September
Basic rate = £4.88 per hour			
Rate	Number of hours	Amount/hour	Total
Basic	124	4.88	◯
Double time	4	◯	◯
Time $+\frac{1}{2}$	11	◯	◯
Total pay			◯

Copy and complete the slip.

6 Steve works in a garage.
His pay slip looks like this.

Copy and complete the slip.

Steve Hicks Pay details – September

Basic rate: £6.26 per hour

Hours worked:

Basic	Double	Time $+\frac{1}{2}$
38	6	7

Pay @ basic rate: £ ◯
Pay @ double time: £ ◯
Pay @ time $+\frac{1}{2}$: £ ◯
Total pay for week: £ ◯

Rounding money

Skill 18D
Rounding money to the
nearest penny

When you do £13.38 ÷ 5 on a calculator you see

$$\boxed{\mathsf{2.676}}$$

To round the screen to the nearest penny

* Look at the third decimal place **2.676**

   ❖ if this number is 5 or more, round up the digit in front
   ❖ if this number is under 5, do not round up.

   So 13.38 ÷ 5 = £2.68 to the nearest penny.

Examples   What is each of these to the nearest penny?

   a £68.42 ÷ 7   **b** £96.26 ÷ 9

The calculator shows $\boxed{\mathsf{9.7742857}}$ $\boxed{\mathsf{10.695556}}$

Look at the 3rd dp   **9.7742857**   **10.695556**

This digit is under 5   This digit is 5 or more,
so do not round.   so round up.

So £68.42 ÷ 7 = £9.77   **So £96.26 ÷ 9 = £10.70**
to the nearest penny   to the nearest penny

Exercise 18.5
Practising Skill 18D

1 Each calculator screen shows an amount of money in £.
Round each amount to the nearest penny.

   a $\boxed{\mathsf{5.26884}}$ **b** $\boxed{\mathsf{57.444444}}$ **c** $\boxed{\mathsf{1.7474747}}$

   d $\boxed{\mathsf{268.6583}}$ **e** $\boxed{\mathsf{0.84358}}$ **f** $\boxed{\mathsf{756.3487}}$

2 Work out each of these with a calculator.
Give each answer to the nearest penny.

   a £56.25 ÷ 8 = ◯   **b** £14.89 ÷ 6 = ◯
   c £78.58 ÷ 5 = ◯   **d** £142.83 ÷ 7 = ◯
   e £2.59 ÷ 9 = ◯   **f** £1463.66 ÷ 3 = ◯

3 Give each answer to the nearest penny.

   a £64.98 ÷ 5 = ◯   **b** £373.47 ÷ 15 = ◯

Exercise 18.6
Using Skill 18D

1 Three people buy a meal. They want to share the bill equally.
The bill comes to £47.36.

   a How much do you think they will each pay?
   b Why might this not total £47.36?

2 A box of 6 eggs costs 76p.
How much does each egg cost, to the nearest penny?

3 Alan buys 50 metres of material for £184.33.

   a What would he pay for 1 metre, to the nearest penny?
   b What should he pay for 5 metres, to the nearest penny?

Part 3b is not as easy as it
seems.

Starting points

You need to know about ...

... so try these questions

A Regular and irregular

- ◆ A regular polygon has:
  - ❖ all its angles equal
  - ❖ all its sides the same length.

Regular polygons   Irregular polygons

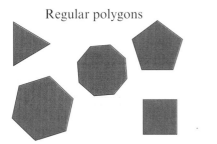 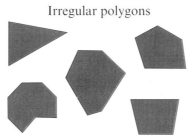

- ◆ A polygon which is not regular is called irregular.

B The names of polygons

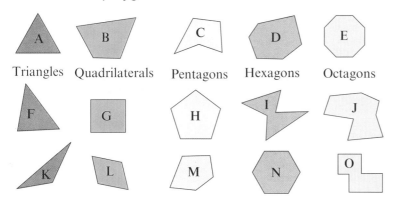

Triangles   Quadrilaterals   Pentagons   Hexagons   Octagons

A1 What is another name for a regular triangle?

A2 Explain why a rhombus is not a regular polygon.

A3 Which of the polygons A to O below left are regular?

B1 Copy and complete this table.

Polygon	No. of sides
Triangle	
Pentagon	
Octagon	
Quadrilateral	
Hexagon	

B2 Draw an irregular pentagon.

The angles of regular polygons

Skill 1A
Ordering whole numbers

'Exterior' means 'outside'.
'Interior' means 'inside'.

The red angles of this pentagon are called its **exterior angles**.
The blue angles are called **interior angles**.

For a regular polygon

- ❖ all the exterior angles are equal
- ❖ all the interior angles are equal.

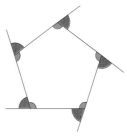

Exercise 19.1
Exterior and interior angles

1   How many exterior angles has a pentagon?

2   What is the name of a polygon with 8 interior angles?

3   Draw a square.
Draw some more lines and colour its exterior angles.

4   Draw a hexagon. Label all its interior angles.

The angles of regular polygons

Skill 19A
Finding an exterior angle

If you move a pencil round the exterior angles of any polygon it turns through one turn of 360°.

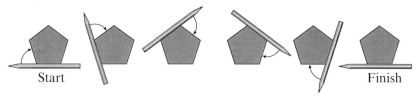

Start   Finish

Example

Find the exterior angle of a regular hexagon.

◆ A regular hexagon has 6 exterior angles.

◆ All the angles are equal.

◆ All six angles must total 360°.

So each exterior angle is 360° ÷ 6 = 60°.

◆ To find the size of an exterior angle of any regular polygon divide 360° by the number of sides.

Exercise 19.2
Practising Skill 19A

1 a How many exterior angles has a regular octagon?
b What is the missing number in this calculation?

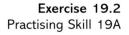

c What is the size of an exterior angle of a regular octagon?

2 Calculate the exterior angle of an equilateral triangle.

3 This table lists some other regular polygons.
Copy and complete the table. Give each angle to the nearest degree.

Examples of rounding
angles to the nearest degree

47.28° to the nearest degree
is 47°.

34.64° to the nearest degree
is 35°.

Regular polygon	No. of sides	Exterior angle
Hexagon	6	60°
Heptagon	7	○
Nonagon	9	○
Decagon	10	○
Dodecagon	12	○
Hexadecagon	16	○

4 Part of a polygon is shown in this frame.
The number of sides it has is not known.
Each exterior angle is 10°.

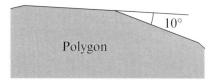

Calculate how many sides the polygon has.

Skill 19B
Finding an interior angle

- In any polygon the interior angle and the exterior angles together make a straight line
- A straight line is 180°.

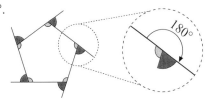

- To calculate the interior angle of a regular polygon
  - ❖ Find the exterior angle
  - ❖ Interior angle = 180° – Exterior angle

Example

Find an interior angle of a regular hexagon.

- ❖ The exterior angle is 360 ÷ 6 = 60°.

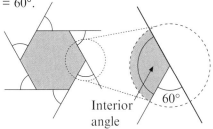

Interior angle

60°

- ❖ The **interior angle** is 180° – 60° = **120°**.

Exercise 19.3
Practising Skill 19B

1 The exterior angle of a regular polygon is 26°.
   What is its interior angle?

2 For a regular pentagon:
   a What is its exterior angle?
   b Calculate its interior angle.

3 Copy and complete this table. Give each angle to the nearest degree.

Regular polygon	No. of sides	Interior angle
Hexagon	6	120°
Heptagon	7	◯
Nonagon	9	◯
Decagon	10	◯
Dodecagon	12	◯
Hexadecagon	16	◯

4 For one regular polygon this equation is true.
      Exterior angle = Interior angle

   What name do we give this polygon?

5 A regular polygon has an interior angle of 60°.
   a What is its exterior angle?
   b How many sides has it?

The angle sum of triangles and quadrilaterals

Skill 19C
Finding missing angles

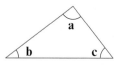

◆ The total of all three angles in any triangle is 180°.

So **a + b + c** = 180°.

◆ Any quadrilateral can be split into two triangles.

So the angles in a quadrilateral add up to 180° × 2 = 360°.

So **p + q + r + s** = 360°.

Example 1

Calculate angle **h** in this quadrilateral.

The other 3 angles add up to 70° + 110° + 50° = 230°.

So angle h = 360° − 230° = 130°.

Example 2

Find the size of angle **y**.

Angle **x** = 180° − 70° − 85° = 25°

Angle **x** and angle **y** make a straight line.
So angle **x** + angle **y** = 180°.

So angle y = 180° − 25° = 155°.

Exercise 19.4
Practising Skill 19C

1 Calculate the angles **a**, **b**, **c** and **d**.

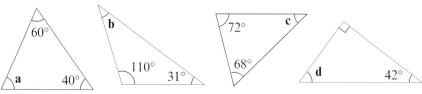

2 Calculate angles **e**, **f**, **g** and **h**.

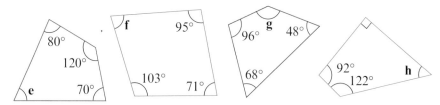

3 Calculate the size of angles **p** and **q**.

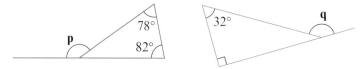

Starting points

You need to know about ...

A Adding with negative numbers

Skill 6C: *see page 36*

B Subtracting with negative numbers

Skill 6D: *see page 36*

C Multiplying with negative numbers

Skill 6E: *see page 37*

... so try these questions

A1 Calculate:

    a $^-5 + ^-6$ **b** $7 + ^-12$

B1 Calculate:

    a $^-5 - 6$ **b** $7 - ^-4$

C1 Calculate

    a $^-5 \times 3$ **b** $7 \times ^-4$

Function machines

◆ A function machine has an input and an output.

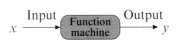

◆ A machine does the same thing to every input number.

Example   This is a ×3 machine.

It is used for the function $y = 3x$.
Every x-value that goes in is multiplied by 3 to give the y-value out.

So if $x = 5$ then $y = 15$
     if $x = 9$ then $y = 27$
     if $x = ^-4$ then $y = ^-12$

◆ Machines can be linked together.

Example   These machines are for the function $y = 4x - 2$

This machine multiplies the x value by 4 then subtracts 2.

So if $x = 6$, then $y = (4 \times 6) - 2 = 24 - 2 = 22$
     if $x = 3$, then $y = (4 \times 3) - 2 = 12 - 2 = 10$
     if $x = ^-8$, then $y = (4 \times ^-8)\, ^-2 = ^-32 - 2 = ^-34$

Exercise 20.1
Function machines

1 For each set of machines say what number is output.

2 Complete this function for the machines in question **1a**: $y =$

3 This is a pair of machines in different orders.
What is the output from each pair when the input is 3?

4 **a** Draw a set of machines for the function $y = 3x + 5$
   b When $x = 8$, what is the value of y?
   c What value of x gives a value of y as 38?

5   What was the input number for each of these?

a ? ⟶ ×7 ⟶ 35   b ? ⟶ −7 ⟶ 6

c ? ⟶ +5 ⟶ 3   d ? ⟶ +2 ⟶ 3

e ? ⟶ ×5 ⟶ −15   f ? ⟶ +3 ⟶ +4 ⟶ 13

Mapping diagrams

A mapping diagram can show the link between x and y values.

Example

Draw a mapping diagram for the function $y = 3x + 1$
Use values of x from 4 to 10.

Mapping Diagram

$y = 3x + 1$

x	⟶	y
4	⟶	13
5	⟶	16
6	⟶	19
7	⟶	22
8	⟶	25
9	⟶	28

This value of y is:
$(3 \times 6) + 1 = 18 + 1$
$= 19$

Exercise 20.2
Mapping diagrams

1   Copy and complete these mapping diagrams.

a $y = 4x - 3$	b $y = 3x + 8$	c $y = 6x + 1$
x ⟶ y	x ⟶ y	x ⟶ y
2 ⟶ 5	3 ⟶ ◯	2 ⟶ ◯
5 ⟶ ◯	7 ⟶ ◯	◯ ⟶ 31
12 ⟶ ◯	8 ⟶ ◯	3 ⟶ ◯
6 ⟶ ◯	9 ⟶ ◯	◯ ⟶ 61
9 ⟶ ◯	11 ⟶ ◯	8 ⟶ ◯
15 ⟶ ◯	12 ⟶ ◯	◯ ⟶ 25

2   Draw a mapping diagram for the function $y = 2x + 7$.
     Use values of x from 1 to 5.

3   Draw a mapping diagram for each set of machines.
     Use x values between 1 and 6.

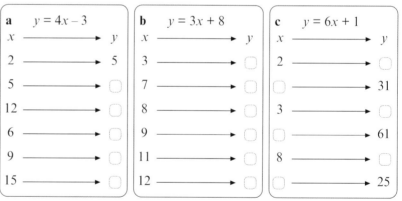

a x ⟶ ×3 ⟶ +5 ⟶ y

b x ⟶ ÷4 ⟶ −3 ⟶ y

4   Draw a mapping diagram for $y = \frac{1}{2}x + 4$.
     Use values of x between 6 and 10.

Inverses

The 'inverse of' means the 'opposite of'.

◆ The inverse of 'open a door' is 'close a door'.

◆ The inverse of [Add 4] is [Subtract 4]

◆ These machines will convert °C to °F, approximately.

$$°C \longrightarrow \boxed{\times 2} \longrightarrow \boxed{+ 32} \longrightarrow °F$$

Example

What is 3°C is in °F?

$$3 °C \longrightarrow \boxed{\times 2} \longrightarrow \boxed{+ 32} \longrightarrow 38 °F$$

So 3°C is about 38°F.

The inverse of '× 2' is '÷ 2' and the inverse of '+ 32' is '– 32'.

◆ To change from °F to °C you must use the inverse machines.

$$°C \longleftarrow \boxed{\div 2} \longleftarrow \boxed{- 32} \longleftarrow °F$$

Example

What is 68°F is in °C?

$$18 °C \longleftarrow \boxed{\div 2} \overset{36}{\longleftarrow} \boxed{- 32} \longleftarrow 68 °F$$

So 68°F is about 18°F.

Exercise 20.3
Inverses

1   Use the machines above to convert:
   a   8°C into °F   **b**   12°C into °F
   c   80°F into °C   **d**   74°F into °C

2   To find the number of hedge plants, H, for a field length of L metres a farmer uses these machines.

$$L \longrightarrow \boxed{\times 3} \longrightarrow \boxed{+ 2} \longrightarrow H$$

   a   How many hedge plants must he buy for a field 100 metres long?
   b   Draw the inverse machines to convert from H to L.
   c   With 185 plants, how long a field can he hedge?

3   These machines are for the function $y = 4x - 5$.

$$x \longrightarrow \boxed{\times 4} \longrightarrow \boxed{- 5} \longrightarrow y$$

   a   What is the value of y when $x = 3$?
   b   Draw the inverse machines.
   c   Use your inverse machines to find x when $y = 47$.

4   These machines are for the function $y = \frac{1}{2}x + 6$.

$$x \longrightarrow \boxed{\div 2} \longrightarrow \boxed{+ 6} \longrightarrow y$$

   a   Draw the inverse machines.
   b   Find x when $y = 21$.

Starting points

You need to know about ...   ... so try these questions

A Frequency

The frequency of some data is:
    the number of times each piece of that data is found.

Example
The number of goals scored by a hockey team in 7 matches were:
    1, 0, 2, 2, 3, 0, 2

Scoring 0 goals has a frequency of   2
Scoring 1 goal has a frequency of   1
Scoring 2 goals has a frequency of   3 (2 goals scored 3 times)
Scoring 3 goals has a frequency of   1

> **A1** This data shows the shoe sizes of a group of students.
>
> 3, 12, 5, 4, 6, 7, 9, 7, 8, 5, 5, 12
>
> What is the frequency of each shoe size?
>
> **A2** This data is for T-shirts on sale in a shop.
>
> M, L, L, S, M, XL, M, L, M
>
> Give the frequency of each size.

Frequency tables

Skill 21A
Making frequency tables

Frequency tables may be called tally tables.

Tally marks can be used to show the data in the table.

Example
Make a frequency table for these ten-pin bowling scores.

    6   8   4   6   9
    3   6   8 10   5
    9   6   7   6   9
    7 10   6   8   4
    6 10   6   7   6
    8   9   4 10   6

> In ten-pin bowling the lowest score is 0, and the highest is 10.

> The frequency shows how many times each score is in the data.
>
> Adding the frequencies gives the total number of pieces of data.

Score	Tally	Frequency
0		0
1		0
2		0
3	/	1
4	///	3
5	/	1
6	ЖЖ ЖЖ	10
7	///	3
8	////	4
9	////	4
10	////	4

Exercise 21.1
Practising Skill 21A

1 a Make a frequency table for these ten-pin bowling scores.

    8 7 8 6 10 5 10 5 4 6 7 6 7 7 8 7

    9 8 5 7 8 9 6 10 8 9 8 10 5 8 7 10

b How many pieces of data are in the list?
c What is the total of the frequencies in your table?

2 a Make a frequency table for these ten-pin bowling scores.

    5 6 7 5 8 9 8 8 7 10 7 8 8 9 6 7 6 8

    7 8 10 9 8 10 9 10 8 7 6 4 7 2 10 9 5 1

b What should be the total of the frequencies in your table?

3 This survey data is for the number of people in cars on a toll bridge.

North Scar Bridge Survey – Number of people in each car

1 3 4 1 2 1 3 1 1 1 2 1 3 2 2 1 1 1 4 3

5 3 1 1 1 1 2 1 3 4 3 2 3 1 1 1 1 1 4 3

3 1 2 1 4 2 1 1 1 3

a How many cars is this data for?
b Make a frequency table for this data.

4 This data gives the shoe sizes for a group of people.

Shoe size

8 8 7 6 9 9 10 13 11 10 9 9 12 10 9 9 13 12

9 8 10 9 12 13 10 9 8 7 9 7 10 10 9 11 10 9

a How many pieces of data for shoe size are there?
b Make a frequency table for the shoe size data.

5 This data gives the birth month for a group of people.

Feb Dec Oct Oct Sept Apr Sept May Mar Feb Jan

Dec Nov Nov Nov Oct June July Oct July Mar Apr

July Aug Mar Feb Aug Dec May Nov Jan Mar June

Dec June Aug Apr Mar May Nov Dec July

Make a frequency table for the data.

Skill 21B
Making grouped
frequency tables

Sometimes data is grouped to make it easier to handle.
Data is grouped using a rule or system.

You might have to decide on the groups to use.

Example This data is for the number of people on a bus.

17 6 31 20 18 47 8 23 45 36 2 47 54 18 21

9 62 51 38 27 17 6 54 19 9 17 11 61 55 44

10 32 20 5 58 31 29 12 3 2 25 39 14

Make a grouped frequency table to show this data.
Use groups of:
0 to 9, 10 to 19, 20 to 29, 30 to 39, 40 to 49, 50 to 59, over 59

Group	Tally	Frequency
0 to 9	JHT JHT	10
10 to 19	JHT IIII	9
20 to 29	JHT II	7
30 to 39	JHT I	6
40 to 49	IIII	4
50 to 59	JHT	5
over 59	II	2

A group like 10 to 19 is
called a 'class of data'.

Exercise 21.2
Practising Skill 21B

1 This data is for the age of seals, in days, when they were rescued.

Age in days of seals when rescued

24, 35, 29, 55, 27, 38, 19, 7, 31, 28, 36, 45, 22, 19, 7, 12, 31, 24,

6, 18, 51, 40, 33, 26, 15, 32, 23, 19, 5, 41, 11, 4, 29, 40, 4

Copy and complete this grouped frequency table for the age of seals.

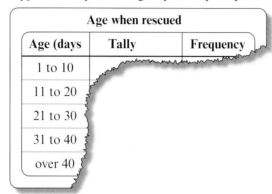

Age when rescued		
Age (days	Tally	Frequency
1 to 10		
11 to 20		
21 to 30		
31 to 40		
over 40		

2 Use the age of seals data in **Question 1**.

Make a different grouped frequency table for the data.
Use groups of:
1 to 5, 6 to 10, 11 to 15, 16 to 20, 21 to 25,
26 to 30, 31 to 35, 36 to 40, over 40.

When data is grouped, the modal class is:
the class with the greatest frequency.

This grouped frequency table shows a modal class of 20 to 29.

Group	Tally	Frequency
0 to 9	////	4
10 to 19	JHT //	7
20 to 29	JHT JHT ///	13
30 to 39	JHT /	6

3 This data shows, the number of items in supermarket trollies at check-out.

Number of items in each trolley at check-out

12, 19, 27, 51, 24, 19, 44, 8, 32, 21, 37, 15, 6, 16, 48, 26, 51,
14, 6, 23, 5, 35, 37, 28, 47, 40, 36, 29, 12, 2, 4, 56, 22, 39, 8

a Make a grouped frequency table for this data.
Use groups of: 1 to 10, 11 to 20, 21 to 30, 31 to 40, 41 to 50, over 50
b What is the modal class for this distribution?
c Make a different grouped frequency table for the trolley data.
This time use groups of: 1 to 5, 6 to 10, 11 to 15, 16 to 20, ..., over 50
d What is the modal class for this distribution?
e Choose a different way to group the trolley data.
f Make a grouped frequency table for the data.
g What is the modal class for your distribution?

The distribution of a set
of data shows how many
pieces if data are in
each class.

This revises the work in Sections 17 to 21

1 Skill 17A

Calculate the angles marked with a letter.

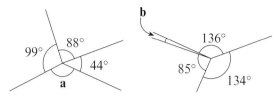

2 Skill 17B

Calculate the angles marked with a letter.

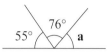
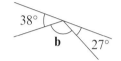

3 Skill 17C

Calculate the angles marked with a letter.

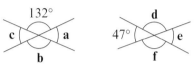

4 Skill 17D

Calculate the angles marked with a letter.

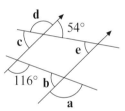

5 Skill 18A

Calculate the answer to each of these.
(Do not use a calculator.)

a £3.75 + £4.01 + 87p
b £235.90 + £17.65 + 92p + £4.18
c £265.45 − £176.88
d £400 − £237.56

6 Skill 18B

Calculate the answer to each of these.
(Do not use a calculator.)

a 58p × 9 **b** 24 × 53p **c** 34p × 45
d £14.72 × 12 **e** 15 × £23.85 **f** £18.72 ÷ 4
g £111.16 ÷ 7 **h** £824.58 ÷ 6 **i** £506.16 ÷ 9

7 Jason buys a CD for £12.49.
He pays with a £10 and a £5 note.
How much change should he get?

8 Ravinda buys a film.
She pays with a £20 note and gets £15.15 change.
How much did the film cost?

9 Skill 18C

Alex earns a basic rate of £4.60 an hour.
How much will she earn each hour at:

a double time **b** time-and-a-half?

10 Skill 18D

Each of these is an amount of money in pounds.
Round each of these to the nearest penny.

a 6.0788 **b** 14.3056 **c** 425.858 585

11 A box of 6 eggs costs 85p.
Find the cost of one egg to the nearest penny.

12 Six friends take a taxi and share the fare equally.
The fare is £8.30.
How much do they each pay to the nearest penny?

13 Skill 19A

A regular dodecagon is a polygon with 12 sides.

a How many exterior angles does it have?
b What is the size of each exterior angle?

14 Skill 19B

The exterior angle of a regular polygon is 72°.
What is its interior angle?

15 Skill 19C

Calculate the angles marked with a letter.

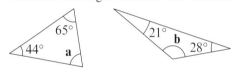

16 Calculate the angles marked with a letter.

17 Give the number output from this function machine.

18 Draw a mapping diagram for the function
$y = 4x - 5$. (Use values of x from 3 to 8.)

19 Skill 21A

Make a frequency table for these bowling scores.

3, 2, 6, 7, 9, 10, 5, 6, 1, 3, 10, 9, 8, 9, 10, 6

1, 4, 7, 8, 9, 9, 8, 5, 4, 10, 3, 6, 8, 9, 8, 2, 5

20 Skill 21B

Make a grouped frequency table for this data.

Age in days of seals when rescued

16, 9, 4, 25, 7, 13, 28, 22, 7, 3, 9, 14, 32, 12, 7

21, 17, 14, 16, 5, 4, 7, 16, 32, 19, 22, 14, 34

Use groups of: 1 to 5, 6 to 10, 11 to 20, 20 to 25, and over 25 days.

About the Cornish Seal Sanctuary

It was founded in 1957.

In 1975, it moved to a site of about 40 acres in Gweek.

It has a fully equipped seal hospital and 10 outdoor pools.

Cafe prices

Coffee		60p
Tea		40p
Cola		50p
Rolls:	Bacon	£1.50
	Sausage	£1.25
	Egg	£1.10
Chips		70p
Beans		40p
Salad		55p

Opening hours
Open every day except Christmas
09 00 to 18 30

Feeding times
11 00 • 13 30 • 16 00

Seals rescued in Cornwall (1990–91)

Reasons for rescue
- Illness
- Caught in nets
- Other injury
- Malnourished

Ratio of male:female seals rescued between Land's End and Porthleven

Year	Ratio
1992–93	1:1
1993–94	1:2
1994–95	2:1

About the grey seals

Weights of pups rescued in December 1992

Name	Weight at rescue (kg)	Weight at release (kg)
Bill	23.4	65.0
Ben	16.8	56.0
Mandy	12.3	66.0
Tony	24.0	98.0
Rory	18.5	85.0

Seals are usually released when they weigh about 60 kg.

Seals at the sanctuary eat over a tonne of fish per week.

Food weight chart (hospital)

Major breeding areas for grey seals

Location	Pups born (1989)	Pups born (1990)	Total population in 1990 (to nearest 100)
Inner Hebrides	2051	2256	7800
Outer Hebrides	9537	9823	34000
Orkney	7038	7319	25400
Isle of May	933	1185	4100
Farne Islands	892	1004	3500

The world population of grey seals is estimated at 120000.

About two thirds of them live around the British coastline.

In water, seals can reach speeds of up to 20 km per hour.

1 How many years is it since the Seal Sanctuary was opened?

2 How long is the Sanctuary open each day?

3 In the cafe, Pritpal buys a cola, bacon roll and chips. How much does this cost?

4 What was wrong with most seals who were rescued in Cornwall in 1990–91?

5 How much did the pup called Rory weigh when he was rescued in 1992?

6 What was the weight of the lightest pup rescued in December 1992?

7 What weight of food does a 20 kg seal pup get per day in hospital?

8 Estimate the weight of food that a 14 kg pup gets per day in hospital.

9 How many pups were born in Orkney in 1990?

10 How long has the Seal Sanctuary been at Gweek?

11 Amy gets to the Sanctuary at 8.25 am.
How many minutes must she wait till it opens?

12 24 seals were rescued in Cornwall in 1990–91.
About how many of these were ill?

13 In the cafe, how much more does a sausage roll cost than a plate of chips?

14 For the pups rescued in December 1992, which one was the heaviest when it was set free?

15 How much weight did the pup Ben put on while he was at the Sanctuary?

16 Which of the pups rescued in December 1992 put on the most weight before being set free?

17 Copy and complete the frequency table to show the ages of seals rescued in 1994.

Age in days	Tally	Frequency
1 to 10		
11 to 20		
21 to 30		
31 to 40		
More than 40		

18 Give the seal feeding times as am and pm times.

19 In a day in hospital, about what weight of food is given to a 15 kg seal pup?

20 A pup in hospital is given 800 grams of food a day. Give the weight of this pup in kilograms.

21 How many grey seal pups were born in the Outer Hebrides in 1990?

22 How many grey seal pups in total were born in the main breeding areas in 1989?

23 Round the number of grey seal pups born in Orkney in 1990 to the nearest thousand.

24 Round the number of grey seal pups born in the Farn Islands in 1989 to the nearest hundred.

25 Out of the main breeding areas, which place had the highest total population of grey seals in 1990?

26 In June about 800 people visit the Seal Sanctuary each day.
About how many people visit in June?

27 About how many of the world's grey seals do not live around the British coast?

28 Susan gets to the Sanctuary 3.15 pm.
How long has she to wait for feeding time?

29 What is the area of the largest pool at the Sanctuary?

30 This table shows the number of male and female seals rescued in different months of 1997.

Month	Male	Female
January	2	1
February	1	1
March	1	0
April	0	0
May	2	0
June	1	1
July	4	1
August	3	2
September	0	4
October	2	5
November	3	2
December	2	4

a Draw a comparative bar chart to show the frequency of male and female rescues.

b How many seals were rescued in 1997?

115

Stage 2 End points

You should be able to ...   ... so try these questions

A Calculate the area of a rectangle
Skill 12A: *see page 68*

A1 Calculate the area of each of these rectangles.

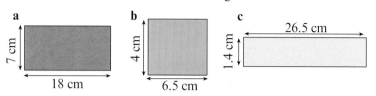

B Calculate the area of a triangle
Skill 12B: *see page 70*

B1 Calculate the area of each of these triangles.

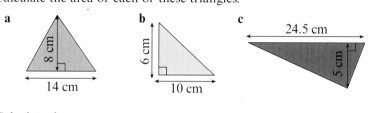

C Calculate the perimeter of shapes
Skill 12C: *see page 71*

C1 Calculate the perimeter of this shape.

5 cm   7 cm   26 cm   9 cm   4 cm   3 cm

D Substitute values in formulas
Skill 13A: *see page 73*

D1 A formula that links k, w and y is:
$y = 3(2k - w)$
Copy and complete this table.

k	w	y
3	4	○
5	9	○
$^-6$	2	○

E Solve equations
Skill 13B: *see page 75*
Skill 13C: *see page 76*

E1 Solve each of these equations.
a $5y + 6 = 41$ **b** $6k - 4 = 38$ **c** $7 + 3m = 22$
d $^-8 + 9h = 73$ **e** $2(g + 3) = 20$ **f** $3(2y - 4) = 24$

F Find multiples of a number
Skill 14A: *see page 79*

F1 Which of these is not a multiple of 6?
14   16   24   42   54   72   76

F2 How can you tell from the digits that a number is a multiple of 5?

G Find the factors of a number
Skill 14B: *see page 78*

G1 List all the factors of 36.

G2 Which factors of 48 are also factors of 56?

H Identify prime numbers
Skill 14C: *see page 78*

H1 Is 35 a prime number? Explain your answer.

H2 List all the prime number between 20 and 40.

I Find prime factors
Skill 14D: *see page 79*

I1 List the prime factors of each of these numbers.
a 72   **b** 75   **c** 18

J Find the square root of a number
Skill 14E: *see page 80*

J1 What is the square root of each of these?
a 100   **b** 144   **c** 225   **d** 81   **e** 400

J2 Calculate the value of:
a $\sqrt{16} + \sqrt{49} - \sqrt{36}$ **b** $\sqrt{100} - \sqrt{64} + \sqrt{121}$

K Draw a comparative bar chart

K1 Draw a comparative bar chart to show this data.

Mark in test	0	1	2	3	4	5	6	7	8
No. in Group A	1	3	2	0	6	8	9	6	5
No. in Group B	2	5	9	6	4	7	4	2	1

L Read a comparative bar chart

L1 This bar chart shows data on drinks chosen by a group.

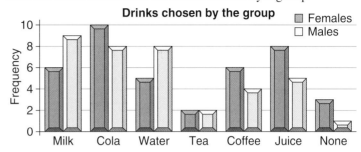

a How many females chose cola?
b How many males chose milk?
c How many females were in the group?
d Which drink was chosen by the same number of males and females?
e What drink was most popular with males?
f What drink was most popular with females?

M Read a split bar chart

M1 The split bar chart shows TV programme watching data for 4 friends.

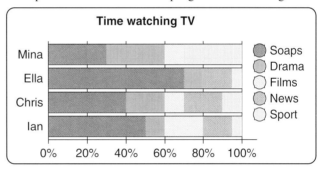

a Who spent more than 50% of the time watching soaps?
b Who spent 20% of their time watching films?
c Estimate the percentage of time spent by each person watching sport.
d Explain how Mina spent her time watching TV.

N Draw a pictogram

N1 The table gives the number of burgers sold by Fastgrill on one week.

Day	Mon	Tues	Wed	Thurs	Fri	Sat	Sun
No. of burgers sold	85	110	78	94	129	155	42

Choose a symbol to stand for 10 burgers and draw a pictogram.

O Draw a pie chart

O1 A survey was done with a group of people.
They were asked where they bought vegetables.
This table gives the data from the survey.

Number of people who bought vegetables from:

Market	Farm shop	Supermarket	Greengrocer	Milkman
5	7	16	6	2

Draw a pie chart to show this data.

P Multiply decimals by powers of 10
Skill **16A**: *see page 87*

Q Divide decimals by powers of 10
Skill **16B** *see page 88*

R Multiply or divide a decimal by a whole number
Skill **16C**: *see page 88*
Skill **16E**: *see page 90*

S Multiply a decimal by a decimal
Skill **16D** *see page 88*

T Calculate angles
Skill **17A**: *see page 94*
Skill **17B**: *see page 95*
Skill **17C**: *see page 95*
Skill **17D** *see page 96*

U Use the properties of polygons
Skill **19A**: *see page 104*
Skill **19B**: *see page 105*
Skill **19C**: *see page 106*

V Work with functions and mapping diagrams

W Make frequency tables for a set of data
Skill **21A**: *see page 110*
Skill **21B**: *see page 111*

X Calculate with money
Skill **18A**: *see page 98*
Skill **18B**: *see page 99*
Skill **18C**: *see page 100*
Skill **18D** *see page 102*

P1 Copy and complete each of these:
  a $1.675\,54 \times 10^3 =$ **b** $0.005\,882 \times 10^2 =$ **c** $12.54 \times 10^4 =$

Q1 Copy and complete each of these. (Do not use a calculator.)
  a $357.25 \div 10^4 =$ **b** $0.75 \div 10^2 =$ **c** $16545.8 \div 10^5 =$

R1 Copy and complete each of these. (Do not use a calculator.)
  a $18.57 \times 6 =$ **b** $238.45 \times 9 =$ **c** $3825.46 \times 3 =$

R2 Copy and complete each of these. (Do not use a calculator.)
  a $1545.48 \div 6 =$ **b** $7477.61 \div 7 =$ **c** $14064.42 \div 3 =$

S1 Copy and complete this table. (Do not use a calculator.)

Calculate	Estimate	Answer
18.6×3.4		
35.8×6.5		
92.4×5.3		

T1 Calculate the angles marked with a letter in each of these.

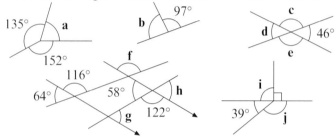

U1 Calculate the exterior angle of a regular octagon (8 sides).

U2 Calculate the interior angle of a regular dodecagon (12 sides).

U3 Calculate the angles marked with a letter in each of these.

V1 Draw a mapping diagram for the function $y = 7x - 9$
Use values of x from 0 to 5.

W1 This data shows the number of days off sick taken by a group.

Number of days sick-leave taken

4, 5, 3, 1, 2, 8, 9, 5, 12, 4, 2, 16, 3, 22, 24, 14, 1, 1, 2, 2, 3, 5,

8, 5, 4, 6, 7, 5, 4, 2, 2, 4, 9, 10, 10, 2, 7, 5, 4, 1, 18

  a Make a frequency table to show this data.
  b Make a grouped frequency table for this data.
  Use groups of: 1 to 5 days, 6 to 10 days, 11 to 15 days, 16 to 20 days and over 20 days.
  c What is the modal class for this distribution?

X1 Copy and complete each of these. (Do not use a calculator.)
  a £3.49 + £7 + 45p + £6.99 + 8p =   **b** £900 − £576.49 =
  c £41.67 × 8 =   **d** £21.88 × 24 =   **e** £270.48 ÷ 7 =

This revises the work in Stages 1 & 2

1 Give the value of the digit 3 in each of these.
  a 230 045   **b** 3 574 202   **c** 12 703 670

2 List these numbers from large to small.
  57 632, 425, 19, 54 881, 1634, 585, 17, 53 085

3 Write each of these numbers in words.
  a 30 607   **b** 230 405   **c** 6 740 050

4 Write each of these numbers in digits.
  a forty thousand and twenty
  b five hundred and six thousand and sixty
  c twelve million and ninety

5 Copy each of these letters and draw in all lines of symmetry.
  V   K   D   T   Y

6 Give the order of rotational symmetry of Shape A.

Shape A

7 How many planes of symmetry has a door?

8 Find an answer to each of these.
  (Do not use a calculator.)
  a $8 + 7 + 4 + 9 + 5 + 6$
  b $34 + 19 + 5$
  c $2575 + 58 + 17840 + 7$
  d $32001 - 8668$
  e 42×14
  f 674×28
  g $3856 \div 16$
  h $33098 \div 13$

9 Give the value of the digit 8 in each of these.
  a 24.813   **b** 9.4785   **c** 9.5068

10 List these numbers in order, smallest first.
  2.012, 0.309. 0.045, 0.4, 2.12, 0.04

11 Find an answer to each of these.
  (Do not use a calculator.)
  a $2.575 + 17.6 + 0.08 + 0.7 + 9$
  b $534.65 + 23 + 0.007 + 5.6$
  c $46.025 - 28.74$

12 Draw each of these angles accurately.
  a 85°   **b** 145°   **c** 265°

13 Which of these angles are obtuse?
  78°, 154°, 64°, 104°, 48°, 199°

14 Copy and complete each of these.
  a $^-7 + {}^-9$ **b** $^-18 + 5$ **c** $9 + {}^-4$
  d $4 - 28$ **e** $^-7 - 9$ **f** $^-5 - {}^-9$
  g $11 - {}^-5$ **h** $^-8 \times 7$ **i** $6 \times {}^-5$
  j $^-8 \times {}^-3$ **k** $72 \div {}^-9$ **l** $^-64 \div {}^-16$

15 Order these numbers with the smallest first.
  a $^-9, 2, {}^-7, 8, {}^-2, 3, 7$
  b $3, {}^-7, {}^-4, 9, 0, {}^-3, 13, {}^-11$

16 The coordinates of two corners of a square are:
  ($^-7, {}^-3$) and ($^-7, 2$).
  Give the coordinates of the other two corners of the square.

17 Collect like terms in each of these.
  a $8k + 4w + 3k + 6w + k$
  b $15f + 6h + f - h - 2h$

18 Expand the brackets in each of these.
  a $6(7w + 3)$
  b $5(9 - 4k)$

19 Expand these brackets and collect like terms to simplify.
  $5(3y + 2g + 4) + 2(5y - 3g - 7)$

20 Round each of these numbers to the nearest thousand.
  a 21 712   **b** 445 478   **c** 5 285 505

21 Round each of these to the nearest 100 000.
  a 703 798   **b** 7 465 466   **c** 5 075 000

22 Find an approximate answer to each of these.
  a 48×73 **b** 67×46 **c** 58×92

23 Construct a triangle with sides of:
    6 cm, 7 cm and 8 cm.

24 Construct triangle ABC where:
    AB = 5 cm, BC = 7 cm, and angle ABC = 55°

25 Write each of these in 24-hour time.
  a 9.50 pm   **b** 4.35 am   **c** 11.15 pm
  d 12.25 pm   **e** 2.05 am   **f** 1.36 pm

26 A train left Manchester at 10:37 and arrived in Glasgow at 15:19.
  What was the journey time for this train?

27 Use the timetable on page 60.
  Jo catches the 11:38 from Andover.
  She travels to Sherborne.
  a When should she get to Sherborne?
  b What is the journey time?

28 Calculate the area of each of these shapes.

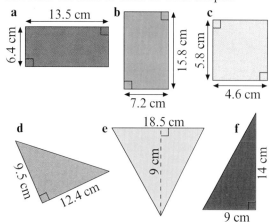

29 A formula that links p, k and t is: $t = 2(3p + 2k)$

Find the value of t when, $p = 5$ and $k = 4$

30 Solve each of these equations.

a $7y + 12 = 40$ b $35 + 4h = 59$
c $5g - 19 = 51$ d $3(f - 4) = 27$

31 a Add all the odd numbers between 24 and 34.
b What square numbers are between 30 and 75?
c Subtract the 9th square number from 100.

32 Which of these is a multiple of 6?

75, 72, 44, 36, 16, 42

33 List all the factors of 56.

34 List all the prime numbers between 10 and 30.

35 This data is about TV viewing in a week.

Ella		Nadim	
Channel	**Hours**	**Channel**	**Hours**
BBC1	5	BBC1	8
BBC2	4	BBC2	5
ITV	8	ITV	8
Ch 4	10	Ch 4	6
Ch 5	12	Ch 5	9
Sky	14	Sky	0

a Draw a comparative bar chart for the data.
b Draw a split bar chart to show the data for each viewer.
c Draw a pie chart to show the data for Nadim.

36 Copy and complete each of these.

a $12.1757 \times 10^2 = \blacksquare$ b $0.0000435 \times 10^4 = \blacksquare$
c $3886.75 \div 10 = \blacksquare$ d $0.0688 \div 10^3 = \blacksquare$

37 Without a calculator find the value of:

a $3169.25 \div 7 = \blacksquare$ b $1503.32 \div 4 = \blacksquare$
c $124.63 \times 5 = \blacksquare$ d $565.38 \times 3 = \blacksquare$

38 Calculate the answer to each of these.
Do not use a calculator.

a £15.79 + £3.99 + 47p + £6
b £5 + £17.99 + 35p + £1.50 + 8p
c £475.39 – £388.75
d £700 – £488.62

39 A box of 8 pencils costs £1.25.

Find the cost of one pencil to the nearest penny.

40 Ed buys a bag of plaster for £7.43.
He pays with a £10 note.

How much change will he get?

41 Alex pays for a brush with a £20 note.
She get £13.51 change.

How much was the brush?

42 Calculate the answer to each of these.
Do not use a calculator.

a $37p \times 9 = \blacksquare$ b $£16.75 \times 7 = \blacksquare$
c $£101.76 \div 8 = \blacksquare$ d $£3949.75 \div 7 = \blacksquare$

43 Draw a mapping diagram for the function
$y = 5x - 2$ (Use values of x from 2 to 7.)

44 Give the number output from this function machine.

45 Calculate each angle marked with a letter.

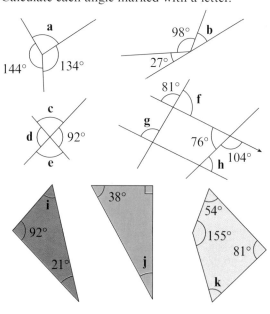

46 Mina earns a basic wage of £7.20 an hour.
How much will she earn at:

a double time   b time-and-a-half?

Starting points

You need to know about ...

... so try these questions

A Simple fractions

These are fractions like a half, and a quarter.

- half $\frac{1}{2}$

we talk about half an hour   [1 hour ÷ 2]
we give half of a chocolate bar away   [1 bar ÷ 2]
we get half marks   [full marks ÷ 2]
we go for half fare   [full fare ÷ 2]
we drink half a can of cola   [can of cola ÷ 2]
...   ...

- quarter $\frac{1}{4}$

we talk about a quarter of an hour   [1 hour ÷ 4]
we get a quarter of the marks   [full marks ÷ 4]
we use a quarter of a tank of petrol   [full tank ÷ 4]
we buy a quarter pounder   [one pound (lb) ÷ 4]
...   ...

B Fractions as part of a whole

- divide a whole into:

2 equal parts – each is $\frac{1}{2}$
3 equal parts – each is $\frac{1}{3}$
4 equal parts – each is $\frac{1}{4}$
5 equal parts – each is $\frac{1}{5}$
...

C Dividing a decimal by a whole number

Skill 16E: *see page 90*

A1 The full-fare on a bus is 74p.
What is the half-fare?

A2 How many minutes in:
   a 1 hour?
   b half an hour?
   c a quarter of an hour?

A3 Full marks in a test was 54.
What was half-marks?

A4 A chocolate bar has
16 squares. You give half the
bar to a friend.
How many squares do you
give away?

A5 A tank holds 20 litres.
How many litres in a $\frac{1}{4}$ tank?

B1 A whole is divided into 8
equal parts.
What fraction is each part?

B2 Emma shaded $\frac{1}{12}$ part of a
whole, blue.
   a How many equal parts was
the whole divided into?
   b How many parts did Emma
not shade?

C1   **a** 25.848 ÷ 4 =
     b 5.7 ÷ 6 =

Showing fractional parts

- One way to show a fractional part is to use shading.

Example 1

Shade $\frac{1}{4}$ of this grid
12 equal parts

Shade 1 of the 4 equal parts

$\frac{1}{4}$ **shaded**

Example 2

Shade $\frac{2}{3}$ of this grid
12 equal parts

Shade 2 of the 3 equal parts

$\frac{2}{3}$ **shaded**

Exercise 22.1
Shading fractional parts

1   Make 2 copies of a grid of 12 equal parts.
   a On one grid shade $\frac{1}{2}$ **b** On the other grid shade $\frac{3}{4}$

2 Make 5 copies of a grid of 16 equal parts.

   a What fraction is one square of the grid?

   b On one copy shade $\frac{1}{8}$ of the grid.

   c On a copy, shade $\frac{5}{8}$ of the grid.

   d Shade and label $\frac{1}{4}$ of a grid.

   e Shade and label $\frac{1}{2}$ of a grid.

   f On a grid shade $\frac{9}{16}$.

3 Make 5 copies of a grid of 20 equal parts.

   a What fraction is one square of the grid?

   b Shade $\frac{2}{5}$ of a grid.

   c Show $\frac{1}{2}$ by shading a grid.

   d On a grid shade $\frac{1}{4}$ of the whole.

   e On a grid shade to show $\frac{1}{10}$.   **f** Shade and label $\frac{7}{10}$ of a grid.

4 For each of these, what part is shaded?

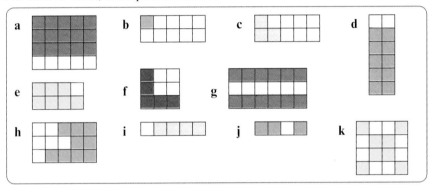

5 A fraction of this 24 square grid is shaded.

   a What fraction is one square of the grid?

   b Give two different fractions for the shaded part.

Calculating a fraction of an amount

Skill 22A
Finding a fraction of
an amount

A fraction is a part of a whole which is divided up.

To calculate a fraction of a whole amount you divide.

Example 1 Calculate $\frac{1}{3}$ of £45.

             To find $\frac{1}{3}$, the whole amount is divided by 3:
             £45 ÷ 3 = £15

             So $\frac{1}{3}$ of £45 is £15.

Example 2 Calculate $\frac{1}{5}$ of £80.50.

             To find $\frac{1}{5}$, the whole amount is divided by 5:
             £80.50 ÷ 5 = £16.10

             So $\frac{1}{5}$ of £80.50 is £16.10.

The fraction tells you what to divide the whole by.

Exercise 22.2
Practising Skill 22A

1 Calculate $\frac{1}{6}$ of £36.84.

2 Find $\frac{1}{8}$ of £60.48.

3 Which is larger: $\frac{1}{4}$ of £27.40   or $\frac{1}{5}$ of £34.40?
Explain your answer.

4 Copy and complete this table. (Change each ■ for a value.)

Amount	Fractions				
	$\frac{1}{2}$	$\frac{1}{4}$	$\frac{1}{3}$	$\frac{1}{5}$	$\frac{1}{8}$
£240	■	■	■	■	■
120 kg	■	■	■	■	■
360 grams	■	■	■	■	■
£4800	■	■	■	■	■
750 tonnes	■	■	■	■	■
42 mm	■	■	■	■	■
£62.40	■	■	■	■	■
£16.50	■	■	■	■	■
£56.80	■	■	■	■	■

5 Calculate $\frac{1}{15}$ of £116.25.

This shape has $\frac{3}{5}$ shaded.

$\frac{3}{5}$ can be thought of as: $\frac{1}{5} + \frac{1}{5} + \frac{1}{5}$ or $3 \times \frac{1}{5}$

Example   Calculate $\frac{3}{5}$ of £14.85.

To find $\frac{1}{5}$ divide the whole amount by 5:
   £14.85 ÷ 5 = £2.97

$\frac{3}{5}$ is $\frac{1}{5} + \frac{1}{5} + \frac{1}{5}$ £2.97 + £2.97 + £2.97 = £8.91

or $\frac{3}{5}$ is $3 \times \frac{1}{5}$ $3 \times$ £2.97 = £8.91

So $\frac{3}{5}$ of £14.85 is £8.91.

Both methods give the same answer £8.91

Most people choose to multiply as it is quicker.

6 Copy and complete each of these.

a $\frac{3}{5}$ of £27.65 =   **b** $\frac{3}{5}$ of 650 tonnes =   **c** $\frac{3}{5}$ of 475 kg =

d $\frac{2}{3}$ of £19.32 =   **e** $\frac{2}{3}$ of 810 tonnes =   **f** $\frac{2}{3}$ of 546 kg =

g $\frac{5}{8}$ of £107.36 =   **h** $\frac{5}{8}$ of 6640 tonnes =   **i** $\frac{5}{8}$ of 336 kg =

7 Find:

a $\frac{3}{4}$ of £40.28   **b** $\frac{4}{5}$ of 915 tonnes   **c** $\frac{5}{12}$ of 186 kg

d $\frac{3}{5}$ of 7.5 cm   **e** $\frac{7}{8}$ of 35 mm   **f** $\frac{7}{16}$ of 68 kg

g $\frac{11}{20}$ of £43   **h** $\frac{7}{10}$ of 142 km   **i** $\frac{3}{10}$ of £15.20

Exercise 22.3
Using Skill 22A

1 In a box of 72 packets of crisps:
$\frac{1}{4}$ were ready salted $\frac{1}{3}$ were salt-and-vinegar
$\frac{3}{8}$ were cheese-and-onion   and the rest were prawn flavour.

a How many packets were salt-and-vinegar?
b How many packets were cheese-and-onion?
c Were there more, or less than 15 packets of ready salted? Explain.
d How many packets were prawn flavour?

2 Last year 132 500 tickets were sold to Blackdown Caves.

Of these, $\frac{2}{5}$ were child tickets, $\frac{3}{10}$ were full price tickets, $\frac{1}{20}$ were 50p tickets and the rest were bargain tickets.

a How many 50p tickets were sold?

b How many of the tickets were sold at full price?

This headline gives an approximate number for child tickets.

> 4   **Blackdown Gazette**
>
> # 50,000 Children Visit Caves
>
> Blackdown Caves are now a firm favourite
> from all over the world

c Is the headline figure for child tickets about right?
Explain your answer.

d How many bargain tickets were sold last year?

3 In a box of 120 biscuits:

$\frac{1}{3}$ were plain, $\frac{2}{5}$ were cream, $\frac{1}{8}$ were chocolate,

$\frac{1}{20}$ were wafer and the rest were iced.

How many of each type of biscuit was in the box?

4 Jake sells walking boots.
On his best week last year he sold 168 pairs.

a How many of each size did Jake sell?

b Do you think most boots were sold
that week to males or females?
Explain your answer.

> 168 pairs of boots
> 1/3 were size 9
> 3/8 were size 10
> 1/6 were size 11
> the rest were size 12

5 There were 320 passengers on a flight to Oslo.

Of the passengers: $\frac{1}{40}$ had no meal $\frac{3}{5}$ had a meal with fish

$\frac{3}{8}$ had a vegetarian meal.

a How many passengers had a meal?

b How many had a vegetarian meal?

c 200 meals with fish were eaten.
How many of the crew had a meal with fish?

6 Eve and Sunny run a market stall.
Last year they sold a total of 48.6 tonnes of potatoes.

Of the potatoes $\frac{1}{3}$ were a type called Wilja

$\frac{4}{9}$ were a type called Maris Piper

$\frac{1}{20}$ were a type called Esteema

the rest were a type called Desiree

How many tonnes of each type did they sell?

7 Shade a grid like this for each of these questions.

a Show that $\frac{2}{3}$ is larger than $\frac{5}{8}$.

b Show that $\frac{3}{4}$ is less than $\frac{11}{12}$.

c Show that $\frac{1}{2}$ is larger than $\frac{3}{8}$.

d Show that $\frac{5}{6}$ is less than $\frac{7}{8}$.

Finding equivalent fractions

Skill 22B
Finding equivalent fractions

> Equivalent means
> the same.

> You must divide both parts
> by the same number.

> Divide by 4 as 8 and 12
> can both be divided exactly
> by 4.

> You can also multiply both
> parts of the fraction. Here
> we multiply by 2.

Equivalent fractions show the same fractional part of a whole.

Here $\frac{8}{12}$ is shaded
which is also $\frac{2}{3}$.
So $\frac{2}{3}$ and $\frac{8}{12}$
show the same fraction.
$\frac{2}{3}$ and $\frac{8}{12}$ are equivalent.

Here $\frac{10}{12}$ is shaded
which is also $\frac{5}{6}$.
So $\frac{5}{6}$ and $\frac{10}{12}$
show the same fraction.
$\frac{5}{6}$ and $\frac{10}{12}$ are equivalent.

You can also think of equivalent fractions in this way.

Start with $\frac{8}{12}$

[÷ both parts by 4] $\frac{8 \div 4}{12 \div 4} = \frac{2}{3}$ So $\frac{8}{12}$ and $\frac{2}{3}$ are equivalent.

Start with $\frac{5}{6}$

[× both parts by 2] $\frac{5 \times 2}{6 \times 2} = \frac{10}{12}$ So $\frac{5}{6}$ and $\frac{10}{12}$ are equivalent.

Exercise 22.4
Practising Skill 22B

1 Copy and complete this table.

Fraction	Divide both parts by	Equivalent fraction
$\frac{10}{15}$	5	$\frac{2}{3}$
$\frac{12}{15}$	■	$\frac{4}{5}$
$\frac{21}{33}$	3	■
$\frac{18}{27}$	9	■
$\frac{15}{21}$	■	$\frac{5}{7}$
$\frac{16}{40}$	8	■
$\frac{24}{27}$	■	$\frac{8}{9}$
$\frac{15}{25}$	■	■
$\frac{14}{35}$	■	
$\frac{27}{63}$	9	■
$\frac{16}{28}$	■	$\frac{4}{7}$
$\frac{24}{44}$	■	$\frac{6}{11}$

2 **a** Divide both parts of $\frac{18}{30}$ by 2.

   b Divide both parts of $\frac{18}{30}$ by 3.

   c Divide both parts of $\frac{18}{30}$ by 6.

   d List three fractions that are equivalent to $\frac{18}{30}$.

3 **a** List three fractions that are equivalent to $\frac{16}{20}$.

   b Are $\frac{24}{42}$ and $\frac{4}{6}$ equivalent fractions?
   Explain your answer.

4 **a** Multiply both parts of $\frac{3}{4}$ by 2.

   b Multiply both parts of $\frac{3}{4}$ by 5.

   c Multiply both parts of $\frac{3}{4}$ by 8.

   d List three fractions that are equivalent to $\frac{3}{4}$.

5 Which of these fractions are equivalent to $\frac{10}{15}$?

$\frac{12}{17}$ $\frac{20}{30}$ $\frac{25}{50}$ $\frac{2}{3}$ $\frac{100}{150}$

6 **a** Show that $\frac{28}{63}$ is equivalent to $\frac{4}{9}$.

   b Show that $\frac{5}{8}$ is equivalent to $\frac{15}{24}$.

   c Show that $\frac{15}{50}$, $\frac{27}{36}$, and $\frac{21}{28}$ are all equivalent to $\frac{3}{4}$.

7 List four fractions that are equivalent to $\frac{9}{15}$.

8 Explain why $\frac{250}{800}$ and $\frac{5}{16}$ are equivalent fractions.

Writing fractions in their lowest terms

Skill 22C
Writing a fraction in its
lowest terms

A fraction in its lowest
terms might be called a
fraction in its simplest
terms.

A fraction is in its lowest terms when:

   a value cannot be found to divide both parts of the fraction

The fraction $\frac{3}{5}$ is in its lowest terms. [3 and 5 cannot both be divided]

Now, $\frac{9}{15}$ is not in its lowest terms. [9 and 15 can both be divided by 3]

$$\frac{9 \div 3}{15 \div 3} = \frac{3}{5} \qquad \text{So } \frac{9}{15} \text{ in its lowest terms is } \frac{3}{5}.$$

Example   Write $\frac{36}{60}$ in its lowest terms.

Divide both parts by 3: $\dfrac{36 \div 3}{60 \div 3} = \dfrac{12}{20}$ [12 and 20 can both be divided by 4]

Divide both parts by 4: $\dfrac{12 \div 4}{20 \div 4} = \dfrac{3}{5}$ [3 and 5 both cannot be divided]

So $\frac{36}{60}$ in its lowest terms is $\frac{3}{5}$.

Exercise 22.5
Practising Skill 22C

1 Write each of these fractions in its lowest terms.

  a $\frac{14}{21}$ **b** $\frac{30}{42}$ **c** $\frac{27}{36}$ **d** $\frac{16}{36}$

  e $\frac{25}{60}$ **f** $\frac{8}{34}$ **g** $\frac{12}{16}$ **h** $\frac{20}{50}$

  i $\frac{56}{63}$ **j** $\frac{24}{72}$ **k** $\frac{19}{50}$ **l** $\frac{18}{90}$

  m $\frac{19}{21}$ **n** $\frac{35}{42}$ **o** $\frac{150}{175}$ **p** $\frac{15}{4500}$

2 Explain why $\frac{45}{81}$ in its lowest terms is not $\frac{15}{27}$.

3 Which of these, in its lowest terms, is $\frac{4}{5}$?

$\frac{12}{20}$ $\frac{28}{35}$ $\frac{44}{50}$ $\frac{24}{36}$ $\frac{48}{60}$

Converting a fraction to a decimal

Skill 22D
Converting a fraction to
a decimal

You will need

Skill 16E: *see page 90*

if you do not use a
calculator

You can convert a fraction into a decimal by:

   dividing the upper part of the fraction by the lower part.

Example   Write $\frac{3}{8}$ as a decimal.

For $\frac{3}{8}$ as a decimal: $8\overline{)3.0^30^60^4}$ $\begin{array}{c}0.375\end{array}$ [Use a calculator: $3 \div 8 = 0.375$]

So $\frac{3}{8}$ as a decimal is 0.375.

Exercise 22.6
Practising Skill 22D

1 Convert each of these fractions to a decimal.
(Do not use a calculator.)

    a $\frac{3}{4}$ **b** $\frac{3}{5}$ **c** $\frac{6}{8}$ **d** $\frac{7}{10}$

    e $\frac{5}{8}$ **f** $\frac{9}{12}$ **g** $\frac{1}{8}$ **h** $\frac{1}{5}$

    i $\frac{3}{10}$ **j** $\frac{4}{5}$ **k** $\frac{7}{8}$ **l** $\frac{3}{15}$

2 Convert each of these to a decimal.
(You may choose to use a calculator.)

    a $\frac{1}{40}$ **b** $\frac{5}{80}$ **c** $\frac{10}{16}$ **d** $\frac{15}{20}$

    e $\frac{12}{20}$ **f** $\frac{9}{20}$ **g** $\frac{12}{50}$ **h** $\frac{18}{30}$

    i $\frac{12}{40}$ **j** $\frac{15}{40}$ **k** $\frac{25}{40}$ **l** $\frac{25}{80}$

Converting a fraction to a percentage

Some fractions are often linked with percentages.

If you get half-marks, you get 50%.   **So $\frac{1}{2}$ and 50% are the same.**

In a sale 25% off means $\frac{1}{4}$ less to pay.   **So $\frac{1}{4}$ and 25% are the same.**

Other fractions and percentages you might know are:

    $\frac{3}{4}$ is the same as 75%

    $\frac{1}{10}$ is the same as 10%

    $\frac{1}{5}$ is the same as 20%

Skill 22E
Converting a fraction to
a percentage.

To convert any fraction to a percentage you can:
    write the fraction as a decimal then multiply by 100.

Example 1   Convert $\frac{7}{20}$ to a percentage.

    As a decimal $\frac{7}{20} = 0.35$

    As a percentage $\frac{7}{20} = 0.35 \times 100 = 35$

    So $\frac{7}{20}$ as a percentage is 35%.

Example 2   Write $\frac{15}{80}$ as a percentage.

    As a decimal $\frac{15}{80} = 0.1875$

    As a percentage $\frac{15}{80} = 0.1875 \times 100 = 18.75$

    So $\frac{15}{80}$ as a percentage is 18.75%.

Exercise 22.7
Practising Skill 22E

1 Write each of these fractions as a percentage.

    a $\frac{15}{50}$ **b** $\frac{24}{64}$ **c** $\frac{15}{75}$ **d** $\frac{36}{80}$

    e $\frac{42}{70}$ **f** $\frac{56}{64}$ **g** $\frac{28}{40}$ **h** $\frac{54}{80}$

    i $\frac{30}{75}$ **j** $\frac{9}{16}$ **k** $\frac{11}{32}$ **l** $\frac{15}{48}$

    m $\frac{144}{200}$ **n** $\frac{125}{160}$ **o** $\frac{250}{800}$ **p** $\frac{1800}{4500}$

2 Which is larger: $\frac{5}{8}$ or 65%? Explain your answer.

Starting points

You need to know about ...

... so try these questions

A Grouped frequency tables

- ◆ A frequency table is a way to organise data.

- ◆ Sometimes the data is collected together in groups.

Example This data shows the ages of 37 people using a shop.

65, 34, 71, 36, 12, 14, 23, 40, 88, 6, 72, 56, 44, 53, 19, 53, 70, 17,
55, 41, 58, 60, 43, 20, 26, 39, 24, 59, 23, 18, 58, 9, 51, 38, 29, 23, 54

Make a grouped
frequency table
using groups of
1 to 19 , 20 to 39,
40 to 59, 60 to 79,
80 or over.

Class	Tally	Frequency
1–19	⦀⦀ //	7
20–39	⦀⦀ ⦀⦀ /	11
40–59	⦀⦀ ⦀⦀ ///	13
60–70	⦀⦀	5
80 or over	/	1
	Total	37

- ◆ Each group that data is put into is called a **class**.

- ◆ The class with the highest frequency is called the **modal class**.

A1 In the shop age survey, which is the modal class?

A2 This data gives the number of miles 30 cyclists travelled in a day:

45, 56, 98, 12, 72, 65, 91, 44,
80, 55, 23, 46, 40, 57, 43, 33,
56, 49, 65, 43, 37, 77, 50, 19,
99, 68, 60, 70, 54, 41

a Make a grouped frequency table using groups of 1–10, 11–20, ... , 91–100

b What is the modal class?

Line graphs

- ◆ A line graph often shows how something changes with time.
- ◆ Points you know are plotted and joined up by a line.

Examples These are both line graphs.

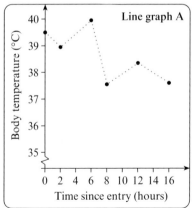

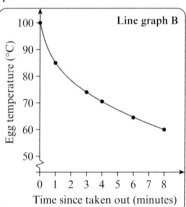

For graph A, points in
between the dots have no
meaning because the man's
temperature will have gone
up or down in between
readings.

For graph B, the
temperature of the egg will
fall in a steady way. So all
points on the line have
meaning.

Graph A shows a man's temperature in hospital.
His temperature has been measured six times.
You **cannot** say what his temperature was after 4 hours.

Graph B shows the temperature of an egg after it is taken from hot water.
The egg's temperature has also been measured six times.
You **can** say that the egg's temperature is about 75 °C after 2 minutes.

Exercise 23.1
Line graphs

1 This table shows the temperature of a radiator from the time it is switched on.

Time (seconds)	0	1	2	3	4	5	6	7	8	9
Temperature (°C)	20	20	22	28	37	50	62	71	77	80

a Copy the axes on to squared paper.
b Plot the points and draw a smooth line graph to show the data.
c From your line, estimate the temperature of the radiator after $4\frac{1}{2}$ seconds.

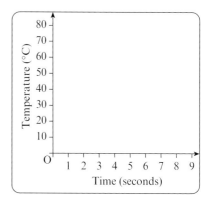

2 This line graph shows the size of a baby inside its mother from the time it is conceived.

A baby is conceived when the egg is fertilised.

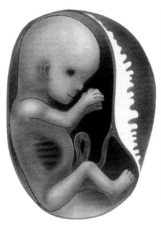

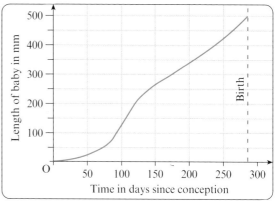

Baby at 70 days
Actual size

a Why does every point on the line have a meaning?
b Measure the length, from head to foot, of the baby shown. After roughly how many days will the baby be this size?
c Estimate the length of the baby at 200 days.
d When does the baby reach 400 mm in length?
e Why does the graph not tell you much about the baby in its first 20 days?
f When is the baby growing fastest?

3 This table gives the weight of a baby in grams from the time it is conceived.

Days since conception	50	100	150	200	250	280
Weights in grams	80	190	375	760	1520	2500

a Draw a smooth line graph to show how the baby's weight changes.
b Estimate the baby's weight after 230 days.
c After roughly how long does the baby weigh 500 grams?

Use these scales for your axes.

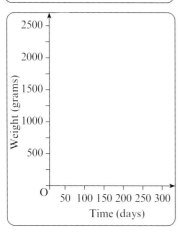

4 This line graph shows the number of birds a watcher saw at times during the day.

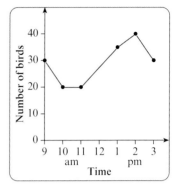

a At what times were the number of birds counted?

b At what times did the watcher see 30 birds?

c About how many birds could the watcher see at 1 pm?

d Explain why it is not possible to say how many birds there were at midday.

e It would be better to use a bar-line graph for this data.
Draw a bar-line graph to show the bird data.

5 This graph shows the heights of two types of wheat after planting.

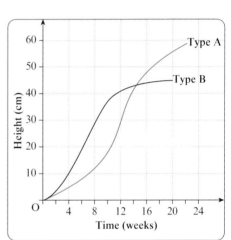

a Which type made the tallest plant when ripe?

b How long did it take type B to grow to full size?

c About how tall was each type after 12 weeks?

d Which type grew more quickly at the start?
How can you tell?

e A farmer plants type A wheat on 26th March.
When can he harvest it?

6 Water flows from a tap at a steady rate.
It fills each of these jars.

These line graphs show how the height of water in the jars changes.
The graphs are muddled up.

You need to decide if a wide jar fills up faster or more slowly than a narrow jar.

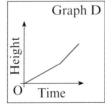 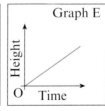 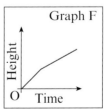

Match each jar to its own graph.

Grouped frequency diagrams

Skill 23A
Drawing a grouped
frequency diagram

- A grouped frequency diagram is a frequency diagram for data which has already been put into groups.

Example

This data shows the scores (out of 30) for a group of 21 people in a competition.
12, 7, 30, 5, 13, 15, 24, 20, 17, 8, 16, 20, 22, 10, 11, 19, 17, 11, 2, 8, 25, 20

Draw a grouped frequency diagram to show this data.
Use class intervals of 0–5, 6–10, 11–15, and so on.

> A class interval is one of the groups into which the data is split.

- Make a grouped frequency table.

- Draw the grouped frequency diagram. Make sure the bars widths go from 0–5, 6–10, and so on.

Class	Tally	Frequency
0–5	//	2
6–10	///	3
11–15	////	5
16–20	//// //	7
21–25	///	3
26–30	/	1

> The gap between bar 0–5 and bar 6–10 is because there are no part-marks between 5 and 6.

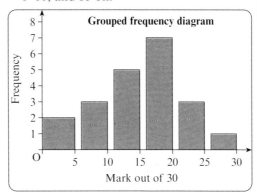

- Note that the bottom scale is continuous.

- In this example the class interval with the highest frequency is 16–20.

  We say that the **modal class** is 16 to 20.

Exercise 23.2
Using skill 23A

1 A group of 20 students ran on a cross-country race.
These are their times. Each is given to the nearest minute.

34, 38, 41, 18, 25, 39, 22, 28, 48, 31, 15, 30, 33, 20, 44, 27, 21, 32, 40, 35

a Make a grouped frequency table.
Use class intervals of 0–9, 10–19, … , 40–49.
b Copy the axes below on to grid paper.
Draw a group frequency diagram.
c Which is the modal class?
d Why do you think the frequency of the 0–9 class is 0 for this race?

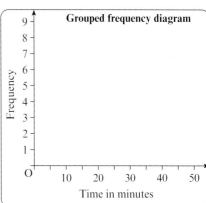

2 A survey of the number of people on National 80-seater buses gave this data.
17, 44, 57, 60, 22, 12, 2, 66, 32, 28, 15, 19, 55, 41, 20, 59, 49, 12, 60, 32, 28, 22, 18, 14, 6, 68, 78, 0, 78, 63, 27, 57, 61, 64, 77

   a Make a grouped frequency table.
      Use class intervals of 0–10, 11–20, 21–30, … , 71–80.
   b On squared paper, draw a grouped frequency diagram.
   c What is the modal class?
   d What does the shape of the diagram tell you about the size of the buses National should run?

Skill 23B
Drawing a grouped
frequency diagram for
continuous data

♦ Some data can have any value, not just whole numbers.
For example, lines could be 4.2 cm long or 3.61 cm long.
We call this continuous data.

♦ Grouped frequency tables and diagrams can be drawn for continuous data.

Example

This data shows the lengths of ten lines in centimetres.
  15 13.4 3 9.6 5 15.2 14 12.9 7.4 10.1

Make a grouped frequency table and a grouped frequency diagram.

Class	Tally	Frequency
$0 \leqslant \text{length} < 5$	/	1
$5 \leqslant \text{time} < 10$	///	3
$10 \leqslant \text{time} < 15$	////	4
$15 \leqslant \text{time} < 20$	//	2

$10 \leqslant \text{length} < 15$
means 10 or greater but
less than 15.

10 **is** included
15 **is not** included.

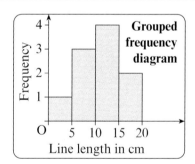

There are no gaps between the bars this time.

Exercise 23.3
Practising skill 23B

1 This data is about the time in minutes that 20 people take to do a task.
23.6 12.2 4 20 24.6 30.1 9.9 28 10 38 23.8 6.6 31 14.61
29.99 39 20.2 18.8 34 30

   a Copy and complete the grouped frequency data with the time data.
   b How many people took 20 minutes or more?

Class	Tally	Frequency
$0 \leqslant \text{time} < 10$		
$10 \leqslant \text{time} < 20$		
$20 \leqslant \text{time} < 30$		
$30 \leqslant \text{time} < 40$		
$40 \leqslant \text{time} < 50$		

2 A survey asked 85 people how much money in pounds they each spent on magazines in a week.

The results of the survey are shown in this table.

Amount spent in pounds	Frequency
$0 \leqslant \text{money} < 0.50$	4
$0.50 \leqslant \text{money} < 1.00$	14
$1.00 \leqslant \text{money} < 1.50$	9
$1.50 \leqslant \text{money} < 2.00$	18
$2.00 \leqslant \text{money} < 2.50$	15
$2.50 \leqslant \text{money} < 3.00$	13
$3.00 \leqslant \text{money} < 3.50$	7
$3.50 \leqslant \text{money} < 4.00$	5

a Copy and complete the grouped frequency diagram.

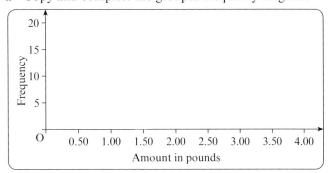

b How many people spent £3 or more?

c How many people spent less than £1.50?

3 This table shows the cost of a car service at different garages.

Cost	£35–	£40–	£45–	£50–	£55–	£60–65
Frequency	1	4	2	5	0	2

£35– means any amount from £35.00 up to £39.99.

£40.00 is in the next class.

a Draw a grouped frequency diagram for the data.

b How many garages were asked in the survey?

c How many garages charged £50 or more?

d What was the modal class?

4 This table shows the heights in inches of a group of men.

Height	Frequency
60–	5
62–	8
64–	16
66–	28
68–	65
70–	42
72–	14
74–76	2

a Copy and complete the grouped frequency diagram.

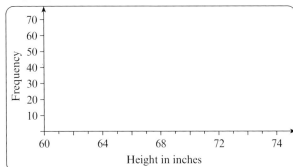

b How many people were 70 inches or more tall?

c How many people were shorter than 66 inches?

Starting points

You need to know about ...   ... so try these questions

A Substituting values in formulas

Skill 13A: *see page 73*

A1 A formula that links k, p and c is: $c = 3p - k$

Copy and complete this table.

p	k	c
5	4	
2	9	
3	2	
7	15	
19	45	

B Solving equations

Skill 13B: *see page 75*

B1 Solve each of these equations.

a $3y - 4 = 17$
b $6 + 4y = 34$
c $5k + 8 = 53$
d $4 + 9k = 22$

C Solving equations with brackets

Skill 13C: *see page 76*

C1 Solve each of these equations.

a $4(2y - 5) = 12$
b $3(5 + 2h) = 51$
c $8(w - 5) = 16$

Solving equations

♦ The unknown in an equation is what you find the value of, when you solve it.

♦ In the equation $3y + 4 = 16$ the unknown y is only on one side.

♦ In the equation $5y + 4 = 3y + 18$ the unknown y is on both sides.

♦ An equation has two sides: a left-hand side (LHS), and a right-hand side (RHS).

$$\begin{array}{cc} \text{LHS} & \text{RHS} \\ 5y + 4 &= 3y + 18 \end{array}$$

Skill 24A
Solving equations with the unknown on both sides

Example Solve the equation $5y + 4 = 3y + 18$.

To keep the equation balanced you must do the same to both sides.

Start with the equation $\quad 5y + 4 = 3y + 18$
[take 4 from both sides] $\quad 5y + 4 - 4 = 3y + 18 - 4$
$\quad 5y = 3y + 14$
[take $3y$ from both sides] $\quad 5y - 3y = 3y - 3y + 14$
$\quad 2y = 14$
[÷ both sides by 2] $\quad y = 7$

$3y$ is on the RHS. When you take $3y$ away this will leave no ys on the RHS.

Exercise 24.1
Practising skill 24A

1 Solve each of these equations.

a $9y + 5 = 3y + 23$ b $15k + 9 = 12k + 24$ c $16h + 8 = 5h + 41$
d $28p + 25 = 16p + 61$ e $11k + 9 = 3k + 41$ f $15y + 8 = 10y + 43$
g $25d = 18d + 56$ h $17a = 55 + 12a$

2 Solve each of these equations.

a $7x - 4 = 3x + 24$ **b** $12y - 8 = 8y + 28$
c $23x - 12 = 18x + 38$ **d** $32k - 37 = 2k + 53$
e $29y - 54 = 18y + 1$ **f** $45y - 9 = y + 79$
g $21k - 1 = 20k + 5$ **h** $52w - 25 = 27w + 75$

3 Solve these equations.

a $9x + 18 = 4x - 7$ **b** $12k - 4 = 9k - 19$
c $15y + 5 = 11y - 11$ **d** $23h + 1 = 15h - 23$
e $30w - 20 = 5w - 70$ **f** $3x - 9 = x - 21$
g $35k - 1 = 5k - 61$ **h** $12n + 45 = 7n - 15$

Skill 24B
Checking the answer when you solve an equation

$5y$ is $5 \times y$

The +4 shows what went wrong when the equation was solved the first time.

When you solve an equation you can check your answer.

This equation has been solved.

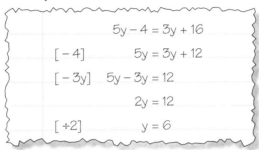

$$5y - 4 = 3y + 16$$
$$[-4] \quad 5y = 3y + 12$$
$$[-3y] \quad 5y - 3y = 12$$
$$2y = 12$$
$$[\div 2] \quad y = 6$$

Now check this answer.

The equation is: $5y - 4 = 3y + 16$

The equation must be balanced:
when $y = 6$ LHS $= 5(6) - 4$ and   RHS $= 3(6) + 16$
                   $= 30 - 4$ $= 18 + 16$
                   $= 26$ $= 34$

The equation is not balanced so:

$y = 6$ is wrong !

Solve the equation again:
$$5y - 4 = 3y + 16$$
$$[+4] \quad 5y - 4 + 4 = 3y + 16 + 4$$
$$5y = 3y + 20$$
$$[-3y] \quad 5y - 3y = 3y - 3y + 20$$
$$2y = 20$$
$$[\div 2] \quad y = 10$$

Check when $y = 10$: LHS $= 5(10) - 4$ and   RHS $= 3(10) + 16$
                     $= 50 - 4$ $= 30 + 16$
                     $= 46$ $= 46$

So, when $y = 10$
the equation is balanced.

$y = 10$ is correct!

Exercise 24.2
Practising **Skill 24B**

1 In which of these equations is $x = 6$?

a $6x - 8 = 4x + 8$ b $9x - 5 = 4x + 25$ c $7x - 4 = 5x + 6$

d $8x + 5 = 6x + 19$ e $7x - 8 = 3x + 16$ f $5x + 4 = 3x - 8$

2 Which of these answers are wrong?

a $12k + 7 = 8k - 9$ $k = {}^-4$

b $20w - 1 = 5w + 29$ $w = 2$

c $18h - 3 = 6h + 27$ $h = 2$

d $35y + 18 = 24y - 9$ $y = {}^-3$

3 Check each of the answers in this table.

No.	Equation	Solution
1	$6y + 4 = 3y + 13$	$y = 3$
2	$8y - 5 = 2y + 7$	$y = 2$
3	$7y + 3 = 5y + 7$	$y = 5$
4	$9y - 3 = 6y - 15$	$y = {}^-4$
5	$8y - 2 = 6y - 14$	$y = {}^-8$
6	$21k + 5 = 15k - 7$	$k = {}^-2$
7	$30x - 8 = 12x + 10$	$x = 1$
8	$35w + 3 = 32w - 15$	$w = {}^-4$
9	$16a - 8 = 12a + 16$	$a = 2$
10	$15x + 25 = 10x - 25$	$x = 10$

a Which of the answers do you think are wrong?

b For each wrong answer:
    ❖ solve the equation
    ❖ check that you have the right answer.

Writing equations

Skill 24C
Forming equations

Often, if you can form and then solve an equation you can find the answer to a problem.

Example

The perimeter of this rectangle is 61 cm.

$x + 4.5$

x

Form an equation and find the length and width of the rectangle.

The perimeter is 61 cm so we can form an equation:

$$61 = x + x + 4.5 + x + x + 4.5$$

[collect like terms] $61 = 4x + 9$

Collect like terms is:

Skill 7A: *see page 42*

Now solve the equation:

$$61 = 4x + 9$$

$[{}^-9]$ $52 = 4x$

$[\div 4]$ $13 = x$

When $x = 13$ $x + 4.5 = 13 + 4.5 = 17.5$

So the length of the rectangle is 17.5 cm and the width is 13 cm.

Exercise 24.3
Practising Skill 24C

1 The perimeter of this rectangle is 91 cm.

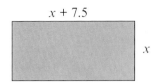

$x + 7.5$

x

 a Form an equation for the perimeter of the rectangle.
 b Solve your equation.
 c What is the width of the rectangle?
 d What is the length of the rectangle?

2 The perimeter of this rectangle is 82 cm

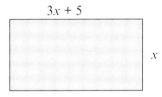

$3x + 5$

x

 a Form an equation for the perimeter of the rectangle.
 b Solve your equation.
 c What is the width of the rectangle?
 d What is the length of the rectangle?
 e Calculate the area of the rectangle.

3 The perimeter of this shape is 93 cm.

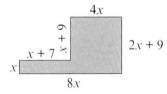

$4x$

$x + 9$

$x + 7$

$2x + 9$

x

$8x$

 a Form an equation for the perimeter of the shape.
 b Solve your equation.
 c Sketch the shape and label each side with its length.

4 These two rectangles have the same perimeter.

15 cm

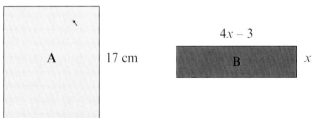

A   17 cm

$4x - 3$

B x

 a Calculate the perimeter of shape A.
 b Form an equation for the perimeter of shape B.
 c Solve your equation.
 d What is the width and the length of shape B?
 e Which shape has the larger area?

> A diagram will help with this question.

5 A rectangle is 4 cm longer than it is wide. It has a perimeter of 76 cm.

Form and solve an equation to find the length of the rectangle.

6   These two rectangles have the same perimeter in cm.

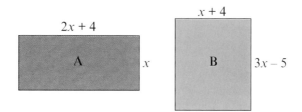

a   If the perimeter of rectangle B is P, complete the equation $P = \ldots$

b   Solve the equation $8x - 2 = 6x + 8$.

c   Find the perimeter of A in centimetres.

d   Find the perimeter of B.

7   The area of rectangle C is 60 cm².

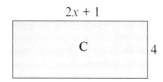

a   The area A of a rectangle is given by: length × width = A
    Which of these equations is for the area of C?
    $(2x + 1) + 4 = 60$ $4 + (2x + 1) = 60$ $4(2x + 1) = 60$

b   Solve the equation for the area of C.

c   Find the perimeter of C.

8   Triangles A and B have the same perimeter, P.

 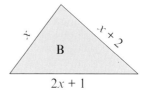

a   Show that $P = 3(x + 3)$ is an equation for the perimeter of A.

b   Explain why: $(2x + 1) + (x + 2) + x = 3(x + 3)$

c   Solve the equation: $(2x + 1) + (x + 2) + x = 3(x + 3)$

d   Find the perimeter of triangle B.

9   The angles in a triangle are given as $2x$, $3x$, and $4x$.

a   Write an equation for the angle sum of this triangle.

b   Solve your equation to find a value for x.

c   Find the size of each angle.

10   The four angles in a quadrilateral are x, $2x$, $3x$ and $4x$.

a   Write an equation for the angle sum of this quadrilateral.

b   Solve your equation and give the size of each angle.

For angle sums:
see page 106.

Starting points

You need to know about ...

... so try these questions

A Rounding to the nearest ten

◆ Numbers can be rounded up or down to give an approximate value.

28	rounded to the nearest 10 is	30	rounded up
143	rounded to the nearest 10 is	140	rounded down
225	rounded to the nearest 10 is	230	rounded up

because half-way numbers are rounded up.
(225 is exactly half-way between 220 and 330.)

◆ When you round to the nearest 10 you must look at the Units digit.

B Rounding to the nearest hundred

◆
245	rounded to the nearest 100 is	200	rounded down
388	rounded to the nearest 100 is	400	rounded up
1150	rounded to the nearest 100 is	1200	rounded up

◆ When you round to the nearest 100 you must look at the Tens digit

C Place value and decimals

The place values for decimal numbers are these.

...	100	10	U	.	$\frac{1}{10}$	$\frac{1}{100}$	$\frac{1}{1000}$	...
			4	.	6	3		
			2	.	0	6		

The value of the digit 6 in 4.62 is $\frac{6}{10}$.

The value of the digit 6 in 12.06 is $\frac{6}{100}$.

A1 Round each of these numbers to the nearest ten.

a	588	b	921	c	17
d	3786	e	585	f	392
g	656	h	891	i	196
j	992	k	3994	l	5997

B1 Round each of these numbers to the nearest hundred.

a	862	b	739	c	849
d	2750	e	3588	f	919
g	8150	h	5949	i	1051
j	323	k	9501	l	1209

B2 Give a number, rounded to the nearest 100, which gives 8500.

C1 Give the value of the digit 4 in each of these numbers:

a 5.475
b 15.004
c 128.142
d 0.00045
e 0.4

Rounding decimal values

Skill 25A
Rounding decimal values to the nearest whole number

Rounding decimal values to the nearest whole number you need to look at the $\frac{1}{10}$ (tenths) digit.

◆ If the $\frac{1}{10}$s digit is 0, 1, 2, 3, or 4
leave the Units digit of the number as it is.

◆ If the $\frac{1}{10}$s digit is 5, 6, 7, 8, or 9
round Units digit up by one.

Example Round 16.385, 12.68, and 31.565 to the nearest whole number.

10	U	.	$\frac{1}{10}$	$\frac{1}{100}$	$\frac{1}{1000}$	
1	6	.	3	8	5	Rounded is 16
1	2	.	6	8		Rounded is 13
3	1		5	6	5	Rounded is 32

Exercise 25.1
Practising Skill 25A

1 Round each of these decimal values to the nearest whole number.

a	37.635	b	128.425	c	7.38	d	8.65	e	17.57
f	20.75	g	125.38	h	57.499	i	56.059	j	130.4
k	78.804	l	39.68	m	109.82	n	300.47	o	999.51

2 Which of these is 35 when rounded to the nearest whole number?
34.685   35.49   34.098   35.199   334.51

3 Round each of these to the nearest whole number.

a 0.675	**b** 0.51	**c** 0.88	**d** 0.6554
e 0.355	**f** 0.49	**g** 0.5	**h** 0.088

Decimal values can have any number of digits after the decimal point.

16.4	1 digit after decimal point
38.75	2 digits …
75.109	3 digits …
94.3684	4 digits …
and so on	and so on

We say these values have a number of decimal places:

1 dp stands for: 1 decimal place.

16.4	has 1 decimal place	1 dp
38.75	has 2 decimal places	2 dp
75.109	has 3 …	3 dp
94.3684	has 4 …	4 dp
and so on	and so on	

Skill 25B
Rounding to one decimal place

The 2nd digit has a place value of $\frac{1}{100}$'s .

A number rounded to 1 dp has only 1 digit after the decimal point.

Rounding to 1 dp you need to look at the 2nd digit after the decimal point.

♦ If the 2nd digit after the decimal point is 0, 1, 2, 3, or 4, leave the 1st digit after the decimal point as it is.

♦ If the 2nd digit after the decimal point is 5, 6, 7, 8, or 9, round the 1st digit up by one.

Example

Round each of these to 1 dp.
44.685   167.349   0.351

(1 dp) tells you that the number has been rounded. You must write the number of decimal places a value has been rounded to.

The rounded values have only 1 digit after the decimal point (1 dp). Look at the digits after the decimal point:

44.685	is 44.7 rounded to 1 dp.	We write	44.7 (1 dp)
167.349	is 167.3 …	…	167.3 (1 dp)
0.351	is 0.4 …	…	0.4 (1 dp)

Exercise 25.2
Practising Skill 25B

1 Round each of these values to 1 dp.

a 345.675	**b** 676.354	**c** 188.649	**d** 1304.707
e 564.715	**f** 60.082	**g** 90.039	**h** 28.36
i 6.351	**j** 11.118	**k** 206.275	**l** 100.05

2 Round each of these values to 1 dp.

a 0.355	**b** 0.61	**c** 0.0815	**d** 0.609
e 0.0175	**f** 0.827	**g** 0.97	**h** 0.084

3 27.4 is a value that is rounded to 1 decimal place. How should you write it?

Skill 25C
Rounding to any number of
decimal places

The number of decimal places you are rounding to, tells you the digits you need to look at.

Rounding to			
1 dp	you look at the	2nd digit after the decimal point
2 dp	...	3rd	...
3 dp	...	4th	...
4 dp	...	5th	...
and so on		and so on.

Example 1 Round 385.604 7 to 3 dp.

The rounded value will have 3 digits after the decimal point (3 dp).
Look at the digits after the decimal point:
385.604 7 rounded to 3 dp is: 385.605 (3 dp).

(3 decimal places)

Example 2 Round 0.065 482 5 to 5 dp

0.065 482 5 rounded to 5 dp is: 0.065 48 (5 dp)

(5 decimal places)

Exercise 25.3
Practising Skill 25C

1 Copy and complete this table.

Decimal value	Rounded to		
	2 dp	3 dp	4 dp
27.685 44			
3.067 45			
158.005 74			
0.607 52			
200.051 88			
61.504 09			
384.958 52			
0.067 58			
3.608 67			
75.757 57			

Exercise 25.4
Using Skill 25C

1 Rewrite this article with every decimal value rounded to 1 dp.

> They walked 258.68 km with temperatures as high as 34.84 °C. They took a total of 988.56 kg of equipment, which included 834.58 metres of rope. Each day they climbed an average of 1045.075 feet, which was 76.85 feet more than they planned.
> Just to get here the team flew 4653.85 km. Then another 608.095 km by road. The trucks used a total of 2856.84 litres of fuel at an average cost of 88.657 pence per litre.

2 **a** Find the perimeter of this rectangular lawn.
b Round the length to 1 dp.
c Round the width to 1 dp.
d Using the rounded figures calculate the perimeter.

16.46 metres

5.25 metres

Starting points

You need to know about ...

... so try these questions

A The terms used to describe likelihood

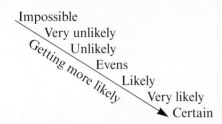

A snow storm in summer is **very unlikely**.
For a person to stay alive, breathing in the next hour is **certain**.
The chance of a boy or a girl being born is about **evens**.

B Outcomes and equally likely outcomes

An outcome is the result of something happening.
'2' is one outcome from rolling a 1 to 6 dice.
'Red' is an outcome from spinning this spinner.

An outcome is equally likely if it has the same chance
as any other outcome of coming up.

Getting a B on the spinner is an equally likely outcome.
Each letter has the same chance of coming up.

Getting a red face on the spinner is not an equally likely outcome.
There are more red faces than any other colour.

A1 Use one of the terms to describe the likelihood that:

  a it will rain some time in the winter

  b the sun will be out when it is dark

  c a 4-year-old will buy a car.

  d you will die some time

  e a coin that is spun will land on heads.

A2 Say one thing which is impossible.

B1 List all the outcomes from rolling a 1 to 6 dice.

B2 **a** What are the outcomes from spinning a coin?

  b Are these outcomes equally likely?

B3 A matchbox is thrown in the air. Is it equally likely to end up on any of its six faces? Explain your answer.

Calculating probability

Skill 26A
Calculating probabilty for equally likely outcomes

♦ For equally likely outcomes you can calculate probability.

Example   This spinner has 12 sections of equal size. What is the probability that the arrow will stop on B?

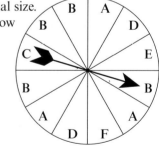

4 sections out of 12 have B on them.

So the probability that the arrow stops on B is $\frac{4}{12} = \frac{1}{3}$.

To find the probability that the arrow stops on either A or B:
♦ count the number of sections with A or B = 7
♦ count the total number of sections = 12
♦ calculate the probability = $\frac{7}{12}$.

Exercise 26.1
Practising skill 26A

Give the probabilities as fractions in their lowest terms.

Skill 22C: *see page 126*

1 Calculate the probability that the arrow above will stop on:

  a C   **b** D   **c** E   **d** F

2 What is the probability that the arrow above stops on G?

3 What is the probability that the arrow stops on a letter of the alphabet?

4 Calculate the probability that the arrow stops on either E or F.

Exercise 26.2
Using skill 26A

This shows all the criminals in Humbleton.

Alf   Edwin   Ian   Mick

Brian   Fred   Jim   Nick

Colin   Graeme   Ken   Owen

Derek   Harry   Liam   Pete

1 What is the probability that a criminal in Humbleton has a beard?

2 Calculate the probability that a criminal has:
   a a moustache   **b** an earring   **c** a necklace.

3 **a** What is the probability that a criminal has a hat?
   b What is the probability that a criminal does not have a hat?
   c Can you find a link between your answers to parts **a** and **b**?

4 The police have brought in all the criminals with beards.
   A man is picked out of this group at random.
   What is the probability that he will have a moustache?

5 A witness said she saw who stole the bag.
   The criminal had fair hair and glasses.
   What is the probability that this is a criminal from Humbleton?

6 The probability that a criminal from Humbleton has _____
   and has _____ is $\frac{1}{16}$.

   What could the missing data be? Explain why.

> Picking at random means picking without choosing.
>
> Every man has an equal chance of being picked.

The probability scale

Skill 26B
Placing probabilities on
a scale

Probabilities can all be placed somewhere on a scale from 0 to 1.

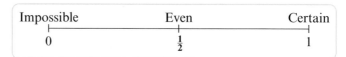

The probability that you will read all of
this book today is unlikely.
It would be placed about here on the
probability scale.

The probability that you will pick, at
random, a blue cube from this bag is $\frac{5}{9}$.
It will be here on the scale.

You can see there is more than an
even chance of picking a blue cube.

Exercise 26.3
Practising skill 26B

1 a For the bag above, what is the probability of picking a red cube?
   b Draw a 0 to 1 scale and show this probability with an arrow.

2 On different 0 to 1 scales show the probability of picking:

   a a yellow cube
   b a cube which is not blue.

3 On a probability scale show the probability that it will snow today.
Give a reason for your answer.

4 On different probability scales show the probability that:

   a you will win the lottery this week
   b you will come to school tomorrow
   c the next teacher to pass the room will be male.

5 This 0 to 1 scale shows the probability of something happening to you.

Decide on something this could be.
Give your reasons

6 You have a full pack of cards (no jokers).
You pick a card at random.
On probability scales show the probility that you pick

   a a red card   **b** a heart   **c** a picture card

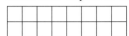
This revises the work in Sections 22 to 26

1 Make four copies of this grid.

a What fraction is one square of the grid?

b On one copy shade $\frac{3}{8}$ of the grid.

c On one copy shade $\frac{3}{4}$ of the grid.

d On one copy shade $\frac{7}{16}$ of the grid.

e On a grid show that $\frac{13}{16}$ is more than $\frac{1}{2}$.

2 **Skill 22A**
Copy and complete each of these.

a $\frac{2}{3}$ of £45.60 =   **b** $\frac{3}{5}$ of 485 kg =

c $\frac{7}{10}$ of 350 km   **d** $\frac{5}{8}$ of £104.72 =

e $\frac{3}{4}$ of 2600 miles =   **f** $\frac{4}{5}$ of 5800 tonnes =

3 **Skill 22B**

a Which of these fractions is equivalent to $\frac{3}{5}$?
$\frac{15}{25}$ $\frac{24}{40}$ $\frac{25}{35}$ $\frac{30}{50}$

b Which of these fractions is equivalent to $\frac{5}{8}$?
$\frac{15}{20}$ $\frac{15}{24}$ $\frac{35}{56}$ $\frac{60}{96}$

4 **Skill 22C**
Write each of these fractions in its lowest terms.

a $\frac{25}{35}$ **b** $\frac{56}{77}$ **c** $\frac{32}{40}$

d $\frac{64}{104}$ **e** $\frac{27}{81}$ **f** $\frac{28}{77}$

g $\frac{54}{63}$ **h** $\frac{24}{40}$ **i** $\frac{36}{54}$

5 **Skill 22D**
Convert each of these fractions to a decimal.
(Do not use a calculator.)

a $\frac{2}{5}$ **b** $\frac{3}{8}$ **c** $\frac{9}{10}$

d $\frac{15}{20}$ **e** $\frac{25}{40}$ **f** $\frac{30}{50}$

6 This graph shows the cost of flour.

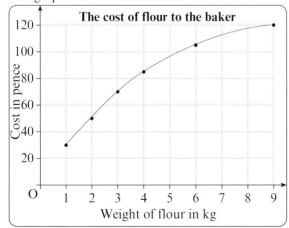

a About how much flour can be bought with 80p?

b Roughly what will 5 kg of flour cost?

c Estimate the cost of 7.5 kg of flour.

7 **Skill 23A**
This data shows the number of people on each bus as it leaves the bus station.

18, 25, 18, 15, 17, 31, 25, 28, 22, 12, 26, 27, 18, 20, 21, 19, 22, 28, 19, 24, 17, 27, 19, 20, 29, 21, 19, 22

a Make a grouped frequency table. Use class intervals of 0–4, 5–9, 10–14, ... , 30–34
b Draw a grouped frequency diagram.
c What is the modal class?

8 **Skill 23B**
This shows the time in minutes people took to finish a task:

12.5, 10.8, 16, 16, 23.5, 8.8, 15.6, 22.5, 24, 19.4, 12, 18.2, 20.5, 21.7, 19.8, 17.5, 20.3, 21, 22, 18, 17.2

a Make a grouped frequency table using these classes.
$0 \leqslant \text{time} < 10$, $10 \leqslant \text{time} < 20$, $20 \leqslant \text{time} < 30$
b How many people took 20 minutes or more to finish the task?

9 **Skill 24A**
Solve each of these equations.

a $12y - 5 = 7y + 35$ **b** $19y + 3 = 12y + 24$
c $35k = 28 + 31k$ **d** $88w - 33 = 66w + 55$

10 **Skill 24B**
Which of these are wrong? Explain why.

a $9w + 3 = 4w + 68$ $w = 11$
b $18k - 6 = 10k - 62$ $k = 6$
c $7y + 1 = 5y - 9$ $y = {}^{-}5$

11 **Skill 24C**
a Form an equation for the perimeter of shape A.
b Solve your equation and find a value for x.

$x + 3$

Shape A
Perimeter 62 cm

x

12 **Skill 25A**
Round these to the nearest whole number.
a 137.724   **b** 28.399   **c** 104.507

13 **Skill 25B** and **Skill 25C**
Round each of these.
a 37.682 (to 1 dp) **b** 0.006 45 (to 3 dp)

14 **Skill 26A**
With a 1 to 6 dice, what is the probability of scoring 5?

15 **Skill 26B**
On a probability scale show the probability that the next person you see will have blue eyes.

The Classifieds

FOR SALE

Mountain bike good condition £60; Aylton 385241

Doors good quality pine doors, 2 metres high and 75cm wide. £45; Stacey's, 37 High Street.

Carpet sale – £150,000 of stock must go!
Look at these examples from our ranges:
Aylesbury cord 3.4 metres by 2.3 metres **£70**
Wellington 5.6 metres by 3.5metres **£255**
Canterbury 4.8 metres by 2.4 metres **£125.99**
Lancaster 3.6 metres by 3.1 metres **£78**
Sale must end 5 pm Sat.
Eurocarpet 775380

Concrete mixer for hire
Why do it the hard way? At our rates you can afford to mix it. £12.50 per day and our weekend rate (Sat + Sun) is only £20.75
The Hire Centre Roford 385855

Want to sell it? Advertise in the *Herald*. Each week you can reach 55000 readers, and where are they?
3/4 of readers live less than 4 miles from Aylton.
4/5 of all readers are on a local bus route.
5/8 of readers read the adverts before the sport!
Ring us today: Ask for Mike on **686 5000**

Cast-iron bath – white. Never been used, cost £475 will accept £280 for quick sale. Newbridge 404277

SEED CITY

SEED CITY for all your gardening needs, Compare our prices. All seeds one price 85p per packet.

	av. contents
Tomatoes	25 seeds
Broad beans	40 beans
Parsnip	50 seeds
Carrot	65 seeds
Sunflower	30 seeds

This is just a few from our amazing range.
At this price be quick !
Newbridge 415363

Sarum Windows will fit 8 UPVC windows, guaranteed for 25 years, for an amazing £2120. Ring us today and make Sarum Windows part of your future.
Newbridge 404358

Scale models See the models on show in the Market Hall until the end of the month. Star of the show is a working 1:40 scale model of a steam engine. More details ring: Roford 386053

SERVICES

Plastering All types of work completed on time. We charge £8.75 per hour plus materials. Phone Bob on Westridge 574

Photographer Weddings and special occasions. Wedding Special £120 plus 55p each extra print.
Phone the **Wedding Line** today on 6865003

Private Hire Luxury cars for your journey. All our drivers are trained to the highest standards. Daily rates of £21.50 plus 15p per mile.
Classic Cars Aylton 386040

PUZZLE LINE
6865001
Ring the Puzzle Line with your solution to these puzzles. The first reader to give the right answer to all the puzzles wins this week's STAR PRIZE.
A Two numbers added together give 117. One number is 5 more than the other. What are the two numbers ?
B Mike rolls a ten-sided dice (numbers 0–9). What is the probability that he will score more than 6 ?
C A map is drawn to a scale of 1:50 000. On the map two railway stations are 2.5 cm apart. In kilometres how far is it from station to station?

PERSONAL
Valentine Messages

KIDNEY BEAN – When we married I thought I'd eat you, but there's nothing on you. All my love. —Cabbage Stump
KEITH – Roses are red, violets are blue. Hope you love me, like I love you. —Angie
MIKE – I love you with all my heart. —Love, Julie
ANDREW – Love you always, Love you lts. Special feelings. —Tracey
WANTED – Brabs, forever. —Duck
MARCIA – Stay my Valentine forever. I love you. —Norman
ALAN – My very special love for you will never die. —Love, your Gremlin
KEITH – Love you now and forever. Your devoted slave.
DARLING GARY – Nothing fancy, nothing smart, just a message from my heart. I love you. —Tracey
TONS and tons of love to my Bug-a-Lug.
TONY and PAUL – Happy Valentine's Day. All our love. —Jane and Voe
LYNDA – Hope you'll be my Valentine always and forever. — Martin
SARAH – Flowers will soon arrive to show I will love you forever non-stop through life.
DARLING SIMON – Love you very much. —From Jackie and daughter Aimee Charlotte
DOOB – Glad you are home. Love from Wig, Pog, Bede.
WATTS – Ed, Happy Valentine's Day. All my love. —Wendy
STEVE – Love you always. Can't wait till 9th March. —Ali
SALLY – Love and need you now and forever. So there. —Alan

Sending a message does not cost a fortune. This is all it costs in the *Herald*
Up to 10 words £3.85, from 11 to 16 words £4.50
Over 16 words, 28p each extra word
Ring Message Line today on **686 5004**

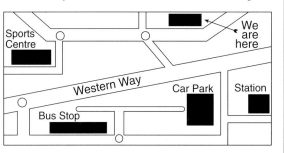

Paint Paint and more Paint we have the colour and finish you want. Our new store is now open.

1 Calculate the area of each door for sale at 37 High Street.

2 **a** Give the area of the Aylesbury cord carpet to the nearest whole number.
  b Estimate the cost of one square metre of Aylesbury cord carpet.

3 **a** Is the area of the Wellington carpet in the advert more or less than 20m²?
  b Linda says the Wellington carpet is about £13 per square metre. Is she right? Explain.

4 Jim wanted to carpet a room 3.4 m by 2.7 m. He bought the Lancaster carpet advertised. What area of carpet did he waste?

5 How many readers live less than 4 miles from Aylton?

6 Ravi calculates that 40 000 readers are on a local bus route. Is he right? Explain.

7 **a** How many readers read the adverts before the sport?
  b Nicole says that 70% of the readers read the adverts before the sport. Is she right? Explain.

8 **a** Give directions from the Bus Stop to the Sports Centre.
  b Give directions from the Sports Centre to the Station.

9 You are at the Car Park. Give two different sets of directions to the Sports Centre.

10 You need to hire a concrete mixer for two days. How much can you save if you choose to hire for a Saturday and a Sunday?

11 Dean decided to test the claims made by Seed City. He bought ten packets of tomato seeds and counted the seeds. This is the data he collected.

  No. tomato seeds in a packet

  28, 25, 26, 25, 25, 22, 24, 25, 27, 29

  a Find the mean number of seeds in a packet.
  b What average do you think Seed City Used? Explain your answer.

12 Jenny did the same for parsnip seeds. This is the data she collected.

  No. parsnip seeds in a packet

  40, 52, 52, 39, 54, 41, 55, 48, 46, 53

  a Find the median number of seeds in a packet.
  b What is the mode for the number of seeds?
  c What is the range for the parsnip seed data?
  d Do you think it would be better to us the mean average for the number of parsnip seeds? Explain your answer.

13 Calculate the mean average price of a window in the Sarum Windows advert.

14 **a** Make a frequency table for the number of words in a Valentine message. Use groups of 1–5, 6–10, 11–15, 16–20.
  b Draw a grouped frequency diagram to show the data in the frequency table.

15 How much did it cost Martin for his message?

16 What did the longest message cost?

17 What was the modal group for the message data?

18 Calculate the mean number of words in a valentines message (to 1 dp).

19 Calculate the total amount paid for all the messages that were printed.

20 Bob did a plastering job. The materials cost £38.65 and it took him $9\frac{1}{2}$ hours.
  Calculate to the nearest penny how much Bob charged for the job.

21 This graph shows the journeys for Private Hire.

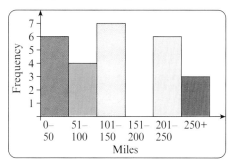

  a How many journeys were 250 miles or more?
  b How many journeys are in the group 151–200?
  c What was the modal group for the data?
  d How many journeys does the diagram show?
  e In which group is the median distance? Explain your answer.

22 Calculate how much Private Hire will charge for a journey of 258 miles in one day.

23 A rod on the model of a steam engine is 35 mm long.
  a How long is this rod on the real steam engine?
  b Is the real rod longer or shorter than 1.5 metres? Explain your answer.

24 The bath was sold for £280. How much was saved on the new price?

25 Solve each of the puzzles.

Starting points
You need to know about ...

... so try these questions

A Simple scales

A scale shows how lengths on a scale drawing compare with lengths on a real object.

A scale can be written in different ways:
  1 cm stands for 5 metres
  1 cm to 5 metres
  1 cm represents 5 metres.
These are all ways of showing the same scale.

With this scale you can compare lengths.

Lengths on:

Scale drawing	Real object
1 cm	5 metres
2.5 cm	12.5 metres
20 cm	100 metres
...	...

A1 Write each of these scales in two different ways.

  a 1 cm to 25 metres
  b 1 metre stands for 2 km
  c 1 mm represents 2 metres

A2 Copy and complete this table.

For a scale of: 1 cm to 4 metres, lengths are:

Scale drawing	Real object
2 cm	
3.5 cm	
10 cm	
25 cm	
40.5 cm	

Different types of scale

Skill 1A
Ordering whole numbers

Sometimes scales are given without units.

A scale might be given as 1:10.

♦ on a drawing with a scale of 1:10
  you can say that lengths are ten times as long as the real object
  or that lengths on the drawing are $\frac{1}{10}$ of the real lengths.

So you can compare lengths to a scale of 1:10.

1 cm = 10 mm

Scale drawing	Real object
1 mm	10 mm (1 cm)
1 metre	10 metres
1 km	10 km
1 mile	10 miles
1 yard	10 yards
...	...

The scale compares lengths in the same units.

Exercise 27.1
Using scales

1 This drawing is to a scale of 1:15.
  a Measure the length AB in mm.
  b What is the length, in mm, of AB on the real object?
  c Measure the length AC in cm.
  d What is the length, in cm, of AC on the real object?

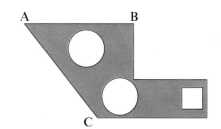

2 Replica Boats make models of sailing boats.
The use a scale of 1:8

Copy and complete this table for a scale of 1:8.

Length on model	Length on real boat
14 cm	■
15 mm	■
55 mm	■
■	64 cm
■	184 mm
0.5 metres	■
3.5 cm	■
■	4 cm

3 On the plan of a garden to a scale of 1:250
a lawn is shown like this.

  a Give the length and width of the lawn on the plan.
    (Use cm.)
  b What will be the length and width of the real lawn?
  c What will be the perimeter of the real lawn?
  d What will be the area of the real lawn?

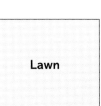

Lawn

4 The plan of a stadium is drawn to a scale of 1:80.
On the plan a seat is 5 mm wide.

How wide is a seat in the stadium?

5 A plan of a sports centre is drawn to a scale of 1:50.
On the plan the changing rooms are 300 mm long.

At the sports centre:
  a How long are the changing rooms in mm?
  b Nina says the changing rooms are 15 metres long.
    Do you agree? Explain your answer.
  c Roughly how long are the changing rooms in feet?

6 A map uses a scale of 1:5000.
On the map the distance between two traffic lights is 8 cm.

  a Are the traffic lights more or less than 0.5 km apart?
    Explain.
  b Ravinda says that the traffic lights are about 400 yards apart.
    Do you think this is a good estimate?
    Explain.

7 The scale used for this map is 1:10000.

Roughly how far is it, in a straight line:
  a from Ash's Farm to
    Nursery farm?
  b from Toll House Farm to
    Bivton College?

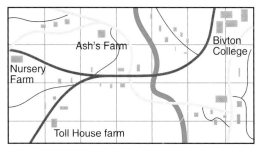

Working from scale drawings

This shows a scale plan of a new garage to be built.

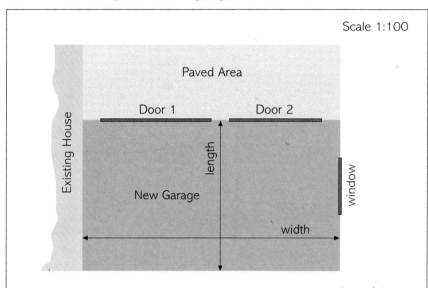

To use the plan for lengths, you need to measure accurately.

As the scale is 1:100 it is probably best to choose to measure in millimetres (mm) or centimetres (cm).

Example 1 How wide is the new garage to be?

♦ Measure the width of the garage in cm, i.e. 7 cm.

As the scale is 1:100 the width of the garage is:
7 cm × 100 = 700 cm = 7 metres

So the new garage is to be 7 metres wide.

Example 2 Calculate the area of the paving.

♦ Measure the paving in cm: length 2 cm   width 7 cm

With a scale of 1:100   length = 2 cm × 100 = 200 cm = 2 m
                            width = 7 cm × 100 = 700 cm = 7 m

Area of paving = Length × Width = 2 m × 7 m = 14 m²

So the area of the paving is 14 m².

Exercise 27.2
Interpreting scales

For questions **1** to **6** use the plan above.

1   How wide is door 2 on the new garage?

2   How long is the window on the new garage?

3   Calculate the area of the floor in the new garage.

4   How much wider is door 1 than door 2?

5   What will be the distance corner-to-corner in the garage?

6   Compare the length of the window and the width of door 1.
    What can you say about these two measurements:
    a on the plan
    b on the garage?

Use this plan for questions **7** to **12**.

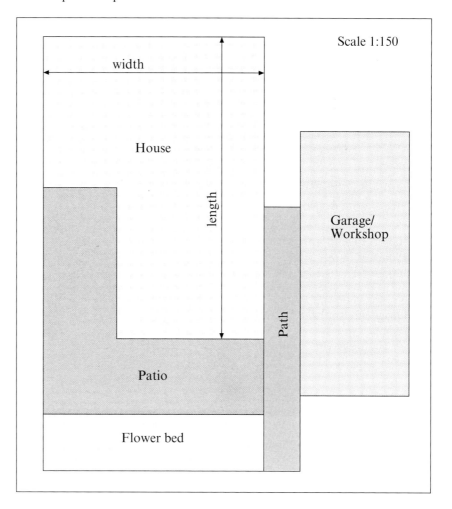

7   **a**   How wide is the house in metres?
       b   What is the length of the real house?

8   Is the path more or less than 2 metres wide?
       Explain your answer.

9   **a**   On the plan, how wide is the flower bed?
               (Measure in cm.)
       b   Calculate the width of the real flower bed.
       c   Calculate the length of the real flower bed.
       d   Find the area of the real flower bed.

10 The builder says the floor area of the garage is about 40 m².
       Is this an underestimate or an overestimate? Explain.

11 **a**   Make a sketch of the patio and label each side with its length.
       b   Calculate the area of the patio.

12 Asif thinks the area taken up by the garage is about half the area
       taken up by the house.
       Is he right? Explain your answer.

Starting points

You need to know about ...   ... so try these questions

A Powers of 10

We can write 100 as 10×10.

We can use a shorthand for 10×10:
we can write $10 \times 10 = 10^2$ (we say 'ten to the power of 2').

So 10^3 is ten to the power of 3
... 10^4 is ten to the power of 4
... and so on.

We can write 100, 1000, 10 000, 100 000 etc. as powers of 10.

$$100 = 10 \times 10 = 10^2$$
$$1000 = 10 \times 10 \times 10 = 10^3$$
$$10\,000 = 10 \times 10 \times 10 \times 10 = 10^4$$
$$100\,000 = 10 \times 10 \times 10 \times 10 \times 10 = 10^5$$
$$1\,000\,000 = 10 \times 10 \times 10 \times 10 \times 10 \times 10 = 10^6$$
...

B Multiplying decimals by powers of ten

Skill 16A: *see page 86*

A1 Copy and complete this table:

No.	is	is
600	6×100	6×10^2
8000	$8 \times$	$\times 10^3$
70 000	$7 \times$	
12 000	$12 \times$	
5000	$5 \times$	
50 000	$5 \times$	
85 000	$85 \times$	
375 000	$375 \times$	
49 000	$49 \times$	
9 200 000	$92 \times$	

B1 Copy and complete each of these.

a 4.875×10^2
b 61.5565×10^3
c 145.577×10^4
d 0.5833×10^2
e $0.008\,875\,7 \times 10^5$

Numbers in standard form

Skill 28A
Writing numbers in
standard form

When a number is in standard form we write it as:

a value (more than 1 and less than ten) $\times 10^{\text{to a number}}$

Example

Write 365 in standard form.

♦ With the digits 3, 6, and 5, in that order write a value that is more than 1 and less than 10.

$$3.65$$

♦ Decide on the power of ten that multiplies 3.65 to give an answer of 365.

$$3.65 \times 10^2 = 365$$

So 365 in standard form is 3.65×10^2.

Exercise 28.1
Practising Skill 28A

1   Copy and complete this table.

Number	Value (between 1 and 10)	Number in standard form
575	5.75	5.75×10^2
6885	○	○
398 766	○	○
325.8	○	○

2   Write each of these numbers in standard form.

a 678	**b** 3455	**c** 38.9	**d** 30 565
e 885.4	**f** 35 688	**g** 8563.5	**h** 50 000
i 3 785 641	**j** 835.68	**k** 100.5	**l** 200 000
m 39.75	**n** 6804.7	**o** 9 million	**p** half-a-million

3   **a**   Which of these answers are wrong?

	Number	In standard form
1	3856.7	3.8567×10^3
2	3455.8	34.558×10^2
3	69845.2	698.452×10^2
4	1887654	1.887654×10^6
5	750000	75.0000×10^4
6	9595.4	9.5954×10^3
7	507.55	50.755×10^2
8	33.333	3.3333×10^3

b   Copy and complete the table with the right answers.

Interpreting calculator displays

Writing numbers in standard form is used in calculator displays.

◆   Use a calculator to find $60\,475 \times 988\,575$

◆   Your calculator display will probably show:

The value of the number in the display is the same as:

$5.978\,41 \times 10^{10}$

(As an ordinary number $5.978\,41 \times 10^{10} = 59\,784\,100\,000$.)

Exercise 28.2
Interpreting displays

1   Each of these calculator displays shows a value.

A   **3.45566 E4**   B   **7.43335102 E5**

C   **9.255455 E6**   D   **6.00755 E5**

E   **6.300008 E7**   F   **2.4655759 E5**

G   **5.636345 E8**   H   **1.990887 E6**

I   **8.677574 E9**

a   Write each display as a number in standard form
b   Write each display as an ordinary number.

Rules of indices

Skill 28B
Using rules of indices

> When there is more than one index number they are called indices.

When we write 10^3, the 3 is called an index number.

For 10^2 and 10^3 we say the indices are 2 and 3.

♦ Multiplying numbers with indices.

Look at this calculation: $3.454 \times 10^3 \times 10^4$
We can write this as: $3.454 \times 10 \times 10 \times 10 \times 10 \times 10 \times 10 \times 10$
We can write this as: 3.454×10^7 [7 = 3 + 4]

There is a rule:

When multiplying by powers of ten you add the indices.

Example

Find the value of $0.005786 \times 10^3 \times 10^2$

Using rules of indices we can write : $0.005786 \times 10^3 \times 10^2 = 0.005786 \times 10^5$

$0.005786 \times 10^5 = 578.6$

Exercise 28.3
Practising Skill 28B

> $10 = 10^1$

1 Copy and complete each of these.
Use rules of indices.

a $10^4 \times 10^2 = 10^■$ **b** $10^3 \times 10^5 = 10^■$ **c** $10^4 \times 10^4 = 10^■$
d $10^2 \times 10^5 = 10^■$ **e** $10^5 \times 10^5 \times 10^2 = 10^■$ **f** $10^4 \times 10 = 10^■$

g $10^2 \times 10^2 \times 10^2 \times 10^2 = 10^■$ **h** $10^3 \times 10^4 \times 10^5 \times 10^6 = 10^■$
i $10^3 \times 10^3 \times 10^4 \times 10^4 = 10^■$ **j** $10^2 \times 10 \times 10^3 \times 10 \times 10^4 = 10^■$

2 Find the value of $0.003455 \times 10^2 \times 10^3$
Do not use a calculator.

3 What does the ■ stand for in each of these calculations?

a $0.035857 \times 10^■ \times 10^2 = 35857$ **b** $0.5662 \times 10 \times 10^■ = 566200$
c $1.42425 \times 10^2 \times 10^■ = 142425000$ **d** $0.0000075 \times 10^3 \times 10^■ = 75$

Indices and trial and improvement

Skill 28C
Using trial-and-improvement.

> 31.5 is half-way between 3.1 and 3.2

Example Solve the equation $x^3 = 30$.

Start with $x = 3$ and give your answer to 1 dp.

Try $x = 3$ $x^3 = 27$
 $x = 3.1$ $x^3 = 29.79...$
 $x = 3.2$ $x^3 = 32.76...$
 $x = 3.15$ $x^3 = 31.25...$ [too big]
 $x = 3.11$ $x^3 = 30.08...$ [just too big]

A value just larger than 3.11^3 will give 30

So when $x^3 = 30$ $x = 3.1$ to 1 dp.

Exercise 28.4
Practising Skill 28C

1 Solve each of these equations to 1 dp.
The starting number is in brackets.

a $x^3 = 40$ (3.2)   **b** $x^3 = 20$ (2)   **c** $x^3 = 70$ (4)

Reflections

Skill 29A
Reflecting a shape

♦ To reflect a shape you need to know where the mirror line is.

Example:

Reflect shape ABCD in
the mirror line PQ.

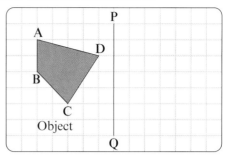

Similar points on the
object and image are often
labelled with the same
letter but with a dash.

A becomes A′ after
reflection.

♦ A point on the image will be the same distance
from the mirror as that point on the object.

(a = b)

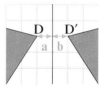

♦ If you join similar points on the object and image,
this line crosses the mirror at right angles.

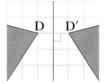

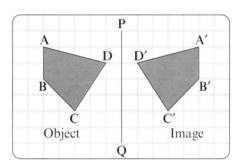

Exercise 29.1
Practising skill 29A

1   Trace the object ABCD above.
Can you fit your tracing over the image A′B′C′D′?
You must not turn over the tracing paper.

2   a   Find the area of ABCD by counting squares.
    b   What is the area of A′B′C′D′?

3   a   Copy the shape PQRS on to square grid paper.
    b   Reflect the shape in the mirror line AB.

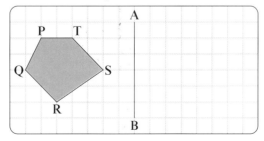

    c   What can you say about the areas of the object and the image?

155

4 **a** Copy the diagram.

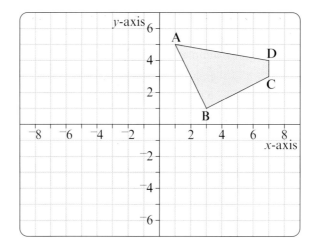

b Reflect ABCD in the *x*-axis. Label this image A′B′C′D′.
c Reflect ABCD in the *y*-axis. Label this image A″B″C″D″.
d List the co-ordinates of point B, point B′ and point B″.
    What do you notice?

5 **a** Copy the shape JKLMN.
b Reflect the shape in the line AB to give the image J′K′L′M′N′.
c What can you say about the position of the line MN and the line M′N′?

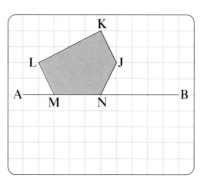

6 Copy the shape ABCD and reflect it in the line ST.

Point D and C will be reflected to the left of the line ST. Points A and B will be reflected to the right of it.

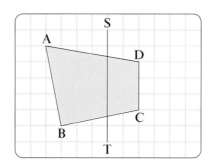

Skill 29B
Rotating a shape

◆ To rotate a shape you need to know:

  ❖ the centre of rotation
  ❖ the direction of rotation
  ❖ the angle the shape is turned through.

◆ It is a good idea to use tracing paper when you rotate a shape.

Example

Rotate the triiangle ABC 90° clockwise
about the point (0, 0).

◆ Centre of rotation = (0, 0)

◆ Direction = clockwise

◆ Angle = 90°

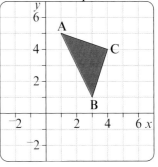

◆ Put the tracing paper over the triangle and the centre of rotation.

◆ Trace the triangle and the two axes.

◆ Put your pencil point on the point (0, 0)

◆ Turn the tracing paper 90° clockwise around the pencil.

◆ Draw in the image A′B′C′.

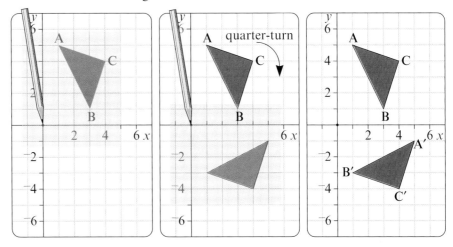

Exercise 29.2
Practising skill 29B

1 a On squared paper draw x and y axes from ⁻6 to ⁺6.
   b Copy triangle ABC above.
   c Rotate triangle ABC 90° clockwise about the point (0, 0).
      Draw and label this image A′B′C′.
   d Rotate triangle ABC 90° anticlockwise about the point (0, 0).
      Draw and label this image A″B″C″.

2 a On squared paper draw x and y axes
      from ⁻6 to ⁺6.
   b Copy the shape PQRS.
   c Rotate PQRS by 180° about the point (0,0).
   d Label the image P′Q′R′S′.
   e What are the coordinates of points S and S′?
      What do you notice?

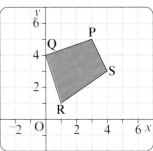

3　**a**　Copy the letter F and the point A.

　　b　Rotate F clockwise by 180°
　　　　about the point A.
　　　　Draw in the image.

　　c　Rotate F anticlockwise by 180°
　　　　about point A.
　　　　What do you notice?

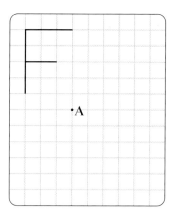

4　**a**　Rotate line AB clockwise by 90°
　　　　about the point P.
　　　　Label the new line A′B′.

　　b　Rotate A′B′ clockwise by 90° about P.
　　　　Label this image A″B″.

　　c　Rotate A″B″ clockwise by 90° about P.
　　　　Label this image A‴B‴.

　　d　What shape have you drawn?

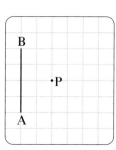

5　**a**　Draw shape A on isometric grid paper.

　　b　Rotate shape A clockwise by 60°
　　　　about the point P.
　　　　Label this image B.

　　c　Rotate shape A anticlockwise by 60°
　　　　about point P.
　　　　Label this image C.

　　d　What rotation will rotate shape A
　　　　on to shape Z?

　　e　What rotation rotates your C
　　　　on to your B?

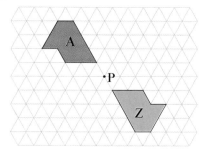

6　**a**　Trace and copy the shapes below.

Remember: when you are
asked for a rotation you
must give:

◆ the centre
◆ the direction
◆ the angle.

　　b　Rotate the shapes 180° about the point P.
　　　　What have you made?

　　c　Show how you can make the word 'pod' by a rotation.

　　d　Mike says he can make DID by a rotation like this.
　　　　Why is Mike wrong?

Identifying transformations

A transformation is a change according to a rule.
Reflection is one type of transformation, rotation is another.

You may need to identify what type of transformation has taken place.

If it is a reflection you must give:
◆ the mirror line.

If it is a rotation you must give:
◆ the centre of rotation
◆ the direction of rotation
◆ the angle of rotation

Show on your diagram any
centres of rotation or
mirror lines.

1 a Copy the diagram.
  b What transformation will map shape A
     on to shape B?
  c What transformation will map shape A
     on to shape C?
  d Would the transformation to map shape B
     on to shape C be a reflection or a rotation?
     Explain your answer.

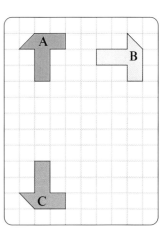

2 The letter **b** can be transformed to the letter **d**.

Could this be a reflection, a rotation, or either?
Explain your answer.

3 The letter **W** can be transformed to the letter **M**.

Could this be a reflection, a rotation, or either?
Explain your answer.

4

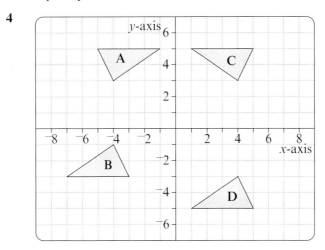

What transformation will map:

a shape A on to shape C
c shape C on to shape D
e shape A on to shape D
g shape B on to shape A

b shape C on to shape A
d shape D on to shape C
f shape D on to shape A
h shape A on to shape B?

Starting points

You need to know about ...   ... so try these questions

A The range of a set of data.

The range of a set of data is:
the difference between the smallest and largest of the data.

This data shows distances travelled to college by members of a group.

Distances (miles)
2, 3, 2, 4, 6, 3, 1, 7, 3, 12, 5, 1, 10, 8, 9, 9, 6

The largest value in the data is: 12 miles
The smallest value in the data is: 1 mile

The range of the data is: 11 miles (12 – 1)

B Rounding to a number of decimal places

Skill 25C: *see page 141*

A1 Find the range of each set of data.

  a scores in an English test:
14, 15, 6, 18, 19, 16, 12, 19, 10, 15, 14,

  b 10-pin bowling scores:
7, 6, 8, 6, 5, 8, 7, 8, 5, 6, 7

  c number of chips in a serving:
22, 31, 24, 27, 21, 25, 32, 24

B1 Round each of these:

  a 27.635 (1dp)
  b 158.345 (2 dp)
  c 0.0354 (3dp)

Finding averages

Skill 30A
Calculating the mean of a set of data

The mean is the average most people think of.

The mean might also be called the arithmetic mean. To calculate the mean of a set of data you:

♦ find the total of all the data

♦ divide the total by the number of pieces if data.

Example

Alison plays snooker.
These are her break scores in a game.
38, 25, 12, 18, 3, 8

Calculate her mean break score.

The data is the 6 break scores.

The answer is rounded to 1 decimal place.

The total of all the data is:
38 + 25 + 12 + 18 + 3 + 8 = 104
The number of pieces of data is: 6

Mean is: 104 ÷ 6 = 17.3 (1 dp)

The mean break score was 17.3 (1 dp).

(The mean is only a value. You cannot have a break score of 17.3.)

Finding the mean

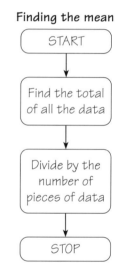

Exercise 30.1
Practising Skill 30A

1 Calculate the mean (to 1dp) for each set of scores.
  a 15, 21, 3, 1, 5, 17, 8, 1
  b 9, 6, 1, 3, 8, 22
  c 17, 31, 8, 19
  d 24, 1, 6, 1, 11, 8, 1, 6

2   Calculate the mean of each set of scores to 1 dp.

   a   17, 23, 16, 44, 18, 9, 12, 7, 25
   b   4, 21, 17, 33, 45, 20, 43, 55
   c   6, 7, 7, 8, 5, 4, 6, 7, 9, 10, 3, 4, 4, 5, 7, 7
   d   54, 56, 65, 42, 53, 58
   e   35, 32, 17, 19, 25, 28, 39, 36, 12, 15, 28, 35

Exercise 30.2
Using Skill 30A

1   Beacon Rovers play in the Superfix League.
These figures show the number of fans at the last six matches.

   443   581   642   319   279   406

Find the mean number of fans at each of these matches.

2   At a crisp tasting a group was asked to give crisps a mark out of ten.
These were the marks given for four brands of crisps.

```
Brand A   5, 6, 4, 7, 6, 8, 5, 6, 4, 5, 8, 6, 5, 9, 3, 4, 6, 7, 8, 3

Brand B   6, 7, 6, 8, 7, 5, 5, 4, 4, 6, 3, 7, 8, 7, 5, 4, 5, 6, 4, 7

Brand C   6, 7, 8, 7, 5, 7, 6, 8, 5, 9, 6, 4, 4, 4, 3, 6, 7, 8, 4, 2

Brand D   5, 6, 7, 8, 4, 5, 6, 9, 2, 9, 8, 5, 4, 7, 9, 7, 8, 5, 6, 6
```

   a   For each brand calculate the mean mark out of ten (to 1 dp).
   b   Which brand was liked best for taste by the group?

3   The company Datafinders was asked to write a questionnaire.
The form should take, on average, no more than 30 seconds to fill in.
A group tested the questionnaire and this data was collected.

       Time taken to fill in. (seconds)

   28, 34, 43, 17, 18, 24, 33, 36, 27, 25, 39, 41,

   29, 30, 32, 26, 30, 20, 22, 27, 28, 32, 19,

   37, 35, 31, 40, 28, 35, 47, 34, 39

   a   How many people tested the form?
   b   Calculate the mean time taken to fill in the form (to 1 dp).
   c   Did the form take, on average, no more than 30 seconds to fill in?

4   Jason drives a delivery van.
This data shows the distances travelled each day.

Day	Distance travelled (miles)
Mon	88
Tues	161
Wed	187
Thurs	154
Fri	204
Sat	63

   a   Calculate the total distance travelled.
   b   Find the mean distance travelled each day (to 1 dp).

5   The mean of 12 numbers is 44.
Eleven of the numbers are: 38, 24, 60, 35, 51, 30, 53, 45, 62, 56, 29.

   a   What is the missing number?
   b   Explain how you calculated the missing number.

Skill 30B
Calculating the median of
a set of data

The median is another type of average.

The median value of a set of data is:
the value of the piece of data that is in the middle of the set

(The set of data must be in size order from smallest to largest.)

Example 1

> Find the median of this set of data.   34, 88, 65, 12, 58, 54, 35, 50, 22

> Sort the data in order: 12, 22, 34, 35, 50, 54, 58, 65, 88

The median is the middle value which here is one of the pieces of data.

> 12, 22, 34, 35, 50, 54, 58, 65, 88

> [middle value]

The median of the set of data is 50.

Example 2   Find the median of this set of data.

> 38, 44, 27, 35, 42, 67, 54, 58, 54, 61

Sort the data in order:
> 27, 35, 38, 42, 44, 54, 54, 58, 61, 67

The median is the middle value which here is between two pieces of data.

> [middle value will be in the middle of this gap]

> 27, 35, 38, 42, 44, 54, 54, 58, 61, 67

> [the value that is half-way between 44 and 54 is 49]

The median of the set of data is 49.

> Most wrong answers for a median are because people forget to sort the data in order first.

> There are two 54's in the data and they must both be put in the order.

> 49 is not one of the pieces of data in the set but it can still be the median value.

Exercise 30.3
Practising Skill 30B

1   Sort each set of data in order, and find the median.
   a   34, 14, 24, 44, 35, 56, 45, 15, 30
   b   58, 14, 15, 45, 32, 30, 44, 25
   c   104, 55, 78, 81, 38, 40, 29, 75, 101, 95, 80
   d   1551, 1384, 1406, 1309
   e   1050, 988, 1304, 675, 808, 1251, 1101

2   Find the median for each set of data.
   a   £35, £300, £85, £125, £55, £95, £90
   b   194 km, 350 km, 256 km, 340 km, 320 km, 125 km, 280 km, 388 km
   c   50.6 cm, 49 cm, 34.6 cm, 51.5 cm, 47.2 cm, 38.3 cm
   d   55.6 kg, 44.5 kg, 28 kg, 13.5 kg, 20.8 kg, 77.8 kg, 62.6 kg

3   Which of these answers for the median are wrong?
   For each wrong answer give the right answer.

	Data	Median
a	88, 56, 41, 92, 75, 63, 75, 42, 31, 29, 30, 50	54
b	136, 112, 148, 132, 136, 140, 120, 124	133
c	205, 200, 235, 240, 250, 260, 250, 220, 225, 230	232.5
d	2, 0, 5, 0, 1, 1, 2, 2, 3, 2, 0, 0, 6, 0, 1, 1, 0, 3, 2, 0	1

Skill 30C
Finding the mode of a set
of data

The mode is a different type of average.

The mode of a set of data is that data which is found most often.

Example

What is the mode for this set of scores?
2, 5, 7, 7, 6, 8, 7, 6, 3, 8, 9, 6, 1, 4, 10, 7, 6, 7, 6, 7, 2, 10

Show the scores in a frequency table:

Score	Tally	Frequency
1	/	1
2	//	2
3	/	1
4	/	1
5	/	1
6	ЖЖ	5
7	ЖЖ /	6
8	//	2
9	/	1
10	//	2

The frequency table shows that there are more scores of 7 than any other score.

So the mode for this set of scores is 7.

Exercise 30.4
Practising Skill 30C

1 Find the mode of the data for each set of scores.
   a 6, 4, 5, 3, 4, 5, 7, 3, 4, 8, 3, 5, 3 ,7, 4, 5, 2, 9, 4, 6, 3
   b 11, 9, 12, 15, 12, 14, 11, 18, 20, 15, 16, 12, 15, 20, 16, 12
   c 23, 34, 35, 26, 19, 24, 25, 28, 24, 21, 30, 24, 23, 25, 32

2 This data shows the sizes of T-shirt sold on a market stall.
   S, M, M, S, L, L, XL, M, L, XL, S, L, L, M, L, XL, S, S, XL, L
   What size is the mode for this data?

3 This data shows the size of trainers sold by a sports shop.
   8, 6, 8, 9, 10, 10, 9, 11, 11, 12, 9, 7, 9, 5, 6, 9, 7, 9, 10, 8, 8, 10
   What size is the mode for this set of data?

Comparing data

You can use an average and the range to compare sets of data.

Example

Starline and Greenbus run buses from the High Street to the Station.
This data is about the time taken.

From High St to the Station:
Starline   Median time 12 min   Range 3 min
Greenbus   Median time 10 min   Range 8 min

Comparing the data:

♦ Greenbus has a shorter journey time on average

♦ Starline has a smaller range.

This tells you that journey times do not vary as much.

As the average times are not very different, Starline is a better service.

163

Exercise 30.5
Comparing data

1 These are the journey times for High Street to the Sports Centre.
The bus service is either Greenbus or Starline.

```
            Journey times in minutes
Greenbus  14, 18, 14, 16, 16, 17, 15, 18, 14, 17,
          15, 17, 15, 17, 17, 14, 18, 17, 16, 15,
Starline  10, 17, 14, 14, 17, 16, 18, 16, 15, 18,
          13, 17, 12, 14, 16, 17, 13, 14, 17, 12
```

a What time is the mode for Greenbus?
b What is the range for the Greenbus data?
c What is the range for the Starline data?
d Calculate the mean journey time for the Greenbus data.
e Calculate the mean journey time for the Starline data.
f Which do you think is the better service?
Use the mean and range to explain your choice.

2 Two groups did the same History test.
This data gives the results.

	History test scores (out of 40)
Group 10HJ	24, 31, 26, 38, 35, 24, 32, 30, 39, 28, 26, 24, 32, 26, 31, 35, 40, 25, 33, 35, 26, 40, 25, 24, 27, 24
Group 10CW	38, 21, 19, 40, 36, 37, 20, 19, 26, 25, 19, 40, 25, 40, 26, 24, 19, 28, 32, 35, 29, 24, 38, 35, 29, 28, 31

a What is the range of the scores for 10HJ?
b Find the range of the scores for 10CW.
c For each group, find the score that is the mode.
d Find the mean score for the 10HJ data.
e What is the mean of the 10CW data?
f Compare the two groups in the History test.
Use the mean and the range to explain which you think is the better group.

3 T-shirt City and Logoshirt both print T-shirts.
Both firms pay a mean wage of £180 per week to their staff.

This data shows how much the firms pay their staff.

```
T-shirt City                    Logoshirt
£155, £75, £115, £280, £272,    £160, £165, £175, £200, £190,
£208, £100, £120, £90, £405,    £165, £155, £215, £180, £195,
£140, £350, £100, £70           £155, £200, £160, £205
```

a For each firm, find the median of their wages data.
b For each firm, find the range of the wages data.
c Liam says that as the mean wage is the same for both firms he wouldn't
mind which of the firms he worked for.
Compare the data. Do you agree with Liam? Explain your answer.

SECTION 31 PLANS AND VIEWS

Starting points

You need to know about ...

... so try these questions

A The points of the compass

This compass rose shows the main 8 points of the compass.

Beware: On a map North does not always point straight up the paper.

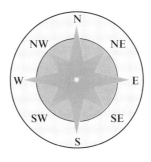

Example
On the map below, what is the direction of Andle from Sandbury?

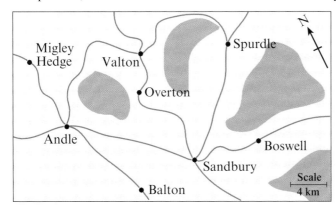

- Turn the page round until North is straight up.
- Imagine the compass on Sandbury and North parallel to the arrow. (You can trace the compass and put its centre on Sandbury.)
- Read off the direction to Andle: North West.

B Scales on maps

A map is a type of scale drawing.

The map above has a scale of 1 cm to 4 km.

Each centimetre on the map stands for 4 km.

A distance that is given **as the crow flies** is the shortest distance. A distance **by road** is the distance a car would have to travel.

Example 1
What is the distance as the crow flies from Boswell to Spurdle?

Measuring from the map, with a ruler, gives the distance as 2.6 cm.

So the distance in real life = 2.6 × 4 = 10.4 km.

Example 2
Find the true distance by road from Valton to Sandbury.

To measure the distance along the road – use a piece of cotton. Length of cotton = 3.8 cm

So distance the in real life = 3.8 × 4 = 15.2 km.

A1 Give the direction of Sandbury from Valton.

A2 Give the direction of:
   a Migley Hedge from Andle
   b Balton from Sandbury
   c Sandbury from Spurdle
   d Spurdle from Andle
   e Sandbury from Andle.

B1 What is the distance in real life between Andle and Spurdle as the crow flies?

B2 What is the distance by road from Boswell to Overton?

B3 What is the distance from Boswell to Andle:
   a as the crow flies
   b by road?

B4 What is the shortest distance by road between Spurdle and Andle?

Giving directions

Skill 31A
Giving directions

◆ To give directions from a map turn the map the way you are going.

◆ Give an instruction when there is a choice to be made.

Example   Give directions from the Red Horse to Market Square.

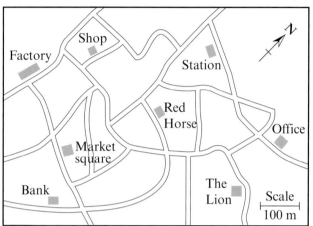

This is one set of directions from the Red Horse to Market Square.

> Turn right outside the Red Horse.
> After about 50 metres, turn left at T junction.
> After about 120 metres turn right at T junction.
> After about 100 metres turn left.
> At the fork after 40 metres stay on the road heading south.
> After about 130 metres you come to a X-roads – turn left.
> Market Square is about 50 metres on your left.

Exercise 31.1
Using skill 31A

1   Give directions for a different route from the Red Horse to Market Square.

2   Denis is a wages clerk at the factory.
Give him directions from the factory to the bank.

3   Mary will arrive at the station tomorrow.
What directions will you send her to get to the office?

4   Bruce has just taken some money out of the bank.
He needs the simplest directions to get him to the station.

5   These are a set of directions from the Lion to Market Square.
There are some mistakes.

> Turn left outside the Lion so you are heading in an easterly direction.
> Take the 3rd turning on your right(after about 400 metres).
> Take the first turning on your right.
> Market Square is about 100 metres on the right.

Write out the directions without mistakes.

6   Sharon is in the office. She asks for directions to the shop.
Write out some directions for her.

7   Andy needs directions to get from the bank to the shop.
He does not know his right from his left. He does have a compass.
Write out directions for him without using right or left.

2D Views

Skill 31B
Showing different views

♦ A 3D object can be looked at from different directions.
Each one may give a different 2D view of the same object.

Example

Sketch views of this object from
the directions A, B and C.

The view from A is called the **plan**.

From B the view is called the **front elevation**.

From C the view is called the **side elevation**.

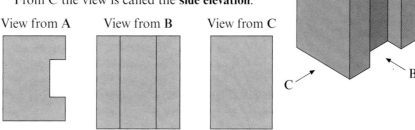

View from **A**   View from **B**   View from **C**

Exercise 31.2
Using skill 31B

1   Match each view to a direction A, B or C.

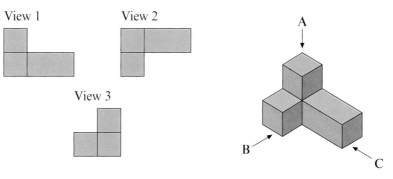

View 1   View 2

View 3

A

B   C

2   Which of these could be views of this church?

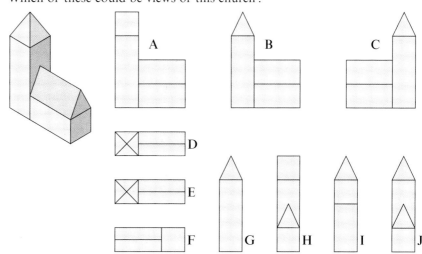

3 Object 1 is made from cubes.
On squared paper, sketch views of the object
from the direction of each arrow.

Object 1

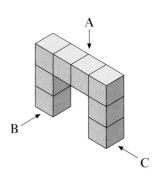

4 **a** How many cubes make up object 2?
b On squared paper, sketch the three views
of this object.

Object 2

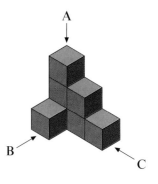

5 **a** If object 3 were made of cubes of this size

how many would there be?
b On squared paper, sketch the
three views of this object.

Object 3

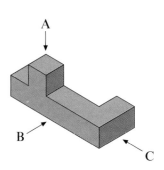

6 Sketch a view of object 4 from each direction
A, B and C.

Object 4

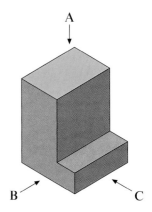

3D Views

Skill 31C
Drawing 3D views

Dotty paper can be used to draw a 3D view of an object.

Example

Draw a 3D view of object 1.

Object 1

When you draw on dotty paper, make sure the dots are this way round: ✔

and **not** this way: ✖

♦ You can imagine the object being made of cubes.

♦ One cube can be drawn on a dotty grid like this. Each corner of the cube is on a dot.

♦ To draw object 1 you can draw each cube in the same way starting from the front.

Some faces of cubes at the back will be hidden.

You can rub out the blue lines or not draw them.

Exercise 31.3
Practising skill 31C

1 Copy and complete the dotty drawing for object 2.

Object 2

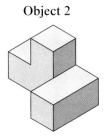

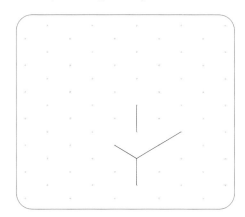

2 Copy and complete the dotty drawing for object 3.

Object 3

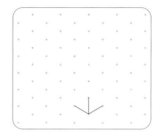

3 This solid is made with 8 cubes.
Use dotty paper to draw the solid.

4 This diagram is drawn full size.

It shows the end of a prism.
The prism is 3 cm long.

On an isometric grid, draw the prism.
The lines BC and CD
have been drawn for you.

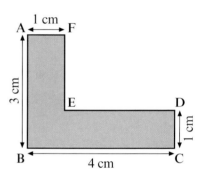

An isometric grid is one
like this :

or like this:

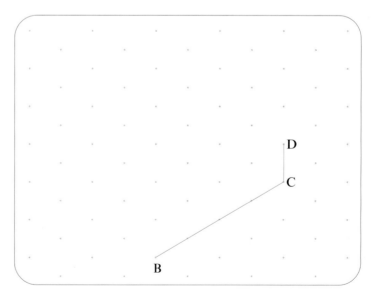

This revises the work in Sections 27 to 31

1 A drawing of a boat is done to a scale of 1 : 25.

  a On the drawing a post is 28 mm long.
  How long is this post on the boat?

  b On the boat a hatch is 1050 mm wide.
  How wide is this hatch on the drawing?

2 A map uses a scale of 1 : 10000.
  On the map the distance between two motorway exits is 12.5 cm.

  Are the exits more, or less than 1.5 km apart? Explain.

3 Skill 28A
  Write each of these numbers in standard form.

  a 34565   **b** 108755.1   **c** 13540.075
  d 205.45   **e** 3989454   **f** 3874.1

4 Each of these calculator displays shows a value.
  A 7.60657 E 5
  B 6.200004 E 6
  C 4.23245 E 4

  a Write each display in standard form.
  b Write each display as an ordinary number.

5 Skill 28B
  Copy and complete each of these.
  Use rules of indices.

  a $10^5 \times 10^2 = 10^{\blacksquare}$ **b** $10^4 \times 10^3 = 10^{\blacksquare}$
  c $10^2 \times 10^3 \times 10^4 = 10^{\blacksquare}$ **d** $10^4 \times 10^{\blacksquare} = 10^6$

6 Skill 28C
  Solve each of these equations to 1dp.
  a $x^3 = 25$ (start with $x = 2.5$)
  b $x^3 = 50$ (start with $x = 3.4$)

7 Skill 29A
  Copy the shape ABCD on to square grid paper.

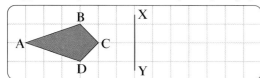

  a Reflect ABCD in the mirror line XY.
  b What can you say about the area of the object and the image?

8 **a** Copy the shape PQRS on to square grid paper.
   b Reflect PQRS in the line AB.

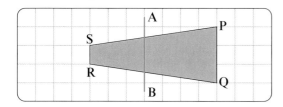

9 Skill 29B
  Copy these axes and the shape ABCD on to a grid.

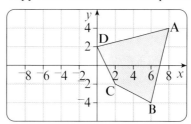

  a Rotate ABCD 180° about the point (0, 0).
  b Give the coordinates of : A′, B′, C′, and D′.

10 Skill 29C
  The letter **p** can be transformed to the letter **d**.

  Could this be a reflection, a rotation, or either? Explain your answer.

11 Skill 30A
  Calculate the mean for each set of data.

  a 55, 90, 85, 160, 255
  b 160, 24, 56, 284
  c 27, 81, 270, 9, 36, 450, 729, 549, 6300

12 Skill 30B
  Find the median for each set of data.

  a 3, 5, 4, 9, 19, 15
  b 21, 12, 35, 27, 40, 35, 55

13 Skill 30C
  Find the mode for this set of scores.
  (Make a frequency table.)

  6, 5, 8, 7, 8, 9, 8, 5, 8, 7, 3, 8, 4, 5, 9, 5, 6, 8, 2, 10,
  3, 8, 6, 7, 9, 8, 10, 4, 5, 8, 4, 8, 9, 10, 5, 8, 3, 8, 9

14 Skill 31A
  Use the map on page 166.

  a Give directions from the Office to the Factory.
  b Is the shop east or west of the Red Horse?

15 Skill 31B
  These are two views of object 3 on page 170.

  Draw a different view of object 3.

16 The diagram shows the end of a prism 4 cm long (cubes are 1 cm).

  On an isometric grid draw the prism.

Toujours Paris

Paris au Quotidien

Arrondissements: Il faut le savoir, Paris est divisé en 20 arrondissements se déroulant en spiraleà partir du 1er (le quartier du Louvre).

Banques: Ouvertes en général du lundi au vendredi de 9h à 16h30, quelques (rares) agences le samedi. Les Caisses d'Epargne ouvrent plus souvent le samedi et ferment le lundi.

Daily Life in Paris

Districts: You should know that Paris is divided into 20 districts numbered in a circular direction, starting with the 1st district (the Louvre area).

Banks: They are generally open from Monday to Friday from 9 am to 4.30 pm, some (rare) branches on Saturday. The savings banks are more often open on Saturday and closed on Monday.

Notre Dame

This cathedral is a good example of a French medieval church. The first stone was laid in 1163 and it was finished in 1330. It is well known for its stained glass windows. This South Window is 13 metres wide.

Notre Dame is open 8 am to 7 pm each day.
In front of Notre Dame is: Point Zéro. This is a mark in the ground from which all distances in France are measured. Each side of the shape is 12 cm long.

Eiffel Tower Factfile

- Built in 1889 for the Universal Exhibition
- Built by Gustave Eiffel (1832–1923)
- Built from pig iron girders
- Total height 320 metres
- The world's tallest building until 1931
- Height to 3rd level is 274 metres
- Height to 1st level is 57 metres
- There are 360 steps to the 1st level, a total of 1060 steps to the 2nd level, and 1652 steps to the 3rd level.
- Two and a half million rivets were used.
- The tower is 15 cm higher on a hot day.
- Its total weight is 10100 tonnes.
- 40 tons of paint are used every 4 years.
- On a clear day you can see Chartres Cathedral, 72 km away to the South West.
- The tower is visited by about 5½ million people every year.
- Open in summer from 9am to 11pm.

Datafile

Population of Paris (in 1982)   2188918
In 1996, £1 was worth about 7.5 French Francs. By 1997 the pound had gone up to 10.3 Francs.
1 kilometre is about 0.6 miles.

Entry fees in Paris – 1996

Eiffel Tower	56 FF
Louvre	45 FF
Pompidou Centre	35 FF
Picasso Museum	28 FF
Museum of Modern Art	27 FF
Versailles Palace	45 FF
Parc de la Villette	45 FF
Cluny Museum	28 FF

DAY TRIPS BY EUROSTAR

Waterloo Station (London) to Paris
Celebrate that special occasion in style with a day trip to Paris!

ADULT	£99
CHILD (4–11 YRS)	£89
Under 4 – free	

Euro Disney

The site was opened in 1992 and is spread over 1500 acres.
It is 32 km east of Paris.
Walt Disney lived from 1901 to 1966.

1 Sharon and Debbie go in the Versailles Palace. What is the total cost of entry in Francs?

2 How many years did Notre Dame take to build?

3 Give the time that the Eiffel Tower closes in 24-hour time.

4 How many lines of symmetry has the large south window of Notre Dame?

5 a What name do we give to the shape of Point Zero?
   b Is it a regular or an irregular polygon?

6 How old was Gustave Eiffel when he died?

7 Who lived longer, Walt Disney or Gustave Eiffel? Explain your answer.

8 How many hours is Notre Dame open each day?

9 The weight of the Eiffel Tower is 10 100 tonnes. Write this number in words.

10 a How many rivets were used in the Eiffel Tower?
   b Write this number in digits.

11 Give the population of Paris in 1982 rounded to:
   a the nearest 10
   b the nearest 1000
   c the nearest million.

12 How many metres is it from the third level to the top of the Eiffel Tower?

13 This family went on a day trip to Paris by Eurostar.

   Jenny   age 36
   Spencer   age 37
   Mark   age 7
   Claire   age 12
   Winston   age 3

   What was the total cost of the fares?

14 a Mark a dot on your paper to show Paris.
   b Draw in a line to show the north direction.
   c Using a scale of 1 cm to 10 kilometres, show the positions of Euro Disney and Chartres Cathedral.

15 If you were at Euro Disney, in what direction would Paris be?

16 If you were at Chartres Cathedral, in what direction would Paris be?

17 For Point Zero, calculate the size of an exterior angle.

18 Paul kept a list of the places he went to in Paris.

   The Eiffel Tower
   The Museum of Modern Art
   The Pompidou Centre
   The Parc de la Villette
   The Louvre

   What was the total cost of his entry fees?

19 About how many people will visit the Eiffel Tower between 1996 and the year 2000?

20 How many steps are there between the first and second levels of the Eiffel Tower?

21 Which of these is about the average (mean) height of a step up to the first level of the Eiffel Tower?
   A 6.3 centimetres   B 1.6 metres
   C 19 centimetres   D 16 centimetres
   E 26 centimetres   F 14 centimetres

22 What is the total charge for each of these sets of tickets?

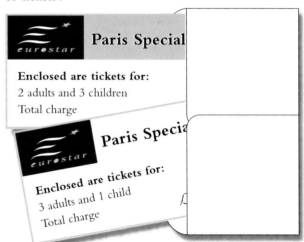

23 By how much in francs did the pound go up between 1996 and 1997?

24 How many planes of symmetry do you think the Eiffel Tower has?

25 In winter the Eiffel Tower opens half an hour later and closes an hour earlier than in summer.
   a At what time does it open in winter?
   b How long is it open each day in winter?

26 How many tons of paint had been used on the Eiffel Tower by the year 1919?

27 Use the note on Daily Life in Paris. Calculate the mean number of letters in a word:
   a in French
   b in English

Stage 3 End points
You should be able to ...

... so try these questions

A Find a fraction of an amount
Skill 22A: *see page 122*

B Find equivalent fractions
Skill 22B: *see page 125*

C Write a fraction in its lowest terms
Skill 22C: *see page 126*

D Convert a fraction to a decimal
Skill 22D: *see page 126*

E Convert a fraction to a percentage
Skill 22E: *see page 127*

F Read a line graph

A1 Calculate $\frac{1}{5}$ of £11.80.

A2 Calculate $\frac{3}{4}$ of £20.60.

B1 List two fractions which are equivalent to $\frac{16}{48}$.

C1 Write each of these fractions in its lowest terms.
  a $\frac{10}{16}$ **b** $\frac{9}{27}$ **c** $\frac{45}{80}$ **d** $\frac{24}{60}$

D1 Convert each of these fractions to a decimal.
  a $\frac{6}{10}$ **b** $\frac{3}{8}$ **c** $\frac{17}{20}$ **d** $\frac{6}{40}$

E1 Write each of these fractions as a percentage.
  a $\frac{2}{5}$ **b** $\frac{3}{8}$ **c** $\frac{7}{20}$ **d** $\frac{9}{40}$

F1 This graph shows the growth of a sunflower.

  a After about how many weeks did the plant reach 1.5 metres?
  b About how high was the plant after 5 weeks?
  c How much did the plant grow between the 10th and 15th week?
  d Estimate the final height of the sunflower.

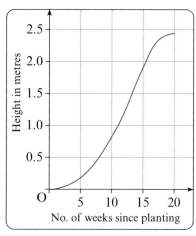

G Draw a grouped frequency diagram
Skill 23A: *see page 131*

G1 A survey tested the time that a group of people took to do a task. This grouped frequency table gives the results

  a How many people took part in the survey?
  b Draw a grouped frequency diagram to show the data.

Time in seconds	Tally	Frequency
$0 \leqslant$ time < 10	/	1
$10 \leqslant$ time < 20	////	4
$20 \leqslant$ time < 30	JHT ///	8
$30 \leqslant$ time < 40	JHT /	6
$40 \leqslant$ time < 50	///	3

H Solve an equation with the unknown on both sides
Skill 24A: *see page 134*
Skill 24B: *see page 135*

H1 Solve each of these equations.
  a $13a + 5 = 6a + 19$ **b** $15s - 2 = 11s + 22$
  c $4p - 7 = 8 - p$ **d** $11t + 5 = 4t - 2$

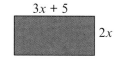

I Forming an equation
Skill 24C: *see page 136*

I1 The perimeteter of this rectangle is 50 cm.

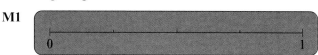

a Form an equation for its perimeter
b Solve your equation to find the value of x.

J Round to the nearest whole number.
Skill 25A: *see page 139*

J1 Round each of these decimal numbers to the nearest whole number.
a 17.865 **b** 7.4 **c** 125.4999 **d** 99.87

K Round a number to a set number of decimal places
Skill 25B: *see page 140*
Skill 25C: *see page 141*

K1 Round 13.2485 to
a 1 decimal place
b 2 decimal places
c 3 decimal places

L Calculate a probability for equally likely outcomes.
Skill 26A: *see page 142*

L1 When you roll a 1 to 6 dice what is the probability of
a getting a 5
b getting an even number
c getting either 1 or 6
d getting a number less than 6?

M Place a probability on a 0 to 1 scale
Skill 26B: *see page 144*

M1

On a probability scale like this, show with arrows the probability that:
a you will leave school today before 3:45
b when you roll a 1 to 6 dice you score 5 or more.

N Use the scale of a map or plan

N1 A plan of a model yacht uses a scale of 1 to 100.
a The mast on the plan is 7 cm high. How high is the real mast?
b On the real yacht the width is 3 metres 80 cm. What will be this distance on the plan?

O Write a number in standard form
Skill 28A: *see page 152*

O1 Write each number in the table in standard form.

Number	In standard form
645	
1843	
42.6	
129 000	
1756.4	

P Interpret a calculator display

P1 A calculator display shows the following answer.

$$7.8546 \; E \; 12$$

Show this as an ordinary number.

Q Use rules of indices
Skill 28B: *see page 154*

Q1 Copy and complete each of these
a $10^5 \times 10^8 = \blacksquare$ **b** $10^6 \times 10^6 \times 10^6 = \blacksquare$
c $10^9 \times 10^{\blacksquare} = 10^{18}$ **d** $10^{\blacksquare} \times 10^6 = 10^9$

R Use trial and improvement
Skill 28C: *see page 154*

R1 Solve the equation $x^3 = 50$. Give your answer to 1 dp.

S   Reflect and rotate a shape on a grid
Skill 29A: *see page 155*
Skill 29B: *see page 157*

T   Identify a transformation
Skill 29C: *see page 159*

U   Find the mean, median or mode for a set of data
Skill 30A: *see page 160*
Skill 30B: *see page 162*
Skill 30C: *see page 163*

V   Give directions from a map or plan
Skill 31A: *see page 166*

W   Show views of an object
Skill 31B: *see page 167*
Skill 31C: *see page 169*

S1   Copy the axes and shape A. Rotate shape A by 90° anticlockwise about the point (0, 0). Label the image B.

S2   Reflect shape A in the *x*-axis. Label the image C.

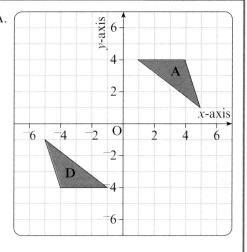

T1   What transformation maps shape A on to shape D?

U1   14 23 5 53 2 5 12 6 17 22 23 5 21

For this set of data find

a   the mean   **b**   the median   **c**   the mode.

V1   Give directions to get from the Red Horse to the office.

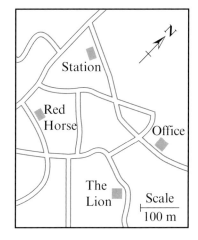

W1   **a**   Sketch a view of object 1 from each direction: A, B and C.
b   Use isometric paper to draw a 3D view of object 1.

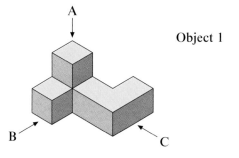

Object 1

This revises the work in Stages 1, 2 and 3

1 Give the value of the digit 3 in each of these.
a 35 045   b 753 004   c 503 977 657

2 List these numbers from large to small.
68 045, 12, 975, 59 897, 3094, 757, 44, 60 998

3 Write each of these numbers in words.
a 50 004   b 610 001   c 13 004 002

4 Write each of these numbers in digits.
a sixty million and sixty
b forty-five thousand and ten
c one million one hundred and one

5 Copy each of these letters and draw in all lines of symmetry.
B   C   U   I   W

6 Give the order of rotational symmetry of Shape A.

Shape A

7 How many planes of symmetry has a mug?

8 Find an answer to each of these.
(Do not use a calculator.)
a $4 + 7 + 9 + 3 + 8 + 5$
b $55 + 39 + 7$
c $3065 + 69 + 12 694 + 11$
d $65 004 - 7886$
e 53×16
f 674×28
g $2286 \div 18$
h $25 215 \div 15$

9 Give the value of the digit 8 in each of these.
a 44.138   b 12.086   c 7.6568

10 List these numbers in order, smallest first.
0.015, 0.62, 0.075, 0.3, 1.02, 0.06

11 Find an answer to each of these.
(Do not use a calculator.)
a $6.104 + 29.3 + 1.07 + 0.09 + 19$
b $807.95 + 41 + 1.082 + 0.65$
c $91.003 - 57.64$

12 Draw each of these angles accurately.
a 35°   b 155°   c 275°

13 Which of these angles are reflex?
88°, 155°, 264°, 304°, 148°, 299°

14 Copy and complete each of these.
a $^-8 + ^-12$ b $^-16 + 9$ c $13 + ^-7$
d $7 - 35$ e $^-8 - 15$ f $^-3 - ^-11$
g $16 - ^-9$ h $^-9 \times 5$ i $12 \times ^-4$
j $^-7 \times ^-9$ k $40 \div ^-8$ l $^-56 \div ^-14$

15 Order these numbers with the smallest first.
a $^-3, 5, ^-5, 1, ^-4, 2, 0$
b $0, ^-9, ^-3, 5, 1, ^-2, 11, ^-12$

16 The coordinates of two corners of a square are:
$(^-7, 0)$ and $(^-1, 0)$.
Give the coordinates of the other two corners of the square.

17 Collect like terms in each of these.
a $13k + 7w + k + 9w + 11k$
b $8f + 14h + f - 3h - 12h$

18 Expand the brackets in each of these.
a $4(9w + 1)$ b $7(14 - 5k)$

19 Expand these brackets and collect like terms to simplify.
$8(4y + 5g + 6) + 4(7y - 9g - 12)$

20 Round each of these numbers to the nearest thousand.
a 40 608   b 375 299   c 6 575 704

21 Round each of these to the nearest 100 000.
a 805 604   b 3 124 492   c 8 014 505

22 Find an approximate answer to each of these.
a 54×82 b 71×48 c 39×88

23 Construct a triangle with sides of:
7 cm, 7 cm and 9 cm.

24 Construct triangle ABC where:
AB = 7 cm, BC = 8 cm, and angle ABC = 65°

25 Write each of these in 24-hour time.
a 8.47 pm   b 3.35 pm   c 11.15 am
d 7.25 pm   e 3.15 am   f 3.36 pm

26 A train left Birmingham at 11:24 and arrived in Glasgow at 16:15.
What was the journey time for this train?

27 Use the timetable on page 59.
Jo catches the 0803 from Waterloo East.
She travels to Ramsgate.
a When should she get to Ramsgate?
b What is the journey time?

28 Calculate the area of each of these shapes.

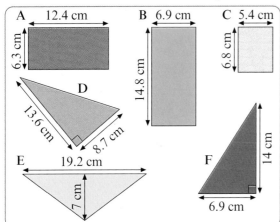

29 A formula that links p, k and t is: $t = 6(4p - 3k)$
Find the value of t when, $p = 3$ and $k = 5$

30 Solve each of these equations.
a $11y + 12 = 56$ b $62 + 7h = 104$
c $8g - 35 = 29$ d $2(2f - 3) = 42$

31 a   Add all the even numbers between 31 and 43.
b   What square numbers are between 80 and 150?
c   Subtract the 7th square number from 55.

32 Which of these is a multiple of 8?
60, 72, 48, 36, 16, 42

33 List all the factors of 72.

34 List all the prime numbers between 20 and 45.

35 This data is about TV viewing in a week.

Ella		Nadim	
Channel	**Hours**	**Channel**	**Hours**
BBC1	4	BBC1	10
BBC2	3	BBC2	3
ITV	9	ITV	6
Ch 4	12	Ch 4	5
Ch 5	9	Ch 5	5
Sky	15	Sky	7

a   Draw a comparative bar chart for the data.
b   Draw a split bar chart to show the data for each viewer.
c   Draw a pie chart to show the data for Nadim.

36 Copy and complete each of these.
a $25.3125 \times 10^2 =$ b $0.000616 \times 10^4 =$
c $546.58 \div 10 =$ d $0.0054 \div 10^3 =$

37 Without a calculator find the value of:
a $3229.1 \div 7 =$ b $2148.32 \div 4 =$
c $207.83 \times 5 =$ d $744.92 \times 3 =$

38 Calculate the answer to each of these.
Do not use a calculator.
a   £12.88 + £6.99 + 88p + £9
b   £7 + £23.99 + 75p + £4.80 + 16p
c   £480.49 – £329.75
d   £1400 – £785.58

39 A box of 8 pens costs £1.95.
Find the cost of one pen to the nearest penny.

40 Ed buys a bag of plaster for £8.38.
He pays with a £10 note.
How much change will he get?

41 Alex pays for a brush with a £20 note.
She gets £14.66 change. How much was the brush?

42 Calculate the answer to each of these.
Do not use a calculator.
a   78p × 9   b   £23.65 × 7 =
c   £305.28 ÷ 8   d   £4048.45 ÷ 7 =

43 Draw a mapping diagram for the function
$y = 3x - 5$ (Use values of x from 1 to 6.)

44 Give the number output from this function machine.

45 Calculate each angle marked with a letter.

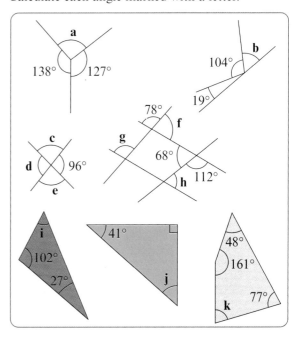

46 Davina earns a basic wage of £6.90 an hour.
How much will she earn at:
a   double time   b   time-and-a-half?

47 Calculate $\frac{3}{8}$ of £45.68.

48 Kamal did a sponsored walk of 42 km.
For $\frac{3}{4}$ of the distance he did not have blisters on his feet.

How far did he walk with blisters on his feet?

49 Which of these fractions is equivalent to $\frac{4}{5}$?

$\frac{28}{35}$ $\frac{36}{45}$ $\frac{44}{60}$ $\frac{60}{75}$

50 **a** Convert $\frac{15}{24}$ to a decimal.
b Put these in order from smallest to largest.

0.8 $\frac{3}{5}$ 0.75 $\frac{5}{8}$ $\frac{1}{4}$

51 Give two different fractions that describe how much of this grid is shaded.

52 This data shows the number of people that travelled in a cable-car.

8, 1, 15, 9, 11, 21, 22, 17, 24, 16, 27, 14, 18, 14, 25, 17, 13, 7, 16, 5, 2, 28, 30, 16, 7, 25, 24, 30, 21, 20, 6

a Make a grouped frequency table for the data.
Groups of: 1 to 5, 6 to 10, 11 to15, ... , 26 to 30
b What is the modal class?
c Draw a grouped frequency diagram to show the data.

53 Solve each of these equations.

a $14y - 6 = 6y + 34$ **b** $9w + 4 = 5w - 8$
c $15x - 28 = 8x + 56$ **d** $15w + 15 = 30 + 5w$

54 Shape A is a rectangle.

12.3 cm

Shape A

3.6 cm

a Calculate the perimeter of shape A.
b Give the perimeter of shape A rounded to the nearest whole number.
c Calculate the area of shape A.
d Give the area rounded to 1 dp.
e Round the length and width to the nearest whole number and use this to find the area.

55 Which of these is 38.07 when rounded to 2 dp?

38.065 48   38.060 99   38.074 95   37.075 02

56 With a 1 to 6 dice:

a What is the probability of scoring 5 or more?
b What is the probability of scoring less than 2?

57 Write each of these numbers in standard form.
a 15 768.75   **b** 70 640 547.65

58 Callum worked out how many seconds there were in 15 years. His calculator display gave:

a Write this number in standard form.
b Write this as an ordinary number.

59 Use the rules of indices to complete each of these.

a $10^5 \times 10^4 = 10^\blacksquare$ **b** $10^3 \times 10^5 \times 10^\blacksquare = 10^{14}$

60 Joel did a survey of the matches in a box.
This data gives the number in each box.

38, 44, 40, 35, 36, 41, 40, 39, 34, 42, 40, 38, 40, 33, 40, 41, 45, 37, 33, 39, 38, 40, 40, 40, 39, 40, 41

a Make a frequency table for the data.
b What number of matches was the mode?
c Find the mean number of matches in a box.
d Find the median number of matches in a box.

61 Make two copies of this grid showing shape A.

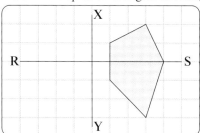

a On one copy show shape A reflected in XY.
b On one copy show shape A reflected in RS.

62 Copy these axes and the shape ABCD on to a grid.

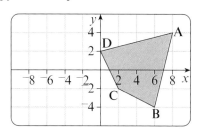

a Rotate ABCD 180° about the point (0, 2)
b Give the coordinates of A′, B′, C′, D′.

63 Object 1 on page 169 is made from 9 cubes. Sketch three different views of object 1.

64 These are two views of an object.

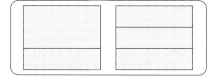

What might be the third view?

Starting points

You need to know about ...

... so try these questions

A Finding a fraction of an amount

Skill 22A: *see page 122*

B Equivalent fractions

Skill 22B: *see page 125*

C Fractions in their lowest terms

Skill 22C: *see page 126*

A1 Find each of these:

    a $\frac{3}{5}$ of £17.50

    b $\frac{5}{8}$ of 216 kg

    c $\frac{7}{10}$ of £50 000

    d $\frac{3}{4}$ of 7500 km

B1 Which of these fractions are equivalent to $\frac{4}{5}$?

    $\frac{16}{20}$ $\frac{32}{35}$ $\frac{76}{95}$ $\frac{14}{15}$

B2 Give two different fractions that are equivalent to $\frac{3}{8}$.

C1 Write each of these fractions in its lowest terms.

    a $\frac{15}{55}$ **b** $\frac{24}{56}$ **c** $\frac{42}{63}$ **d** $\frac{18}{81}$

Percentages and decimals

Skill 32A
Converting a percentage to a decimal

A percentage describes part of a whole.
The whole is 100%.

As the whole is 100%
any percentage less than 100% is only part of the whole.

We can think of 28% as 28 of the 100 parts of the whole.
This diagram shows 28%.

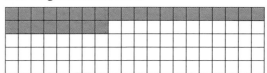

As there are 100 parts, each small square shows $\frac{1}{100}$.

In the place value system we can show $\frac{1}{100}$ in this way:

U	.	$\frac{1}{10}$	$\frac{1}{100}$
0	.	0	1

So $1\% = \frac{1}{100}$, which is 0.01 as a decimal.

We can think of 28% as $28 \times 1\%$ but we know that 1% is 0.01.
So, $28\% = 28 \times 0.01 = 0.28$ as a decimal.

Example   Convert 74% to a decimal.

    $74\% = 74 \times 0.01 = 0.74$

So 74% as a decimal is 0.74.

Exercise 32.1
Practising Skill 32A

1 Convert each of these to a decimal.

    a 26%   **b** 54%   **c** 61%   **d** 14%   **e** 95%

2 Convert each of these to a decimal.

a 4%	**b** 22%	**c** 67%	**d** 91%	**e** 34%
f 8%	**g** 88%	**h** 9%	**i** 7%	**j** 99%
k 16%	**l** 3%	**m** 25%	**n** 75%	**o** 50%

We can also convert percentages like $26\frac{1}{2}\%$ to a decimal.

$26\frac{1}{2}\%$ is half-way between 26% and 27%.

As a decimal $26\frac{1}{2}\%$ is half way between 0.26 and 0.27.

We can think of these decimals on a number line.

> 26% is 0.26 and
> 27% is 0.27

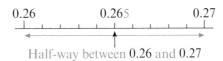

The half-way value between 0.26 and 0.27 is 0.265.

So, as a decimal, $26\frac{1}{2}\%$ is 0.265.

3 Write each of these as a decimal.

a $35\frac{1}{2}\%$	**b** $12\frac{1}{2}\%$	**c** $40\frac{1}{2}\%$	**d** $81\frac{1}{2}\%$
e $66\frac{1}{2}\%$	**f** $20\frac{1}{2}\%$	**g** $6\frac{1}{2}\%$	**h** $17\frac{1}{2}\%$
i $7\frac{1}{2}\%$	**j** $3\frac{1}{2}\%$	**k** $1\frac{1}{2}\%$	**l** $99\frac{1}{2}\%$

Skill 32B
Converting a decimal to a percentage

As a percentage the decimal 0.64 is 64%.

We can think of this conversion in this way:

0.01 is 1%

So if we divide 0.64 by 0.01 that will tell us how many lots of 1% there are

0.64 ÷ 0.01 = 64

So, as a percentage, 0.64 is 64%.

Exercise 32.2
Practising Skill 32B

1 Convert each of these decimals to a percentage.

a 0.29	**b** 0.96	**c** 0.83	**d** 0.77	**e** 0.49
f 0.19	**g** 0.33	**h** 0.69	**i** 0.11	**j** 0.07
k 0.02	**l** 0.09	**m** 0.15	**n** 0.41	**o** 0.87

2 Convert each of these decimals to a percentage.

a 0.165	**b** 0.275	**c** 0.065	**d** 0.375	**e** 0.625
f 0.875	**g** 0.615	**h** 0.105	**i** 0.025	**j** 0.085
k 0.305	**l** 0.255	**m** 0.505	**n** 0.005	**o** 0.045

3 Copy and complete this table.

Percentage	72		$61\frac{1}{2}$	18		$37\frac{1}{2}$	72
Decimal		0.57			0.135		0.89

4 Put this list of decimals and percentages in order.
Start with the smallest.

37% 0.38 0.18 0.72 65% 27% 0.04 $12\frac{1}{2}\%$ 0.565

Percentages of amounts

Skill 32C
Calculating a percentage
of an amount

Thinking of a percentage as a decimal is a help when you need to calculate a percentage of an amount.

Example 1 Calculate 65% of 350 km.

65% as a decimal is 0.65
65% of 350 is given by: $350 \times 0.65 = 227.5$

So, 65% of 350 km is 227.5 km.

Example 2 Calculate 18% of £2450.

18% as a decimal is 0.18
18% of 2450 is given by: $2450 \times 0.18 = 441$

So, 18% of £2450 is £441.

Example 3 Calculate $17\frac{1}{2}$% of £65.

$17\frac{1}{2}$% as a decimal is 0.175

$17\frac{1}{2}$% of 65 is given by: $65 \times 0.175 = 11.375$

So $17\frac{1}{2}$% of £65 is £11.38 (to the nearest penny).

> When an answer is an amount of money it is best to round to the nearest penny. To the nearest penny £11.375 is £11.38.

Exercise 32.3
Practising Skill 32C

> When an answer is an amount of money, round it to the nearest penny.

1 Copy and complete each of these.

a	16% of 4575 miles =	**b**	38% of 75 km =	**c**	85% of £420 =
d	24% of 1685 kg =	**e**	42% of £2654 =	**f**	8% of 260 km =
g	92% of £35620 =	**h**	6% of 472 kg =	**i**	22% of £35.20 =
j	84% of £6.44 =	**k**	8% of 1805 km =	**l**	3% of £45.60 =

2 Calculate each of these.

a $12\frac{1}{2}$% of 1350 km   **b** $21\frac{1}{2}$% of 380 kg   **c** $15\frac{1}{2}$% of £80

d $50\frac{1}{2}$% of £385   **e** $6\frac{1}{2}$% of 42 miles   **f** $32\frac{1}{2}$% of £168

g $17\frac{1}{2}$% of £78.40   **h** $2\frac{1}{2}$% of 36458 km   **i** $5\frac{1}{2}$% of £92

j $28\frac{1}{2}$% of 16 million   **k** $7\frac{1}{2}$% of 94 miles   **l** $1\frac{1}{2}$% of £3.88

> 62.5 is the same as $62\frac{1}{2}$.

3 Find 62.5% of half a million.

4 Calculate 3.5% of £7560.32.

5 What is 15.5% of 85p?

Exercise 32.4
Using Skill 32C

1 In a batch of 24680 light bulbs $2\frac{1}{2}$% of the bulbs were faulty.
How many bulbs in the batch were faulty?

2 Last year Citybus carried 565000 passengers to London.
27% of these passengers were children.
How many of these Citybus passengers were children?

3 Zenta buys beads to make necklaces.
Her last order was for 3760 beads.
15% of the beads were made of wood, 45% were made of glass, and the rest were made of porcelain.
How many of each type of bead did Zenta order?

4 In Westridge there are 7680 households with a TV.
Records show that 15% of them do not have a TV licence.

    a How many households in Westridge do not have a TV licence?
(Use the data from the records.)

    b How many households in westridge do have a TV licence?

5 This table gives data on the complaints to a bus company.

Complaints Record	Month: **APRIL**
Total number of complaints: **875**	

Type of complaint	Percentage
Fares	16%
Late running	20%
Overcrowding	8%
Cancelled buses	32%
Dirty buses	4%
Driving too fast	12%
Dirty bus shelters	8%

Calculate the number of each type of complaint.

6 A cake weighs 875 grams.
$22\frac{1}{2}$% of the weight of the cake is made up by sugar.

How many grams of sugar are in the cake?
Give your answer to the nearest whole number.

7 Last year at an accident black-spot there were 560 accidents.

35% of the accidents involved cyclists
12.5% of the accidents involved people walking
$37\frac{1}{2}$% involved motorcycle riders
2.5% involved lorries
The rest involved just cars.

    a How many accidents involved a cyclist?
    b How many accidents involved a lorry?
    c Jake says that 75 accidents involved people walking.
Is he right? Explain.
    d How many accident involved motorcycle riders?
    e What percentage of accidents just involved cars?
    f How many of the accidents just involved cars?

8 A football ground has 21 000 seats.

45% are season ticket seats
32% of the seats have a ticket price of £15
15.5% have a ticket price of £21
7.5% of the seats are for guests of the club.

    a How many seats are for guests of the club?
    b How may seats have a ticket price of £15?
    c How many seats have a ticket price of £21?

This headline was in the
match programme.

All 10,000 season ticket seats sold!

    d Every ticket was sold.
How accurate is the headline?
Explain.

9 A forest was planted with 34 800 trees.
Larch, pine, Douglas fir, and spruce trees were used.

This data is for the numbers planted.

Type of tree	Percentage	Number
Larch	28.5	⬭
Pine	34	⬭
Douglas fir	16.5	⬭
Spruce	⬭	⬭

  a How many pine trees were planted?
  b The foresters were told to plant about 10 000 larch trees.
   Did they do as they were told? Explain.
  c How many of the trees were Douglas fir?
  d What percentage of the trees were spruce?
   How many trees is this?

10 Westover District Council gave this data for recycled glass bottles.

Bottle bank	Colour of glass			No. of bottles
	Green	Brown	Clear	
West End car park	54%	28.5%	17.5%	16 800
Market Square	44%	37%	19%	24 300
Station Car Park	38.5%	34%	27.5%	31 400
Recycling Centre	62%	23%	15%	75 100
Total number of bottles	⬭	⬭	⬭	⬭

  a How many green bottles were in the West End car park bank?
  b How many clear bottles were in the Station car park bank?
  c Make a copy of the table:
   • with each percentage changed for a number of bottles
   • with all the totals filled in.

One number as a percentage of another number

To compare two numbers you can think of:
 one number as a percentage of the other.

 ◆ Say you compare the numbers 18 and 36:

   18 is half of 36
   18 is 50% of 36

$\frac{1}{2} = 50\%$

We can write: **18 as a percentage of 36 is 50%.**

 ◆ Say you compare the numbers 14 and 56:

   14 is a quarter of 56
   14 is 25% of 56

$\frac{1}{4} = 25\%$

We can write: **14 as a percentage of 56 is 25%.**

Exercise 32.5
One number as a percentage of another

1 Compare each pair of numbers and write the first as a percentage of the second.

  a 28 and 56   **b** 15 and 60   **c** 27 and 36   **d** 50 and 200

2 What is 35 as a percentage of 70?

3 What is 16 as a percentage of 64?

4 Roughly what is 15 as a percentage of 32?

5 In a group of 32 students 24 were right-handed.

Give the right-handed students as a percentage of the group.

Skill 32D
Writing one number as a percentage of another

To find 18 as a percentage of 36 we can think of it in this way:

18 is half of 36   or $18 \div 36 = 0.5$
18 is 50% of 36   or $0.5 \times 100 = 50\%$

This can be one calculation: $(18 \div 36) \times 100 = 50\%$

Example 1

Write 54 as a percentage of 80.
$(54 \div 80) \times 100 = 67.5\%$

Example 2

What is £12.60 as a percentage of £44?
$(12.6 \div 44) \times 100 = 28.636 \dots$

The answer $28.636 \dots$ needs to be rounded.

So £12.60 as a percentage of £44 is £28.64 (to the nearest penny).

Exercise 32.6
Practising Skill 32D

1 Calculate each of these and give your answers correct to 1 dp.

   a 16 as a percentage of 36   **b** 52 as a percentage of 80
   c 14 as a percentage of 48   **d** 85 as a percentage of 184
   e 12 as a percentage of 15   **f** 5 as a percentage of 12
   g 8 as a percentage of 20   **h** 16 as a percentage of 25
   i 12 as a percentage of 64   **j** 75 as a percentage of 250

Exercise 32.7
Using Skill 32D

Give your answers correct to 1 dp.

1 At a driving test centre 55 people took their test last Monday.
Only 38 of them passed.

What percentage of the people who took their test passed?

2 A hockey club played 42 matches last season.
They won 25 of the matches.

What is the number of wins as a percentage of all the matches played?

3 A bus has 22 seats and 8 people are allowed to stand.
Give the number of people allowed to stand, as a percentage
of the number of seats.

4 A sports club was sent a bill for repairs to its video camera.
The parts cost £9.20 and the total bill was for £65.70

What was the cost of parts as a percentage of the total bill?

5 Of the first 80 customers at a supermarket, 44 were female.

Give the number of male customers as a percentage of the 80 customers.

6 A ferry carried 1088 people.
Of these, 856 were French and 134 were Italian.
Gary says that about 75% of the passengers were French and 10% Italian.

Do you agree? Explain your answer.

Starting points

You need to know about ...

... so try these questions

A Odd and even numbers

- ◆ Even numbers: 2, 4, 6, 8, 10, ...
- ◆ Odd numbers: 1, 3, 5, 7, 9, ...

A1 Which of these are odd numbers?
14, 21, 53, 70, 87, 105

A2 How many even numbers are there between 101 and 201?

B Square and triangle numbers

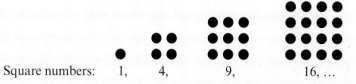

- ◆ Square numbers: 1,   4,   9,   16, ...

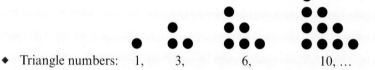

- ◆ Triangle numbers: 1,   3,   6,   10, ...

B1 Draw a pattern of dots to show that 25 is a square number.

B2 What is the next square number after 25?

B3 List four square numbers that are odd.

B4 List the first six triangle numbers.

C Sequences from powers of numbers

2^3 is called 2 to the power of 3. It means $2 \times 2 \times 2 = 8$

2^4 means $2 \times 2 \times 2 \times 2 = 16$

- ◆ Powers of 2: 2, 4, 8, 16, 32, ... (this is $2^1, 2^2, 2^3, 2^4, 2^5, ...$)
- ◆ Powers of 3: 3, 9, 27, 81, 243, ... (this is $3^1, 3^2, 3^3, 3^4, 3^5, ...$)

C1 What is the next number in the powers of 2 sequence?

C2 List the first five powers of 4.

D Fibonacci numbers

- ◆ Fibonacci sequence: 1, 1, 2, 3, 5, 8, 13, ...

The Fibonacci sequence starts 1, 1, ...

You can find more numbers by adding the two numbers to the left. For example, the next Fibonacci number is 8 + 13 = 21.

D1 What are the next three numbers in this Fibonacci sequence?
1, 1, 2, 3, 5, 8, 13, ... , ... , ...

D2 Each number in this sequence is found by adding the two numbers to the left of it
1, 3, 4, 7, 11, 18, ... , ... , ...
Find the next three numbers in this sequence.

E Terms of a sequence

- ◆ A number in a sequence is called a term.

2, 5, 8, 11, 14, 17, ...

The first term in this sequence is 2, and the 4th term is 11.

E1 What is the 5th term of the sequence 1, 3, 5, 7, 9, 11, 13?

E2 What is the 7th term in this sequence?
2, 5, 8, 11, 14, 17, ...

Sequences from patterns

Skill 33A
Making sequences
from patterns

As new parts are added to a pattern a sequence may develop.

For example, these patterns are made from matches.

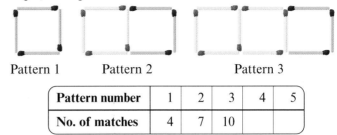

Pattern 1   Pattern 2   Pattern 3

Pattern number	1	2	3	4	5
No. of matches	4	7	10		

The number of matches in each pattern makes a sequence: 4, 7, 10, …

Each time, 3 matches like this are added.

Match sequence A

Exercise 33.1
Practising skill 33A

1 How many matches will there be in pattern 4 above?

2 **a** Draw pattern 5.
    b How many matches are in pattern 5?

3 For match sequence A:
    a Make a table to show the number of matches for each pattern.
    b How many matches are added for each new pattern?
    c Draw pattern 4.
    d How many matches are there in pattern 5?

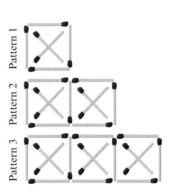

4 This shows another sequence made from matches.

Pattern 1   Pattern 2   Pattern 3   Pattern 4

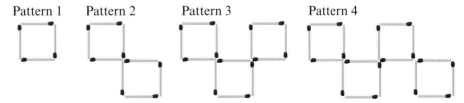

    a Make a table to show the sequence for the number of matches.
    b How does the sequence grow?
    c Draw pattern 5.
    d How many matches are in pattern 5?
    e Predict how many matches there will be in pattern 6.
    f Draw pattern 6 to test your prediction.
    g How many matches will there be in pattern 20?
       Describe how you found your answer.

Sequences from rules

Skill 33B
Making a sequence when you know the rule

◆ A rule can be used to describe the next term in a sequence.

Example 1

Look at sequence 1:

Sequence 1   2, 5, 8, 11, 14, ...

The rule is: **Multiply the term number by 3, then take away 1**.

This shows how it works.

Term no.	1	2	3	4 ...
Working out	$(3 \times 1) - 1$	$(3 \times 2) - 1$	$(3 \times 3) - 1$	$(3 \times 4) - 1$
Sequence	2	5	8	11 ...

◆ Other sequences are made from different types of rule.

Example 2

Look at sequence 2.

The numbers 1, 2, 3 are needed to start it off.

Sequence 2   1, 2, 3, 6, 11, 20, 37, ...

From term 4, the rule is: **Add the last three terms.**

$$(1 + 2 + 3) \quad (2 + 3 + 6) \quad (3 + 6 + 11) \quad (6 + 11 + 20)$$

1, 2, 3,   6,   11,   20,   37, ...

Exercise 33.2
Practising skill 33B

1   For sequence 1 show why the 5th term is 14.

2   For sequence 1, what are the next two terms after 14?

3   For sequence 2, what are the next two terms after 37?

4   This sequence uses the rule Multiply the last term by 6.
      1, 6, 36, 216, ...

   What are the next two terms in the sequence?

5   The sequence below uses the rule Multiply the term number by 2 then add 1.
      3, 5, 7, 9, ...

   The 4th term of this sequence is 9. What is:

   a   the 5th term   **b**   the 10th term   **c**   the 43rd term?

6   Look at this sequence of numbers 9, 14, 19, 24, 29, ...
   Write down the rule for getting each number from the one before it.

7   The rule Multiply the term number by 5 then subtract 3 is used for this
   sequence: 2, 7, ...
   What are the next two terms in the sequence?

8   These are three terms in a sequence: ... , ... , 128, 64, 32, ... , ... , ... , ... , ...
   Write down all ten terms of the sequence.

Rules from sequences

Skill 33C
Finding a rule from a
sequence pattern

◆ You can find the rule by looking at how a pattern grows.

Example

You can think of this pattern growing like this:

For pattern 2,
$n = 2$ and the number of
matches $m = 7$

So a rule for the number of matches m in the nth pattern is $\boldsymbol{m = 1 + 3n}$.

Exercise 33.3
Practising skill 33C

1 Use the rule $\boldsymbol{m = 1 + 3n}$ above to work out the number of matches in the
   10th pattern.

2 This shows three patterns in a sequence.

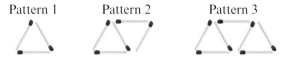

For pattern 1, an expression for the number of matches is $1 + (2 \times 1)$.
   a What is an expression for pattern 2?
   b What is an expression for pattern 3?
   c What is an expression for the number of matches in pattern 10?
   d Use your expression to find how many matches there are in pattern 10.
   e Write a rule for the number of matches in pattern n.

3 This sequence is similar to the one in question **2**.

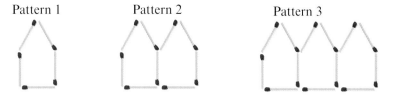

   a By how many matches does the sequence grow each time?
   b Write an expression for the number of matches in pattern 2.
   c Write a rule for the number of matches in pattern n.
   d Use your rule to find the number of matches in pattern 20.

4 a For this sequence, write a rule for the number of matches in pattern n.
   b Use your rule to find the number of matches in pattern 20.

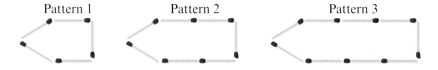

Skill 33D
Using differences to find a rule

◆ You do not always have a picture for terms in a sequence. To find the rule you then need to look at differences.

Example   Find a rule for the nth term in sequence A.

Sequence A   7, 10, 13, 16, …

◆ Look at the differences between terms.

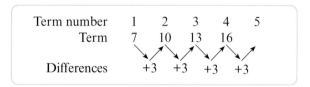

Term number	1	2	3	4	5
Term	7	10	13	16	
Differences		+3	+3	+3	+3

Every term goes up by 3 each time.

So the rule for the nth term is $3n$ …

Compare the sequence above with the sequence where the nth term is $3n$.

Term number	1	2	3	4
$3n$	3	6	9	12
	$\downarrow +4$			
Sequence A	7	10	13	16

Each term in sequence A is 4 more than for the $3n$ sequence.

So the rule for the nth term of sequence A is $3n + 4$

Check the rule for a term you know:

Term 4 … rule gives $(3 \times 4) + 4 = 12 + 4 = 16$ ✔

Exercise 33.4
Practising skill 33D

1   Use the rule $3n + 4$ above to find the value of:

   a   term 8   **b**   term 20   **c**   term 100

2   For the sequence 3, 5, 7, 9, 11, … :

   a   what is the difference between terms each time?
   b   what is the value of ▲ in this rule ▲ n + ●?
   c   what is the value of ● in this rule ▲ n + ●?
   d   write the rule for the nth term of the sequence?

3   Find the rule for the nth term in each of these sequences.

   a   6, 10, 14, 18, 22, …   **b**   9, 15, 21, 27, 33, …
   c   2, 5, 8, 11, 14, …   **d**   2, 6, 10, 14, 18, …
   e   1, 6, 11, 16, 21, …   **f**   5, 8, 11, 14, 17, …

Starting points
You need to know about ...   ... so try these questions

A The nets of a cube

A net is a group of joined polygons which folds up to make a solid.

There are six different nets for a cube. Here are three of them.

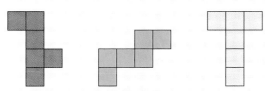

You do not need to show glue flaps on a net

B The area of a rectangles and a triangle

Area of rectangle = Length × Width

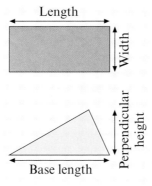

Area of triangle =
Base length × Perpendicular height

> **A1 a** On squared paper copy the three nets shown.
>
> **b** Cut each one out and check that it folds to make a cube.
>
> **A2** Find and draw the other three nets of a cube.
>
> **B1** Calculate the area of a rectangle 8 cm long by 6.5 cm wide.
>
> **B2** Calculate the area of this triangle.
>
>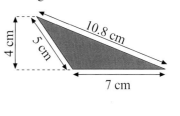

The net of a cuboid

Skill 34A
Drawing the net of a cuboid

◆ Every cuboid has 6 faces, so its net must have 6 rectangles or squares.

Example

Draw a net for this cuboid

◆ Think about the size of each face.

There are: two faces like F ... 4 cm by 1 cm
two faces like T ... 4 cm by 3 cm
two faces like S ... 3 cm by 1 cm

◆ Think about how the faces are joined on the cuboid
F joins to T along a 4 cm edge and so on.

◆ Draw the net.

◆ Make sure edges that will join each other are the same length.

Join red to red and blue to blue.

> This shows only one net for the cuboid. Others are possible.

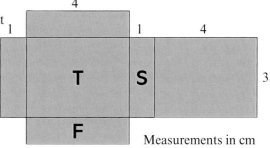

Measurements in cm

Exercise 34.1
Practising skill 34A

1   For cuboid A,

   a what is the size of face T?
   b give the size of face F
   c give the size of face S
   d on squared paper, draw a net full size.

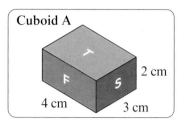

2   Draw a net for each of these cuboids

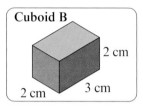

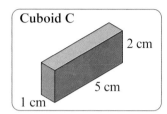

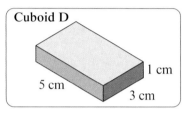

3   One of these is not the net of a cuboid. (All drawings are to scale.)
   Which one is it? Give your reason.

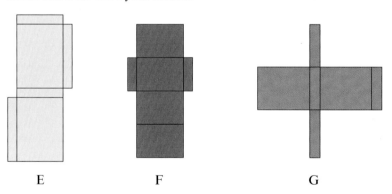

       E   F   G

♦ The surface area of a solid is the total area of all its outside surfaces.

Example

What is the surface area of cuboid C above?
It has: two faces of area 2 cm² (2 cm × 1 cm)   =   4 cm²
           two faces of area 10 cm² (5 cm × 2 cm) = 20 cm²
           two faces of area 5 cm² (5 cm × 1 cm)   = 10 cm²

           So the surface area of cuboid C = 34 cm².

4   Calculate the surface area of cuboid A above.
   Show all your working.

Your nets can help you
work out the surface areas.

5   Rob says the surface area of cuboid B is 16 cm².
   What has he done wrong?

6   Calculate the surface area of cuboid D.

The net of a prism

Skill 34B
Drawing the net of a prism

> The cuboid is a special type of prism which has a rectangular or square end face.

A prism has two parallel end faces which are the same shape. For all its length it has this shape as its cross-section.

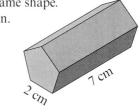

Example

Draw the net of this prism.
Each end face is a regular pentagon.

♦ Look at the number of faces the prism has (this one has 7 faces).

So the net must have 7 faces …
… two faces are pentagons
… five faces are rectangles 2 cm by 7 cm.

♦ Draw the net.

♦ Check that the edges that meet have the same length.
Join red to red;
red length = red length.

All measurements in cm

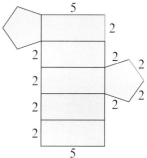

Exercise 34.2
Practising skill 34B

1 This prism has an end face which is a right-angled triangle.

  a How many rectangular faces are there?
  b Give the sizes of the rectangular faces.
  c Draw the net of the prism.
  d What is the area of a triangular end?
  e Calculate the surface area of the prism.

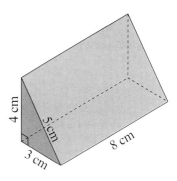

2 This prism has an end face which is an equilateral triangle.

Draw the net of this prism.

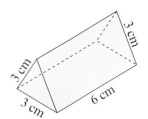

3 Which one of these is a net of a triangular prism?

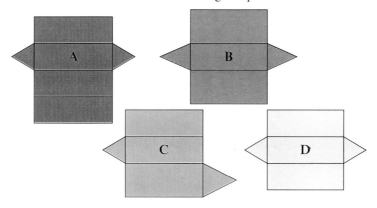

The net of a pyramid

Skill 34C
Drawing the net of
a pyramid

A **pyramid** has a polygon as a base.
All its other faces are triangles which meet at one top vertex.

Example

Draw the net of this right pyramid.

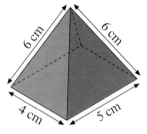

- ◆ Look at the number of faces
  the pyramid has (this one has 5 faces).

So the net must have 5 faces …
… the base is a rectangle 4 cm by 5 cm
… two faces are isosceles triangles
  (base of 4 cm, other sides 6 cm).
… two faces are isosceles triangles
  (base of 5 cm, other sides 6 cm).

- ◆ Draw the net

Note that this is not the only
net for the pyramid, but it is
easiest to draw the base first
then place the triangles
around this.

A right pyramid is one
where its top vertex is
exactly over the centre of
its base.

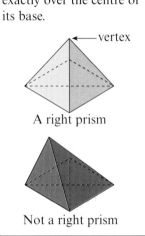

A right prism

Not a right prism

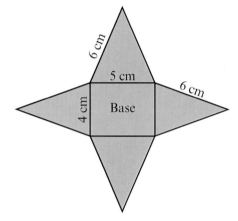

Exercise 34.3
Practising skill 34C

1 This right pyramid has a square base of side 4 cm.
    Each triangular side has a sloping height of 5 cm.

  a Draw a net for the pyramid.
  b Calculate the area of one
      triangular face.
  c What is the total surface area of
      the pyramid?

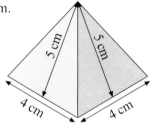

2 This solid is a special type of pyramid.
    Each face is an equilateral triangle of side 4 cm.

  a How many faces has the pyramid?
  b What name do we give this solid?
  c Draw a net for this pyramid.

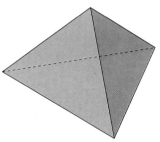

Starting points
You need to know about ...   ... so try these questions

A Calculating probability from equally likely outcomes

When outcomes are equally likely you can calculate the probability of something happening.

Example

For this 0 to 9 dice, what is the probability of getting a multiple of 4?

There are 10 numbers
(0, 1, 2, 3, 4, 5, 6, 7, 8, 9)

2 numbers are multiples of 4 (i.e. 4, 8).

So the probability of getting a

multiple of 4 is $\frac{2}{10} = \frac{1}{5}$

> **A1** For the 0 to 9 dice, what is the probability of getting:
>
> **a** a 5
> **b** a multiple of 3
> **c** an even number
> **d** a factor of 12?
>
> **A2** When you roll a 1 to 6 dice, what is the probability of getting a number less than 5?
>
> **A3** A drum has 12 equally sized sections. On 3 sections are apples, on 4 sections are potatoes and on 5 sections are bananas.
> What is the probability that the drum will stop on a fruit?

Calculating probability

Skill 35A
Calculating probabilty from data

◆ For outcomes which are not equally likely a probability has to be found in another way.

◆ When you have some data or have done an experiment you can use the results to find a probability.

Example

These are the results of a car survey in Hueton.

What is the probability that a car picked at random is blue?

Car colour	Tally	Frequency
Blue	ЖЖ ЖЖ ||	12
Red	ЖЖ ЖЖ ЖЖ |||	18
Black	ЖЖ		6
Green	|||	3
White	ЖЖ ||||	9
Silver	||||	4

The total number of cars is 12 + 18 + 6 + 3 + 9 + 4 = 52
The number of blue cars is 12.

So the probability of picking a blue car = $\frac{12}{52} = \frac{6}{26} = \frac{3}{13}$

This type of probability is often shown as a decimal.

So the probability of picking a blue car = $\frac{12}{52}$ = 0.23 (to 2 dp).

> To convert a fraction to a decimal you can use
>
> Skill 22D: *see page 126*

Exercise 35.1
Practising skill 35A

1 For the car survey above, what is the probability that a red car is picked at random:

a as a fraction   **b** as a decimal to 2 dp.

> To write a fraction in its lowest terms you can use
>
> Skill 22C: *see page 126*

2 Write the probability of picking a black car as a fraction in its lowest terms.

3 Give the probability of picking either a white or silver car as a decimal.

4 About 0.12 is the probability of picking one colour car.
What colour is this?

Combinations

Skill 35B
Listing combinations

♦ When you have to choose one thing from two or more groups there are many different combinations possible.

Example

List all the different combinations of activities you could choose.

Rangate Hall – Outdoor Pursuits Centre

Group A		Group B	
Rock climbing	**(R)**	Canoeing	**(C)**
Hiking	**(H)**	Water skiing	**(W)**
Pot holing	**(B)**	Archery	**(A)**
Poney treking	**(P)**	Sailing	**(S)**

Choose *one* activity from each group.

♦ Use a system to make sure

❖ you have not missed out any combination
❖ you have not counted any twice.

♦ Start from one in group A (R) and list all the others from B:
RC, RW, RA, RS

♦ Now take the next one in group A (H): HC, HW, HA, HS, and so on …

♦ Put all the combinations together:
RC, RW, RA, RS, HC, HW, HA, HS, BC, BW, BA, BS, PC, PW, PC, PS

So there are 16 different combinations.

> A combination is an arrangement of items in any order. So R + A is the same as A + R

Exercise 35.2
Using skill 35B

1 This is the menu at a hostel. Visitors must choose a main course and a sweet.

  a List all the combinations possible.

  b How many different combinations are there?

  c List all the combinations that a vegetarian could have.

BELLE VIEW HOSTEL

Main course		Sweet	
Beef casserol	(B)	Rice pudding	(R)
Veggi lasagne	(V)	Fruit salad	(F)
Pork ribs	(P)	Mangoes	(M)
Lamb chops	(L)		
Cheese salad	(C)		

2 You have only these symbols to use:

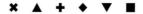

List all the different two-symbol combinations you can make with them.

> Check that you have not used the same combination twice.
>
> Remember ▲ ✚ counts the same as ✚ ▲.

3 These two spinners are spun.

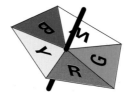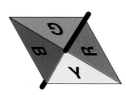

List all the **different** colour combinations possible.

4 a List all the different combinations of flavours you could have.

b How many combinations are there?

c Antonio's Parlour is up the road. Here you have to choose any three different flavours from a list of four.

How many combinations are now possible?

Luigi's Ice Cream Parlour
Any three different flavours from the following in a giant cornet:

Rum
Vanilla   Toffee
Strawberry   Kiwi

Sample-space diagrams

Skill 35C
Making a sample-space diagram

◆ When two events happen the combinations can be shown in a table. This type of two-way table is called a sample-space diagram.

Example

This spinner and a 1 to 6 dice are spun together.
Show all the possible outcomes in a sample-space diagram.

By outcomes here they mean combinations.
Red and 3 is one outcome.

In the table, label one axis with the spinner's colours and one with the number on the dice.

Sample-space diagram

Colour on spinner						
G	G1	G2	G3	G4	G5	G6
R	R1	R2	R3	R4	R5	R6
Y	Y1	Y2	Y3	Y4	Y5	Y6
B	B1	B2	B3	B4	B5	B6
W	W1	W2	W3	W4	W5	W6
	1	2	3	4	5	6

Number on dice

Exercise 35.3
Using skill 35C

1 Look at the sample space diagram above.
What link is these between:

• the number of colours on the spinner
• the number of numbers on the dice
• the total number of outcomes?

2 This spinner and a 1 to 8 dice are spun together.

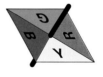 

a Make a sample-space diagram to show all the possible outcomes.

b How many of the outcomes have even numbers?

c How many outcomes have red in them?

3 A coin and 1 to 6 dice are spun together.

a Show the different outcomes on a sample-space diagram.

b How many different outcomes are there?

Probabilities for two events

Skill 35D
Finding a probability for two events

◆ A sample-space diagram helps you find probabilites with two events.

Example

This spinner is spun once and the number recorded. Then it is spun again and the score recorded again.

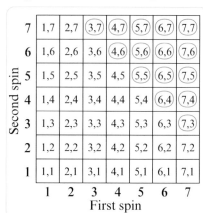

What is the probability that the total will greater than 9?

◆ Make a sample-space diagram for the first and second spin.

◆ Circle the outcomes where the total is greater than 9.

Total = 10

◆ Calculate the probability:
Total number of outcomes = 49
Number of outcomes with totals greater than 9 is 15

So the probability of getting a total greater than 9 is $\frac{15}{49}$.

	1	2	3	4	5	6	7
7	1,7	2,7	(3,7)	(4,7)	(5,7)	(6,7)	(7,7)
6	1,6	2,6	3,6	(4,6)	(5,6)	(6,6)	(7,6)
5	1,5	2,5	3,5	4,5	(5,5)	(6,5)	(7,5)
4	1,4	2,4	3,4	4,4	5,4	(6,4)	(7,4)
3	1,3	2,3	3,3	4,3	5,3	6,3	(7,3)
2	1,2	2,2	3,2	4,2	5,2	6,2	7,2
1	1,1	2,1	3,1	4,1	5,1	6,1	7,1

Second spin / First spin

Exercise 35.4
Using skill 35D

1 Use the sample-space diagram above to help you give these probabilities for two spins of the spinner.
The probability of:

a a total of exactly 6
b a total of 4 or less
c a score of six in either the first or second spin, or in both.

2 A red 1 to 6 dice and a blue 1 to 6 dice are rolled together.

	1	2	3	4	5	6
6						
5					4,5	
4		2,4				
3						
2		2,2				
1						

Blue dice / Red dice

a Copy and complete this sample-space diagram.
b Circle all the outcomes which give a total which is a multiple of 3.
c Calculate the probability that in a roll of both dice the total will be a multiple of 3.

3 Make another copy of the sample space diagram in question 2.

a Circle those outcomes which give a total less than 7.
b Calculate the probability of getting a total less than 7.

4 This spinner is spun twice and the letter recorded each time.

a Copy and complete the sample-space diagram.

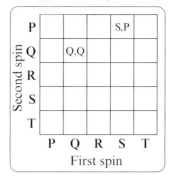

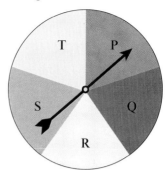

To write a fraction in its lowest terms you can use:

Skill 22C: *see page 126*

b Calculate the probability of getting two letters the same. Give your answer as a fraction in its lowest terms.

c Calculate the probability that the two letters will be different.

d What should the answers to parts **b** and **c** add up to?

5 You spin these two spinners together.

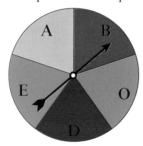

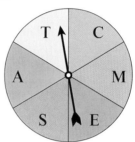

a Make a sample space diagram to show the outcomes.

b Give the probability that the two letters you get can be made into an English word.

6 Anna's combination bike lock has two rings.

On ring 1 are the digits 1, 2, 3, 4, 5, 6
On ring 2 are the digits 2, 3, 4, 5

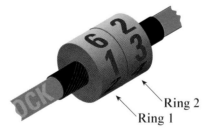

Ring 2
Ring 1

a The two rings are spun at random
Show all the possible combinations on a
sample-space diagram.

Anna has forgotten the combination.

b She sets a number at random.
What is the probability that she will get the right combination?

c What is the probability that the two digits are the same?

d What is the probability that the second digit is one more than the first?

e What is the probability that the second digit is one less than the first?

Starting points

You need to know about ...

... so try these questions

A The angle sum of triangles and quadrilaterals

Skill 19C: *see page 106*

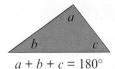

$a + b + c = 180°$

$p + q + r + s = 360°$

B Angles at a point, on a line and between parallel lines

Skill 17A, 17B, 17C, 17D: *see pages 94–97*

$p + q = 180°$ $f + g + h + i = 360°$

Equal angles are shown in the same colour:

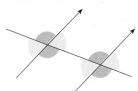

C The interior angles of a regular polygon

Skill 19B: *see page 105*

A1 Calculate the labelled angles in each of these polygons.

B1 Calculate the labelled angles in each of these.

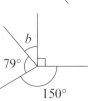

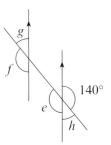

C1 Calculate the interior angle of a regular hexagon.

Tessellations

A tessellation is an arrangement of shapes which fit together.
There must be no overlaps or gaps.

Tessellations can be seen in tiling patterns in palaces from ancient times.

Here are some examples:

This photo shows tiling patterns used in the Alhambra Palace in Spain.

They were made by the Moors who came from North West Africa.

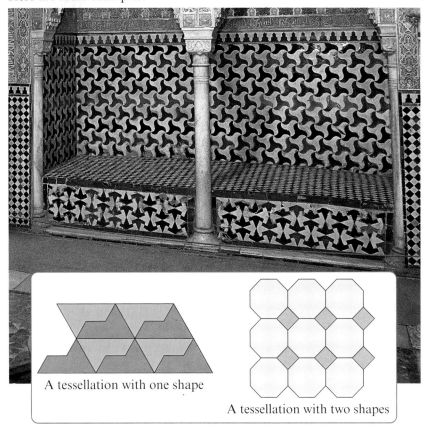

A tessellation with one shape

A tessellation with two shapes

Exercise 36.1
Making tessellations

1 Trace each of these shapes.
Show part of a tessellation with each one.

a   **b**   **c**

 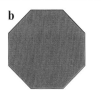 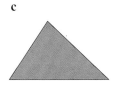

2 This is one tessellation with rectangles.
Find three other tessellations for
the same shaped rectangle.

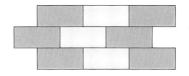

You can use

Skill 5A: *see page 31*

to measure an angle.

3 This regular pentagon will not tessellate on its own.
  a By fitting copies of the pentagon together,
     find one other shape
     which will tessellate with it.
  b What sizes are the internal angles of this shape?

Skill 36A
Finding if a shape
will tessellate

> The interior angles of a
> regular polygon can be
> found using
>
> Skill 19B: *see page 105*

♦ Most regular polygons do not tessellate on their own.

To see why some shapes tessellate you need to think about their
interior angles.

♦ Regular hexagons **will** tessellate

The interior angles of a regular hexagon are
each 120°.

In this tessellation, three of these angles meet
at a point.

So the angles at this point are
120° + 120° + 120° = 360°

The angles at a point must total 360°

So this means there are no gaps between the
hexagons and …
… the hexagons tessellate.

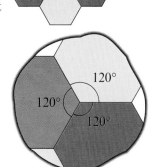

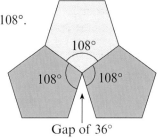

♦ Regular pentagons **will not** tessellate.

The interior angle of a regular pentagon is 108°.

When you fit these together at a point
you get 108° + 108° + 108° = 324°

So there is a gap of 360° – 324° = 36°

So the pentagons do not tessellate.

Gap of 36°

Exercise 36.2
Practising Skill 36A

1 This shows equilateral triangles as
part of a tessellation.
 a How many triangles meet at point P?
 b Calculate the size of angle **s**.

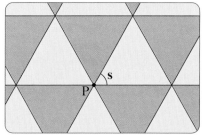

2 This shows part of a tessellation of
squares and a shape A.
 a What is the name of shape A?
 b What size is angle **p**?

Four **q**'s and two **p**'s meet at one point.

 c What must these six angles
 add up to?
 d Calculate the size of angle **q**.

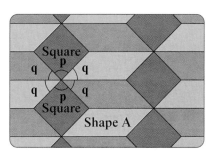

3 This is a tessellation of squares and octagons.
Calculate the size of angle **a**.

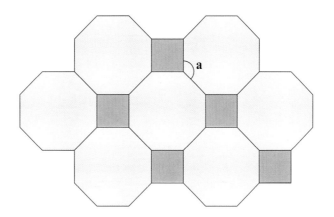

4 This is a tessellation of parallelograms.

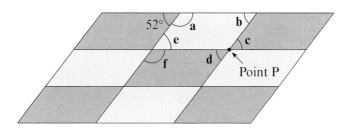

a Calculate the size of angle **a**. Give your reason.
b For each other angle, find its size and give a reason for your answer.

5 **a** Trace this triangle and show that it will tessellate.
b Calculate the size of angle **a**.
c Show, with a diagram, why the angles
of this triangle tell you it must tessellate.

6 **a** Draw any quadrilateral with one side about 5 cm long.
b Measure and list all its interior angles.
c Make a tessellation with your quadrilateral.
d By looking at the angles at a point in your tessellation, show
that it must tessellate.

7 **a** Draw a triangle, any shape.
b See if your triangle will tessellate.
c Try it with another triangle.
What do you discover?
d Show that any triangle, what ever its angles, will tessellate.

When you are asked for
your reason in problems
like this you need to say
something like:

Vertically opposite
angles: *see page 95*

alternate angles:
see page 96

corresponding angles:
see page 96

angles at a point:
see page 94

angles on a line:
see page 95

angle sum of a
triangle: *see page 106*

angle sum of a
quadrilateral:*see page 106*

and so on.

Congruent shapes

♦ Congruent shapes are ones that are the same shape and size as each other. One shape can be fitted exactly over the other by turning or by reflection.

These triangles are all congruent.

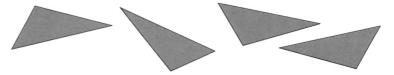

♦ You can use tracing paper to test if two shapes are congruent.

♦ Most tessellations use congruent shapes.

Exercise 36.3
Finding congruent shapes

1 Which of the polygons (B to E) are congruent to polygon A?

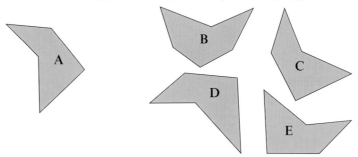

2 Which two of these shapes are congruent?

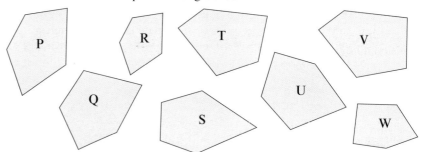

3 List the pairs of congruent shapes in this glass window.

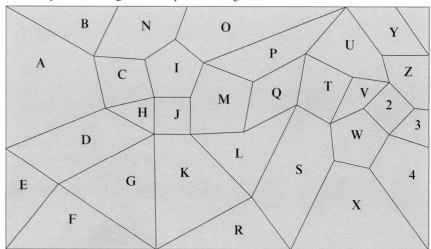

This revises the work in Sections 32 to 36

1 **Skill 32A** and **Skill 32B**

   a Convert 28% to a decimal.

   b Convert 0.35 to a percentage.

2 **Skill 32C**

Calculate 8% of £387.50

3 **Skill 32D**

Write 15 as a percentage of 25.

4 **Skill 33A**

Pattern 1   Pattern 2   Pattern 3

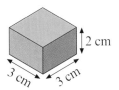

   a How does the pattern grow each time?

   b How many matches will be in pattern 8?

5 **Skill 33B**

This sequence uses the rule:

    Multiply by 5 then add 2

    7, 12, 17, …, …, …

List the next three terms in the sequence.

6 **Skill 34A**

   a Draw the net of this cuboid.

2 cm

3 cm   3 cm

   b Calculate its surface area.

7 **Skill 35A**

This table shows the results of a favourite colour survey.

Colour	Frequency
Red	12
Green	6
Blue	8
Yellow	10
Purple	4
Pink	0
Brown	2

What is the probability that a person chosen at random will have blue as their favourite colour?

8 **Skill 35B**

Three red cards have these symbols on them.

Four blue cards have these symbols

One red and one blue card are picked.

List all the different combinations possible.

9 **Skill 35C** and **Skill 35D**

A coin and a 1 to 5 spinner are thrown together.

   a Copy and complete the sample space diagram to show all the possible outcomes.

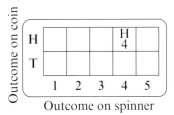

   b What is the probability of getting a tail and a number less than 3?

10 Trace this triangle and show that you can make a tessellation with it.

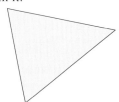

11 **Skill 36A**

An irregular pentagon and a rhombus will tessellate.

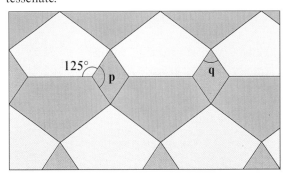

   a Calculate the size of angle **p**.

   b Use your answer to part **a** to calculate the size of angle **q**.

Seager Travel – Disneyland Paris

Welcome to the Magical Land of Dreams
20 miles to the East of Paris

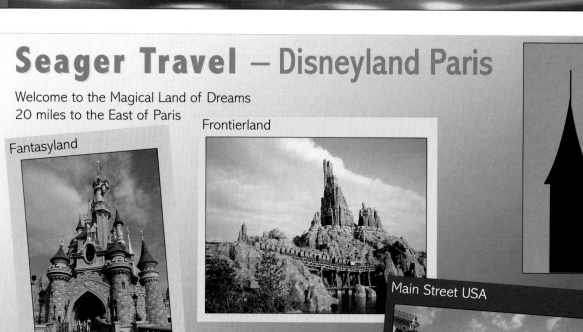

Fantasyland

Frontierland

Main Street USA

Non-discounted park ticket prices 27 March to 26 September		
No. of days	Adult	Child (3–11)
3 Day	£68.00	£52.00
2 Day	£48.00	£37.25
1 Day	£25.00	£19.00

Park opening hours

1 Jan to 19 June	...	Monday – Friday 10 am – 6 pm; Weekends 9 am – 8 pm
20 June to 10 July	...	Daily 9 am – 8 pm
11 July to 31 August	...	Daily 9 am – 11pm
1 September to 31 December	...	Monday – Friday 10 am – 6 pm; Weekends 9 am – 8 pm

All-inclusive Holidays

You pay us, we pay for your Total World of Adventure

With Seager you can either go by car, by train or by air.

The price includes either: your ferry costs, Eurostar train fair or your air fair.

✔ Entry to Disneyland for all your stay.

✔ Your stay at the hotel.

✔ Breakfast each day.

All prices in the table are in pounds.

	No. of adults				child	No. of adults				child	No. of adults				child
	2	3	4	1		2	3	4	1		2	3	4	1	
By Car															
No. of nights 2	179	149	137	259	56	179	149	137	259	56	179	149	137	259	56
3	225	187	165	335	67	225	187	165	335	67	225	187	165	335	67
4	269	216	197	405	76	269	216	197	405	76	269	216	197	405	76
Extra night	37	24	18	65	3	37	24	18	65	3	37	24	18	65	3
By Train															
No. of nights 2	259	245	235	315	123	259	245	235	315	123	259	245	235	315	123
3	307	277	267	385	299	307	277	267	385	299	307	277	267	385	299
4	349	309	289	456	144	349	309	289	456	144	349	309	289	456	144
Extra night	37	24	18	65	3	37	24	18	65	3	37	24	18	65	3
By Air															
No. of nights 2	269	249	237	317	135	269	249	237	317	135	269	249	237	317	135
3	315	285	269	399	159	315	285	269	399	159	315	285	269	399	159
4	355	317	295	465	168	355	317	295	465	168	355	317	295	465	168
Extra night	37	24	18	65	3	37	24	18	65	3	37	24	18	65	3

Prices are for each person   Child price: from age 3 to 14

☐ October–March   ☐ April–June & Sept.   ☐ July–August

1   a   Copy the tower logo.
    b   Draw on all its lines of symmetry.
    c   What is the order of rotational symmetry of
        the logo?

2   The tower logo is in a rectangle 2.6 cm by 6 cm.
    a   Calculate the perimeter of the rectangle.
    b   Calculate the area of the rectangle.

3   At what time does the Disneyland park open
    on 19 July?

4   What is the cost of a 2-day adult ticket to
    Disneyland?

5   a   At what time does the park close on 30 June?
    b   Give this time in 24-hour time.

6   Tracey and Ahmed, and their son Joel who is 8, go
    to Disneyland for a 3-day visit at the end of July.
    a   How much must they pay for tickets to get in?
    b   How many hours could they stay in the park
        each day?

7   Look at Seager Travel's prices.
    What colour would you look up if you wanted to
    go to Disneyland in:
    a   July   b   January   c   June

8   a   With Seager Travel is it cheaper to go by car,
        by train or by air?
    b   Why do you think this is?

9   Look at Seager Travel's 'by car' prices.
    What is the total cost for 1 adult for 4 nights in
    November?

10 Emma and Derek want to fly to Paris for their
    honeymoon at Disneyland in October.
    They go by Seager Travel and stay for 2 nights.
    What will be the total cost?

11 This family is going to Disneyland by train in May:
    Jim (aged 42), Becky (aged 15), Jason (aged 13)
    and Anna (aged 2).
    a   Which of these people count as children with
        Seager Travel?
    b   What colour is the table for May?

    They want to stay for 3 nights.
    c   How much will it cost for the children?
    d   How much will it cost for the adults?
    e   How much will it cost them in total?

12 a   How far is Disneyland from Paris in miles?
    b   1 mile is about 1.6 kilometres.
        How far is Disneyland from Paris in km?

13 a   What time does Disneyland close on a
        Thursday in January?
    b   How many hours is Disneyland open on a
        Thursday in January?
    c   How many more hours is it open on a Saturday
        in January?

14 Here is a receipt for a holiday with Seager Travel.

Seager Travel
Disneyland Holiday

Means of travel	Air
Date of departure	19 July
Length of stay	4 nights
Disneyland Tickets	Free
No. of adults	2 – £ _____
No. of children	2 – £ _____
TOTAL	£ _____

    a   How much is the cost for the adults?
    b   What is the cost for the children?
    c   What is the total cost?

15 For this receipt, calculate the total cost.

Seager Travel
Disneyland Holiday

Means of travel	Train
Date of departure	22 February
Length of stay	5 nights
Disneyland Tickets	Free
No. of adults	1 – £ _____
No. of children	0 – £ _____
TOTAL	£ _____

16 Copy this receipt and fill in the missing amounts.

Seager Travel
Disneyland Holiday

Means of travel	Car
Date of departure	2 August
Length of stay	2 nights
Disneyland Tickets	Free
No. of adults	1 – £ _____
No. of children	3 – £ _____
TOTAL	£ _____

Starting points

You need to know about ...   ... so try these questions

A Converting between metric units

You need to know these conversions:

- **Length**   10 mm = 1 cm   100 cm = 1 metre   1000 m = 1 km

- **Mass**   1000 grams = 1 kg   1000 kg = 1 tonne

- **Capacity**   1 cm³ = 1 millilitre (ml)   1000 ml = 1 litre

B Converting between Imperial units

You need to know these conversions:

- **Length**   12 inches = 1 foot   3 feet = 1 yard   1760 yards = 1 mile

- **Mass**   16 ounces (oz) = 1 pound (lb)   14 pounds = 1 stone

- **Capacity**   1 gallon = 8 pints

- **Time**   60 seconds = 1 minute   60 minutes = 1 hour
       24 hours = 1 day   7 days = 1 week   52 weeks = 1 year

C Approximate conversions between metric and Imperial units

Length   1 foot ≈ 30 cm   1 mile ≈ 1.6 km

Mass   1 kg ≈ 2.2 pounds

Capacity   1 gallon ≈ 4.5 litres

A1   Convert these units:

 a 55 mm to centimetres
 b 80 000 metres to km
 c 5 tonnes to kg
 d 5.6 metres to centimetres
 e 14.2 kg to grams

B1   Convert these units:

 a 96 feet to yards
 b 5 feet 2 inches to inches
 c 2 days to minutes
 d 6 stone 5 pounds to pounds
 e 1 mile to feet
 f 240 gallons to pints
 g 240 pints to gallons

C1   Convert these units:

 a 8 miles to km
 b 8 km to miles
 c 15 kg to pounds
 d 150 cm to feet
 e 27 litres to gallons

Units in problems

Skill 37A
Using units in problems

You may need to use the conversions above in word problems.

Example

A box contains 24 bars of Choc-stix.
Each bar weighs 150 grams.

Does the full box weigh
more or less
than 8 pounds?

- Calculate the weight of 24 bars in grams:

   24 × 150 = 3600 grams

- Convert this to kilograms: 3600 grams = 3600 ÷ 1000 kg
                                              = 3.6 kg

- Convert the kilograms to pounds: 1 kg ≈ 2.2 pounds

   So 3.6 kg = 3.6 × 2.2 pounds
             = 7.92 pounds

So the weight of the box is just less than 8 lb.

Exercise 37.1
Using skill 37A

1 Darren is 6 feet tall. About how tall is he in metres?

2 Mandy weighs 60 kg. Alison weighs 8 stone 10 pounds.

  a Who is heavier, Mandy or Alison?
  b By how much is she heavier?

3 **a** How many ounces of this paste
     must be mixed with 1 gallon of water?
  b How many ounces of paste should be
     mixed with 1 pint of water?

4 Sharron and Wayne are flying to Greece.
They are allowed a total baggage weight of 40 kg.
These are the weights of their bags.

28 lb 4 oz means
28 pounds and 4 ounces.

11 lb 11 oz   28 lb 4 oz   29 lb 8 oz   14 lb 9 oz

  a What is the total weight of their bags in lb and oz?
  b Are they above or below their allowance? Explain your answer.

5 Mike works on a production line.
He must fill an average of 4 boxes with sweets every minute.
He works 7 hours a day and 5 days a week.

How many boxes must he fill with sweets in a week?

Compound units

Skill 37B
Using compound units

◆ A compound unit is one which uses two or more other units.
For example, **miles per hour** uses both **miles** and **hours**.

Other examples include kg per litre, metres per second,
tonnes per square centimetre, and there are many others.

◆ Some other units also count as compound units – for example,
population density, which is measured in people per square km.

Example 1

The population density of Hong Kong is 5308 people per
square kilometre.
The land area of Hong Kong is 1072 square kilometres.
How many people live in Hong Kong?

In each square km there are 5308 people.
So the number of people in Hong Kong is $5308 \times 1072 = 5\,690\,176$
(or just less than 5.7 million).

Example 2

An elephant weighs 12 tonnes and has a total foot area of 800 cm^2.
What is the pressure under the elephant's foot in kg per cm^2?

◆ The elephant's weight is 12×1000 kg $= 12\,000$ kg

◆ The pressure under his feet is Weight ÷ Area $= 12000 \div 800$
$= 15$ kg per cm^2

Exercise 37.2
Using skill 37B

The table shows the population density in different places.

Place	No. of people per km^2
UK	234
Australia	2.1
France	102
Macao	25 882
Norway	10.8
Hong Kong	5308
Mongolia	1.3

1 Which area is most crowded?

2 France and the UK have roughly the same population.

From the table, how do you think their land areas compare?

3 In Mongolia, roughly how many people would live in an area of 100 km^2?

4 In the UK, roughly what area would be used by 700 people?

5 The island of Majorca has an area of about 5000 km^2.
How many people would live on it if it had the population density of:

   a the UK   **b** Macao   **c** Australia?

6 Mark, Amy and Afzal pack boxes in a factory.
They work 8 hours a day for 5 days a week.
Mark's work rate is 24 boxes an hour.

   a Amy packs a box every two minutes.
   What is her work rate in boxes per hour?
   b Afzal packs 224 boxes a day.
   What is his work rate in boxes per hour?
   c How many boxes will each person pack in a week?

7 Denise weighs $8\frac{1}{2}$ stone.
She wears high heels with a total area of 2 cm^2.

   a Calculate her weight in pounds (lb).
   b Convert this weight to kilograms.
   c She stands on her heels.
   What is the pressure underneath in kg per square cm?

You should find that the pressure under Denise's heels is greater than the pressure under the elephant's foot on page 207.

This is not because Denise is very heavy but because the area of her heels is very small.

8 A grape vine grows at the rate of 28 cm a week.

   a How far will the vine grow in 6 weeks?
   b How far will it grow in 6 hours?

The Russian Vine is called the 'mile-a-minute vine' because it grows so fast.

   c If this were true, what would be its speed in miles per hour?
   d How far would Russian Vine grow in a full day?

9 Compost is sold in 80 litre packs.
Each pack costs £4.40.

   a How much does this compost cost in pence per litre?
   b At this rate, what would a 60-litre pack cost?

Gro-rite
ONLY
£4.40
COMPOST
80 litres

Conversion graphs

Skill 37C
Reading a conversion
graph

A conversion graph is used to convert one measure into another.

The peseta is the coin used in Spain and Majorca.

Example

This graph
will convert
pounds to
pesetas ...
or ...
pesetas to
pounds.

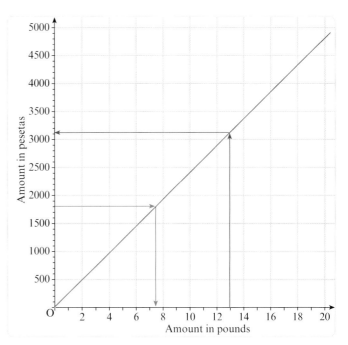

- ◆ To change £13 to pesetas:
  - ❖ Go up from £13 to the line (blue arrow)
  - ❖ Go across to peseta axis
  - ❖ Read off the number of pesetas ... about 3150 pesetas.

- ◆ To change 1800 pesetas to pounds:
  - ❖ Go across from 1800 pesetas (green arrow)
  - ❖ Go down to pounds axis
  - ❖ Read off the number of pounds ... about £7.40.

Exercise 37.3
Practising skill 37C

1 Simon wants to change £10 into Spanish money.
About how many pesetas is £10 worth?

2 Maria has 4000 pesetas to change into pounds.
Roughly what is this worth in pounds?

3 Convert these amounts

    a £4 into pesetas   **b** £12 into pesetas
    c £18 into pesetas   **d** 3500 pesetas into pounds
    e 1500 pesetas into pounds   **f** 4600 pesetas into pounds

4 **a** What is £20 in pesetas?
    b Use your answer to part **a** to say how many pesetas there are to £1.
    c Use the graph to find the value of £1 in pesetas.
    d Which method, **b** or **c**, is more accurate when finding the value of £1?

5 Debbie has £100 to change into pesetas.
How can you use the graph to do this?

6 Use the graph to find the value of 6500 pesetas in pounds.

Exercise 37.4
Using skill 37C

This conversion graph is used to change between a weight in grams and a weight in ounces.

1   This is a recipe:

Mix together:

8 ounces of flour

4 ounces of sugar

3 ounces of nuts

$1\frac{1}{2}$ ounces of butter

Copy this recipe but convert all weights to grams.

2   A recipe asks for 140 grams of flour.
    What is this in ounces?

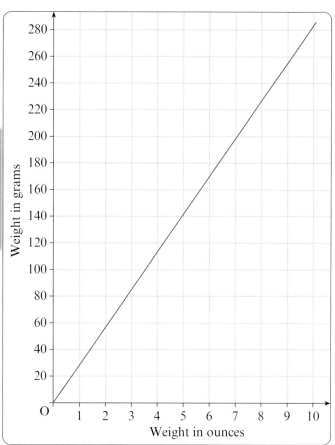

3   Mo has caught a rabbit which weighs 260 grams.
    What is this weight to the nearest ounce?

4   A balloon will lift a maximum weight of 9 ounces.
    How many blocks weighing 40 grams each can the balloon lift?

Fuel consumption measures the amount of fuel a car uses.
A large car or sports car has a higher petrol consumption than a small mini.

This shows that a conversion graph is not always a straight line.

mpg is short for 'miles per gallon'.

5   In the UK, fuel consumption for a car is measured in miles per gallon.
    In Europe they use litres per 100 kilometres as their measure.

    A new car from France has a fuel consumption of 7 litres/100 km.

    What is this in mpg?

6   A Series 1 Land Rover did about 18 mpg. Give this in litres/100 km.

7   The new Ecocar uses 20 litres per 100 km.
    Why does it not deserve its name?

8   The Triumph Herald did about 32 mpg. Give this in litres/100 km.

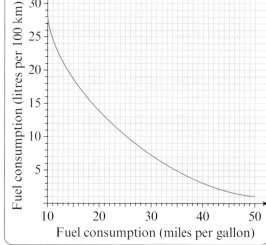

Starting points

You need to know about ...

... so try these questions

A Writing times in the 24-hour clock system

Skill 11A: *see page 56*

A1 Write each time as a 24-hour time.

    a 5.45 pm   **b** 6.46 am
    c 9.35 pm   **d** 3.34 am
    e 12.40 pm   **f** 12.40 am

B Calculating time intervals

Skill 11B: *see page 58*

B1 These times show when lights were turned on and off.

For each light calculate for how long it was on.

On	Off
19:00	21:30
06:25	13:10
15:55	23:30

C Reading timetables

PAIGNTON	0625	0825	0955	1145	1345	1700
TORQUAY	0640	0840	1010	1205	1400	1715
Newton Abbot	0700	0900	1030	1225	1425	1735
EXETER................................	0730	0930	1100	1300	1500	1805
Taunton						1855
Calcot Coachway			1345		1745	
HEATHROW AIRPORT............	1105	1310	1440	1635	1840	2145

C1 Does the 1145 from Paignton get to Heathrow at 3.35 pm or 4.35 pm?

C2 You arrive at Torquay bus station at 1130.

How long must you wait for a bus to Heathrow?

C3 You leave Newton Abbot at 1425 to travel to Heathrow.

  a When should you get there?
  b What is the journey time?

Distance, time and constant speed

Skill 1A
Ordering whole numbers

> mph stands for miles per hour

> mm stands for millimetres

A constant speed is a steady speed.
If you travel at a constant speed you do not slow down or get faster.

The units of speed tell you about how far you will travel in a fixed time.

At a constant speed of		you travel			
56 mph		56 miles	in	1 hour	
...	126 kph	...	126 km	in	1 hour
...	34 m/s	...	34 metres	in	1 second
...	15.5 ft/s	...	15.5 feet	in	1 second
...	65 mm/s	...	65 mm	in	1 second

If you know:
◆ your constant speed,   [Speed]
  and
◆ for how long you travel,   [Time]
  you can calculate
◆ how far you travel.   [Distance]

Example   At a constant speed of 67 mph, how far will you travel in $4\frac{1}{2}$ hours?
              In 1 hour you travel 67 miles.

> $4\frac{1}{2} = 4.5$ miles per hour

So in $4\frac{1}{2}$ hours you travel (67 × 4.5) miles = 301.5 miles.

Exercise 38.1
Calculating distances

1   At a constant speed of 43 mph, how far will you travel in 5 hours?

2   The White Lady Chairlift travels at a constant speed of 2.5 m/s.
    On this chair lift how far will you travel in:

    a 5 seconds   **b** 7.5 seconds   **c** 12 seconds   **d** $21\frac{1}{2}$ seconds

3   Copy and complete this table:

Constant speed	Time travelled	Distance travelled
38 mph	7 hours	■ miles
86 kph	9 hours	■ km
14 m/s	15 seconds	■ metres
12.5 m/s	35 seconds	■ metres
$8\frac{1}{2}$ m/s	21.5 seconds	■ metres
31 mm/s	55 seconds	■ mm
52.5 mph	4 hours	■ miles
0.5 m/s	17 seconds	■ metres
25.4 mph	6 hours	■ miles
38.6 mph	5.5 hours	■ miles

Skill 38A
Finding distance travelled
using a formula

The formula is :   **D**istance = **S**peed × **T**ime

Example

At a constant speed of 9.5 m/s, how far
will a car travel in 17 seconds?

Speed = 9.5 m/s   Time = 17 seconds
$D = S \times T$
$D = 9.5 \times 17$
$D = 161.5$

So at a speed of 9.5 m/s, in 17 seconds a car will travel 161.5 metres.

Exercise 38.2
Practising Skill 38A

1   At a constant speed of 428 kph, find the distance travelled in:

    a 3 hours   **b** 24 hours   **c** $5\frac{1}{2}$ hours   **d** 12.5 hours
    e 15 hours   **f** half an hour   **g** 1hour 30 minutes.

2   At a constant speed of 84 mph, find the distance travelled in:

    a 4 hours   **b** 6.5 hours   **c** 30 minutes
    d 9.5 hours   **e** 15 minutes   **f** 3 hours 15 minutes
    g three-quarters of an hour.

> Think of 15 minutes as a
> fraction of one hour.
> Then think of that fraction
> as a decimal.
>
> 15 minutes is **not**
> 0.15 hours !

3   A Douglas DC-10 jet cruises at a constant speed of 620 mph.
    How far will the jet travel in:

    a 3 hours   **b** 5 hours   **c** $1\frac{1}{2}$ hours   **d** 2.5 hours
    e 15 minutes   **f** 30 minutes   **g** 45 minutes   **h** 3.25 hours
    i $4\frac{3}{4}$ hours   **j** 3 hours 45 minutes?

4   Concorde cruises at a constant speed of 1350 mph.
    At this speed how far will Concorde travel in:

    a 2 hours   **b** 3 hours   **c** 1.5 hours   **d** $2\frac{1}{2}$ hours
    e $\frac{1}{2}$ hour   **f** $\frac{1}{4}$ hour   **g** 3 hours 15 minutes?

5   A snail travels at a speed of 145 mm per minute.
    At this constant speed how far could it travel in 30 minutes?

Average speed

For a journey or part of a journey:

> Average speed = Total distance ÷ Total time

You can think of this with a simple case:

If you travel 40 miles in 4 hours what is your average speed?

40 miles in 4 hours gives an average speed of 10mph.
(40 miles in 4 hours is 10 miles in each hour or 10 miles an hour.)

Skill 38B
Finding average speed using a formula

The formula is

$$\text{Average Speed} = \text{Distance} \div \text{Time}$$

Example 1

A train travelled 342 miles in 5 hours.
Calculate its average speed for the journey.

Distance = 342 miles   Time = 5 hours
$S = D \div T$
$S = 342 \div 5$
$S = 68.4$

So the average speed of the train was 68.4 mph.

Example 2

A taxi travelled 128 miles in 3 hours 30 minutes.
Calculate its average speed for the journey.

Distance = 128 miles   Time = 3.5 hours
$S = D \div T$
$S = 128 \div 3.5$
$S = 36.571... = 36.6$ to 1 dp

So the average speed of the taxi was 36.6 mph (1 dp).

> 36.571... needs to be rounded. Round to 1 dp unless you are told to round in a different way.

Exercise 38.3
Practising Skill 38B

1 Copy and complete this table.
Give average speeds to 1 dp.

Distance travelled	Journey time	Average speed
400 miles	9 hours	■ mph
260 miles	7 hours	■ mph
585 km	8 hours	■ kph
46 metres	2.5 seconds	■ m/s
125 metres	10.5 seconds	■ m/s
455 km	8.5 hours	■ kph
16.6 miles	0.25 hours	■ mph
0.8 metres	0.5 seconds	■ m/s
118 miles	3.75 hours	■ mph
1050 miles	1.75 hours	■ mph

2 A car travels 30 miles in 50 minutes.
   a Is its average speed more or less than 1 mile per minute?
   b What is the average speed of this car in miles per minute.

3 What is the average speed for a journey of 25 miles in 18 minutes?

Time

Converting a fraction to a decimal is:

Skill 22D: *see page 126*

The units of time you use are important.

Say you travel 35 miles in 42 minutes.
The time is less than 1 hour. As a fraction it is $\frac{42}{60}$ of an hour.

$\frac{42}{60}$ as a decimal is 0.7

You travelled 35 miles in 0.7 hours.

So 42 minutes is 0.7 of an hour.

You might need to know what a decimal of an hour is in minutes:
Some decimals you know:
    0.25 hours = 15 minutes
    0.5   hours = 30 minutes
    0.75 hours = 45 minutes

To convert any decimal of an hour to minutes you: multiply by 60.

Say you want 0.56 hours as minutes:
    $0.56 \times 60 = 33.6$ [round this to the nearest minute]

So 0.56 hours is 34 minutes (to the nearest minute).

Exercise 38.4
Calculating with minutes as decimal parts of one hour

1 Find each of these numbers of minutes as a decimal of an hour.
Give each decimal to 2 dp.

a	24	**b**	18	**c**	14	**d**	28	**e**	7	**f**	5	**g**	10
h	35	**i**	25	**j**	32	**k**	48	**l**	12	**m**	56	**n**	6

2 Convert each of these decimals of an hour to minutes.
Give each answer to the nearest minute.

a	0.74	**b**	0.22	**c**	0.48	**d**	0.35	**e**	0.16	**f**	0.36	**g**	0.90
h	0.56	**i**	0.27	**j**	0.85	**k**	0.92	**l**	0.14	**m**	0.16	**n**	0.08

Skill 38C
Finding journey time using a formula

The formula is :
    Time = Distance ÷ Speed

Example   A train travelled 385 miles at an average speed of 54 mph.
How long did this journey take?

Distance = 385 miles   Speed = 54 mph
    $T = D \div S$
    $T = 385 \div 54$
    $T = 7.129... = 7.13$ to 2 dp.

This is 7.13 hours. (0.13 hours in minutes is given by:
    $0.13 \times 60 = 7.8$)

So the journey took 7 hours 8 minutes (to the nearest minute).

Round the 7.8 minutes to 8 minutes.

Exercise 38.5
Practising Skill 38C

1 A car travelled 164 miles at an average speed of 35 mph.
How long did this journey take? Answer to the nearest minute.

2 A plane travelled 2500 miles at an average speed of 570 mph.
How long did this journey take?
Give your answer in hours and minutes.

3 Copy and complete this table.

Distance	Average speed	Time taken (nearest minute)
420 km	70 kph	■
585 miles	130 mph	■
76 miles	32 mph	■
344 km	66 kph	■
3763 km	142 kph	■
550 km	88 kph	■
414 miles	72 mph	■
294 miles	46 mph	■
729 km	108 kph	■
256.15 km	27.25 kph	■

Exercise 38.6
Using Skills 38A, 38B and 38C

1 The bus from Swansea to Cardiff travels 40 miles.
A bus leaves Swansea at 14:28 and gets to Cardiff at 15:43.

a How long did this journey take in hours and minutes?
b What is this time as a decimal?
c Calculate the average speed of the bus.

2 Cara travels from Dover to Leeds to watch her team play.
This is a journey of 247 miles.
Cara does the journey in $4\frac{3}{4}$ hours.

a Give the journey time as a decimal.
b Calculate her average speed for the journey.

For the return journey she says her average speed is 40 mph.

c Find the time taken for this journey in hours and minutes.

3 Ian drives from Paris to Basel.
Paris to Basel is 590 km.
He leaves Paris at 14:50 and arrives in Basel at 9.20 pm.

a What is Ian's journey time?
b Find the average speed for this journey to 1 dp.

4 This table shows distances in miles.

a How far is it from Sheffield to London?
b Lisa lives in Glasgow.
She drove to one of the cities in the table.
She travelled about 400 miles?
Which city did she drive to? Explain.
c The Virgin Cross-Country train from Plymouth to Glasgow takes $8\frac{1}{2}$ hours.
Calculate the average speed of this train.
(Give the speed to the nearest whole number.)

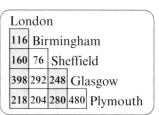

5 Intercity Bus say that their buses average 46 mph.
They plan a journey of 161 miles to Lancaster.
The bus is planned to leave at 16:55.

When should the bus get to Lancaster?

6 In a traffic jam a bus travels 320 metres in half an hour.

At this speed how long will it take the bus to travel 3 kilometres?

Starting points

You need to know about ...   ... so try these questions

A Write fractions in their lowest terms

Skill 22C: *see page 126*

B Convert fractions to decimals

Skill 22D: *see page 126*

C convert fractions to percentages

Skill 22E: *see page 127*

A1 Write each of these fractions in its lowest terms:

a $\frac{12}{15}$ b $\frac{28}{36}$ c $\frac{42}{63}$

d $\frac{55}{132}$ e $\frac{18}{48}$ f $\frac{36}{81}$

B1 Convert each of these fractions to a decimal.

a $\frac{7}{8}$ b $\frac{12}{16}$ c $\frac{12}{15}$

d $\frac{24}{40}$ e $\frac{8}{32}$ f $\frac{3}{24}$

C1 Convert each of these fractions to a percentage.

a $\frac{16}{25}$ b $\frac{5}{8}$ c $\frac{15}{24}$

d $\frac{35}{40}$ e $\frac{18}{48}$ f $\frac{4}{5}$

Percentages to fractions

Skill 39A
Converting a percentage to a fraction

A percentage describes part of a whole.
The whole is 100%.

In the diagram:

♦ 32% is shaded
♦ each small square is $\frac{1}{100}$
♦ $\frac{32}{100}$ is shaded

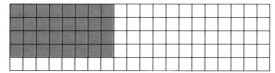

So 32% and $\frac{32}{100}$ describe the same shaded area.

Now $32\% = \frac{32}{100}$ [this fraction is not in its lowest terms]

$= \frac{8}{25}$ [as a fraction in its lowest terms]

So as a fraction 32% is $\frac{8}{25}$.

In words, to convert a percentage to a fraction
you put the percentage over 100 and write the fraction in its lowest terms.

Exercise 39.1
Practising Skill 39A

1 Write each of these percentages as a fraction in its lowest terms.

a 64%   b 72%   c 38%   d 88%   e 90%
f 30%   g 15%   h 18%   i 55%   j 32%
k 45%   l 8%   m 5%   n 44%   o 61%

2 Which of these percentages is the same as $\frac{14}{25}$?

72%   42%   36%   56%   28%

3 Copy and complete this table.

CJ Supplies	Summer sale reductions	
Item	% off	Fraction off
Bath towels	20%	$\frac{1}{5}$
Hand towels	30%	
Flannels	12%	
Sheets	16%	
Tea towels	24%	

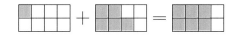
Addition of fractions

Skill 39B
Adding fractions with the same denominator

The denominator is the bottom number of a fraction.

$\frac{3}{4}$ denominator is 4

$\frac{5}{8}$ denominator is 8

$\frac{7}{15}$ denominator is 15

Adding fractions when the denominators are the same.

Say you want to add $\frac{1}{8}$ and $\frac{5}{8}$.

One way to show this is:

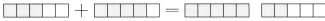

So $\frac{1}{8} + \frac{5}{8} = \frac{6}{8}$.

Examples

$\frac{3}{8} + \frac{1}{8} = \frac{4}{8} = \frac{1}{2}$ [in its lowest terms] $\frac{2}{5} + \frac{1}{5} = \frac{3}{5}$

$\frac{2}{7} + \frac{3}{7} = \frac{5}{7}$ $\frac{5}{16} + \frac{7}{16} = \frac{12}{16} = \frac{3}{4}$ [in its lowest terms]

Sometimes when you add fractions with the same denominator, you get an answer more than a whole one.

Say you add $\frac{3}{5}$ and $\frac{4}{5}$.

One way to show this is:

So $\frac{3}{5} + \frac{4}{5} = \frac{7}{5} = 1\frac{2}{5}$.

Examples

$\frac{2}{3} + \frac{2}{3} = \frac{4}{3} = 1\frac{1}{3}$ $\frac{4}{5} + \frac{4}{5} = \frac{8}{5} = 1\frac{3}{5}$

$\frac{5}{8} + \frac{7}{8} = \frac{12}{8} = 1\frac{4}{8} = 1\frac{1}{2}$ [in its lowest terms]

$\frac{9}{16} + \frac{13}{16} = \frac{22}{16} = 1\frac{6}{16} = 1\frac{3}{8}$ [in its lowest terms]

Exercise 39.2
Practising Skill 39B

1 Add these fractions.
Give each answer in its lowest terms.

a $\frac{2}{9} + \frac{5}{9}$ **b** $\frac{3}{8} + \frac{1}{8}$ **c** $\frac{7}{16} + \frac{5}{16}$ **d** $\frac{3}{5} + \frac{1}{5}$

e $\frac{5}{12} + \frac{11}{12}$ **f** $\frac{3}{8} + \frac{7}{8}$ **g** $\frac{7}{10} + \frac{9}{10}$ **h** $\frac{3}{4} + \frac{3}{4}$

i $\frac{5}{9} + \frac{7}{9}$ **j** $\frac{9}{16} + \frac{11}{16}$ **k** $\frac{3}{10} + \frac{9}{10}$ **l** $\frac{1}{12} + \frac{7}{12}$

m $\frac{4}{9} + \frac{8}{9}$ **n** $\frac{11}{12} + \frac{7}{12}$ **o** $\frac{5}{16} + \frac{7}{16} + \frac{9}{16}$

2 Which of these gives an answer of $1\frac{3}{4}$? (In its lowest terms.)

a $\frac{7}{8} + \frac{7}{8}$ **b** $\frac{15}{16} + \frac{13}{16}$ **c** $\frac{5}{12} + \frac{11}{12} + \frac{5}{12}$ **d** $\frac{7}{10} + \frac{6}{10}$

Skill 39C
Adding fractions when the denominators are not the same

Finding equivalent fractions is:

Skill 22B: *see page 125*

Adding fractions when the denominators are not the same.

Here equivalent fractions can help.

Example $\frac{5}{8} + \frac{3}{4}$

Now $\frac{3}{4} = \frac{6}{8}$

 or

So $\frac{5}{8} + \frac{3}{4} = \frac{5}{8} + \frac{6}{8}$

$= \frac{11}{8}$

$= 1\frac{3}{8}$

So $\frac{5}{8} + \frac{3}{4} = 1\frac{3}{8}$.

Exercise 39.3
Practising Skill 39C

1 Add these fractions.
Give each answer in its lowest terms.

a $\frac{3}{4} + \frac{3}{8}$ **b** $\frac{1}{4} + \frac{5}{8}$ **c** $\frac{3}{4} + \frac{7}{8}$ **d** $\frac{3}{4} + \frac{1}{8}$

e $\frac{3}{4} + \frac{5}{12}$ **f** $\frac{3}{4} + \frac{7}{12}$ **g** $\frac{1}{4} + \frac{11}{12}$ **h** $\frac{1}{4} + \frac{5}{12}$

i $\frac{3}{8} + \frac{5}{16}$ **j** $\frac{5}{8} + \frac{3}{16}$ **k** $\frac{5}{8} + \frac{7}{16}$ **l** $\frac{7}{8} + \frac{9}{16}$

2 Give each of these answers in its lowest terms.

a $\frac{3}{5} + \frac{7}{10}$ **b** $\frac{3}{10} + \frac{1}{5}$ **c** $\frac{4}{5} + \frac{7}{10}$ **d** $\frac{2}{5} + \frac{9}{10}$

3 Give each of these answers in its lowest terms

a $\frac{3}{4} + \frac{5}{16}$ **b** $\frac{1}{4} + \frac{7}{16}$ **c** $\frac{3}{4} + \frac{9}{16}$ **d** $\frac{1}{4} + \frac{3}{16}$

4 Give each of these answers in its lowest terms.

a $\frac{1}{4} + \frac{1}{3}$ **b** $\frac{3}{4} + \frac{2}{3}$ **c** $\frac{3}{4} + \frac{2}{5}$ **d** $\frac{1}{4} + \frac{4}{5}$

e $\frac{3}{5} + \frac{3}{4}$ **f** $\frac{4}{5} + \frac{1}{3}$ **g** $\frac{2}{3} + \frac{2}{5}$ **h** $\frac{1}{5} + \frac{1}{4}$

i $\frac{1}{3} + \frac{1}{5}$ **j** $\frac{2}{3} + \frac{3}{5}$ **k** $\frac{3}{5} + \frac{2}{3}$ **l** $\frac{4}{5} + \frac{1}{3}$

Skill 39D
Subtracting fractions

Sometimes we want to subtract fractions when the denominators are the same.

Examples $\frac{5}{8} - \frac{3}{8} = \frac{2}{8} = \frac{1}{4}$ [in its lowest terms]

$\frac{7}{16} - \frac{5}{16} = \frac{2}{16} = \frac{1}{8}$ [in its lowest terms]

$\frac{7}{10} - \frac{3}{10} = \frac{4}{10} = \frac{2}{5}$ [in its lowest terms]

Where there are whole numbers.

Examples $1\frac{3}{8} - \frac{7}{8} = \frac{11}{8} - \frac{7}{8}$

$\qquad\qquad = \frac{4}{8} = \frac{1}{2}$ [in its lowest terms]

$2\frac{3}{5} - \frac{4}{5} = \frac{13}{5} - \frac{4}{5}$

$\qquad\qquad = \frac{9}{5}$

$\qquad\qquad = 1\frac{4}{5}$

Sometimes we want to subtract fractions when the denominators are not the same.

Example $\frac{7}{8} - \frac{3}{16} = \frac{14}{16} - \frac{3}{16}$

$\qquad\qquad = \frac{11}{16}$

Exercise 39.4
Practising Skill 39D

1 Subtract these fractions.
Give each answer in its lowest terms.

a $\frac{11}{16} - \frac{5}{16}$ **b** $\frac{7}{8} - \frac{3}{8}$ **c** $\frac{9}{10} - \frac{3}{10}$ **d** $\frac{9}{16} - \frac{7}{16}$

e $\frac{15}{16} - \frac{9}{16}$ **f** $\frac{9}{10} - \frac{7}{10}$ **g** $\frac{11}{12} - \frac{7}{12}$ **h** $\frac{7}{12} - \frac{5}{12}$

2 Give each of these answers in its lowest terms.

a $1\frac{5}{8} - \frac{7}{8}$ **b** $1\frac{3}{16} - \frac{11}{16}$ **c** $1\frac{7}{10} - \frac{9}{10}$ **d** $2\frac{1}{8} - \frac{5}{8}$

e $3\frac{1}{4} - \frac{3}{4}$ **f** $1\frac{3}{8} - \frac{5}{8}$ **g** $2\frac{1}{10} - \frac{7}{10}$ **h** $3\frac{3}{5} - \frac{4}{5}$

3 Give each of these answers in its lowest terms.

a $\frac{9}{16} - \frac{3}{8}$ **b** $\frac{3}{4} - \frac{3}{8}$ **c** $\frac{4}{5} - \frac{7}{10}$ **d** $\frac{5}{8} - \frac{3}{16}$

Starting points

You need to know about ...

... so try these questions

A Calculating the area of a rectangle

Skill 12A: *see page 68*

A1 Calculate the area of each rectangle.

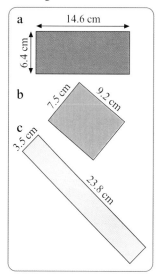

a 14.6 cm 6.4 cm

b 7.5 cm 9.2 cm

c 3.5 cm 23.8 cm

B Calculating the area of a triangle

Skill 12B: *see page 70*

B1 Calculate the area of each triangle.

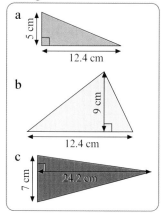

a 5 cm 12.4 cm

b 9 cm 12.4 cm

c 7 cm 24.2 cm

C The difference between volume and capacity.

You can think of it in this way:

Capacity is the space inside a container
Volume is the amount of space that something takes up

A bottle might have a capacity of 250 ml, but
the volume of liquid inside the bottle might be only 120 ml.

Capacity and volume are not the same!
(The same units are used for both, for example cm³.)

C1 Copy this sentence filling in the missing words.

A bucket has a ◯ of 15 litres. I didn't fill it. I just put a ◯ of 12 litres in the bucket.

C2 A bottle has a capacity of 225 ml. A volume of 220 ml of liquid is put in the bottle. Is the bottle full? Explain.

C3 An oil tank has a capacity of 300 litres; it is half full.

What is the volume of oil in the tank?

The volume of cuboids

| When you count cubes, you have to think of the cubes you can't see in the diagram. |

The simplest way to work out a volume is to count cubes.

Example

Calculate the volume of this block of cubes.

You might see 3 layers of 16 cubes which gives a count of 48 cubes.

You might see 4 rows of 12 cubes which gives a count of 48 cubes.

If each cube is a 1 cm cube then:

The volume of the block is 48 cm³.

| Volume is given in cubic units. cm³ stands for cubic centimetres. |

Skill 40A
Calculating the volume of a cuboid using the formula

The formula for the volume of a cuboid is:

Volume = $L \times W \times H$

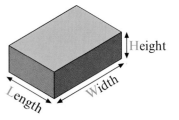

Example

Calculate the volume of this box.

Volume = $L \times W \times H$

$V = 4.5 \times 6 \times 7.5$
$V = 202.5$

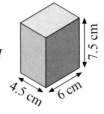

So the volume of the cuboid is 202.5 cm³.

Exercise 40.1
Practising Skill 40A

1 Calculate the volume of each cuboid.
Give each answer to 1 dp.

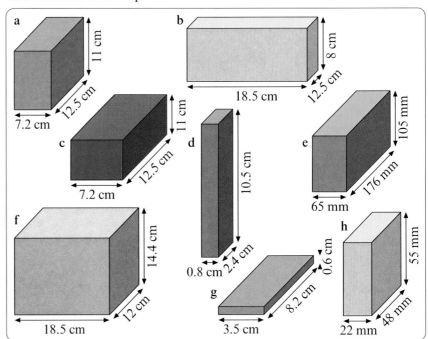

Exercise 40.2
Using Skill 40A

1 A matchbox measures 32 mm by 12 mm by 40 mm.

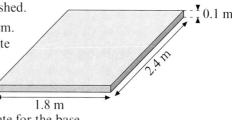

a Calculate the volume of the box.

These boxes are sold in packs of 12.
The boxes are packed in 3 layers of 4 boxes.

b Sketch a pack of 12 boxes.
c What does a pack of 12 boxes measure?
d Show that the volume of the pack is 184 320 mm³.

2 A concrete base is put down for a shed.

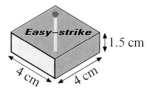

a Give the height of the base in cm.
b Calculate the volume of concrete used for the base.

Readymix concrete was used, at a price of £65 per m³.

c Calculate the cost of the concrete for the base.

3 Easy-strike Matches want a box with a volume of 24 cm³.

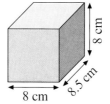

a Show that this box has a volume of 24 cm³.

Jenny designed a box with a volume of 24 cm³ with a height of 3 cm.

b Sketch and show the measurements of two possible boxes for Jenny's design.

Javed designed a box that measured 4.2 cm by 1.8 cm by 3.2 cm.
He said that his design had a volume of 24 cm³ when rounded to the nearest whole number.

c Do you agree with Javed? Explain your answer.

4 Connor was asked to design a milk carton.
The carton was to hold 550 ml of milk.
This was his design. It was rejected.

a Calculate the volume of the carton.
b Explain why you think Connor's design was rejected.

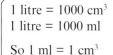

1 litre = 1000 cm³
1 litre = 1000 ml

So 1 ml = 1 cm³

5 This box has a volume of 219 375 mm³.

a Find the height of the box.
b Give the measurements of the box in cm.
c Give the volume of the box in cm³.

The box is filled with seeds that weigh 2 grams per cm³. 65 mm · 45 mm

d Give the weight of the seeds in the box to the nearest 10 grams.

6 A freezer in a supermarket is 3.5 metres long, 1 metre wide and 80 cm high.

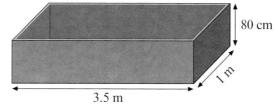

a What is the height of the freezer in metres?
b Calculate the volume of the freezer in cubic metres.

The volume of a prism

A cross-section is the shape you make when you slice a solid in one direction.

A prism is a solid with a cross-section that does not change.

That is, in the same direction, each cross-section is the same.

Sometimes this is called: a uniform cross-section.

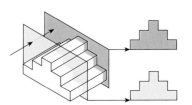

Skill 40B
Calculating the volume of a prism using the formula

The volume of a prism is given by:

Volume = Area of cross-section × Length

Example 1

Calculate the volume of this prism.

The cross-section is a triangle.

V = Area cross-section × Length
$V = 0.5 \times 15 \times 7 \times 12$
$V = 630$

So the volume of the prism is 630 cm³.

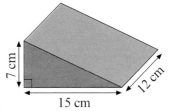

Finding the area of a triangle is:

Skill 12B: *see page 70*

Example 2

Calculate the volume of this prism.

V = Area of cross-section × Length
$V = 15 \times 3.5$
$V = 52.5$

So the volume of the prism is 52.5 cm³.

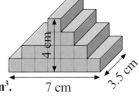

Exercise 40.3
Practising Skill 40B

1 Calculate the volume of each prism.
Give each answer to 1 dp.

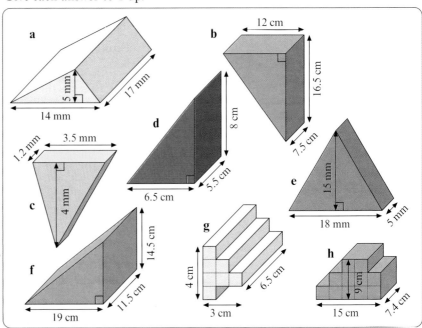

Starting points

You need to know about ...   ... so try these questions

A Rounding to the nearest 10, 100, 1000 etc.

Skill 9A: *see page 49*

A1 Round each of these numbers to the nearest 1000.
  a 15602   **b** 2485   **c** 838

A2 Round each of these numbers to the nearest 10.
  a 5704   **b** 6997   **c** 996

B Rounding to find approximate answers.

Skill 9B: *see page 50*

B1 By rounding, find an approximate answer to each of these:
  a 34×58 **b** 18×72
  c 27×96 **d** 46×62
  e 14×88 **f** 38×75

C Rounding decimal values to the nearest whole number.

Skill 25A: *see page 139*

C1 Round each of these decimal values to the nearest whole number.
  a 27.616   **b** 134.488
  c 6.503   **d** 12.089
  e 257.395   **f** 799.765

D Rounding to decimal places.

Skill 25B: *see page 140*
Skill 25C: *see page 141*

D1 Round each of these to the number of dp shown.
  a 34.639 (1 dp)
  b 138.0881 (2 dp)
  c 0.067 45 (3 dp)
  d 5.600 572 (4 dp)

Rounding in calculations

You can round numbers in calculations:
♦ before you start to calculate
♦ at the end [the answer]

With each method you will have a different approximate answer.

You can see the difference with these calculations for area.
Calculate the area of this rectangle.

19.4 cm — 3.7 cm

≈ stands for:
is approximately equal to

Rounding at the start
Area = 19.4×3.7
$A \approx 19 \times 4$
$A \approx 76$

So area is approx. 76 cm².

Rounding at the end
Area = 19.4×3.7
$A = 71.78$
$A \approx 72$

So area is approx 72 cm².

Exercise 41.1
Rounding in calculations

1 Calculate the area of shape A.
  a Round at the start of the calculation.
  b Round at the end of the calculation.

21.8 cm

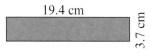
Shape A — 5.4 cm

2 Calculate the area of shape B.
  a Round at the start of the calculation
  b Round at the end of the calculation.

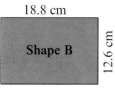

18.8 cm

Shape B

12.6 cm

3 Calculate the area of shape C.
  a Round at the start of the calculation.
  b Round at the end of the calculation.

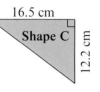

16.5 cm

Shape C

12.2 cm

4 Calculate the area of shape D.
  a Round at the start of the calculation.
  b Round at the end of the calculation.

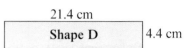

21.4 cm

Shape D

4.4 cm

5 **a** Calculate the volume of this solid.
  b Round your answer to 1 dp.
  c Round the length, width, and height of the solid to the nearest whole number.
  d Use these rounded measurements and calculate the approximate volume of the solid.
  e Which rounded answer do you think gives the better approximate volume of the solid? Explain.

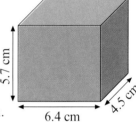

5.7 cm

6.4 cm

4.5 cm

Errors in calculations

Rounding at the start of a calculation is fine as a rough approximation.
For a better approximation round at the end.
Rounding will always give an error.

This shows the rounding error when finding area.

Round all numbers to 1 dp at the start.
  Area ≈ 3.2 × 6.4
    ≈ 20.48 m^2

6.38 m

3.15 m

Without rounding:
  Area = 3.15 × 6.38
    = 20.097 m^2

The error made by rounding to 1 dp is:
  20.48 – 20.097 = 0.383

So the error made by rounding to 1 dp ≈ 0.383 m^2.

1 **a** Calculate the area of shape E.
  b Round the length and the width to 1 dp.
  c Calculate the area using the rounded values.
  d Calculate the error made by rounding to 1 dp.

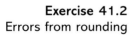

5.72 m

Shape E

4.28 m

2 **a** Round the length and width of shape F to 1 dp.
  b With these rounded values calculate the area and perimeter of shape F.
  c Calculate the area and perimeter of shape F.
  d What is the error from rounding in the area?
  e What is the error from rounding in the perimeter?

12.38 m

Shape F

3.44 m

3 A pane of glass is 3.65 m long and 2.82 m wide.

   a Round the measurements to the nearest whole number.

   b Round the measurements to 1 dp.

   c What is the area of the pane of glass?

   d What is the error in the area when the measurements are rounded to 1 dp at the start?

4 Jake rounds the measurements of this rectangle. The length and width are to the nearest whole number.

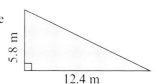

   a Copy and complete: The longest the two measurements could have been is 5.■ m, and 3.■ m.

   b What is the largest the area might be?

   c What is the shortest the measurements might have been?

   d What is the smallest the area might be?

5 Sam says that the approximate area of this triangle is 36 m².

   a Explain any rounding you think she has done.

   b Calculate the error in what Sam says.

6 Darren bought 14 m² of wall tiles.
Darren was told that the wall was approximately 7 metres long and 2 metres high.

He measured the wall and found it to be:
only 6.5 m long, but 2.4 metres high.

   a Will he have enough tiles for the wall?

   b Explain your answer, and any error you find.

7 This diagram shows Asa's sketch of a car park.

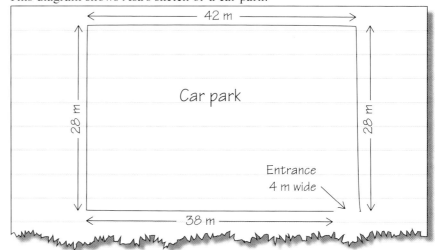

Asa approximates to the nearest whole number.

The car park is to be fenced.
Asa ordered 136 metres of fencing.
Jane said he would either have too much or too little fencing.
Derek said that he should have ordered 138 m to be sure to have enough.

   a Explain what you think Jane meant.

   b Explain how you think Derek came up with a figure of 138 m.

Asa said that he expected to have fence left over.

   c What can you say about the measurements before rounding?

Starting points
You need to know about ...

... so try these questions

A Area and perimeter

see page 68

This is the total distance around the edge of a shape.

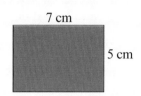
7 cm
5 cm

The periemeter of this rectangle is:
5 cm + 7 cm + 5 cm + 7 cm = 24 cm

A1 Estimate the shaded area.

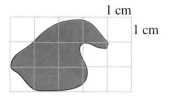
1 cm
1 cm

A2 Find the perimeter.

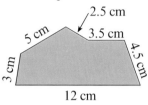
2.5 cm
5 cm
3.5 cm
3 cm
4.5 cm
12 cm

B Calculating the area of a rectangle

Skill 12A: *see page 68*

This is the amount of surface covered by a shape.

To find the area of shape A:
put a centimetre grid over the shape, it shows that the area is about 6 cm².

(cm² stands for square centimetres.)

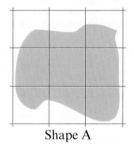

Shape A

B1 Calculate the areas.

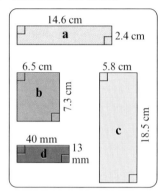
14.6 cm
a
2.4 cm
6.5 cm
b
7.3 cm
5.8 cm
c
18.5 cm
40 mm
d
13 mm

B2 A rectangle has an area of 51 cm². Its length is 7.5 cm. Calculate its width.

C Calculating the area of a triangle

Skill 12B: *see page 70*

C1 Calculate the areas.

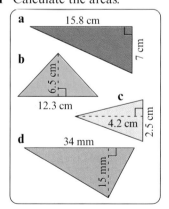
a
15.8 cm
7 cm
b
6.5 cm
12.3 cm
c
4.2 cm
2.5 cm
d
34 mm
15 mm

C2 A triangle has a base of 15 cm.
Its area is 142 .5 cm².

Calculate the height of the triangle.

Area of composite shapes

A composite shape is a shape made up of two or more other shapes.

Shape A is a composite shape.
It is made up of a rectangle and a triangle.

Skill 42A
Calculating the area of a
composite shape

One way to find the area of a composite shape is to:

♦ split the composite shape into shapes you can find the area of
[you might need to draw a new diagram]

♦ calculate the area of each shape part
[you might have to work out some lengths]

♦ add the areas of all the shape parts.

Example

You can split shape B into
two rectangles in 2 ways.

Calculate the area of Shape B

Shape B can be split into
two rectangles:
part 1 and part 2.

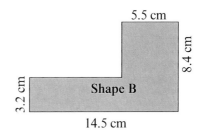

You need to find
the length of part 1

Length of shape B =
Length of Part 1 + Length of part 2

$14.5 = ■ + 5.5$
$■ = 9$

Area of part 1
$A = L \times W$
$A = 9 \times 3.5$
$A = 31.5$

Area of part 2
$A = L \times W$
$A = 5.5 \times 8.4$
$A = 46.2$

Area of part 1 + Area of part 2 = 31.5 + 46.2 = 77.7

So the area of shape B is 77.7 cm².

Exercise 42.1
Practising Skill 42A

1 Calculate the area of each shape.

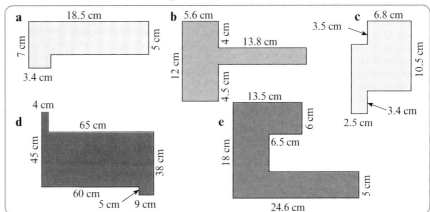

A composite shape can be made up of different shapes.

Example

Calculate the area of shape C.

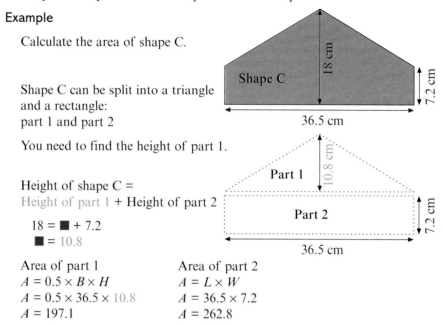

Shape C can be split into a triangle
and a rectangle:
part 1 and part 2

You need to find the height of part 1.

Height of shape C =
Height of part 1 + Height of part 2

$18 = \blacksquare + 7.2$

$\blacksquare = 10.8$

Area of part 1	Area of part 2
$A = 0.5 \times B \times H$	$A = L \times W$
$A = 0.5 \times 36.5 \times 10.8$	$A = 36.5 \times 7.2$
$A = 197.1$	$A = 262.8$

Area of part 1 + Area of part 2 = 197.1 + 262.8 = 459.9

So the area of shape C is 459.9 cm².

2   Calculate the area of each shape.

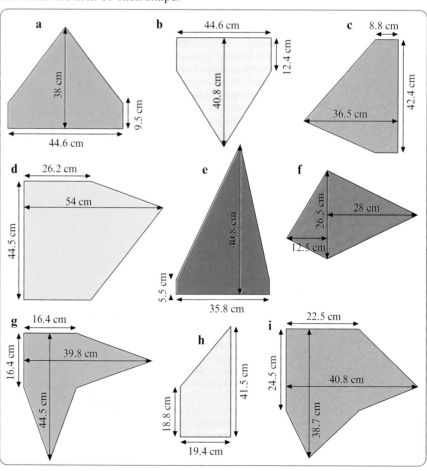

Perimeter of composite shapes

Skill 42B
Calculating the perimeter of a composite shape

The **perimeter** is the total distance around the edges of a shape.

You might need to work out the length of one or more edges before you can find the perimeter.

Example

Calculate the perimeter of shape D.

To calculate length 1:
    Length 1 + 5.5 = 13.8
So   Length 1 = 8.3

To calculate length 2:
    Length 2 + 3.8 = 12.6
So   Length 2 = 8.8

The perimeter of shape B is given by:
    P = 5.5 + 12.6 + 13.8 + 3.8 + 8.3 + 8.8 = 52.8

So the perimeter of shape D is 52.8 cm.

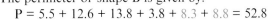

Exercise 42.2
Practising Skill 42B

1   Calculate the perimeter of each shape.

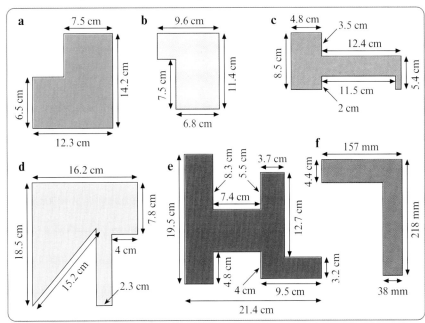

Exercise 42.3
Using Skills 42A and 42B

1   **a** Calculate the area of this lawn.

        Turf for the lawn was £6.80 per square metre.

    b Calculate the total cost of the turf.
        Give your answer to the nearest penny.
    c Calculate the perimeter of the lawn.

        A metal edge is put around the lawn.
        The metal strip costs £6.99 per metre.
    d Calculate the total cost of the metal strip (to the nearest pound).

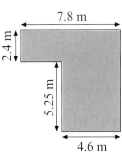

2 The diagram shows the plan of a room.

   a Sketch the shape and show that it can be split into 2 rectangles and a triangle.

   b Calculate the floor area.

The room is carpeted with carpet that costs £11.99 per m².

   c Find the total cost of carpet for the room. Give your answer to the nearest pound.

Alex estimates the perimeter of the floor as 25 m.

A cable is fixed around the edge of the floor. The cable costs 99p per metre.

   d To the nearest pound, estimate the total cost of the cable.

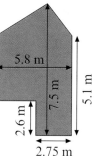

3 The diagram shows the glass for a shop window.

   a Calculate the area of the sheet of glass.

A sealing strip is put on the edge of the glass.

   b Calculate the total length of strip needed.

A security wire is fixed to the glass. It is fixed 20 cm from the edges of the glass.

   c How much security wire is needed?

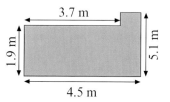

Composite shapes and volume

Example

Calculate the volume of this solid.

Volume V = Area of cross-section × Length

Area of cross-section is:
Part 1   12.8 × 10.4 = 133.12
Part 2   14.1 × 7.5 = 105.75

Part 1 + Part 2 = 133.12 + 105.75
                   = 238.87

Length = 18 cm
V = 238.87 × 18
V = 4299.66

So the volume of the solid is 4299.66 cm³.

> Calculating the volume of a prism is:
>
> Skill 40B: *see page 222*

> 14.1 cm is the length of part 2. (24.5 − 10.4 = 14.1)

Exercise 42.4
Calculating volume

1 Calculate the volume of each solid.

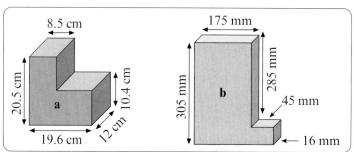

This revises the work in Sections 37 to 42

1 Skill 37A
Ian weighs 72 kg, Kim weighs 11 stone 12 pounds.
a Who is heavier?
b By how much?

2 Skill 37B
The population density of an island is
3658 people per square kilometre.
The island has a land area of 374 km².
How many people live on the island?

3 Skill 37C
Use the conversion graph on page 211.
a Convert 4000 pesetas to pounds.
b Convert £6.50 to pesetas.
c Convert £42.50 to pesetas.
d On holiday in Palma, Javed bought a camera.
The camera cost 6600 pesetas.
He saw the same model camera in York for £25.99.
Which camera was cheaper? Explain.

4 At a constant speed of 58 kph how far will you travel in 6 hours?

5 Skill 38A
An aircraft cruises at a constant speed of 568 mph.
At this speed how far will it travel in:
a 5 hours **b** $3\frac{1}{2}$ hours **c** 15 minutes?

6 Skill 38B
A car travels 95 miles in $2\frac{1}{2}$ hours.
What is the average speed of the car?

7 A train did a journey of 508.5 miles in 9 hours.
Calculate the average speed of the train.

8 Find each of these as a decimal of an hour to 2 dp.
a 35 min **b** 55 min **c** 9 min

9 Convert each of these to a number of minutes
(to the nearest minute).
a 0.55 hours **b** 0.24 hours **c** 0.39 hours

10 Skill 38C
A car did 188 miles at an average speed of 75 mph.
Calculate the time taken for the journey:
a in hours (as a decimal)
b in hours and minutes.

11 Skill 39A
Write each of these percentages as a fraction in its lowest terms.
a 56% **b** 24% **c** 85% **d** 8% **e** 5%

12 Skill 39B
Add these fractions. Give lowest terms answers.
a $\frac{7}{8} + \frac{3}{8} =$ **b** $\frac{2}{9} + \frac{4}{9} =$ **c** $\frac{7}{16} + \frac{11}{16} =$

13 Skill 39C
Add these fractions.
Give each answer in its lowest terms.
a $\frac{3}{4} + \frac{5}{8} =$ **b** $\frac{2}{3} + \frac{7}{10} =$ **c** $\frac{3}{5} + \frac{7}{8} =$

14 Skill 39D
Subtract these fractions.
Give each answer in its lowest terms.
a $\frac{5}{8} - \frac{1}{8} =$ **b** $\frac{7}{12} - \frac{5}{12} =$ **c** $\frac{9}{16} - \frac{5}{16} =$
d $1\frac{5}{8} - \frac{3}{4} =$ **e** $2\frac{1}{2} - \frac{3}{5} =$ **f** $3\frac{1}{4} - \frac{7}{10} =$

15 Skill 40A
Find the volume of each cuboid to 1 dp.

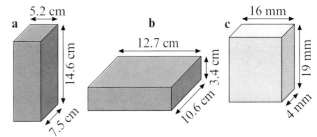

16 Skill 40B
Calculate the volume of each prism to 1 dp.

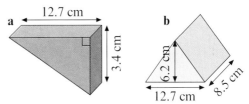

17 **a** Calculate the area of this rectangle.

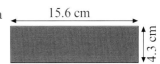

b Round the length and width to the nearest whole number.
c Find the area with the rounded values.
d Find the error caused by rounding.

18 A playground is a rectangle 15.75 metres long and 12.45 metres wide.
a Calculate the area of the playground.
b Give the area of the playground to 2 dp.
c Give the area to the nearest whole number
d Give the measurements rounded to 1 dp.
e Calculate the area using the rounded values.
f Find the error in the area by rounding the length and the width to 1 dp.

19 Coaches take fans to a match. Each coach carries 58 fans and there are 44 coaches.

Approximately how many fans went by coach?

—— Airport News ——

Early morning service started by Station/Air Link

Now you can travel from the airport to the station before 8am thanks to this new service.
This new timetable starts on Thursday 1 September.

Station/Air Link Coaches					
AIRPORT	BRIDGE ST	BANK	MOTEL	HIGH ST	STATION
0610	0624	0630	0636	0648	0655
0640	0654	07000	0706	0718	0725
0700	——	——	——	0720	0730
0720	0735	——	0750	0805	0815
0750	0805	0810	——	0825	0835

Passenger numbers still rise

In June this year a total of 36 600 foreign visitors use the airport. ¼ of the visitors came from the USA, ⅝ came from Europe and the rest came from Canada.
Car hire figures for June show that 14% of all foreign visitors hired a car for at least a day.

June spending by foreign visitors tops £7½ million.

The tourist board tells us that in June each foreign visitor spent an average of £200 each in our shops and hotels at the airport. Business is definitely booming !

Design a new airport logo and win £500

It's so simple! All you have to do is to draw your logo design inside a rectangle that is 22.5 cm long and 16.5 cm wide.
Colour or black-and-white? Well, that's up to you!
Remember all entries must be in by 30 November.
How will you spend the £500?

New baggage wagons arrive.

No more wet baggage! From 1 August we will be using our new covered wagons.
This is just another way that we are improving our services.
Passengers to fly from here because we care!

Security checks out !

With our new staff and machines we are proud to announce that we can now check up to 1350 passengers an hour.

Baggage waiting times cut

Spending on baggage handling is paying off. Our latest survey shows that the average waiting time for baggage is now only 21.5 minutes.

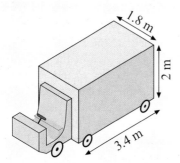

1.8 m
2 m
3.4 m

Weight when empty 232 kg.

1 **a** What is the journey time for the 06:10 bus from the Airport to the Station?

 b Write this time as a decimal of one hour.

2 From the Airport to the Station is 12 miles. Calculate the average speed of the 06:10 bus from the airport to the station.

3 Calculate the average speed of:

 a the 07:00 from the Airport to the Station

 b the 07:20 from the Airport to the Station.

4 You arrive at the Airport bus stop at four minutes past seven.

 a How long will you have to wait for a bus to the High St?

 b At what time will you get to the High St?

5 What is the shortest journey time from Bridge St to High St?

6 Kim looked at the timetable and said that the 06:10 bus, and the 06:40 from the Airport to the Station had the same average speed.

 How could she tell? Explain.

7 Swiftlink Buses started a service from the Airport to the Station.
 They said their buses would average a speed of 20 mph for the journey.

 Calculate the journey time in minutes.

8 How many visitors came into the airport from Europe?

9 How many visitors came in from Canada?

10 How many foreign visitors hired a car for at least one day?

11 In June, how much was spent in total by foreign visitors in the airport shops and hotels?

12 Do you agree with the headline about visitors spending £7$\frac{1}{2}$ million in June? Explain.

13 Calculate the area of the rectangle that the new airport logo must fit inside.

14 If Alison wins the logo competition she will convert the £500 into pesetas for her holiday in Spain.
 She expects to get 242 pesetas to the pound.
 At this rate, how many pesetas will the £500 buy?

15 Alison started her design on 15 July and finished it on 8 November. How many days is this?

16 Alison worked out that she did an average of 2.5 hours a day on her design.

 Calculate how long in total she spent on the design.

17 Calculate the volume of one of the new covered luggage trolleys in m^3.

18 A case has a volume of about 0.11m^3.
 Roughly how many cases can be fitted in one of the new covered baggage trolleys?

 Explain how you worked out your answer.

19 On average a case weighs 40 lb.
 Calculate the weight of a new baggage trolley when it is loaded with 85 cases.
 Give your answer to the nearest 100 kg.

20 This data shows the number of minutes people had to wait for their baggage.

Waiting times in minutes

16, 29, 22, 24, 16, 19, 22, 18, 15, 15, 24, 20, 14,

23, 25, 26, 25, 17, 24, 20, 25, 26, 24, 21, 22, 18,

23, 14, 18, 17, 21, 20, 18, 14, 28, 29, 28, 15, 12, 13

 a Make a frequency table for this data.
 Use groups of 11–15, 16–20, 21–25, 26–30

 b Which is the modal group?

 c What is the median waiting time?

 d Calculate the mean waiting time.

 e Which average would you have used for the headline? Explain.

21 In June 1.5% of the spending by foreign visitors was in the Duty-Free shop.
 Misha said this was over £100 000.
 Do you agree? Explain.

22 **a** How many security checks can be carried out in 20 minutes?

 b Security were working as fast as possible. They checked 1215 people.
 How many minutes did this take?

23 In a very busy time in August, over 3 days security checked 92 736 passengers.

 a At a steady rate, how many passengers an hour was this?

 b Security checks cost 38p per passenger. How much an hour was spent on security checks (to the nearest 50p)?

 c About 2$\frac{1}{2}$% of the passengers had their cases searched.
 About how many passengers was this?

 d About 7% of the passengers did not lock their cases.
 About how many passengers was this?

24 You arrive at the airport at 07:28 and have the average waiting time for your baggage.

 How many minutes have you to catch the next bus to the station?

Stage 4 End points

You should be able to ...   ... so try these questions

A Convert a percentage to a
      decimal
      Skill 32A: *see page 180*

A1 Convert each of these to a decimal.
       a 58%   **b** 74%   **c** 7%   **d** $12\frac{1}{2}\%$ **e** 62.5%

B Convert a decimal to a
      percentage
      Skill 32B: *see page 181*

B1 Convert each of these decimals to a percentage.
       a 0.31   **b** 0.09   **c** 0.135
       d 0.065   **e** 0.105   **f** 0.01

C Calculate a percentage of an
      amount
      Skill 32C: *see page 185*

C1 Calculate each of these.
       a 16% of £35 000   **b** 12% of 42 km   **c** 16.5% of 4200 miles

D Write one number as a
      percentage of another
      Skill 32D: *see page 185*

D1 Calculate each of these. Give your answers to 1 dp.
       a 64 as a percentage of 400   **b** 75 as a percentage of 6000
       c 48 as a percentage of 55   **d** 108 as a percentage of 180

E Make sequences from patterns
      Skill 33A: *see page 187*

E1 This is the start of a pattern of matchsticks.

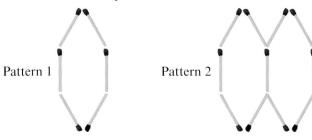

Pattern 1   Pattern 2

       a How many matches will be in pattern 4?
       b Predict how many matches will be in pattern 8
       c How many matches will be in pattern 16? Explain your answer.

F Make a sequence when you
      know the rule
      Skill 33B: *see page 188*

F1 The rule for a sequence is :
       Multiply the term number by 8 and subtract 5.

       a Write the first 6 terms of the sequence.
       b Find term 34 of the sequence.

F2 The rule for a sequence is:
       Add 3 to the term number and multiply by 4.

       a Write the first 5 terms of the sequence.
       b Find term 75 of the sequence.

G Find a rule from a sequence
      pattern
      Skill 33C: *see page 189*

G1 Look at the matchstick pattern in question **E1**.
       Write a rule for the number of matches in pattern n.

H Use differences to find a rule
      Skill 33D: *see page 190*

H1 Find the rule for the nth term of each of these sequences.
       a 1, 4, 7, 10, ...   **b** 6, 11, 16, 21, 26, ...   **c** 9, 12, 15, 18, ...

I Draw the net of a cuboid
      Skill 34A: *see page 191*

I1 Draw a net of a cube.

I2 Draw a net for this cuboid.
       Show measurements.
       Do not show tabs or flaps.

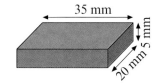

35 mm

5 mm

20 mm

J	Draw the net of a prism **Skill 34B**: *see page 193*	**J1** Draw a net of this prism. 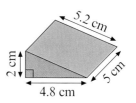

K calculate probability from data
Skill 35A: *see page 195*

K1 This data shows the results of a survey on what people choose to drink when they watch TV.

Drink	Frequency
Tea	12
Coffee	28
Milk	6
Cola	54
Orange juice	2
None	8

For each drink, calculate the probability that someone chosen at random would choose that drink.

L List combinations
Skill 35B: *see page 196*

L1 People were asked to choose any two of the choices in the list for question **K1**.

List all the possible combinations when choosing any two.

M Draw a sample space diagram
Skill 35C: *see page 197*

M1 Draw a sample-space diagram to show the outcomes from spinning a coin and rolling a 1 to 6 dice.

M2 With a coin and a 1 to 6 dice what is the probability of:
a head and a score of 4 or more?

N Use tesselations
Skill 36A: *see page 202*

N1 Explain why a square and a parallelogram will tesselate.

O Use units in problems
Skill 37A: *see page 206*

O1 Jason had the choice of buying 56 lb, or 25 kg of potatoes for £1.99.
Which weight should he choose to buy for best value?

P Use compound units
Skill 37B: *see page 207*

P1 The base of a pole has an area of 4 cm². The pole weighs 55 kg.
Calculate the pressure at the foot of the pole in kg per cm².

Q Read conversion graphs
Skill 37C: *see page 209*

Q1 Use the conversion graph on page 209 to convert:
a £10.50 to pesetas   **b** 3600 pesetas to pounds
c 9000 pesetas to pounds

R Find distances travelled
Skill 38A: *see page 214*

R1 At a constant speed of 275 mph find the distance travelled in:
a 4 hours   **b** 3 hours 15 min   **c** $5\frac{1}{2}$ hours
d 45 minutes   **e** $\frac{1}{4}$ of an hour   **f** 6 minutes

S Find average speeds
Skill 38B: *see page 215*

S1 A train left Birmingham at 14:03 and got to Doncaster at 16:18
Birmingham to Doncaster is a journey of 153 km.
Calculate the average speed of the train.

S2 On a 6-day cycle tour, Carina cycled for $5\frac{1}{2}$ hours each day.
On the tour she cycled a total of 742.5 km.
Calculate her average speed for the tour.

T Calculate with minutes as decimal parts of one hour.

T1 Find each of these as a decimal of an hour to 1 dp.
a 52 min   **b** 38 min   **c** 7 min   **d** 12 min

T2 Give each of these parts of an hour to the nearest minute.
a 0.36   **b** 0.88   **c** 0.56
d 0.12   **e** 0.08   **f** 0.6

U Find journey times
Skill 38C: *see page 216*

U1 A car travelled 340 km at an average speed of 68 kph.
Calculate the time for this journey.

U2 A train travelled 175.5 miles at an average speed of 78 mph.
Calculate the time for this journey.

V Convert a percentage to a fraction
Skill 39A: *see page 218*

V1 Write each of these as a fraction in its lowest terms.
a 85%   **b** 14%   **c** 36%   **d** 74%   **e** 2%   **f** 18%

W Add fractions with the same denominator
Skill 39B: *see page 219*

W1 Add these fractions. Give each answer in its lowest terms.
a $\frac{5}{16} + \frac{9}{16}$ **b** $\frac{5}{15} + \frac{13}{15}$ **c** $\frac{7}{12} + \frac{11}{12}$
d $\frac{4}{9} + \frac{7}{9}$ **e** $\frac{11}{20} + \frac{17}{20}$ **f** $\frac{7}{10} + \frac{9}{10}$

X Add fractions when the denominators are not the same
Skill 39C: *see page 219*

X1 Add these fractions. Give each answer in its lowest terms.
a $\frac{3}{4} + \frac{5}{12}$ **b** $\frac{2}{3} + \frac{7}{8}$ **c** $\frac{1}{4} + \frac{7}{12}$ **d** $\frac{1}{2} + \frac{2}{3}$
e $\frac{1}{3} + \frac{2}{5}$ **f** $\frac{1}{2} + \frac{1}{5}$ **g** $\frac{3}{4} + \frac{3}{5}$ **h** $\frac{1}{2} + \frac{7}{8}$.

Y Subtract fractions
Skill 39D: *see page 220*

Y1 Subtract these fractions. Give each answer in its lowest terms.
a $\frac{7}{12} - \frac{5}{12}$ **b** $\frac{3}{4} - \frac{2}{5}$ **c** $1\frac{1}{2} - \frac{5}{8}$ **d** $2\frac{1}{4} - \frac{5}{16}$

Z Calculate the volume of a cuboid
Skill 40A: *see page 222*

Z1 Calculate the volume of each cuboid to 1 dp.

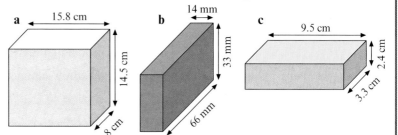

AA Calculate the volume of a prism
Skill 40B: *see page 224*

AA1 Calculate the volume of each prism to 1 dp.

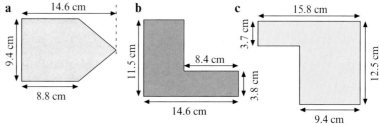

BB Calculate the area of a composite shape
Skill 42A: *see page 229*

BB1 Calculate the area of each shape to 1 dp.

a 14.6 cm, 9.4 cm, 8.8 cm
b 11.5 cm, 8.4 cm, 14.6 cm
c 15.8 cm, 3.7 cm, 3.8 cm, 12.5 cm, 9.4 cm

CC Calculate the perimeter of a composite shape
Skill 42B: *see page 231*

CC1 Calculate the perimeter of shapes **b** and **c** in question **BB1**.

CC2 A rectangular picture has a perimeter of 320 cm.
The picture is 92 cm long.
  a Calculate the width of the picture.
  b Find the area of the picture.

This revises the work in Stages 1, 2, 3 and 4

1 Give the value of the digit 5 in each of these.
   a 35047   **b** 753004   **c** 503977637

2 List these numbers from smallest to largest.
   8045, 123, 1975, 58997, 394, 7507, 4009, 60008

3 Write each of these numbers in words.
   a 61007   **b** 390004   **c** 25006001

4 Write each of these numbers in digits.
   a three million and three
   b fifty-thousand and five
   c one hundred million one hundred and one

5 Copy each of these letters and draw in all lines of symmetry.

A   K   D   E   H

6 Give the order of rotational symmetry of shape A.

Shape A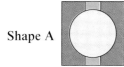

7 How many planes of symmetry has a spoon?

8 Find an answer to each of these.
   (Do not use a calculator.)
   a 6 + 5 + 8 + 4 + 9 + 3
   b 64 + 29 + 5
   c 5205 + 88 + 20975 + 43
   d 90003 − 5964
   e 72 × 15
   f 674 × 28
   g 2278 ÷ 17
   h 54800 ÷ 16

9 Give the value of the digit 9 in each of these.
   a 40.198   **b** 31.079   **c** 4.0359

10 List these numbers in order, smallest first.
   0.034, 0.175, 0.059, 0.2, 1.001, 0.05

11 Find an answer to each of these.
   (Do not use a calculator.)
   a 5.603 + 37.4 + 21.07 + 2.09 + 0.17
   b 594.95 + 38 + 2.0052 + 0.135
   c 55.001 − 48.766

12 Draw each of these angles accurately.
   a 75°   **b** 125°   **c** 205°

13 Which of these angles are acute?
   108°, 55°, 204°, 34°, 108°, 29°

14 Copy and complete each of these.
   a $^-3 + ^-19 =$ **b** $^-24 + 18 =$ **c** $23 + ^-14 =$
   d $17 − 44 =$ **e** $^-11 − 21 =$ **f** $^-6 − ^-23 =$
   g $31 − ^-8 =$ **h** $^-8 × 7 =$ **i** $8 × ^-8 =$
   j $^-4 × ^-7 =$ **k** $36 ÷ ^-9 =$ **l** $^-81 ÷ ^-27 =$

15 Order these numbers with the smallest first.
   a $^-7, 2, ^-11, 4, ^-4, 1, 3$
   b $1, ^-8, ^-2, 6, 0, ^-5, 4, ^-9$

16 The coordinates of two corners of a square are:
   ($^-3$, 5) and ($^-1$, 5).
   Give the coordinates of the other two corners of the square.

17 Collect like terms in each of these.
   a $21k + 4w + k + 19w + 15k$
   b $11f + 3h + f − h − 12h$

18 Expand the brackets in each of these.
   a $5(7w + 6)$ **b** $8(15 − 6k)$

19 Expand these brackets and collect like terms to simplify.
   $5(3y + 7g + 6) + 8(3y − 6g − 12)$

20 Round each of these numbers to the nearest thousand.
   a 37504   **b** 568329   **c** 8382805

21 Round each of these to the nearest 100000.
   a 609556   **b** 5307504   **c** 6018495

22 Find an approximate answer to each of these.
   a 67 × 33   **b** 91 × 27   **c** 69 × 48

23 Construct a triangle with sides of:
   6 cm, 6 cm and 5 cm.

24 Construct triangle ABC where:
   AB = 6 cm, BC = 9 cm, and angle ABC = 55°.

25 Write each of these in 24-hour time.
   a 6.07 pm   **b** 2.45 pm   **c** 12.25 am
   d 8.35 pm   **e** 2.25 am   **f** 4.06 pm

26 A train left Birmingham at 13:57 and arrived in Glasgow at 19:05.
   What was the journey time for this train?

27 Use the timetable on page 59.
   Jo catches the 2003 from Waterloo East.
   She travels to Walmer.
   a When should she get to Walmer?
   b What is the journey time?

28 Calculate the area of each of these shapes.

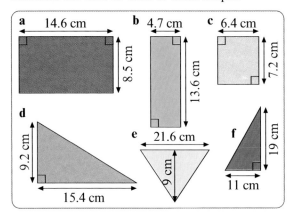

29 A formula that links p, k and t is: $t = 9(2p - 5k)$.
Find the value of t when, $p = 8$ and $k = 3$.

30 Solve each of these equations.
  a $8y + 19 = 75$ **b** $88 + 5h = 103$
  c $6g - 15 = 27$ **d** $3(4f - 5) = 45$

31 **a**   Add all the even numbers between 21 and 53.
    b   What square numbers are between 50 and 160?
    c   Subtract the 9th square number from 90.

32 Which of these is a multiple of 7?
    57, 84, 35, 17, 28, 42

33 List all the factors of 60.

34 List all the prime numbers between 40 and 60.

35 This data is about TV viewing in a week.

Ella		Nadim	
Channel	**Hours**	**Channel**	**Hours**
BBC1	5	BBC1	7
BBC2	6	BBC2	4
ITV	9	ITV	6
Ch 4	15	Ch 4	6
Ch 5	9	Ch 5	5
Sky	6	Sky	8

  a   Draw a comparative bar chart for the data.
  b   Draw a split bar chart to show the data for
      each viewer.
  c   Draw a pie chart to show the data for Nadim.

36 Copy and complete each of these.
  a $66.3027 \times 10^3 =$ **b** $0.005\,34 \times 10^5 =$
  c $300.16 \div 10 =$ **d** $0.1062 \div 10^3 =$

37 Without a calculator find the value of:
  a $3229.6 \div 8$ **b** $5148.36 \div 6$
  c 408.78×5 **d** 365.78×3

38 Calculate the answer to each of these.
Do not use a calculator.
  a   £15.04 + £12.99 + 35p + £6
  b   £12 + £217.99 + 9p + £5.75 + 23p
  c   £560.38 – £485.66
  d   £2500 – £964.77

39 A box of 6 pens costs £2.05.
Find the cost of one pencil to the nearest penny.

40 Ed buys a bag of tile grout for £7.71.
He pays with a £10 note.
How much change will he get?

41 Denise pays a bill with a £20 note.
She gets £3.05 change.
How much was the bill?

42 Calculate the answer to each of these.
Do not use a calculator.
  a   57p × 8   **b**   £34.28 × 5 =
  c   £616.36 ÷ 4   **d**   £3506.49 ÷ 9 =

43 Draw a mapping diagram for the function
$y = 2x - 7$. (Use values of x from 1 to 5.)

44 Give the number output from this function
machine.

$-8 \longrightarrow \boxed{+3} \longrightarrow \boxed{\times 3} \longrightarrow$

45 Calculate each angle marked with a letter.

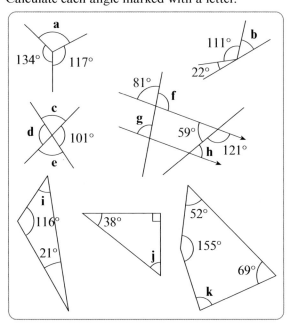

46 Davina earns a basic wage of £7.30 an hour.
How much will she earn at:
  a   double time   **b**   time-and-a-half?

47 Calculate $\frac{3}{5}$ of £78.15.

48 Kamal did a sponsored walk of 42km.
For $\frac{5}{7}$ of the distance he did not have blisters on his feet.

How far did he walk with blisters on his feet?

49 Which of these fractions is equivalent to $\frac{1}{4}$?
$\frac{28}{112}$ $\frac{36}{114}$ $\frac{144}{160}$ $\frac{60}{250}$

50 **a** Convert $\frac{7}{56}$ to a decimal.
b Put these in order from smallest to largest.
0.7 $\frac{4}{5}$ 0.65 $\frac{7}{8}$ $\frac{3}{4}$

51 Give two different fractions that describe how much of this grid is shaded.

52 This data shows the number of people that travelled in a cable-car.

4, 11, 16, 7, 21, 21, 12, 27, 14, 6, 17, 24, 8, 15, 24, 16, 21, 10, 6, 8, 3, 26, 16, 30, 9, 15, 22, 30, 7, 23, 8

a Make a grouped frequency table for the data.
Groups of: 1–5, 6–10, 11–15, … , 26–30
b What is the modal class?
c Draw a grouped frequency diagram to show the data.

53 Solve each of these equations.

a $19y - 4 = 12y + 31$ **b** $15w + 8 = 7w - 8$
c $25x - 37 = 18x + 61$ **d** $9w + 12 = 48 + 5w$

54 Shape A is a rectangle.

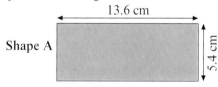

a Calculate the perimeter of shape A.
b Give the perimeter of shape A rounded to the nearest whole number.
c Calculate the area of shape A.
d Give the area rounded to 1 dp.
e Round the length and width to the nearest whole number and use this to find the area.

55 Which of these is 57.05 when rounded to 2 dp?

57.05399   57.05601   57.05495   57.05702

56 With a 1 to 6 dice:

a What is the probability of scoring 3 or more?
b What is the probability of scoring less than 5?

57 Write each of these numbers in standard form.

a 3204.66   **b** 6573007.55

58 Callum worked out how many seconds there were in 9 years. His calculator display gave:

a Write this number in standard form.
b Write this as an ordinary number.

59 Use the rules of indices to complete each of these.

a $10^6 \times 10^2 = 10^{\blacksquare}$ **b** $10^4 \times 10^3 \times 10^{\blacksquare} = 10^{14}$

60 Joel did a survey of the matches in a box.
This data gives the number in each box.

43, 37, 36, 40, 38, 42, 40, 36, 34, 40, 40, 39, 40, 34, 45, 36, 44, 40, 36, 39, 37, 40, 40, 40, 35, 40, 42

a Make a frequency table for the data.
b What number of matches was the mode?
c Find the mean number of matches in a box.
d Find the median number of matches in a box.

61 Make two copies of this grid showing shape A.

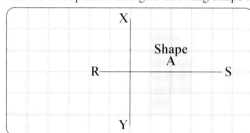

a On one copy show shape A reflected in XY.
b On one copy show shape A reflected in RS.

62 Copy these axes and the shape ABCDE on to a grid.

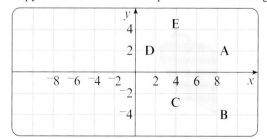

a Rotate ABCDE 180° about the point (0, 2).
b Give the coordinates of A′, B′, C′, D′, E′.

63 The mean of 8 numbers is 17.

a What is the total of the 8 numbers?

Seven of the numbers are:
14, 23, 12, 15, 19, 21, 16

b What is the missing number?

64 Use the map on page 176.
Give directions to get from the Station to the Lion.
What might be the third view?

65 Convert each of these to a decimal.
  a 65%   **b** 12%   **c** 4%   **d** 1%

66 Write each of these as a decimal.
  a $15\frac{1}{2}\%$ **b** $30\frac{1}{2}\%$ **c** $\frac{1}{2}\%$

67 Convert each of these decimals to a percentage.
  a 0.66   **b** 0.07   **c** 0.02   **d** 0.145
  e 0.585   **f** 0.065   **g** 0.015   **h** 0.875

68 Find:
  a 17% of £4500   **b** 38% of 650 kg
  c 45% of £45   **d** 6% of 365 000
  e 18% of 60 miles   **f** $7\frac{1}{2}\%$ of £4000

69 **a** Write 55 as a percentage of 80.
  b Write 180 as a percentage of 750.
  c Write 45 000 as a percentage of half a million.

70 The rule for a sequence is:
   Multiply the term number by 4 and add 3.
The sequence starts: 7, 11, 15, …
Write the next 4 terms of the sequence.

71 The nth term of a sequence is given by:
   $5n - 3$
Write the first 5 terms of the sequence.

72 Draw a net for a cube (without tabs or flaps).

73 Draw a net for
this cuboid.
Label your net with
measurements.
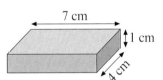

74 Sketch a net of a triangular prism.

75 Sketch a net of a square-based pyramid.

76 This data shows the results of
a survey of sizes of T-shirt
for sale by a trader.

Size	Frequency
S	15
M	22
L	40
XL	18

  a Calculate the probability that a T-shirt picked
  at random will be size S.
  (Give the answer as a fraction and a decimal.)
  b Gita calculates that the probability of picking
  one size is 0.23. Which size is this?
  c Calculate the probability for the other sizes of
  T-shirt.

77 At an activities centre students must choose two
activities from this list:
Climbing, Sailing, Walking, Diving, Archery
List all the possible combinations there are.

78 **a** Draw a sample space diagram for the scores on
  two 1-to-6 dice.
  b Show on your diagram total scores of 8 or more.
  c What is the probability of scoring a total of 8
  or more with two dice?

79 Explain why a triangle will tessellate.
(You will need to draw diagrams.)

80 At a constant speed of 76 kph, how far will you
travel in $7\frac{1}{2}$ hours?

81 At a steady speed of 256 kph find the distance
travelled in:
  a 45 min   **b** half an hour   **c** 15 min.

82 You travel 176 miles in 2 hours 30 minutes.
Calculate your average speed.

83 Write each of these as a fraction.
  a 44% **b** 72% **c** 84% **d** 16% **e** 4%

84 Find: **a** $\frac{5}{9} + \frac{7}{9}$ **b** $\frac{15}{16} - \frac{9}{16}$ **c** $\frac{2}{3} - \frac{1}{4}$

85 Calculate the volume of
each cuboid to 1 dp.
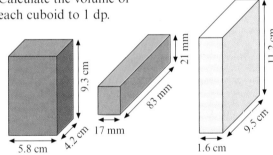

86 Easy-strike Matches want a box with a volume
of 30 cm³.
Sketch two possible boxes showing measurements.

87 Calculate the volume of each prism to 1 dp.
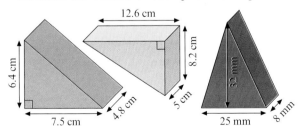

88 A park is a rectangle 224.56 m by 188.55 m.
Calculate the approximate area of the park.
Explain any rounding you did.

Starting points
You need to know about ...

... so try these questions

A Measuring and drawing angles

Skill 5A and 5B: *see pages 31 and 32*

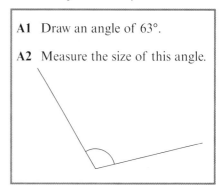

A1 Draw an angle of 63°.

A2 Measure the size of this angle.

Three-figure Bearings

Skill 43A
Using 3-figure bearings

- ◆ Bearings can be given either as compass bearings or as 3-figure bearings.

- ◆ 3-figure bearings are always:
  - ❖ written with three digits
  - ❖ measured from the North line
  - ❖ measured in a clockwise direction.

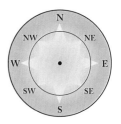

Examples

This map shows the position of 4 villages which can be seen from a hill.

What is the 3-figure bearing of each one from the hill?

The bearing of each village is shown in this table.

The bearing of Creech is measured clockwise from the North line.
This is 40° but all bearings must have 3 figures so it is written as 040°.

Village	Working out	Bearing
Creech		040°
Radway	40°+85°	125°
Ganning	40°+85°+100°	225°
Voland	40°+85°+100°+92° or 360° − 43°	317°

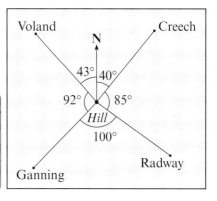

Exercise 43.1
Using Skill 43A

1 This map shows the position of five boats and a rock.

Copy and complete this table to show the 3-figure bearing of each boat from the rock.

Boat	Bearing
Viking	
Freelander	
Daisy Rue	
Marlene	
Seasprite	

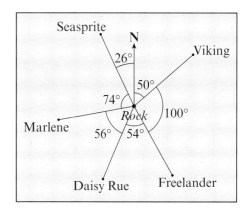

2 This diagram shows 8 compass bearings.

Copy and complete the table to show each compass bearing as a 3-figure bearing.

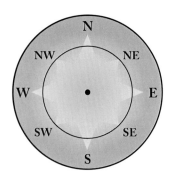

Compass bearing	Three-figure bearing
North	000°
North-East	
East	
South-East	
South	
South-West	225°
West	
North-West	

This map shows the position of 3 boats.

3 Measure the bearing of Dimple from Ellie May.

4 Measure the bearing of Daisy from Ellie May.

5 What is the bearing of Daisy from Dimple?

6 Find the bearing of Ellie May from Dimple.

7 Measure the bearing of
  a Dimple from Daisy
  b Ellie May from Daisy.

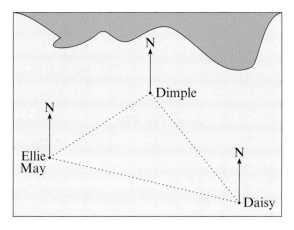

> To find the bearing of Dimple from Ellie May, put the centre of your angle measurer on Ellie May with zero on the North line.

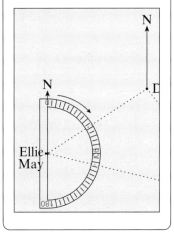

8 Two rescue ships, A and B, are shown on this map
A life raft R can be seen from each ship. It is not marked on the map.

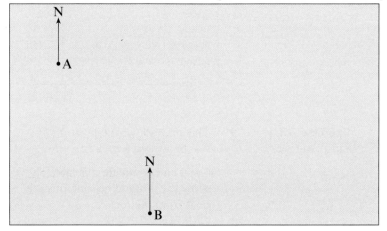

  a Trace the map into your book.
  b From ship A the bearing of the raft is 097°.
    From ship B the bearing of the raft is 055°.

Mark the position of R accurately on your map.

> You need to draw a line at 097° from A and 055° from B. Where the lines cross is the postion of R.

Bearings and scales

Skill 43B
Solving problems with
bearings and scales

◆ Bearings are often used on a scale drawing to fix a position.

Example

A lighthouse can be seen from a ship.
It is on a bearing of 135° and at a distance of 10 km.

Draw a map to show their positions.
Use a scale of 1 cm to 2 km.

◆ First mark a point for the position
of the ship, S.

◆ Draw a north line from S.

◆ Draw a line at a bearing of 135°
from S.

◆ Measure along this line a
distance of 5 cm.
Mark this as the position of the
lighthouse, L.

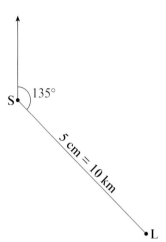

Exercise 43.2
Using Skill 43B

1 A church can be seen from a hill.
Its bearing is 075° from the hill and it is 6 km away.

Draw a map to show their positions. Use a scale of 1 cm to 1 km.

2 A radar screen on a tanker
shows the position of six other ships.
The scale is 1 cm to 4 km.

Copy and complete this table.

Ship	Bearing	Distance
A		
B		
C		
D		
E		
F		

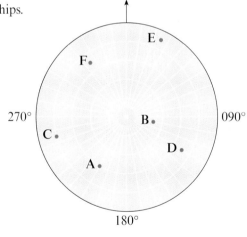

Use a scale of 1 cm to
1 km for question 3.

3 The positions of three boats, P, Q and R are given by this data:

Q is 8 km from P on a bearing of 090°

R is 8 km from P on a bearing of 030°.

a Mark a dot for boat P then mark the postions of boats Q and R.
b From your diagram give the bearing of Q from R.
c What is the distance of Q from R in km?

Routes

Skill 43C
Drawing routes

When a boat sets a route it uses different bearings and distances.
Each stage in the course is called a leg.
Here is one route.

Farland Queen   Plan of voyage

Cast off from Saltham Quay

Leg 1   60 miles on bearing 050°
Leg 2   70 miles on bearing 140°
Leg 3   30 miles on bearing 075°

You must draw a new
North line at the start of
each new leg

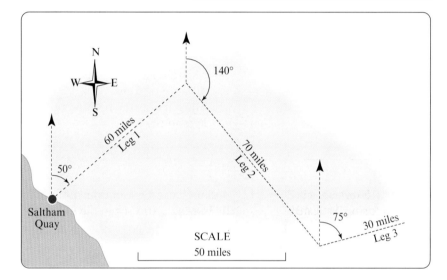

Exercise 43.3
Using Skill 43C

1   Copy and complete the route of the Farland Queen.

2   This diagram shows three legs on a route.

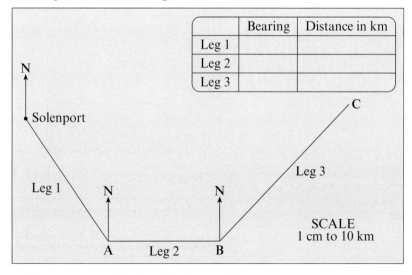

	Bearing	Distance in km
Leg 1		
Leg 2		
Leg 3		

a   Copy and complete the table for each leg.
b   As the crow flies, how far is point C from Solenport?

3 The sailing boat Belle Fleur sets off from Stanton Head.
This is the route she follows.

Belle Fleur Plan of voyage

Cast off from Stanton Head

Leg 1 6000 metres on a bearing of 160°
Leg 2 8000 metres on a bearing of 050°
Leg 3 5000 metres on a bearing of 320°
Leg 4 3500 metres on a bearing of 280°

Remember:

A scale of 1:100 000 means
1 cm stands for 100 000 cm
so
1 cm stands for 1000 metres.

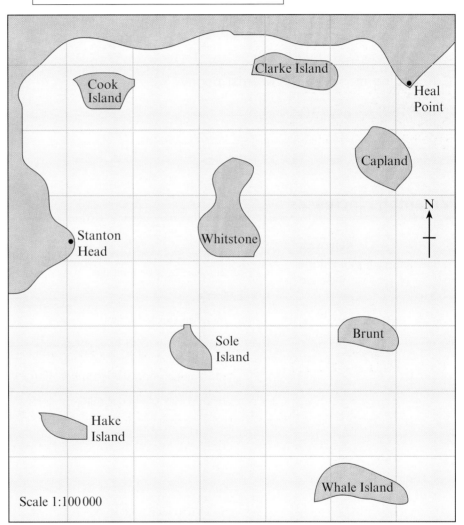

Scale 1:100 000

a Trace the map.
b Plot the course of the Belle Fleur.
c At which island does she stop at the end of her course?

4 a Trace another copy of the map above.
b Plot this course from Heal Point.

Leg 1 6000 metres on a bearing of 259°
Leg 2 8000 metres on a bearing of 193°
Leg 3 5000 metres on a bearing of 085°
Leg 4 3500 metres on a bearing of 235°

---

c At which island does the course finish?

Starting points
You need to know about ...   ... so try these questions

A Converting a percentage to a decimal

Skill 32A: *see page 180*

B Calculating a percentage of an amount

Skill 32C: *see page 182*

C Rounding money to the nearest penny

Skill 18D: *see page 102*

A1 Convert each of these to a decimal value.

   a 34%   **b** 65%   **c** 4%
   d 6%   **e** $5\frac{1}{2}$%   **f** 1%
   g $12\frac{1}{2}$%   **h** 55.5%   **i** $\frac{1}{2}$%

B1 Calculate each of these:

   a 35% of £35 000
   b 12% of £875
   c 4% of 460 tonnes
   d $2\frac{1}{2}$% of 66 km
   e 6.5% of £280 000

C1 Round each of these amounts to the nearest penny.

   a £45.688   **b** £1.304
   c £0.067   **d** £4.008
   e £52.1288   **f** £0.1062

Percentage increases

Skill 44A
Calculating a percentage increase

Thinking of percentages as decimals will help when you want to increase an amount by a percentage.

Example

Increase £65.50 by 8%.

Start with all of £65.50, which is 100%.
Increase by 8%
and you end up with a total of 100% + 8% = 108%.

To find 108% as a decimal:

$$108\% \text{ is } 100\% + 8\%$$
$$100\% = 1.00$$
$$\underline{8\% = 0.08}$$
$$108\% = 1.08$$

108% of £65.50 is given by: $65.50 \times 1.08 = 70.74$

So £65.50 increased by 8% is £70.74.

Exercise 44.1
Practising Skill 44 A

1 Increase each of these amounts by 8%.
   a £24   **b** £56   **c** £188   **d** £341   **e** £12

2 Increase each of these by 6%.
   a £85   **b** £6   **c** £823   **d** £9500   **e** £17

3 Increase each of these by 15%.
   a 450 miles   **b** 120 kg   **c** 6400 km   **d** 380 cm²   **e** 160 g

4 Increase each of these by $21\frac{1}{2}$%.
   a £16   **b** 2600 km   **c** £18 500   **d** 2 kg   **e** 300 g

Sometimes you will need to round your answer to the nearest penny.

Example

Increase £44.85 by $18\frac{1}{2}\%$.

An increase by $18\frac{1}{2}\%$ gives a total of $118\frac{1}{2}\%$.
$118\frac{1}{2}\%$ as a decimal is 1.185.

$118\frac{1}{2}\%$ of £44.85 is given by:
$44.85 \times 1.185 = 53.147\ldots$

£53.147… is £53.15 to nearest penny.

So £44.85 increased by $18\frac{1}{2}\%$ is £53.15 (to the nearest penny).

5   Calculate each of these to the nearest penny.

   a   Increase £56.85 by 12%   **b**   Increase £272.66 by 9%

   c   Increase £388.75 by 16%   **d**   Increase £450.55 by 21%

   e   Increase £16.94 by 4%   **f**   Increase £1.08 by 68%

   g   Increase £4002.38 by 7%   **h**   Increase £2537 by 41%.

6   Calculate each of these to the nearest penny.

   a   Increase £85.56 by $12\frac{1}{2}\%$ **b**   Increase £97.99 by $4\frac{1}{2}\%$

   c   Increase £549.99 by $5\frac{1}{2}\%$ **d**   Increase £19.99 by $7\frac{1}{2}\%$

   e   Increase £12.49 by $2\frac{1}{2}\%$ **f**   Increase £10.99 by $15\frac{1}{2}\%$.

Exercise 44.2
Using Skill 44A

1   Last year the ferry Vista carried a total of 26 788 passengers.
Next year Vista's owners plan for passenger numbers to increase by 8%.

How many passengers are they planning for next year?
Your answer must be to the nearest whole number.

2   Jake prints T-shirts.
Last year he bought 12 700 T-shirts.
This year he will increase his order by $12\frac{1}{2}\%$.

How many T-shirts will to order this year?

3   A stadium with 23 570 seats is being worked on.
The plan is to increase the number of seats by about 14%.

When the work is finished how many seats will there be?
Give your answer to the nearest 10.

4   Last year Jodie went on holiday to Spain. The holiday cost £365.
This year prices have increased by $7\frac{1}{2}\%$.

How much will the same holiday cost this year?

5   In the low season the ferry fare for a car and 4 people is £76.
In the high season the fares are increased by 8%.

Calculate the high season fare for a car and 4 people.
Give your answer to the nearest penny.

6   Iain sells ice-cream on a beach.
Last year he sold a total of 4234 litres.
This year he expects to increase his sales by 17%.

How much ice-cream does Iain expect to sell this year?

7   A club has 18 654 season-ticket holders. It wants to increase this by 12%.

After the increase, how many season-ticket holders do they hope for?

Percentage decreases

Skill 44B
Calculating a percentage decrease

When you decrease an amount by a percentage:
    you subtract from the 100% that you start with.

Example   Decrease £47.85 by 6%.

Start with all of £47.85, which is 100%.
Decrease by 6%:
and you end up with 100% − 6% = 94%.

As a decimal 94% = 0.94.

94% of £47.85 is given by: 47.85 × 0.94 = 44.979

£44.979 is £44.98 to nearest penny.

So £47.85 decreased by 6% is £44.98 (to the nearest penny).

Exercise 44.3
Practising Skill 44B

1   Decrease each of these amounts by 6%. Give answers to the nearest penny.
    a £34.75   **b** £58.99   **c** £458.56   **d** £135.99   **e** £7.49

2   Decrease each of these amounts by 15%. Give answers to the nearest penny.
    a £75.55   **b** £21.85   **c** £75.49   **d** £128.21   **e** £6.25

3   Decrease each of these by 31%. Give answers to the nearest penny.
    a £3.99   **b** £425.60   **c** £855.85   **d** £12.99   **e** £7.35

4   Decrease each of these by 5%. Give answers to the nearest whole number.
    a 85 kg   **b** 425 lb   **c** 27.5 km   **d** 16.8 metres   **e** 54 mm

5   Calculate each of these to the nearest penny.
    a Decrease £69.99 by 20%   **b** Decrease £355.49 by 18%
    c Decrease £3.85 by 15%   **d** Decrease £575.65 by 12%
    e Decrease £2655.44 by 8%   **f** Decrease £3501.75 by 21%
    g Decrease £1.99 by 7%   **h** Decrease 99p by 15%.

6   Calculate each of these to the nearest penny.
    a Decrease £5.85 by $4\frac{1}{2}$%   **b** Decrease £355.99 by $12\frac{1}{2}$%
    c Decrease £3.99 by $7\frac{1}{2}$%   **d** Decrease £485.62 by $3\frac{1}{2}$%
    e Decrease £4.75 by $15\frac{1}{2}$%   **f** Decrease £604.49 by $6\frac{1}{2}$%.

Exercise 44.4
Using Skill 44B

1   Last year a garden centre sold 15.8 tonnes of weedkiller.
    Next year they think sales of weedkiller will decrease by 7%.
    How much weedkiller do they think they will sell next year (to the nearest tonne)?

2   Last year in Ashleigh 188 cyclists were injured in road accidents.
    Next year they hope to decrease injuries to cyclists in road accidents by 18%.
    How many cyclists do they expect to be injured next year on the road?

3   Jade wants to buy a motorbike that is priced at £3995.
    If she pays cash the price will be decreased by 5%.
    a If she pays cash how much will she pay for the bike?
    b How much will she save by paying cash?

4   Decrease three-and-a-half million by 8.5%.

VAT (Value Added Tax)

♦ VAT is a tax added to goods or services.
♦ VAT was introduced on 1 April 1973 at a standard rate of 10%
♦ VAT was increased to 15% on 18 June 1979
♦ VAT was increased to $17\frac{1}{2}\%$ (17.5%) on 1 April 1994

Check on the standard rate of VAT today and use that in your working.

Skill 44C
Calculating VAT

To calculate the total price of things including VAT is the same as:
increasing the cost price by the percentage VAT.

Example   A shed is advertised for: £114.99 + VAT at 17.5%
Calculate the total charge for the shed.

Think of the total charge for the shed as: cost price + VAT

That is: 100% of the cost price + 17.5% VAT = 117.5%
The total charge is: 117.5% of the cost price.

117.5% as a decimal is 1.175.

117.5% of £114.99 is given by: $114.99 \times 1.175 = 135.113\ldots$

So the total charge for the shed, with VAT, is £135.11 (to the nearest penny).

Exercise 44.5
Practising Skill 44C

1   The cost of these items is given without VAT.
Calculate the charge, with VAT, for each item to the nearest penny.

a camera £18	**b** trainers £48.75	**c** bike £195
d toaster £12.50	**e** pen 85 pence	**f** TV £455
g fridge £315	**h** mower £32.60	**i** CD £11.50
j bag £18.25	**k** telephone £16.75	**l** stapler £3.80
m disc 36 pence	**n** tent £175.35	**o** chocolates £4.15

Exercise 44.6
Using Skill 44C

Give each answer in this exercise to the nearest penny.

1   Pia bought a cycle tyre and was charged £12.75 + VAT.
    a   What did she pay in total for the tyre?
    b   How much VAT did she pay?

2   Connor fits carpets. He said a carpet would cost £85 + VAT to fit.
    Calculate the total charge for Connor to fit the carpet.

3   Ria was told that repairs to her car would cost £265.50.
    When she paid she found that VAT had to be added to the cost.
    a   How much did Ria pay in total with VAT?
    b   How much VAT was added to her bill?

4   In the High Street two shops advertised CD's.
    SuperCD advertised all CD's at: Only £13.49 (including VAT)
    CDcity advertised all CD's at: Only £11.50 (+ VAT)
    a   Which price was cheaper? Explain your answer.
    b   How much will you save if you buy 3 CD's at the cheaper shop?

5   Jenny needs 4 new tyres on her car. She has £85 to spend.
    She sees tyres priced at £20.99 (including VAT) each or £18.99 (+ VAT) each.
    a   Which tyres can she afford? Explain.
    b   She buys 4 tyres. How much has she left over from her £85?

Starting points

You need to know about ...   ... so try these questions

A Calculating probability from equally likely outcomes

When outcomes are equally likely you can calculate the probability of something happening.

Example For this 0 to 9 dice, what is the probability of getting a multiple of 4?

There are 10 numbers
 (0, 1, 2, 3, 4, 5, 6, 7, 8, 9)

2 numbers are multiples of 4 (they are 4 and 8).

So the probability of getting a multiple of 4 is
 $\frac{2}{10} = \frac{1}{5}$

This way of finding probability is called **theoretical probability**.

A1 For the 0 to 9 dice, what is the probability of getting:

 a a 5
 b a multiple of 3
 c an even number
 d a factor of 12?

A2 When you roll a 1 to 6 dice, what is the probability of getting a number less than 5?

A3 A bag holds 7 sweets. 4 sweets are red, 2 are blue and 1 is green.

 You pick a sweet at random. What is the probability that it will be blue?

Experimental probability

Skill 45A
Doing probability experiements

◆ A probability can also be found by doing an experiment. This is called **experimental probability**.

Example

What is the probability of scoring a 4 with a 1 to 6 dice?

This can be found in two ways
◆ by using theoretical probability
◆ by using experimental probability.

◆ By theory – there are six equally likely outcomes:
 ❖ 1 outcome gives 4
 ❖ the probability of a 4 is $\frac{1}{6}$ or about **0.17**

◆ By experiment – throw a dice many times and record the outcomes.

These are the results of an experiment. A dice was thrown 280 times.

The probability of a 4 by experiment $= \frac{53}{280} =$ **0.19**

Note that the two probabilities are nearly the same but not quite.

Outcome	Frequency
1	38
2	45
3	49
4	53
5	41
6	54
Total	**280**

To change $\frac{1}{6}$ to a decimal divide 1 by 6.

This gives 0.1666666... or 0.17 to 2 dp.

To change $\frac{53}{280}$ to a decimal divide 53 by 280.

This gives 0.189 28... or 0.19 to 2 dp.

Exercise 45.1
Practising skill 45A

1 **a** Do the dice experiment.
 Throw a dice 100 times. Put the outcomes in a table.
 b Calculate the probability of a 4 from your results.

2 Four people do the dice experiment.

Sadie throws her dice 350 times and gets 0.18 as her probability.
Leroy throws his dice 180 times and gets 0.19 as his probability.
Pragna throws her dice 1000 times and gets 0.17 as her probability.
Carla throws her dice 8 times and gets 0.38 as her probability.

Whose results would you choose to rely on?
Explain why.

3 Choose one of these experiments to do.

Experiment A
To find the probability that a drawing pin lands point up
When you drop a drawing pin it can land ...

    point up   or point down

Drop a pin 100 times and record the results in a frequency table.

Position of pin	Tally	Frequency
Point up		
Point down		

Calculate the probability that a pin will land point up.

Experiment B
To find the probability that a shape will land side down
When you drop this L shape it can land ...

  side down   flat down   on its edges

Drop the shape 100 times and record the results in a frequency table.

Position of shape	Tally	Frequency
Side down		
Flat down		
On its edges		

Calculate the probability that the shape willl land side down.

---

4 How could you make the probability from each
experiment above more reliable?

5

Experiment C
To find the probability that a coin will give heads
When you spin a coin it can land showing Heads or Tails.
Drop a coin many times and record the results in a frequency table.

Side showing	Tally	Frequency
Heads		
Tails		

Calculate the probability that the coin willl land showing heads.

---

a Find the probability of heads after 10 throws.
b Find the probability of heads after 100 throws.
c Find the probability of heads after 200 throws.
d Which of these, **a**, **b** or **c**, is likely to be the most reliable?
e You spin a coin 100 million times.
   What do you think the probability of a head will be?

6

Experiment D
To find the probability that you will pick a red cube from a bag
- Put 3 blue cubes, 2 red cubes and 1 yellow cube in an envelope.
- Pick out a cube without looking.
  Record its colour.
  Then put the cube back.
- Do this 100 times.

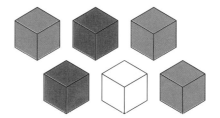

Colour of cube	Tally	Frequency
Blue		
Red		
Yellow		
	Total	100

Calculate the probability that you will pick a red cube at random.

---

a Do Experiment D.
b What is the theoretical probability that you would pick a red cube?

Starting points

You need to know about ...

... so try these questions

A Finding a fraction of an amount

Skill 22A: *see page 122*

B Finding equivalent fractions

Skill 22B: *see page 125*

C Writing a fraction in its lowest terms

Skill 22C: *see page 126*

A1 Find:

a $\frac{3}{5}$ of 317.50   **b** $\frac{3}{4}$ of £15.84

c $\frac{5}{8}$ of £100.88   **d** $\frac{7}{10}$ of £45000

e $\frac{2}{3}$ of £450.18

B1 Which of these are equivalent to $\frac{2}{3}$? $\frac{14}{21}, \frac{25}{35}, \frac{20}{30}, \frac{5}{7}, \frac{30}{45}$

B2 Which of these are equivalent to $\frac{4}{5}$? $\frac{10}{12}, \frac{24}{30}, \frac{36}{45}, \frac{11}{16}, \frac{12}{15}$

C1 Write each of these fractions in its lowest terms.

a $\frac{12}{20}$ **b** $\frac{15}{36}$ **c** $\frac{30}{42}$

d $\frac{24}{32}$ **e** $\frac{56}{63}$ **f** $\frac{14}{25}$

Writing ratios

Skill 46A
Writing ratios

A ratio compares the size of two or more amounts.

Example   Orange paint is made by mixing red and yellow paint.
5 parts of red paint are mixed with 2 parts of yellow.

Give the ratio red paint : yellow paint
and the ratio yellow paint : red paint

The ratio of red : yellow is 5 : 2
The ratio of yellow : red is 2 : 5

> The ratio compares the parts of red paint used to the parts of yellow paint used, in the order red : yellow

Exercise 46.1
Practising Skill 46A

1 To make salad oil, 7 parts of sunflower oil are mixed with 3 parts of olive oil.
For salad oil, give the ratio of:

a sunflower oil : olive oil   **b** olive oil : sunflower oil.

2 To make green paint, 8 parts of blue paint are mixed with 5 parts of yellow.
For the green paint, give the ratio of:

a blue paint : yellow paint   **b** yellow : blue.

3 In the Spartans A hockey team there are 6 males and 5 females.
For the Spartans A hockey team, give the ratio of:

a females : males   **b** males to females

4 Last week at a driving centre, 320 people passed their test and 183 failed.
For the driving centre, give the ratio of:

a fails : passes   **b** passes : fails.

5 On a bus there were 37 adults and 9 children.
Give the ratio of:

a children : adults   **b** adults : children.

Ratios in their lowest terms

Skill 46B
Writing ratios in their
lowest terms

A ratio in its lowest terms
might be called a ratio in
its simplest terms.

A ratio in its lowest terms is written
with the smallest whole numbers possible.

Example 1   Write the ratio $15:24$ in its lowest terms.

To get the smallest possible whole numbers you need to divide
each part of the ratio by the same number.

To find the ratio $15:24$, you see that 15 and 24 can each be divided by 3.

So to find the ratio
in its lowest terms
divide by 3:

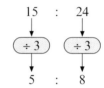

So 15:24 in its lowest terms is 5:8.

Example 2   Write the ratio $3:\frac{1}{2}:5$ in its lowest terms.

For the smallest whole numbers in this ratio
you need to multiply each part.

For the ratio $3:\frac{1}{2}:5$ (multiply parts by 2 as $2 \times \frac{1}{2} = 1$)

You multiply as you need
to change the fraction to a
whole number.

To find the ratio
in its lowest terms
multiply by 2:

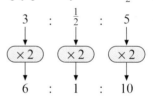

So $3:\frac{1}{2}:5$ in its lowest terms is 6:1:10.

Exercise 46.2
Practising Skill 46B

1   Write each of these ratios in its lowest terms.

a $6:10$	**b** $12:15$	**c** $21:35$	**d** $42:60$
e $21:33$	**f** $24:42$	**g** $25:75$	**h** $28:36$
i $12:27$	**j** $14:16$	**k** $21:24$	**l** $15:30$
m $12:18$	**n** $5:8$	**o** $35:63$	**p** $75:300$

2   Write each of these in its lowest terms.

a $2:\frac{1}{3}:3$	**b** $3:\frac{1}{5}:4$	**c** $1:\frac{1}{4}:5$	**d** $4:\frac{1}{6}:3$
e $1:\frac{1}{8}:2$	**f** $2:\frac{1}{10}:5$	**g** $3:\frac{1}{12}:7$	**h** $1:\frac{1}{100}:4$

3   Write each of these in its lowest terms.

a $2:4:6$	**b** $12:20:24$	**c** $15:25:35$	**d** $14:28:35$
e $50:60:70$	**f** $18:27:45$	**g** $35:42:56$	**h** $16:12:28$
i $120:36:60$	**j** $40:32:72$	**k** $45:10:55$	**l** $18:21:33$

Exercise 46.3
Using Skill 46B

1   An athletics club has 420 female athletes and 385 male athletes.

Give the ratio female athletes : male athletes in its lowest terms.

2   On a train there are 136 first-class seats and 728 standard-class seats.

What is the seat ratio first-class : standard-class in its lowest terms?

3   On a plane there were 12 crew and 324 passengers.

Give the ratio passengers : crew in its lowest terms.

4 In a car park there were 265 cars. Of these 55 were red.
   a How many cars in the car park were not red?
   b Give the ratio red cars : not red cars in its lowest terms.

5 In a cinema there are 420 seats. Of these, 180 are superior-club seats and the rest are standard-club seats.
   a How many standard-club seats are there?
   b Give the seat ratio standard : superior in its lowest terms.

6 On one trip of a cross-channel ferry there were 374 cars and 128 lorries.
   Give the ratio lorries : cars in its lowest terms.

7 A tropical fruit juice is made by blending orange, lemon and lime juice.
   In the blend 200 litres of orange juice is mixed with 80 litres of lemon juice, and 120 litres of lime juice.
   Give the ratio for the blend in its lowest terms.

8 In a box of 50 felt-tipped pens, 15 were black, 25 were blue and the rest were red.
   Give the ratio that shows the colours of pens in its lowest terms.

Equivalent ratios

Skill 46C
Writing equivalent ratios

The ratio $6:8$ in its lowest terms is $3:4$.

We can also say that $6:8$ and $3:4$ are equivalent ratios.

You can think of equivalent ratios in this way.
Starting with one ratio:
   by multiplying or dividing, you can make the other ratio.

Example 1 Complete this set of equivalent ratios.

   $5:2:3:7$
   ■ : 6 : ■ : ■

Here the **6** can be made by multiplying the 2 by 3.

To find the equivalent ratio multiply by 3:

   $5:2:3:7$
   $15:6:9:21$ $\downarrow \times 3$

So $5:2:3:7$ and $15:6:9:21$ are equivalent ratios.

Example 2 Complete this set of equivalent ratios.

   $15:24:27$
   ■ : 8 : ■

Here the 8 can be made by dividing the 24 by 3.

To find the equivalent ratio divide by 3:

   $15:24:27$
   $5:8:9$

So $15:24:27$ and $5:8:9$ are equivalent ratios.

Exercise 46.4
Practising Skill 46C

1 Copy and complete each set of equivalent ratios.

  a 12:30   b 18:45   c 42:35   d 40:56
     2:■   ■:5   6:■   5:■

  e 15:27   f 42:15   g 36:63   h 56:24
     5:■   ■:5   4:■   ■:3

  i 21:35   j 9:81   k 17:51   l 36:32
     ■:5   1:■   ■:3   ■:8

2 Copy and complete each set of equivalent ratios.

  a 15:35:65   b 27:36:45   c 18:36:42   d 63:28:49
     ■:7:■   3:■:■   ■:■:7   ■:4:■

  e 9:15:36   f 45:21:36   g 56:24:64   h 98:14:63
     ■:5:■   ■:7:■   ■:■:8   ■:■:9

3 Copy and complete each set of equivalent ratios.

  a 3:5   b 3:7:9   c 5:11   d 9:2:7
     ■:35   ■:28:■   ■:66   ■:18:■

  e 1:4:7   f 7:11:15   g 12:17   h 21:5:13
     ■:28:■   ■:■:60   ■:51   ■:60:■

  i 12:5   j 1000:75   k 275:50:350   l 1200:1000
     ■:35   ■:3   ■:2:■   ■:5

Sharing by ratio

Skill 46D
Dividing in a given ratio

When you divide an amount in a ratio, it is not the same as dividing the amount equally.

Example

Orange dye is a mix of red and yellow in the ratio 2:3.
How much of each colour is used to mix 675 litres of orange dye?

The mix is: Red:Yellow
               2 : 3   (a total of 5 parts)

> The ratio 2:3 compares 2 parts with 3 parts. This is a total of 5 parts.

To find the value of 1 part.
   675 litres has to be divided into 5 parts
   that is   675 ÷ 5 = 135
   So 1 part of the mix is 135 litres.

Red dye is 2 parts, which is   2 × 135 = 270
Yellow dye is 3 parts, which is   3 × 135 = 405

So 270 litres of red dye and 405 litres of yellow dye are used.

Exercise 46.5
Practising Skill 46D

1 Divide 364 litres in the ratio 5:8.

2 Divide 150 km in the ratio 3:7.

3 Divide 112 kg in the ratio 5:9.

4 Divide £3744 in the ratio 5:4.

5 Divide £675 in the ratio 13:12.

6 Divide 1500 kg in the ratio 1:1:6.

7 Divide £1250 in the ratio 4:1:5.

8 Divide 1575 litres in the ratio 5:13:7.

9 Divide 114 metres in the ratio 3:2:1.

10 Divide £35000 in the ratio 13:11:14:12.

Exercise 46.6
Using Skill 46D

1 Green dye is a mix of blue and yellow in the ratio 7:11.
A mix of 810 litres of green dye is made.

  a How much blue dye is in the mix?
  b How much yellow dye is in the mix?

2 Tropical Juice is a mix of orange and pineapple juice in the ratio 5:7.
A mix of 2100 litres of Tropical Juice is made.

  a How much orange juice is in the mix?
  b How much pineapple juice is in the mix?

3 The Orion B hockey team scored a total of 56 goals last season.
Goals at home and away goals were in the ratio 9:5.

  a How many away goals did they score last season?
  b How many home goals did they score?

4 Josh and Mia are doing a sponsored swim of 5000 metres.
They decide to share the distance so that:
    Josh and Mia swim the distance in the ratio 17:23.

  a What share of the distance will Josh swim?
  b What distance will Mia swim?

5 There are 408 pages in a book.
The ratio of pages with pictures to pages without pictures is 5:19.

  a How many pages do not have pictures?
  b How many pages do have pictures?

6 Stuart teaches people to dive. Last year he taught 589 people to dive.
The ratio of females to males was 7:12.

  a How many males did he teach to dive?
  b How many females did he teach to dive?

7 The fuel for a mower is a mix of petrol and oil.
Petrol and oil is mixed in the ratio 18:1.
The tank holds 950 ml of fuel.

  a How much petrol is used in a mix to fill the tank?
  b How much oil is used?

8 Jo and Emma share £75 in the ratio 7:8. How much does each get?

9 The length and width of rectangle A are in the ratio 13:3.

Rectangle A
Perimeter 224 m

  a Find the length of the rectangle.
  b Find the width of the rectangle.
  c Calculate the area of the rectangle.

Translations

Skill 47A
Translating a shape

A vector is written with two numbers in a bracket.

The top number gives the move across:

$$- \longleftrightarrow +$$

The bottom number gives the move up or down.

$$\begin{array}{c} + \\ \uparrow \\ \downarrow \\ - \end{array}$$

So the vector $\binom{-3}{5}$ means a slide of 3 left and 5 up.

◆ A **translation** is one type of transformation.

◆ When a shape slides on a grid we say it has been translated.

This diagram shows a quadrilateral PQRS which has been translated.

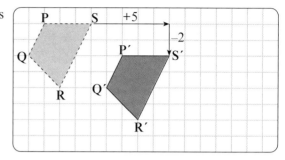

Each point has moved 5 squares to the right and 2 squares down

We say the quadrilateral has been translated by the vector $\binom{5}{-2}$.

Note that a translation does not
◆ change the object's size or shape.
◆ rotate or reflect the object.

Exercise 47.1
Practising skill 47A

1 a Copy the triangle ABC on to squared paper.

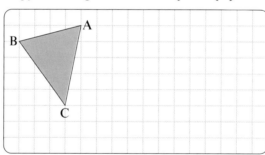

b Translate the triangle by the vector $\binom{7}{3}$ and draw the image A′B′C′.

2 a Copy the quadrilateral STUV.

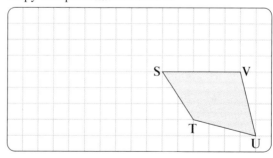

b Translate STUV by the vector $\binom{-7}{3}$ and draw the image S′T′U′V′.
c What translation would take S′T′U′V′ back to STUV?

When you are asked what translation does something, you must give the vector.

3 This diagram shows six similar triangles.

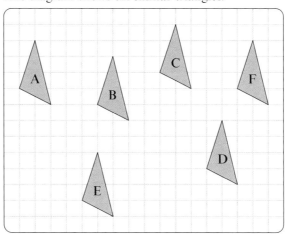

a What translation would slide triangle D on to triangle F?

b Copy and complete this table.

Slide		Translation
from triangle	to triangle	
D	A	$\binom{-12}{5}$
E	D	■
C	A	■
B	F	■
F	■	$\binom{-9}{-1}$
B	■	$\binom{4}{2}$
C	D	■

4 **a** Copy shape A.

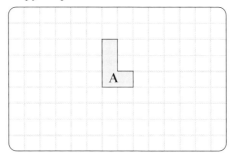

b Translate A by the vector $\binom{4}{-1}$. Give this shape the label B.

c Translate B by the vector $\binom{-7}{-2}$. Give this shape the label C.

d Translate C by the vector $\binom{3}{3}$.
What do you discover?

5 When a shape is translated by the vectior $\binom{0}{0}$, what happens to it?

6 A shape P is translated by the vector $\binom{4}{-3}$ to give shape Q.
What translation will slide Q back on to P?

Enlargements

Skill 47B
Enlarging a shape

♦ Enlargement is another type of transformation.

♦ When a shape is enlarged the angles stay the same but the lengths change.

♦ When a shape is enlarged by a scale factor of 2, every length on the image will be twice as long as on the object.

Example

Draw an enlargement of shape ABCDE with a scale factor of 2.

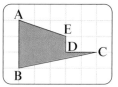

The length AB is 3 units, so on the image A´B´ will be 6 units.
Length CD is 2 units, so C´D´ will be 4 units on the image.

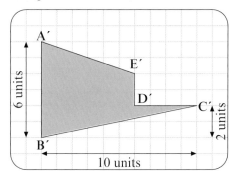

On the object BC is 5 across and 1 up.
So on the image B´C´ will be 10 across and 2 up.

Exercise 47.2
Practising skill 47B

1 Draw an enlargement of shape P with a scale factor of 2.

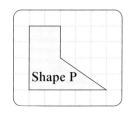

2 Draw an enlargement, with scale factor 3, of shape Q.

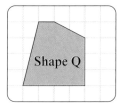

3 **a** What is the area of shape R in square units?
   b Draw an enlargement of shape R with a scale factor of 2.
   c Find the area of the image. What do you notice?

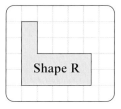

Skill 47C
Enlarging a shape from the
centre of enlargement

♦ Sometimes you will know the **centre of enlargement**.
All parts of the image are enlarged from this point.

Example

Enlarge shape ABCDE with scale factor 3
from the centre of enlargement P.

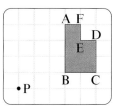

♦ Join the centre P with a straight line
through point A.
♦ Measure the length PA.
♦ Multiply the length of PA by 3 – this
is the length of PA′.
♦ Mark point A′.

♦ Do the same for each other point: B, C, D, E and F.
♦ Join up the points of the image.

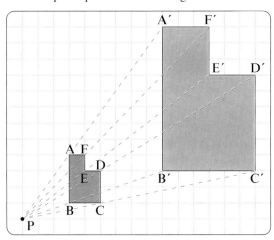

Exercise 47.3
Practising Skill 47C

1 a Copy the diagram below.
It shows the start of an enlargement of shape ABCD with a
scale factor 2, from the centre of enlargement P.

b Complete the enlargement to show all the image A′B′C′D′.
The side A′D′ has been drawn for you.

When you finish your
image A′B′C′D′, check
that all its sides are twice as
long as on shape ABCD.

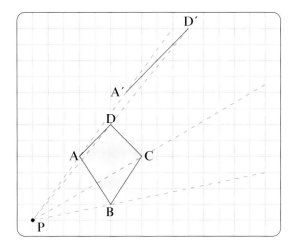

2   Enlarge triangle PQR with scale factor 3 from the centre of enlargement C.

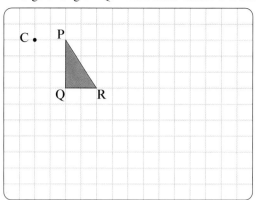

3   Shape RSTU is enlarged with scale factor 2 from the centre of enlargement C.

    a   Will the image be on the left or the right of the shape?
    b   Show the enlargement.

You will find that the image R′S′T′U′ overlaps the shape RSTU.
This is OK.

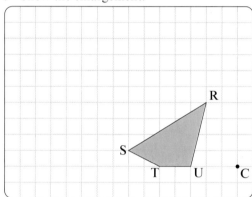

When the centre of enlargement C is inside the object, the image will be around the outside.

Example

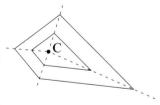

4   For this enlargement, the centre of enlargement C is inside the object.
Enlarge JKLM with scale factor 3 from point C.

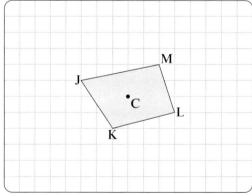

This revises the work in Sections 43 to 47

This shows the position of three boats.

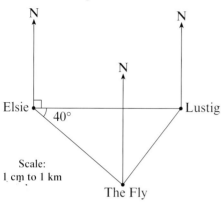

Scale:
1 cm to 1 km

1 Skill 43A

  a Calculate the bearing of The Fly from Elsie.
  b Measure the bearing of The Fly from Lustig.

2 Skill 43B

Give the bearing and distance of:

  a Elsie from Lustig
  b Elsie from The Fly.

3 Skill 44A

The prices in a shop are all increased by 20%.
Copy and complete the table.

Item	Old price	New price
Lead	£4.00	■
Video	£256	■
Remote	£16.20	■

4 Skill 44B

Decrease each amount by 5%.

  a £6.00   **b** £424   **c** £24.80

5 Skill 44C

Rachel bought a carpet for £420.
She found that she had to add VAT at 17.5%.

  a What was the total price including VAT?
  b How much VAT did she pay?

6 Skill 45A

These results came from 100 spins of a spinner with coloured sections.

Colour	Frequency
Red	32
Green	23
Yellow	16
Blue	29

What is the probability of the spinner landing on Blue?

7 Skill 46A

These are the items used in a wood treatment.

Linseed oil	1 litre
Stain	$\frac{1}{2}$ litre
White spirit	2 litres

Write the ratio of:

  a white spirit to linseed oil
  b stain to white spirit.

8 Skill 46B

Write each of these ratios in its lowest terms.

  a $12:48$ **b** $2:\frac{1}{2}:4$ **c** $15:25:100$

9 Skill 46C

Which two of these ratios are equivalent to each other?

$30:40$ $6:8$ $12:18$ $4:8$
$4:5$ $44:60$ $20:30$ $9:18$

10 Skill 46D

  a Divide 20 in the ratio $3:1$.
  b Divide £56 in the ratio $1:2:5$.

11 Skill 47A

  a Make a copy of the diagram below.
  b Show the image of PQR after the translation $\left(\begin{smallmatrix}6\\-2\end{smallmatrix}\right)$.

12 Skill 47B

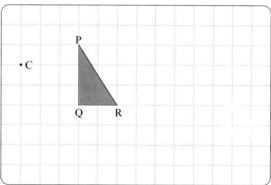

  a Make another copy the diagram above.
  b Enlarge triangle PQR with scale factor 2 from the centre of enlargement C.

On 31 May 1682 there was a storm in Oxford which gave 60 cm of water in about a quarter of an hour.

A slight shower!

Bananananananananananananananananananananana
On 30 April 1988 in Selinsgrove Pennsylvania USA a banana split was made which was 7.32 km long.

Jo's always on hand
In 1900 Johann Hurlinger of Austria walked 871 miles from Vienna to Paris on his hands. His average speed was 1.6 mph. He walked for 10 hours each day.

OH! WHAT A LITTLE ONE-WHEEL
In March 1994 in Las Vegas Peter Rosendahl of Sweden rode a unicycle 20 centimetre high for a distance of 3.6 metres. The wheel diameter was only 2.5 cm.

Up the pole !
Mellissa Sanders lived in a hut at the top of a pole in the USA for two years. She started on 10 October 1986. Her hut was 1.8 metres wide by 2.1 metres deep by 1.8 metres tall.

Michael Lotito was born in France in 1950. He found he could eat 2 pounds of metal per day. He has been seen to eat 10 bicycles, 7 TV sets and a small aeroplane.

Number types
On 14 October 1993 Mikhail Shestov set a record when he had typed the numbers 1 to 795 in 5 minutes. He had made no errors.

Em25
The world's longest bypass is the M25 around London. It has a total length of 195.5 km (121.5 miles)

The circumference of the Earth at the equator is 40075 km and its mass is 5880 000 000 000 000 000 000 tons.

Weight watchers

Piece on earth
A jigsaw with 1500 pieces was made for the photo on the cover of a magazine. The jigsaw was done in 1985 by students from schools in Canterbury.

It was a rectangle about 22 metres long by 14 metres wide.

Can beans be hasbeens?
Baked beans were first sold in the UK in 1928. By 1992 they were selling at the rate of 55.8 million cans per year.

Tall stories
The tallest man in the world was Robert Wadlow from the USA who was 2.72 metres tall. The tallest man in Scotland was Angus Macaskill who was 2.36 metres tall. The highest mountain in the USA is Mount McKinley at 6194 metres and the highest one in Scotland is Ben Nevis at 1344 metres.

Jagged line
In 1992 the Jaguar XJ220 set the land speed record for a road car of 217 miles per hour.

Barmy salami
In Norway in July 1992 a giant salami was made. It had a diameter of 20 cm and was about 21 metres long.

Can can or cannot
A square-based pyramid tower of 4900 cans was built by 5 adults and 5 children at Dunhurst School, Petersfield on 30 May 1994 in a time of 25 minutes 54 seconds.

AMAZING FACTS
p9

1 **a** How much higher is Mount McKinley than Ben Nevis?

  b How many times higher is Mount McKinley than Ben Nevis? Give your answer to 1 dp.

2 The jigsaw in Canterbury had 1500 pieces.

Write this number in words.

3 **a** For baked beans, after how many years were they selling at 55.8 million cans a year?

  b Write 55.8 million in digits.

4 If the Jaguar XJ220 went flat-out round the M25 would it take:

  A just over a quarter of an hour

  B just over half an hour

  C just over an hour and three quarters

  D just under an hour?

5 1 mile is about 1.6 km.

Roughly how long was the Selinsgrove banana split in miles?

6 For roughly how many days did Mellissa Sanders live in her hut at the top of the pole?

7 Mellissa Sander's hut was this size.

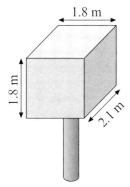

1.8 m

1.8 m

2.1 m

Calculate the capacity of the hut.
Give your answer in m³ to 1 dp.

8 What was the area of the Canterbury jigsaw?

9 A bicycle weighs about 28 pounds.

How many days would it take Michael Lotito to eat ten of these bicycles?

10 About how many Selinsgrove banana splits could be laid end to end around the M25 motorway?

11 How much taller was Robert Wadlow in the USA than Angus Macaskill in Scotland?

12 For the Oxford storm in 1682:

  a How many centimetres of rain fell per minute?

  b 1 inch is equal to 2.54 cm.
  About how many inches of rain fell in the quarter of an hour?

13 **a** Peter Rosendahl rode his unicycle 3.6 metres. How many centimetres is this?

  b Calculate the circumference of the unicycle wheel. Give your answer to the nearest cm.

14 Which of these is the approximate radius of the Earth at the equator?

  A 12 756 km   **B** 125 900 km

  C 6295 km   **D** 6378 km

  E 20 038 km   **F** 113 km

15 This shows the cross-section of the giant Norway salami.

20 cm

  a Calculate the circumference of the salami.

  b Calculate the area of this cross-section.

16 **a** When Johann Hurlinger walked on his hands, how far could he walk in one day?

  b How many days would it take Johann to walk round the M25 on his hands?

17 The shows the top of the pyramid of cans.

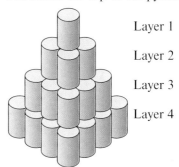

Layer 1

Layer 2

Layer 3

Layer 4

  a Copy and complete this table.

Layer	1	2	3	4	5	6
No. of cans	1	4	9	■	■	■
Total from top	1	5	14	■	■	■

  b How many cans will be in layer 10?

Starting points

You need to know about ...   ... so try these questions

A Writing times in the 24-hour clock system

Skill 11A: *see page 56*

A1 Write each time as a 24-hour time:

a 3:15 pm	b 2:10 am
c 12:45 pm	d 11:35 am
e 9:25 pm	f 8:45 pm
g 9:35 am	h 1 am
i 11:05 pm	j 4:18 am

B Calculating time intervals

Skill 11B: *see page 58*

B1 Copy and complete this table.

Start time	Stop time	Time interval
12:25	14:05	■
16:40	19:10	■
07:35	13:20	■
02:05	07:50	■
12:22	15:08	■
14:48	19:07	■

C Reading timetables

Skill 11C: *see page 59*

C1 Use the timetable on page 59.

a Leave Tonbridge at 19:42 . When do you get to Deal?

b Leave Sandling at 08:45. When do you get to Deal?

D Finding average speed using a formula

Skill 38B: *see page 215*

D1 Calculate the average speed for each journey (to 1 dp).

a 600 miles in 8 hours

b 420 miles in 7.5 hours

c 184 miles in $4\frac{1}{4}$ hours

d 140 miles in 3 hours 45 min

Reading travel graphs

Exercise 48.1

This timetable shows the journeys of three buses from the Station to Bell Cross.

The D column gives distances, in miles, from the Station.

D	Stop	Bus 1	Bus 2	Bus 3
0	Station	08:20	08:40	09:00
2	High Street	08:30	—	09:10
4	King's Square	08:45	09:00	09:20
5	Oak Lane	08:55	09:05	—
7	Blue Star	09:10	09:15	—
10	Bell Cross	09:20	09:25	09:30

1   How far is it from the Station to King's Square?

2   How far is it from the Station to Bell Cross?

3   How far is it from King's Square to Bell Cross?

4   Calculate the journey time for each bus from the station to Bell Cross.

5   What is the average speed of bus 1 for the journey?

6   What is average speed of bus 3 for the journey?

Skill 48A
Interpreting a travel graph

You can think of a travel graph as a picture of a journey.
A travel graph shows distances and times on its axes.

Example

This graph shows the journeys of the 3 buses in the timetable on page 268.

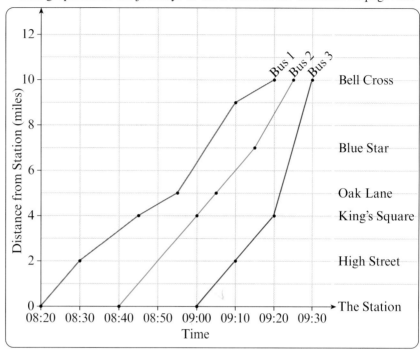

♦ The graphs can also tell you about the speed of travel:

   ❖ The steeper the line of the graph, the faster the speed of travel.

   The graph for bus 1 shows that:
   the journey from High Street to Kings Square was slower than
   the journey from Blue Star to Bell Cross.

♦ The graphs can tell you how far from the Station buses are at
   a certain time.

   From the Station:
   at 09:15 bus 1 was about   8.5 miles away
             bus 2 was   7 miles away
             bus 3 was about   3 miles away.

♦ The graph can tell you at what time each bus passes a fixed point.

   A speed camera is fixed exactly 6 miles from the Station.
   At what time did each bus pass the speed camera?

   The speed camera was passed by: bus 1 at about 09:02
                                    bus 2 at about 09:10
                                    bus 3 at about 09:24

> We have to say *about* as
> we are reading from the
> graph. The value will not
> be exact unless it is one of
> the plots.

Exercise 48.2
Practising Skill 48A

1   Use the graph above.

    a How far was each bus from the station at 09:05?
    b At what time was each bus exactly 8 miles from the station?
    c For bus 3, which part of the journey was fastest?
           Explain how you know.

2   This graph shows the journeys of 3 buses from the Station to Church End.

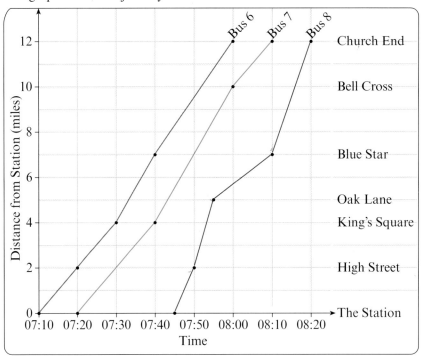

a   How far is it from Church End to the Station?
b   How far is it from Oak Lane to Church End?
c   At what time did bus 8 leave the Station?
d   At what time was bus 7 at Bell Cross?
e   Is Blue Star more, or less, than half way between
    the Station and Church End? Explain.

3   At what time was each bus exactly 8 miles from the Station?

4   A new speed camera has been set up exactly 3 miles from the Station.
    At about what time did each bus pass the speed camera?

5   At 07:55 how far was each bus from the Station?

6   Kamal travelled on bus 7.
    He saw a sign post that said Church End 3 miles.
    He looked at his watch.

    What time do you think his watch showed?

7   Copy and complete this timetable.

D	Stop	Bus 1	Bus 2	Bus 3
0	Station	07:10	■	■
2	High Street	■	—	■
4	King's Square	■	07:40	■
5	Oak Lane	■	■	■
7	Blue Star	07:40	■	■
10	Bell Cross	■	■	■
12	Church End	■	■	■

8   For the journey of bus 8:
    a   Which part of the journey was quickest? Explain.
    b   Which part of the journey was the slowest? Explain.
    c   In minutes, how long was the whole journey?

This travel graph shows the journey of 4 buses:
three buses from the Station to Church End, and one
from Church End to the Station.

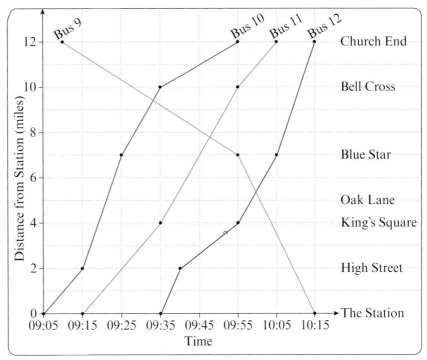

♦ The graph for bus 9 crosses the graphs for buses 10, 11, and 12.

This shows that bus 9 passes buses 10, 11, and 12.
Reading from the graph:
Bus 9 passes bus 10 at about 09:33
about 9.5 miles from the Station
(about 2.5 miles from Church End)

9 From the graph above, roughly where, and when did bus 9 pass:
a bus 11
b bus 12?

10 At what time was each bus at the half-way point of its journey?

11 At 09:50 a bus was caught in a speed trap 9 miles from Church End.
Which bus was this?

12 Which had the faster average speed for the journey: bus 10 or bus 11?
Explain how you decided.

13 At what time was bus 9 exactly ten miles from Church End?

14 Copy and complete this timetable for the graph above.

D	Stop	Bus 10	Bus 11	Bus 12
0	Station	■	■	■
2	High Street	■	■	■
4	King's Square	■	■	■
5	Oak Lane	■	■	■
7	Blue Star	■	■	■
10	Bell Cross	■	■	■
12	Church End	■	■	■

Drawing travel graphs

Skill 48B
Drawing a travel graph

To draw a travel graph you need data about time and distance.

This can be:
    the time and distance for a whole journey
    or times and distances for each part of a journey.

Example

Emma, Steve and Ravi all cycle to college.
On one day:
Ravi cycled home from college non-stop. He left college
    at 12:15 and got home at 13:30.
Emma left home at 12:15, at 13:00 she stopped at a shop
    8 miles from home for 10 minutes. She got to college at 13:35.
Steve left home at 12:00. He stopped 4 miles away for a 15 minute rest.
    Then he set off for for the bike shop 10 miles from home.
    He was in the shop 15 minutes and got to college at 13:45.

Draw a travel graph to show these three journeys.

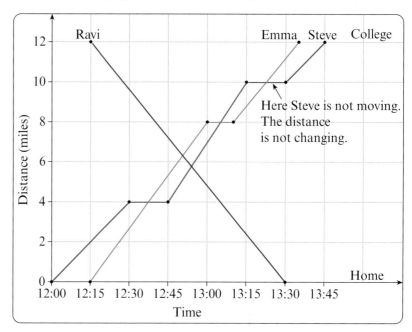

Exercise 48.3
Practising Skill 48B

1   Make a copy of the travel graph above.

2   From your graph at where and when did Ravi pass:

   a   Emma   **b**   Steve?

3   **a**   At what time did Emma pass Steve?
     b   Where was Steve at the time?

4   Kim left college at 12:00 and got to the cycle shop at 12:15.
    She was in the shop for 15 minutes and got home at 13:45.

   a   On your axes draw a graph to show Kim's journey home.
   b   Who did Kim pass first on her way home: Emma or Steve?
         Explain how you decided.
   c   Calculate the time each person's journey took.

Starting points

You need to know about ...

... so try these questions

A Rounding money to the nearest penny

Skill 18D: *see page 102*

A1 Round each of these amounts to the nearest penny.
  a £34.878   b £2.494
  c £15.996   d £1.375
  e £234.076   f £3.008

A2 Calculate $\frac{1}{3}$ of £20 to the nearest penny.

B Converting a percentage to a decimal

Skill 32A: *see page 180*

B1 Convert each of these to a decimal value.
  a 72%   b 6%   c 88%
  d $34\frac{1}{2}$%   e $8\frac{1}{2}$%   f 1%
  g 25.5%   h 10.5%   i $\frac{1}{2}$%

C Calculating a percentage of an amount

Skill 32C: *see page 182*

C1 Calculate each of these to the nearest penny.
  a 42% of £27 650
  b 18% of £65 000
  c 37% of £55
  d $14\frac{1}{2}$% of £9
  e $7\frac{1}{2}$% of £12.50
  f 17% of £125.65

D Calculting a percentage increase

Skill 44A: *see page 248*

D1 Increase each of these by 17% (answers to the nearest penny).
  a £55   b £180   c £6
  d £82.45 e £2.99   f £1.39

D2 Calculate each of these to the nearest penny.
  a Increase £14.55 by 6%
  b Increase £300.99 by 7%
  c Increase £3.99 by 45%
  d Increase £199.99 by 12%
  e Increase £350.55 by 15%.

E Calculating a percentage decrease

Skill 44B: *see page 250*

E1 Decrease each of these by 14% (answers to the nearest penny).
  a £55   b £180   c £6
  d £82.45 e £2.99   f £1.39

E2 Calculate each of these to the nearest penny.
  a Decrease £55.14 by 6%
  b Decrease £105.99 by 7%
  c Decrease £35.65 by 15%
  d Decrease £255.99 by 10%
  e Decrease £349.99 by 18%

E3 A regular size cola is 350 ml. A super size is regular +12%, how many ml is this?

Buying on credit

There are rules for credit.
These rules can be changed
by the government to:

  make credit easier to get
  make credit harder to get.

When you buy on credit, you buy something and only pay a deposit
The rest of the price is paid off with a loan.

The deposit is an amount you pay in cash.

The deposit can be:

- a sum of money, say £30
- a percentage of the full price, say 20%.

It may be possible to buy on credit with no deposit.

When you have paid the deposit and signed the credit forms,
you can take the item you have bought on credit from the shop.

Skill 49A
Calculating a deposit

You may have to calculate a deposit as a percentage of the price of an item.

Example

A TV is priced at £219.99.
To buy the TV on credit you must pay a deposit of 17%.
Calculate the deposit to the nearest penny.

To the nearest penny is the
same as to 2 dp.

To calculate 17% of £219.99
        17% as a decimal is 0.17

The deposit is given by: $219.99 \times 0.17 = 37.3983$
                          $= 37.40$ (to 2 dp)

So the deposit paid on the TV is £37.40 (to the nearest penny).

Exercise 49.1
Practising Skill 49A

1 Copy and complete this table.
   Give the deposit paid to
   the nearest penny.

Item	Price	Deposit	Deposit paid
TV	£219.99	17%	£37.40
Video	£349.99	15%	■
Camcorder	£499.99	22%	■
Cooker	£359.99	8%	■
Fridge	£234.99	7%	■
Scooter	£2395	18%	■
Bike	£7995	21%	■
CD player	£189.99	$7\frac{1}{2}$%	■
Sound system	£679.99	$15\frac{1}{2}$%	■
Holiday	£438.65	22%	■
Microwave	£279.99	35%	■

You may also have to pay a deposit when you book or reserve something.

- If you book a holiday, you will have to pay a deposit.
- If you book tickets for something, you may have to pay a deposit.
- If you hire something, say a car, you may have to pay a deposit.

Exercise 49.2
Using Skill 49A

1 Jade booked a holiday with her friends. The total cost was £1657.75.
   They had to pay a deposit of 15%.

   a How much was the deposit, to the nearest penny?
   b How much was left to pay before they went?

2 A freezer is advertised for £309.99.
To buy it on credit you have to pay a deposit of 7%.

  a To the nearest penny calculate the deposit for credit.
  b How much is left to pay by credit?

3 Darren wants to buy a new bike priced at £259.99.
To buy it on credit he must pay a deposit of 18%.

  a To the nearest penny calculate the deposit he must pay.
  b How much is left to pay by credit.

4 Mia saw a CD system advertised for £249.99.
To buy the system on credit she had to pay a deposit of $7\frac{1}{2}$%.

  a Calculate the deposit to the nearest penny.
  b How much did she have to pay by credit?

5 Shelly bought a car that was priced at £2995.
She needed a 15% deposit and could pay the rest by credit.

  a Calculate the deposit she needed to the nearest penny.
  b How much did she have to pay by credit?

Skill 49B
Calculating with interest
for credit

The amount you borrow on credit will have interest added to it.
◆ Interest is a charge made for borrowing the money.
◆ Interest is charged at a percentage rate for each year of the loan.
◆ Interest is calculated on the amount borrowed.
◆ Interest is added at the start of the loan.

Example

pa stands for 'per annum'.

This means 'each year'.

When you calculate with money, round to the nearest penny (to 2 dp).

Carla borrows £385 on credit over 2 years. The rate of interest is 18% pa
Calculate how much Carla has to pay back in total.

The money to pay back is: Year 1 Year 2
100% of money borrowed + 18% + 18% which is 136%
136% as a decimal is 1.36

136% of £385 is given by: $385 \times 1.36 = 523.60$

So the total amount to pay back on credit is £523.60.

Exercise 49.3
Practising skill 49B

1 Copy and complete this table.
Calculate the total to be paid back to the nearest penny.

Loan	Interest rate	Years	Total payback
£45	22%	2	£64.80
£275	14%	2	■
£455	23%	2	■
£850	17%	2	■
£1200	$15\frac{1}{2}$%	2	■
£725	21%	1	■
£2265	16%	3	■
£3435	18%	3	■
£6125	12.5%	4	■
£638.55	15%	5	■
£424.80	21%	6	■
£375.75	22%	4	■

Skill 49C
Calculating credit payments by instalment

To pay on credit you make a number of payments, or instalments.
♦ Instalments may be once a week or once a month.
♦ Instalments are equal amounts.

The amount of each instalment is:
The total to be paid back on credit ÷ The number of instalments

Example

Jim has a loan of £675 for 3 years at 14% pa.
He will pay it back in 36 instalments (once a month).
Calculate what he pays each instalment.

The money to pay back is:
100% of loan + 14% + 14% + 14% which is 142%
142% as a decimal is 1.42

142% of £675 is given by:
$675 \times 1.42 = 958.50$
The total to be paid back is £958.50.

Each instalment is   £958.50 ÷ 36 = £26.625
= £26.63 (to the nearest penny)

So each instalment is £26.63 (to the nearest penny).

Exercise 49.4
Practising Skill 49C

1   Copy and complete this table.
Calculate each instalment to the nearest penny.

Loan	Interest rate	Years	Total payback	No. of instalments	Each instalment
£675	14%	3	£958.50	36	£39.94
£850	22%	2	■	24	■
£945	15%	4	■	48	■
£1655	18%	5	■	60	■

2   Calculate the monthly instalment for:
a loan of £875
at a rate of interest of 21% for 3 years
paid back in 36 instalments.

For these questions, answers should be:
to the nearest penny.

3   Ella took a loan of £1235 to pay for her first car.
She took the loan over 4 years at a rate of interest of 15% pa.
She will pay back with 48 equal monthly instalments.

Calculate how much she pays each month.

4   Rita took a loan of £485 over 3 years to buy a video camera.
The rate of interest was 18% and she is paying 36 monthly instalments.

Calculate how much she pays each month.

5   Ky decided on a holiday and took a loan to pay for it.
The loan was for £955 at an interest rate of 22% over 2 years.
There were 24 instalments to be paid.

   a   How much in total did he have to pay back on the loan?
   b   Calculate the amount of each instalment.
   c   How much interest did he pay back on the loan?

Skill 49D
Calculating a discount

A discount is a sum of money that is taken off an original amount. When you get a discount, you pay less for something.

♦ You might get a discount for paying in cash.

♦ You might get a discount for paying by a certain date.

♦ In all sales you get a discount on the price of goods.

♦ A discount is often a percentage of the original price.

Example

A watch is priced at £34.99.
A discount of 7% is given for cash.
Calculate the discount price of the watch to the nearest penny.

£34.99 is 100% of the price of the watch.
The discount for cash is 7%.
The price after discount is: 100% − 7% = 93% of £34.99

93% as a decimal is 0.93

93% of £34.99 is given by:
34.99 × 0.93 = 32.5407

So the discount price of the watch is £32.54 (to the nearest penny).

Exercise 49.5
Practising Skill 49D

1 Copy and complete this table.
Calculate the discount price to the nearest penny.

Item	Price	Discount	Discount price
Watch	£34.99	7%	£32.54
Bike	£219.99	8%	■
TV	£349.99	15%	■
Camera	£79.99	12%	■
Toaster	£12.99	5%	■
Holiday	£579.99	18%	■
Drill	£169.99	17%	■
Microwave	£229.99	25%	■
Fridge	£219.99	20%	■
CD player	£349.99	$17\frac{1}{2}$%	■
Clarinet	£269.99	5.5%	■

Exercise 49.6
Using Skill 49D

For this exercise answers should be:
to the nearest penny.

1 Mina saw a cycle helmet priced at £49.99.
She waited until the shop had a sale and got a discount of 12%.
How much did she pay for the helmet?

2 A shop had water filters priced at £28.49.
If you bought one before 31 March, you could get a discount of 15%.
How much would you pay for a filter on 30 March?

3 A holiday is advertised for £379.99.
If you book before 1 November, you get a discount of 8%.
You book this holiday on 31 October, how much should you pay?

4 A TV is priced at £189.99, and a video recorder at £269.99.
If you buy them both, at the same time, you get a discount of 18%.
Find the total charged for a TV and video recorder bought together.

5 Explain how to calculate a price after a discount of $12\frac{1}{2}$%.

Savings and simple interest

Skill 49E

Calculating with the simple interest formula

---

pa stands for per annum.
This means each year.

When you save money in a savings account you are paid interest.
One type of interest is called 'simple interest'.

◆ Simple interest is calculated:

❖ on the sum of money you save: this is called the Principal
❖ as a percentage pa: this is called the Rate
❖ over a number of years: this is called the Time.

The formula in words is:
    $Interest = Principal \times Rate \times Time$
In this formula:
    the Rate must be used as a decimal
    the Time is in years.

Example

Calculate the interest paid on £320 saved for 4 years at a simple interest rate of 6%.

$Interest = Principal \times Rate \times Time$
    Principal = £320
    Rate = 6% = 0.06
    Time = 4 years
    $I = P \times R \times T$
       $= 320 \times 0.06 \times 4$
       $= 76.8$

So the interest on £320 saved for 4 years at 6% is £76.80.

Exercise 49.7

Practising Skill 49E

1 Copy and complete this table.
Calculate the simple interest to the nearest penny.

Principal (£)	%	Rate (decimal)	Time (years)	Interest (£)
20	6	0.06	4	76.80
450	7	■	3	■
275	4	■	6	■
620	5	■	2	■
280	8	■	5	■
660	9	■	3	■
810	7	■	5	■
1200	3	■	12	■
2250	11	■	15	■
1750	6.5	■	8	■
3550	4.5	■	7	■

Exercise 49.8

Using Skill 49E

1 Ky won £365 in a prize draw.
He saved this money for 6 years at a simple interest rate of 4%.

  a Calculate the interest paid on these savings.
  b At the end of 6 years what were these savings in total?

2 Raisa was left £865 in a will.
She saved this money for 12 years at a simple interest rate of 7%.

  a Calculate the interest paid on these savings.
  b At the end of 12 years what were these savings in total?

3 A sports club is given a grant of £12 500.
The grant is not used for 2 years and the club saves the money for this time at a simple interest rate of 6%.

  a How much interest will the club get at the end of the 2 years?
  b What will the grant be worth in total at the end of 2 years?

4 Calculate the simple interest paid on a sum of £478 saved at 7% pa for 6 years.

5 Dave is saving for a bike. He wants to spend about £750.
Five years ago he saved £525 at a simple interest rate of 8%.

  a With the interest does Dave have the amount he wants to spend? Explain your answer.

  Dave decides to save his money for another 2 years.

  b How much will he then have in total for his bike?

Profit and loss

Skill 49F
Calculating profit and loss

You make a profit if you gain money in some way.
You make a loss if you lose money in some way.

Example 1

A sports club printed 5000 programmes which cost them £2350.
Each programme is sold for £2.50.
If they sell every programme, how much profit will they make?

Total for selling 5000 programmes at £2.50 each is:
  $5000 \times £2.50 = £12\,500$

The cost of the programmes is £2350.

Profit = Total from sales – Cost of programmes
  $= £12\,500 – £2350$
  $= £10\,150$

So if they sell every programme they will make £10 150 profit.

Example 2

A 52-seater coach is hired to take fans to a match.
The charge for the coach is £382.
The coach fare will be £7.50.
If only 47 fans go on the coach, what loss is made on coach hire?

Total fares paid by the fans is:
  $47 \times £7.50 = £352.50$

The cost of coach hire is £382.

Loss = Cost of coach hire – Total from fares
  $= £382 – £352.50$
  $= £29.50$

So the loss made on the coach hire is £29.50.

Exercise 49.9
Using Skill 49F

1 Jake has a market stall.
He buys 150 tapes at 80p each and sells them at £1.99 each.
If he sells all the tapes, how much profit will he make?

2 For a match Emma buys 250 cans of cola at 14p each.
She sells them at 25p each but only sells 87 cans at the match.

   a Calculate the loss Emma makes on the match.
   b If Emma did sell all the cans, how much profit would she make?

3 Jake bought 450 flowerpots for 16p each.
He sold them all at 49p each.

   Calculate the total profit Jake made on the flowerpots.

4 Asa bought 30 tickets for a match at £6.50 each.
He planned to sell them at £8 each but only managed to sell 17 tickets.

   Calculate the loss Asa made on the tickets.

Value for money

Skill 49G
Calculating value
for money

'Value for money' is one way to compare prices.
When you compare items you must compare equal amounts of the items.

Example

A 500 g box of cereal costs 89p. A 750 g box costs £1.39.
Which box is better value for money?

For the 500 g box
Cost of 100 g is:
   89p ÷ 5 = 17.8p

For the 750 g box
Cost of 100 g is:
   139p ÷ 7.5 = 18.5p

17.8p is less than 18.5p.
This shows that:
each 100 g in the 500 g box costs less than each 100 g in the 750 g box.

So the 500 g box is better value for money.

Exercise 49.10
Using Skill 49G

You will need to use all the digits shown in your calculator display. Rounding answers does not help when you compare in this way.

1 A 500 g box of biscuits costs £1.39, and a 750 g box costs £1.99.

   Which box is better value for money? Explain.

2 A 2 litre bottle of olive oil costs £6.99.
A 4.5 litre can of the same oil costs £15.99.

   Which is better value for money: the bottle or the can? Explain.

3 A case of cat food holds 24 cans and sells for £11.49.

   a Calculate the cost of one tin in the case.
      (Record all the calculator display for your answer.)

   A crate of cat food holds 50 cans and sells for £23.99.

   b Which is better value for money: the case or the crate?

4 Two shops advertise tapes for sale.
Supersounds advertises 10 tapes for £8.99.
Sound City advertises 12 tapes for £9.85.

   Which shop is better value for tapes? Explain.

5 A garden centre sells compost in 3 different size bags.
   Standard pack: holds 60 litres and costs £1.99
   Large pack: holds 80 litres and costs £2.69
   Value pack: holds 110 litres and costs £3.49

   a Calculate the cost of one litre of compost in each size bag.
   b Which bag gives better value for money?

Starting points

You need to know about ...   ... so try these questions

A Mathematical terms for some parts of a circle

- On the diagram these parts of a circle are labelled:
  Centre
  Diameter
  Radius
  Circumference

Circumference
Diameter
Radius
Centre

Also note that:

- ❖ a diameter must go through the centre of the circle
- ❖ the length of a diameter is twice the length of the radius
- ❖ the radius is a straight line from the centre to the edge
- ❖ the circumference is the distance around the edge of the circle.

A1 Copy and complete this table.

Radius	Diameter
6 cm	■
■	18 cm
■	15 cm
12 mm	■
5.5 mm	■
8.4 m	■
■	22.5 cm
4.6 cm	■
■	6.5 cm
■	1.6 m
0.05 m	■

Terms for parts of a circle

A chord

A chord is a straight line drawn across a circle from edge to edge.

Each straight line in the diagram is a **chord**.

A tangent

A tangent to a circle is a line that touches a circle at only one point.

Each straight line in the diagram is a **tangent**.

An arc

An arc of a circle is any piece of the edge of the circle.
An arc can be any length.

Each red part of the circle is an **arc**.

A sector

A sector is part of a whole circle.

A sector is the shape made by an arc and the two radii at the ends of the arc.

In the diagram, the part of the circle shaded red is a **sector**, called the major (or larger) sector. The other sector is called the minor (or smaller) sector.

Exercise 50.1
Parts of a circle

1 a Draw a circle of radius 30 mm.
   b Label the radius.
   c What is the length of the diameter?
   d Draw and label a tangent to the circle.

2 a Draw a circle with a diameter of 7 cm.
   b Label the diameter.
   c Is the radius of the circle more or less than 40 mm?

3 a Draw a circle.
   b Measure its radius.
   c On the circle, show and label an arc.

4 Draw a diagram to show a sector of a circle.

5 Use a diagram to show that the diameter is the longest chord of a circle.

6 Explain why the red part of this diagram is **not** a sector.

The circumference of a circle

Skill 50 A
Calculating the circumference of a circle

π is the Greek letter 'pi'. It is said as 'pie'.

π does not have an exact value so use:
either π = the value on the π key of a calculator
or π = 3.142

The formula for the circumference of a circle is:

Circumference = π × diameter

or you can think of it as:
Circumference = π × 2 × radius

The circumference of a circle is its perimeter.

Example 1

Calculate the circumference of a circle of diameter 7.5 cm.

The formula is: $C = \pi d$
$C = \pi \times 7.5$
$= 23.561 \ldots$
$= 23.56$ (to 2 dp)

So the circumference of a circle of diameter 7.5 cm is 23.56 cm (to 2 dp).

Example 2

Calculate the circumference of a circle of radius 4.2 cm.

The formula is: $C = \pi \times 2 \times r$
$C = \pi \times 2 \times 4.2$
$= 26.389 \ldots$
$= 26.39$ (to 2 dp)

So the circumference of a circle of radius 4.2 cm is 26.39 cm (to 2 dp).

Exercise 50.2
Practising Skill 50A

1 Calculate the circumference of each circle.

   a Diameter 6.8 cm   b Diameter 3.4 cm   c Radius 2.7 cm
   d Radius 6.5 cm   e Diameter 12.5 cm   f Radius 1.8 cm
   g Diameter 15.2 cm   h Radius 22 mm   i Radius 3.15 m

2 A circle has a radius of 6.75 metres.

   a What is the diameter of the circle?

   b Calculate the circumference of the circle.

3 Copy and complete this table.

Radius	Diameter	Circumference
4.5 cm	■	■
■	10.4 cm	■
■	15.8 cm	■
0.75 m	■	■
■	1.3 m	■

Exercise 50.3
Using Skill 50A

1 A wheel has a radius of 15 cm.

   a Calculate the circumference of the wheel.

   The wheel is on a moving trolley. The wheel makes 8 full turns.

   b How far has the trolley moved (to 1 dp)?

2 A can of beans has a radius of 3.9 cm.

   a Calculate the circumference of the can.

   A label 6 cm wide fits exactly around the can.

   b Calculate the area of the label (to 1 dp).

3 This tin of travel sweets is sealed with tape.
The tin has a diameter of 7.2 cm.
The ends of the tape overlap by 0.6 cm.

Find the length of tape used for one tin (to 1 dp).

4 The Classic Cake Co. ties a ribbon around
each cake it makes.
An extra 12 cm of ribbon is allowed for each bow.

Copy and complete this table.

Diameter of cake	Total length of ribbon (to nearest cm)
16 cm	62 cm
17.5 cm	■
20 cm	■
22.5 cm	■
24 cm	■

5 This oil drum has a radius of 27.5 cm.
A white band 4 cm wide is to be painted
around the top of the drum.

   a Calculate the circumference of the drum.

   b Calculate the area of the white band (to 1 dp).

6 A £1 coin had a diameter of 22mm.

   a Calculate its circumference.

   For charity, Ravi is going to roll a £1 coin for 1 km.

   b How many turns will the coin make (to the nearest 10)?

The area of a circle

Skill 50B
Calculating the area of
a circle

$r^2 = r \times r$

For any circle:
radius = diameter ÷ 2

The formula for the area of a circle is:

Area = $\pi \times r^2$ (*r* is the radius of the circle)

Example 1

Calculate the area of a circle of radius 6.5 cm.

The formula is: $A = \pi \times r^2$
$A = \pi \times 6.5^2$
$= 132.732 \dots$
$= 132.73$ (to 2 dp)

So the area of a circle of radius 6.5 cm is 132.73 cm² (to 2 dp).

Example 2

Calculate the area of a circle of diameter 8.5 cm.

The formula is: $A = \pi \times r^2$

The radius $r = 8.5 \div 2$
$r = 4.25$

$A = \pi \times 4.252$
$= 56.745 \dots$
$= 56.75$ (to 2 dp)

So the area of a circle of diameter 8.5 cm is 56.75 cm² (to 2 dp).

Exercise 50.4
Practising Skill 50B

1 Calculate the area of each circle.

a Radius 6.8 cm | b Diameter 5.4 cm | c Radius 2.9 cm
d Radius 6.5 cm | e Diameter 12.5 cm | f Radius 1.8 cm
g Diameter 15.2 cm | h Radius 22 mm | i Radius 3.15 m

2 Copy and complete this table.

Radius	Diameter	Area
4.5 cm	■	■
■	6.8 cm	■
10.5 cm	■	■
■	14.6 cm	■
8.1 cm	■	■
■	21.4 cm	■
0.6 m	■	■

Exercise 50.5
Using Skill 50B

1 A circular lawn has a diameter of 7.5 metres.
Calculate the area of the lawn.

2 Jemma has two parking permits.
One is circular in shape with a radius of 3.5 cm.
The other is square, with a side of 3.5 cm.
Which permit has the larger area? By how much?

3 The label on a jar of honey is circular. It has a diameter of 42 mm.
Show that its area is 14 cm² to the nearest whole number.

4   Music House FM serves an area within a 40 km radius of its transmitter.
    Calculate the area served by Music House FM.

5   The cross-section of a steel cable is a circle of diameter 35 cm.
    Calculate the area of the cross-section.

6   A rope has a circular cross-section with a radius of 0.4 cm.
    Calculate the area of the cross-section of the rope.

Composite shapes with circles

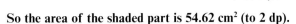

Composite shapes are made up from more than one shape.

Example 1

Find the shaded area.

The area of the shaded part is:
   Area of rectangle – Area of circle

Area of rectangle $= 9.5 \times 9.8 = 93.1$

Area of circle $= \pi \times 3.5^2$
                     $= 38.484 \ldots$
                     $= 38.48$ (to 2 dp)

Area of shaded part $= 93.1 - 38.48$
                                 $= 54.62$ (to 2 dp)

So the area of the shaded part is 54.62 cm² (to 2 dp).

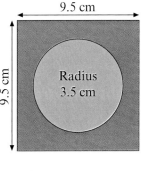

Example 2

Find the shaded area

The area of the shaded part is:
   Area of large circle – Area of small circle

Area large circle $= \pi \times 5.2^2$
                     $= 84.948 \ldots$
                     $= 84.95$ (to 2 dp)

Area small circle $= \pi \times 4.5^2$
                     $= 63.617 \ldots$
                     $= 63.62$ (to 2 dp)

Area of shaded part $= 84.95 - 63.62$
                                 $= 21.33$

So the area of the shaded part is 21.33 cm² (to 2 dp).

Exercise 50.6   1   Find the area of the shaded part in each diagram.

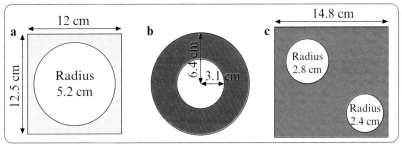

Starting points
You need to know about ...

... so try these questions

A Substituting values in formulas

Skill 13A: *see page 73*

Skill 13A: *see page 73*

A1 A formula that links w, p and k is:
$$w = 5p - 2k$$
Copy and complete this table.

p	k	w
4	5	■
2	8	■
1	6	■
4	9	■
2	11	■
0	4	■
⁻2	3	■
⁻1	0	■

Straight line graphs

Skill 51A
Drawing straight line graphs from a table of values

A straight line graph has a rule that links the x and y coordinates. This rule is called the equation of the line.

A table of values can help you to work out the coordinates to plot. You need to decide on the x-coordinates you are going to use.

Example

Make a table of values with x from ⁻2 to 4 for the line $y = 2x + 1$
Draw a graph of $y = 2x + 1$

The table of values:

x	⁻2	⁻1	0	1	2	3	4
y	⁻3	⁻1	1	3	5	7	9

The y-coordinate is worked out with the equation $y = 2x + 1$.
The y-coordinate is:
$2 \times$ the x-coordinate $+ 1$.

For $x = ⁻2$
$y = (2 \times ⁻2) + 1$
$y = ⁻4 + 1$
$y = ⁻3$

The coordinates of points to plot are: (⁻2, ⁻3)
(⁻1, ⁻1)
(0, 1)
(1, 3)
(2, 5)
(3, 7)
(5, 9)

The graph of $y = 2x + 1$ is drawn on the axes.

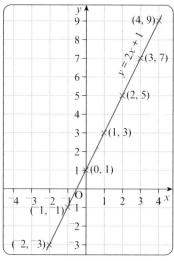

Exercise 51.1
Practising Skill 51A

1 This is a table of values for the graph of $y = 2x + 2$.

x	⁻2	⁻1	0	1	2	3	4
y	⁻2	■	2	■	■	8	■

a Draw and label a pair of axes like those above.
b Copy and complete the table of values.
c Draw and label the graph of $y = 2x + 2$.

2 a Draw and label a pair of axes with:
    x values from $^{-}1$ to 5
    y values from 0 to 14.

This is the table of values for a graph of $y = 2x + 4$.

x	$^{-}1$	0	1	2	3	4	5
y	■	4	■	■	10	■	■

  b Copy and complete the table of values.
  c Draw and label a graph of $y = 2x + 4$.

3 a Draw and label a pair of axes with:
    x values from $^{-}1$ to 4
    y values from $^{-}1$ to 20.

This is the table of values for a graph of $y = 4x + 3$.

x	$^{-}1$	0	1	2	3	4
y	■	3	■	■	15	■

  b Copy and complete the table of values.
  c Draw and label a graph of $y = 4x + 3$.

4 a Draw and label a pair of axes with:
    x values from $^{-}2$ to 4
    y values from $^{-}8$ to 6.

This is the table of values for a graph of $y = 2x - 3$.

x	$^{-}2$	$^{-}1$	0	1	2	3	4
y	■	$^{-}5$	■	■	■	3	■

  b Copy and complete the table of values.
  c Draw and label a graph of $y = 2x - 3$.

5 a Draw and label a pair of axes with:
    x values from $^{-}2$ to 4
    y values from $^{-}6$ to 12.

This is the table of values for a graph of $y = 3x - 2$.

x	$^{-}2$	$^{-}1$	0	1	2	3	4
y	■	■	$^{-}2$	■	■	■	■

  b Copy and complete the table of values.
  c Draw and label a graph of $y = 3x - 2$.

> The y values in the table will show the values you need for the y-axis.

6 This is a table of values for a graph of $y = x + 2$.

x	$^{-}3$	$^{-}2$	$^{-}1$	1	2	3	4
y	$^{-}1$	■	■	■	■	■	■

  a Copy and complete the table of values.
  b Draw and label a graph of $y = x + 2$.

7 This is a table of values for a graph of $y = 2x + 3$.

x	$^{-}4$	$^{-}3$	$^{-}2$	0	2	3	4
y	$^{-}5$	■	■	■	■	■	■

  a Copy and complete the table of values, and draw a graph of $y = 2x + 3$.
  b From your graph, what is the value of y when $x = ^{-}1$?

Exercise 51.2
Using Skill 51A

1 This graph shows the line $y = 5 - 2x$.

a Copy the axes, plot the points, and draw the graph of $y = 5 - 2x$.

b Copy and complete this table of values for a graph of $y = 2x - 1$.

x	$^-1$	0	1	2	3
y	■	■	■	■	■

c On your axes draw and label a graph of $y = 2x + 1$.

d From your graph, give the coordinates of the point where the two lines cross.

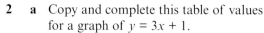

2 a Copy and complete this table of values for a graph of $y = 3x + 1$.

x	$^-1$	0	1	2	3
y	■	■	■	■	■

b Copy and complete this table of values for a graph of $y = 2x + 3$.

x	$^-1$	0	1	2	3
y	■	■	■	■	■

c Copy and label the axes used in question **1**.

d On your axes draw graphs of $y = 3x + 1$ and, $y = 2x + 3$.

e Give the coordinates of the point where the two lines cross.

3 a Draw a pair of axes with:
x values from $^-2$ to 6
y values from $^-8$ to 8.

b Copy and complete this table of valies for $y = 2x - 4$.

x	$^-2$	$^-1$	0	1	2	3	4	5	6
y	■	■	■	■	■	■	■	■	■

c Copy and complete this table of values for $y = x + 1$.

x	$^-2$	$^-1$	0	1	2	3	4	5	6
y	■	■	■	■	■	■	■	■	■

d On your axes draw a graph of $y = 2x - 4$, and a graph of $y = x + 1$.

e Give the coordinates of the point where $y = 2x - 4$ crosses $y = x + 1$.

4 a Draw a pair of axes with:
x values from 0 to 6
y values from 0 to 20

b Copy and complete this table of values for $y = 20 - 3x$.

x	0	1	3	5	6
y	20	■	■	■	■

c Draw a graph of the straight line $y = 20 - 3x$.

5 **a** Draw a pair of axes with:
  x values from $^-6$ to 3
  y values from $^-3$ to 6

b Copy and complete this table of values for $y = x + 3$.

x	$^-6$	$^-5$	$^-4$	$^-3$	$^-2$	$^-1$	0	1	2	3
y	■	$^-2$	■	■	■	■	3	■	■	■

c Plot and join the points given in your table.
d From your graph estimate the value of x when $y = 2.5$.
e From your graph estimate the values of x when $y = 4.5$.

Curved graphs

Skill 51B
Drawing curved graphs

There are different types of curved graphs.
This type has x^2 in its rule or equation.

Example

Complete this table of values for $y = x^2 + 1$ and draw
a graph of $y = x^2 + 1$.

x	$^-4$	$^-3$	$^-2$	$^-1$	0	1	2	3	4
y	17	■	5	2	1	■	■	■	■

$^-3^2 = ^-3 \times ^-3 = 9$

For the table of values:
when $x = ^-3$ $y = ^-3^2 + 1 = 9 + 1 = 10$
  $x = 1$ $y = 1^2 + 1 = 1 + 1 = 2$
  $x = 2$ $y = 2^2 + 1 = 4 + 1 = 5$
  $x = 3$ $y = 3^2 + 1 = 9 + 1 = 10$
  $x = 4$ $y = 4^2 + 1 = 16 + 1 = 17$

This is the set of points to plot:
  $(^-4, 17), (^-3, 10), (^-2, 5), (^-1, 2), (0, 1), (1, 2), (2, 5), (3, 10), (4, 17)$

The graph should be a
smooth curve, so you must
try to draw it in that way.
Do not use a ruler to join
the points you plot.

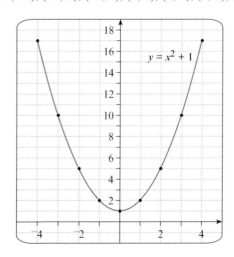

Note that the graph is a smooth curve.

289

Exercise 51.3
Practising Skill 51B

1 a Draw a pair of axes like those used in the example on page 289.
b Copy and complete this table of values for $y = x^2 + 2$.

x	−4	−3	−2	−1	0	1	2	3	4
y	18	■	■	3	2	■	■	■	■

c From your table, list the points to plot.
d Draw and label a graph of $y = x^2 + 2$.

2 a Draw and label a pair of axes with:
x values from −4 to 4
y values from 0 to 25.
b Copy and complete this table of values for $y = x^2 + 5$.

x	−4	−3	−2	−1	0	1	2	3	4
y	■	■	9	6	5	■	■	■	■

c From your table, list the points to plot.
d Draw and label a graph of $y = x^2 + 5$.

3 a Draw and label a pair of axes with:
x values from −3 to 4
y values from −2 to 16.
b Copy and complete this table of values for $y = x^2 - 1$.

x	−3	−2	−1	0	1	2	3	4
y	■	■	■	−1	0	■	■	■

c From your table, list the points to plot.
d Draw and label a graph of $y = x^2 - 1$.

4 a Draw and label a pair of axes with:
x values from −3 to 4
y values from −4 to 15.
b Copy and complete this table of values for $y = x^2 - 3$.

x	−3	−2	−1	0	1	2	3	4
y	■	■	■	−3	−2	■	■	■

c From your table, list the points to plot.
d Draw and label a graph of $y = x^2 - 3$.

5 a Draw and label a pair of axes with:
x values from −3 to 4
y values from −6 to 15.
b Copy and complete this table of values for $y = x^2 - 5$.

x	−3	−2	−1	0	1	2	3	4
y	■	■	■	−5	−4	■	■	■

c From your table, list the points to plot.
d Draw and label a graph of $y = x^2 - 5$.
e From your graph estimate the value of y when $x = 2.5$.
f From your graph estimate two values of x when $y = 10$.

Drawing a scatter diagram

Skill 52A
Plotting points on a
scatter diagram

♦ A scatter diagram has single points plotted – usually with crosses. The points are not joined up.

♦ It is used when there may be a link between two sets of data.

Example

The table shows data collected in a survey on how far 18 people travelled to their holiday last year and what they earn each week.

Draw a scatter diagram to show the data.

£/week	Distance (miles)
100	900
450	500
400	600
125	1200
350	800
325	1100
150	200
250	1300
475	200
100	1100
75	50
275	1000
325	300
175	1300
400	300
125	1400
200	1500
425	800

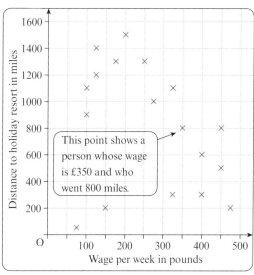

This point shows a person whose wage is £350 and who went 800 miles.

Exercise 52.1
Practising skill 52A

1 Which of these do you think the scatter diagram above shows?

A The more you earn, the further you go on holiday.
B The less you earn, the further you go on holiday.
C People earning about £400 a week go further.
D Poorer people cannot afford to go far on holiday.
E People earning about £200 a week go further.

2 This table shows the shoe size and height of ten men.

5' 6" means 5 foot 6 inches.

Since 1 foot = 12 inches, then 5' 6" = 66"

Shoe size	Height
9	5' 6"
11	5' 10"
8	6' 0"
10	5' 11"
12	6' 0"
7	5' 8"
10	5' 7"
11	6' 2"
8	5' 4"
9	5' 8"

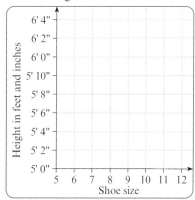

a Copy the axes and draw a scatter diagram to show the data.
b What link does your diagram show?

3 Sadie wants to buy a second-hand Ford Fiesta.
The figures in this table show the prices of 8 cars she sees in a paper.

Age of car (years)	6	9	1	3	5	10	2	7
Price (£)	5000	3000	8500	6000	4000	1200	6500	3000

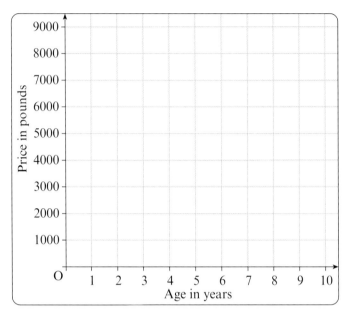

a On a copy of these axes, draw a scatter diagram to show the data.
b From your diagram, estimate what an 8-year-old car would cost.

4 This table shows the birth weights of 7 babies and the number of weeks each one spent in the womb before birth.

Weeks in the womb	38	42	27	35	45	40	25
Birth weight in kg	2.2	2.5	2.1	2.6	3.0	3.0	1.3

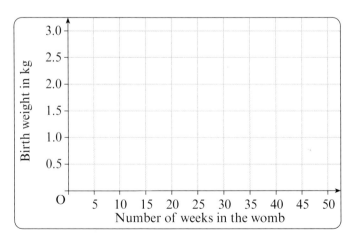

a On axes like this, draw a scatter diagram to show the data.
b Babies are usually born between 36 and 40 weeks.
How many of these babies were born premature?

A premature baby is one born before 36 weeks.

Links shown by a scatter diagram

♦ A scatter diagram can show if there
is a link between two sets of data.

This diagram shows how a girl's
heartbeat changes with her walking
speed.

It shows a **positive** link:
  as her speed goes up …
  … her heartbeat also goes up.

This link between two sets
of data is called
correlation.

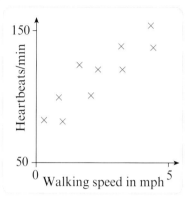

This diagram shows the walking
speeds of 11 people of different
ages.

It shows a **negative** link (correlation):
  as their ages go up …
  … their speeds go down.

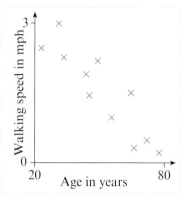

This diagram shows the walking
speeds of 10 people and their marks
in a maths test

It shows **no** link (no correlation):
  A person's walking speed does
  not seem to affect how they do in
  a maths test.

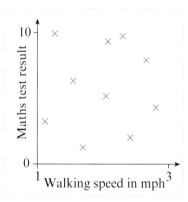

1 This diagram has two labels missing.
Which pair of labels best fits the diagram?

A Label 1 The engine size of a car.
   Label 2 The top speed of a car.

B Label 1 The engine size of a car.
   Label 2 The fuel economy of the car.

C Label 1 The engine size of a car.
   Label 2 The height of the driver.

Fuel economy is measured
in mpg, which stands for the
number of miles a car will
go on 1 gallon of petrol.

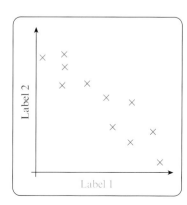

2   For each scatter diagram say if you would expect a positive link, a negative link, or no link at all.

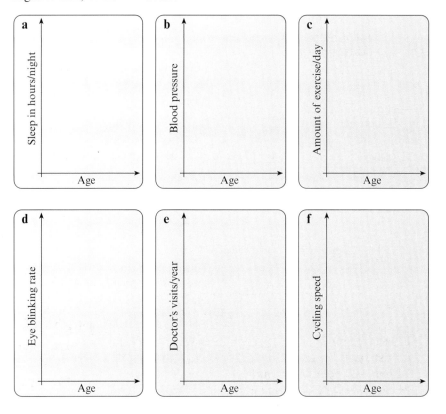

3   Look at these two true statements.

> Heavier lorries tend to wear out roads more quickly.
>
> Heavier lorries tend to go at slower speeds than lighter ones.

     a   Copy each of the sets of axes below.
     b   On each one mark where ten crosses might be.

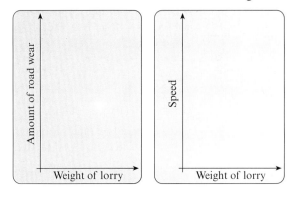

4   Sonia wrote this statement.

> People who are taller have a greater head circumference.

     a   Collect some data on height and head circumference.
     b   Draw a scatter diagram to show your data.
     c   Decide if Sonia was right in her statement.

This revises the work in Sections 48 to 52

1 Skill 48A

This travel graph shows the journeys of 4 buses.

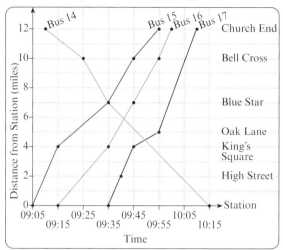

a Which bus was going from Church End to the Station?

b Where and when did bus 14 pass bus 15?

c Estimate the time when each bus was at the half-way point in its journey.

d One of the buses was in a speed trap 3 miles from the Station at about 10:00.
Which bus was this?

e Make a timetable to show buses 15, 16, and 17.

2 Skill 48B

a Make a copy of the axes for the graph in question **1**.

b On the axes draw graphs to show the journeys of these 3 buses.

D	Stop	Bus 15	Bus 16	Bus 17
0	Station	09:10	09:20	09:25
2	High Street	——	09:25	09:30
4	King's Square	09:20	——	09:45
5	Oak Lane	09:25	09:35	——
7	Blue Star	——	——	——
10	Bell Cross	——	10:05	——
12	Church End	09:45	10:15	10:05

3 Skill 49A

Copy and complete this table.
Give the deposit paid to the nearest penny.

Item	Price	Deposit	Deposit paid
Bike	£6975	15%	■
TV	£249.99	12%	■
Video	£399.99	7%	■
Holiday	£466.75	20%	■
Fridge	£199.99	6%	■

4 Skill 49B

Jim took a loan of £2250 at an interest rate of 9% pa for 3 years. Calculate the total he has to pay back.

5 Skill 49C

Ella took a loan of £4280 for 5 years at 14% pa.

a Calculate the total she has to pay back.

She is paying back in 60 instalments.

b Calculate the amount of each instalment.

6 Skill 49D

A freezer was advertised for £219.99.
If you pay by cash, you get a 15% discount.
You pay by cash. How much do you pay?

7 Skill 49E

Calculate the simple interest paid on a sum of £580 saved for 6 years at a rate of interest of £4%.

8 Skill 49F

Jake buys 230 tapes at 60p each.
He sold them all at £1.99 each.
How much profit did he make in total?

9 Skill 49G

A 500 g box of sweets costs £2.25.
A 750 g box of the same sweets costs £3.45.
Which box is better value? Explain.

10 Skill 50A and 50B

Calculate the circumference and the area of a circle of radius 7.4 cm. (Give answers to 1 dp.)

11 Skill 51A

a Copy and complete this table for $y = 3x - 2$.

x	-3	-2	-1	0	1	2	3	4
y	-11	5	■	-2	■	■	■	■

b Draw a pair of axes with:
x from -3 to 4, and y from -11 to 11

c On the axes draw a graph of $y = 3x - 2$

12 Skill 51B

a Copy and complete this table for $y = x^2 + 1$.

x	-3	-2	-1	0	1	2	3
y	■	5	■	■	■	■	■

b On the axes you drew for Question 11, draw and label graph of $y = x^2 + 1$.

13 Skill 52A and 52B

a Sketch a scatter diagram that shows a positive link.

b Sketch a scatter diagram that shows a negative link.

SUMMER

NINE ELMS GARDEN CENTRE

Watering cans – plastic			
5 litre	8 litre	10 litre	12 litre
99p	£1.29	£1.69	£1.99
Watering cans – traditional			
1 gallon	1.5 gallon	2 gallon	2.5 gallon
£4. 99	£6.49	£7.99	£9.99

Special offers for July

Nine Elms Mulchbags

Large	£1.49
Super	£1.99
Major	£2.99
Professional	£4.99

15% OFF THESE PRICES

Mower Madness !!! Can you believe this offer ?

- 20% deposit
- 15% interest over 3 years
- 6 equal monthly payments

Super Hover	**Mowhog**	**Mastermow**
£179.99	**£199.99**	**£249.99**

New Opening Hours

Mon–Fri
9 am to 6 pm
Saturday
8.30 am to 7 pm
Sunday
10 am to 4.30 pm

LIQUIDGRO
Add one scoop
(15 grams) per gallon
£3.99 1 kg Pack

Superbraid
50 metre rolls £12.99
30 metre rolls £7.49
Connectors 75p each
Any length in bulk: just 28p per metre

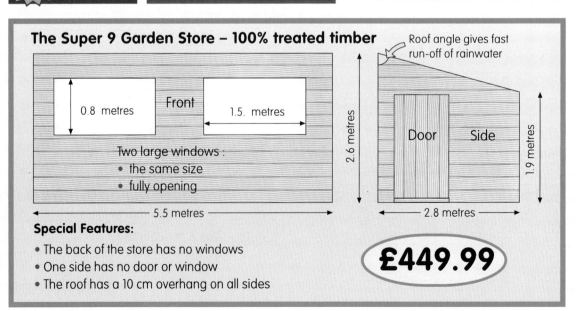

The Super 9 Garden Store – 100% treated timber

0.8 metres Front 1.5. metres

Two large windows :
- the same size
- fully opening

5.5 metres

Roof angle gives fast run-off of rainwater

2.6 metres

Door Side

1.9 metres

2.8 metres

Special Features:
- The back of the store has no windows
- One side has no door or window
- The roof has a 10 cm overhang on all sides

£449.99

1   Copy and complete this table.
Give discount prices to the nearest penny.

Mulchbags size	Price	Discount price
Large	£1.49	■
Super	■	■
Major	■	■
Professional	■	■

2   Asa goes to Nine Elms to buy 8 Major size Mulchbags.
He takes a £20 note with him.
How much does he have to borrow from his friend to buy the 8 bags? Explain your answer.

3   To 1 dp the cost of a 5 litre plastic watering can works out at 19.8p per litre.

   a   Calculate the cost per litre of 8 litre plastic watering can to 1 dp.
   b   Len saya that the cost of the 10 litre plastic can works out at about 17p per litre.
Do you agree? Explain your answer.
   c   Does the cost of the 12 litre plastic can work out at more or less than 15p per litre? Explain.
   d   Which size plastic watering can is better value for money? Explain your answer.

4   What size traditional watering can is better value for money? Explain your answer.

5   For the new opening hours:

   a   Give the closing time on a Sunday in 24-hour time.
   b   For how many hours is Nine Elms open on a week day?
   c   For how many hours is Nine Elms open each week (9 am Monday to 4.30 pm Sunday)?

6   Jason works weekends (Sat. and Sun.) at Nine Elms.
Each day he gets 1 hour off for lunch and two 15 minute tea-breaks.

   a   For how many hours is Jason paid?

Jason is paid at a normal rate of £4.18 an hour.

   b   How much is Jason paid for a weekend?

At a bank holiday weekend he is paid at time-and-a-half.

   c   How much an hour is this?
   d   How much is Jason paid for working a bank holiday weekend in total?

7   Meg wants to add Liquidgro to 14 litres of water.
Roughly how many grams should she add?
Explain how you decided.

8   Jim needs 150 metres of Superbraid.

   a   If he buys 50 metre rolls, how many connectors will he need to buy?
   b   If he buys 30 metre rolls how many connectors will he need?
   c   Including the cost of connectors, which is cheaper to buy for a 150 metre run of Superbraid: three 50 metre rolls or five 30 metre rolls?
   d   By how much is it cheaper?
   e   Would Jim save any money if he bought 150 metres in bulk? Explain your answer.

9   Calculate the area of one window of the Super 9 Garden Store.

10   Calculate the area of one side of the Super 9. (The side without a door or window.)

11   Measure the roof angle of the Super 9.

12   **a**   Roughly how long is the Super 9 in feet?
   b   Roughly how wide is the Super 9 in yards?

13   How much more expensive is the Mastermow than the Super Hover?

14   Jan decides to buy a Mastermow.

   a   To the nearest penny, calculate the deposit she has to pay.
   b   To the nearest pound, how much will she have to borrow on credit for the mower?
   c   What is the total Jan will pay back for the credit?
   d   Calculate the amount of each monthly payment. (Calculate to the nearest penny.)
   e   How much, in total, will the mower have cost Jan? (Calculate to the nearest £1.)

15   Ian is saving to buy a Mastermow.
He has savings of £145 that have been saved at a simple interest rate of 7% for 3 years.

   a   Calculate the interest Ian will have made on his savings.
   b   With the interest how much are the savings worth in total?
   c   How much more does he need to buy a Mastermow?

Ian gets a job working at Nine Elms at the same rate of pay as Jason.

   d   How many hours will Ian have to work to have enough, with his savings, to buy a Mastermow?

16   Which watering can holds more water?
A 12 litre plastic can or a 2.5 gallon traditional? Explain how you decided.

Stage 5 End points

You should be able to ...   ... so try these questions

A Use 3-figure bearings
Skill 43A: *see page 243*

A1 Give the bearing of each of these directions.
   a South-West   **b** North-East   **c** North
   d West   **e** North-West

B Solve problems with bearings and scales
Skill 43B: *see page 245*

B1 The positions of three boats R, S, and T are given by this data:
   R is 5 km from S on a bearing of 125°
   T is 4 km from S on a bearing of 235°.
   a Draw a diagram to show the position of the three boats.
         Use a scale of 1cm = 1 km
   b How far is R from T as the crow flies?

C Draw routes
Skill 43C: *see page 246*

C1 A boat sets off from a point P. This is the route it follows.
      5 km on a bearing of 080°
      4 km on a bearing of 165°
      3.5 km on a bearing of 280°
   Plot this course. Use a scale of 1 cm = 1 km.

D Calculate a percentage increase
Skill 44A: *see page 248*

D1 Increase each of these amounts by 15%.
   a £650000   **b** £ half-a-million   **c** 35.5 km

E Calculate a percentage decrease
Skill 44B: *see page 250*

E1 Calculate each of these.
   a Decrease £12.75 by 16%.   **b** Decrease 2650 miles by 8%.
   c Decrease 1660 mm by 20%.   **d** Decrease 80p by 5%.

F Calculate VAT
Skill 44C: *see page 251*

F1 The cost of these items is given without VAT.
   Calculate the charge for each item with VAT to the nearest penny.
   a Toaster £23.99   **b** Bike £189.99
   c TV £359.99   **d** Battery 68p

G Do a probability experiment
Skill 45A: *see page 252*

G1 **a** Roll a dice 100 times and record your results in a frequency table.
   b From your results calculate the probability of rolling a 2.

G2 Terry said he rolled a dice about 20 times and the probability of a 2 worked out at 0.3.
   Explain why this result is not one to rely on.

H Write ratios
Skill 46A: *see page 255*

H1 In the Isis B hockey team there are 7 male and 4 female players.
   a Give the ratio Female players : Male players.
   b Give the ratio Male players : Female players.

I Write ratios in their lowest terms
Skill 46B: *see page 256*

I1 Write each of these in its lowest terms.
   a 28 : 16   **b** 15 : 56   **c** 12 : 60   **d** 81 : 27

I2 In a car park there were 216 cars. Of these 96 were red.
   a How many cars in the car park were not red?
   b Give the ratio red cars : not red cars in its lowest terms.

J1 Write equivalent ratios
Skill 46C: *see page 257*

J1 Copy and complete each set of equivalent ratios.
   a 45 : 63   **b** 18 : 81   **c** 24 : 5 : 9   **d** 35 : 56 : 84
       ■ : 7   2 : ■   ■ : 60 : ■   ■ : 8 : ■

K Translate a shape
Skill 47A: *see page 260*

K1 Copy shape A on to squared paper.
Translate the shape by (2, ⁻2)

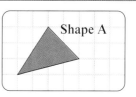

L Enlarge a shape
Skill 47B: *see page 262*

Skill 47C: *see page 263*

L1 Copy shape B on to squared paper.
Enlarge shape B with a
scale factor of 3.

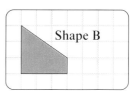

L2 Copy shape C and point P on to
squared paper.
Enlarge shape C with a
scale factor of 2.
Use P as the centre of enlargement.

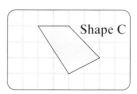

M Interpret a travel graph
Skill 48A: *see page 269*

M1 This travel graph shows 3 buses.

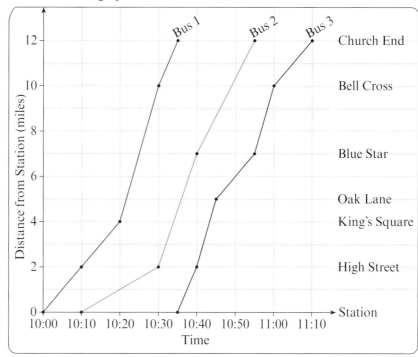

   a At what time did bus 1 get to Kings Square?
   b How long did it take bus 3 to get from the Station to Church End?
   c Which was the fastest part of the journey for bus 2?
      Explain how you decided.
   d At 10:45, how far was bus 2 from the Station?
   e Make a timetable for these 3 buses.

N Draw a travel graph
Skill 48A: *see page 269*

N1 **a** Copy the travel graph for Question M1.
   b Add a graph for bus 4 if: bus 4 leaves Church End at 10:05, gets to
      Blue Star at 10:45, to High Street at 11:00 and the Station at 11:10.

O Calculate a deposit
Skill 49A: *see page 274*

O1 Jade booked a holiday with friends. The total cost was £1065.75.
They had to pay a 12% deposit.

Calculate the deposit.

299

P Calculate with interest
for credit
Skill 49B: *see page 275*

P1 Shelley took a loan of £280 for 4 years at an interest rate of 7%.
Calculate the total Shelley has to pay back on the loan.

P2 Fergal borrowed £755 for 3 years at 11% interest.
Calculate the total Fergal has to pay back.

Q Calculate credit payments
by instalment
Skill 49C: *see page 276*

Q1 Kit took a loan of £1755 to pay for his first car.
He took the loan over 2 years at a rate of interest of 18%.
He will pay back in 24 instalments.
Calculate the amount of each instalment.

R Calculate a discount
Skill 49D: *see page 277*

R1 Jeff saw a cycle helmet priced at £34.99.
He waited for the sales and got a discount of 15%.
How much did he pay for the helmet (to the nearest penny)?

S Calculate with the simple
interest formula
Skill 49E: *see page 278*

S1 Calculate the simple interest pa on £850 saved for 7 years at a simple
interest rate of 4%.

T Calculate profit and loss
Skill 49F: *see page 279*

T1 Jake has a market stall.
He buys 245 tapes at 65p each and sells them at £2.49.

  a Calculate the profit he makes if he sells all the tapes.

He only sells 47 tapes.

  b Calculate the loss Jake has made.

U Calculate value for money
Skill 49G: *see page 280*

U1 A 600 g box of biscuits costs £1.85, and a 750 g box costs £2.35.
Which box is better value for money? Explain your answer.

V Calculate the circumference and
area of a circle
Skill 50A: *see page 282*

Skill 50B: *see page 283*

V1 A circle has a diameter of 9.4 cm.

  a Calculate its circumference to 2 dp.
  b Calculate its area to 1 dp.

W Draw a straight line graph from
a table of values
Skill 51A: *see page 286*

W1 **a** Copy and complete this table of values for $y = 3x - 2$.

x	−3	−2	−1	0	1	2	3	4
y	■	■	■	■	■	■	■	■

  b Draw axes with x from −3 to 4 , and y from −12 to 15.
  c On your axes draw a graph of $y = 3x - 2$.

X Draw curved graphs
Skill 51B: *see page 289*

X1 **a** Copy and complete this table of values for $y = x^2 - 2$.

x	−3	−2	−1	0	1	2	3	4
y	■	■	■	■	■	■	■	■

  b Draw axes with x from −3 to 4, and y from −3 to 15.
  c On your axes draw a graph of $y = x^2 - 2$.

Y Use scatter diagrams
Skill 52A: *see page 291*

Skill 52B: *see page 293*

Y1 Looking at a scatter diagram Mark said that:
'taller men wear shorter shorts'.

  a Sketch what the scatter diagram might have looked like.
  b Does the diagram show a positive or a negative link?

This revises the work in Stages 1, 2, 3, 4 and 5

1 Give the value of the digit 5 in each of these.
   a 11 508   **b** 56 671   **c** 354 667 662

2 List these numbers from smallest to largest.
636, 4052, 3999, 61 075, 199, 3088, 9004, 100 001

3 Write each of these numbers in words.
   a 30 504   **b** 4 300 603   **c** 170 270

4 Write each of these numbers in digits.
   a nine thousand and five
   b thirty-five thousand two hundred and one
   c one million ten thousand and one

5 Copy each of these letters and draw in all lines of symmetry.
   V   W   T   X   A

6 What is the order of rotational symmetry of shape A?

Shape A

7 How many planes of symmetry has a screwdriver?

8 Find an answer to each of these.
(Do not use a calculator.)
   a $7 + 9 + 4 + 6 + 8 + 5$
   b $57 + 44 + 6$
   c $3714 + 67 + 15\,304 + 88$
   d $160\,001 - 79\,352$
   e 64×13
   f 573×37
   g $5520 \div 16$
   h $46\,134 \div 18$

9 Give the value of the digit 9 in each of these.
   a 37.009   **b** 1.907   **c** 0.0904

10 List these numbers in order, smallest first.
0.075, 1.175, 0.057, 0.57, 1.0075, 0.0705

11 Find an answer to each of these.
(Do not use a calculator.)
   a $8.347 + 55.8 + 46.62 + 1.08 + 0.06$
   b $65 + 83.665 + 4.0027 + 0.04$
   c $76.0033 - 58.3657$

12 Draw each of these angles accurately.
   a 75°   **b** 125°   **c** 205°

13 Which of these angles are acute?
75°, 155°, 235°, 48°, 122°, 15°

14 Copy and complete each of these.
   a $^-7 + {}^-21$ **b** $^-38 + 15$ **c** $44 + {}^-17$
   d $19 - 52$ **e** $^-18 - 35$ **f** $^-7 - {}^-44$
   g $13 - {}^-88$ **h** $^-5 \times 12$ **i** $9 \times {}^-7$
   j $^-15 \times {}^-3$ **k** $54 \div {}^-6$ **l** $-96 \div {}^-32$

15 Order these numbers with the smallest first.
   a $^-8, 1, {}^-10, 3, {}^-1, 0, 2$
   b $2, {}^-3, {}^-5, 4, 1, {}^-1, 0, {}^-7$

16 The coordinates of two corners of a square are:
($^-1$, 4) and ($^-1$, 7).
Give the coordinates of the other two corners of the square.

17 Collect like terms in each of these.
   a $21k + 4w + k + 19w + 15k$
   b $11f + 3h + f - h - 12h$

18 Expand the brackets in each of these.
   a $3(8w + y + 1)$ **b** $5(4 - 5k + p)$

19 Expand these brackets and collect like terms to simplify.
$4(3a + 2b + 6c) + 8(5a - 3b - 9)$

20 Round each of these numbers to the nearest thousand.
   a 9409   **b** 347 504   **c** 3 436 398

21 Round each of these to the nearest 100 000.
   a 506 479   **b** 2 316 044   **c** 51 547 882

22 Find an approximate answer to each of these.
   a 58×22 **b** 74×38 **c** 79×55

23 Construct a triangle with sides of:
5 cm, 5 cm and 7 cm.

24 Construct triangle ABC where:
AB = 6 cm, BC = 8 cm, and angle ABC = 65°

25 Write each of these in 24-hour time.
   a 5.24 pm   **b** 9 pm   **c** 11.53 am
   d 10.05 pm   **e** 3.40 am   **f** 1.08 pm

26 A train left Birmingham at 15:44 and arrived in Glasgow at 20:06.
What was the journey time for this train?

27 Use the timetable on page 59.
Jo catches the 0842 from Tonbridge.
She travels to Ramsgate.
   a When should she get to Ramsgate?
   b What is the journey time?

28 Calculate the area of each of these shapes.

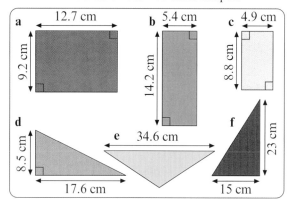

a 12.7 cm, 9.2 cm
b 5.4 cm, 14.2 cm
c 4.9 cm, 8.8 cm
d 8.5 cm, 17.6 cm
e 34.6 cm
f 23 cm, 15 cm

29 A formula that links p, k and t is: $t = 4(5p - k)$.
Find the value of t when, $p = 3$ and $k = 12$.

30 Solve each of these equations.

a $11y + 19 = 96$ b $43 + 8h = 107$
c $5g - 135 = 125$ d $5(2f - 8) = 120$

31 a Add all the even numbers between 41 and 51.
b What square numbers are between 60 and 200?
c Subtract the 12th square number from 400.

32 Which of these is a multiple of 8?
56, 82, 38, 96, 28, 40

33 List all the factors of 72.

34 List all the prime numbers between 50 and 80.

35 This data is about TV viewing in a week.

Ella		Nadim	
Channel	Hours	Channel	Hours
BBC1	8	BBC1	9
BBC2	6	BBC2	2
ITV	7	ITV	10
Ch 4	14	Ch 4	3
Ch 5	11	Ch 5	8
Sky	4	Sky	4

a Draw a comparative bar chart for the data.
b Draw a split bar chart to show the data for each viewer.
c Draw a pie chart to show the data for Nadim.

36 Copy and complete each of these.

a $5.0045 \times 10^3 =$ b $0.00121 \times 10^5 =$
c $2344.5 \div 10 =$ d $10.044 \div 10^3 =$

37 Without a calculator find the value of:

a $666.8 \div 4 =$ b $20747.4 \div 6 =$
c $354.65 \times 5 =$ d $1075.8 \times 3 =$

38 Calculate the answer to each of these.
Do not use a calculator.

a £30.08 + £17.49 + 75p + £9.50
b £38 + £523.99 + 24p + £17.65 + 14p
c £712.35 – £675.88
d £6700 – £866.68

39 A box of 9 pens costs £2.14.
Find the cost of one pencil to the nearest penny.

40 Ed buys a tub of tile cement for £8.49.
He pays with a £10 note.
How much change will he get?

41 Denise pays a bill with a £20 note.
She gets £4.27 change.
How much was the bill?

42 Calculate the answer to each of these.
Do not use a calculator.

a 65p × 7   b £58.34 × 7 =
c £831.42 ÷ 6   d £324 449.84 ÷ 8 =

43 Draw a mapping diagram for the function
$y = 5x - 9$ (Use values of x from 1 to 5.)

44 Give the number output from this function machine.

$^-9 \rightarrow \boxed{- 5} \rightarrow \boxed{\times 7} \rightarrow$

45 Calculate each angle marked with a letter.

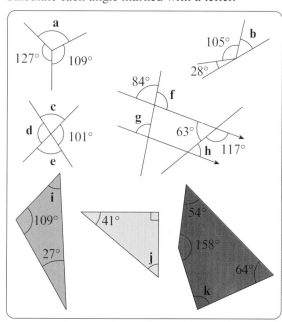

127° a 109°
105° b
28°
84° f
c
d 101°
g 63°
e
h 117°
i 109°
27°
41°
54°
158°
64°
j
k

46 Connor earns a basic wage of £6.80 an hour.
How much will he earn at:

a double time   b time-and-a-half?

47 Calculate $\frac{3}{4}$ of £66.08.

48 Kamal did a sponsored walk of 49 km.
For $\frac{4}{7}$ of the distance he did not have blisters on his feet.
How far did he walk with blisters on his feet?

49 Which of these fractions is equivalent to $\frac{1}{5}$?
$$\frac{25}{125} \qquad \frac{15}{55} \qquad \frac{120}{600} \qquad \frac{60}{240}$$

50 **a** Convert $\frac{3}{8}$ to a decimal.
b Put these in order from smallest to largest.
$$0.4 \qquad \frac{3}{8} \qquad 0.35 \qquad \frac{3}{5} \qquad \frac{7}{10}$$

51 Give two different fractions that describe how much of this grid that is shaded.

52 This data shows the number of people that travelled in a cable-car.

8, 21, 16, 17, 11, 18, 13, 26, 24, 12, 16, 24, 8, 18, 22, 19, 20, 14, 16, 9, 3, 6, 18, 31, 9, 16, 15, 28, 8, 21, 8

a Make a grouped frequency table for the data.
Groups of: 1 to 5, 6 to 10, 11 to 15, ... , 26 to 30.
b What is the modal class?
c Draw a grouped frequency diagram to show the data.

53 Solve each of these equations.
a $23y - 4 = 8y + 59$ **b** $29w + 4 = 17w - 56$
c $44x - 35 = 19x + 40$ **d** $7w + 19 = 37 + 5w$

54 Shape A is a rectangle.

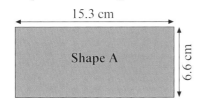

a Calculate the perimeter of shape A.
b Give the perimeter of shape A rounded to the nearest whole number.
c Calculate the area of shape A.
d Give the area rounded to 1 dp.
e Round the length and width to the nearest whole number and use this to find the area.

55 Which of these is 61.05 when rounded to 2 dp?
61.05099   61.05594   61.05449   61.05395

56 With a 1 to 6 dice:
a What is the probability of scoring 4 or more?
b What is the probability of scoring less than 2?

57 Write each of these numbers in standard form.
a 15616.66   **b** 3805542.5

58 Callum worked out how many seconds there were in 15 years. His calculator display gave:

a Write this number in standard form.
b Write this as an ordinary number.

59 Use the rules of indices to complete each of these.
a $10^5 \times 10^4 = 10^{\blacksquare}$ **b** $10^3 \times 10^3 \times 10^{\blacksquare} = 10^{18}$

60 Joel did a survey of the matches in a box.
This data gives the number in each box.

43, 39, 38, 41, 37, 41, 40, 35, 38, 40, 40, 42, 40, 33, 44, 37, 40, 40, 36, 38, 36, 40, 40, 40, 34, 40, 41

a Make a frequency table for the data.
b What number of matches was the mode?
c Find the mean number of matches in a box.
d Find the median number of matches in a box.

61 Make two copies of this grid showing shape A.

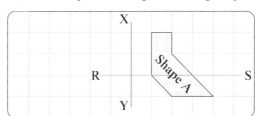

a On one copy show shape A reflected in XY.
b On one copy show shape A reflected in RS.

62 Copy these axes and the shape ABCD on to a grid.

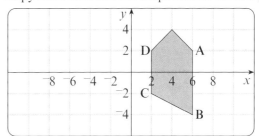

a Rotate ABCD 180° about the point (0, 2).
b Give the coordinates of A′, B′, C′, D′.

63 The mean of 9 numbers is 28.
a What is the total of the 9 numbers?

Eight of the numbers are:
24, 29, 31, 25, 19, 38, 22, 40

b What is the missing number?

64 Use the map on page 176.
Give directions to get from the Station to the Lion.

65 Convert each of these to a decimal.
    a 78%   **b** 9%   **c** 27%   **d** 3%

66 Write each of these as a decimal.
    a $5\frac{1}{2}\%$ **b** $24\frac{1}{2}\%$ **c** $1\frac{1}{2}\%$

67 Convert each of these decimals to a percentage.
    a 0.35   **b** 0.06   **c** 0.4   **d** 0.545
    e 0.155   **f** 0.06   **g** 0.085   **h** 0.175

68 Find:
    a 27% of £4500   **b** 58% of 650 kg
    c 66% of £45   **d** 4% of 365 000
    e 39% of 60 miles   **f** $12\frac{1}{2}\%$ of £4000

69 **a** Write 64 as a percentage of 84
    b Write 320 as a percentage of 780
    c Write 165 000 as a percentage of half a million.

70 The rule for a sequence is:
    'Multiply the term number by 8 and add 1.'

    The sequence starts: 9, 17, 25, ..

    Write the next 4 terms of the sequence.

71 The nth term of a sequence is given by:
    $2n - 9$

    Write the first 5 terms of the sequence.

72 Draw a net for a cube (without tabs or flaps).

73 Draw a net for this cuboid. Label your net with measurements.

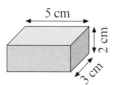

74 Sketch a net of a triangular prism.

75 Sketch a net of a square-based pyramid.

76 This data shows the results of a survey of sizes of T-shirt for sale by a trader.

Size	Frequency
S	25
M	42
L	3
XL	3

    a Calculate the probability that a T-shirt picked at random will be size S.
    (Give the answer as a fraction and a decimal.)
    b Gita calculates that the probability of picking one size is $\frac{21}{50}$. Which size is this?
    c Calculate the probability for the other sizes of T-shirt.

77 At an activities centre students must choose two activities from this list:

    Climbing, Skiing, Canoeing, Diving

    List all the possible combinations there are.

78 **a** Draw a sample space diagram for the scores on two 1 to 6 dice.
    b Show on your diagram total scores of 9 or more.
    c What is the probability of scoring a total of 9 or more with two dice?

79 Explain why a hexagon will tessellate.
(You will need to draw diagrams.)

80 At a constant speed of 82 kph, how far will you travel in $6\frac{1}{2}$ hours?

81 At a steady speed of 174 kph find the distance travelled in:
    a 45 min   **b** $1\frac{1}{2}$ hours   **c** 15 min.

82 You travel 235 miles in 2 hours 30 minutes.
    Calculate your average speed.

83 Write each of these as a fraction.
    a 36%   **b** 58%   **c** 24%   **d** 8%   **e** 2%

84 Find:
    a $\frac{4}{9} + \frac{7}{9}$ **b** $\frac{13}{16} - \frac{7}{16}$ **c** $\frac{1}{3} - \frac{1}{6}$

85 Calculate the volume of each cuboid to 1 dp.

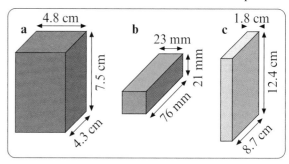

86 Easy-strike Matches want a box with a volume of 36 cm³.

    Sketch two possible boxes showing measurements.

87 Calculate the volume of each prism to 1 dp.

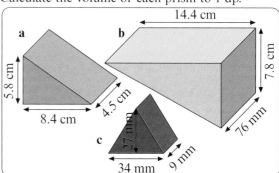

88 A park is a rectangle 300.56 m by 199.55 m.

    Calculate the approximate area of the park.
    Explain any rounding you did.

89 Give a 3-figure bearing for each of these:

    a East   **b** North West   **c** North East

90 From the boat Sea Seeker three others are seen.
The Maybug is 4 km away on a bearing of 075°.
The Baru is 6.5 km away on a bearing of 220°.
The Ryde is 5 km away on a bearing of 100°.

    a Draw a diagram to show the position of the four boats. Use a scale of 1 cm = 1 km.

    b In a straight line, how far is Baru from Ryde?

91 Increase each of these amounts by 12%.

    a £6500   **b** £588   **c** £1245.25 **d** £1.75

92 In 1996 a sponsored walk raised £2658.
In 1997 the money raised increased by 6%.

Calculate the amount raised in 1997.
Give your answer to the nearest £1.

93 Decrease each of these amounts by 7%

    a 45 000 km   **b** £3 million   **c** £32

94 In high season, a fare on a ferry is £96.80.
In low season, fares are reduced by 15%.

Calculate this fare in the low season.

95 Last year damage by visitors to a new bridge was estimated to cost £35000.
This year a fall of 18% in the damage is hoped for.

Estimate the cost of the damage this year.

96 What is the standard rate of VAT today?

97 The cost of these items is given without VAT.
Find the cost with VAT (to the nearest penny).

    a cooker £259.99   **b** tent £119.99
    c telephone £18.75   **d** pen 38p

98 Pia bought a tyre for £34.99 + VAT.

How much did she pay in total?

99 **a** Roll a dice 100 times and list the outcomes in a frequency table.

    b From your results calculate the probability of rolling a 5.

100 To make green paint, 9 parts of blue paint are mixed with 5 parts of yellow paint.

    a Give the ratio of Blue : Yellow.

    b Give the ratio of Yellow : Blue.

101 Last week a snack bar sold 388 cans of cola and 265 cans of diet cola.

Give the ratio of diet cola sales : cola sales.

102 Give each of these ratios in its lowest terms.

    a 25 : 40   **b** 36 : 45   **c** 150 : 175

103 Copy and complete each set of equivalent ratios.

    a 14 : 63   **b** 8 : 15 : 3   **c** 3 : 12 : 5
       ■ : 9   ■ : 60 : ■   ■ : ■ : 40

104 Divide £3450 in the ratio 1 : 4 : 5

105 There are 360 pages in a book.
The ratio of pages with pictures to pages without pictures is 11 : 13.

    a How may pages have pictures?

    b How many pages do not have pictures?

106 **a** Copy shape A on to squared paper.

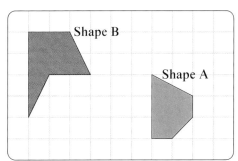

    b Translate shape A by the vector $\binom{-3}{2}$.

    c Copy shape B.

    d Translate shape B by the vector $\binom{2}{-3}$.

107 **a** Copy shape A on to squared paper.

    b Enlarge shape A with a scale factor of 2.

108 **a** Copy shape B on to squared paper.

    b Mark one point outside shape B and label the point P.
With P as the centre of enlargement, enlarge shape B with a scale factor of 3.

109 **a** Draw a travel graph to show these buses:

Distance	Stop	Bus 1	Bus 2
0	High St.	06:00	06:20
3	Mill St.	06:10	06:25
8	Kings Head	06:25	06:35
10	Well End	06:30	——
14	St Mary's	06:40	06:45

    b At what time was each bus at the half-way point of its journey?

110 Calculate the simple interest paid in a saving of £240 for 9 years at 4%.

111 Calculate the circumference and area of a circle of radius 8.6 cm. (Give your answers to 2 dp.)

112 Draw a graph of $y = 2x + 3$.

Formula sheet

In the GCSE examination you will be given a formula sheet like this one.

You should use it as an aid to memory, and it will be useful to become familiar with the information on the sheet.

The formula sheet is the same for all Examining Groups.

Area of triangle $= \frac{1}{2} \times \text{Base} \times \text{Height}$

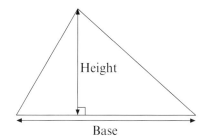

Circumference of circle $= \pi \times \text{diameter}$
$= 2\pi \times \text{diameter}$

Area of circle $= \pi \times (\text{radius})^2$

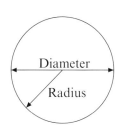

Volume of cuboid $= \text{Length} \times \text{Width} \times \text{Height}$

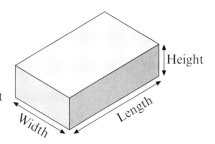

Number

N1		
Whole number arithmetic	**N1.1**	**a** A machine makes 7836 dice each day. They are packed in boxes of 10. How many boxes can be fully filled?

N1 **Whole number arithmetic**

N1.1 **a** A machine makes 7836 dice each day. They are packed in boxes of 10. How many boxes can be fully filled?

b Another machine makes 3825 larger dice each day. These are packed in boxes of 10. How many boxes can be completely filled?

N1.2 Do not use a calculator when answering this question. (All working must be shown.)

A lorry carries 23 tonnes when fully loaded. How many journeys must it make to move 598 tonnes of sand?

N1.3 Without using your calculator find 583×47. (Show all working clearly).

N1.4 The cards $\boxed{3}$ $\boxed{8}$ $\boxed{2}$ and $\boxed{6}$ are used to make different numbers. Each card can only be used once. All the cards must be used each time.

a Write down the largest number.
b Write down the smallest number.

N1.5 The temperature inside a building was $17\,°C$ and outside it was $^-9\,°C$. How many degrees warmer was it inside than outside?

N1.6 Sian knows that when a certain number is doubled the answer is 58. Explain in words, starting with 58, how she can work out the number.

N1.7 At a hockey match there were twenty-three thousand fans.

a Write this number in figures.
b Twelve thousand seven hundred were female. How many were male?

N1.8 **a** Multiply 45 by 100.
b Write the number two thousand and seventy three in figures.
c Add the number in part **b** to your answer for part **a**.

N1.9 Here are the rules for a number trick.

Rule 1   Think of a number
Rule 2   Double it
Rule 3   Add 6
Rule 4   Halve the total
Rule 5   Take away the number you first thought of.

a Vaughan picks the number 4. He follows the rules. What number should he end up with?
b Rhian picks 72. What number should she end with?
c **i** Pick a starting number of your own. Work out your finishing number. (Show your working.)
     ii Write down anything you find out about the finishing numbers.

N1.10 Andreas says that $437 \div 23$ is about 20.

a Without using a calculator, explain why 20 is a good estimate for $437 \div 23$.
b Without using a calculator, find the exact value of $437 \div 23$. You must show all your working.

N2
Units, conversions and compound measures

You are expected to know that 5 miles is about 8 kilometres.

You should know that:

1.76 pints is about 1 litre
and
1 kg is about 2.2 pounds.

You should know that:

1 metre is about 39 inches
and
12 inches = 1 foot.

N2.1 The distance between two towns is 24 km.
Approximately what is this distance in miles?

N2.2 Two radio masts are 30 miles apart.
Roughly how many kilometres is this?

N2.3 Joanna saved £240 for her holiday in Corfu.
How many Drachma would she get when the exchange rate was 334 Drachma to the pound?

N2.4 Kelvin types, on average, 20 words per minute.
He can get 280 words on a page.
  a How long will it take him to type 2 pages?
  b How many full pages can he type in 1 hour?

N2.5 David's dad sends him to the shops to buy 4 pounds of potatoes and 2 pints of milk. He buys 2 kilograms of potatoes and a litre of milk.
Does he buy enough potatoes and milk?
You must give reasons for your answer.

N2.6 When at rest, Zoe's heart beats at a rate of 50 beats per minute.
  a How many times will her heart beat while she is asleep for 8 hours?
  b When she rides her bike, Zoe's heart beats rise to an average of 80 beats per minute. How long would she be riding her bike for her heart to beat 1000 times?

N2.7 The speed limit on UK motorways is 70 mph.
  a What is this speed in kilometres per hour (kph)?
  b In France trailers have a limit of 80 kph.
    What is this speed in mph?

N2.8 On the way to Alton Towers, the bus driver takes a short cut.
He comes to a low bridge with height limit of 3 metres.
The driver knows his bus is 9 feet 10 inches high.
Can the bus go under the bridge?

N2.9 Deon spent £10 on petrol.
She saw that the pump showed 16.4 litres.
  a What was the price per litre for the petrol (to the nearest penny)?
  b Given that 1 gallon = 4.55 litres:
    How many gallons did Deon buy for her £10?
    Give your answer correct to 1 dp.
  c Deon travelled 125 miles on the £10 worth of petrol.
    Calculate her petrol cost per mile.

N2.10 Lennie makes a book shelf.
He needs a piece of wood 45 inches long.
His tape measure is metric. He knows that 2.54 cm = 1 inch.
To the nearest millimetre, how long is the piece of wood he needs?

N2.11 Given that 1 mile = 5280 feet:
Convert a speed of 50 mph to a speed in feet per second.
Give your answer to 1 dp.

N3
Estimation, degrees of accuracy

N3.1   There are 5700 people, to the nearest hundred, at a rugby match.
   a   What is the smallest number that the crowd could be?
   b   What is the largest number that it could be?

N3.2   Sam and Nia describe the same whole number.
   Sam says that it is bigger than 3.
   Nia says that it is smaller than 9.
   Write down all possible values of the number.

N3.3   A village hall has 32 rows of seats. Each row has 49 seats.
   The total number of seats is given by 32×49.
   a   Write down the numbers you could use to get an approximate answer to 32×49.
   b   Write down your approximate answer.
   c   Use a calculator to find the difference between your approximate answer and the exact answer.

N3.4   **a**   Write down the numbers you would use to find an estimate for $1991 \div 42$.
   b   Write down your estimate for $1991 \div 42$.

N3.5   Do not use a calculator for this question.

   Estimate the value of $\dfrac{417 \times 82}{42}$.

   Show all your working.

N3.6   George always measures in imperial units.
   He uses a tape marked in tenths of an inch.
   He measures the width of a table as 27 inches (to the nearest inch).
   a   **i**   What is the widest the table could be?
      ii   What is the narrowest the table could be?
   b   George wants to convert his measurements to millimetres:
      i   what is the widest the table could be?
      ii   what is the smallest the width of the table could be?

You are expected to know that:

1 inch = 25.4 millimetres.

N3.7   For a bicycle, estimate:
   a   its length in metres
   b   its weight, in kilograms.

N3.8   Cans of Fiz cost 29p each. Estimate the cost of 132 cans.
   Show how you found your estimate.

N3.9   Bart works out that the average speed of trains from Manchester to London is 4 kilometres per hour.
   Is this sensible? Explain your answer.

N3.10   For a school trip 148 students pay £19.50 each.
   Without using a calculator:
   a   **i**   Estimate the total amount paid by students.
      ii   Show your working and explain any rounding you use.
   b   **i**   Is your estimate more, or less, than the actual total?
      ii   Explain how you decided.
   c   Calculate, without a calculator the exact total paid by students.
      You must show all your working.

You must show enough working to convince someone that you did not use a calculator.

N4
Types of number

N4.1 Evan uses four of the digits 2, 3, 4, 7, 8, 9 to make a four-digit number, for example 7423.

    a What is the smallest four-digit odd number that he can make?
    b He now makes a three-digit number using each of the numbers 3, 4, 8.

He finds that it is a multiple of 8.
What is his number?

N4.2 Use one of these words **cube, factor, multiple, odd, prime, square** to complete these sentences.

    a 4 is a .... of 8.   **b** 9 is a .... of 3.
    c 2 is a .... number.   **d** 4 is a .... number.

N4.3 Jill thinks of a number.
It is less than 10.
It can be divided exactly by 2.
It is a multiple of 3.

What is Jill's number?

N4.4

1	2	3	4	5	6	7	8	9	10
11	12	13	14	15	16	17	18	19	20
21	22	23	24	25	26	27	28	29	30

From the numbers in the box, write down:
    a the square of 4   **b** all of the multiples of 8
    c the prime factors of 60   **d** the values of 2^3
    e the values of $\sqrt{25}$

N4.5 Keir is thinking about a number. Its square is 169.
What number is Keir thinking of?

N4.6   **a** Is 46 a multiple of 6? Explain your answer.
    b Write down two factors of 27.

N4.7 5, 7, 11, 13, ... are prime numbers.

    a What is the next prime number?
    b Explain why 2 is the only even prime number.

N4.8 Write down:
    a the square of 4
    b the multiples of 7 which lie between 1 and 25.

N4.9 These steps form a number chain.

Step 1	Write down a whole number.
Step 2	If the number is even divide by 2, if the number is odd add 1 to it.
Step 3	Write down the new number.
Step 4	Repeat 2 and 3 until the new number is 1 or $^-1$.

    a Write down the chain that begins with the number 13.
    b Write down the chain that begins with the number $^-11$.

N5
Fractions

N5.1 What fraction of this rectangle is shaded?
Give your fraction in its lowest terms

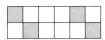

N5.2 **a** Of the 200 pupils attending a school,
40 went home for dinner.
What fraction went home?
b Copy this grid and shade $\frac{2}{3}$ of it.

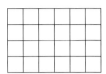

N5.3 A fruit drink is made by mixing water with concentrated fruit juice.
$\frac{3}{4}$ of the drink is water.
How many litres of water will there be in 12 litres of the fruit drink?

N5.4 The petrol tank in Laura's car holds 80 litres.
The drawing shows the car's petrol gauge when
she arrived at a garage.

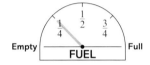

a How many litres were in the tank when
she arrived?
b At the garage Laura filled the tank to the $\frac{3}{4}$ mark.
How many litres of petrol did she buy?

N5.5 **a** $\frac{1}{4}, \frac{1}{2}, \frac{5}{16}, \frac{3}{8}$.
List these fractions in order of size. Start with the smallest.
b Add the four fractions to find the total.

N5.6 In a test of memory, four students were given fifteen seconds to read
from a list of numbers.
• Claire read out $\frac{3}{4}$ of the numbers
• Rob read out $\frac{3}{5}$ of the numbers
• Joel read out $\frac{5}{8}$ of the numbers
• Nicole read out $\frac{7}{10}$ of the numbers
a **i** Which student read out most numbers?
ii Which student read out the fewest numbers?
You must show, and explain, all your working.
There were 40 numbers in the list.
b How many numbers did Joel read out?
c How many more numbers did Claire read out than Rob?

N5.7 Ian packs and labels pizzas.
He starts his shift with a sheet of 1000 labels.
After working for an hour he has used 150 labels.
a **i** What fraction of the labels had Ian used after an hour?
ii Write this fraction in its lowest terms.
During the second hour Ian used $\frac{1}{5}$ of the labels that were left over.
b How many labels did Ian use in the second hour?
During the third hour Ian used $\frac{1}{2}$ of the labels that he had left.
c How many pizzas did Ian pack in the first three hours of his shift?

N6
Decimals

N6.1   **a**   While on holiday, Denise hired a motor-bike.
She bought petrol three times.
The first time she bought 5.4 litres, next time she had 4.6 litres
and then she bought 3.9 litres.
What was the total amount of petrol Denise bought?
  b   The total cost of the petrol was £9.54.
How much change did Denise get from a £20 note?

N6.2   200 pages inside a book were found to be 2.78 cm thick.

  a   Calculate the thickness, in cm, of one page.
  b   Calculate the thickness of 280 pages in the same book.

N6.3   Howard is baking apple tarts and blackberry tarts.
He uses 1.22 kg of flour in the blackberry tarts.
He uses 0.95 kg of flour in the apple tarts.

How much flour will he have left from a 3 kg bag of flour?

N6.4   Jaff's Fruit Juice is sold in boxes containing 2.75 litres.
Heather wants to fill 8 jugs. Each jug holds 1.5 litres.

How many boxes of fruit juice must she buy?

N6.5   Richard buys a 10 m roll of tape to mend cracks in his shed roof.
He uses 3.75 m on one crack and 3.6 m on the other.

How much tape is left on the roll after he has done both cracks?

N6.6   Sheets of glass are stacked on top of each other.
The height of 26 identical sheets of glass is 16.9 cm.

  a   Find the thickness of one sheet of the glass.
  b   Calculate the height of 37 sheets of this glass.

N6.7   Using a calculator and giving your answer correct to 1 decimal place,
find the value of:

  a $4.52 + 1.23^2$ **b** $\sqrt{3.24} - 1.25$ **c** $1.27 + 2.98 \times 3.27$
  d $2.17 \times (2.98 + 2.37)$ **e** 7.35×10^3

N6.8   **a**   Read the scale below and write down the value of A.

  b   Copy this scale and mark the position of 3.25 on your copy.

N7
Percentages

N7.1 A class test is marked out of 70 marks.

   a Mike gets 60%. How many marks does he get?

   b Georgina gets 49 marks. What percentage does she get?

N7.2   **a** In a class of 30 pupils 12 are girls.
      What percentage of the class are girls?

   b Write $\frac{7}{20}$ as a percentage.

N7.3 The rate of interest given by a bank is 6%.

   a Explain what 6% means.   **b** Find 6% of £200.

N7.4 A cake weighs 750 grams.
20% of its weight is sugar.

What is the weight of sugar in the cake?

N7.5 The entry fee to a theme park is £14. Youth clubs get a 15% discount.
What is the cost of entry for a member of a youth club?

N7.6

Local Accident Statistics	
Type of casualty	Number of casualties
Car driver	154
Car passenger	155
Cyclist	65
Motorcyclist	167
Pedestrian	79
Other	5
Total	625

What percentage of the casualties were cyclists?

N7.7 Sam earns £12.50 a week delivering newspapers.
He is given a 6% pay rise.

How much will Sam now earn each week?

N7.8 A gas bill comes to £106 before VAT at 8% is added.

   a How much VAT at 8% has to be added to this bill?

   b What is the total bill including VAT?

N7.9 A computer is priced at £998 plus VAT at $17\frac{1}{2}$%.

   a What is $17\frac{1}{2}$% of £998?

   b What is the full cost of buying this computer?

N7.10 A sports stadium has seating for 60 000 people.
For the semifinals of a tournament the seats are priced in this way:

     20% of the seats £22.50
     28% of the seats £18
     17% of the seats £12.50
     30% of the seats £8.50
     the remaining seats .... NO CHARGE

   a **i** For what percentage of the seats is no charge made?
       ii How many seats is this?

   b How many seats are to be sold for £12.50?

Every seat in the stadium was full for the semifinal.

   c How much, in total, was taken from ticket sales?

N8
Fractions, decimals and percentages

N8.1 Susan buys a bag of 24 sweets.
She eats 4 sweets.

a What fraction of the bag of sweets has she eaten?

Later, she eats $\frac{3}{5}$ of the sweets that are left.

b How many sweets have been eaten altogether?
c What percentage of the sweets have not been eaten?

N8.2 Copy and complete the following table:

Fraction	Decimal	Percentage
$\frac{1}{2}$	0.5	50%
		25%
	0.6	
$\frac{3}{8}$		

N8.3 Here is a list of decimals, fractions and percentages
43%, $\frac{3}{4}$, 0.7, 35%, 0.4, $\frac{5}{8}$.

Rewrite the list in order of size. Start with the largest.

N8.4 Work out 46% of 350 grams.

N8.5 Lisa works at the checkout of a supermarket.
This shows the hours she worked in the week before her holidays.

Mon	$5\frac{1}{2}$
Tues	$4\frac{3}{4}$
Wed	5
Thurs	$5\frac{3}{4}$
Fri	$4\frac{1}{2}$

a How many hours, in total, did Lisa work in the week?

Lisa is paid £3.85 per hour.

b How much did Lisa earn in total for the week's work?
Give your answer to the nearest penny.

After her holiday Lisa's pay was increased to £3.90 per hour.

c Roughly, what is this pay rise as a percentage?

N8.6 This diagram shows how the total price of a pair of trainers is made up.

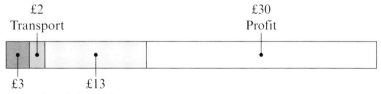

£2
Transport

£30
Profit

£3
Cost to make

£13
Advertising

a What is the total price of a pair of these trainers?
b What fraction of the total price is what it costs to make the trainers?
c Approximately what percentage of the price goes to advertising?
d **i** What fraction of the price does profit represent?
   ii What percentage of the total price is profit?

N9
Mixtures, ratio and proportion

N9.1 Ben buys 3 raffle tickets and Bill buys 2.
They win £600.
They share the £600 in the ratio of the number of tickets they bought.
How much should Bill get?

N9.2 A cake for three people needs 45g of sugar.
Sam makes a similar cake for five people.
Calculate the weight of sugar he needs.

N9.3 A 27 g packet of crisps costs 24 pence.
Calculate the cost of a 36 g packet of crisps (at the same price per gram).

N9.4 To estimate the number of miles in a number of kilometres you can:
MULTIPLY THE NUMBER OF KILOMETRES BY 5
THEN DIVIDE BY 8
a Use this estimate to change 40 kilometres into miles.
b Write down a similar sentence which estimates the number of miles
in a given number of kilometres.

N9.5 Onion soup can be made from these ingredients.

For two people use:	
450 ml	Stock
325 g	Onions
25 g	Butter
25 g	Grated cheese

a List the ingredients needed to make this soup for six people.

When a cook uses 200 g of butter to make this soup:

b How much stock will he need?
c What weight of onions will he need?

N9.6 Bronze can be made by mixing copper and tin by weight
in the ratio of 4 : 1.
A bronze coin weighs 25 g.
What weight of copper does it contain?

N9.7 Ann, Graham and Elwyn sit on the same table in the Bingo hall.
They decide to share any winnings in the ratio of the number of cards
they have each filled in.
When their winnings come to £36, Ann has filled in 5 cards, Graham 4
and Elwyn 3 cards.
What share of the £36 should each get?

N9.8 Out of 600 pupils going to a school, 400 are girls.
What is the ratio of girls to boys?

N9.9 The plan of a house has been drawn using a scale of 1 : 25.
On the plan the length of the lounge is 20 cm.
a What is the real length of the lounge in metres?
b The width of the lounge is 3 metres.
How wide is the lounge on the plan?

N10
Speed distance and time

N10.1 Zara catches a bus to Luton airport.
It leaves her home town at 12 48 and arrives at the airport at 13 13.

a What was her arrival time in 12-hour clock time?
b How long did the journey take?

N10.2 If the first day of June is a Monday:

a which day of the week is 12 June?
b which day of the week is the last day in June?

N10.3 Jim travelled from Bridgwater to Bristol by bus.
The distance from Bridgwater to Bristol is 40 miles.
The bus left Bridgwater at at 12 34 and arrived in Bristol at 14 25.

a How many minutes did the journey take?

Sharon left Bridgwater at 11 00 and travelled to Bristol by car.
Her average speed was 30 mph.

b What time did Sharon get to Bristol?

N10.4

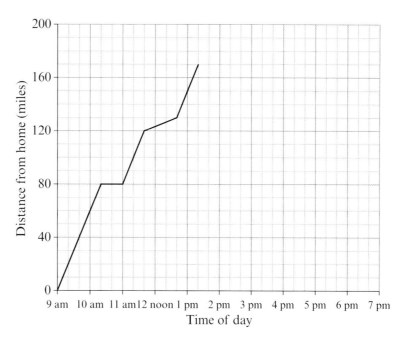

Mr Beaton's journey from home to Exeter is shown on the graph above.
After driving for a while Mr Beaton stopped for a rest.

a Write down the time he stopped for his rest.
b Write down how long his rest lasted.

Mr Beaton slowed down for part of the journey because of heavy traffic .

c For how many miles did he travel at this slower speed?
d On arriving in Exeter, Mr Beaton had half an hour for lunch and then
spent one and a half hours at a meeting.
He then went home at a steady speed of 50 miles per hour.
Copy the graph and complete the whole of his journey.

N11
Personal and
household finance

N11.1 You have £5 to buy floppy disks which cost 45p each.
  a How many disks can you buy?
  b How much change will you get?

N11.2 In the local market Freda's stall sells 12 oranges for £1.08.
Bert sells oranges at 10 for £1.
  a At which stall was the price of one orange cheaper?
  b By how much was one orange cheaper?

N11.3 Andrew buys a camcorder.
He pays £115 deposit and 12 monthly installments of £31.62.
Work out the total amount that Andrew pays.

N11.4 Nia earns £9 a week doing a paper round.
She also gets £3 pocket money each week.
She wants to buy a bike which costs £230 so she saves all her money.
Calculate how many weeks she will have to save before she can
buy the bike.

N11.5 Ellie buys a pack of four batteries for £2.34.
How much does one battery cost to the nearest penny?

N11.6 Sarah bought a new car for £8500.
She paid a deposit of $\frac{2}{5}$ of this price and paid the rest by
12 monthly payments.
  a What deposit did she pay when she bought the car?
  b What was her monthly payment for the next twelve months?

N11.7 To hire a stone cutting machine it costs £12.40 per day plus a delivery
charge of £8.
  a How much will it cost to hire the cutter for three days?
  b Tom hired the stone cutter to make a patio.
He was charged £107.20 including delivery.
For how many days did Tom hire the cutter?

N11.8 A small tube of toothpaste contains 76 ml and costs 50 pence.
A large tube contains 125 ml and costs 80 pence.
Which size of toothpaste gives better value for money?
You must show all your working.

N11.9 The details of a gas bill for the quarter January to March are as follows:

Previous meter reading	66 156
Present meter reading	67 343
Cost per unit is 9 pence	
Fixed standing charge per quarter	£12.05

  a Show all your calculations and write down the total cost of the gas
for the January to march quarter.
  b The rate of VAT on gas bills is 8%.
What is the total bill for gas including VAT?

N12
Reading scales

N12.1　This scale is in metres.

　　a　What is Adrian's height?

　　b　How tall will Adrian be
　　　　when he has grown
　　　　4 cm taller?

N12.2　The point 0.5 has been marked on the number line below.
　　Copy the diagram and mark the following numbers in the same way.

　　a　$^{-}1.5$　　　**b**　$1\frac{1}{3}$　　　**c**　2.7　　　**d**　$-\frac{3}{4}$

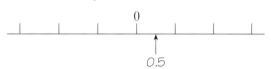

N12.3　What temperature is this thermometer showing when:

　　a　it is at position A　　　　　　**b**　it moves to position B
　　c　it moves to position C.
　　d　how many degrees has the temperature risen as it moved from
　　　　position A to position C?

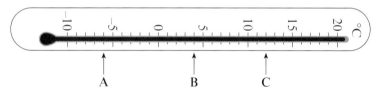

N12.4　The diagram below shows a parking meter.

　　a　How much time is left before the arrow reaches zero?

　　b　Parking costs 10p for 30 minutes. The motorist puts 30p in this meter.
　　　　How much time will he now have before the arrow reaches zero?

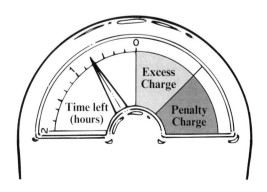

N13
Miscellaneous

N13.1 From this list of numbers
       2, 3, 4, 5, 6, 7, 8, 9
   write down the numbers that are:
   a odd numbers   **b** multiples of 4   **c** square numbers

N13.2 The value of 7 in the number 375 is seventy.
   a What is the value of 5 in this number?
   The number 375 is multiplied by 100.
   b What is the value of 7 in the answer?
   The number 3750 is divided by 100.
   c What is the value of 3 in the answer?

N13.3 Rhys catches a train from Swansea to Cardiff.
   The temperature in the train was 15 °C.
   When he got out in Cardiff he noticed that the temperature was ‾3 °C
   a How many degrees warmer was it inside the train than outside?
   The train left Swansea at 13.45 and arrived in Cardiff at 14.33.
   b How many minutes did the journey take?
   c Write the time that Rhys arrived in Cardiff in 12-hour clock time.

N13.4 Heather measures the length of a pen with the top on.

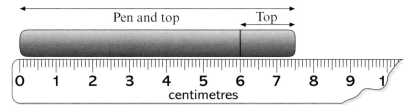

   a What is the length of the pen and top?
   b What is the length of the top?
   c What is the length of the top as a fraction of the
      total length of the pen and top?

13.5 Christopher's television is faulty.
   He calls out a repair man who replaces some parts which cost £18.60.
   Copy out and complete the bill.

T**REPAIR**V	
Fixed call-out charge	£40.00
$\frac{3}{4}$ hours at £20 per hour	£
Parts	£18.60
Total before VAT	£
VAT at 17.5%	£
Total due	£

N13
Miscellaneous continued

N13.6 To go on holiday to Spain, Tom exchanged
£200 for 50 000pts (pesetas).
At the same exchange rate, Heather changed £250 into pesetas.

a How many pesetas did Heather receive?
b Tom spent $\frac{3}{4}$ of his pesetas. How many did he have left?
c Tom changed these pesetas back into pounds at a rate of 240 pts = £1.
Calculate how much, in pounds, he received.

N13.7 **a** Write down the fraction of the rectangle that is shaded.

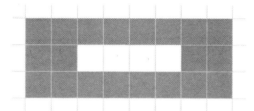

b On squared paper draw a similar rectangle of 24 squares
and shade in $\frac{3}{4}$ of it.

N13.8 **a** Calculate 65% of 530 kg.
b Find $\frac{3}{8}$ of £960.
c Change $\frac{3}{8}$ into a decimal.
d Write down your answer to part **c** correct to 2 decimal places.

N13.9 There are 20 metres of curtain material left on a roll.
A customer buys 15 metres of the material.

a What fraction of the original roll has the customer bought?
b What percentage of the original roll is left?
The curtain material costs £14.75 per square metre and is
1.8 metres wide.
c Estimate what the customer will pay for the material.
You must show your working out.

N13.10 The recommended price of a computer game is £14.99.
Two shops have special offers.
The first shop offers $\frac{1}{3}$ off the recommended price.
The second shop offers 35% off the recommended price.

At which shop is the computer game cheaper?
You must show all your working out.

N13.11 There were 648 pupils in a school.
The ratio of the number of girls to the number of boys was 5 : 4.

a Copy and complete the following statement
Five out of every _____ pupils in the school were girls.
b Find the number of girls in the school.

N13.12 This timetable shows the weekday train times from Taunton to London

| Taunton | 0636 | 0706 | 0740 | then every | 2040 | 2114 |
| London | 0850 | 0918 | 0955 | hour until | 2255 | 2330 |

a How long does it take the 06 36 train to travel to London?
b Liam wants to get to London just before three o'clock in the afternoon.
Which would be the best train to catch from Taunton?

**N13
Miscellaneous continued**

N13.13 Calculate the exact value of 453×76 without using a calculator. You must show all your working.

N13.14 You must show all your working in this question.
Without using a calculator work out $986 \div 29$.

N13.15 When Graham took his car for its MOT the car had 44005 miles on the clock. He noticed that exactly one year earlier, on his previous MOT certificate, the mileage was recorded as 34232 miles.
How many miles had Graham's car travelled during the year?

N13.16 a Write one hundred and fifty thousand and forty six as a number.
b How many digits are there in this number?
c Write this number to the nearest hundred.

N13.17 Write out these statements and put brackets in to make the answers correct.
a $12 + 9 \div 3 \times 2 = 30$
b $12 + 9 \div 3 \times 2 = 14$
c $12 + 9 \div 3 \times 2 = 18$

N13.18 What is the value of:
a $3^2 \times 3^4$
b $4^4 \div 4^3$

N13.19 The value of 2^n is 64.
a What is the value of n?
b What is the value of n^3?
c i Is n^3 a square number?
ii Explain your answer.

N13.20 Write the following numbers in standard form:
a 140   b 200   c 2300
d 6500000   e 30300

N13.21 Write the following standard form numbers as integers:
a 1.3×10^2 b 2.4×10^3 c 5.6×10^5
d 1.04×10^2 e 9.14×10^6

N13.22 It has been estimated that by the year 2050, the population of India will be greater than the population of China.
Population estimates for 2050 are given as: India 1.6×10^9.
China 1554875000
In 2050, roughly how many more people will live in India than in China?

N13.23 United Nations estimates show that in the 1980s the population of the world increased from 4.4×10^9 to 5.2×10^9.
a How many people does this increase represent?
Give your answer in standard form.
b Roughly, what is this increase as a percentage?

Algebra

A1
Letters to represent unknowns

A1.1 Write down an expression, using x, for the total length of the bar drawn below.

$$2x \qquad\qquad x$$

A1.2
a If 8 centimetres is cut from a piece of string 13 centimetres long, how much is left?
b If d centimetres is cut off a piece of string 20 centimetres long, how much is left?
c If g centimetres is cut from a piece of string h centimetres long, how much is left?

A1.3
a A number is multiplied by 3 and then 5 is added to the result. The answer is 29. What is the starting number?
b Find the value of $3c + 2d$ when $c = {}^{-}1$ and $d = 3$.

A1.4 Emma buys a car.
She pays £m deposit and 36 monthly instalments of £n each.

Write down an expression for the total amount that Emma pays.

A1.5 The length of each side of a regular hexagon is f centimetres.

Write down a formula for the perimeter P of the regular hexagon.
Write your answer in its simplest form.

A1.6 The three angles of a triangle are given as x, $2x$ and $3x$.

Calculate the value of x.

A1.7 A rectangle is m centimetres long and w centimetres wide.

Write down an expression using m and w to show
a the area of the rectangle
b the perimeter of the rectangle.

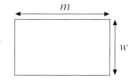

A1.8 The machine in this diagram is balancing 10 packets of peas and 2 weights.
Each packet of peas weighs p kilograms.

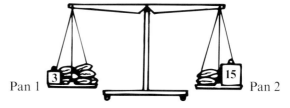

Pan 1   Pan 2

In pan 1 there are 7 packets of peas and a 3 kg weight.
The total weight in pan 1 can be written as $7p + 3$ kilograms.

a In pan 2 there are 3 packets of peas and a weight of 15 kg.
Write down an expression in terms of p for the total weight in pan 2.

The total weight in each pan is the same.

b Show this information as an equation in terms of p.
c Use your equation to calculate the weight, p kilograms, of one packet of peas.

A2
**Number patterns and
sequences**

A2.1 The rule for the following sequence that starts 1, 2, 3, … is:

The next number is the previous three numbers added together.

1, 2, 3, 6, 11, 20, …

a Write down the next three numbers in this sequence.

The numbers also seem to follow the pattern
odd, even, odd, even, odd, even, …

b Does the 'odd, even, odd, …' sequence carry on?
Give examples to support your answer.

A2.2 Here is a number sequence
4, 8, 12, 16, 20, …, …, 32

a Write down the two missing numbers.

From the following list
cube   factor   multiple   prime   square
use one to correctly complete each of these sentences about the sequence.

b Each of the numbers 4 and 8 is a _____ of 16.
c Each number is a _____ of 4.
d The numbers 4 and 16 _____ numbers.

A2.3 Bill builds fences with panels made up of pieces of wood.

 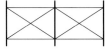 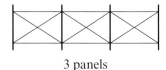

1 panel   2 panels   3 panels

a Sketch the fence made up with 5 panels.

Bill draws up a table to show how many pieces of wood he
needs for each fence.

Panel length	1	2	3	4	5	6
Number of pieces	5	9	13			

b Copy and complete the table to show how many pieces of wood he
would use for fences using 4, 5, and 6 panels.
c Write down how you would work out the number of pieces of wood
Bill would need to build a fence with 20 panels.

A2.4 This is the rule that Ivor used to get each number of a sequence from the
number before it:

Multiply by 2 then add 1.

Starting with 1 we get these numbers 1, 3, 7, 15, …

a Write down the next number.
b When he used the same rule with a different starting number, the
second number was 17.
What was his starting number?
c A different rule is used to get each number from the number before it,
the result is:
1, 3, 9, 27, …
Write down the new rule.

A2
Number patterns and sequences continued.

A2.5

```
Input    Function A   Output
 0  ───────────────▶  0
 1  ───────────────▶  2
 2  ───────────────▶  4
 3  ───────────────▶  6
 4  ───────────────▶  8
```

```
Input    Function B   Output
 0  ───────────────▶  0
 1  ───────────────▶  1
 2  ───────────────▶  4
 3  ───────────────▶  9
 4  ───────────────▶  16
```

The diagrams above show the result of functions A and B on the numbers 0 to 4.

a What does function A do to each of the numbers 0 to 4?
b What does function B do?

A2.6 **a** Write down the next two numbers in this sequence
               2, 6, 10, 14, ..., ...
       b Write down, in words, the rule for getting each number from the one before it.
       c Write down the rule for finding the nth number in the pattern.

A2.7

Line 1		1		total = 1 = 1^3
Line 2		3 5		total = 8 = 2^3
Line 3		7 9 11		total = 27 = 3^3

a Write down the numbers and the total which continue the pattern in line 4.
b Which line will have a total equal to 1000?
c What is the total of line 20?
d The first number in a line is n.
      What is the second number in this line?
      Give your answer in terms of n.

A2.8 One week the winning lottery numbers, with the bonus number, were:

3   4   6   9   13   17   24

When one of these numbers is changed the numbers will form a pattern.

Write down the number which must be changed and say what you would change it to.
Give a reason why your numbers form a pattern.

A3
Formulas

A3.1   Denzil works each weekend. His wages are worked out using this rule:

Wages in pounds equals the number of hours worked multiplied by five.

a   Last weekend Denzil worked for 9 hours.
    What were his wages for last weekend?
b   The weekend before Denzil earned £60.
    How many hours did he work that weekend?

A3.2   The cost of advertising, C pence, is worked out using the formula

$$C = 20w + 50$$

where w is the number of words in the advertisement.

a   Work out the cost of an advertisement of 25 words.
b   Kay put in an advertisement which cost £3.50.
    i   Use this cost, and the formula, to write an equation in w.
    ii Solve the equation to find the number of words in Kay's
        advertisement.

A3.3   a   Use the formula

$$s = at$$

to find the value of s when $a = 4$ and $t = 7$.
b   Given that

$$3y - 5 = 13$$

work out the value of

$$2y - 1$$

A3.4   For this sequence of numbers:

3, 7, 11, 15, 19, ...

a   Write down, in words, the rule for getting each number
    from the one before it.
b   Write down a formula, in terms of n, for the nth number in
    the sequence.

A3.5   The total cost of using a computer repair company called to your home
can be calculated using the following formula:

Cost (in pounds) = 60 + 40 × Number of hours worked.

a   Calculate the cost of repairing a computer when the work took
    half an hour.
b   The cost of repairing a computer was £160.
    How long did it take to repair?
c   The cost of repairing another computer was £145 which included
    £15 for parts. How long did this computer take to repair?

A3
Formulas continued

A3.6 A pattern is formed by arranging black and white tiles as shown below:

1 white   2 white   3 white

If b is the number of black tiles and w is the number of white tiles

a Write down a formula that links b and w.

Below is shown another way of arranging the tiles.

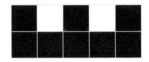

This time the formula connecting b and w is
$$b = 3w + 2$$

b Use this formula to work out the number of black tiles needed when 20 white tiles are used.

c When 173 black tiles are used an equation involving w is
$$173 = 3w + 2$$
Solve this equation to work out the number of white tiles needed.

A3.7 A rough guide to your 'ideal weight' states:
Your weight in kilograms is equal to
your height in centimetres minus 100.

a Jenny's height is 179 cm.
What is her 'ideal weight'?

b Will's weight is 83 kilograms.
What is his height if he fits this rule?

c Do you think this rule works for everyone?
Give reasons for your answer.

A3.8 One formula used to calculate velocity (v) is: $v = u + ft$.

a Calculate the value of v when $u = 0$, $f = 8$ and $t = 12$.

b Calculate the value of v when $u = 3.5$, $f = 15.6$ and $t = \frac{1}{4}$.

c **i** Rearrange the formula to express t in terms of v, u and f.
    ii Calculate t when $u = 6.2$, $v = 30.7$ and $f = 5$.

A3.9 The diagram shows how boards in a fence are nailed together – with some nails just for decoration!
A single board needs 5 nails, two boards need 8 nails, three boards need 11 nails, and so on.

a How many nails are needed for a fence of 15 boards?

b **i** If b is the number of boards, and n the number of nails, write a formula for the total number of nails for any number of boards.
    ii Use your formula to calculate the number of nails needed for a fence with 1484 boards.

A4
Manipulation

A4.1 Simplify the following:

   a $y + 2y + 3y + 2y$ **b** $2x + 2 + 2x + 2$ **c** $2x + y - 2x + 2$

   d $x + 2y - 2xy + x$ **e** $2x - x^2 + x + 2x^2$ **f** $2xy - 2x - y$

A4.2 **a** Simplify $2a + 4b - 3a$.
   b Simplify $3x + 2(x - 2y)$.
   c Find the value of $2x + 3y$ when $x = ^-1$ and $y = 3$.

A4.3 The area of this figure can
be found using this formula:
Area $= 16 + 2 \times$ Length.

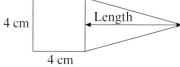

   a Work out what the area will be
when the length is 4 cm.
   b What will the length be when the total area is 40 cm²?

A4.4 Given that $v = \frac{1}{2}$, $w = \frac{3}{4}$, $x = 3$ and $y = 2$ evaluate:

   a vw **b** wx **c** $v + w$ **d** $\dfrac{v + w}{x}$ **e** $x + vy$

A4.5 Multiply out:

   a $3(2x - 3)$ **b** $2(3x^2 + 2)$ **c** $2y(y - 3)$
   d $2x(x + y)$ **e** $x(x^2 - 2x + 3)$

A5
Functions

A5.1 Copy and complete these mapping diagrams:

A5.2 The effect of functions A, B and C on the numbers 0 to 4 is shown.
Describe each of these functions.

a (Function A)

Input	Output
0 →	0
1 →	2
2 →	4
3 →	6
4 →	8

b (Function B)

Input	Output
0 →	0
1 →	1
2 →	4
3 →	9
4 →	16

c (Function C)

Input	Output
0 →	2
1 →	4
2 →	6
3 →	8
4 →	10

A5.3 Copy and complete the following mappings:

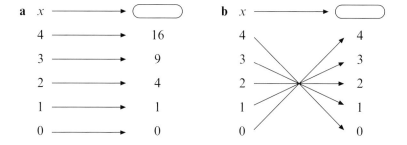

A5
Functions continued

A5.4

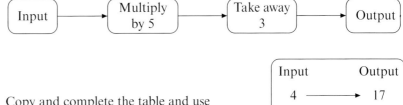

Copy and complete the table and use
the instructions above to
fill in the blanks.

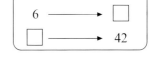

A5.5

a   When the input is 9, what is the output?
b   If the number you input was n, write down the output as an
   expression in n.

A5.6   Equilateral triangles are made with matchsticks.

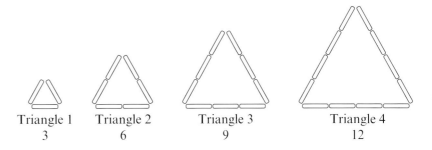

Triangle 1   Triangle 2   Triangle 3   Triangle 4
   3   6   9   12

The first triangle uses three matches, one for each side of the triangle.
The second triangle uses six matches, two for each side of the triangle.
The triangles continue to grow in this way.

a   Write down the values x and y which should appear in the boxes below.

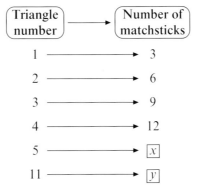

b   Explain, in words, your rule for finding
   the number of matches for each triangle.

c

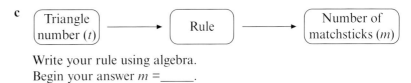

Write your rule using algebra.
Begin your answer $m =$ _____.

A6
Solving equations

A6.1 Solve each equation.

a $x + 9 = 17$ **b** $y - 3 = 5$ **c** $4 + z = 9$ **d** $8 - x = 3$
e $3y = 27$ **f** $2z + 3 = 15$ **g** $\frac{1}{2}x - 5 = 3$

A6.2 Jenny thinks of a number.
She doubles it then subtracts five from the result.

a What was her number when the answer is 21?
b What was her number when the answer is ⁻3?

A6.3 Solve these equations

a $6 = x - 4$ **b** $2(2x - 3) = 10$ **c** $11 = 3x - 1$
d $12 = 3(x - 1)$ **e** $3(4x - 1) = 15$ **f** $3x + 3 = 11 - x$

A6.4 Pia is 5 years older than Sean.
If Pia is n years old, write an expression in n for Sean's age.

A6.5 Liam and Neil have ages that total 33 years. Liam is 5 years older than Neil.

a If Neil is j years old, write an equation in j for their total ages.
b Solve your equation to find each of their ages.

> An expression in n is an expression that uses the letter n – for example: $n + 2$ or $3n - 7$.

A6.6 The following rule changes a temperature in degrees Celsius (C), into an approximate temperature in degrees Fahrenheit (F).

Double the Celsius temperature, then add thirty.

a Write this rule as a formula for F in terms of C.
b Find F when $C = 32$.
c Find C when $F = 54$.

A6.7

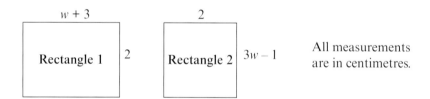

All measurements are in centimetres.

a Write down an expression in w for the perimeter of rectangle 1.
Put it in its simplest form
b The areas of the two rectangles are the same. By solving the equation $2(w + 3) = 2(3w - 1)$ find the area of each rectangle.

A6.8 I start with a number, k.
I double my number.

a Write an expression, in k, for the number I now have.

I start with k, treble it, and subtract 5.
b Write an expression, in k, for the number I now have.

With one starting number k, when I double it, it gives exactly the same answer as trebling it and subtracting 5.
c **i** Show this as an equation in k.
ii Solve your equation to find this starting number.

A7
Trial and improvement

A7.1 Jane wants to solve this problem using a trial-and-improvement method.
Number × 3.1 = 8.4
The first two lines of her working are shown below.

Continue Jane's working until you know the number correct to 1 dp.
Write down this number.

Try 3   3 × 3.1 = 9.3   too big.
Try 2.5   2.5 × 3.1 = 7.75   too small.

A7.2

A   B

500 m²

D   C

a   The square ABCD has an area of 500 m².
    The length AB is √500 m.

Mira wants to find the length of AB using trial and improvement.
Her first two trials were:

23 × 23 = 529   (too big)
22 × 22 = 484   (too small).

Show your working clearly and continue for at least two more trials
until you have found the length of AB correct to 1 dp.

b   Change your answer to part **a** into centimetres.

A7.3 The length of a rectangle is 3 cm more than its width.

a   Calculate the area of the rectangle when the width is 4 cm.
b   Calculate the area when the width is 5 cm.
c   Using a trial and improvement method,
    find the width of the rectangle if its area is 35 cm².
    Give your answer in centimetres correct to 1 dp.
    You must show all your trials.

A7.4 a   Continue this table to find x if $3x + 6 = 57$.

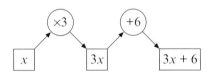

x	$3x$	$3x + 6$	
12	36	42	Too small
20	60	66	Too big

b   Using the same method, find y if $y^2 + 3 = 9.25$.

y	y^2	$y^2 + 3$	
2			

A8
Graphs

A8.1   On graph paper, with the x axis and y axis numbered from 0 to 6.

    a Plot the points (0, 6), (1, 4), and (3, 0) and draw a line through them.

    b Draw the line $y = x + 3$ on the same grid.
        Write the coordinates of the point where the two lines cross.

A8.2   **a** Copy and complete the table of values below for $y = x - 2$.

x	⁻5	⁻4	⁻3	⁻2	⁻1	0	1	2	3	4	5
y					⁻2						3

    b Draw the graph of $y = x - 2$.

    c On the same graph, plot the points A (⁻5, 2) and B (1, ⁻4).

    d Join the points A and B with a straight line and write down where this line crosses the graph of $y = x - 2$.

A8.3   On squared paper draw x and y axes with values 0 to 9.

    a Plot the points (1, 3) and (6, 8) and join them with a straight line.

    b The point $(a, 6)$ lies on this line. What is the value of a?

    c This line can be extended.

Copy and complete this mapping for points on the extended line.

$$1 \longrightarrow 3$$
$$6 \longrightarrow 8$$
$$8 \longrightarrow \square$$
$$x \longrightarrow \square$$

    d On the same axes draw the graph of $y = 6 - x$.

    e Solve the equation $x + 2 = 6 - x$.

A8.4   **a** Copy and complete this table of values for $y = x^2 + 1$.

x	0	1	2	3	4	5	6	7
$y = x^2 + 1$			5			26		

    b Plot these points on graph paper and draw the graph of $y = x^2 + 1$.

    c Use your graph to find the value of x when $y = 45$.

A8.5   The distance y metres a car travels in x seconds is given by the formula
        $y = 2x^2$

    a Copy and complete the following table of values

Time x	0	1	2	3	4	5	6	7
Distance y	0			18			72	

    b On graph paper plot the points shown in the table and draw a smooth curve through your points.

    c Use your graph and write down an estimate of the distance travelled by the car in the first 5.5 seconds.

    d Use your graph to write down an estimate of how long it takes the car to travel the first 30 metres.

A9
Miscellaneous

A9.1

Input → Multiply by 9 → Subtract 7 → Output

a When the input is 5, what is the output?
b The input is x. Write down the output in terms of x.

A9.2
a When a number is multiplied by three and then four is taken away from the result the answer is five. What is the number?
b Simplify
   i $a + 3b + 2a$
   ii $3a + 2(3b - a)$
c Find the value of $3c + 2d$ when $c = 3$ and $d = {}^-2$.

A9.3
a Write down the next two numbers in the following number pattern
   2, 6, 10, 14, 18, __, __,
b Write down, in words, the rule for finding the next number in the pattern from the one before it.
c Write down the rule for finding the nth number in the pattern.

A9.4 The cost of servicing a domestic appliance can be calculated using the following formula:
   Cost (in pounds) = 40 + 36 × Number of hours worked

a Calculate the cost of servicing a dishwasher when the work took half an hour.
b The total cost of servicing a washing machine was £85. This included a £9 charge for parts. How long did it take to service the machine?

A9.5
a Solve the equation $4x + 3 = 23$.
b Use the formula $A = wb$ to work out the value of A when $w = 6$ and $b = 4$.

A9.6 Sue buys x nails and $x - 9$ screws. Altogether she has 37 nails and screws.

a Use this information to form an equation in x.
b Solve your equation to find out how many screws Sue bought.

A9.7 Simplify:
a $3x + 4y - 2x$
b $4a + 2(3a - 2b)$

A9.8 The graph of $y = x^2 + 2$ can be drawn by plotting the points in the following table.

x	0	1	2	3	4	5	6	7
y	2	3	6	11	18	27	38	51

a On graph paper plot the points in the table.
b Join the points with a smooth curve to draw the graph of $y = x^2 + 2$.
c Mark the position of
   i A (3,30)
   ii B (6,15) on your graph.
d Join A to B and write down the coordinates of the point where line AB meets the curve $y = x^2 + 2$.

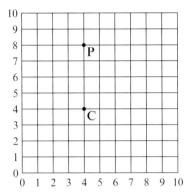
Shape, space and measures

S1 **S1.1** A player in a television game had to follow instructions and move to the
Fixing position correct spot on a floor marked in metre squares as shown below.

At the start the contestant is at
C (4, 4) facing **P**.

The instructions were:

Forward 3 metres.
Turn clockwise through 90°.
Forward 4 metres.
Turn anticlockwise through 270°.
Forward 3 metres.

a Copy the diagram and draw the path the player should have followed.
b Write down the coordinates of the final position of the player.
c Write down two further instructions which will take the player
back to the start point.

S1.2 Three places are close to each other on a map.
The Castle (C) is due South of the Market (M).
The Cross (X) is due East of the Castle.
The Cross is South East of the Market.

a Draw a North line and sketch the positions of the three places.
Mark them C, M and X.
b What is the bearing of M from C?
c What is the bearing of C from X?
d What is the bearing of M from X?

S1.3 This diagram shows a square.

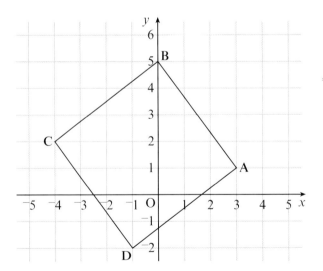

Write down the coordinates of the corners A, B, C and D.

S1
Fixing position
continued

S1.4   The four points A (1, 2), B (4, 6), C (7, 4) and D (x, y)
are the corners of a rectangle.

a   Draw a grid with x (horizontal) values from 0 to 8
and y (vertical) values from 0 to 7.
b   Plot the four points A, B, C and D on your grid.
c   Write down the coordinates of D.
d   Write down the coordinates of the point where the diagonals of
rectangle ABCD meet.

S1.5   A field was surveyed and the dimensions recorded on the following
diagram.

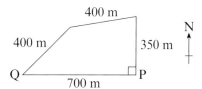

a   Using 1 cm square grid paper, draw an accurate scale drawing of the
field using a scale of 1 cm to represent 50 m.
b   There is a large boulder in the field.
The bearing of the boulder from corner P is 315°
and from corner Q the bearing is 070°.
Mark the position of the boulder on your drawing.
Show all your working.

S1.6   The diagram shows a radar screen which scans an area of the North Sea.
The radii of the circles, measured from base B, are 10 km, 20 km,
30 km, etc.

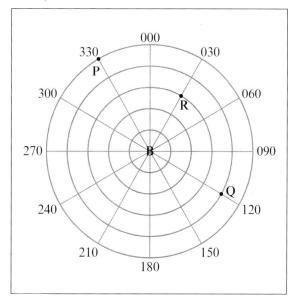

An oil rig R is 30 km from B on a bearing of 030°.
This is written as (30, 030).

a   Write down the position of ship Q.

A submarine appears on the surface at (20, 120).

b   How far is it from ship Q?
c   Write down the position of ship P.
d   Use your protractor to measure the bearing of ship P from ship Q.
e   Calculate the area of sea, in km², that is scanned by this radar screen.

S2
Compound measures and graphs

S2.1 At the start of a journey the mileometer on Jed's bike showed 0163 miles.
The journey lasted 30 minutes.
At the end of the journey the mileometer showed 0188 miles.

a How far did he travel?
b What was Jed's average speed for the journey?

S2.2 Albert types at an average speed of 40 words per minute.
His son Frank types words at a speed of 9 words per minute.

a How many more words would Albert type than Frank in 1 hour?

A book has 340 pages with an average of 35 lines per page and 10 words per line.

b How many words are there, on average, on one page of the book?
c Approximately how many words are there in the whole book?
d How many hours, to the nearest hour, would it take Albert to type out the whole book?

S2.3 This sketch graph shows the journey of a car and a cycle.
The cyclist travelled from Leeds to York.
The car driver took the same route to York but returned to Leeds.

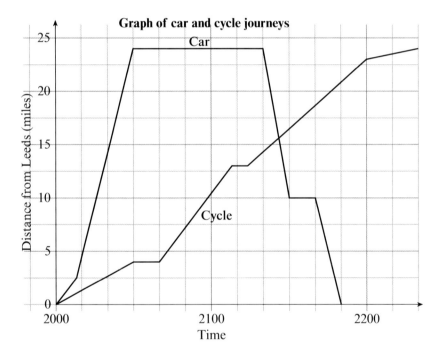

a How far did the cyclist travel in the first 20 minutes?
b How long did it take the car to travel the first 20 miles?
c How many times did the cyclist stop on her journey to York?
d What was the cyclist's average speed for this journey in mph, correct to 1 dp?

S2
Compound measures and graphs continued.

S2.4   Water flows out of a pipe at a constant rate.
In 30 minutes, 924 litres flow out.

In litres per minute at what rate is water flowing out of the pipe?

S2.5   Graphs that help you change from one unit to another are called **conversion graphs**.

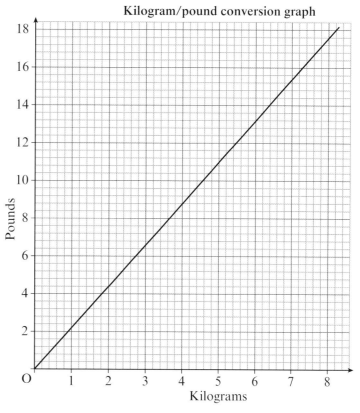

Kilogram/pound conversion graph

a Use the graph to give an estimate, in kilograms, of:
  i   11 pounds
  ii 6 pounds

b Use the graph to give an estimate, in pounds, of:
  i   6 kilograms
  ii 1.2 kilograms

S2.6   You must show all your working out for this question.
Alison bought a 250 ml tube of cream for £4.00.
Brett bought a 200 ml bottle of the same cream for £3.40.

a Work out what Alison paid for 1 ml of cream from the tube.
b Work out what Brett paid for 1 ml of cream from the bottle.
c Who had the best value for money: Brett buying a bottle or Alison buying a tube?

S2.7   Claire wants to buy a 500 gram bag of nuts for 80p for the bird feeder.
Her brother Damian sees mixed seeds on offer at 6 grams for 1p and says they could save money by buying the mixed seeds.

a Was Damian correct?
    (You must show working out to support your answer.)
b If the bird feeder only holds 120 grams, would you buy the nuts or the mixed seed? (Give a reason for your choice.)

S3
Angles and polygons

S3.1 Write down the size of the angles marked x in each of these diagrams.

a **b** **c**

S3.2 **a** What is the special name given to the quadrilateral below?

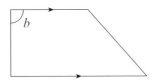

b Measure angle b and write down your result.
c What is the special name of the angle b?

S3.3 This drawing has not been drawn accurately.
AEC is a straight line.
Angle BED is a right angle
$x + y + z = 203°$.
Work out the sizes of angles x and z.

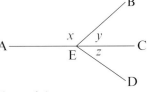

S3.4 The three angles of a triangle are given as $2x$, $3x$ and $4x$.
Calculate the value of each angle in degrees

S3.5 ABCD is a rectangle with H
halfway between A and B.

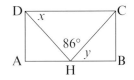

a What type of triangle is CDH?
b Calculate the size of angle x and angle y.
c Calculate the area of triangle CDH when
AB = 13 cm and AD = 6 cm.

Sketch a diagram to work on.

Label any angle or distance you know or have calculated on your sketch. Show which (if any) lines are parallel or equal.

When you are asked to explain or give reasons it is important to do so clearly. In this way you will gain the maximum number of marks.

S3.6 The diagram below shows a frame which is symmetrical about FB.
Angle HFI = 55°, angle AHI = 105° and angle HAI = 30°.
The bars AC, HD and GE are parallel.

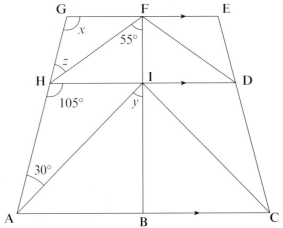

a What is the size of angle x?
b Work out the size of angle y?
c Giving reasons, work out the size of angle z.
d Write down two lines which are equal, and say why they are equal.

S3
Angles and polygons
continued

S3.7   Here are the names of some shapes:
　　　Square　Cone　Cube　Trapezium　Rectangle
　　　Pyramid　Cylinder　Kite　Circle　Triangle

Use the list to help you write down the names of these shapes:

a

b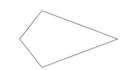

c

d

S3.8   **Regular polygons**

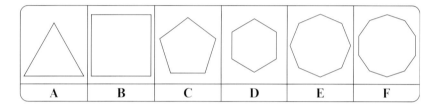

a Name each regular polygon in the table.
b For polygons A, B and C, give the sum of the interior angles.
c For polygons D, E and F, give the size of one interior angle.
d **i** A regular heptagon has how many sides?
　　ii Calculate the size of one interior angle of a regular heptagon.
e Calculate the size of an exterior angle of polygon F.
f Which of these polygons are shapes that will tessellate?
　　Explain your answer.

S3.9   O is the centre of ABCDEF which is a regular hexagon.

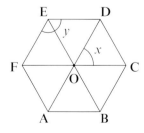

a Write down the order of rotational symmetry of the regular hexagon,
b Write down the number of lines of symmetry of triangle EFO.
c Work out the size of angle x.
d Work out the size of angle y.

S4
Measures

S4.1 At the Regent Cinema the main film starts at 19:55.

a Write this time in 12-hour clock notation.

The main film lasts for 1 hour 52 minutes.

b At what time will the film end?
Give your answer in 24-hour time.

S4.2 **a** **i** Which train has the shortest journey time between Exeter and London?
ii What is the journey time?
b What is the longest journey time?
c How long does it take the 0837 from Exeter to travel to Taunton?

Exeter to London Paddington is a distance of 193 miles.

d Find the average speed of the 0756 from Exeter to London Paddington. Give your answer correct to 2 sf.

Mondays to Fridays		
Exeter St Davids	Taunton	London Paddington
Depart	Depart	Arrive
0600	0628	0835
0620	0648	0920
0659	0726	0930
0756	0820	1002
0837	0904	1110
0950	1024	1225
1131	1158	1350

Colin calculates that the average speed of the 0600 from Exeter to London must be less than 90 mph.

e Explain whether you agree or disagree with Colin.
Show all your calculations, and do not use a calculator.

S4.3 **a** Draw a rectangle with sides of length 5 cm and 7 cm.
b Write down the perimeter of your rectangle.
c Calculate the area of your rectangle.

S4.4 In this question take $\pi = 3.14$ or use the π button on your calculator.

a Measure and record the diameter of the circle below.
Give your answer
i in centimetres
ii in millimetres.

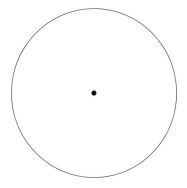

b Calculate the circumference of the circle.
c Find the area of the circle.

S4.5 A cuboid is 10 cm long, 4 cm wide and 2 cm high.

a Sketch this cuboid and label the three dimensions given above.
b Calculate the surface area of the cuboid.

S4
Measures continued

S4.6 The diagram, which is not drawn accurately, is part of a net of a triangular prism.

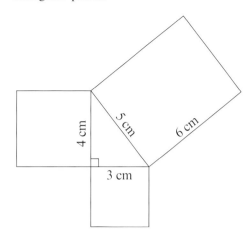

a Draw an accurate diagram using the dimensions given.
b Complete your diagram to show an accurate net of the triangular prism.
c Sketch the triangular prism.
d Using the dimensions shown on the diagram, calculate the total area of the five faces of the prism.
e Calculate the volume of the prism.

S4.7 Tiles measure 10 cm by 10 cm.
Asif was tiling his kitchen.
He had to tile this surface.

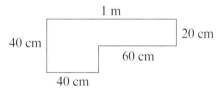

a How many tiles does he need for this surface?
b Calculate the area of this surface.
c Asif wants to put a plastic edging strip around the perimeter of this surface.
Allowing 20 cm extra for the corners, how many metres of plastic strip will he need?

S4.8 a Work out the volume of this tin of sardines.
b Sketch another tin with different dimensions which has the same volume.
c Give the dimensions of your tin
Length = ?
Width = ?
Height = ?

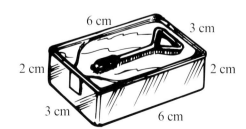

S5
Nets and polyhedra

S5.1 The diagram shows a box
in the form of a triangular prism.
The sides of the triangular
cross-section are 3 cm, 4 cm
and 5 cm long.
The length of the prism is 6 cm.

a For the triangular prism
write down the number of:
i faces
ii edges
iii vertices.

b Draw the net of the prism accurately.

The cross section is a right-angled triangle.

c Calculate the area of the triangular end, ABC of the prism.
d Calculate the volume of the prism.

State clearly the units of your answers to parts **c** and **d**.

S5.2 This is a net of a cube.

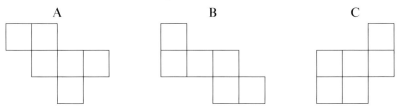

a Which one of the following will **not** fold into a cube?

      A   B   C

b On 1 cm squared dotty paper draw a different net of a cube.

S5.3 Jim decided to make a cardboard model of a drawer from a chest of
drawers. The diagrams below show the chest and Jim's sketch of the
model drawer he wanted to make.

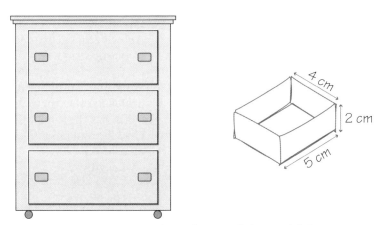

a On 1 cm squared paper draw the net of the model drawer.
b How many square centimetres of card do you need to make the
model drawer?

S5
Nets and polyhedra
continued

S5.4 This diagram shows one end of a prism.
The diagram is drawn to scale and
all measurements are in centimetres.
The prism is 2 centimetres long.

On spotty isometric grid paper
draw the prism.

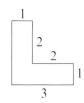

S5.5 On spotty isometric paper draw a diagram of a cuboid.

S5.6 A cube is joined to
a square-based pyramid
to make this shape.
For the complete shape
write down the number of

a faces
b edges
c vertices.

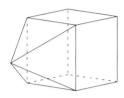

S6
Transformations

S6.1

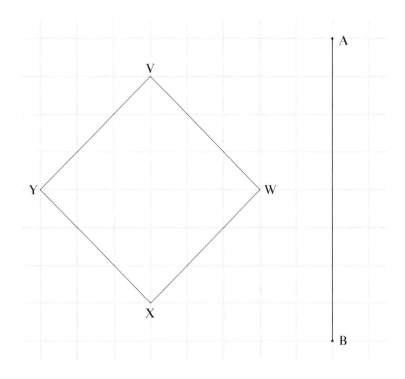

Copy this diagram on to 1 cm squared paper.

a Draw a reflection of VWXY in the mirror line AB.
b On your drawing mark the centre of rotation of VWXY.

S6
Transformations
continued

S6.2

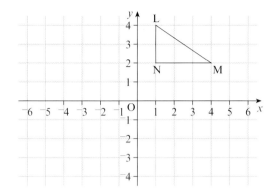

Copy the drawing above on squared paper.

a Rotate triangle LMN 90° clockwise about (0,0).
Label the new triangle ABC.

b Reflect triangle ABC in the y-axis.
Label the new triangle DEF.

c Translate triangle LMN five units to the left.
Label the new triangle RST.

d Give the coordinates of the point R.

S6.3 Describe as fully as possible
the transformation which maps
triangle A on to the triangle B.

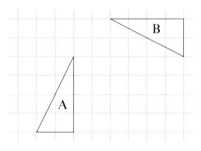

S6.4 Copy the pentagon PQRST and the point
marked C on to squared paper.
Draw an enlargement of PQRST with
scale factor 2.

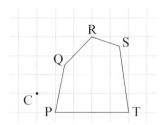

S6.5

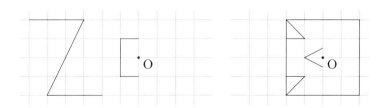

Only half of each of these symmetrical designs has been drawn.
When fully drawn each design will look the same when it is rotated
through a half turn about the point marked O.
Copy each drawing on to squared paper and complete each design.

S7
Similarity and congruence

S7.1 The diagram shows a matchbox with a volume of 24 cm³.

a On isometric spotty paper sketch another box with different dimensions which also has a volume of 24 cm³.

b Write down the length, width and height of your box.

c On the isometric spotty paper draw a box with each dimension twice that of the original matchbox.

d What is the largest number of matchboxes that will fit into this box?

S7.2 Write down which of the shapes below are congruent to shape C.

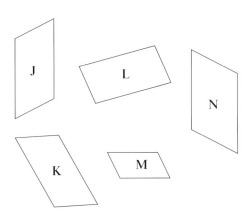

S7.3 Copy this diagram on to squared paper. With C the centre, enlarge the figure using a scale factor of 3.

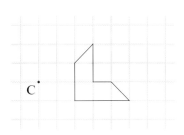

S7.4 Write down which one of the triangles (A, B, C or D) is congruent to the triangle marked G.

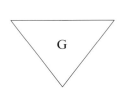

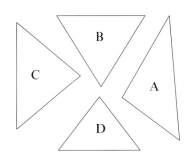

S8
Symmetry

S8.1   Copy the following drawings out on squared paper.
Complete each of your drawings so that the line AB is a line of symmetry.

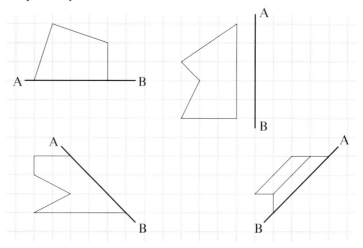

S8.2   Write down the names of the tiles below which have line symmetry.

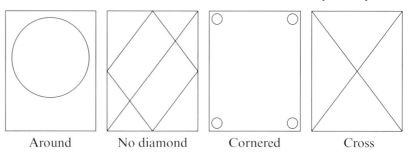

Around   No diamond   Cornered   Cross

S8.3   Write down the order of rotational symmetry of each of these shapes.

a

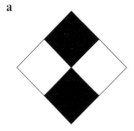

b

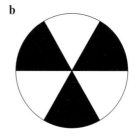

S8.4   Gail has to make up a crossword for her French homework.
She begins by making a blank crossword with lines x and y its two lines of symmetry.

Copy the diagram out on squared paper and complete the crossword blank.

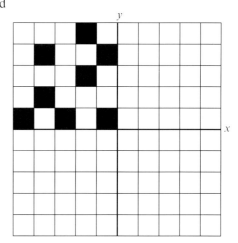

S8
Symmetry continued

S8.5 This diagram shows one quarter of the pattern of a tile.
When complete the tile has symmetry about the lines AB and CD.

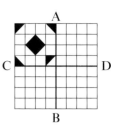

a Copy the pattern on squared paper and complete the design.

b The complete tile pattern has another symmetry.
Describe this symmetry as fully as possible.

S8.6 A square piece of paper six centimetres long is folded in half horizontally, then folded in half vertically as shown in the diagram.
A triangle is then cut through all four sections of the folded paper. The paper is then opened out.

a On squared paper draw the shapes you see when the paper is opened out.

b On your diagram draw any lines of symmetry.

S8.7 Copy the diagram on the right.
(You are allowed to use tracing paper.)

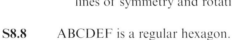

a Complete your diagram so that it has rotational symmetry.

b Draw a shape which has exactly two lines of symmetry and rotational symmetry.

S8.8 ABCDEF is a regular hexagon.
O is the centre of the hexagon.

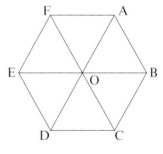

a Write down the order of rotational symmetry of the regular hexagon.

b Write down the number of lines of symmetry of triangle DOC.

S8.9 Only one of the shapes below has **no** rotational symmetry.

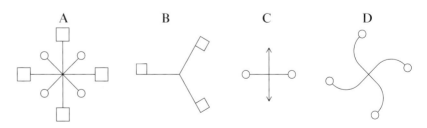

Which shape is it?

S8.10 These are the initials of the Wildlife International Conference on Kangaroos.

W I C K

Which of these letters has rotational symmetry?

S9
Circles

In these questions take π as 3.14 or use the π button on your calculator.

S9.1 Draw a semicircle with a radius of 6 cm.

S9.2 An engineer wants to make a wire circle with a diameter of 16 cm.
  a How much wire will he need?
  b Write your answer to part **a** to the nearest millimetre.

S9.3 A circle has a radius of 13 cm.
  Calculate the area of the circle.

S9.4 The radius of the large rear wheel of a wheelchair is 30 cm.

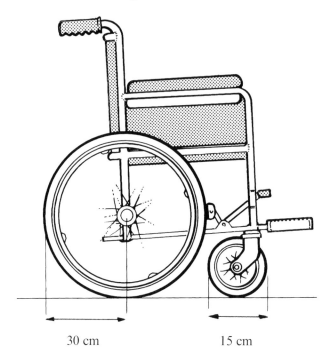

30 cm   15 cm

The rear wheel makes one full turn.
  a Calculate the distance the wheelchair moves.
  b The small front wheel has a diameter of 15 cm.
    How many full turns will the small wheel make for each full turn of the rear wheel?

S9.5 Jade's mountain bike has 70 cm diameter wheels.
  How many times does a wheel go round when the bike travels 20 metres?

S9.6 Name tags for pets are made by stamping discs from rectangular sheets of metal.
  Each metal sheet is 48 cm long and 36 cm wide
  The diagram shows part of a sheet
  with discs cut out of it.
  The radius of each disc is 3 cm.

  a How many discs can be cut from one sheet?
  b Calculate the total area of all the discs that can be cut from one sheet.
  c How much waste metal is left from each sheet after the discs have been cut out?

S10
Construction and scale drawing

S10.1 This diagram shows the end of a house.

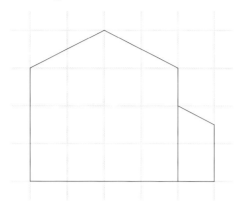

On 1 cm squared paper draw an enlargement of it with scale factor 2.

S10.2 Use your ruler, compasses and protractor to construct this triangle.

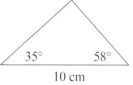

S10.3 This sketch shows the plan of a garden.

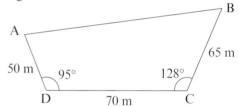

   a Using a scale of 1 centimetre to 10 metres, make an accurate scale drawing of the garden.
   b Write down the length of side AB on your drawing.
   c Write down the length of side AB of the garden, to the nearest metre.

S10.4 The plan of a house is drawn to a scale of 1:50.

   a On the plan the length of the kitchen is 7 cm. What is the actual length of the kitchen in metres?
   b A room is $7\frac{1}{2}$ metres long. What length is it on the plan of the house?

S10.5 Copy the diagram below (you may use tracing paper). On your copy:

   a Draw a line through the point C which is parallel to AB.
   b Draw a line through the point D which is perpendicular to AB.

S10.6 A map has a scale of 1:5000.
The distance between two places on the map is 8 cm.

What is the real-life distance, in metres, between these two places?

S11
Miscellaneous

S11.1 Two hexagons have been drawn on the isometric grid below.

    a Copy this drawing on to a half sheet of A4 isometric paper, and continue the drawing to show how regular hexagons tessellate.

    b Explain why regular pentagons will not tessellate.

S11.2 This diagram shows a rectangle WXYZ with A the mid point of WX.

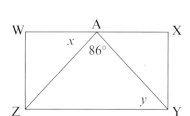

    a Calculate:
       i angle x
       ii angle y.

    b What kind of triangle is AYZ?

    When WX = 13 cm and XY = 5 cm:

    c Calculate the area of:
       i rectangle WXYZ
       ii triangle AYZ.

S11.3 The diagram shows a regular hexagon ABCDEF with centre O.

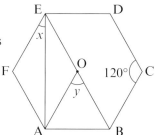

    a Work out the sizes of the following angles giving reasons for your answers:
       i angle x
       ii angle y.

    b What name is given to the quadrilaterals
       i AOEF
       ii ABEF?

S11.4   **a** Draw a circle with a radius of 3 cm.
    b Mark the centre point clearly and label it O.
    c Draw in a chord and label it.
    d Draw in a diameter of your circle and label it.
    e Write down an estimate of the length of the circumference of your circle.

S11.5 This drawing is made up of 1 cm squares.

    a Work out and write down the perimeter of the shape.

    b Work out and write down the area of the shape.

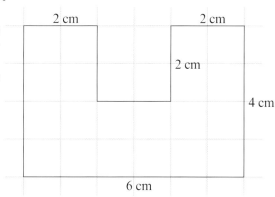

S11
Miscellaneous
continued

S11.6 Lorna and Mike try out a new game.
Mike puts on a blindfold and Pat directs him around a course.

COURSE

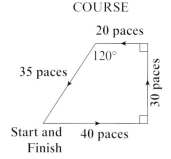

DIRECTIONS

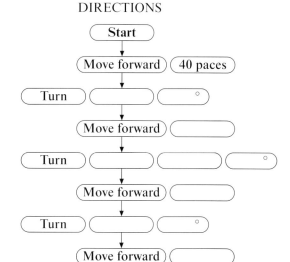

Copy out the directions and use
some of these boxed terms to fill
in the blank spaces. You can use
each box only once. You do not
have to use all the boxes.

right	30°	clockwise
anti-	90°	35 paces
left	60°	20 paces
left	90°	30 paces

S11.7 This diagram represents a rectangular box
made to carry wooden blocks.

  a Write down how many:
   i   faces
   ii edges
   iii vertices
   the box has.
  b Calculate the volume of
   the box.
   The wooden blocks which go
   into the box each has a volume
   of 3 cm³.

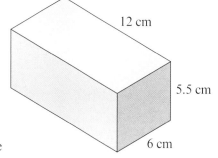

  c If there is no wasted space inside the box when it is full of blocks,
   how many wooden blocks will fit into the box?

S11.8

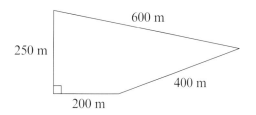

  a Using a scale of 1 cm to represent 50 m, on 1 cm squared paper,
   draw an accurate scale drawing of the field shown above.
   Leave all construction lines on your drawing.

Handling data

D1
Probability

D1.1 Copy the probability scale below.

| 0 | 0.1 | 0.2 | 0.3 | 0.4 | 0.5 | 0.6 | 0.7 | 0.8 | 0.9 | 1 |

Half of the counters in a box are blue.
One counter is picked at random.

a Mark your copy of the scale with an arrow
to show the probability of picking a blue counter.

b A quarter of the counters in the box are red.
Mark your copy of the scale with an X to show the probability of
picking a red counter.

D1.2 Three events are described .
  X I spin a coin and it comes down tails.
  Y I will win the jackpot in the National Lottery next Wednesday.
  Z There will be ice at the North Pole tomorrow.
Draw a probability scale like this.

| 0 | 1 |

a Mark X on your probability scale at the point where you think the
probability of event X occurring is.

b Mark Y at the point where you think the probability of Y occurring
is and Z where you think the probability of event Z occurring is.

D1.3 'The probability that Manchester United will win the cup is 1.4.'
'The probability that Cardiff City will win the cup is ⁻0.3.'

Explain why the value of the probability in each of these statements is
not possible.

D1.4 Sonya has five videos in a drawer. They are labelled A, B, C, D and E.

a She takes two videos out of the box at random.
List all the possible combinations of videos that she might pick.

b Sonya puts the videos back in the drawer.
She now takes one video at random.
What is the probability that she takes video E?

D1.5 This table shows the results of a survey of a group of students.

Hair colour	Boys	Girls
Fair	9	7
Auburn	2	4
Dark	14	14

a What is the probability that one of the girls has fair hair?
b What is the probability that one of the students has dark hair?

D1.6 Ravi has 3 blue, 1 red, 2 green and 2 black pens.
He takes one pen without looking at it.
What is the probability that it is:

a green   **b** red or black   **c** not blue.

D1
Probability
continued

D1.7   To raise money a school held a raffle. The tickets were numbered 1 to 500.
There was one main prize, and 500 children bought 1 ticket each.
The winning ticket will be drawn from a drum.
Aaron had ticket number 275.

    a What is the probability that Aaron will win the main prize?

    b Two brothers and their sister each had a ticket.
What is the probability that one of them will win the main prize?

    c Nicole says that the probability that a girl will win is $\frac{1}{2}$ because
either a boy or a girl must win. Explain why she might be wrong.

    d What is the probability that the winning ticket number will be
greater than 400?

There are also some smaller prizes to be won in the same raffle.
The probability that Aaron wins any prize with his ticket is $\frac{1}{50}$.

    e How many prizes are there altogether?

D1.8   Jessica uses a spinner with seven edges.
It has an equal chance of landing on any
one of it's edges when it has been spun.

    a What is the probability that it lands
on the edge marked 2?

    b What is the probability that it lands on
an edge marked with an odd number?

Jack makes a seven sided spinner. He spins it 35 times.
This table shows the result.

Score	1	2	3	4	5	6	7
Frequency	4	3	5	6	3	10	4

    c Is Jack's spinner fair? Give a reason for your answer.

D1.9   Ten cards are numbered 0 to 9. Peter takes **one** card without looking.

    a What is the probability that it is the 3?

    b What is the probability that it is an odd number?

Esther has a different pack of cards.
Some cards have the same number on them.
The probability that she chooses a 7 is 0.3.

    c What is the probability that she does not choose a 7?

D1.10   On a stall at a school fete players spin a coin and throw a dice.
The two winning scores are 6 on the dice with Heads on the coin (6, H)
and 1 on the dice with tails on the coin (1, T).
These scores are shown on the diagram below.

Head						6 H
Tail	1 T					
Score on dice	1	2	3	4	5	6	6

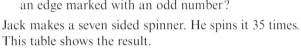

    a Copy and complete the table above to show all possible outcomes.

    b Jeremy has one turn at the game.
What is the probability that he wins a prize?

D2
Collecting and organising
data

D2.1 Kurt decides to find out which food dog-owners buy.
He carries out a survey at a pet store.
The store sells:
    Doggo, Fido's Favourite, Best Boneo and Marrowbisk.

Design a table in which Kurt can record his results.

D2.2 The table shows some results recorded
when a red dice and a blue dice are thrown.
If the score on both dice is the same then
this score is recorded otherwise the highest
score showing on the red or the blue dice
is recorded.

Copy and complete the table
to show all possible scores.

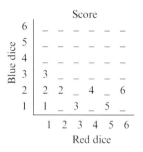

D2.3 Ravinder has two fair spinners with five equal sectors.

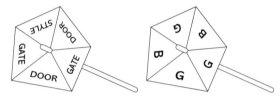

The first spinner has three green sectors and two brown sectors.
The second spinner has sectors labelled GATE (2 sectors),
DOOR (2 sectors) and STYLE (1 sector).

She spins each spinner once . List all the possible outcomes.

D2.4 The destinations of 90 people arriving
at an airport are shown in the table.
Alistair must draw a pie chart to
show this data.

List each destination and next to it
the angle that this destination will take up
in the pie chart.

Destination	Number of travellers
Australia	9
USA	25
Canada	15
Europe	30
India	11

D2.5 Stephen and Tessa are each doing a survey to find out what people think
about sport on TV.

Stephen's Questions   Tessa's Questions

There is too much sport on
television.

☐   ☐
I agree   I disagree

Is the time given to sport on TV:

☐   ☐   ☐
Too little?   About right?   Too much?

a Which set of questions do you think is better?
b Give a reason for your answer.
c Write down, with a reason, one other question that could be asked
in this survey.

D2.6 Design an observation sheet that you could use to collect data to find out
which colours of cars are popular.

D2.7 Design a questionnaire to collect data on the numbers of brothers and
the number of sisters of the students in your maths group.

D2
Collecting and organising data continued

D2.8   A class of students had their heights measured in centimetres. The results are shown below.

163	171	154	165	159	152	172	156	155	147
164	167	173	182	162	159	168	172	166	144
157	153	162	168	149	173	163	154	164	168

a   What was the height of the tallest student in this class?
b   How much taller was the tallest student than the shortest student?

Copy and complete the following frequency table for these results.

Height (centimetres)	Tally	Frequency
140–149		
150–159		
160–169		
170–179		
180–189		

c   How many students were in the class?
d   How many students were taller than 169 cm?
e   On squared paper draw a frequency diagram using the complete frequency table.

D2.9   A survey was carried out on the shoe sizes of 20 women. The results are listed below.

6	7	5	4	6	4	5	6	6	5
6	4	5	6	7	6	4	5	6	1

a   What is the median of the shoe sizes?
b   What is the mode of the shoe sizes?

This frequency diagram shows the results of a shoe size survey of 20 men.

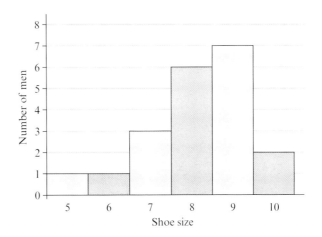

c   Use your answers to parts **a** and **b** to make two comparisons between the shoe sizes of women and men.

D3
Drawing and interpreting
graphs and charts

D3.1   The graph shows the average height for different weights of women and men.

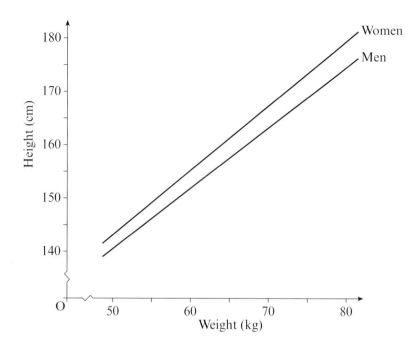

a   For the average man and average woman with the same weight, what does the graph tell us about their height?
b   Mary and Phil both weigh 60 kg.
Use the graphs to decide who is the taller and by how much.
c   Sam and his wife Sasha are both 170 cm tall.
From the graphs, what are their weights?

D3.2   A drink was heated in a microwave and its temperature was recorded every 10 seconds.

Time (seconds)	0	10	20	30	40	50	60	70	80	90	100
Temperature (°C)	30	32	35	40	48	55	66	76	88	92	94

Plot these points on graph paper and join them up with a curve.

What was the temperature of the drink:
a   when it was put into the microwave
b   after 30 seconds
c   after 55 seconds?
d   How long did it take the drink to reach a temperature of 70 °C?

D3.3   Nigel asked the boys in his group what type of transport they would use to travel to their holiday destination.
The result of his survey was:

Coach   4
Train   7
Car   5

a   How many boys were in Nigel's group?
b   Draw a pictogram to show the above data.
c   What type of transport was the mode?

D3
Drawing and interpreting graphs and charts continued

D3.4 These are the test marks of a group of students.

18	32	70	60	51	40	32	23	26	42
35	18	17	19	62	47	48	39	34	27
53	32	29	33	28	26	36	47	46	43

a Copy and complete the following frequency table.

Mark	Tally	Frequency
11–20		
21–30		
31–40		
41–50		
51–60		
61–70		

a How many students were in the group?
b Draw a bar chart for the frequency table.

D3.5 This graph shows the number of pupil attendances, in thousands, at a comprehensive school each month from January to December.

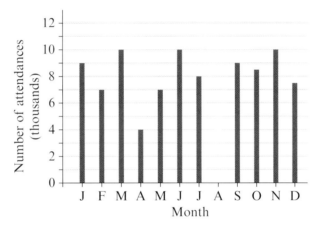

a How many attendances were there in
  i April
  ii February
  iii October
  iv December?
b Which were the modal months?

The months January, February, March and April make up the Spring term.
May, June and July make up the Summer term.
September, October, November and December make up the Autumn term.

c Copy and complete this table to show the total attendances, in thousands, for each term.

Spring	Summer	Autumn
30		

d Draw and label a pie chart to show the attendances by terms.
You must show how you calculate the angles of your pie chart.

D4
Scatter diagrams and correlation

D4.1 Data was collected from a group of lorry drivers.
The data was used to plot these scatter graphs.

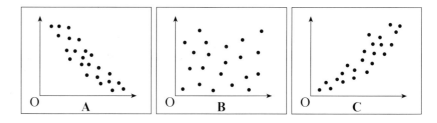

Match each of the following sentences to the graph it best describes.

1 This graph describes the distance the driver has driven in a week plotted against his shoe size.

2 This graph describes the height of the driver (in centimetres) plotted against his weight.

3 This graph describes the age of the lorry plotted against the value of the lorry.

D4.2 Megan carried out a survey of her tutor group.
She asked about the hours spent doing homework and the time spent on leisure activities.
Here is a scatter diagram that Megan drew to show the results.

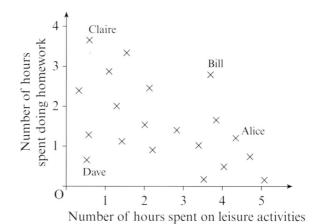

a Write down which of the four students you think is making each statement.
  i I went to the cinema last night and I also did a lot of homework.
  ii I only watched one programme on TV and then spent most of my evening doing homework.
  iii I felt unwell and stayed in, so I didn't do much homework or watch much TV.
  iv I played with my computer most of the evening but did some homework.
b What does the scatter diagram that Megan drew tell us about the link between the time spent doing homework and time spent on leisure activities?
c Megan drew a scatter diagram which showed that younger students spent less time doing homework than older students.
Show what Megan's scatter diagram may have looked like.

D4
Scatter diagrams and correlation continued

D4.3   These are the results of 22 candidates who sat exams in French and German.

Candidate No.	1	2	3	4	5	6	7	8	9	10	11	12	13	14	15	16	17	18	19	20	21	22
French mark	11	14	22	25	27	35	38	44	37	44	49	55	62	69	19	45	64	54	29	72	13	40
German mark	17	26	26	34	40	43	36	26	41	48	48	45	53	41	48	21	34	50	49	36	16	30

a   Show these results on a scatter diagram.
b   What does your graph tell you about the link between the French marks and the German marks?
c   George scored 55 marks on the French paper.
     How many marks would you expect him to score on the German paper? Give your reason for this choice of marks.

D4.4   Lorraine asked some students to weigh some ingredients both in metric (grams) and in imperial (pounds) measures.
She drew a scattergram of the results and drew in the line of best fit.
Lorraine's graph can be used to change weights between Metric and Imperial scales.

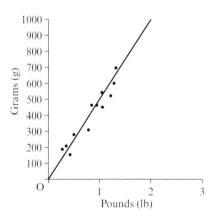

a   Change 2 lb into grams.
b   Change 450 grams into pounds.

D4.5   The ten finalists in a competition were marked by two judges. This table shows the marks given by each of the judges.

Competitor	1	2	3	4	5	6	7	8	9	10
Judge A	2.2	9.6	2.8	10	9	3.5	2.5	5	7	4.5
Judge B	2	7.8	3.2	8.4	7.5	3	3	3.2	6.5	4

a   On graph paper draw a scatter diagram with the marks given by judge A on the horizontal axis, and the marks given by judge B on the vertical axis.
b   Does your diagram show a link between the two judges' marks? Give a reason for your answer.
c   Write down the number of the winning competitor.

D4.6   This table shows the heights and scores of 10 people who took an intelligence test.

Height (cm)	175	185	155	165	170	165	154	180	177	165
IQ score	120	115	80	90	110	98	110	95	110	115

a   Draw a scatter diagram to show these results.
b   What does the scatter diagram tell you about height and intelligence scores?

D5
Averages and measures
of spread

D5.1   Kelly is investigating the number of occupied seats per car travelling
along a main road which passes a school.
She collects data by tallying.
This is the result of her survey taken between 8.15 am and 9.00 am on a
weekday morning.

No. of seats occupied	Tally, number of cars
1	卌 I
2	卌 III
3	卌 卌 卌 II
4	卌 卌 卌 卌 III
5	卌 卌 卌 卌 卌 III
6	卌 卌 卌 I
7	II

a   How many cars were involved in the survey?
b   What is the range of the number of seats occupied per car?
c   Write down the modal number of occupied seats.
d   Work out the median number of occupied seats per car.

Kelly carried out the same survey at the same time
on the following Sunday morning.

e   For this survey, what do you think would be
the modal number of occupied seats per car?
Give a reason for your answer.

D5.2   These are the goals scored by the school Hockey team this season.
1 0 1 1 2 3 0 2 3 3 5 2 3

For the number of goals scored, work out and write down:

a   the mode   b   the range
c   the median   d   the mean.

D5.3   Mrs Phitt and Mr Strong both teach PE.
They each kept a record of the time (in minutes) taken for students
in their group to complete a cross-country run.

Mrs Phitt's group									
29	21	28	23	31	22	27	22	24	25
19	28	26	25	33	24	26	24	25	18

Mr Strong's group									
32	29	31	29	27	33	30	24	33	33
32	31	25	31	31	33	31	23	31	31

a   For each group calculate:
   i   the mean
   ii   the range.
b   Which group did best in the cross-country run?
   Explain your choice, using both the range and the mean
   in your answer.

D5
Averages and measures of spread continued

5.4 In her weekly maths test, Kim scored these marks out of ten:

5 8 6 5 8 9 8

a What was her average (mean) mark?
b What was the range of Kim's marks?

She wanted to improve her performance so that after the next test the mean of her marks was the same as the median mark.

c Calculate whether this is possible. You must show your working.
d There were to be ten tests altogether that term.
What was the highest average (mean) mark that Kim could get?

5.5 In ice skating competitions there are eight judges.
Each judge gives the skater a mark out of six.
Martina is given the following marks:

5.3 5.8 5.9 5.5 4.4 5.8 5.7 5.6

a work out: **i** the range **ii** the mean of these marks.

The rules say that the highest and the lowest mark do not count for the final total.

b For the six other marks, find: **i** the range **ii** the mean.
c Use the ranges and the means you have calculated to decide if you think it is better to count all eight marks or to count only the six other marks to decide the final score.

5.6 Isha measures the lengths of carrots in a gardening competition.
The lengths of the ten longest carrots are given in centimetres:

27, 36, 27, 25, 27, 37, 30, 29, 27, 35

a Calculate the mean length of these carrots.
b Write down the range in the lengths of the carrots.

Isha's father measured the carrots in last year's competition and he found that the mean length of the ten longest carrots was 31 cm and the range was 7 cm.

c Explain how the lengths of the carrots differ this year from last year.

5.7 The number of pupils in each set in year 10 is:

Set	N	E	T	R	A	F	Y
Number of pupils	29	25	29	24	30	29	30

a What is the mode of the set sizes?
b What is the range of the set sizes for year 10?
c Calculate the mean of the set sizes.
d On graph paper, draw a bar chart to show the set sizes.

5.8 John, Ivan and Tracey calculate that their average weight (mass) is 86 kg.

a What is the total weight of all three?
b If John and Ivan weigh 179 kg how much does Tracey weigh?

D6
Estimating and evaluating results

D6.1 A survey to find the most effective washing powder was carried out by questioning five children aged between ten and eleven.

Do you think the results would be useful?
Give **two** reasons for your answer.

D6.2 Val collected information and drew a scatter diagram which showed that there was no relationship between the time students spent watching TV and their exam results.
Len's project found there was a direct relationship between time spent doing homework and students' scores in weekly test results.

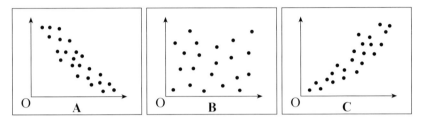

Write down which diagram represents:

a Val's scatter diagram.
b Len's results plotted as a scatter diagram.
c Describe an investigation which you would expect to give the results shown in the remaining scatter diagram.

D6.3 These are the sizes of the shoes worn by the thirteen members of Tuesday's after school netball club:
7 6 6 3 8 7 8 7 5 3 5 6 7

a For these sizes find:
 i the mean ii the median iii the mode iv the range.

The thirteen members of Wednesday's basketball club were asked for their shoe sizes.
From their replies Rekha calculated that the median was 7, the mode was 8 and the range was 3.

b Write down how the shoe sizes for Wednesday's basketball club compare with the shoe sizes of Tuesday's netball club.

D6.4 The heights of a group of year 11 boys were recorded and a bar chart drawn of the results.

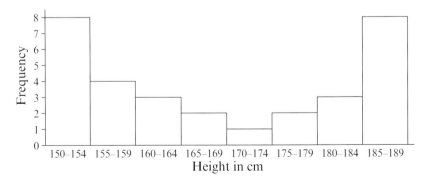

a How many boys were in the group?
b Is the bar chart the shape you would expect to see for a group of year 11 students?
Give reasons for your answer.

D6
Estimating and evaluating results continued

D6.5   Claud carried out a survey. He asked three groups of 100 people the question 'Do you think the railways should carry more freight to reduce the number of lorries on the road?'.

Group A   Lorry drivers in a transport cafe
Group B   People leaving a car park
Group C   Primary school children during morning break

Here are the results

Set 1   Yes 73   No 27
Set 2   Yes 9   No 91
Set 3   Yes 55   No 45

a   Which set of results belongs to which group of people?
        Give a reason for each match.
b   How would you carry out an unbiased survey which would give a representative view of public opinion on this question?

D6.6   The circumference around the head and heights of ten pupils, measured in centimetres, were recorded for a hat making competition.
The results are shown in this table.

Height	182	169	176	157	190	154	188	166	140	189
Head	52	50	55	48	58	47	56	51	41	59

a   Plot a scatter graph using this data.
b   Daisy gives her height as 165 cm. Use your scatter graph to estimate the circumference of Daisy's head.
c   Explain why your answer can only be an estimate.
d   Write down any relationship you can see between the head circumferences and heights of the pupils.

D6.7   A six-sided dice was rolled and the number of times each of the numbers 1 to 6 appeared was recorded.
This frequency diagram shows the result.

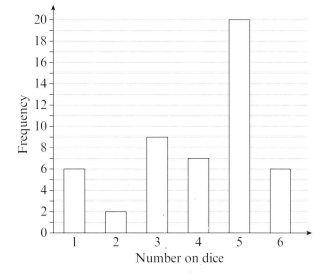

a   How many times was the dice rolled?
b   Would you describe the dice as a fair dice on these results?
        Give a reason for your answer.
c   What is the modal number on the frequency diagram?

D7
Miscellaneous

D7.1   A school sells 520 raffle tickets for their fund-raising draw.
There is one major prize.

a   Sonia buys 1 ticket. What is the probability that she wins the prize?
b   Terry buys 10 tickets. What is the probability that he will win?
c   Geeta works out that her family have a $\frac{1}{40}$ chance of winning
the prize. How many tickets have they bought between them?

D7.2   A bag contains 36 beads.
There are 18 red beads, 5 green beads, 4 blue beads and 9 white beads.
A bead is taken at random from the bag.

a   What is the probability that it is red?
b   What is the probability that it is blue or green?
c   What is the probability that it is **not** white?

D7.3   The probability that Sue will be selected for a netball team is 0.89.
What is the probability that she will not be selected for the netball team?

D7.4   In a school fete contestants throw two fair dice, one red and one blue.
The two numbers showing are added together.

a   Copy and complete the table
to show all the possible
outcomes for the game.
b   What is the probability
that Tim will score a
total of 5 with his turn?
c   What is the probability
that Tim will score
10 or more with one turn?
d   Prizes are given to all contestants whose
total score each turn adds up to 7.
What is the probability that Tina wins a prize when she has one turn?
e   At the fete 390 people each play the game once.
Approximately how many are likely to win a prize?

D7.5   Misha arranged for her friend to call for her at 8.15 am so that they
could walk to school together.
Her friend was not always on time, so Misha kept a record of how many
minutes late she was.
This bar chart shows the results of her record-keeping.

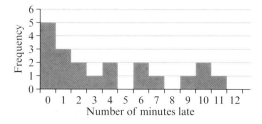

a   For how many school days did Misha keep her records?
b   What was the longest time Misha had to wait for her friend?
c   What is the probability that her friend will be on time the next
school day she calls?
d   What is the probability that the next time Misha's friend calls
she will be more than 6 minutes late?

D7
Miscellaneous continued

D7.6   Denzil keeps a daily diary. He has five identical diaries for the years
1995, 1996, 1997, 1998, 1999 which he keeps in a drawer.
Denzil takes two diaries out of the drawer at random.

a   List all the possible combinations of diaries that he might take.

Denzil replaces the diaries in a drawer.
He now takes one diary at random.

b   What is the probability that he takes the 1997 diary?

D7.7   Kay counted out 16 blue beads, 9 green beads and 11 red beads.
She put all 36 beads into a bag.

a   Kay is going to take one bead at random from the bag.
  i   What colour will she be most likely to get?
  ii Explain your answer.

b   Copy the line below and mark on your copy the probability
that Kay will take a green bead.

```
|---------------------|---------------------|
0                     1/2                    1
```

c   Write down the probability that Kay will take
a red bead from the bag.

d   Write down the probability that the bead Kay takes will **not** be blue.

D7.8   Some students were asked to estimate the length of a line.
Their answers, in centimetres, are recorded below.
6, 13, 14, 13, 14, 4, 11.5, 8, 13, 7, 12, 12.5, 11, 10.5 10, 9, 8, 10, 12, 9.5

a   Copy and complete this frequency table for their estimates.

Estimate of length (cm)	Tally	Frequency
4 ⩽ length of line < 6		
6 ⩽ length of line < 8		
8 ⩽ length of line < 10		
10 ⩽ length of line < 12		
12 ⩽ length of line < 14		
14 ⩽ length of line < 16		

b   On graph paper draw a frequency diagram
for the estimated line lengths.

c   What was the modal length estimated by the students?

d   What was the mean length estimated by the students?

D7.9   As part of Jan's work she collects data on the value of cars.
The data is for two groups of cars:
    Group A, from new to 5 years old
    Group B, from 30 to 80 years old.
She sketches scatter graphs for the data in each group.

a   Sketch a scatter graph that could show Group A.

b   Sketch a possible scatter diagram for Group B.

c   Explain any differences you think your two sketch graphs show.

Using and applying mathematics

U1
Gridlock

A grid of squares can be made by drawing straight lines.
This 3 by 4 grid is made from 9 straight lines.

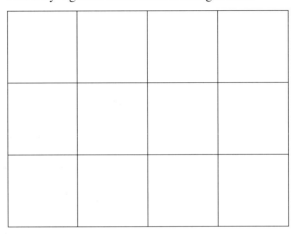

U1.1 **a** How many squares are there on the grid?
       b What shape is the grid?

U1.2 **a** How many lines are used to make a 3 by 5 grid?
       b How many lines are used for a 4 by 5 grid?

U1.3 **a** Investigate different size grids, record your results, and find a rule for the number of lines used for a grid.
       b Use your rule to work out the number of lines in a 70 by 82 grid, without drawing the grid!

In this grid there are 10 straight lines.

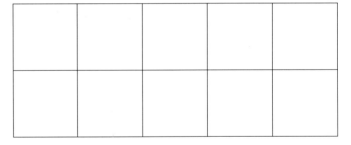

U1.4 **a** How many squares are there in the grid ?
       b Investigate other grids made with 10 straight lines.
          How many squares can be in grids made from 10 straight lines?
       c Try grids with different numbers of straight lines.
          How many squares can be in the grids?
          Can you predict the numbers of squares if you know the number of lines?
          Explain how you work out your prediction.

U2
Triple totals

U2.1 (1, 4, 1) is a number triple. It has a triple total of 6.
       a How many other triples have a total of 6?
          (You can use a number more than once but you cannot use 0 in a triple.)
       b Investigate different triple totals.

U3
Number strips

For this pair of numbers on a strip of five squares …

… the blank squares are filled so that each number is the sum of the two numbers on its left.

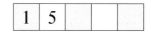

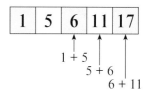

U3.1   On a strip of five squares:
a   Find the number in the last square, if the numbers in the first two squares are 6 and 3.
b   Try different pairs of numbers in the first two squares. Find a rule to calculate the last number from the first two numbers without calculating the numbers in between.
c   Investigate rules for longer strips.

U3.2   **a**   Find all the numbers in a strip of five squares with 5 as the first number and 16 as the last number.
b   Investigate methods to complete a strip when you know the first and last number.

U4
A set of weights

U4.1   Emma is making a set of weights.
The set of weights will allow the user to weigh objects from 1 gram to 100 grams. (Weights are in whole numbers of grams only.)
a   What weights would you put in the set?
b   Show how your weights can be used for all weights from 1 gram to 100 grams. (Weights are in whole numbers of grams only.)

U4.2   **a**   What is the smallest number of weights you need in the set?
b   List the weights in the smallest set.
c   Show that the smallest set can cope with all the weights needed.

U5
About diagonals

U5.1   These diagrams show two polygons with all the diagonals drawn in.

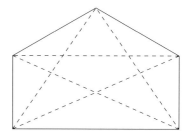

a   How many diagonals can be drawn in a hexagon?
b   What shape has no diagonals?
Explain with a diagram.
c   Investigate the number of diagonals in other polygons.

U5.2   **a**   Can you predict how many diagonals a polygon will have? Explain.
b   Find a rule to work out the number of diagonals if you know the number of sides.
c   Use your rule to work out the number of diagonals in a 25-sided polygon.

Section 1

Starting points
A1 b
A2 **a** 4 **b** 5 **c** 7 **d** 9
A4 100

Exercise 1.1
1 **a** 6 **b** 60 **c** 600 **d** 600
   e 60 **f** 6000 **g** 600 **h** 6
   i 60 **j** 6 **k** 6000 **l** 60 000
   m 600 000 **n** 6 000 000 **o** 6 **p** 6000

2 b, c, e, h

Exercise 1.2
1 40 000, 5000, 600, 20, 7   **2** 100 000, 20 000, 40, 3

3 645   **4** 2394   **5** 28 673

6 **a** 40 000, 5000, 200, 30, 6 **b** 500 000, 10 000, 2000, 600, 7
   c 5 000 000, 800 000, 20 000, 1000, 700, 60, 3

Exercise 1.3
1 **a** 21, 34, 58, 189, 567, 2362, 5332
   b 14, 16, 384, 495, 509, 630, 1244
   c 75, 81, 88, 385, 592, 636, 1304, 4425
   d 5, 17, 38, 112, 488, 675, 846, 9224, 10 566
   e 3, 15, 88, 327, 565, 875, 3224, 4342, 4553, 18 455
   f 9, 16, 1047, 3005, 3502, 7802, 11 000, 12 883, 14 562

Exercise 1.4
1 **a** 752 **b** 257 **c** 257, 275, 572, 527, 725, 752
   d 257, 275, 527, 572, 725, 752

2 **a** 839, 893, 398, 389, 983, 938 **b** 389, 398, 839, 893, 938, 983

3 **a** 4100 **b** 1004 **c** 4100, 4010, 4001, 1400, 1040, 1004

4 **a** 9500 **b** 0059
   c 9500, 9050, 9005, 5900, 5090, 5009
   (0950, 0905, 0590, 0509, 0095, 0059 are 3-digit and 2-digit numbers.)

Exercise 1.5
1 **a** six hundred and seventy five
   b one thousand five hundred and forty two
   c twelve thousand four hundred and fifty eight
   d five thousand six hundred and seven
   e one thousand and four
   f twenty six thousand eight hundred and four
   g four thousand and forty
   h fifty six thousand four hundred and ten
   i two hundred and sixty five thousand six hundred and twelve
   j four million eight hundred and seventy two thousand
      four hundred and fifty three
   k one million three hundred and seven thousand five hundred
      and twenty six
   l thirty seven million and two

Exercise 1.6
1 **a** 3067 **b** 5240 **c** 9506 **d** 8001
   e 6029 **f** 9310 **g** 1101

2 **a** 21 056 **b** 32 608 **c** 75 045 **d** 91 016
   e 60 024 **f** 10 010 **g** 9909

3 Only **45** of those on board were children. **1062** holiday makers chose to
fly the **11 305** kilometres back to London.
Repairs will cost **£2 342 000**. The ship will be in dry dock for about **8040**
hours and will be worked on by **1500** men and women. A new ship
costing **367 000 000** dollars will be started next year. The new ship will
weigh about **35 000** tonnes.

Section 2

Starting points
A1 **a** horizontal **b** vertical **c** vertical **d** horizontal
A2 It slopes a little so that the water drains away.

A3 only a jump-jet
   Most planes move horizontally as well as up when they take off.

Exercise 2.1
1 **a** horizontal **b** none **c** none **d** none
   e vertical **f** horizontal **g** none **h** vertical
   i none **j** vertical and horizontal
   k horizontal **l** horizontal

Exercise 2.2
1 H, I, N, S

3 **a** 3 **b** 4 **c** 6 **d** 2 **e** 5 **f** 1 **g** 3 **h** 3

4 2 (4 only when it is a square) **7** **a** 3 **b** none

9 **b** left to right: 3, 1, 2, 1, 2

Exercise 2.3
1 **a, b, d, f, h** **c** handset usually on one side
   e numbers or winder different **g** steering wheel on one side

2 6   **3** 3

4 The usual answers are:
   a vertical **b** vertical **c** vertical
   d horizontal **e** vertical **f** horizontal.

5 It fits either a left or a right foot, not both.

6 **a** 4 **b** 3   **7** 9

Section 3

Exercise 3.1
1 **a** 32 **b** 31 **c** 36 **d** 37 **e** 48 **f** 39
2 **a** 71 **b** 101 **c** 164 **d** 162 **e** 159
   f 110 **g** 85 **h** 228
3 **a** 133 **b** 137 **c** 92 **d** 96 **e** 107
   f 104 **g** 116 **h** 152 **i** 137

Exercise 3.2
1 **a** 613 **b** 691 **c** 650 **d** 1802 **e** 6807
   f 35 370 **g** 13 182 **h** 170 719 **i** 31 062
2 **a** 190 **b** 1445 **c** 1298 **d** 4484 **e** 5836
   f 9243 **g** 17 309 **h** 18 877 **i** 391 101 **j** 155 047

Exercise 3.3
1 37   **2** **a** 419 cars **b** 1229 passengers
3 **a** 1853 **b** 1421
4 **a** 17 334 **b** 22 133 **c** 2862 **d** 38 699
5 **a** 166 276 **b** 166 870 **c** 168 526 **d** 171 333 **e** 5345

Exercise 3.4
1 **a** 189 **b** 129 **c** 134 **d** 89 **e** 5855
   f 866 **g** 3767 **h** 6648 **i** 25 157
2 **a** 3 536 048 **b** 1 124 376 **c** 26 664 403
   d 7 378 167 **e** 24 477 **f** 5 495 739

Exercise 3.5
1 **a** end of the day **b** 474 miles
   c four hundred and seventy four
2 18 238 males **3** 3617 cartons **4** 2 973 226 adults
5 2 775 324 **6** 63 539 **7** 20 127 435 litres

Exercise 3.6
1 **a** 368 **b** 348 **c** 504 **d** 234
   e 335 **f** 182 **g** 666 **h** 270
2 **a** 1904 **b** 4526 **c** 1334 **d** 3915
   e 2574 **f** 2090 **g** 1554 **h** 5022
3 **a** 1160 **b** 1855 **c** 752 **d** 2056
   e 1620 **f** 5616 **g** 1771 **h** 5715
4 **a** 2232 **b** 3744 **c** 9994 **d** 12 584
   e 16 790 **f** 27 474 **g** 33 170 **h** 54 604

Exercise 3.7
1 3000 **2** 882 **3** 3360 **4** 1632
5 828 **6** 3034 **7** 71 040

Exercise 3.8

1 a 95   **b** 54   **c** 47   **d** 73
   e 83 rem 8   **f** 67 rem 2   **g** 66 rem 1   **h** 85 rem 2
   i 73 rem 4   **j** 58 rem 2   **k** 56   **l** 88

2 a 58   **b** 57   **c** 57   **d** 78
   e 64 rem 3   **f** 47 rem 7   **g** 46 rem 3   **h** 34 rem 4
   i 68 rem 10   **j** 35   **k** 75 rem 8   **l** 49 rem 8

3 a 186   **b** 256   **c** 157   **d** 585 rem 2
   e 547   **f** 954 rem 2   **g** 596   **h** 562 rem 5

4 a 18   **b** 21 rem 21   **c** 21   **d** 34
   e 65   **f** 96   **g** 75 rem 4   **h** 62 rem 7

Exercise 3.9

1 87   **2** 64   **3** 14

4 a 152   **b** 1

5 a 64   **b** 9   **c** 56

SECTION 4

Starting points

A1 30   **A2** 90   **A3 a** 70   **b** 23

Exercise 4.1

1 a nought point three seven one
   b nought point two eight
   c nought point five nought six
   d nought point nought four nought nine

2 Sam has written the decimal using the wrong place values.
The right way is 'nought point four eight five'.

3 0.372   0.9703   0.076   **4** 0.3366   **5** 0.4945

6 five-thousandths or 0.005   **7** 0.482

Exercise 4.2

1 9.67 seconds   **2** 9.94 seconds   **3 a** 5.82 m   **b** 7 cm or 0.07 m

Exercise 4.3

1 4.358 m   4.355 m   4.356 m   **2** 7.12 m   7.152 m   7.116 m

3 a 6.4 cm   **b** 7.8 cm   **c** 5 cm

4 7 cm and 7.0 cm are the same length; the extra '0' does not change the
length 7 cm because it stands for **no** tenths (unless the answer is rounded).

Exercise 4.4

1 0.006   0.2   0.729   0.75   1.82   1.905

2 a 0.02   0.571   0.92   1.2175   1.26   2.1
   b 0.037   0.0391   0.052   0.4   0.72   1.07   1.093
   c 0.06   0.601   0.7019   0.706   1.2   2   2.145

3 0.317   0.34   1.2   8.07   11.125   12.6

4 11   1.51   1.5   1.053   0.0613   0.06   0.0032

Exercise 4.5

1
Alex	52.325
Nasser	52.3
Graham	32.525
Michael	32.5
John	23.75
Mark	23.1875

2
Getaway	9.02
Going Abroad	9.015
Travelfar	9.005
Flysave	9.0025
Summer Breaks	9.0

Exercise 4.6

1 a 9.77   **b** 7.79   **c** 4.419   **d** 6.1   **e** 4.81
   f 9.692   **g** 37.6   **h** 11.64   **i** 10.36   **j** 18.06
   k 28.41   **l** 41.43   **m** 35.935

2 a 9.86   **b** 9.54   **c** 12.719   **d** 10.017   **e** 20.05
   f 21.978   **g** 21.17   **h** 44.138   **i** 25.147   **j** 25.769

Exercise 4.7

1 £213.07   **2** 176.59 seconds   **3** £507.48

Exercise 4.8

1 a 3.61   **b** 12.25   **c** 4.51   **d** 3.16
   e 5.7   **f** 6.29   **g** 4.82   **h** 0.085
   i 0.085   **j** 5.99   **k** 26.8   **l** 12.287

2 a 11.5   **b** 15.6   **c** 3.65   **d** 2.79
   e 22.38   **f** 5.57   **g** 10.05   **h** 5.542
   i 5.293   **j** 2.634   **k** 10.77   **l** 10.763

Exercise 4.9

1 a 0.47 seconds   **b** 0.70 seconds   **c** 1.72 seconds
   d 0.67 seconds   **e** final, 0.57 seconds

2 47.30 seconds   **3** £16.35   **4** 14.22 seconds

SECTION 5

Starting points

A1 a 90°   **b** 180°   **c** 270°

A2 $\frac{3}{4}, \frac{1}{2}, \frac{1}{4}$

Exercise 5.1

1 165° is obtuse, 188° is reflex, 75° is acute, 104° is obtuse, 16° is acute,
304° is reflex, 197° is reflex

2 a acute   **b** right angle   **c** obtuse   **d** acute
   e reflex   **f** obtuse   **g** right angle   **h** right angle
   i reflex

Exercise 5.2

1 a 65°   **b** 85°   **c** 132°   **d** 275°   **e** 88°
   f 70°   **g** 89°   **h** 215°   **i** 322°

2 a 66°   **b** 128°   **c** 99°   **d** 67°

3 b and c   **4** 360°   **5** 194°   **6** 166°

7 a 88°   **b** 46°   **c** 130°   **d** 42°   **e** 113°   **f** 97°
   g 67°   **h** 22°   **i** 113°   **j** 42°   **k** 26°

8 c, e, f, i

SECTION 6

Starting points

A1 5080, 5800, 8005, 8050, 8500   **A2** 8740

B1 a 756 < 2365   **b** 143 > 134   **c** 4564 < 4645   **d** 108 < 1800
   e 9 million < 11 020 400

C1 a 49   **b** 62   **C2 a** 24   **b** 8

Exercise 6.1

1 a true   **b** true   **c** false   **d** false
   e true   **f** false   **g** true   **h** false

2 a ⁻6 < ⁻4   **b** 0 > ⁻3   **c** ⁻3 > ⁻9   **d** 5 > ⁻6
   e ⁻2 < 2   **f** ⁻10 > ⁻67

3 a ⁻4, ⁻2, 2   **b** ⁻12, ⁻7, ⁻5, ⁻3, ⁻2, 0
   c ⁻8, ⁻6, ⁻5, ⁻4, 2, 4, 5, 6   **d** ⁻56, ⁻12, ⁻4, ⁻3, 7, 45

4 Mark has ignored the signs. The correct order is: ⁻6, ⁻4, ⁻2, 7, 8, 9.

5 5, 0, ⁻4, ⁻6, ⁻7, ⁻12

Exercise 6.2

1 ⁻8°C   **2** ⁻2°C

3 Vladivostok, Helsinki, Warsaw, New York, London, Bombay, Sydney

4 B, A, D, E, C

Exercise 6.3

1 a 3°C   **b** ⁻5°C   **c** ⁻8°C   **d** ⁻2°C
   e 1°C   **f** ⁻4°C   **g** ⁻10°C   **h** 18°C
   i ⁻35°C   **j** ⁻12°C   **k** 14°C   **l** ⁻43°C

2 a ⁻2°C   **b** ⁻8°C   **c** ⁻7°C   **d** a fall of 6 degrees
   e a rise of 5 degrees   **f** 2°C   **g** a fall of 2 degrees
   h a rise of 12 degrees   **i** ⁻10°C

3 a ⁻8, ⁻6, ⁻4, ⁻2, 0, 2   **b** 10, 7, 4, 1, ⁻2, ⁻5
   c ⁻15, ⁻11, ⁻7, ⁻3, 1, 5   **d** 17, 10, 3, ⁻4, ⁻11, ⁻18

Exercise 6.4

1 7 degrees   **2** 60 degrees

3 New York: the change was 21 degrees.

4 It rose 24 degrees between 2 am and 8 am;
it rose 8 degrees between 8 am and 2 pm;
it fell 35 degrees between 2 pm and 8 pm.

5 a 7 °C   **b** 7 °C, 1 °C, ⁻5 °C, ⁻11 °C, ⁻17 °C

6 ⁻17 °C

Exercise 6.5

2 b ⁻2

3 a ⁻2   **b** ⁻6   **c** 2   **d** ⁻6

4 a ⁻8   **b** 1   **c** ⁻1   **d** ⁻9   **e** ⁻4   **f** 0   **g** 0   **h** ⁻6

Exercise 6.6

1 a ⁻6   **b** ⁻2   **c** ⁻6   **d** 2

2 a ⁻2   **b** 11   **c** ⁻7   **d** 1   **e** 10   **f** ⁻6   **g** 10   **h** 6

Exercise 6.7

1 a positive   **b** negative   **c** negative   **d** positive
e positive   **f** negative   **g** positive   **h** negative

2 a 3 × ⁻5 = ⁻15   **b** ⁻2 × 6 = ⁻12   **c** 5 × ⁻4 = ⁻20
d ⁻3 × ⁻6 = 18   **e** ⁻12 × ⁻3 = 36   **f** ⁻8 × 4 = ⁻32
g 24 × ⁻6 = ⁻144   **h** ⁻40 × 5 = ⁻200

3 c should be 20, **d** should be ⁻8, **e** should be ⁻32,
f should be 15, **h** should be ⁻35.

Exercise 6.8

1 a positive   **b** positive   **c** negative   **d** positive
e positive   **f** negative   **g** positive   **h** negative

2 a 35 ÷ ⁻5 = ⁻7   **b** ⁻6 ÷ 2 = ⁻3   **c** 16 ÷ ⁻4 = ⁻4   **d** ⁻36 ÷ ⁻6 = 6
e ⁻12 ÷ ⁻3 = 4   **f** ⁻8 ÷ 4 = ⁻2   **g** 24 ÷ ⁻6 = ⁻4   **h** ⁻40 ÷ 5 = ⁻8

3 correct answers:
a 1   **b** 2   **c** ⁻9   **d** ⁻3   **e** 3   **f** ⁻2   **g** $\frac{1}{2}$ **h** 1

Exercise 6.9

1 P(⁻4, 2) Q(4, ⁻4) R(⁻3, ⁻2) S(2, ⁻2) T(2, 1) U(⁻2, 1)

3 a (3, ⁻2)   **b** (2, ⁻3)   **c** (3, ⁻1)   **d** (⁻3, 2)

4 (⁻5, 7)   **5** (2, ⁻2) (8, ⁻2)   **6** right

7 above   **8** above   **9** C(4, 3) D(4, ⁻2)

10 (⁻6, 4) (⁻2.9, ⁻4) (⁻2.3, ⁻4) (0, ⁻4) (4.5, ⁻4) (5, ⁻4)

11 (0, 6.7) (⁻5, 3) (15, ⁻2.6) (2, ⁻4)

REVIEW 1A

1 a 40   **b** 400   **c** 4   **d** 4000000
e 400   **f** 40000000

2 a 6, 14, 63, 157, 575, 1053, 1305
b 51, 108, 15677, 15766, 106540, 150405, 160504

3 a eight hundred and sixty three
b three thousand five hundred and four
c sixteen thousand and fifty two
d seven million eighty two thousand two hundred and seven
e eight hundred and thirty four thousand nine hundred and two
f sixty five million eight hundred and two thousand three hundred and one

4 a 8017   **b** 1000005   **c** 2220000

H — O — O — D

5 horizontal
(There are an infinite number of axes through each of the O's.)

7 two   **8** one

9 a 29   **b** 134   **c** 153

10 a 453   **b** 1505

11 a 84549   **b** 13667

12 a 3196   **b** 4704   **c** 22776

13 a 373   **b** 273   **c** 331 rem 20

14 a zero point five zero four
b zero point zero two five
c zero point three eight

15 a $\frac{8}{100}$ **b** $\frac{8}{1000}$ **c** $\frac{8}{10}$ **16** 6.58 m

17 a 0.0506, 0.26, 0.35, 0.6, 1.08, 2.01
b 0.007, 0.17, 0.701, 0.71, 1.07, 7.1

18 a 16.89   **b** 178.58

19 a 13.93   **b** 26.685

20 a acute   **b** reflex   **c** acute   **d** obtuse   **e** acute

23 a ⁻8, ⁻6, ⁻3, 4, 5   **b** ⁻18, ⁻9, ⁻1, 5, 6, 23

24 a 1° C   **b** ⁻5° C   **25** above

26 a ⁻3   **b** ⁻11   **c** ⁻21   **d** ⁻20   **e** ⁻17   **f** ⁻10   **g** ⁻3   **h** ⁻11

27 a ⁻20   **b** 48   **c** ⁻21   **d** 63   **e** ⁻4   **f** 8   **g** 5   **h** ⁻9

SKILLS BREAK 1

1 31 pence   **2** £1.79   **3** £16   **4** £17.89   **5** £28.98

6 £32.94   **7** £5.06   **8 a** £45.43 **b** £4.57   **9** £17.10

10 a one 5 litre tin **b** 11 pence   **11** 20 pence

12 a 5 spare tiles   **b** £373.78

13 a 447   **b** 44 boxes   **c** 7   **d** £849.49   **e** 51 pence

14 a obtuse   **b** 5   **c** 108°   **d** larger   **e** 540°

15 90°, a right angle   **17 b** larger (120°)

18 15 square metres   **19** You need to buy 14 tubs (15 × 13 = 195).

20 a 12   **b** £92.28

21 $\frac{1}{4}$ off   **22** £63   **23** £2352

24 a 250000, 107500, 107050, 104520, 95040, 94880
b 758990 tiles

SECTION 7

Starting points

A1 5

A2 a 1   **b** 9   **c** 1   **d** ⁻3

A3 a 7   **b** 2   **c** ⁻2   **d** 0

Exercise 7.1

1 a 2k + 4w   **b** 4f + 4h   **c** 3a + 4n   **d** 5a + 3y   **e** 2a
f 2a + 3b + 2c   **g** 4e + 2t + 2w   **h** 3r + t + v + 2w

2 a 12w   **b** 4y   **c** 3k   **d** 4a + 8b
e 3f + 44h   **f** 16b + 13y   **g** 29w − 2b   **h** 45h − 50k

3 a ⁻13y   **b** ⁻55k   **c** ⁻41h   **d** ⁻18n

Exercise 7.2

1 a 16k + 6c   **b** 15w   **c** 25k
d 21h + 21p   **e** 22f + 8h   **f** 20a + 13c
g 32b + 30y   **h** 13a + 37c + 13k   **i** 3a + b + 6c + 4y
j 40c + 8d + 29k + 35y **k** 26a + 18b + 13h   **l** 16a + 14k + 11n + 2y

2 a 8y   **b** 11v   **c** 16f

3 a 2y   **b** 12k

Exercise 7.3

1 a 12y − 20k   **b** 30h − 15   **c** 48f + 84v
d 108v + 81n   **e** 88y − 16   **f** 16h + 20k
g 63v + 7   **h** 5y − 5f   **i** 6k + 18a − 6y

2 a 24n − 30v + 6w   **b** 7h − 56y + 63k   **c** 7a + 7y − 7k
d 10n + 5w − 60a   **e** 15w − 15a + 30b   **f** 72 − 6h + 18w + 36b
g 20f − 4y − 4w + 4   **h** 50 − 30v + 10w − 50c **i** 150a − 150 + 50y

3 a 40k − 5w + 5   **b** 63f + 21 − 7y + 35w **c** 15 − 5h − 5k + 25w
d 6w + 18 − 6y + 18n **e** 100 − 75a + 200n   **f** 450 + 600a − 150w

Exercise 7.4

1 a 30k + 6y   **b** 36k + w   **c** w + 5y + 33f
d 5a + 36n + 52   **e** a + 8y

SECTION 8

Exercise 8.3

1 a Different people are likely to have different ideas of what is meant by 'early' and 'late'.

2 a The question seems to expect the answer 'yes'.

3 a The question could have more than one meaning.

4 a Question 1 is a leading question.
Question 2 is not clear; the word 'frequent' is likely to have different meanings for different people.
Question 3 is not clear; the 'courts' could refer to several different types such as squash, badminton, etc.
Question 4 does not give a box for people to tick between £1.50 and £2.50.

SECTION 9

Starting points

A1 a 330 **b** 680 **c** 10 **d** 1050 **e** 270 **f** 190
g 770 **h** 990 **i** 1000 **j** 1280 **k** 2000 **l** 3900

B1 a 500 **b** 800 **c** 400 **d** 1600 **e** 2000 **f** 700
g 3000 **h** 9700 **i** 1100 **j** 200 **k** 5600 **l** 9000

Exercise 9.1

1 a 7000 **b** 7000 **c** 3000 **d** 3000
e 6000 **f** 8000 **g** 3000 **h** 9000
i 13 000 **j** 25 000 **k** 16 000 **l** 34 000
m 37 000 **n** 123 000 **o** 345 000 **p** 651 000

2 a 30 000 **b** 60 000 **c** 20 000 **d** 20 000
e 50 000 **f** 40 000 **g** 30 000 **h** 70 000
i 90 000 **j** 70 000 **k** 240 000 **l** 300 000
m 140 000 **n** 250 000 **o** 540 000 **p** 620 000

3 a 400 000 **b** 400 000 **c** 700 000 **d** 600 000
e 700 000 **f** 900 000 **g** 100 000 **h** 500 000
i 1 300 000 **j** 2 500 000 **k** 2 600 000 **l** 800 000

4 a 4 000 000 **b** 4 000 000 **c** 5 000 000 **d** 12 000 000
e 49 000 000 **f** 7 000 000 **g** 10 000 000 **h** 35 000 000
i 20 000 000 **j** 17 000 000 **k** 100 000 000 **l** 56 000 000

Exercise 9.2

1 a 64 **b** 55

2 a 35 400 **b** 35 000 **c** 40 000

3 a 364 999 **b** 355 000 **c** 280 000

4 a D, F and G **b** 4493 g **c** 4500 g

Exercise 9.3

1 a 2000 **b** 2100 **c** 3000 **d** 7200 **e** 1600 **f** 2100
g 3000 **h** 2400 **i** 400 **j** 4000 **k** 4500 **l** 4000

2 a, b, d, g **3 a, b** **4 a** 54 **b** 45

5 a 2000 **b** 6000 **c** 2000 **d** 4000
e 2000 **f** 6000 **g** 8000 **h** 5000

Exercise 9.4

1

Stock Sheet			
Item	No. of Cases	No. in a case	No. in stock Approximately
Beans	44	48	**2000**
Pears	75	36	**3200**
Peaches	116	24	**2400**
Tomatoes	152	12	**1500**
Peas	97	16	**2000**

2 There were **1700** people on the train for the **900** mile trip. During the day a total of **2200** cans of cola, **1900** bags of crisps, and **300** gallons of coffee were sold. Ticket sales were **£32 300** and the organisers expect to give **£20 800** to local charities. There were **300** children on board and **200** of them spent time with the drivers.
The train used **14 600** litres of fuel for the trip. Wessex Oil donated **12 600** litres of fuel on the day of the trip.

3 £1800 **4** £1500

5 a 1200 miles **b** 1092 miles **c** probably too large

SECTION 10

Starting points

A1 a All angles are equal. **b** Two angles are equal.

A2 A rhombus must have all sides equal in length.

A5 Opposite angles are equal.

Exercise 10.2

1 b Angle ACB is a right angle. **3 b** isosceles

5 b The two short sides added together (6 cm + 3 cm = 9 cm) make less than 10 cm.

6 c and **e** are impossible.

Exercise 10.4

3 b Both angles are 70°. **c** isosceles

4 b AB = 8.9 cm **c** angle ABC = 54°

Exercise 10.5

2 b isosceles

3 c Both are the same – they are congruent (i.e. they are both equilateral triangles of the same size).

Exercise 10.6

2 a parallelogram **3 b** Both are about 9 cm.

4 a trapezium **7 b** about 5.7 cm **c** 570 metres

SECTION 11

Exercise 11.1

1 16 40, 17 30, 06 15, 03 44

2 a 04 20 **b** 19 25 **c** 08 19 **d** 12 42 **e** 01 35
f 21 05 **g** 11 47 **h** 19 08 **i** 12 55 **j** 10 18
k 18 04 **l** 23 52 **m** 06 57 **n** 01 10 **o** 12 27

Exercise 11.2

1 a C **b** B

2 a no **b** 15 44

3 04 20 **4** Late: 9.35 pm is 21 35.

5 The team was up by **05 25**. They had gone to bed at **23 15** the night before. The bus to the airport was booked for **06 40**, this was the only bus on the island. The plane had left London at **21 45** to arrive here at **08 10**. The plane was late, it got here at **13 28** and it finally took off at **17 30**. The team should be in Rome at about **03 00** tomorrow.

Exercise 11.3

1 4, 15, 9, 9, 5

Exercise 11.4

1 time intervals: 2 hours 42 minutes, 3 hours 25 minutes, 2 hours 37 minutes, 2 hours 41 minutes, 7 hours 51 minutes, 9 hours 47 minutes, 8 hours 33 minutes, 12 hours 46 minutes

Exercise 11. 5

1 3 hours 53 minutes **2** 6 hours 35 minutes

3 7 hours 50 minutes **4** 4 hours 15 minutes

5 10 hours 20 minutes

Exercise 11.6

1 a 0845 **b** 1001 **c** 0743 **d** 0923 **e** 0834 **f** 0933

2

Leave	at	Leave	at
Tonbridge	0842	Walmer	**0956**
Dover Priory	0941	Ramsgate	**1019**
Ashford	0734	Deal	**0826**
Martin Mill	2055	Sandwich	**2109**
Sandling	0745	Margate	**0857**
Tonbridge	**0811**	Sandling	0908
Folkestone West	**0750**	Deal	0826
Ashford	**2014**	Ramsgate	2122
Walmer	**0923**	Ramsgate	0945
Walterloo East	**1903**	Sandwich	2109

Exercise 11.7
1 2044   **2** 0915   **3** 0915

Exercise 11.8
1 0755   **2** 1302   **3** 1357

4 3 hours 19 minutes   **5** 1 hour 41 minutes

6 1241   **7** Crewkerne

8 a no   **b** 1732   **c** 1 hour 35 minutes

9 a 25 minutes   **b** 1752   **c** 1 hour 52 minutes

10 a 1744   **b** 1814   **c** 2 hours 23 minutes

REVIEW 1B

1 a $2b + 2c$ **b** $5s + 3b$ **c** $5t + 4g$ **d** $19h + 5f + 4j$

2 a $2a + 4b$ **b** $20s + 24$ **c** $25g - 10r$ **d** $15a + 30b - 20c$

3 $9a + 19b + 3c$

5 a It does not tell you what often means (is it once a week, once a day, or what ?).
   c It is a leading question. Most people will say 'yes'.

7 a 160   **b** 200

8 a 4000   **b** 9000   **c** 9754000
   d 37000   **e** 70000   **f** 10000

9 a 40000   **b** 38000000   **c** 3460000   **d** 3000000

15 a 16.45   **b** 11.30   **c** 20.55
   d 12.15   **e** 00.15   **f** 06.40

16 a 7:20 pm   **b** 6:20 am   **c** 12:45 pm
   d 4:30 pm   **e** 12:38 am   **f** 4:50 am

17 4 hours 45 minutes   **18** 10.06

SKILLS BREAK 2

1 2208 people   **2** 400   **3** 711

4 a 1316   **b** 499   **c** 817

5 The Titanic sank in 1912.

6 b T I T A N I C

    c I, N

7 1898   **8** 22 40   **9** It was warmer by 3°.

10 vertical   **11** 3 hours 40 minutes

12 a 3500   **b** 4000

13 4000 tons   **14** 30000000   **15** £295800   **16** 01 10

17 a 128   **b** 155   **c** 534

18 223

19 a angle ABC = 18°   **b** angle BAC = 102°   **c** angle ACB = 60°

20 02 20

21 a 2 appears in 2 boxes, as does 5.
   b It is a leading question – it expects the answer 'yes'.
   c No real alternatives are given – the question is very subjective.

22 6 tenths or $\frac{6}{10}$

STAGE 1 END POINTS

A1 a 500   **b** 5000   **c** 5000000   **d** 50000

B1 a 104, 206, 3252, 4553, 35143, 54532
   b 9, 18, 126, 564, 654, 1053, 2513, 3054
   c 67, 93, 120, 341, 25182, 26654, 100342, 110020

B2 2575, 2403, 2304, 562, 136, 81, 48, 17

C1 a one thousand and forty five
   b twenty three thousand one hundred and six
   c three million four hundred and fifty thousand and two
   d twenty four million and one

D1 a 4005   **b** 163660   **c** 8000357

E1 b 3 lines of symmetry

E2 H, 2   C, 1   M, 1   Y, 1   I, 2

F1 three   **F2** two   **G1** two

H1 a 31   **b** 38   **c** 97   **d** 142   **e** 73   **f** 110
   g 851   **h** 4612   **i** 681171   **j** 2460   **k** 165652

I1 a 297   **b** 47736   **c** 5767728   **d** 1013869   **e** 8700000

J1 a 168   **b** 536   **c** 2610   **d** 4104
   e 2160   **f** 8092   **g** 22824   **h** 52234

K1 a 148   **b** 357 rem 2   **c** 453   **d** 26
   e 54   **f** 123   **g** 187 rem 4   **h** 454

L1 0.005, 0.403, 0.6028, 0.604, 1.3, 2, 2.271

M1 a 60.88   **b** 17.874   **c** 1.1804   **d** 19.351   **e** 4.505

N1 a 5.397   **b** 8.65   **c** 1.62   **d** 11.994   **e** 1.694

O1 a acute   **b** obtuse   **c** acute   **d** reflex   **e** acute   **f** reflex

P1 a 40°   **b** 305°

R1 a ⁻6, ⁻5, ⁻4, ⁻1, 3, 5   **b** ⁻9, ⁻6, ⁻3, ⁻2, 1, 4, 7, 12

R2 a ⁻2 °C   **b** ⁻7 °C

S1 a ⁻2   **b** ⁻9   **c** ⁻13   **d** ⁻1

S2 a ⁻16   **b** ⁻15   **c** 3   **d** 11

T1 a 40   **b** ⁻27   **c** ⁻84   **d** 0

T2 a ⁻5   **b** ⁻9   **c** 1   **d** ⁻31

U1 a $10b + 4y$ **b** $4w + 8y$ **c** $9k + f$

U2 a $2y$ **b** $⁻3h$ **c** $⁻99k$

V1 a $15k + 5$ **b** $28y - 21x$ **c** $24f + 32 - 40p$
   d $27y - 15 + 21x$

X1 a 9000   **b** 12000   **c** 10000   **d** 14000

X2 a 40000   **b** 60000   **c** 10000   **d** 28000

X3 a 13000000   **b** 36000000   **c** 15000000   **d** 37000000

Y1 a 1600   **b** 1800   **c** 3200   **d** 6000

CC1 a 06 15   **b** 14 35   **c** 19 45   **d** 12 50

DD1 2 hours 53 minutes

EE1 a 11 18   **b** 18 20   **c** 2 hours 3 minutes

REVISION 1

1 a 3 thousand   **b** thirty thousand   **c** 3 million

2 55241, 54362, 3058, 1064, 585, 342, 16, 8

3 a twenty five thousand six hundred and four
   b four hundred and twenty thousand three hundred and eight
   c forty million five hundred and two thousand and six

4 a 50062   **b** 204008   **c** 5000007

5 T A H M X   **6** two   **7** one

8 a 39   **b** 48   **c** 24060   **d** 15459
   e 578   **f** 20831   **g** 248   **h** 563 rem 2

9 a 8 hundredths   **b** 8 ten thousandths   **c** 8 thousandths

10 0.05, 0.094, 0.409, 0.41, 2.004, 2.1

11 a 19.265   **b** 348.084   **c** 17.285

13 144°, 148°, 99°

14 a ⁻13   **b** ⁻5   **c** 1   **d** ⁻8   **e** ⁻14   **f** 2
   g 11   **h** ⁻30   **i** ⁻36   **j** 63   **k** ⁻7   **l** 6

15 a ⁻9, ⁻8, ⁻5, ⁻1, 1, 3, 4   **b** ⁻10, ⁻6, ⁻2, ⁻1, 0, 3, 4, 12

16 (⁻1, ⁻1) (⁻1, 5) or (⁻11, ⁻1) (⁻11, 5)

17 a $3k + 10w$ **b** $6f + h$ **18 a** $20w + 28$ **b** $12 - 18k$

19 $32y + 6g + 1$

20 a 16000   **b** 235000   **c** 2365000

21 a 300000   **b** 2600000   **c** 1100000

22 a 4200   **b** 2700   **c** 5000

25 a 19 55   **b** 06 25   **c** 22 20   **d** 12 35   **e** 02 45   **f** 13 56

26 6 hours 38 minutes   **27 a** 1912   **b** 51 minutes

SECTION 12

Starting points
A1 24 cm   **B1 a** 8 square units   **b** 8 square units

Exercise 12.1
1 UVWY = 56 cm²   EFGH = 42.32 cm²

2 a 50.4 cm² **b** 97.86 cm² **c** 89 cm² **d** 108.1 cm² **e** 240 cm²
   f 100.44 cm² **g** 66.8 cm² **h** 43.2 cm² **i** 43.96 cm²

3 8 cm   **4** 12 cm

Exercise 12.2
1 94.24 m²   **2 a** 8.82 m²   **b** £57.33

3 a 1120 cm² **b** 134 cm   **4 a** 700 mm²   **b** 128 mm

5 616 ORCO (screen area 899 cm²)   **6** less than 3100 (3080 mm²)

Exercise 12.3
1 a 96 cm²   **b** 105 cm²   **c** 93.5 cm²   **d** 100 cm²
   e 90 cm²   **f** 74 cm²   **g** 67.5 cm²

2 a 66.5 cm²   **b** 162.5 cm²   **c** 40.7 cm²
   d 110.49 cm²   **e** 68.625 cm²

Exercise 12.4
1 a 28 mm   **b** 12 mm   **c** 168 mm²

2 a 44 m²   **b** £395.56

3 a 1787.5 mm² **b** 750 mm²   **c** 3212.5 mm²

4 a 1.56 m²   **b** 1.56 m²   **c** 6.24 m²   **d** 3.12 m²

Exercise 12.5
1 a 62.6 cm   **b** 78 cm   **c** 42.6 cm
   d 89 cm   **e** 77.2 cm   **f** 59.3 cm

Exercise 12.6
1 a 6 cm   **b** 30 cm   **2** 25 cm²

3 a 6 cm   **b** 22 cm   **4 a** 8 cm **b** 3 cm

5 20 cm, 28 cm, 36 cm   **6** 15 cm   **7** 127.5 cm²

SECTION 13

Starting Points
A1 4

A2

a	*b*	*c*	**Score**
5	4	2	**3**
6	5	3	**4**
3	4	5	**4**
6	2	6	**10**
5	1	3	**7**
1	5	2	**⁻2**
3	6	1	**⁻2**
2	5	6	**3**

B1 a 20k – 8   **b** 12 + 15w   **c** 42w + 28n   **d** 40g – 15y

Exercise 13.1
1

w	*l*
15	35
18	**41**
23	**51**
34	**73**

2

p	*r*	*t*
5	2	19
7	4	**23**
12	15	**15**
35	24	**103**
6.5	4	**20.5**
8	7.5	**17.5**
6.4	8.5	**6.5**

3 a 34   **b** 100   **c** 62   **d** 64

4 a 24   **b** 132   **c** 84   **d** 0

5 a 11   **b** 1.5   **c** 37   **d** 38

Exercise 13.2
1 a £160   **b** £250   **c** £340

2 a £6.80   **b** £16.40   **3 a** 22   **b** 13

Exercise 13.3
1 a 5   **b** 8   **c** 14   **d** 25   **e** 34
   f 15   **g** 21   **h** 56   **i** 129

2 a n = 11   **b** w = 15   **c** t = 15   **d** k = 5   **e** n = 50
   f b = 33   **g** a = 212   **h** n = 220   **i** c = 130

3 a 4   **b** 9   **c** 12   **d** 8   **e** 9
   f 8   **g** 4   **h** 3   **i** 15

Exercise 13.4
1 a n = 5   **b** n = 5   **c** n = 4   **d** n = 9   **e** n = 8
   f n = 7   **g** n = 6   **h** n = 74   **i** n = 6.5

2 a n = 5   **b** n = 5   **c** n = 2   **d** n = 2   **e** n = 8
   f n = 7   **g** n = 8   **h** n = 4.5 **i** n = 7.5

3 a n = 6   **b** n = 16   **c** n = 8

Exercise 13.5
1 a n = 3   **b** y = 6   **c** a = 7   **d** p = 5   **e** w = 3
   f h = 5   **g** c = 6   **h** t = 5   **i** m = 8

2 a n = 3   **b** n = 14   **c** n = 5   **d** n = 2   **e** n = 7
   f n = 5   **g** n = 1   **h** n = 8   **i** n = 9

3 a n = 4   **b** n = 7   **c** n = 5   **d** n = 12   **e** n = 6
   f n = 6   **g** n = 2   **h** n = 2   **i** n = 4

Exercise 13.6
1 a P = l + l + 9 + 9   **b** 42 = 2l + 18   l = 12

2 a 4(w – 3) = 12 **b** w = 6   **c** 4(w – 3) = 4   **d** w = 4

SECTION 14

Starting points
B1 (any two from) 25, 36, 49   **B2** 64

Exercise 14.1
2 26, 38   **3 a** yes **b** because 6 × 7 = 42 (or equivalent)

4 a 9, 18, 27, 36, 45   **5** 12

6 The answer can be any number that ends in 0.   **7** It will end in 0.

Exercise 14.2
1 3   **2** 1, 2, 4, 8   **3** 36, 63, 72

4 a 1, 2, 7, 14   **b** 1, 2, 3, 5, 6, 10, 15, 30
   c 1, 5, 25   **d** 1, 2, 3, 6, 9, 18

5 a 1, 2, 4, 5, 10. 20   **b** six   **6** four

7 any prime number such as 2, 3, 5, 7, 11, 13, 17, …

8 one   **9 a** 60 **b** 12

Exercise 14.3
1 a 1,11   **b** Yes: it has only two different factors.

2 It only has one factor.   **3** No: it has factors 1, 3, 7, 21.

4 2, 3, 5, 7   **5** 41   **6** 97   **7** 105, 111

Exercise 14.4
1 2, 3   **2** 10 is not prime   **3** 21 is not prime

4 a 2, 7 **b** 2,3,7 **c** 2,7 **d** 2, 3 **e** 2 **f** 3, 5 **6** 147

Exercise 14.5

1 a 10 **b** 4 **c** 9 **d** 5 **e** 8 **f** 11

2 124 **3** 20 **4 a** 5 **b** 1 **c** 4

5 289 **6** 60

Exercise 14.6

1

			2 1	3 2			
	1 1		4 3	5 3	0		
	6 4	0	0		2		
7 1	4			4		9 2	
1		8 1			10 1	9	
	2		11 1	4	9		
12 9	0	13 9		6			
	14 8	4					

SECTION 15

Starting points

A1
A	2	G	2	N	2	U	3
B	16	H	3	O	13	V	2
D	1	I	5	R	3	W	2
E	8	L	2	S	2	Y	6
F	1	M	3	T	5		

B1 25 **B2** badger **B3 a** rabbit **b** badger

B4 29 **B5** hare **B6** 9 **B7** 172

Exercise 15.1

1 Jan and Oct **2** Apr, May, July, Sept, Nov, Dec

3 3 males, 5 females **4** August **5** 0 **6** March

7 a 62 **b** 117 **8 b** 33 **c** 16

Exercise 15.2

1 a Shane **b** 40% **2 a** Sam **b** 10%

3 Mark, 40% spent on travel **4** Mark, 15% spent on shelter

5 Sam, 40% Mark, 15% Vicky, 35% Shane, 20%

Exercise 15.4

1 a 24 **b** Spain 90°, Greece 120°, Turkey 75°, Malta 45°, UK 30°

2 120

Exercise 15.5

1 A, table 4 B, table 1 C, table 3 D, table 2

2 a Fiona **b** Kate **c** £60 **d** £60

SECTION 16

Starting points

A1
500	5 × 100	5 × 10²
6000	6 × 1000	6 × 10³
8000	8 × 1000	8 × 10³
20 000	2 × 10 000	2 × 10⁴
50 000	5 × 10 000	5 × 10⁴
600 000	6 × 100 000	6 × 10⁵
300 000	3 × 100 000	3 × 10⁵
4 000 000	4 × 1 000 000	4 × 10⁶
9 000 000	9 × 1 000 000	9 × 10⁶

Exercise 16.1

1 a 316.5 **b** 27 560 **c** 10 524 **d** 4105.6 **e** 2315.5

f 346.18 **g** 544 **h** 1534 **i** 11 655.2 **j** 347 500

k 6250 **l** 554.51 **m** 158 750 **n** 85 000 **o** 166 670

2 a 65.75 **b** 54.5 **c** 0.0558 **d** 67.5 **e** 0.752

f 86.8 **g** 3575 **h** 8610 **i** 1750 **j** 0.924

k 10.5 **l** 5.0605 **m** 50.06 **n** 40 **o** 0.0005

Exercise 16.2

1 a 0.046 52 **b** 0.1355 **c** 235.265 **d** 0.0125 **e** 0.013 575

f 38.54 **g** 0.003 65 **h** 2.775 **i** 0.003 054 **j** 0.001 204

k 0.065 004 **l** 8.7525 **m** 0.0005 **n** 0.035 41 **o** 0.003 85

2 a 0.045 **b** 0.000 125 **c** 0.002 75 **d** 0.004

e 0.000 0725 **f** 0.000 05 **g** 0.007 55 **h** 0.0004

i 0.015 **j** 0.004 05 **k** 0.0006 **l** 0.000 075

Exercise 16.3

1 a 49.4 **b** 165.33 **c** 706.56 **d** 172.5

e 789 **f** 21.525 **g** 837.2 **h** 144.675

i 621.44 **j** 443.375 **k** 5444.28 **l** 12 912.21

Exercise 16.4

1
24.3 × 6.4	144	155.52
45.2 × 3.6	135	162.72
66.2 × 5.3	330	350.86
78.4 × 6.2	468	486.08
94.6 × 7.1	658	671.66
75.5 × 8.5	600	641.75

2 a 167.04 **b** 185.22 **c** 384.82 **d** 643.5 **e** 287.32

f 550.9 **g** 1378.62 **h** 1421.7 **i** 3429.75

Exercise 16.5

1 a 315 **b** Kim **c** 332.15 **d** Kim

2 123.2 seconds

3 a 4556.5 **b** less than 5000 seconds

4 more than 6000 hours, 6354.6 hours

5 a 10 000 = 10⁴ **b** 0.367 45 seconds

6 a 100 000 **b** One hundred thousand is ten to the power of five.

c 358 500 seconds = 5975 minutes = 99 hours 35 minutes

7 a no **b** Weight is 100.96 kg.

8 a divided by 10³ not multiplied in question 16,
multiplied by 10³ not 10⁴ in question 17

b 1345.54 × 10³ = 1345 540 0.575 41 × 10⁴ = 5754.1

Exercise 16.6

1 a 7.164 **b** 18.872 **c** 95.376 **d** 64.306

e 321.68 **f** 273.15 **g** 304.05 **h** 247.28

i 144.885 **j** 1327.255 **k** 1306.836 **l** 118.815

2 a 323.81 **b** 61.383 **c** 132.541 **d** 274.312 **e** 165.325

f 4030.2 **g** 25.362 **h** 473.02 **i** 342.223

Exercise 16.7

1 76.35 km **2** 406.35 grams

3 24.175 seconds **4** 53.125 ml

REVIEW 2A

1 area ABCD = 91 cm² area EFGH = 52.9 cm²

2 width = 4.5 cm **3** area KLM = 48 cm² area CDE = 31.5 cm²

4 28.8 cm

5

w	t	l
4	5	7
7	6	26
3.5	3	13
50	40	200

6 a n = 8 **b** y = 7 **c** k = 5 **d** n = 4

e w = 7 **f** h = 7 **g** m = 2 **h** d = 1

7 a 20   **b** 25   **c** 81 and 49

8 56, 49, 35 and 42   **9** 15

10 a 1, 2, 3, 6, 9, 18   **b** 1, 2, 3, 4, 6, 8, 12, 24   **c** 1, 2, 4, 7, 14, 28

11 2, 3, 5, 7, 11, 13, 17, 19   **12** 2, 5

13 a 12   **b** 3   **c** 80

17 a 13 840.0   **b** 566.0   **c** 1.5862   **d** 0.002 3405

18 a 94.78   **b** 105   **c** 67.68

19 a 34.245   **b** 13.76

SKILLS BREAK 3

1 4 square miles   **2** 30 square miles

3 a no   **b** 18 square miles

4 right   **5** Silchurch

6 a 1 May   **b** 30 September   **c** 153 days

7 a 15:05   **b** 35 minutes

8 a 14:45   **b** 1 hour 55 minutes   **c** 15:20

9 a 16:10   **b** 55 minutes   **c** 16:45

10 50 minutes

11

Calverton	10.00 am	12.00	2.30 pm
Robridge	10.12 am	12.12 pm	2.45 pm
Char Falls	10.25 am	12.25 pm	3.05 pm
Silchurch	10.40 am	12.40 pm	3.20 pm
Silchurch	11.05 am	1.30 pm	4.10 pm
Char Falls	11.20 am	1.45 pm	4.28 pm
Robridge	11.35 am	2.00 pm	4.45 pm
Calverton	11.45 am	2.10 pm	5.00 pm

12 10 tons

13 a May   **b** Aug

     c

May	June	July	Aug	Sept
155 tons	192 tons	219 tons	256 tons	229 tons

14 The water for the locomotive is 5×10^2 gallons.   **15** 60 480 lb

16 a 123 200 lb

     b one hundred and twenty three thousand two hundred pounds

17 a 7 May   **b** 9 May   **c** 12.48 tons **d** 0.87 tons   **e** 8 May

18 group A, £20; group B, £17.50; group C, £21; group D, £31.50; group E, £40

19 19 children   **20** £123.50

21 a 67 adult   **b** 93 senior citizens

22 £883.50   **23** £1844.50

SECTION 17

Starting points

A1 a obtuse   **b** reflex   **c** obtuse   **d** acute   **e** reflex   **f** acute

A2 a two   **b** four

Exercise 17.1

1 a 74°   **b** 103°   **c** 126°   **d** 33°   **e** 111°

   f 35°   **g** 91°   **h** 121°   **i** 156°   **j** 133°

Exercise 17.2

1 a 76°   **b** 66°   **c** 25°   **d** 40°   **e** 69°

   f 49°   **g** 41°   **h** 60°   **i** 121°   **j** 52°

Exercise 17.3

1 a 114°   **b** 114°   **c** 66°   **d** 133°   **e** 47°   **f** 47°

   g 39°   **h** 141°   **i** 39°   **j** 88°   **k** 92°   **l** 92°

   m 121°   **n** 143°   **o** 37°   **p** 121°   **q** 59°   **r** 143°

   s 121°   **t** 117°   **u** 59°   **v** 117°   **w** 59°   **x** 63°

   y 147°   **z** 125°

Exercise 17.4

1 $k = 94°$, $m = 104°$

2 a 78°   **b** 42°   **c** 108°   **d** 67°   **e** 96°

   f 56°   **g** 124°   **h** 64°   **i** 98°

Exercise 17.5

1 a 85°   **b** 82°

2 a XY and CB   **b** 37°   **c** 68°

   d more than 100° (105°)

3 a vertically opposite and obtuse   **b** 23° and angle i

   c 46°, vertically opposite   **d** 134°, angle on a straight line

   e no: 23°, alternate angle

4 a m and w; and 39° and k **b** 45°   **c** 39°, alternate angle

   d $y + 39° = 90°$ **e** $m = 45°$

SECTION 18

Starting points

A1 a 43.712   **b** 12.684   **c** 100.991

B1 a 33.05   **b** 57.644

C1 a 13.5   **b** 10.8   **D1 a** 21.5   **b** 5.719

Exercise 18.1

1 a £43.66   **b** £6.91   **c** £7.83   **d** £22.54

   e £135.59   **f** £97.11   **g** £401.61   **h** £386.24

2 a £9.07   **b** £435.99   **c** £40.65   **d** £56.34

   e £35.42   **f** £46.02   **g** £5.55   **h** £259.79

Exercise 18.2

1 a £3.36   **b** £7.83   **c** £6.46   **d** £32.16   **e** £16.15   **f** £19.32

2 a £4.51   **b** £5.76   **c** £2.37   **d** £7.86   **e** £16.45   **f** £18.47

3 a £22.80   **b** £90.72   **c** £98.47   **d** £125.70   **e** £1464.64 **f** £56.13

4 a 8   **b** 6   **c** £45.72   **d** £5.38

Exercise 18.3

1 Sharp's Chemist cash total = £83.32

   Staples Newsagents Yachting Times cost £3.56

   Ringway DIY   4 @ £2.59 cost £10.36 and sale total =£23.19

2 £6.24   **3** £15.42

4 a $8 \times £0.16$

   b

```
Vole Malley Farm Supplies
Item Ref.  Description              Quantity   Each     Cost
0261       Grease - chainsaw        1          3.85     3.85
0564       Starter cord sold per metre  8      0.16     1.28
0435       Sprayer                  1          16.49    16.49
0134       Fence post               6          5.23     31.38
0957       Spark plug BMR7A                    1.55     3.10
0963       Spark plug BPMR6Y        3          1.86     5.58
                                               Total    £61.68
```

Exercise 18.4

1 a A = £549.24   B = £63.36   C = £255.42   **b** D = £868.02

2 a £8   **b** £6   **3 a** £11.60   **b** £8.70

4

Winston Landers	Pay details		September
Basic rate = £4.50 per hour			
Rate	Number of hours	Amount/hour	Total
Basic	138	4.50	621
Double time	10	9	90
Time $+\frac{1}{2}$	25	6.75	168.75
Total pay			£ 879.75

5

Amanda Rogers	Pay details		September
Basic rate = £4.88 per hour			
Rate	Number of hours	Amount/hour	Total
Basic	124	4.88	605.12
Double time	4	9.76	39.04
Time $+\frac{1}{2}$	11	7.32	80.52
Total pay			£ 724.68

6

```
Steve Hicks    Pay details – September

Basic rate: £6.26 per hour

Hours worked:

Basic          Double         Time + ½
  38             6                7

Pay @ basic rate:        237.88
Pay @ double time:        75.12
Pay @ time + ½:           65.73
Total pay for week:     £378.73
```

Exercise 18.5

1 **a** £5.27   **b** £57.44   **c** £1.75
     d £268.66   **e** £0.84   **f** £756.35

2 **a** £7.03   **b** £2.48   **c** £15.72
     d £20.40   **e** £0.29   **f** £487.89

3 **a** £13.00   **b** £24.90

Exercise 18.6

1 **a** £15.79   **b** rounding   **2** 13p

3 **a** £3.69   **b** £18.43

SECTION 19

Exercise 19.1

1 5   **2** octagon

Exercise 19.2

1 **a** 8   **b** 8   **c** 45°   **2** 120°

3

Regular polygon	No. of sides	Exterior angle
Hexagon	6	60°
Heptagon	7	**51°**
Nonagon	9	**40°**
Decagon	10	**36°**
Dodecagon	12	**30°**
Hexadecagon	16	**23°**

4 36

Exercise 19.3

1 154°   **2** **a** 72° **b** 108°

3

Regular polygon	No. of sides	Interior angle
Hexagon	6	120°
Heptagon	7	**129°**
Nonagon	9	**140°**
Decagon	10	**144°**
Dodecagon	12	**150°**
Hexadecagon	16	**158°**

4 square   **5** **a** 120° **b** 3

Exercise 19.4

1 $a = 80°$ **b** $39°$ **c** $40°$ **d** $48°$
2 $e = 90°$ **f** $91°$ **g** $148°$ **h** $56°$
3 $p = 160°$ **q** $122°$

SECTION 20

Starting points

A1 **a** $^-11$ **b** $^-5$ **B1** **a** $^-11$ **b** 11
C1 **a** $^-15$ **b** $^-28$

Exercise 20.1

1 **a** 21   **b** 7   **c** 25   **d** 27   **e** 4   **f** 12

---

2 **a** $y = 5x + 1$ **b** $y = 6x - 5$ **c** $y = (x + 2) \times 5$
     d $y = (x \div 2) \times 3$ **e** $y = 3x + 10$ **f** $y = (x - 3) \times 6$

3 **a** 22   **b** 42   **4** **b** $y = 29$ **c** $x = 11$

5 **a** 5   **b** 13   **c** $^-2$ **d** 6   **e** $^-3$ **f** 27

Exercise 20.2

1

a $x \longrightarrow y$	**b** $x \longrightarrow y$	**c** $x \longrightarrow y$
2 → 5	3 → 17	2 → 13
5 → 17	7 → 29	5 → 31
12 → 45	8 → 32	3 → 19
6 → 21	9 → 35	10 → 61
9 → 33	11 → 41	8 → 49
15 → 57	12 → 44	4 → 25

2

$x \longrightarrow y$
1 → 9
2 → 11
3 → 13
4 → 15
5 → 17

3

a $x \longrightarrow y$	**b** $x \longrightarrow y$
1 → 8	1 → $^-2.75$
2 → 11	2 → $^-2.5$
3 → 14	3 → $^-2.25$
4 → 17	4 → $^-2$
5 → 20	5 → $^-1.75$
6 → 23	6 → $^-1.5$

4

$x \longrightarrow y$
6 → 7
7 → 7.5
8 → 8
9 → 8.5
10 → 9

Exercise 20.3

1 **a** 48 °F   **b** 56 °F   **c** 24 °C   **d** 21 °C
2 **a** 302   **b** $- 2 \ldots \div 3$ **c** 61
3 **a** 7   **b** $+ 5 \ldots \div 4$ **c** 13
4 **a** $- 6 \ldots \times 2$ **b** 30

SECTION 21

Starting points

A1

Size	3	4	5	6	7	8	9	12
Frequency	1	1	3	1	2	1	1	2

A2

Size	S	M	L	XL
Frequency	1	4	3	1

Exercise 21.1

1 **a**

Score	4	5	6	7	8	9	10
Frequency	1	4	4	7	8	3	5

b 32   **c** 32

2

Score	1	2	3	4	5	6	7	8	9	10
Frequency	1	1	0	1	3	4	7	9	5	5

b 36

3 **a** 50

b

Number of people in car	1	2	3	4	5
Frequency	25	8	11	5	1

4 a 36

b

Shoe size	6	7	8	9	10	11	12	13
Frequency	1	3	4	12	8	2	3	3

5

Month	Frequency	Month	Frequency
Jan	2	July	4
Feb	3	Aug	3
Mar	5	Sept	2
Apr	3	Oct	4
May	3	Nov	5
June	3	Dec	5

Exercise 21.2

1

Age	Frequency
1–10	6
11–20	7
21–30	9
31–40	9
over 40	4

2

Age	Frequency
1–5	3
6–10	3
11–15	3
16–20	4
21–25	4
26–30	5
31–35	5
36–40	3
over 40	5

3 a

Items	Frequency
1–10	7
11–20	7
21–30	8
31–40	7
41–50	3
over 50	3

c

Items	Frequency
1–5	3
6–10	4
11–15	4
16–20	3
21–25	4
26–30	4
31–35	2
36–40	5
41–45	1
46–50	2
over 50	3

b 21 to 30 is the modal group.

d The modal class is 36 to 40.

REVIEW 2B

1 a 129°   **b** 5°   **2 a** 49°   **b** 115°

3 a 48°   **b** 132°   **c** 48°   **d** 133°   **e** 47°   **f** 133°

4 a 116°   **b** 64°   **c** 54°   **d** 126°   **e** 54°

5 a £8.63   **b** £258.65   **c** £88.57   **d** £162.44

6 a £5.22   **b** £12.72   **c** £15.30   **d** £176.64   **e** £357.75

　　f £4.68   **g** £15.88   **h** £137.43   **i** £56.24

7 £2.51   **8** £4.85   **9 a** £9.20 **b** £6.90

10 a £6.08   **b** £14.31   **c** £425.86

11 14p   **12** £1.38   **13 a** 12 **b** 30°

14 108°   **15 a** 71° **b** 131°

16 a 72°   **b** 22°   **17** 20

18

x		y
3	⟶	7
4	⟶	11
5	⟶	15
6	⟶	19
7	⟶	23
8	⟶	27

19

Score	Frequency
1	2
2	2
3	3
4	2
5	3
6	4
7	2
8	5
9	6
10	4

20

Group	Frequency
1 to 5	4
6 to 10	6
10 to 15	5
16 to 20	5
2 to 25	4
Over 25 days	4

SKILLS BREAK 4 – SEALS

1 This year – 1957 = answer   **2** $9\frac{1}{2}$ hours   **3** £2.70

4 They were underfed.   **5** 18.5 kg   **6** 16.8 kg (Ben)

7 1.1 kg   **8** 0.77 kg   **9** 7319

10 This year – 1975 = answer   **11** 35 minutes

12 8   **13** 55 pence   **14** Tony

15 39.2 kg   **16** Tony

17

Age in days	Tally	Frequency
1 to 10	卌 卌 卌 III	18
11 to 20	卌 卌 I	11
21 to 30	卌 卌 I	11
31 to 40	II	2
More than 40	I	1

18 11:00 am, 1:30 pm, 4:00 pm   **19** 0.81 kg   **20** 14.5 kg

21 9823   **22** 20451   **23** 7000   **24** 900

25 Outer Hebrides   **26** 24000   **27** 40000   **28** 45 minutes

29 96 square metres   **30 b** 42

STAGE 2 END POINTS

A1 a 126 cm²   **b** 26 cm²   **c** 37.1 cm²

B1 a 56 cm²   **b** 30 cm²   **c** 61.25 cm²

C1 68 cm

D1

k	w	y
3	4	6
5	9	3
⁻6	2	⁻42

E1 a $y = 7$ **b** $k = 7$ **c** $m = 5$ **d** $h = 9$ **e** $g = 7$ **f** $y = 6$

F1 14, 16, and 76   **F2** It ends with a 0 or a 5.

G1 1, 2, 3, 4, 6, 9, 12, 18, 36   **G2** 1, 2, 4, 8

H1 no (because $7 \times 5 = 35$)   **H2** 3, 29, 31, 37

I1 a 2, 3   **b** 3, 5   **c** 2, 3

J1 a 10   **b** 12   **c** 15   **d** 9   **e** 20

J2 a 5   **b** 13

L1 a 8   **b** 6   **c** 37   **d** tea   **e** cola   **f** milk

M1 a Ella **b** Ian **c** Mina, 30%   Ella, 0%   Chris, 10%   Ian, 20%

d soaps, 30%   drama, 30%   films, 10%   news, 0%   sport, 30%

P1 **a** 1675.54 **b** 0.5882 **c** 125400

Q1 **a** 0.035725 **b** 0.0075 **c** 0.165458

R1 **a** 111.42 **b** 2146.05 **c** 11476.38

S1

Calculate	Estimate	Answer
18.6×3.4	$19 \times 3 = 57$	63.24
35.8×6.5	$36 \times 7 = 252$	232.7
92.4×5.3	$92 \times 5 = 460$	489.72

T1 **a** 73° **b** 83° **c** 134° **d** 46° **e** 134°
f 116° **g** 58° **h** 58° **i** 90° **j** 141°

U1 45° **U2** 150° **U3** **a** 139° **b** 126°

V1

x		y
0	⟶	⁻9
1	⟶	⁻2
2	⟶	5
3	⟶	12
4	⟶	19
5	⟶	26

W1 **a**

Days	Frequency
1	4
2	7
3	3
4	6
5	6
6	1
7	2
8	2
9	2
10	2
11	0
12	1
13	0
14	1
15	0
16	1
17	0
18	1
19	0
20	0
21	0
22	1
23	0
24	1

b

1 to 5	26
6 to 10	9
11 to 15	2
16 to 20	2
Over 20	2

c 1 to 5

X1 **a** £18.01 **b** £323.51 **c** £333.36 **d** £525.12 **e** £38.64

REVISION 2

1 **a** thirty thousand **b** three million **c** three thousand

2 57632, 54881, 53085, 1634, 585, 425, 19, 17

3 **a** thirty thousand six hundred and seven
b two hundred and thirty thousand four hundred and five
c six million seven hundred and forty thousand and fifty

4 **a** 40026 **b** 506060 **c** 12000090

5 V̶ K̶ D̶ T̶ Y̶ **6** two

7 one (forgetting hinges, handle, etc.)

8 **a** 39 **b** 58 **c** 20480 **d** 23333
e 588 **f** 18872 **g** 241 **h** 2546

---

9 **a** $\frac{8}{10}$ **b** $\frac{8}{1000}$ **c** $\frac{8}{10\,000}$

10 0.04, 0.045, 0.309, 0.4, 2.012, 2.12

11 **a** 29.955 **b** 563.257 **c** 17.285

13 154°, 104°

14 **a** ⁻16 **b** ⁻13 **c** 5 **d** ⁻24 **e** ⁻16 **f** 4
g 16 **h** ⁻56 **i** ⁻30 **j** 24 **k** ⁻8 **l** 4

15 **a** ⁻9, ⁻7, ⁻2, 2, 3, 7, 8
b ⁻11, ⁻7, ⁻4, ⁻3, 0, 3, 9, 13

16 (⁻2, 2) and (⁻2, ⁻3) or (⁻12, 2) and (⁻12, ⁻3)

17 **a** $12k + 10w$ **b** $16f + 3h$

18 **a** $42w + 18$ **b** $45 - 20k$

19 $25y + 4g + 6$

20 **a** 22000 **b** 445000 **c** 5286000

21 **a** 700000 **b** 7500000 **c** 5080000

22 **a** 3500 **b** 3500 **c** 5400

25 **a** 21:50 **b** 04:35 **c** 23:15 **d** 12:25 **e** 02:05 **f** 13:36

26 4 hours 42 minutes

27 **a** 12:35 **b** 57 minutes

28 **a** 86.4 cm² **b** 113.76 cm² **c** 26.68 cm²
d 58.9 cm² **e** 83.25 cm² **f** 63 cm²

29 $t = 46$

30 **a** $y = 4$ **b** $h = 6$ **c** $g = 14$ **d** $f = 13$

31 **a** 145 **b** 36, 49, 64 **c** 19

32 72, 42, 36 **33** 1, 2, 4, 7, 8, 14, 28, 56

34 11, 13, 17, 19, 23, 29

36 **a** 1217.57 **b** 0.435 **c** 388.675 **d** 0.0000688

37 **a** 452.75 **b** 375.83 **c** 623.15 **d** 1696.14

38 **a** £26.25 **b** £24.92 **c** £86.64 **d** £211.38

39 16p **40** £2.57 **41** £6.49

42 **a** £3.33 **b** £117.25 **c** £12.72 **d** £564.25

43

x		y
2	⟶	8
3	⟶	13
4	⟶	18
5	⟶	23
6	⟶	28
7	⟶	33

44 36

45 **a** 82° **b** 55° **c** 88° **d** 92° **e** 88° **f** 99°
g 81° **h** 76° **i** 67° **j** 52° **k** 70°

46 **a** £14.40 **b** £10.80

SECTION 22

Starting points

A1 37p **A2** **a** 60 **b** 30 **c** 15

A3 27 **A4** 8

A5 5 litres **B1** $\frac{1}{8}$ **B2** **a** 12 **b** 11 parts

C1 **a** 6.462 **b** 0.95

Exercise 22.1

4 **a** $\frac{3}{4}$ or $\frac{15}{20}$ **b** $\frac{1}{10}$ **c** $\frac{3}{10}$ **d** $\frac{5}{6}$ or $\frac{10}{12}$ **e** $\frac{7}{8}$
f $\frac{5}{9}$ **g** $\frac{2}{3}$ or $\frac{12}{18}$ **h** $\frac{9}{15}$ or $\frac{3}{5}$ **i** $\frac{4}{5}$ **j** $\frac{3}{4}$
k $\frac{8}{16}$ or $\frac{1}{2}$

5 **a** $\frac{1}{24}$ **b** $\frac{15}{24}$ or $\frac{5}{8}$

Exercise 22.2

1 £6.14 **2** £7.56

3 $\frac{1}{5}$ of £34.40 is larger £6.88 ($\frac{1}{4}$ of £27.40 = £6.85)

4 £240   £120   £60   £80   £48   £30
120 kg   60 kg   30 kg   40 kg   24 kg   15 kg

360 g	180 g	90 g	120 g	72 g	45 g
£4800	£2400	£1200	£1600	£960	£600
750 t	375 t	187.5 t	250 t	150 t	93.75 t
42 mm	21 mm	10.5 mm	14 mm	8.4 mm	5.25 mm
£62.40	£31.20	£15.60	£20.80	£12.48	£7.80
£16.50	£8.25		£5.50	£3.30	
£56.80	£28.40	£14.20		£11.36	£7.10

5 £7.75

6 **a** £16.59   **b** 390 t   **c** 285 kg   **d** £12.88   **e** 540 t
   f 364 kg   **g** £67.10   **h** 4150 t   **i** 210 kg

7 **a** £30.21   **b** 732 t   **c** 77.5 kg   **d** 4.5 cm
   e 30.625 mm   **f** 29.75 kg   **g** £23.65   **h** 99.4 km
   i £4.56

Exercise 22.3

1 **a** 24   **b** 27   **c** more than 15 (18)   **d** 3

2 **a** 6625   **b** 39 750   **c** yes: 53 000 child tickets sold   **d** 33 125

3 plain, 40   cream, 48   chocolate, 15   wafer, 6   iced, 11

4 **a** 56 of size 9, 63 of size 10, 28 of size 11, 21 of size 12
   b males (because not many females have size 9, 10, 11 or 12 feet)

5 **a** 312   **b** 120   **c** 8

6 Wilja, 16.2 tonnes   Maris Piper, 21.6 tonnes
   Esteema, 2.43 tonnes   Desiree, 8.37 tonnes

Exercise 22.4

1

Fraction	Divide both parts by	Equivalent fraction
$\frac{10}{15}$	5	$\frac{2}{3}$
$\frac{12}{15}$	3	$\frac{4}{5}$
$\frac{21}{33}$	3	$\frac{7}{11}$
$\frac{18}{27}$	9	$\frac{2}{3}$
$\frac{15}{21}$	3	$\frac{5}{7}$
$\frac{16}{40}$	8	$\frac{2}{5}$
$\frac{24}{27}$	3	$\frac{8}{9}$
$\frac{15}{25}$	5	$\frac{3}{5}$
$\frac{14}{35}$	7	$\frac{2}{5}$
$\frac{27}{63}$	9	$\frac{3}{7}$
$\frac{16}{28}$	4	$\frac{4}{7}$
$\frac{24}{44}$	4	$\frac{6}{11}$

2 **a** $\frac{9}{15}$ **b** $\frac{6}{10}$ **c** $\frac{3}{5}$ **d** $\frac{9}{15}, \frac{6}{10}, \frac{3}{5}$

3 **b** no: $\frac{24}{42} = \frac{4}{7}$

4 **a** $\frac{6}{8}$ **b** $\frac{15}{20}$ **c** $\frac{24}{32}$ **d** $\frac{6}{8}, \frac{15}{20}, \frac{24}{32}$

5 $\frac{20}{30}, \frac{2}{3}, \frac{100}{150}$

Exercise 22.5

1 **a** $\frac{2}{3}$ **b** $\frac{5}{7}$ **c** $\frac{3}{4}$ **d** $\frac{4}{9}$ **e** $\frac{5}{12}$ **f** $\frac{4}{17}$
   g $\frac{3}{4}$ **h** $\frac{2}{5}$ **i** $\frac{8}{9}$ **j** $\frac{1}{3}$ **k** $\frac{1}{6}$ **l** $\frac{1}{5}$
   m $\frac{19}{21}$ **n** $\frac{5}{6}$ **o** $\frac{6}{7}$ **p** $\frac{1}{300}$

3 $\frac{28}{35}, \frac{48}{60}$

Exercise 22.6

1 **a** 0.75   **b** 0.6   **c** 0.75   **d** 0.7   **e** 0.625   **f** 0.75
   g 0.125   **h** 0.2   **i** 0.3   **j** 0.8   **k** 0.875   **l** 0.2

2 **a** 0.025   **b** 0.0625   **c** 0.625   **d** 0.75   **e** 0.6   **f** 0.45
   g 0.24   **h** 0.6   **i** 0.3   **j** 0.375   **k** 0.625   **l** 0.3125

Exercise 22.7

1 **a** 30%   **b** 37.5%   **c** 20%   **d** 45%   **e** 60%   **f** 87.5%
   g 70%   **h** 67.5%   **i** 40%   **j** 56.25%   **k** 34.375%   **l** 31.25%
   m 72%   **n** 78.125%   **o** 31.25%   **p** 40%

2 65% because $\frac{5}{8} = 62.5\%$

SECTION 23

Starting Points

A1 40–59

A2 41–50 (frequency of 8)

Exercise 23.1

1 **c** about 43 °C

2 **a** A baby will grow continuously.   **b** 50 mm, about 70–80 days
   c about 350 mm   **d** at about 240 days
   e The scales on the axes are too small.
   f between about 80 and 120 days

3 **b** about 1200 grams   **c** 170 days

4 **a** 9 am, 10 am, 11 am, 1 pm, 2 pm, 3 pm
   b 10 am and 11 am   **c** about 37 birds
   d No reading was taken – he may even have been having lunch at that time.

5 **a** type A   **b** 20 weeks
   c 30 cm and 40 cm   **d** type B (steepest line)
   e 26 March + 22 weeks = 28 August

6 jar A, graph E   jar B, graph F   jar C, graph D

Exercise 23.2

1 **a**

Class	Tally	Frequency
0–9		0
10–19	II	2
20–29	卌 I	6
30–39	卌 III	8
40–49	IIII	4

   c The modal class is 30–39.
   d The race was too long for anyone to finish in less that 10 minutes.

2 **a**

Class	Tally	Frequency
0–10	III	3
11–20	卌 III	8
21–30	卌	5
31–40	II	2
41–50	III	3
51–60	卌 I	6
61–70	卌	5
71–80	III	3

   c The modal class is 11–20.
   d The graph has two peaks (at 11–20 and at 51–60) so it would make more sense to run some small buses as well as the 80-seater ones.

Exercise 23.3

1 **a**

Class	Tally	Frequency
0 ⩽ time < 10	III	3
10 ⩽ time < 20	IIII	4
20 ⩽ time < 30	卌 II	7
30 ⩽ time < 40	卌 I	6
40 ⩽ time < 50		0

   b 13 people took 20 minutes or more.

2 **b** 12   **c** 27

3 **b** 14   **c** 7   **d** £50 –

4 **b** 58   **c** 29

SECTION 24

Starting points

A1

p	k	c
5	4	11
2	9	⁻3
3	2	7
7	15	6
19	45	12

B1   **a** $y = 7$ **b** $y = 7$ **c** $k = 9$ **d** $k = 2$

C1   **a** $y = 4$ **b** $h = 6$ **c** $w = 7$

Exercise 24.1

1   **a** $y = 3$ **b** $k = 9$ **c** $h = 3$ **d** $p = 3$
    e $k = 4$ **f** $y = 7$ **g** $d = 8$ **h** $a = 11$

2   **a** $x = 7$ **b** $y = 7$ **c** $x = 8$ **d** $k = 3$
    e $y = 5$ **f** $y = 2$ **g** $k = 6$ **h** $w = 4$

3   **a** $x = ⁻5$ **b** $k = ⁻5$ **c** $y = ⁻4$ **d** $h = ⁻3$
    e $w = ⁻2$ **f** $x = ⁻6$ **g** $k = ⁻2$ **h** $n = ⁻12$

Exercise 24.2

1 **b** and **e**   **2** **c** and **d**

3   **a** Nos 3, 5, 9, and 10
    b No. 3, $y = 2$ No. 5, $y = ⁻6$ No. 8, $w = ⁻6$
    No. 9, $a = 6$ No. 10, $x = ⁻10$

Exercise 24.3

1   **a** $91 = 4x + 15$ **b** $x = 19$ **c** 19 cm   **d** 26.5 cm

2   **a** $82 = 8x + 10$ **b** $x = 9$ **c** 9 cm
    d 32 cm   **e** 288 cm²

3   **a** $93 = 17x + 25$ **b** $x = 4$

4   **a** 64 cm   **b** $64 = 10x - 6$ **c** $x = 7$
    d width 7 cm, length 25 cm   **e** shape A (255 cm²), (B = 175 cm²)

5 length = 21 cm

6   **a** $P = 8x - 2$ **b** $x = 5$ **c** 38 cm   **d** 38 cm

7   **a** $4(2x + 1) = 60$ **b** $x = 7$ **c** 38 cm

8   **c** $x = 6$ **d** 27 cm

9   **a** $180 = 9x$ **b** $x = 20$ **c** 40°, 60°, 80°

10   **a** $360 = 10x$ **b** $x = 36$ angles: 36°, 72°, 108°, 144°

SECTION 25

Starting points

A1   **a** 590   **b** 920   **c** 20   **d** 3790   **e** 590   **f** 390
    g 660   **h** 890   **i** 200   **j** 990   **k** 3990   **l** 6000

B1   **a** 900   **b** 700   **c** 800   **d** 2800   **e** 3600   **f** 900
    g 8200   **h** 5900   **i** 1100   **j** 300   **k** 9500   **l** 1200

C1   **a** $\frac{4}{10}$ **b** $\frac{4}{1000}$ **c** $\frac{4}{100}$ **d** $\frac{4}{10\,000}$ **e** $\frac{4}{10}$

Exercise 25.1

1   **a** 38   **b** 128   **c** 7   **d** 9   **e** 18
    f 21   **g** 125   **h** 57   **i** 56   **j** 130
    k 79   **l** 40   **m** 110   **n** 300   **o** 1000

2 34.685, 35.49, 35.199

3   **a** 1   **b** 1   **c** 1   **d** 1
    e 0   **f** 0   **g** 1   **h** 0

Exercise 25.2

1   **a** 345.7 **b** 676.4 **c** 188.6 **d** 1304.7 **e** 564.7 **f** 60.1
    g 90.0 **h** 28.4 **i** 6.4 **j** 11.1 **k** 206.3 **l** 100.1

2   **a** 0.4   **b** 0.6   **c** 0.1   **d** 0.6
    e 0.0   **f** 0.8   **g** 1.0   **h** 0.1

3 27.4 (to 1dp)

Exercise 25.3

1

Decimal value	Rounded to		
	2 dp	3 dp	4 dp
27.685 44	27.69	27.685	27.6854
3.067 45	3.07	3.067	3.0675
158.005 74	158.01	158.006	158.0057
0.607 52	0.61	0.608	0.6075
200.051 88	200.05	200.052	200.0519
61.504 09	61.50	61.504	61.5041
384.958 52	384.96	384.959	384.9585
0.067 58	0.07	0.068	0.0676
3.608 67	3.61	3.609	3.6087
75.757 57	75.76	75.758	75.7576

Exercise 25.4

1 258.7 km   34.8 °C   988.6 kg   834.6 metres   1045.1 feet
    76.9 feet   4653.9 km   76.9 feet   4653.9 km   608.1 km
    2856.8 litres   88.7p per litre

2   **a** 43.42 metres   **b** 16.5 metres   **c** 5.3 metres   **d** 43.6 metres

SECTION 26

Starting Points

A1   **a** very likely   **b** impossible   **c** very unlikely
    d certain   **e** evens

B1 1, 2, 3, 4, 5, 6   **B2**   **a** heads, tails   **b** yes

B3 No: the faces are not all the same size; it is less likely to land on an end.

Exercise 26.1

1   **a** $\frac{1}{12}$ **b** $\frac{2}{12} = \frac{1}{6}$ **c** $\frac{1}{12}$ **d** $\frac{1}{12}$

2 0   **3** 1   **4** $\frac{2}{12} = \frac{1}{6}$

Exercise 26.2

1 $\frac{4}{16} = \frac{1}{4}$

2   **a** $\frac{7}{16}$ **b** $\frac{5}{16}$ **c** $\frac{6}{16} = \frac{3}{8}$

3   **a** $\frac{4}{16} = \frac{1}{4}$ **b** $\frac{12}{16} = \frac{3}{4}$ **c** They add up to 1.

4 $\frac{3}{4}$ **5** 0

6 Different answers are possible (e.g. 'has a hat and has dark hair').

Exercise 26.3

1   **a** $\frac{3}{9} = \frac{1}{3}$

2 scales to show **a** $\frac{1}{9}$ and **b** $\frac{4}{9}$

6 scales to show **a** $\frac{1}{2}$, **b** $\frac{1}{4}$ and **c** $\frac{12}{52} = \frac{6}{26}$

REVIEW 3A

1   **a** $\frac{1}{16}$

2   **a** £30.40   **b** 291 kg   **c** 245 km   **d** 65.45
    e 1950 miles   **f** 4640 tonnes

3   **a** $\frac{15}{25}$ $\frac{24}{40}$ $\frac{30}{50}$ **b** $\frac{15}{24}$ $\frac{35}{56}$ $\frac{60}{96}$

4   **a** $\frac{5}{7}$ **b** $\frac{8}{11}$ **c** $\frac{4}{5}$ **d** $\frac{8}{13}$ **e** $\frac{1}{3}$
    f $\frac{4}{11}$ **g** $\frac{6}{7}$ **h** $\frac{3}{5}$ **i** $\frac{2}{3}$

5   **a** 0.4   **b** 0.375   **c** 0.9   **d** 0.75   **e** 0.625   **f** 0.6

6   **a** 3.8 kg   **b** 98p   **c** £1.18

7 a

Class	Frequency
0–4	0
5–9	0
10–14	1
15–19	10
20–24	8
25–29	8
30–34	1

Total frequency 28

c modal class 15–19

8 a

Group	Frequency
$0 \leqslant$ time < 10	1
$10 \leqslant$ time < 20	12
$20 \leqslant$ time < 30	8

b 8

9 a $y = 8$ **b** $y = 3$ **c** $k = 7$ **d** $w = 4$

10 a wrong: $w = 13$ **b** wrong: $k = {}^-7$ **c** correct

11 $x = 14$ **12 a** 138 **b** 28 **c** 105

13 a 37.7 **b** 0.006 **14** $\frac{1}{6}$ **15** arrow to show less than 0.5

SKILLS BREAK 5

1 1.5 m² **2 a** 8 m² **b** £8.95

3 a less than 20 m² (19.6 m²) **b** yes (because 255 ÷ 19.6 = £13.01 …)

4 1.98 m² **5** 41 250 **6** No: there are 44 000.

7 a 34 375 **b** No: the answer is 62.5%.

10 £4.25 **11 a** 25.6 **b** the median (25)

12 a 50 **b** 52 **c** 16

d yes, from customer point of view (because the mean is only 48)

13 £265 **15** £3.85 **16** £5.62 **17** 6–10

18 11.6 **19** £71.77 **20** £121.78

21 a 3 **b** zero **c** 101–150 **d** 26 **e** 101–150

22 £60.20 **23 a** 1400 mm **b** shorter than 1.5 metres (1.4 m)

24 £195 **25** A 56 and 61 B $\frac{3}{10}$ C 1.25 km

SECTION 27

Starting points

A1 a 1 cm represents 25 metres, 1 cm stands for 25 metres.

b 1 metre to 2 km, 1 metre represents 2 km.

c 1 mm to 2 metres, 1 mm stands for 2 metres.

A2

Scale drawing	Real object
2 cm	**8 metres**
3.5 cm	**14 metres**
10 cm	**40 metres**
25 cm	**100 metres**
40.5 cm	**162 metres**

Exercise 27.1

1 a 28 mm **b** 420 mm **c** 3 cm **d** 45 cm

2

Length on model	Length on real boat
14 cm	**112 cm**
15 mm	**120 mm**
55 mm	**440 mm**
8 cm	64 cm
23 mm	184 mm
0.5 metres	**4 metres**
3.5 cm	**28 cm**
0.5 cm	4 cm

3 a length 3 cm, width 2.5 cm **b** length 7.5 metres, width 6.25 metres
c 27.5 metres **d** 46.875 m²

4 400 mm

5 a 15 000 mm **b** yes (15 000 mm = 15 m) **c** about 49 ft

6 a less than 0.5 km (0.4 km) **b** yes, because 1 yd is approx 1 metre

7 a 2.4 km **b** 5 km

Exercise 27.2

1 2.5 metres **2** 1.5 metres **3** 26 m² **4** 50 cm **5** 8 metres

6 a width of window = $\frac{1}{2}$ width of door

b width of window = $\frac{1}{2}$ width of door

7 a 9 metres **b** 12 metres

8 less than 2 metres wide (1.5 metres)

9 a 6 cm **b** 9 metres **c** 2.25 metres **d** 20.25 m²

10 underestimate (44.1 m²) **11 b** 45 m²

12 area of house = 96 m²
no (because it is less than $\frac{1}{2}$)

SECTION 28

Starting points

A1

No.	is	is
600	6×100	6×10^2
8000	8×1000	8×10^3
70 000	7×10000	7×10^4
12 000	12×1000	12×10^3
5000	5×1000	5×10^3
50 000	5×10000	5×10^4
85 000	85×1000	85×10^3
375 000	375×1000	375×10^3
49 000	49×1000	49×10^3
9 200 000	92×100000	92×10^5

B1 a 487.5 **b** 61556.5 **c** 1455770 **d** 58.33 **e** 887.57

Exercise 28.1

1

Number	Value (between 1 and 10)	Number in standard form
575	5.75	5.75×10^2
6885	**6.885**	**6.885×10^3**
398 766	**3.98766**	**3.98766×10^5**
325.8	**3.258**	**3.258×10^2**

2 a 6.78×10^2 **b** 3.455×10^3 **c** 3.89×10 **d** 3.0565×10^4
e 8.854×10^2 **f** 3.5688×10^4 **g** 8.5635×10^3 **h** 5.0×10^4
i 3.785641×10^6 **j** 8.3568×10^2 **k** 1.005×10^2 **l** 2.0×10^5
m 3.975×10 **n** 6.8047×10^3 **o** 9.0×10^6 **p** 5.0×10^5

3 a 2, 3, 5, 7, 8

b

	Number	In standard form
1	3856.7	3.8567×10^3
2	3455.8	3.4558×10^3
3	69845.2	6.98452×10^4
4	1887654	1.887654×10^6
5	750000	7.5×10^5
6	9595.4	9.5954×10^3
7	507.55	5.0755×10^2
8	33.333	3.3333×10

Exercise 28.2

1 **a** A 3.45566×10^4 B 7.4335102×10^5 C 9.255455×10^6
  D 6.00755×10^5 E 6.300008×10^7 F 2.4655759×10^5
  G 5.636345×10^8 H 1.990887×10^6 I 8.677574×10^9
 b A 34556.6   B 743351.02   C 9255455
  D 600755   E 63000080   f 246557.59
  G 563634500   H 1990887   I 8677574000

Exercise 28.3

1 **a** 10^6 **b** 10^8 **c** 10^8 **d** 10^7 **e** 10^{12}
 f 10^5 **g** 10^8 **h** 10^{18} **i** 10^{14} **j** 10^{11}

2 345.5

3 **a** 4   **b** 5   **c** 6   **d** 4

Exercise 28.4

1 **a** $x = 3.4$ **b** $x = 2.7$ **c** $x = 4.1$

SECTION 29

Exercise 29.1

1 The image will not fit on the object.

2 **a** about 9 square units   **b** about 9 square units

3 **c** The areas are equal.

4 **d** B (3, 1), B' (3, ⁻1), B" (⁻3, 1)
  One coordinate has been multiplied by ⁻1.

5 **c** They are on top of each other.

Exercise 29.2

2 **e** S (4, 3), S' (⁻4, ⁻3). Both coordinates have been multiplied by ⁻1.

3 **c** Both F's are in the same position.

4 **d** a square

5 **d** 180° about the point P   **e** 120° anticlockwise about the point P

6 **b** the word **MOW**   **d** It would make **D I ⵡ**, not **DID**.

Exercise 29.3

1 **b** rotation 90° clockwise (centre marked at 5 across to right 8 up)
 c reflection (mirror line marked horizontally at 6.5 up)
 d reflection because C is the mirror image of B

2 reflection   3 either

4 **a** reflection in the y-axis   **b** reflection in the y-axis
 c reflection in the x-axis   **d** reflection in the x-axis
 e rotation 180° about (0, 0)   **f** rotation 180° about (0, 0)
 g rotation 180° about (⁻4, 1)   **h** rotation 180° about (⁻4, 1)

SECTION 30

Starting points

A1 a 13   **b** 3   **c** 11

B1 a 27.64   **b** 158.35   **c** 0.035

Exercise 30.1

1 **a** 8.9   **b** 8.2   **c** 18.8   **d** 7.3

2 **a** 19   **b** 29.8   **c** 6.2   **d** 54.7   **e** 26.8

Exercise 30.2

1 445

2 **a** brand A, 5.8   brand B, 5.7   brand C, 5.8   brand D, 6.3
 b Brand D

3 **a** 32   **b** 30.8 seconds   **c** no: slightly longer than 30 seconds

4 **a** 857 miles   **b** 142.8   **5 a** 45

Exercise 30.3

1 **a** 34   **b** 31   **c** 78   **d** 1395   **e** 1050

2 **a** £90   **b** 300 km   **c** 48.1 cm   **d** 44.5 kg

3 **a** wrong (correct answer, 53)   **b** wrong (correct answer, 134)
 c correct

Exercise 30.4

1 **a** 4   **b** 12   **c** 24

2 L (large)   3 9

Exercise 30.5

1 **a** 17 minutes   **b** 4 minutes   **c** 8 minutes
 d 16 minutes   **e** 15 minutes
 f The mean journey time is almost the same. The range of times is smaller for Greenbus. Greenbus is more consistent and probably provides the better service.

2 **a** 16   **b** 22   **c** 10HJ mode, 24   10CW mode, 19
 d 30   **e** 29
 f Group 10HJ is probably the better group. It has a slightly better average and the range of the marks is smaller.

3 **a** T-shirt City, £130   Logoshirt, £177.50
 b T-shirt City, £335   Logoshirt, £60
 c No: it is better to work for Logoshirt as the range of wages is much smaller.

SECTION 31

Starting Points

A1 South

A2 a North   **b** West   **c** South West
 d East   **e** South East

B1 20 km   **B2** 18 km

B3 a 21 km   **b** 24 km   **B4** 31 km

Exercise 31.1

Many different answers are possible to questions in this exercise.

5 This is one answer:
  Turn **left** outside the Lion so you are heading in an **easterly** direction.
  Take the third turning on your **left** (after about 400 metres).
  Take the **second** turning on your right.
  Market Square is about 100 metres on the right.

Exercise 31.2

1 view 1, B   view 2, A   view 3, C

2 C, D, G, J   **5 a** 7 cubes

REVIEW 3B

1 **a** 700 mm   **b** 42 mm

2 less than 1.5 km apart (1.25 km apart)

3 **a** 3.4565×10^4 **b** 1.087551×10^5 **c** 1.3540075×10^4
 d 2.0545×10^2 **e** 3.989454×10^6 **f** 3.8741×10^3

4 **a** A 7.60657×10^5 B 6.200004×10^6 C 4.23245×10^4
 b A 760657   B 6200004   C 42324.5

5 **a** 10^7 **b** 10^7 **c** 10^9 **d** 10^2

6 **a** $x = 2.9$ **b** $x = 3.7$

7 **b** The areas of object and image are the same.

9 **b** A' (⁻8, ⁻4), B' (⁻6, 4), C' (⁻2, 2), D' (0, ⁻2)

10 rotation

11 **a** 129   **b** 131   **c** 939

12 **a** 7   **b** 35   **13** 8

SKILLS BREAK 6

1 90 francs **2** 167 years **3** 23:00 **4** 12

5 a octagon **b** regular **6** 91

7 Gustave Eiffel, by 26 years **8** 11 hours

9 ten thousand one hundred tonnes **10 a** $2\frac{1}{2}$ million **b** 2500000

11 a 2188920 **b** 2189000 **c** 2 million

12 46 metres **13** £386 **15** West **16** North East

17 45° **18** 208 francs **19** 22 million **20** 700 steps

21 D, 16 centimetres **22 A** £465 **B** £386 **23** 2.8 francs

24 4 **25 a** 9:30 **b** $12\frac{1}{2}$ hours

26 320 tons (40 tons in each of these years: 1889, 1893, 1897, 1901, 1905, 1909, 1913, 1917)

27 a 5.1 **b** 4.7

STAGE 3 END POINTS

A1 £2.36 **A2** £15.45

B1 Examples are $\frac{8}{24}, \frac{4}{12}, \frac{2}{6}, \frac{1}{3}, \frac{32}{96}, \frac{48}{144}, \cdots$.

C1 a $\frac{5}{8}$ **b** $\frac{1}{3}$ **c** $\frac{9}{16}$ **d** $\frac{2}{5}$

D1 a 0.6 **b** 0.375 **c** 0.85 **d** 0.15

E1 a 40% **b** 37.5% **c** 35% **d** 22.5%

F1 a 13 weeks **b** 0.2 metres **c** 1 metre **d** 2.4 metres

G1 a 22

H1 a $a = 2$ **b** $s = 6$ **c** $p = 3$ **d** $t = ^-1$

I1 a $10x + 10 = 50$ or $x + 1 = 5$ **b** $x = 4$

J1 a 18 **b** 7 **c** 125 **d** 100

K1 a 13.2 **b** 13.25 **c** 13.249

L1 a $\frac{1}{6}$ **b** $\frac{3}{6} = \frac{1}{2}$ **c** $\frac{2}{6} = \frac{1}{3}$ **d** $\frac{5}{6}$

N1 a 7 metres **b** 3.8 cm or 38 mm

O1

Number	In standard form
645	6.45×10^2
1843	1.843×10^3
42.6	4.26×10
129 000	1.29×10^5
1756.4	1.7564×10^3

P1 7854600000000

Q1 a 10^{13} **b** 10^{18} **c** 9 **d** 3

R1 3.7 **T1** rotation of 180° about the point (0, 0)

U1 a 16 **b** 14 **c** 5

V1 Different answers are possible.

REVISION 3

1 a thirty thousand **b** three thousand **c** 3 million

2 68045, 60998, 59897, 3094, 975, 757, 44, 12

3 a fifty thousand and four
   b six hundred and ten thousand and one
   c thirteen million four thousand and two

4 a 60000060 **b** 45010 **c** 1000101

5

6 two

7 one (with a handle)

8 a 36 **b** 101 **c** 15839 **d** 57118
   e 848 **f** 18872 **g** 127 **h** 1681

9 a $\frac{8}{1000}$ **b** $\frac{8}{100}$ **c** $\frac{8}{10000}$

10 0.015, 0.06, 0.075, 0.3, 0.62, 1.02

11 a 55.564 **b** 850.682 **c** 33.363

13 264°, 304°, 299°

14 a $^-20$ **b** $^-7$ **c** 6 **d** $^-28$ **e** $^-23$ **f** 8
   g 25 **h** $^-45$ **i** $^-48$ **j** 63 **k** $^-5$ **l** 4

15 a $^-5, ^-4, ^-3, 0, 1, 2, 5$ **b** $^-12, ^-9, ^-3, ^-2, 0, 1, 11$

16 $(^-7, 6)$ and $(^-1, 6)$ or $(^-7, ^-6)$ and $(^-1, ^-6)$

17 a $25k + 16w$ **b** $9f - h$ **18 a** $36w + 4$ **b** $98 - 35k$

19 $60y + 4g$

20 a 41000 **b** 375000 **c** 6576000

21 a 800000 **b** 3100000 **c** 8000000

22 a 4000 **b** 3500 **c** 3600

25 a 20:47 **b** 15:35 **c** 11:15 **d** 19:25 **e** 03:15 **f** 15:36

26 4 hours 51 minutes

27 a 1019 **b** 2 hours 16 minutes

28 a 78.12 cm² **b** 102.12 cm² **c** 36.72 cm² **d** 59.16 cm²
   e 67.2 cm² **f** 63 cm²

29 $^-18$

30 a $y = 4$ **b** $h = 6$ **c** $g = 8$ **d** $f = 12$

31 a 222 **b** 81, 100, 121, 144 **c** 6

32 72, 48, and 16 **33** 1, 2, 3, 4, 6, 8, 9, 12, 18, 24, 36, 72

34 23, 29, 31, 37, 41, 43

36 a 2531.25 **b** 6.16 **c** 54.658 **d** 0.0000054

37 a 461.3 **b** 537.08 **c** 1039.15 **d** 2234.76

38 a £29.75 **b** £36.70 **c** £150.74 **d** £614.42

39 24 pence **40** £1.62 **41** £5.34

42 a £7.02 **b** £165.55 **c** £38.16 **d** £578.35

43

x	$\longrightarrow$	$3x - 5$
1	$\longrightarrow$	$^-2$
2	$\longrightarrow$	1
3	$\longrightarrow$	4
4	$\longrightarrow$	7
5	$\longrightarrow$	10
6	$\longrightarrow$	13

44 32

45 a 95° **b** 57° **c** 84° **d** 96° **e** 84° **f** 102°
   g 78° **h** 68° **i** 51° **j** 49° **k** 74°

46 a £13.80 **b** £10.35 **47** £17.13 **48** 10.5 km

49 $\frac{28}{35}, \frac{36}{45}, \frac{60}{75}$

50 a 0.625 **b** $\frac{1}{4}, \frac{3}{5}, \frac{5}{8}, 0.75, 0.8$

51 $\frac{15}{24}$ or $\frac{5}{8}$

52 a

Group	Frequency
1–5	3
6–10	5
11–15	4
16–20	8
21–25	7
26–30	4

b 16–20

53 a $y = 5$ **b** $w = ^-3$ **c** $x = 12$ **d** $w = 1.5$

54 a 31.8 cm **b** 32 cm **c** 44.28 cm² **d** 44.3 cm² **e** 48 cm²

55 38.06548, 38.07495

56 a $\frac{2}{6}$ or $\frac{1}{3}$ **b** $\frac{1}{6}$

57 a 1.576875×10^4 **b** 7.064054765×10^7

58 a 4.7304×10^8 **b** 473040000

59 a 10^9 **b** 10^6

60 a   **b** 40   **c** 39   **d** 40

Matches	Frequency
33	3
34	1
35	1
36	1
37	1
38	3
39	3
40	9
41	3
42	1
43	0
44	1
45	1

SECTION 32

Starting points

A1 a £10.50   **b** 135 kg   **c** £35 000   **d** 5625 km

B1 $\frac{16}{20}$ $\frac{76}{95}$

C1 a $\frac{3}{11}$ **b** $\frac{3}{7}$ **c** $\frac{2}{3}$ **d** $\frac{2}{9}$

Exercise 32.1

1 a 0.26   **b** 0.54   **c** 0.61   **d** 0.14   **e** 0.95

2 a 0.04   **b** 0.22   **c** 0.67   **d** 0.91   **e** 0.34
   f 0.08   **g** 0.88   **h** 0.09   **i** 0.07   **j** 0.99
   k 0.16   **l** 0.03   **m** 0.25   **n** 0.75   **o** 0.5

3 a 0.355   **b** 0.125   **c** 0.405   **d** 0.815   **e** 0.665   **f** 0.205
   g 0.065   **h** 0.175   **i** 0.075   **j** 0.035   **k** 0.015   **l** 0.995

Exercise 32.2

1 a 29%   **b** 96%   **c** 83%   **d** 77%   **e** 49%
   f 19%   **g** 33%   **h** 69%   **i** 11%   **j** 7%
   k 2%   **l** 9%   **m** 15%   **n** 41%   **o** 87%

2 a 16.5%   **b** 27.5%   **c** 6.5%   **d** 37.5%   **e** 62.5%
   f 87.5%   **g** 61.5%   **h** 10.5%   **i** 2.5%   **j** 8.5%
   k 30.5%   **l** 25.5%   **m** 50.5%   **n** 0.5%   **o** 4.5%

3

Percentage	72	57	$61\frac{1}{2}$	18	$13\frac{1}{2}$	$37\frac{1}{2}$	89
Decimal	**0.72**	0.57	**0.615**	**0.18**	0.135	**0.375**	0.89

4 0.04, $12\frac{1}{2}$%, 0.18, 27%, 37%, 0.38, 0.565, 65%, 0.72

Exercise 32.3

1 a 732 miles   **b** 28.5 km   **c** £357   **d** 404.4 kg
   e £1114.68   **f** 20.8 km   **g** £32 770.40   **h** 28.32 kg
   i £7.74   **j** £5.41   **k** 144.4 km   **l** £1.37

2 a 168.75 km   **b** 81.7 kg   **c** £12.40   **d** £194.43
   e 2.73 miles   **f** £54.60   **g** £13.72   **h** 911.45 km
   i £5.06   **j** 4560 000   **k** 7.05 miles   **l** 6p

3 312 500   **4** £264.61   **5** 13p

Exercise 32.4

1 617   **2** 152 550

3 Wood, 564   Glass, 1692   Porcelain, 1504

4 a 1152   **b** 6528

5

Type of complaint	Number
Fares	140
Late running	175
Overcrowding	70
Cancelled	280
Dirty buses	35
Driving too fast	105
Dirty bus shelters	70

6 197 grams

7 a 196   **b** 14   **c** no (70)   **d** 210   **e** 12.5%   **f** 70

8 a 1575   **b** 6720   **c** 3255
   d unreasonable journalistic rounding (9450)

9 a 11 832   **b** yes (9918)   **c** 5742   **d** 21% 7308 trees

10 a 9072   **b** 8635

   c

Bottle bank	Colour of glass			No. of bottles
	Green	**Brown**	**Clear**	
West End car park	**9072**	**4788**	**2940**	16 800
Market Square	**10 692**	**8991**	**4617**	24 300
Station Car Park	**12 089**	**10 676**	**8635**	31 400
Recycling Centre	**46 562**	**17 273**	**11 265**	75 100
Total no. of bottles	**78 415**	**41 728**	**27 457**	**147 600**

Exercise 32.5

1 a 50%   **b** 25%   **c** 75%   **d** 25%

2 50%   **3** 25%   **4** 50%   **5** 75%

Exercise 32.6

1 a 44.4%   **b** 65%   **c** 29.2%   **d** 46.2%   **e** 80%
   f 41.7%   **g** 40%   **h** 64%   **i** 18.8%   **j** 30%

Exercise 32.7

1 69.1%   **2** 59.5%   **3** 36.4%   **4** 14%   **5** 45%

6 yes (French, 78.7%   Italian, 12.3%)

SECTION 33

Starting points

A1 21, 53, 87, 105   **A2** 50

B2 36   **B3** One example is 9, 25, 49, 81.   **B4** 1, 3, 6, 10, 15, 21

C1 64   **C2** 4, 16, 64, 256

D1 21, 34, 55   **D2** 29, 47, 76   **E1** 9   **E2** 20

Exercise 33.1

1 13   **2 b** 16

3 a

Pattern no.	1	2	3
No. of matches	6	11	16

   b 5   **d** 26

4 a

Pattern no.	1	2	3	4
No. of matches	4	8	12	16

   b It goes up by 4 each time.   **d** 20   **e** 24   **g** 80

Exercise 33.2

1 $(3 \times 5) - 1 = 15 - 1 = 14$

2 17, 20   **3** 68, 125   **4** 1296, 7776

5 a 11   **b** 21   **c** 87

6 Add 5.   **7** 12, 17   **8** 512, 256, 128, 64, 32, 16, 8, 4, 2, 1

Exercise 33.3

1 31

2 a $1 + (2 \times 2)$ **b** $1 + (2 \times 3)$ **c** $1 + (2 \times 10)$
   d 21   **e** $1 + 2n$

3 a 4   **b** $1 + (4 \times 2)$ **c** $1 + 4n$ **d** 81

4 a $3 + 2n$ (or $2n + 3$)   **b** 43

Exercise 33.4

1 a 28   **b** 64   **c** 304

2 a 2   **b** 2   **c** 1   **d** $2n + 1$

3 a $4n + 2$ **b** $6n + 3$ **c** $3n - 1$ **d** $4n - 2$
   e $5n - 4$ **f** $3n + 2$

SECTION 34

Starting points

B1 52 cm²   **B2** 14 cm²

Exercise 34.1

1 a 3 cm by 4 cm   **b** 2 cm by 4 cm   **c** 3 cm by 2 cm

3 b is not the net of a cuboid: the side faces are not deep enough.

4 $6 + 6 + 8 + 8 + 12 + 12 = 52$ cm²

5 He has only used three faces. The true answer is 32 cm².   **6** 46 cm²

Exercise 34.2

1 a 3   **b** 8 cm by 3 cm, 8 cm by 5 cm, 8 cm by 4 cm
   d 6 cm²   **e** $6 + 6 + 24 + 40 + 32 = 108$ cm²

3 B is a net of a triangular prism.

Exercise 34.3

1 b 10 cm²   **c** 56 cm²   **2 a** 4   **b** tetrahedron

SECTION 35

Starting points

A1 a $\frac{1}{10}$ **b** $\frac{3}{10}$ **c** $\frac{5}{10} = \frac{1}{2}$ (with 0 counting as an even number)
   d $\frac{5}{10} = \frac{1}{2}$

A2 $\frac{4}{6} = \frac{2}{3}$ **A3** $\frac{8}{12} = \frac{2}{3}$

Exercise 35.1

1 a $\frac{18}{52} = \frac{9}{26}$ **b** 0.35   **2** $\frac{3}{26}$ **3** 0.25   **4** black

Exercise 35.2

1 a BR, BF, BM, VR, VF, VM, PR, PF, PM, LR, LF, LM, CR, CF, CM
   b 15   **c** VR, VF, VM, CR, CF, CM

2 ✗▲ ✗+ ✗◆ ✗▼ ✗■ ▲+ ▲◆ ▲▼ ▲■ +◆ +▼ +■ ◆▼ ◆■ ▼■

3 WG, WR, WY, WB, GG, GR, GY, GB, RR, RY, RB, YY, YB, BB

4 a RVS, RVT, RVK, VST, VSK, SRT, SRK, TKS, TKV, TKR
   b 10   **c** 4

Exercise 35.3

1 no. of colours × no. of numbers = no. of outcomes

2 a

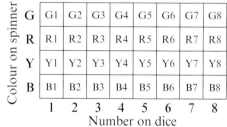

   b 16   **c** 8

3 a

	1	2	3	4	5	6
Heads	H1	H2	H3	H4	H5	H6
Tails	T1	T2	T3	T4	T5	T6

Number on dice

   b 12

Exercise 35.4

1 a $\frac{5}{49}$ **b** $\frac{6}{49}$ **c** $\frac{13}{49}$

2 c $\frac{12}{36} = \frac{1}{3}$ **3 b** $\frac{15}{36} = \frac{5}{12}$

4 b $\frac{1}{5}$ **c** $\frac{4}{5}$ **d** 1

5 b $\frac{5}{30} = \frac{1}{6}$ (AT, TO, ME, BE, SO)

---

6 b $\frac{1}{24}$ **c** $\frac{4}{24} = \frac{1}{6}$ **d** $\frac{4}{24} = \frac{1}{6}$ **e** $\frac{4}{24} = \frac{1}{6}$

SECTION 36

Starting points

A1 a 65°   **b** 125°

B1 a 140° **b** 41° **c** 30° **d** 150° **e** 140° **f** 140° **g** 40° **h** 40°

C1 120°

Exercise 36.1

3 b 108°

Exercise 36.2

1 a 6   **b** 60°

2 a parallelogram **b** 90°   **c** 360°   **d** 45°

3 135°

4 a 128°, angles on a straight line   **b** 52°, corresponding angles
   c 52°, alternate angles   **d** 52°, vertically opposite angles
   e 52°, alternate angles   **f** 128°, angles on a straight line

5 b 85°   **7 c** All triangles will tessellate.

Exercise 36.3

1 C and E   **2** Q and U   **3** C and T, I and W, Q and Y

REVIEW 4A

1 a 0.28   **b** 35%   **2** £31   **3** 60%

4 a 2 matches are added.   **b** 17 matches

5 22, 27, 32   **6 b** 42 cm²   **7** $\frac{8}{42} = \frac{4}{21}$

8 ●▲ ●▼ ●♣ ●♠   ◆▲ ◆▼ ◆♣ ◆♠   ▼▲ ▼▼ ♣▲ ♣▼

9 b $\frac{2}{10} = \frac{1}{5}$ **11 a** 110°   **b** 70°

SKILLS BREAK 7

1 c 1   **2 a** 10.4 cm   **b** 6.76 cm²

3 9 am   **4** £48

5 a 8 pm   **b** 20:00   **6 a** £188   **b** 14 hours

7 a green   **b** blue   **c** yellow

8 a by car
   b You pay for fuel and do not need transport from station or airport.

9 £405   **10** £538 (which is £269 × 2)

11 a Jason only   **b** yellow   **c** £0
   d £299 × 2 = £598   **e** £598

12 a 20 miles   **b** 32 km

13 a 6 pm   **b** 8 hours   **c** 3 hours more

14 a £774   **b** £336   **c** £1110

15 £521 (£456 + £65)

16 1 adults, £299   3 children, £168   Total cost, £467

SECTION 37

Starting points

A1 a 5.5 cm   **b** 80 km   **c** 5000 kg   **d** 560 cm   **e** 14 200 g

B1 a 32 yards   **b** 62 inches   **c** 2880 minutes   **d** 89 pounds
   e 5280 ft   **f** 1920 pints   **g** 30 gallons

C1 a 12.8 km   **b** 5 miles   **c** 33 pounds **d** 5 ft   **e** 6 gallons

Exercise 37.1

1 1.8 metres   **2 a** Mandy   **b** by 10 pounds (or about 4.5 kg)

3 a 32 oz   **b** 4 oz

4 a 84 lb   **b** below allowance (total ≈ 38 kg)   **5** 8400 boxes

Exercise 37.2

1 Macao

2 France has a larger land area (more than twice as much as the UK)

3 130 people   **4** 3 km²

5 a 1 170 000   **b** 129 410 000   **c** 10 500

6 a 30 boxes per hour   **b** 28 boxes per hour
  c Mark, 960 boxes   Amy, 1200 boxes   Afzal, 1120 boxes

7 a 119 pounds   **b** 54.1 kg (to 1 dp)   **c** about 27 kg/cm²

8 a 168 cm   **b** 1 cm   **c** 60 mph   **d** 1440 miles

9 a 5.5 pence/litre   **b** £3.30

Exercise 37.3

1 2400 pesetas   **2** £17 (to the nearest pound)

3 a 1000 pesetas   **b** 2800 pesetas   **c** 4300 pesetas
  d about £15   **e** £6   **f** £19

4 a 4800 pesetas   **b** 240 pesetas   **d** method **b**

5 24 000 pesetas   **6** about £27

Exercise 37.4

1 Mix together: 225 g of flour, 112 g of sugar, 82 g of nuts, 40 g of butter.

2 5 oz   **3** 9 oz   **4** 6 blocks   **5** 40 mpg

6 15 litres/100 km

7 14 mpg: this is not economical; it is a 'gas-guzzler'!

8 8.5 litres/100 km

SECTION 38

Starting points

A1 a 17:45   **b** 06:46   **c** 21:35   **d** 03:34   **e** 12:40   **f** 00:40

B1 a 2 hours   30 minutes
   b 6 hours   45 minutes
   c 7 hours   35 minutes

C1 4.35 pm   **C2** 35 minutes

C3 a 18:40   **b** 4 hours 15 minutes

Exercise 38.1

1 215 miles

2 a 12.5 metres   **b** 18.75 metres   **c** 30 metres   **d** 53.75 metres

3

Constant speed	Time travelled	Distance travelled
38 mph	7 hours	**266** miles
86 kph	9 hours	**774** km
14 m/s	15 seconds	**210** metres
12.5 m/s	35 seconds	**437.5** metres
$8\frac{1}{2}$ m/s	21.5 seconds	**182.75** metres
31 mm/s	55 seconds	**1705** mm
52.5 mph	4 hours	**210** miles
0.5 m/s	17 seconds	**8.5** metres
25.4 mph	6 hours	**152.4** miles
38.6 mph	5.5 hours	**212.3** miles

Exercise 38.2

1 a 1284 km   **b** 10 272 km   **c** 2354 km   **d** 5350 km
  e 6420 km   **f** 214 km   **g** 642 km

2 a 336 miles   **b** 546 miles   **c** 42 miles   **d** 798 miles
  e 21 miles   **f** 273 miles   **g** 63 miles

3 a 1860 miles   **b** 3100 miles   **c** 930 miles   **d** 1550 miles
  e 155 miles   **f** 310 miles   **g** 465 miles   **h** 2015 miles
  i 2945 miles   **j** 2325 miles

4 a 2700 miles   **b** 4050 miles   **c** 2025 miles   **d** 3375 miles
  e 675 miles   **f** 337.5 miles   **g** 4387.5 miles

5 4350 mm

Exercise 38.3

1

Distance travelled	Journey time	Average speed
400 miles	9 hours	**44.4 mph**
260 miles	7 hours	**37.1 mph**
585 km	8 hours	**73.1 kph**
46 metres	2.5 seconds	**18.4 m/s**
125 metres	10.5 seconds	**11.9 m/s**
455 km	8.5 hours	**53.5 kph**
16.6 miles	0.25 hours	**66.4 mph**
0.8 metres	0.5 seconds	**0.4 m/s**
118 miles	3.75 hours	**31.5 mph**
1050 miles	1.75 hours	**600 mph**

2 a more than one mile per minute   **b** 1.7 miles per minute

3 1.4 miles per minute

Exercise 38.4

1 a 0.40   **b** 0.30   **c** 0.23   **d** 0.47   **e** 0.12
  f 0.08   **g** 0.17   **h** 0.58   **i** 0.42   **j** 0.53
  k 0.80   **l** 0.20   **m** 0.93   **n** 0.10

2 a 44   **b** 13   **c** 29   **d** 21   **e** 10
  f 22   **g** 54   **h** 34   **i** 16   **j** 51
  k 55   **l** 8   **m** 10   **n** 5

Exercise 38.5

1 4 hours 41 minutes   **2** 4 hours 23 minutes

3

Distance	Average speed	Time taken (nearest minute)
420 km	70 kph	**6 hours**
585 miles	130 mph	**4 hours 30 minutes**
76 miles	32 mph	**2 hours 23 minutes**
344 km	66 kph	**5 hours 13 minutes**
3763 km	142 kph	**26 hours 30 minutes**
550 km	88 kph	**6 hours 15 minutes**
414 miles	72 mph	**5 hours 45 minutes**
294 miles	46 mph	**6 hours 23 minutes**
729 km	108 kph	**6 hours 45 minutes**
256.15 km	27.25 kph	**9 hours 24 minutes**

Exercise 38.6

1 a 1 hour 15 minutes   **b** 1.25   **c** 32 mph

2 a 4.75 hours   **b** 52 mph   **c** 6 hours 11 minutes

3 a 6 hours 30 minutes   **b** 90.8 kph

4 a 160 miles   **b** London (398 is approx. 400)   **c** 56.5 mph

5 20:25

6 4 hours 41 minutes.

SECTION 39

Starting points

A1 a $\frac{4}{9}$ **b** $\frac{7}{9}$ **c** $\frac{2}{3}$ **d** $\frac{5}{12}$ **e** $\frac{3}{8}$ **f** $\frac{4}{9}$

B1 a 0.875   **b** 0.75   **c** 0.8   **d** 0.6   **e** 0.25   **f** 0.125

C1 a 64%   **b** 62.5%   **c** 62.5%   **d** 87.5%   **e** 37.5%   **f** 80%

Exercise 39.1

1 a $\frac{16}{25}$ **b** $\frac{18}{25}$ **c** $\frac{19}{50}$ **d** $\frac{22}{25}$ **e** $\frac{9}{10}$
  f $\frac{3}{10}$ **g** $\frac{3}{20}$ **h** $\frac{9}{50}$ **i** $\frac{11}{20}$ **j** $\frac{8}{25}$
  k $\frac{9}{20}$ **l** $\frac{2}{25}$ **m** $\frac{1}{20}$ **n** $\frac{11}{25}$ **o** $\frac{61}{100}$

2 56%

3

CJ Supplies	Summer sale reductions	
Item	% off	Fraction off
Bath towels	20%	$\frac{1}{5}$
Hand towels	30%	$\frac{3}{10}$
Flannels	12% .	$\frac{3}{25}$
Sheets	16%	$\frac{4}{25}$
Tea towels	24%	$\frac{6}{25}$

Exercise 39.2

1 a $\frac{7}{9}$ **b** $\frac{1}{2}$ **c** $\frac{3}{4}$ **d** $\frac{4}{5}$ **e** $1\frac{1}{3}$ **f** $1\frac{1}{4}$ **g** $1\frac{3}{5}$ **h** $1\frac{1}{2}$
 i $1\frac{1}{3}$ **j** $1\frac{1}{4}$ **k** $1\frac{1}{5}$ **l** $\frac{2}{3}$ **m** $1\frac{1}{3}$ **n** $1\frac{1}{2}$ **o** $1\frac{5}{16}$

2 a, b, c

Exercise 39.3

1 a $1\frac{1}{8}$ **b** $\frac{7}{8}$ **c** $1\frac{5}{8}$ **d** $\frac{7}{8}$ **e** $1\frac{1}{6}$ **f** $1\frac{1}{3}$
 g $1\frac{1}{6}$ **h** $\frac{2}{3}$ **i** $\frac{11}{16}$ **j** $\frac{13}{16}$ **k** $1\frac{1}{16}$ **l** $1\frac{7}{16}$

2 a $1\frac{3}{10}$ **b** $\frac{1}{2}$ **c** $1\frac{1}{2}$ **d** $1\frac{3}{10}$

3 a $1\frac{1}{16}$ **b** $\frac{11}{16}$ **c** $1\frac{5}{16}$ **d** $\frac{7}{16}$

4 a $\frac{7}{12}$ **b** $1\frac{5}{12}$ **c** $1\frac{3}{20}$ **d** $1\frac{1}{20}$ **e** $1\frac{7}{20}$ **f** $1\frac{2}{15}$
 g $1\frac{1}{15}$ **h** $\frac{9}{20}$ **i** $\frac{8}{15}$ **j** $1\frac{4}{15}$ **k** $1\frac{4}{15}$ **l** $1\frac{2}{15}$

Exercise 39.4

1 a $\frac{3}{8}$ **b** $\frac{1}{2}$ **c** $\frac{3}{5}$ **d** $\frac{1}{8}$ **e** $\frac{3}{8}$ **f** $\frac{1}{5}$ **g** $\frac{1}{3}$ **h** $\frac{1}{6}$
2 a $\frac{3}{4}$ **b** $\frac{1}{2}$ **c** $\frac{4}{5}$ **d** $1\frac{1}{2}$ **e** $2\frac{1}{2}$ **f** $\frac{3}{4}$ **g** $1\frac{2}{5}$ **h** $2\frac{4}{5}$
3 a $\frac{3}{16}$ **b** $\frac{3}{8}$ **c** $\frac{1}{10}$ **d** $\frac{7}{16}$

Section 40

Starting points

A1 a 93.44 cm² **b** 69 cm² **c** 83.3 cm²

B1 a 31 cm² **b** 74.25 cm² **c** 84.7 cm²

C1 A bucket has a **capacity** of 15 litres.
I didn't fill it. I just put a **volume** of 12 litres in the bucket.

C2 not quite: an extra 5 ml needed to fill the bottle **C3** 150 litres

Exercise 40.1

1 a 990 cm³ **b** 1864.8 cm³ **c** 11 136 mm³ **d** 20.2 cm³
 e 1201 200 mm³ **f** 3196.8 cm³ **g** 17.2 cm³ **h** 58 080 mm³

Exercise 40.2

1 a 15 360 mm³ **c** 64 mm by 80 mm by 36 mm
2 a 10 cm **b** 0.432 m³ **c** £28.08
3 a 4 × 4 × 1.5 = 24 **c** yes (4.2 × 1.8 × 3.2 = 24.192)
4 a 544 cm³ **b** It does not have a capacity of 550 ml.
5 a 75 mm **b** 6.5 cm by 4.5 cm by 7.5 cm **c** 219.375 cm³
6 a 0.8 metres **b** 2.8 m³

Exercise 40.3

1 a 595 mm³ **b** 742.5 cm³ **c** 8.4 mm³ **d** 143 cm³
 e 675 mm³ **f** 1584.1 cm³ **g** 45.5 cm³ **h** 732.6 cm³

Section 41

Starting points

A1 a 16 000 **b** 2000 **c** 1000
A2 a 5700 **b** 7000 **c** 1000
B1 a 1800 **b** 1400 **c** 3000 **d** 3000 **e** 900 **f** 3200
C1 a 28 **b** 134 **c** 7 **d** 12 **e** 257 **f** 800
D1 a 34.6 **b** 138.09 **c** 0.067 **d** 5.6006

Exercise 41.1

1 a 110 cm² **b** 118 cm² **2 a** 247 cm² **b** 237 cm²
3 a 102 cm² **b** 101 cm²
4 a 84 cm² **b** 94 cm² (approx.)
5 a 164.16 cm³ **b** 164.2 cm³ **c** 6 cm, 6 cm, 5 cm

d 180 cm³ **e** b (164.2 cm³)

Exercise 41.2

1 a 24.4816 cm² **b** 5.7 m, 4.3 m **c** 24.51 cm² **d** 0.0284 cm²
2 a 12.4 m, 3.4 m **b** area, 42.16 m² perimeter, 31.6 m
 c area, 42.5872 m² perimeter, 31.64 m
 d 0.4272 m² **e** 0.04 m
3 a 4 m, 3, m **b** 3.7 m, 2.8 m **c** 10.293 m² **d** 0.067 m²
4 a The longest the two measurements could have been is 5.4 m and 3.4 m.
 b 18.36 m² **c** 4.5 m. 2.5 m **d** 11.25 m²
5 a rounded to nearest whole number **b** 0.04 m²
6 a no **b** The area of the wall is 15.6 m².
   So the approximation created an error of 1.6 m².
7 a Rounding some numbers up and some numbers down could give
   a total of just less than that required or just more than that required.
 b Rounding 38 to 40 and 28 to 30 gives: 40 + 30 + 30 + 42 = 142.
   Deduct 4 for entrance: 142 – 4 = 138.
 c Measurements are rounded up.

Section 42

Starting points

A1 7 square units **A2** 30.5 cm

B1 a 35.04 cm² **b** 47.45 cm² **c** 107.3 cm² **d** 520 mm² **B2** 6.8 cm

C1 a 55.3 cm² **b** 39.975 cm² **c** 5.25 cm² **d** 255 mm² **C2** 19 cm

Exercise 42.1

1 a 99.3 cm² **b** 115.5 cm² **c** 97.4 cm² **d** 3308 mm² **e** 253 cm²
2 a 1059.25 cm² **b** 965.58 cm² **c** 960.36 cm²
 d 1784.45 cm² **e** 1104.43 cm² **f** 536.625 cm²
 g 639.6 cm² **h** 584.91 cm² **i** 935.175 cm²

Exercise 42.2

1 a 53 cm **b** 42 cm **c** 56.2 cm
 d 85.4 cm **e** 102.7 cm **f** 750 mm

Exercise 42.3

1 a 42.87 m² **b** £291.52 **c** 30.9 m **d** £216
2 b 28.34 m² **c** £343 **d** £25
3 a 8.95 m² **b** 13.8 m **c** 12.2 m

Exercise 42.4

1 a 3476.28 cm³ **b** 868 400 mm³

Review 4b

1 a Kim **b** by about 3 lb **2** 1368 092 people
3 a £16.60 to £16.70 **b** 1560 pesetas
 c 10200 **d** the one in York (because it cost only 6238 pesetas)
4 348 km **5 a** 2840 miles **b** 1988 miles **c** 142 miles
6 38 mph **7** 56.5 mph
8 a 0.58 **b** 0.92 **c** 0.15
9 a 33 min **b** 14 min **c** 23 min
10 a 2.51 h **b** 2 h 30 min
11 a $\frac{14}{25}$ **b** $\frac{6}{25}$ **c** $\frac{17}{20}$ **d** $\frac{2}{25}$ **e** $\frac{1}{20}$
12 a $1\frac{1}{4}$ **b** $\frac{2}{3}$ **c** $1\frac{1}{8}$
13 a $1\frac{3}{8}$ **b** $1\frac{11}{30}$ **c** $1\frac{19}{40}$
14 a $\frac{1}{2}$ **b** $\frac{1}{6}$ **c** $\frac{1}{4}$ **d** $\frac{7}{8}$ **e** $1\frac{9}{10}$ **f** $2\frac{11}{20}$
15 a 569.4 cm³ **b** 457.7 cm³ **c** 1216 mm³
16 a 215 cm³ **b** 245.1 cm³
17 a 67.08 cm² **b** length 16 cm, width 4 cm **c** 64 cm² **d** 3.08 cm²
18 a 196.0875 m² **b** 196.09 m² **c** 196 m²
 d 15.8 m, 12.5 m **e** 197.5 m² **f** 1.4125 m²
19 2400

SKILLS BREAK 8

1 a 45 minutes **b** 0.75 hours **2** 16 mph

3 a 24 mph **b** 13 mph **4 a** 16 minutes **b** 08 05

5 20 minutes **6** They have the same journey time.

7 36 minutes **8** 22 875 **9** 4575 **10** 5124

11 £7 320 000 **12** no (because the amount is less than £7.5 million)

13 371.25 cm² **14** 121 000 pesetas **15** 148 days

16 370 hours **17** 12.24 m³

18 roughly 110 (actually 111.27...) **19** 1500 kg

20 b 21–25 **c** 21.5 minutes **d** 20.5 minutes

21 yes (£109 800) **22 a** 450 **b** 54 minutes

23 a 1288 **b** £489.50 **c** 2320 (2318.4) **d** 6500 (6491.52)

24 half a minute

STAGE 4 END POINTS

A1 a 0.58 **b** 0.74 **c** 0.07 **d** 0.125 **e** 0.625

B1 a 31% **b** 9% **c** 13.5% **d** 6.5% **e** 10.5% **f** 1%

C1 a £5600 **b** 5.04 km **c** 693 miles

D1 a 16% **b** 1.25% **c** 87.3% **d** 60%

E1 a 21 **b** 41 **c** 81 (from the rule 5n + 1)

F1 a 3, 11, 19, 27, 35, 43 **b** 267

F2 a 16, 20, 24, 28, 32 **b** 312 **G1** 5n + 1

H1 a 3n − 2 **b** 5n + 1 **c** 3n + 6

K1 tea, 0.11 coffee, 0.25 milk, 0.05 cola, 0.49
orange juice, 0.02 none, 0.07

L1 TC, TM, TCo, TO, TN, CM, CCo, CO, CN, MCo, MO, MN, CoO, CoN, ON

M2 0.25

O1 There is no difference: 56 lb and 25 kg can be regarded as equivalent.

P1 13.75 kg/cm²

Q1 a 2520 pesetas **b** £15 **c** £37.50

R1 a 1100 miles **b** 893.75 miles **c** 1512.5 miles
d 206.25 miles **e** 68.75 miles **f** 27.5 miles

S1 68 kph **S2** 22.5 kph

T1 a 0.9 **b** 0.6 **c** 0.1 **d** 0.2

T2 a 22 min **b** 53 min **c** 34 min **d** 7 min **e** 5 min **f** 36 min

U1 5 hours **U2** 2 h 15 min

V1 a $\frac{17}{20}$ **b** $\frac{7}{50}$ **c** $\frac{9}{25}$ **d** $\frac{37}{50}$ **e** $\frac{1}{50}$ **f** $\frac{9}{50}$

W1 a $\frac{7}{8}$ **b** $1\frac{2}{5}$ **c** $1\frac{1}{2}$ **d** $1\frac{2}{9}$ **e** $1\frac{2}{5}$ **f** $1\frac{3}{5}$

X1 a $1\frac{1}{6}$ **b** $1\frac{13}{24}$ **c** $\frac{5}{6}$ **d** $1\frac{1}{6}$ **e** $\frac{11}{16}$ **f** $\frac{7}{10}$ **g** $1\frac{7}{20}$ **h** $1\frac{3}{8}$

Y1 a $\frac{1}{6}$ **b** $\frac{7}{20}$ **c** $\frac{7}{8}$ **d** $1\frac{15}{16}$

Z1 a 1832.8 cm² **b** 30 492 mm² **c** 75.2 cm²

AA1 a 138.6 cm² **b** 128.52 cm² **c** 226.1 cm²

BB1 a 110 cm² **b** 103.2 cm² **c** 141.2 cm²

CC1 shape **b**, 44.5 cm shape **c**, 55.8 cm

CC2 a 68 cm **b** 6256 cm²

REVISION 4

1 a 5000 **b** 50 000 **c** 500 000 000

2 123, 394, 1975, 4009, 7507, 8045, 58 997, 60 008

3 a sixty-one thousand and seven
b three hundred and ninety thousand and four
c twenty-five million six thousand and one

4 a 3 000 003 **b** 50 005 **c** 100 000 101

5 A K D E H **6** two **7** one

8 a 35 **b** 98 **c** 26 311 **d** 84 039
e 1080 **f** 18 872 **g** 134 **h** 3425

9 a $\frac{9}{100}$ **b** $\frac{9}{1000}$ **c** $\frac{9}{10\,000}$ **10** 0.034, 0.05, 0.059, 0.175, 0.2, 1.001

11 a 66.333 **b** 635.0902 **c** 6.235 **13** 55°, 34°, 29°

14 a ⁻22 **b** ⁻6 **c** 9 **d** ⁻27 **e** ⁻32 **f** 17
g 39 **h** ⁻56 **i** ⁻64 **j** 28 **k** ⁻4 **l** 3

15 a ⁻11, ⁻7, ⁻4, 1, 2, 3, 4 **b** ⁻9, ⁻8, ⁻5, ⁻2, 0, 1, 4, 6

16 (⁻3, 3) and (⁻1, 3) or (⁻3, 7) and (⁻1, 7)

17 a 37k + 23w **b** 12f − 10h **18 a** 35w + 30 **b** 120 − 48k

19 39y − 13g − 66

20 a 38 000 **b** 568 000 **c** 8 383 000

21 a 600 000 **b** 5 300 000 **c** 6 000 000

22 a 2100 **b** 2700 **c** 3500

25 a 18:07 **b** 14:45 **c** 12:25 **d** 20:35 **e** 02:25 **f** 16:06

26 5 hours 8 minutes

27 a 21:59 **b** 56 minutes

28 a 124.1 cm² **b** 63.92 cm² **c** 46.08 cm²
d 70.84 cm² **e** 97.2 cm² **f** 104.5 cm²

29 t = 9

30 a y = 7 **b** h = 3 **c** g = 7 **d** f = 5

31 a 592 **b** 64, 81, 100, 121, 144 **c** 9

32 84, 35, 28, 42

33 1, 2, 3, 4, 5, 6, 10, 12, 15, 20, 30, 60

34 41, 43, 47, 53, 59

36 a 66 302.7 **b** 534 **c** 30.016 **d** 0.001 062

37 a 403.7 **b** 858.06 **c** 2043.9 **d** 1097.34

38 a £34.38 **b** £236.06 **c** £74.72 **d** £1535.23

39 34p **40** £2.29 **41** £16.95

42 a £4.56 **b** £171.40 **c** £154.09 **d** £389.61

43 x ⟶ y
1 ⟶ ⁻5
2 ⟶ ⁻3
3 ⟶ ⁻1
4 ⟶ 1
5 ⟶ 3

44 ⁻15

45 a 109° **b** 47° **c** 79° **d** 101° **e** 79° **f** 99°
g 81° **h** 59° **i** 43° **j** 52° **k** 84°

46 a £14.60 **b** £10.95 **47** £46.89 **48** 12 km

49 $\frac{28}{112}, \frac{36}{144}$ **50 a** 0.125 **b** 0.65, 0.7, $\frac{3}{4}, \frac{4}{5}, \frac{7}{8}$

51 $\frac{20}{24}$ or $\frac{5}{6}$

52 a

Group	Frequency
1–5	2
6–10	9
11–15	5
16–20	4
21–25	7
26–30	4

b 6–10

53 a y = 5 **b** w = ⁻2 **c** x = 14 **d** w = 9

54 a 38 cm **b** 38 **c** 73.44 cm² **d** 73.0 cm² **e** 70 cm²

55 57.053 99, 57.054 95 **56** **a** $\frac{4}{6}$ or $\frac{2}{3}$ **b** $\frac{4}{6}$ or $\frac{2}{3}$

57 a 3.204 66 × 10³ **b** 6.573 007 55 × 10⁶

58 a 2.8382 × 10⁸ **b** 283 820 000

59 a 10⁸ **b** 10⁷

60 a

Number	Frequency
34	2
35	1
36	4
37	2
38	1
39	2
40	10
41	0
42	2
43	1
44	1
45	1

b 40   **c** 39   **d** 40

63 a 136   **b** 16

65 a 0.65   **b** 0.12   **c** 0.04   **d** 0.01

66 a 0.155   **b** 0.305   **c** 0.005

67 a 66%   **b** 7%   **c** 2%   **d** 14.5%
e 58.5%   **f** 6.5%   **g** 1.5%   **h** 87.5%

68 a £765   **b** 247 kg   **c** £20.25
d 21 900   **e** 10.8 miles   **f** £300

69 a 68.75%   **b** 24%   **c** 9%

70 19, 23, 27, 31   **71** 2, 7, 12, 17, 22

76 a $\frac{15}{95}$ or 0.158   **b** M   **c** L, 0.42   XL, 0.19

77 CS, CW, CD, CA, SW, SD, SA, WD, WA, DA

78 c $\frac{15}{36} = \frac{5}{12}$ **80** 570 km

81 a 192 km   **b** 128 km   **c** 64 km   **82** 70.4 mph

83 a $\frac{11}{25}$ **b** $\frac{18}{25}$ **c** $\frac{21}{25}$ **d** $\frac{4}{25}$ **e** $\frac{1}{25}$

84 a $1\frac{1}{3}$ **b** $\frac{3}{8}$ **c** $\frac{5}{12}$

85 a 226.5 cm³   **b** 29631 mm³   **c** 170.24 cm³

87 a 115.2 cm³   **b** 258.3 cm³   **c** 3200 cm³

88 area = 42 340.788 m²
42 525 m², rounding to nearest whole no. at start
42 359.56 m², rounding to 1 dp at start
40 000 m², rounding to nearest hundred at start

SECTION 43

Starting points
A2 108°

Exercise 43.1

1

Boat	Bearing
Viking	**050°**
Freelander	**150°**
Daisy Rue	**204°**
Marlene	**260°**
Seasprite	**334°**

2

Compass bearing	Three-figure bearing
North	000°
North East	**045°**
East	**090°**
South East	**135°**
South	**180°**
South West	225°
West	**270°**
North West	**315°**

3 057° (within 2 degrees)   **4** 102°   **5** 140°
6 238°   **7 a** 318°   **b** 280°

Exercise 43.2

2

Ship	Bearing	Distance
A	**210°**	**6 km**
B	**100°**	**3 km**
C	**255°**	**8 km**
D	**120°**	**7 km**
E	**025°**	**9 km**
F	**325°**	**7 km**

3 c 8 km

Exercise 43.3

2 a

	Bearing	Distance
Leg 1	**145°**	**40 km**
Leg 2	**090°**	**30 km**
Leg 3	**045°**	**50 km**

b 89 km

3 c Cook Island   **4 c** Sole Island

SECTION 44

Starting points
A1 a 0.34   **b** 0.65   **c** 0.04   **d** 0.06   **e** 0.055
f 0.01   **g** 0.125   **h** 0.555   **i** 0.005

B1 a £12 250   **b** £105   **c** 18.4 tonnes **d** 1.65 km   **e** £18 200

C1 a £45.69   **b** £1.30   **c** £0.07   **d** £4.01   **e** £52.13   **f** £0.11

Exercise 44.1

1 a £29.92   **b** £60.48   **c** £203.04   **d** £368.28   **e** £12.96

2 a £90.10   **b** £6.36   **c** £872.38   **d** £10070   **e** £18.02

3 a 517.5 miles **b** 138 kg   **c** 7360 km   **d** 437 cm²   **e** 184 g

4 a £19.44   **b** 3159 km   **c** £22477.5   **d** 2.43 kg   **e** 364.5 g

5 a £63.67   **b** £297.20   **c** £450.95   **d** £545.17   **e** £17.62
f £1.81   **g** £4282.55   **h** £3577.17

6 a £96.26   **b** £102.40 **c** £580.24 **d** £21.49   **e** £12.80   **f** £12.69

Exercise 44.2

1 28 931   **2** 14 287 or 14 288 (14 287.5)   **3** 26 870

4 £392.38   **5** £82.08   **6** 4954 litres (4953.78)

7 20 892 (20 892.48)

Exercise 44.3

1 a £32.67   **b** £55.45   **c** £431.05   **d** £127.83   **e** £7.04

2 a £64.22   **b** £18.57   **c** £64.17   **d** £108.98   **e** £5.31

3 a £2.75   **b** £293.66   **c** £590.54   **d** £8.96   **e** £5.07

4 a 81 kg   **b** 404 lb   **c** 26 km   **d** 16 metres   **e** 51 mm

5 a £55.99   **b** £291.50   **c** £3.27   **d** £506.57   **e** £2443
  f £2766.38   **g** £1.85   **h** 84p

6 a £5.59   **b** £311.49   **c** £3.69   **d** £468.62
  e £4.01   **f** £565.20

Exercise 44.4

1 15   **2** 154 or 155 (154.16)

3 a £3795.25   **b** £199.75   **4** 3202 500

Exercise 44.5

1 a £21.15   **b** £57.28   **c** £229.13   **d** £14.69   **e** £1
  f £534.63   **g** £370.13   **h** £38.31   **i** £13.51   **j** £21.44
  k £19.68   **l** £4.47   **m** 42p   **n** £206.04   **o** £4.88

Exercise 44.6

1 a £14.98   **b** £2.23   **2** £99.88

3 a £311.96   **b** £46.46

4 SuperCD £13.49 CDcity £13.51 (SuperCD cheaper by 2p per CD)
  b 6p

5 a £20.99, because £18.99 + VAT (17.5%) = £22.31   **b** £1.04

SECTION 45

Starting points

A1 a $\frac{1}{10}$ **b** $\frac{3}{10}$ **c** $\frac{5}{10} = \frac{1}{2}$ (0 counts as even)   **d** $\frac{5}{10} = \frac{1}{2}$

A2 $\frac{4}{6} = \frac{2}{3}$ **A3** $\frac{2}{7}$

Exercise 45.1

2 Pragna's results will probably give a more reliable answer because she has done more throws.

4 Do more drops of the pin or the shape.

5 d **c** will probably be more reliable because it has more throws.
  e The value should be $\frac{1}{2}$ or 0.5000

6 b $\frac{1}{3}$ or 0.33 (to 2 dp)

SECTION 46

Starting points

A1 a £190.50   **b** £11.88   **c** 363.05   **d** £31 500   **e** £300.12

B1 $\frac{14}{21}, \frac{20}{30}, \frac{30}{45}$

B2 $\frac{24}{30}, \frac{36}{45}, \frac{12}{15}$

C1 a $\frac{3}{5}$ **b** $\frac{5}{12}$ **c** $\frac{5}{7}$ **d** $\frac{3}{4}$ **e** $\frac{8}{9}$ **f** $\frac{14}{25}$

Exercise 46.1

1 a 7:3   **b** 3:7   **2 a** 8:5   **b** 5:8

3 a 5:6   **b** 6:5   **4 a** 183:320   **b** 320:183

5 a 9:37   **b** 37:9

Exercise 46.2

1 a 3:5   **b** 4:5   **c** 3:5   **d** 7:10   **e** 7:11   **f** 4:7
  g 1:3   **h** 7:9   **i** 4:9   **j** 7:8   **k** 7:8   **l** 1:2
  m 2:3   **n** 5:8   **o** 5:9   **p** 1:4

2 a 6:1:9   **b** 15:1:20   **c** 4:1:20   **d** 24:1:18
  e 8:1:16   **f** 20:1:50   **g** 36:1:84   **h** 100:1:400

3 a 1:2:3   **b** 3:5:6   **c** 3:5:7   **d** 2:4:5
  e 5:6:7   **f** 2:3:5   **g** 5:6:8   **h** 4:3:7
  i 10:3:5   **j** 5:4:9   **k** 9:2:11   **l** 6:7:11

Exercise 46.3

1 12:11   **2** 17:91   **3** 27:1

4 a 210   **b** 11:42   **5 a** 240   **b** 4:3

6 64:187   **7** Orange:Lemon:Lime is 5:2:3

8 Black:Blue:Red is 3:5:2

Exercise 46.4

1 a 2:5   **b** 2:5   **c** 6:5   **d** 5:7   **e** 5:9   **f** 14:5
  g 4:7   **h** 7:3   **i** 3:5   **j** 1:9   **k** 1:3   **l** 9:8

2 a 3:7:13   **b** 3:4:5   **c** 3:6:7   **d** 9:4:7
  e 3:5:12   **f** 15:7:12   **g** 7:3:8   **h** 14:2:9

3 a 21:35   **b** 12:28:36   **c** 30:66   **d** 81:18:63
  e 7:28:49   **f** 28:44:60   **g** 36:51   **h** 252:60:156
  i 84:35   **j** 40:3   **k** 11:50:14   **l** 6:5

Exercise 46.5

1 140 litres:224 litres   **2** 45 km:105 km   **3** 40 kg:72 kg

4 £2080:£1664   **5** £351:£324

6 187.5 kg:187.5 kg:1125 kg   **7** £500:£125:625

8 315 litres:819 litres:441 litres   **9** 57 m:38 m:19 m

10 £9100:£7700:£9800:£8400

Exercise 46.6

1 a 315 litres   **b** 495 litres   **2 a** 875 litres   **b** 1225 litres

3 a 20   **b** 36   **4 a** 2125 m   **b** 2875 m

5 a 323   **b** 85   **6 a** 372   **b** 217

7 a 900 ml   **b** 50 ml   **8** Jo, £35   Emma, £40

9 a 91 mm   **b** 21 mm   **c** 1911 mm^2

SECTION 47

Exercise 47.1

2 c $\begin{pmatrix} 7 \\ -3 \end{pmatrix}$

3 a $\begin{pmatrix} 2 \\ 5 \end{pmatrix}$ **b**

Slide		Translation
from triangle	to triangle	
D	A	$\begin{pmatrix} -12 \\ 5 \end{pmatrix}$
E	D	$\begin{pmatrix} 8 \\ 2 \end{pmatrix}$
C	A	$\begin{pmatrix} -9 \\ -1 \end{pmatrix}$
B	F	$\begin{pmatrix} 9 \\ 1 \end{pmatrix}$
F	**B**	$\begin{pmatrix} -9 \\ -1 \end{pmatrix}$
B	C	$\begin{pmatrix} 4 \\ 2 \end{pmatrix}$
C	D	$\begin{pmatrix} 3 \\ -6 \end{pmatrix}$

4 d The final shape lies exactly on shape A.

5 The shape does not move.   **6** $\begin{pmatrix} 4 \\ 3 \end{pmatrix}$

Exercise 47.2

3 a 11 square units   **c** 44 square units: 4 times as great

Exercise 47.3

3 a left

REVIEW 5A

1 a 130°   **b** about 218°   **2 a** 270°, 4 km   **b** 310°, 3.2 km

3

Item	Old price	New price
Lead	£4.00	**£4.80**
Video	£256	**£307.20**
Remote	£16.20	**£19.44**

4 a £5.70   **b** £402.80   **c** £23.56

5 a £493.50   **b** £73.50

6 $\frac{29}{100}$

7 a 2:1   **b** $\frac{1}{2}$:2 (or 1:4)

8 a 1:4   **b** 4:1:8   **c** 3:5:20

9 12:18 and 20:30 (both ratios being equivalent to 2:3)

10 a 15 and 5   **b** £7 and £14 and £35

SKILLS BREAK 9

1 a 4850 m   **b** 4.6   **2** one thousand five hundred

3 a 64 years   **b** 55 800 000   **4 B**

5 4.6 miles   **6** 730 days   **7** 6.8 m³   **8** 308 m²

9 140 days   **10** almost 27   **11** 0.36 m

12 a 4 cm/min   **b** almost 24 inches

13 a 360 cm   **b** 8 cm   **14 D**

15 a 63 cm (to nearest whole number)
  b 314 cm² (to nearest whole number)

16 a 16 miles   **b** 13 days (12.2 days)

17 a

Layer	1	2	3	4	5	6
No. of cans	1	4	9	**16**	**25**	**36**
Total from top	1	5	14	**30**	**55**	**91**

b 100

SECTION 48

Starting points

A1 a 15:15   **b** 02:10   **c** 12:45   **d** 11:35   **e** 21:25
  f 20:45   **g** 09:35   **h** 01:00   **i** 23:05   **j** 04:18

B1

Start time	Stop time	Time interval
12:25	14:05	**1 h 40 min**
16:40	19:10	**2 h 30 min**
07:35	13:20	**5 h 45 min**
02:05	07:50	**5 h 45 min**
12:22	15:08	**2 h 46 min**
14:48	19:07	**4 h 19 min**

C1 a 21:02   **b** 09:26

D1 a 75 mph   **b** 56 mph   **c** 43.3 mph   **d** 37.3 mph

Exercise 48.1

1 4 miles   **2** 10 miles   **3** 6 miles

4 bus 1, 1 hour   bus 2, 45 minutes   bus 3, 30 minutes

5 10 mph   **6** 20 mph

Exercise 48.2

1 a bus 1, about 6.5 miles   bus 2, 5 miles   bus 3, about 1 mile
  b bus 1, about 09:13   bus 2, about 09:18   bus 3, about 09:26
  c Between King's Square and Bell Cross (steepest part of the graph)

2 a 12 miles   **b** 7 miles   **c** 07:45   **d** 08:00
  e more than half way (7 miles from the station)

3 bus 6, about 07:45   bus 7, about 07:52   bus 8, about 08:12

4 bus 6, about 07:25   bus 7, about 07:35   bus 8, about 07:52

5 bus 6, about 11 miles   bus 7, about 9 miles   bus 8, 5 miles

6 about 08:15

7

D	Stop	Bus 1	Bus 2	Bus 3
0	Station	07:10	**07:20**	**07:45**
2	High Street	**07:20**	——	**07:50**
4	King's Square	**07:30**	07:40	——
5	Oak Lane	——	——	**07:55**
7	Blue Star	07:40	——	**08:10**
10	Bell Cross	——	**08:00**	——
12	Church End	**08:00**	**08:10**	**08:20**

8 a High Street to Oak Lane (steepest part of graph)
  b Oak Lane to Blue Star (shallowest part of graph)
  c 35 minutes

9 a bus 11, roughly 4 miles from Church End at 09:47
  b bus 12, roughly 7 miles from Church End at 10:00

10 bus 9, about 09:58   bus 10, about 09:24
  bus 11, about 09:40   bus 12, about 10:02

11 bus 12   **12** bus 10 (shorter journey time)   **13** about 10:10

14

D	Stop	Bus 10	Bus 11	Bus 12
0	Station	**09:05**	**09:15**	**09:35**
2	High Street	**09:15**	——	**09:40**
4	King's Square	——	**09:35**	**09:55**
5	Oak Lane	——	——	——
7	Blue Star	**09:25**	——	**10:05**
10	Bell Cross	**09:35**	**09:55**	——
12	Church End	**09:55**	**10:10**	**10:15**

Exercise 48.3

2 a about 12:50   **b** about 12:55

3 a about 13:25   **b** in the cycle shop

4 b Emma, because the graphs cross before graphs of Ravi and Steve
  c Ravi, 1 hour 15 minutes   Emma, 1 hour 35 minutes
    Steve, 1 hour 30 minutes   Kim, 1 hour 30 minutes

SECTION 49

Starting points

A1 a £34.88 **b** £2.49 **c** £16.00 **d** £1.38 **e** £234.08 **f** £3.01

A2 £6.67

B1 a 0.72 **b** 0.06 **c** 0.88 **d** 0.345 **e** 0.085
  f 0.01 **g** 0.255 **h** 0.105 **i** 0.005

C1 a £11613 **b** £11700 **c** £20.35 **d** £1.31 **e** 94p **f** £21.36

D1 a £64.35 **b** £210.60 **c** £7.02 **d** £96.47 **e** £3.50 **f** £1.63

D2 a £15.42 **b** £322.06 **c** £5.79 **d** £223.99 **e** £403.13

E1 a £47.30 **b** £154.80 **c** £5.16 **d** £70.91 **e** £2.57 **f** £1.20

E2 a £51.83 **b** £98.57 **c** £30.30 **d** £230.39 **e** £286.99

E3 392 ml

Exercise 49.1

1

Item	Price	Deposit	Deposit paid
TV	£219.99	17%	£37.40
Video	£349.99	15%	**£52.50**
Camcorder	£499.99	22%	**£110.00**
Cooker	£359.99	8%	**£28.80**
Fridge	£234.99	7%	**£16.45**
Scooter	£2395	18%	**£431.10**
Bike	£7995	21%	**£1678.95**
CD player	£189.99	$7\frac{1}{2}$%	**£14.25**
Sound system	£679.99	$15\frac{1}{2}$%	**£105.40**
Holiday	£438.65	22%	**£96.50**
Microwave	£279.99	35%	**£98.00**

Exercise 49.2

1 a £248.66 **b** £1409.09   **2 a** £21.70 **b** £288.29
3 a £46.80 **b** £213.19   **4 a** £18.75 **b** £231.24
5 a £499.25 **b** £2545.75

Exercise 49.3

1

Loan	Interest rate	Years	Total payback
£45	22%	2	£64.80
£275	14%	2	**£352.00**
£455	23%	2	**£664.30**
£850	17%	2	**£1139**
£1200	$15\frac{1}{2}$%	2	**£1572**
£725	21%	1	**£877.25**
£2265	16%	3	**£3352.20**
£3435	18%	3	**£5289.90**
£6125	12.5%	4	**£9187.50**
£638.55	15%	5	**£1117.46**
£424.80	21%	6	**£960.05**
£375.75	22%	4	**£706.41**

Exercise 49.4

1

Loan	Total payback	Each instalment
£675	£958.50	£39.94
£850	**£1244**	**£51**
£945	**£1512**	**£31.50**
£1655	**£3144.50**	**£52.41**

2 £39.62   **3** £41.17   **4** £20.75
5 a £1375.20 **b** £57.30 **c** £420.20

Exercise 49.5

1

Item	Price	Discount	Discount price
Watch	£34.99	7%	£32.54
Bike	£219.99	8%	**£202.39**
TV	£349.99	15%	**£297.49**
Camera	£79.99	12%	**£70.39**
Toaster	£12.99	5%	**£12.34**
Holiday	£579.99	18%	**£475.59**
Drill	£169.99	17%	**£141.09**
Microwave	£229.99	25%	**£172.49**
Fridge	£219.99	20%	**£175.99**
CD player	£349.99	$17\frac{1}{2}$%	**£288.74**
Clarinet	£269.99	5.5%	**£255.14**

Exercise 49.6

1 £43.99   **2** £24.22   **3** £349.59   **4** £377.18

Exercise 49.7

1

Principal (£)	%	Rate (decimal)	Interest (£)
20	6	0.06	76.80
450	7	**0.07**	**94.50**
275	4	**0.04**	**66**
620	5	**0.05**	**62**
280	8	**0.08**	**112**
660	9	**0.09**	**178.20**
810	7	**0.07**	**283.50**
1200	3	**0.03**	**432**
2250	11	**0.11**	**3712.50**
1750	6.5	**0.065**	**910**
3550	4.5	**0.045**	**1118.25**

Exercise 49.8

1 a £87.60 **b** £452.60   **2 a** £726.60 **b** £1591.60
3 a £1500 **b** £14000   **4** £200.76
5 a probably yes because he has £735 in total
  b £819

Exercise 49.9

1 £178.50   **2 a** £13.25 **b** £27.50
3 £148.50   **4** £59

Exercise 49.10

1 750 g is better value for money.
  (500 g box, £0.139 for 50 g   750 g box, £0.132... for 50 g)
2 2 litre bottle is better value for money.
  (2 litre bottle, £3.495 per litre   4.5 litre can, £3.553... per litre)
3 a £0.478 75
  b The case is better value for money.
    (cost of 1 can in case, £0.47875   cost of 1 can in crate, £0.4798)
4 Sound City offers better value.
  (cost of one tape in Supersounds, £0.899
  cost of one tape in Sound City, £0.820...)
5 a standard, £0.0331...   large, £0.0336...   value, £0.0317...
  b The value pack is better value for money.

SECTION 50

Starting points

A1

Radius	Diameter
6 cm	**12 cm**
9 cm	18 cm
7.5 cm	15 cm
12 mm	**24 mm**
5.5 mm	**11 mm**
8.4 m	**16.8 m**
11.25 cm	22.5 cm
4.6 cm	**9.2 cm**
3.25 cm	6.5 cm
0.8 m	1.6 m
0.05 m	**0.1 m**

Exercise 50.2

1 a 21.36 cm **b** 10.68 cm **c** 16.96 cm **d** 40.84 cm **e** 39.27 cm
f 11.31 cm **g** 47.75 cm **h** 138.23 cm **i** 19.79 cm
2 a 13.5 cm **b** 42.41 cm
3

Radius	Diameter	Circumference
4.5 cm	**9 cm**	**28.27 cm**
3.1 cm	10.4 cm	**32.67 cm**
7.9 m	15.8 cm	**49.64 m**
0.75 m	**1.5 m**	**4.71 m**
0.68 m	1.3 m	**4.08 m**

Exercise 50.3

1 a 94.25 cm **b** 754.0 cm **2 a** 24.50 cm **c** 147.0 cm^2
3 23.2 cm
4

Diameter of cake	Total length of ribbon
16 cm	62 cm
17.5 cm	**67 cm**
20 cm	**75 cm**
22.5 cm	**83 cm**
24 cm	**87 cm**

5 a 172.79 cm **b** 691.2 cm^2 **6 a** 69.12 cm **b** 1450

Exercise 50.4

1 a 145.27 cm^2 **b** 22.90 cm^2 **c** 26.42 cm^2
d 132.73 cm^2 **e** 122.72 cm^2 **f** 10.18 cm^2
g 181.46 cm^2 **h** 1520.53 cm^2 **i** 31.17 cm^2
2

Radius	Diameter	Area
4.5 cm	**9 cm**	**63.62 cm^2**
3.4 cm	6.8 cm	**36.32 cm^2**
10.5 cm	**21 cm**	**346.36 cm^2**
7.3 cm	14.6 cm	**167.42 cm^2**
8.1 cm	**16.2 cm**	**206.12 cm^2**
10.7 cm	21.4 cm	**359.68 cm^2**
0.6 m	**1.2 m**	**1.13 m^2**

Exercise 50.5

1 44.18 m^2
2 The circle is larger by 26.23 cm^2 (circle, 38.48 cm^2 square, 12.25 cm^2).
4 5026.55 km^2 **5** 962.11 cm^2 **6** 0.50 cm^2

Exercise 50.6

1 a 65.05 cm^2 **b** 98.49 cm^2 **c** 161.51 cm^2

SECTION 51

Starting points

A1

p	k	w
4	5	**10**
2	8	**⁻6**
1	6	**⁻7**
4	9	**2**
2	11	**⁻12**
0	4	**⁻8**
⁻2	3	**⁻16**
⁻1	0	**⁻5**

Exercise 51.1

1

x	⁻2	⁻1	0	1	2	3	4
y	⁻2	**0**	**2**	**4**	**6**	**8**	**10**

2 b

x	⁻1	0	1	2	3	4	5
y	**2**	**4**	**6**	**8**	10	**12**	**14**

3 b

x	⁻1	0	1	2	3	4
y	**⁻1**	3	7	**11**	**15**	**19**

4 b

x	⁻2	⁻1	0	1	2	3	4
y	**⁻7**	**⁻5**	**⁻3**	**⁻1**	**1**	**3**	**5**

5 b

x	⁻2	⁻1	0	1	2	3	4
y	**⁻8**	**⁻5**	**⁻2**	1	**4**	**7**	**10**

6 a

x	⁻3	⁻2	⁻1	1	2	3	4
y	**⁻1**	**0**	**1**	**3**	**4**	**5**	**6**

7 a

x	⁻4	⁻3	⁻2	0	2	3	4
y	**⁻5**	**⁻3**	**⁻1**	3	**7**	**9**	**11**

Exercise 51.2

1 b

x	⁻1	0	1	2	3
y	**⁻3**	**⁻1**	**1**	**3**	**5**

d (1, 3)

2 a

x	⁻1	0	1	2	3
y	**⁻2**	**1**	**4**	**7**	**10**

b

x	⁻1	0	1	2	3
y	**1**	**3**	**5**	**7**	**9**

e (2,7)

3 b

x	⁻2	⁻1	0	1	2	3	4	5	6
y	**⁻8**	**⁻6**	**⁻4**	**⁻2**	**0**	**2**	**4**	**6**	**8**

c

x	-2	-1	0	1	2	3	4	5	6
y	-1	0	1	2	3	4	5	6	7

e (5, 6)

4 b

x	0	1	3	5	6
y	20	17	11	5	2

5 b

x	-6	-5	-4	-3	-2	-1	0	1	2	3
y	-3	-2	-1	0	1	2	3	4	5	6

d $x \approx -0.5$
e $x \approx 1.5$

Exercise 51.3

1 b

x	-4	-3	-2	-1	0	1	2	3	4
y	18	11	6	3	2	3	6	11	18

2 b

x	-4	-3	-2	-1	0	1	2	3	4
y	21	14	9	6	5	6	9	14	21

3 b

x	-3	-2	-1	0	1	2	3	4
y	8	3	0	-1	0	3	8	15

4 b

x	-3	-2	-1	0	1	2	3	4
y	6	1	-2	-3	-2	1	6	13

5 b

x	-3	-2	-1	0	1	2	3	4
y	4	-1	-4	-5	-4	-1	4	11

e $x \approx 1.25$ f $y \approx 2.25$

SECTION 52

Exercise 52.1

1 Alternative answers are possible – for discussion.
B, all but two points show this link   E, strongly shown
(D, only two points show this link)

2 b As the shoe size gets larger, height also tends to get larger.

3 b about £3000   4 b 3

Exercise 52.2

1 B: cars with larger engines tend to use more fuel, so are less economical.

2 a negative   b positive   c negative   d none
e positive   f negative

REVIEW 5B

1 a bus 14   b Blue Star at 09:35
c bus 14, about 09:40   bus 15, about 09:27
bus 16, about 09:40   bus 17, about 09:57
d bus 14

3

Item	Price	Deposit	Deposit paid
Bike	£6975	15%	**£1046.25**
TV	£249.99	12%	**£30.00**
Video	£399.99	7%	**£28.00**
Holiday	£466.75	20%	**£93.35**
Fridge	£199.99	6%	**£12.00**

4 £2857.50   5 a £7276   b £121.27

6 £186.99   7 £139.20   8 £319.70

9 The 500 g box is better value for money.
(500 g box, £0.225/50 g)   750 g box, £0.23/50 g).

10 circumference, 46.5 cm (to 1 dp)   area, 172.0 cm² (to 1 dp)

11 a

x	-3	-2	-1	0	1	2	3	4
y	-11	-8	-5	-2	1	4	7	10

12 a

x	-3	-2	-1	0	1	2	3
y	10	5	2	1	2	5	10

SKILLS BREAK 10

1

Mulchbags size	Price	Discount price
Large	£1.49	**£1.27**
Super	**£1.99**	**£1.69**
Major	**£2.99**	**£2.54**
Professional	**£4.99**	**£4.24**

2 £2.54 × 8 = £20.32, so he will have to borrow 32p.

3 a 16.1p per litre   b yes (£1.69 ÷ 10 ≈ 17p)
c more than 15p (£1.99 ÷ 12 ≈ 17p)
d The 8 litre plastic can is better value for money: it costs
approximately 16.1p per litre.

4 Traditional watering cans:
1 gal   £4.99 per gal
1.5 gal   £4.33 per gal
2 gal   £4 per gal (£3.995)
2.5 gal   £4 per gal (£3.996)
To be accurate the 2 gal is better value !!!

5 a 16:30   b 9 hours   c 62 hours

6 a 14 hours   b £58.52   c £6.27   d £87.78

7 14 litres is about 3 gallons, so for 3 gallons Meg should add about
3 × 1.5 g = 4.5 g of Liquidgro.

8 a 2   b 4   c five 30 metre rolls   d 2p
e no (because 150 m costs £42 at bulk rate)

9 1.2 m²   10 6.3 m²   11 77°

12 a 18 feet   b 3 yards   13 £70

14 a £50   b £200   c £260   d £7.22   e £310

15 a £30.45   b £175.45   c £74.54   d 18 hours

16 the 12 litre plastic can (because 2.5 gal ≈ 11.3 litres)

STAGE 5 END POINTS

A1 **a** 225°   **b** 045°   **c** 000°   **d** 270°   **e** 315°

B1 **b** 7.4 km

D1 **a** £747 500   **b** £575 000   **c** 40.825 km

E1 **a** £10.71   **b** 2438 miles   **c** 1328 mm   **d** 76p

F1 with VAT at 17.5%:
    a £28.19   **b** £223.24   **c** £422.99   **d** 80p

H1 **a** 4:7   **b** 7:4

I1 **a** 7:4   **b** 15:56   **c** 1:5   **d** 3:1

I2 **a** 120   **b** 4:5

J1 **a** 5:7   **b** 2:9   **c** 288:60:108   **d** 5:8:12

M1 **a** 10:20   **b** 35 minutes **c** High Street to Blue Star (steepest)
    d bus 2, about 9 miles
    e

D	Stop	Bus 1	Bus 2	Bus 3
0	Station	10:00	10:10	10:35
2	High Street	10:10	10:30	10:40
4	King's Square	10:20	——	——
5	Oak Lane	——	——	10:45
7	Blue Star	——	10:40	10:55
10	Bell Cross	10:30	——	11:00
12	Church End	10:35	10:55	11:10

O1 £127.89   **P1** £358.40   **P2** £1004.15   **Q1** £99.45

R1 £29.74   **S1** £238   **T1** **a** £450.80   **b** £42.22

U1 The 600 g box is the better value (600 g box, £0.1541... per 50 g
    750 g box, £0.1566... per 50 g).

V1 **a** 29.53 cm   **b** 69.4 cm^2

W1 **a**

x	$^-3$	$^-2$	$^-1$	0	1	2	3	4
y	$^-11$	$^-8$	$^-5$	$^-2$	1	4	7	10

X1 **a**

x	$^-3$	$^-2$	$^-1$	0	1	2	3	4
y	7	2	$^-1$	$^-2$	$^-1$	2	7	14

REVISION 5

1 **a** 500   **b** 50 000   **c** 50 000 000

2 199, 636, 3008, 3999, 4052, 9004, 61 075, 100 001

3 **a** thirty thousand five hundred and four
    b four million three hundred thousand six hundred and three
    c one hundred and seventy thousand two hundred and seventy

4 **a** 9005   **b** 35 201   **c** 1 010 001

5 V W T X A   **6** 2   **7** 2

8 **a** 39   **b** 107   **c** 19 173   **d** 80 649
    e 832   **f** 21 201   **g** 345   **h** 2563

9 **a** $\frac{9}{1000}$ **b** $\frac{9}{10}$ **c** $\frac{9}{100}$

10 0.057, 0.0705, 0.075, 0.57, 1.0075, 1.175

11 **a** 111.907   **b** 152.7077   **c** 17.6376

13 75°, 48°, 15°

14 **a** $^-28$ **b** $^-23$ **c** 27   **d** $^-33$ **e** $^-53$ **f** 37
    g 101   **h** $^-60$ **i** $^-63$ **j** 45   **k** $^-9$ **l** 3

15 **a** $^-10$, $^-8$, $^-1$, 0, 1, 2, 3
    b $^-7$, $^-5$, $^-3$, $^-1$, 0, 1, 2, 4

16 (2, 4) and (2, 7) or ($^-1$, 1) and (2, 1)

17 **a** $37k + 23w$ **b** $12f - 10h$ **18** **a** $24w + 3y + 3$ **b** $20 - 25k + 5p$

19 $52a - 16b + 24c - 72$

20 **a** 9000   **b** 348 000   **c** 3 436 000

21 **a** 500 000   **b** 2 300 000   **c** 51 500 000

22 **a** 1200   **b** 2800   **c** 4800

25 **a** 17:24   **b** 21:00   **c** 11:53   **d** 22:05   **e** 03:40   **f** 13:08

26 4 hours 22 minutes

27 **a** 10:19   **b** 2 hours 23 minutes

28 **a** 116.84 cm^2 **b** 76.68 cm^2 **c** 43.12 cm^2
    d 74.8 cm^2 **e** 190.3 cm^2 **f** 172.5 cm^2

29 12

30 **a** $y = 7$ **b** $h = 8$ **c** $g = 52$ **d** $f = 16$

31 **a** 230   **b** 64, 81, 100, 121, 144, 169, 196   **c** 256

32 56, 96, 40   **33** 1, 2, 3, 4, 6, 8, 9, 12, 18, 24, 36, 72

34 53, 59, 61, 67, 71, 73, 79

36 **a** 5004.5   **b** 121.0   **c** 234.45   **d** 0.010044

37 **a** 166.7   **b** 3457.9   **c** 1773.25   **d** 3227.4

38 **a** £57.82   **b** £580.02   **c** £36.47   **d** £5833.32

39 24p   **40** £1.51   **41** £15.73

42 **a** £4.55   **b** £408.38   **c** £183.57   **d** £40 556.23

43 $x \longrightarrow y$ **44** $^-98$
    1 $\longrightarrow$ $^-4$
    2 $\longrightarrow$ 1
    3 $\longrightarrow$ 6
    4 $\longrightarrow$ 11
    5 $\longrightarrow$ 16

45 **a** 124°   **b** 47°   **c** 79°   **d** 101°   **e** 79°   **f** 96°
    g 84°   **h** 63°   **i** 44°   **j** 49°   **k** 84°

46 **a** £13.60   **b** £10.20   **47** £49.56   **48** 21 km

49 $\frac{25}{125}, \frac{120}{600}$ **50** **a** 0.375   **b** 0.35, $\frac{3}{8}$, 0.4, $\frac{3}{5}$, $\frac{7}{10}$

51 $\frac{18}{24}, \frac{9}{12}, \frac{3}{4}$ or 0.75

52 **a**   **b** modal class, 16–20

No. in car	Frequency
1–5	1
6–10	7
11–15	5
16–20	10
21–25	5
26–30	3

53 a $y = 4$ **b** $w = {}^-5$ **c** $x = 3$ **d** $w = 9$

54 a 43.8 cm **b** 44 cm **c** 100.98 cm² **d** 101.0 **e** 105 cm²

55 61.05099, 61.05449, 61.05395 **56 a** $\frac{1}{2}$ **b** $\frac{1}{6}$

57 a 1.561666×10^4 **b** 3.8055425×10^6

58 a 4.7304×10^9 **b** 4730400000

59 a 10^9 **b** 10^{12}

60 a

Number	Frequency
33	1
34	1
35	1
36	2
37	2
38	3
39	1
40	10
41	3
42	1
43	1
44	1

b 40 **c** 39 **d** 40

63 a 252 **b** 24

65 a 0.78 **b** 0.09 **c** 0.27 **d** 0.03

66 a 0.055 **b** 0.245 **c** 0.015

67 a 35% **b** 6% **c** 40% **d** 54.5%
e 15.5% **f** 6% **g** 8.5% **h** 17.5%

68 a £1215 **b** 377 kg **c** £29.70 **d** 14600
e 23.4 miles **f** £500

69 a 76.2% (to 1 dp) **b** 41.0% (to 1 dp) **c** 33%

70 33, 41, 49, 57 **71** $^-7, ^-5, ^-3, ^-1, 1$

76 a 0.25 **b** M **c** Large, $\frac{3}{10}$ XL, $\frac{3}{100}$

77 Cl S, Cl Ca, Cl D, S Ca, S D, Ca D

78 c $\frac{6}{36}$ or $\frac{1}{6}$ **80** 533 km

81 a 130.5 km **b** 261 km **c** 43.5 km

82 94 mph

83 a $\frac{9}{25}$ **b** $\frac{29}{50}$ **c** $\frac{6}{25}$ **d** $\frac{2}{25}$ **e** $\frac{1}{50}$

84 a $1\frac{2}{9}$ **b** $\frac{6}{16}$ or $\frac{3}{8}$ **c** $\frac{1}{6}$

85 a 154.8 cm² **b** 36708 mm² **c** 194.184 cm²

87 a 109.62 cm³ **b** 336.96 cm³ **c** 4131 mm³

88 about 60000m² (which is 300 m × 200 m)

89 a 090° **b** 315° **c** 045°

91 a £7280 **b** £658.56 **c** £1394.68 **d** £1.96

92 £2817

93 a 41850 km **b** £2790000 **c** £29.76

94 £82.28 **95** £28700

97 with VAT at 17.5%:
a £305.49 **b** £140.99 **c** £22.03 **d** 45p

98 £41.11 **100 a** 9:5 **b** 5:9

101 265:388

102 a 5:8 **b** 4:5 **c** 6:7

103 a 2:9 **b** 32:60:12 **c** 24:96:40

104 £345:£1380:£1725 **105 a** 165 **b** 195

110 £86.40 **111** circumference, 54.04 cm area, 232.35 cm²

EXAM-STYLE QUESTIONS

N1.1 **a** 783 **b** 382   **N1.2** 26

N1.3 27 401   **N1.4** **a** 8632 **b** 2368

N1.5 26 degrees   **N1.6** Divide 58 by 2.

N1.7 **a** 23 000 **b** 10 300

N1.8 **a** 4500 **b** 2073 **c** 6573

N1.9 **a** 3 **b** 3   **N1.10** **b** 19

N2.1 about 15 miles   **N2.2** 48 km

N2.3 80 160   **N2.4** **a** 28 minutes **b** 4

N2.5 enough potatoes but not enough milk

N2.6 **a** 24 000 **b** $12\frac{1}{2}$ min   **N2.7** **a** 112 kph **b** 50 mph

N2.8 no, because the bus is too high

N2.9 **a** 61p **b** 3.6 gallons   **c** 8 pence/mile

N2.10 114.3 cm   **N2.11** 73.3 feet per second

N3.1 **a** 5650 **b** 5750   **N3.2** 4, 5, 6, 7, 8

N3.6 **a i** 27.5 inches **ii** 26.5 inches **b i** 699 mm **ii** 673 mm

N3.8 ≈ £39 (30p × 130)   **N3.9** no, because it is too slow

N4.1 **a** 2347 **b** 348 or 384

N4.2 **a** factor **b** multiple **c** prime **d** square

N4.3 6

N4.4 **a** 16 **b** 8, 16, 24 **c** 2, 3, 5 **d** 8 **e** 5

N4.5 13

N4.6 **a** no, because it is not divisible exactly by 6 **b** any two from 1, 3, 9, 27

N4.7 **a** 17 **b** All other evens are divisible by 2 and are therefore not prime.

N4.8 **a** 16 **b** 7, 14, 21

N4.9 **a** 13 → 14 → 7 → 8 → 4 → 2 → 1 **b** ⁻11 → ⁻10 → ⁻5 → ⁻4 → ⁻2 → ⁻1

N5.1 $\frac{1}{3}$ **N5.2** **a** $\frac{40}{200} = \frac{1}{5}$

N5.3 9 litres   **N5.4** **a** 20 litres **b** 40 litres

N5.5 **a** $\frac{1}{4}, \frac{5}{16}, \frac{3}{8}, \frac{1}{2}$ **b** $1\frac{7}{16}$ or $\frac{23}{16}$

N5.6 **a i** Claire **ii** Rob **b** 25 **c** 6 words

N5.7 **a i** $\frac{150}{1000}$ **ii** $\frac{3}{20}$ **b** 170 **c** 660

N6.1 **a** 13.9 litres **b** £10.46   **N6.2** **a** 0.0139 cm **b** 3.892 cm

N6.3 0.83 kg   **N6.4** 5 boxes

N6.5 2.65 metres   **N6.6** **a** 0.65 cm **b** 24.05 cm

N6.7 **a** 6.0329 **b** 0.55 **c** 11.0146 **d** 11.6095 **e** 7350

N6.8 **a** 0.26

N7.1 **a** 42 **b** 70%   **N7.2** **a** 40% **b** 35%

N7.3 **a** 6p in every pound **b** £12 **N7.4** 150 grams

N7.5 £11.90   **N7.6** 10.4%

N7.7 £13.25   **N7.8** **a** £8.48 **b** £114.48

N7.9 **a** £174.65 **b** £1172.65

N7.10 **a i** 5% **ii** 3000 **b** 10 200 **c** £852 900

N8.1 **a** $\frac{1}{6}$ **b** 16 **c** 33.3% (to 1 dp)

N8.2

Fraction	Decimal	Percentage
$\frac{1}{2}$	0.5	50%
$\frac{1}{4}$	**0.25**	25%
$\frac{3}{5}$	0.6	**60%**
$\frac{3}{8}$	**0.375**	**37.5%**

N8.3 $\frac{3}{4}$, 0.7, $\frac{5}{8}$, 43%, 0.4, 35%   **N8.4** 161 grams

N8.5 **a** 25.5 hours **b** £98.18 **c** 1%

N8.6 **a** £48 **b** $\frac{1}{16}$ **c** about 25% (27.08%) **d i** $\frac{5}{8}$ **ii** 62.5%

N9.1 £240   **N9.2** 75 grams

N9.3 32 pence

N9.4 **a** 25 miles **b** Multiply the number of miles by 8, then divide by 5.

N9.5 **a** stock, 1350 g   onions, 975 g   butter, 75 g   cheese, 75 g **b** 3600 grams **c** 2600 grams

N9.6 20 grams

N9.7 Ann, £15   Graham, £12   Elwyn, £9

N9.8 2 : 1   **N9.9** **a** 5 metres **b** 12 cm

N10.1 **a** 1:13 pm **b** 25 minutes **N10.2** **a** Friday **b** Tuesday

N10.3 **a** 111 minutes **b** 12:20

N10.4 **a** 10:20 am **b** 40 minutes **c** 10 miles

N11.1 **a** 11 **b** 5p   **N11.2** **a** Freda's **b** 1p

N11.3 £494.44   **N11.4** 20 weeks

N11.5 59p   **N11.6** **a** £3400 **b** £425

N11.7 **a** £45.20 **b** 8 days **N11.8** the 125 ml tube

N11.9 **a** £118.88 **b** £128.39 (to the nearest penny)

N12.1 **a** 1.58 metres **b** 1.62 metres

N12.3 **a** ⁻6 °C **b** 4 °C **c** 12 °C **d** 18 degrees

N12.4 **a** 40 minutes **b** 2 hours 10 minutes

N13.1 **a** 3, 5, 7, 9 **b** 4, 8 **c** 4, 9

N13.2 **a** 5 units **b** 7 thousand **c** thirty

N13.3 **a** 18 degrees **b** 48 minutes **c** 2:33 pm

N13.4 **a** 7.5 cm **b** 1.5 cm **c** $\frac{1}{5}$

N13.5 £40.00 + £15 + £18.60 = £73.60 (total before VAT), VAT = £12.88, total due = £86.48

N13.6 **a** 62 500 pesetas **b** 12 500 pesetas **c** £52.08 (to the nearest penny)

N13.7 **a** $\frac{20}{24} = \frac{5}{6}$

N13.8 **a** 344.5 kg **b** £360 **c** 0.375 **d** 0.38

N13.9 **a** $\frac{3}{4}$ **b** 25% **c** about £400

N13.10 at the second shop

N13.11 **a** Five out of every 9 pupils in the school were girls. **b** 360 girls

N13.12 **a** 2 hours 14 minutes **b** 12:40 train

N13.13 34 428

N13.14 34   **N13.15** 9773 miles

N13.16 **a** 150 046 **b** 6 **c** 150 000

N13.17 **a** 12 + (9 ÷ 3) × 2 = 30 **b** (12 + 9) ÷ 3 × 2 = 14 **c** 12 + ((9 ÷ 3) × 2) = 18

N13.18 **a** 3⁶ or 729 **b** 4   **N13.19** **a** 6 **b** 216 **c i** no

N13.20 **a** 1.4×10^2 **b** 2.0×10^2 **c** 2.3×10^3 **d** 6.5×10^6 **e** 3.03×10^4

N13.21 **a** 130 **b** 2400 **c** 560 000 **d** 104 **e** 9 140 000

N13.22 45 125 000   **N13.23** **a** 8×10^8 **b** about 18%

A1.1 $3x$ **A1.2** **a** 5 cm **b** $20 - d$ **c** $h - g$

A1.3 **a** 8 **b** 3   **A1.4** $£m + £36n$

A1.5 $P = 6f$ **A1.6** 30°

A1.7 **a** mw **b** $2(m + w)$

A1.8 **a** $3p + 15$ **b** $7p + 3 = 3p + 15$ **c** $p = 3$

A2.1 **a** 37, 68, 125 **b** yes

A2.2 **a** 24, 28 **b** factor **c** multiple **d** square

A2.3 **b**

Panel length	1	2	3	4	5	6
Number of pieces	5	9	13	**17**	**21**	**25**

c Bill needs 81 pieces ($4n + 1$).

A2.4 **a** 31 **b** 8 **c** Multiply by 3.

A2.5 **a** It doubles each number. **b** It squares each number.

A2.6 **a** 18, 22 **b** Add 4. **c** $4n - 2$

A2.7 **a** 13, 15, 17, 19, total = 64 = 4³ **b** line 10 **c** 8000 **d** $n + 2$

ANSWERS

A2.8 17 changes to 18.

A3.1 **a** £45   **b** 12 hours

A3.2 **a** £5.50   **b i** $w = \dfrac{C - 50}{20}$ **ii** 15 words

A3.3 **a** 28   **b** 11   **A3.4** **a** Add 4.   **b** $4n - 1$

A3.5 **a** £80   **b** $2\frac{1}{2}$ hours   **c** $1\frac{3}{4}$ hours

A3.6 **a** $b = 3w$ **b** 62   **c** 57

A3.7 **a** 79 kg   **b** 183 cm   **c** no

A3.8 **a** 96   **b** 7.4   **c i** $t = \dfrac{v - u}{f}$ **ii** $t = 4.9$

A3.9 **a** 47   **b i** $n = 3b + 2$ **ii** 4254

A4.1 **a** $8y$ **b** $4x + 4$ **c** $y + 2$
        d $2x + 2y - 2xy$ **e** $x^2 + 3x$ **f** $2xy - 2x - y$

A4.2 **a** $4b - a$ **b** $5x - 4y$ **c** 7

A4.3 **a** 24 cm²   **b** 12 cm

A4.4 **a** $\frac{3}{8}$ **b** $\frac{9}{4}$ **c** $1\frac{1}{4}$ **d** $-\frac{5}{8}$ **e** 2

A4.5 **a** $6x - 9$ **b** $6x^2 + 4$ **c** $2y^2 - 6y$
        d $2x^2 + 2xy$ **e** $x^3 - 2x^2 + 3x$

A5.1 **a** 4 ⟶ 9   **b** 4 ⟶ 7
          2 ⟶ 5   2 ⟶ 9
          1 ⟶ 3   1 ⟶ 10
          0 ⟶ 1   0 ⟶ 11

A5.2 **a** It doubles.   **b** It squares.   **c** It doubles and adds 2.

A5.3 **a** $x \rightarrow x^2$ **b** $x \rightarrow 4 - x$

A5.4

Input		Output
4	⟶	17
6	⟶	**27**
9	⟶	42

A5.5 **a** 21   **b** $3n - 6$

A5.6 **a** $x = 15, y = 33$ **b** a triangle number × 3   **c** $m = 3t$

A6.1 **a** $x = 8$ **b** $y = 8$ **c** $z = 5$ **d** $x = 5$
        e $y = 9$ **f** $z = 6$ **g** $x = 16$

A6.2 **a** 13   **b** 1

A6.3 **a** $x = 10$ **b** $x = 4$ **c** $x = 4$ **d** $x = 5$
        e $x = 1.5$ **f** $x = 2$

A6.4 $n - 5$

A6.5 **a** $2j + 5$ **b** Neil, 14   Liam, 19

A6.6 **a** $F = 2C + 30$ **b** $F = 94°$ **c** $C = 12°$

A6.7 **a** $2w + 10$ **b** Area of rectangle 1 = 10 cm²
              $w = 2$, giving: Area of rectangle 2 = 10 cm²

A6.8 **a** $2k$ **b** $3k - 5$ **c i** $2k = 3k - 5$ **ii** 5

A7.1 2.7   **A7.2** **a** 22.4   **b** 2240 cm

A7.3 **a** 28 cm²   **b** 40 cm²   **c** 4.6 cm

A7.4 **a** $x = 17$ **b** $y = 2.5$

A8.1 **b** (1, 4)

A8.2 **a**

x	$^-5$	$^-4$	$^-3$	$^-2$	$^-1$	0	1	2	3	4	5
y	$^-7$	$^-6$	$^-5$	$^-4$	$^-3$	$^-2$	$^-1$	0	1	2	3

        d $\left(-\frac{1}{2}, -2\frac{1}{2}\right)$

A8.3 **b** 4   **c** 1 ⟶ 3   **e** $x = 2$
                    6 ⟶ 8
                    8 ⟶ **10**
                    x ⟶ $x + 2$

A8.4 **a**

x	0	1	2	3	4	5	6	7
$y = x^2 + 1$	1	**2**	5	**10**	**17**	26	**37**	**50**

        c 6.6

A8.5 **a**

Time x	0	1	2	3	4	5	6	7
Distance y	0	**2**	**8**	18	**32**	**50**	72	**98**

        c 60.5 m   **d** 3.9 ± 0.1 s

A9.1 **a** 38   **b** $9x - 7$

A9.2 **a** 3   **b i** $3a + 3b$ **ii** $a + 6b$ **c** 5

A9.3 **a** 22, 26   **b** Add 4.   **c** $4n - 2$

A9.4 **a** £58   **b** one hour   **A9.5** **a** $x = 5$ **b** 24

A9.6 **a** $2x - 9 = 37$ **b** 14 screws

A9.7 **a** $x + 4y$ **b** $10a - 4b$

A9.8 **d** about (4.5, 22)

S1.1 **b** (8, 4)   **c** Turn clockwise by 90°, then forward 4 metres.

S1.2 **b** 000°   **c** 270°   **d** 315°

S1.3 A(3, 1),   B(0, 5),   C($^-$4, 2),   D($^-$1, $^-$2)

S1.4 **c** (4, 0)   **d** (4, 3)

S1.6 **a** (40, 120)   **b** 20 km   **c** (50, 330)
        d about 320°   **e** 7854 km² (to the nearest whole number)

S2.1 **a** 25 miles   **b** 50 mph

S2.2 **a** 1860   **b** 350   **c** 119 000   **d** 50 hours

S2.3 **a** 2.5 miles   **b** 26 minutes   **c** twice
        d about 10.3 mph

S2.4 30.8 litres per minute

S2.5 **a i** 5 kg **ii** 2.33 kg   **b i** 13.2 lb **ii** 2.6 lb

S2.6 **a** 1.6 pence/ml   **b** 1.7 pence/ml   **c** Alison

S2.7 **a** no

S3.1 **a** 40°   **b** 75°   **c** 25°

S3.2 **a** trapezium   **b** 90°   **c** right angle

S3.3 $x = 113°$ $z = 23°$ **S3.4** 40°, 60°, 80°

S3.5 **a** isosceles   **b** $x = 47°, y = 47°$ **c** 39 cm²

S3.6 **a** $x = 105°$ **b** $y = 45°$ **c** $z = 40°$
        d AI = IC or HF = FD or …

S3.7 **a** cube   **b** rectangle **c** kite   **d** cylinder

S3.8 **a** A, equilateral triangle   B, square   C, pentagon
              D, hexagon   E, octagon   F, decagon
        b A, 180° B, 360° C, 540°   **c** D, 120° E, 135° F, 144°
        d i 7 **ii** 128.6° (to 1 dp)   **e** 36°

S3.9 **a** 6   **b** 3   **c** 60°   **d** 120°

S4.1 **a** 7:55 pm   **b** 21:47

S4.2 **a i** 07:56 from Exeter **ii** 2 hours 6 minutes   **b** 0620 train
        c 27 minutes   **d** 92 mph (to the nearest whole number)

S4.3 **b** 24 cm   **c** 35 cm²

S4.4 **b** about 14 cm   **c** about 15 cm²

S4.5 **b** 136 cm²   **S4.6** **d** 84 cm²   **e** 36 cm³

S4.7 **a** 28 tiles   **b** 2800 cm²   **c** 3 metres

S4.8 **a** 36 cm³

S5.1 **a i** 5 **ii** 9 **iii** 6   **c** 6 cm²   **d** 36 cm³

S5.2 **a** C   **S5.3** **b** 56 cm²

S5.6 **a** 9   **b** 16   **c** 9

S6.2 **d** ($^-$4, 4)

S6.3 rotation of 90° anticlockwise (the centre of rotation being 2 squares above the top vertex of triangle A)

S7.1 **d** 8   **S7.2** J and K   **S7.4** C

S8.2 around, cornered, cross   **S8.3** **a** 2   **b** 3

S8.5 **b** rotational symmetry of order 4

S8.8 **a** 6   **b** 3   **S8.9** B   **S8.10** I

S9.2 **a** 50.265 cm   **b** 503 mm

S9.3 531 cm^2 (to the nearest whole number)

S9.4 **a** 188.5 cm (to 1 dp)   **b** 4   **S9.5** just over 9 times

S9.6 **a** 48   **b** 1357 cm^2 (to the nearest cm)   **c** 371 cm^2

S10.3 **b** 11.3 cm   **c** 113 metres

S10.4 **a** 3.5 metres   **b** 15 cm   **S10.6** 400 metres

S11.1 **b** The interior angle is 108°, which is not a factor of 360°.

S11.2 **a i** $x = 47°$ **ii** $y = 47°$ **b** isosceles
c i 65 cm^2 **ii** 32.5 cm^2

S11.3 **a i** $x = 30°$ **ii** $y = 60°$ **b i** rhombus   **ii** trapezium

S11.5 **a** 24 cm   **b** 20 cm^2

S11.6 move forward 40 paces, turn left 90°, move forward 30 paces, turn anticlockwise 90°, move forward 20 paces, turn left 60°, move forward 35 paces

S11.7 **a i** 6   **ii** 12   **iii** 8   **b** 396   **c** 132

D1.3 You cannot have a probability greater than 1 (certain) or less than 0 (impossible).

D1.4 **a** AB, AC, AD, AE, BC, BD, BE, CD, CE, DE   **b** $\frac{1}{5}$

D1.5 **a** $\frac{7}{25}$ **b** $\frac{28}{50} = \frac{14}{25}$

D1.6 **a** $\frac{2}{8} = \frac{1}{4}$ **b** $\frac{3}{8}$ **c** $\frac{5}{8}$

D1.7 **a** $\frac{1}{500}$ **b** $\frac{3}{500}$
c You don't know that equal numbers of boys and girls bought tickets.
d $\frac{100}{500} = \frac{1}{5}$

D1.8 **a** $\frac{1}{7}$ **b** $\frac{4}{7}$
c It does not look fair, but you can only be certain by doing many more spins.

D1.9 **a** $\frac{1}{10}$ **b** $\frac{5}{10} = \frac{1}{2}$ **c** 0.7

D1.10 **a**

Head	1H	2H	3H	4H	5H	6H	6H
Tail	1T	2T	3T	4T	5T	6T	6T
Score on dice	1	2	3	4	5	6	6

b $\frac{2}{12} = \frac{1}{6}$

D2.3 GREEN + GATE (6 times), BROWN + GATE (4 times), GREEN + DOOR (6 times), BROWN + DOOR (4 times), GREEN + STYLE (3 times), BROWN + STYLE (2 times)

D2.4 Australia, 36°   USA, 100°   Canada, 60°   Europe, 120°   India, 44°

D2.5 **a** Tessa's

D2.8 **a** 182 cm   **b** 38 cm   **c** 30   **d** 6

D2.9 **a** 5.5   **b** 6

D3.1 **a** Women of a fixed weight are, on average, taller than men of the same weight.
b Mary is taller by about 3 cm.
c Sam, about 75 kg   Sasha, about 72 kg

D3.2 **a** 30 °C   **b** 40 °C   **c** about 61 °C
d about 64 seconds

D3.3 **a** 16   **c** train   **D3.4** **a** 30

D3.5 **a i** 4000   **ii** 7000   **iii** 8500   **iv** 7500
b March, June, November   **c** Summer, 25   Autumn, 35

D4.1 1, B   2, C   3, A

D4.2 **a i** Bill   **ii** Claire   **iii** Dave   **iv** Alice
b People who spend more time on leisure activities do less homework.

D4.3 **b** There is a slight link: people who do better in French tend to do better in German too.
c a little over 40 marks in German

D4.4 **a** 900 grams   **b** 1 lb   **D4.5** **c** no. 4

D4.6 **b** There is not much of a link. For this sample taller people appear slightly more intelligent.

D5.1 **a** 100   **b** 6   **c** 5   **d** 4

D5.2 **a** 3   **b** 5   **c** 2   **d** 2

D5.3 **a i** Mrs Phitts' group, 25   Mr Strong's group, 30
ii Mrs Phitts' group, 15   Mr Strong's group, 10

D5.4 **a** 7   **b** 4
c no because she would have to score $\frac{15}{10}$ to do this   **d** 7.9

D5.5 **a i** 1.5   **ii** 5.5   **b i** 0.5   **ii** 5.6 (to 1 dp)

D5.6 **a** 30 cm   **b** 12 cm
c They were more reliable and longer last year.

D5.7 **a** 29   **b** 6   **c** 28

D5.8 **a** 258 kg   **b** 79 kg

D6.2 **a** B   **b** C

D6.3 **a i** 6   **ii** 6   **iii** 7   **iv** 5
b The Wednesday team had larger feet.

D6.4 **a** 31   **D6.5** **a** A2, B1, C3

D6.7 **a** 50   **b** It does not appear to be fair because there are too many 5's.
c 5

D7.1 **a** $\frac{1}{520}$ **b** $\frac{1}{52}$ **c** $\frac{1}{13}$

D7.2 **a** $\frac{18}{36} = \frac{1}{2}$ **b** $\frac{9}{36} = \frac{1}{4}$ **c** $\frac{27}{36} = \frac{3}{4}$

D7.3 0.11

D7.4 **a**

Number on blue dice

6	7	8	9	10	11	12
5	6	7	8	9	10	11
4	5	6	7	8	9	10
3	4	5	6	7	8	9
2	3	4	5	6	7	8
1	2	3	4	5	6	7
	1	2	3	4	5	6

Number on red dice

b $\frac{4}{36} = \frac{1}{9}$ **c** $\frac{6}{36} = \frac{1}{6}$ **d** $\frac{6}{36} = \frac{1}{6}$ **e** 65

D7.5 **a** 20   **b** 11 minutes   **c** $\frac{5}{20} = \frac{1}{4}$ **d** $\frac{5}{20} = \frac{1}{4}$

D7.6 **a** 1995 and 1996, 1995 and 1997, 1995 and 1998, 1995 and 1999, 1996 and 1997, 1996 and 1998, 1996 and 1999, 1997 and 1998, 1997 and 1999, 1998 and 1999
b $\frac{1}{5}$

D7.7 **a i** blue   **ii** There are more blue beads than any other colour.
b

0	$\frac{1}{4}$	$\frac{1}{2}$	1

(green bead)

c $\frac{11}{36}$ **d** $\frac{20}{36} = \frac{5}{9}$

D7.8 **a**

Estimate of length (cm)	Tally	Frequency
4 ≤ length of line < 6	I	1
6 ≤ length of line < 8	II	2
8 ≤ length of line < 10	IIII	4
10 ≤ length of line < 12	IIII	4
12 ≤ length of line < 14	IIII II	7
14 ≤ length of line < 16	II	2

c $12 \leq l < 14$ **d** 10.4 cm

Acknowledgements

The publisher and authors are grateful to the following for permission to reproduce material.

Illustrators Moondisks Ltd, Oxford Illustrators, Nick Hawken, Pat Moffett, Phillip Reeve, Tony Dover

Photographers Mike Dudley, Martin Sookias, Andrew Ward

Photographic Libraries Mary Evans Picture Library, J. Allan Cash Ltd, World Pictures, The Science Photographic Library (cover)

Suppliers Eurostar

Every reasonable effort has been made to contact copyright owners, but we apologise for any unknown errors or omissions.

Oxford University Press, Great Clarendon Street, Oxford OX2 6DP

Oxford New York
Athens Auckland Bangkok Bogota Buenos Aires
Calcutta Cape Town Chennai Dar es Salaam
Delhi Florence Hong Kong Istanbul Karachi
Kuala Lumpur Madrid Melbourne
Mexico City Mumbai Nairobi
Paris São Paulo Singapore
Taipei Tokyo Toronto Warsaw

and associated companies in
Berlin Ibadan

Oxford is a trade mark of Oxford University Press

© Oxford University Press 1998

First published 1998

ISBN 0 19 914717 5

Typeset and designed by Moondisks Ltd, Cambridge

Printed in Spain by Graficas Estella S.A.